PARADISE NOW

SBL

Society of Biblical Literature

Symposium Series

Victor H. Matthews,
Series Editor

Number 11

PARADISE NOW
Essays on Early Jewish
and Christian Mysticism

PARADISE NOW

Essays on Early Jewish and Christian Mysticism

Edited by

April D. DeConick

Society of Biblical Literature
Atlanta

PARADISE NOW
Essays on Early Jewish and Christian Mysticism

Library of Congress Cataloging-in-Publication Data

Paradise now : essays on early Jewish and Christian mysticism / edited by April D. DeConick.
p. cm. — (Society of Biblical Literature symposium series ; no. 11)
Includes bibliographical references and index.
ISBN-13: 978-1-58983-257-2 (paper binding : alk. paper)
ISBN-10: 1-58983-257-4 (paper binding : alk. paper)
1. Mysticism—Judaism—History. 2. Mysticism—History. I. De Conick, April D. II. Series: Symposium series (Society of Biblical Literature) ; no. 11.
BM723 .P368 2006
296.8'1—dc22 2006034373

14 13 12 11 10 09 08 07 06 5 4 3 2 1
Printed in the United States of America on acid-free, recycled paper conforming to ANSI/NISO Z39.48-1992 (R1997) and ISO 9706:1994 standards for paper permanence.

IN MEMORY OF GILLES QUISPEL (1916–2006)

Contents

Abbreviations

Primary Sources

'Abod. Zar.	*'Abodah Zarah*
'Abot R. Nat.	*'Abot of Rabbi Nathan*
Abr.	Philo, *De Abrahamo*
Aen.	Virgil, *Aeneid*
Ag. Ap.	Josephus, *Against Apion*
Agr.	Philo, *De agricultura*
Alc.	Euripides, *Alcestis*
Ant.	Josephus, *Jewish Antiquities*
Apoc. Abr.	*Apocalypse of Abraham*
Apoc. Mos.	*Apocalypse of Moses*
Asc. Isa.	*Ascension of Isaiah*
Autol.	Theophilus of Antioch, *Ad Autolycum*
b.	Babylonian Talmud
2 Bar.	*2 Baruch* (*Syriac Apocalypse*)
B. Bat	*Baba Batra*
Bapt.	Tertullian, *De baptismo*
Ber.	*Berakot*
Cant. Rab.	*Canticles Rabbah*
CD	Cairo Genizah copy of the *Damascus Document*
Cher.	Philo, *De cherubim*
Com. Jo.	Origen, *Commentarii in evangelium Joannis*
Conf.	Philo, *De confusione linguarum*
Cong.	Philo, *De congressu eruditionis gratia*
Contempl.	Philo, *De vita contemplativa*
Dec.	Philo, *De decalogo*
Demon.	Irenaeus, *Demonstratio*
Det.	Philo, *Quod deterius potiori insidari soleat*
Deus	Philo, *Quod Deus sit immutabilis*
Deut. Rab.	*Deuteronomy Rabbah*
Did. Apost.	*Didascalia Apostolorum*
Ebr.	Philo, *De ebrietate*

El.	Euripides, *Electra*
Elench.	Hippolytus, *Elenchus*
1 En.	*1 Enoch*
2 En.	*2 Enoch*
3 En.	*3 Enoch* (*Sefer Hekhalot*)
Ep.	Philostratus, *Epistulae*
Eugn.	*Eugnostos the Blessed*
Eum.	Nepos, *Eumenes*
Exag.	Ezekiel the Tragedian, *Exagoge*
Exod. Rab	*Exodus Rabbah*
Ezek. Trag.	Ezekiel the Tragedian
Fug.	Philo, *De fuga et inventione*
Gen. Rab.	*Genesis Rabbah*
Gig.	Philo, *De gigantibus*
Gos. Heb.	*Gospel of Hebrews*
Gos. Pet.	*Gospel of Peter*
Gos. Phil.	*Gospel of Philip*
Gos. Thom.	*Gospel of Thomas*
Gos. Truth	*Gospel of Truth*
Haer.	Irenaeus, *Adversus haereses*
Hag.	*Hagigah*
Hec.	Euripides, *Hecuba*
Hekh. Rab.	*Hekhalot Rabbati*
Hekh. Zut.	*Hekhalot Zutarti*
Her.	Philo, *Quis rerum divinarum heres sit*
Herm. Vis.	Shepherd of Hermas, *Vision*
Herm. Sim.	Shepherd of Hermas, *Similitude*
Herm. Mand.	Shepherd of Hermas, *Mandate*
Hom. Ezech.	Origen, *Homiliae in Ezechielem*
Hom. Luc.	Origen, *Homiliae in Lucam*
Hyp. Arch.	*Hypostasis of the Archons*
Hypoth.	Philo, *Hypothetica*
Insomn.	Aristotle, *De insomniis*
Ios.	Philo, *De Iosepho*
Is. Os.	Plutarch, *De Iside et Osiride*
Jos. Asen.	*Joseph and Aseneth*
Jub.	*Jubilees*
L.A.B.	*Liber antiquitatum biblicarum*
Lad. Jac.	*Ladder of Jacob*
Lam. Rab.	*Lamentations Rabbah*
Leg.	Philo, *Legum allegoriae*
Legat.	Philo, *Legatio ad Gaium*
Leuc. Clit.	Achilles Tatius, *Leucippe and Clitophon*

Lev. Rab	*Leviticus Rabbah*
m.	Mishnah
Meg.	*Megillah*
Men.	*Menahot*
Metam.	Apuleius, *Metamorphoses*
Mid.	*Middot*
Mig.	Philo, *De migratione Abrahami*
Mos.	Philo, *De vita Mosis*
Mut.	Philo, *De mutatione nominum*
Myst.	Ambrose, *De mysteriis*
Num. Rab.	*Numbers Rabbah*
Odes. Sol.	*Odes of Solomon*
Opif.	Philo, *De opificio mundi*
Orest.	Euripides, *Orestes*
Orig. World	*On the Origin of the World*
Pan.	Epiphanius, *Panarion*
Pesiq. Rab. Kah.	*Pesiqta de Rab Kahana*
Phaedr.	Plato, *Phaedrus*
Pirqe R. El	*Pirqe Rabbi Eliezer*
Plant.	Philo, *De plantatione*
Post.	Philo, *De posteritate Caini*
Praem.	Philo, *De praemiis et poenis*
Praep. ev.	Eusebius, *Praeparatio evangelica*
Prob.	Philo, *Quod omnis probus liber sit*
Prov.	Philo, *De providentia*
QE	Philo, *Quaestiones et solutiones in Exodum*
QG	Philo, *Quaestiones et solutiones in Genesin*
Ref.	Hippolytus, *Refutatio omnium haeresium*
Resp.	Plato, *Respublica*
Rom.	Ignatius, *Letter to Romans*
Roš. Haš.	*Roš Haššanah*
Sacr.	Philo, *De sacrificiis Abelis et Caini*
Sanh.	*Sanhedrin*
Smyrn.	Ignatius, *Letter to the Smyrneans*
Somn.	Philo, *De somniis*
Spec.	Philo, *De specialibus legibus*
Sym.	Plato, *Symposium*
T. Job	*Testament of Job*
T. Jos.	*Testament of Joseph*
T. Levi	*Testament of Levi*
T. Napht.	*Testament of Naphtali*
T. Reu.	*Testament of Reuben*
Tanh. Qed.	*Tanhuma Qedusha*

Tg. Onq.	*Targum Onqelos*
Tg. Prov.	*Targum of Proverbs*
Theaet.	Plato, *Theaetetus*
Trad. ap.	Hippolytus, *Traditio apostolica*
Vir. Ill.	Jerome, *De viris illustribus*
Virt.	Philo, *De virtutibus*
War	Josephus, *Jewish War*
y.	Jerusalem Talmud
Yebam.	*Yebamot*

Secondary Sources

AB	Anchor Bible
ABD	*Anchor Bible Dictionary*. Edited by D. N. Freedman. 6 vols. New York: Doublday, 1992.
ABRL	Anchor Bible Reference Library
AfO	*Archiv für Orientforschung*
AGJU	Arbeiten zur Geschichte des antiken Judentums und des Urchristentums
AGWG	Abhandlungen der Königlichen gesellschaft der wissenschaften zu Göttingen
AJS Review	*Association for Jewish Studies Review*
AJSL	*American Journal of Semitic Languages and Literature*
ALGHJ	Arbeiten zur Literatur und Geschichte des hellenistischen Judentums
AnBib	Analecta biblica
ANRW	*Aufstieg und Niedergang der römischen Welt: Geschichte und Kultur Roms im Spiegel der neueren Forschung*. Edited by H. Temporini and W. Haase. Berlin: de Gruyter, 1972–.
AOAT	Alter Orient und Altes Testament
AR	*Archiv für Religionswissenschaft*
BEATAJ	Beiträge zur Erforschung des Alten Testaments und des antiken Judentum
BETL	Bibliotheca Ephemeridum theologicarum Lovaniensium
Bib	*Biblica*
Bijdr	*Bijdragen: Tijdschrift voor filosofie en theologie*
BJRL	*Bulletin of the John Rylands University Library of Manchester*
BJS	Brown Judaic Studies
BR	*Biblical Research*
BZNW	Beihefte zur Zeitschrift für die neutestamentliche Wissenschaft
CBQ	*Catholic Biblical Quarterly*
CBQMS	Catholic Biblical Quarterly Monograph Series
CH	*Church History*

CNT	Commentaire du Nouveau Testament
ConBOT	Coniectanea biblica: Old Testament Series
CRINT	Compendia rerum iudaicarum ad Novum Testamentum
CSCO	Corpus scriptorum christianorum orientalium
CWS	Classics of Western Spirituality
DDD	*Dictionary of Deities and Demons in the Bible.* Edited by K. van der Toorn, B. Becking, and P. W. van der Horst. Leiden: Brill, 1995.
DJD	Discoveries in the Judaean Desert
DSD	*Dead Sea Discoveries*
EJM	Etudes sur le judaïsme médiéval
EPRO	Etudes préliminaires aux religions orientales dans l'empire romain
ETS	Erfurter theologische Studien
ExAud	*Ex auditu*
ExTim	*Expository Times*
FJB	*Frankfurter Judaistische Beiträge*
FOTL	Forms of Old Testament Literature
Hen	*Henoch*
HNT	Handbuch zum Neuen Testament
HNTC	Harper's New Testament Commentaries
HSM	Harvard Semitic Monographs
HSS	Harvard Semitic Studies
HTR	*Harvard Theological Review*
HTS	Harvard Theological Studies
HUCA	*Hebrew Union College Annual*
HUCM	Monographs of the Hebrew Union College
IBC	Interpretation: A Bible Commentary for Teaching and Preaching
ICC	International Critical Commentary
Imm	*Immanuel*
JAOS	*Journal of the American Oriental Society*
JBL	*Journal of Biblical Literature*
JCS	*Journal of Cuneiform Studies*
JJS	*Journal of Jewish Studies*
JNES	*Journal of Near Eastern Studies*
JQR	*Jewish Quarterly Review*
JRelS	*Journal of Religious Studies*
JRS	*Journal of Roman Studies*
JSJ	*Journal for the Study of Judaism in the Persian, Hellenistic, and Roman Periods*
JSJSup	Supplements to Journal for the Study of Judaism
JSNT	*Journal for the Study of the New Testament*
JSNTSup	Journal for the Study of the New Testament Supplement Series
JSOTSup	Journal for the Study of the Old Testament Supplement Series
JSP	*Journal for the Study of the Pseudepigrapha*

JSPSup	Journal for the Study of the Pseudepigrapha Supplement Series
JSQ	*Jewish Studies Quarterly*
JSS	*Journal of Semitic Studies*
JTS	*Journal of Theological Studies*
Jud	*Judaica*
LCL	Loeb Classical Library
Neot	*Neotestamentica*
NICNT	New International Commentary on the New Testament
NIGTC	New International Greek Testament Commentary
NovT	*Novum Testamentum*
NovTSup	Supplements to Novum Testamentum
NTOA	Novum Testamentum et Orbis Antiquus
NTS	*New Testament Studies*
OBO	Orbis biblicus et orientalis
ÖBS	Österreichische biblische Studien
OTL	Old Testament Library
OTP	*Old Testament Pseudepigrapha.* Edited by J. H. Charlesworth. 2 vols. New York: Doubleday, 1983–85.
OtSt	Oudtestamentische Studiën
PIBA	*Proceedings of the Irish Biblical Association*
PVTG	Pseudepigrapha Veteris Testamenti Graece
RB	*Revue biblique*
RevQ	*Revue de Qumran*
RHist	*Reflexions historiques*
RlA	*Reallexikon der Assyriologie.* Edited by Erich Ebeling et al. Berlin: de Gruyter, 1928–.
RSR	*Recherches de science religieuse*
SAA	State Archives of Assyria
SBLBMI	Society of Biblical Literature The Bible and Its Modern Interpreters
SBLDS	Society of Biblical Literature Dissertation Series
SBLEJL	Society of Biblical Literature Early Judaism and Its Literature
SBLSBS	Society of Biblical Literature Sources for Biblical Study
SBLSP	Society of Biblical Literature Seminar Papers
SBLTT	Society of Biblical Literature Texts and Translations
SBT	Studies in Biblical Theology
Sem	*Semitica*
SemeiaSt	Semeia Studies
SHR	Studies in the History of Religions (supplement to *Numen*)
SJLA	Studies in Judaism and Late Antiquity
SNTSMS	Society for New Testament Studies Monograph Series
SPhilo	*Studia philonica*
STDJ	Studies on the Texts of the Desert of Judah
SVTP	Studia in Veteris Testamenti pseudepigraphica

SVTQ	*St. Vladimir's Theological Quarterly*
TAPS	Transactions of the American Philosophical Society
TBT	*The Bible Today*
TSAJ	Texte und Studien zum antiken Judentum
TU	Texte und Untersuchungen
VC	*Vigiliae christianae*
VCSup	Supplements to Vigiliae christianae
VT	*Vetus Testamentum*
VTSup	Supplements to Vetus Testamentum
WBC	Word Biblical Commentary
WMANT	Wissenschaftliche Monographien zum Alten und Neuen Testament
WUNT	Wissenschaftliche Untersuchungen zum Neuen Testament
WZKM	*Wiener Zeitschrift für die Kunde des Morgenlandes*
ZA	*Zeitschrift für Assyriologie*
ZAW	*Zeitschrift für die alttestamentliche Wissenschaft*

Preface

The papers in this volume were collected in celebration of the tenth anniversary of the Early Jewish and Christian Mysticism group of the Society of Biblical Literature. The group was conceived in December 1995, when I convened with Jarl Fossum a symposium at the University of Michigan. The conference was held in the beautiful Rackham amphitheater in Ann Arbor. Our subject was "Early Jewish and Christian Mysticism: Vision and Audition." Over a two-day period, an international group of scholars presented pioneering papers and held ground-breaking discussions about pre-Kabbalistic Jewish and pre-Dionysiac Christian mysticism. The scholars included April DeConick, David Evans, Jarl Fossum, Naomi Janowitz, Dan Merkur, Chris Morray-Jones, Phillip Munoa, and Alan Segal.

At the conclusion of the symposium, the group met for dinner at the famous converted train station, the Gandy Dancer, where, over fine wine and a delicious meal, the conversation turned to discussing the possibility of launching a Society of Biblical Literature group. I spoke to the group about the need to create a national venue for the exploration of mysticism in this early period, across the traditional boundaries that have separated the study of Judaism and Christianity from each other. I felt that the study of mysticism in this early period had been ignored, neglected, and marginalized for far too long. Others in the group agreed. So, over dessert, we mapped out an initial proposal for the group, and the Early Jewish and Christian Mysticism group was born the following year.

From 1996 to 1998, we functioned as a Society of Biblical Literature Consultation. Since the field that we were proposing to study was so new, at the time we could not even form a good definition of our topic. So we decided to approach the matter by examining various traditions, that is, mystical themes in literature of the Second Temple Period and the *hekhalot*. Since we did not wish to impose an *etic* definition on these materials, we thought that, if we explored various themes in the period-literature, eventually an *emic* definition might emerge. Even when we became a Society of Biblical Literature Group, three years later in 1999, we continued the thematic approach with the aim of coming to a better understanding of the nature and perforations of mysticism in the early period.

Over a ten-year period the group explored many themes, including, "Vision and Knowledge of God," "Esoteric Temple Traditions," "The Body of God," "The Chariot," "The Use of Scripture in Mystical Texts and Practice," "Angelology and the Heavenly World," "Ritual And Practices," "Death and the Afterlife," "Gendered Images," "Cosmology," and "The Problem of Rabbinic Mysticism." Scholars who contributed papers or reviewed books included Ron Afzal, Philip Alexander, Daphna Arbel, Matthew Baldwin, Kelley Coblentz Bautch, Adam Becker, Ra'anan Abusch Boustan, Bogdan Bucur, Elizabeth Clark, Jim Davila, April DeConick, Kindalee Pfremmer DeLong, Celia Deutsch, Nathaniel Deutsch, Jonathan Draper, Rachel Elior, Frances Flannery-Daily, Crispin Fletcher-Louis, Charles Gieschen, Alexander Golitizin, Alon Goshen-Gottstein, Bob Hall, David Halperin, Larry Hurtado, Rebecca Lesses, Andrea Lieber, Mark Kinzer, Jonathan Klawans, Jonathan Knight, Kathryn Muller Lopez, Edmondo Lupieri, James McGrath, Dan Merkur, Philip Munoa, Andrei Orlov, Birger Pearson, Catherine Playoust, Seth Sanders, Jane Schaberg, Alan Segal, Michael Swartz, Jonah Steinberg, Kevin Sullivan, John Turner, Michael Williams, and Elliot Wolfson. The vitality of the group and its success is due to each of these scholars, who have presented over the years very fine, even ground-breaking, contributions.

One of the loveliest meetings, in my memory, was the Denver roundtable session in 2001, when members of the group each contributed 500-word essays on their own working definitions of early Jewish and Christian mysticism, which I "stitched" together for the Society of Biblical Literature Seminar Papers. It was a session in which members with very different approaches and understandings gathered and genuinely talked with each other. I learned many things that Tuesday morning, mostly about the willingness to share and the kindness of the people who sat around that table. It was the day when many of us became friends, not just colleagues. The next year we started a tradition to carry on that comradery. Since then, every Saturday night at the Annual Convention, we have met for a meal at a local restaurant. Together we have drunk lots of wine and broken lots of bread and told lots of stories!

The present volume attempts to provide an overview of the work that members of the group delivered in one format or another but that has not been published previously in other venues. I have attempted, in the first essay, to offer an *emic* definition of "early Jewish and Christian mysticism" as it unfolded in the thematic work of this group and my own musings as an independent scholar. Not everyone in the group would agree with my definition, but I offer it as my understanding of what the work of the group as a whole has brought to table and what insights I have gained from my interactions with members of the group.

The various parts of the volume build off this definition. The section on "Hermeneutics and Experience" consists of three papers that offer discussions about the intersection of exegesis and religious experience. Each scholar attempts to move the discussion beyond the roadblock that has stood in the field for some time: that the period-literature represents either imaginative fiction or actual experiences. Alan Segal addresses the issue from the angle of neurology, culture, and religiously interpreted experiences. Christopher Rowland applies the innovative work of Mary Carruthers, the "craft of memory," as well as cross-cultural studies to the problem. Seth Sanders turns to the study of performance and interpretation as a way to lead us out of this ambivalence.

In the second part of the book, “Communal Identities,” three essays offer provocative ways to imagine the identities of communities of mystics responsible for various strands of the period-literature. Rachel Elior explores the emergence of the early *merkabah* traditions within the community of deposed priests at Qumran. Jim Davila compares the “fictional” experiences of the heroes in the ancient Jewish apocalypses to shamanistic techniques illustrated in the later *hekhalot* texts, concluding that the apocalypses represent magico-religious ritual traditions that are, in some way, ancestral to the *hekhalot*. To conclude this section of the book, Ra‘anan Boustan offers a paper that attempts to negotiate conflicting opinions about Rabbi Ishmael as constructions of differing socioreligious contexts that produced constituent components of the Hekhalot corpus.

Part 3, “Cosmology,” is composed of four important essays that describe various aspects of the cosmology that undergrids the period-literature. Christopher Morray-Jones contributes a chapter that systematically describes the celestial temple as the seven heavens as well as the human body. He thus offers a new and provocative theory about the meaning of the phrase “descender to the chariot.” Andrei Orlov explores the idea of the face of God, whether it can be seen by the devotee and what dangers are involved. Ron Afzal focuses on the *merkabah* visions in Revelation as innovative reinterpretations of a “communal icon” that invoke the passage of time, the movement of the four seasons, authenticating the revelations given to John as one who has seen the creator in his cosmic role as the “director of history.” Finally, Kevin Sullivan pulls together a wide array of sources to address the thorny problem of sexuality and angels. He concludes that the overwhelming descriptions of angels as male in the period-literature helped to foster ascetic and encratic practices of some early mystics who wished to gain access to God through imitation of the angels.

In the fourth section of the volume, “Apocalypticism,” Frances Flannery-dailey offers a paper that reassesses scholarly approaches to “apocalypticism” and “mysticism” by stressing the importance of dreams to the period-literature. She points to the previous lack of understanding among scholars that apocalypticism is as much about mysticism as it is about eschatology. In the next essay, Kelley Coblentz Bautch studies the geography and eschatology of the Book of the Watchers, comparing the location of places associated with death and judgment with other Near Eastern cosmologies. She thinks that the journeys described in this book may be evidence for religious experience, although she finds nothing about transformative experiences. In the last paper of the section, Rebecca Lesses discusses the theological effort of the Jewish mystics to understand the destruction of the temple and the exile of the Jewish people and their prayer for an end to Jewish suffering through divine redemption.

In the final section of the book, “Practices,” Celia Deutsch uses the Therapeutae as a case study for the exploration of the interaction between the study of sacred texts and the use of rituals to evoke mystical experiences in a religious community. Andrea Lieber examines the emergence of meal rituals in Jewish and Christian communities as a way in which the structured boundaries between the divine and human worlds is collapsed. Charles Gieschen looks at baptism in Revelation as a foundational "priestly" preparation for early Christian mystical experience of God's presence, especially in the Eucharist. The book concludes with the essay by Daphna Arbel who compares traditions of divination in ancient Mesopotamia with similar traditions in the *hekhalot* literature, suggesting that the old traditions were reconfigured in *3 Enoch* to show that humans are able to access deeper and concealed dimensions of reality through inner revelation directly from God.

It is a pioneering volume, the first ever to collect international voices that are mapping this field of study. Unfortunately, it could not hold all of the papers delivered in this ten-year period. The range of papers given over this time was vast, and a large number of them were published independently in journals or became the basis for monographs, many of which were reviewed in sessions by the group. For these previously published and/or reviewed works, consult the following bibliography. I have tried to be exhaustive but fear that I may have missed a piece or two (for which I apologize wholeheartedly).

Arbel, Daphna. *Beholders of Divine Secrets: Myth and Mysticism in the Hekhalot and Merkavah Literature.* New York: State University of New York Press, 2003.

Buckley, Jorunn. *The Mandaeans: Ancient Text and Modern People.* Oxford: Oxford University Press, 2002.

Bucur, Bogdan. "On Climbing the Cosmic Ladder: Clement of Alexandria's Hierarchical Cosmology and Its Innovations." *VC* 60 (2006): 251–68.

Boustan, Ra'anan Abusch. *From Martyr to Mystic: the Story of the Ten Martyrs, Hekhalot Rabbati, and the Making of Merkavah Mysticism.* Tübingen: Möhr Siebeck, 2005.

Flannery-Dailey, Frances. *Dreamers, Scribes and Priests: Jewish Dreams in the Hellenistic and Roman Eras.* JSJSup 90. Leiden: Brill, 2004.

Davila, James R. *Descenders to the Chariot: The People behind the Hekhalot Literature.* JSJSup 70. Leiden: Brill, 2001.

DeConick, April D. "The Great Mystery of Marriage: Sex and Conception in Ancient Valentinian Traditions." *VC* 57 (2003): 307–42.

———. "The True Mysteries: Sacramentalism in the Gospel of Philip." *VC* 55 (2001): 225–61.

———. *Recovering the Original Gospel of Thomas: A History of the Gospel and Its Growth.* JSNTSup 286. London: T&T Clark, 2005.

———. Pages 109–32 in *Voices of the Mystics: Early Christian Discourse in the Gospels of John and Thomas and Other Ancient Christian Literature.* JSNTSup 157. Sheffield: Sheffield Academic Press.

Draper, Jonathan. "Practicing the Presence of God in John: Ritual Use of Scripture and the *Eidos Theou* in John 5:37." Pages 155–70 in *Orality, Literacy, and Colonialism in Antiquity*. Edited by J. A. Draper. SemeiaSt 47. Atlanta: Society of Biblical Literature, 2004.

———. "What Did Isaiah See? Angelic Theophany in the Tomb in John 20:11-18." *Neot* 36 (2002): 63–76.

Elior, Rachel. *The Three Temples: On the Emergence of Jewish Mysticism*. Translated by David Louvish. Oxford: Littman Library of Jewish Civilization, 2004.

———. "You Have Chosen Enoch from among Human Beings: Enoch the Scribe of Righteousness and the Scroll's Library of the Priests the Sons of Zadok." Pages 15–64 in *Creation and Re-creation in Jewish Thought: Festschrift in Honor of Joseph Dan on the Occasion of His Seventieth Birthday*. Edited by Rachel Elior and Peter Schäfer. Tubingen: Mohr Siebeck, 2005.

Fletcher-Louis, Crispin H. T. *All the Glory of Adam: Liturgical Anthropology in the Dead Sea Scrolls*. STDJ 42. Leiden: Brill, 2002.

Golitzin, Alexander. " 'The Demons Suggest an Illusion of God's Glory in a Form': Controversy over the Divine Body and Vision of Glory." *Studia Monastica* 44 (2002): 13–43.

———. " 'Earthly Angels and Heavenly Men': The Old Testament Pseudepigrapha, Niketas Stethatos, and the Tradition of 'Interiorized Apocalyptic' in Eastern Christian Ascetical and Mystical Literature." *Dumbarton Oaks Papers* 55 (2001): 125–53.

Klawans, Jonathan. Review of Rachel Elior, *The Three Temples: On the Emergence of Jewish Mysticism*. *Association for Jewish Studies Review* 29 (2005): 376–78.

Lesses, Rebecca. *Ritual Practices to Gain Power: Angels, Incantations, and Revelation in Early Jewish Mysticism*. HTS 44. Harrisburg, Pa.: Trinity Press International, 1998.

Lieber, Andrea. "Angels That Kill: Mediation and the Threat of Bodily Destruction in the Hekhalot Narratives." *Studies in Spirituality* 14 (2004): 17–35.

———. "I Set a Table before You: The Jewish Mystical Character of Aseneth's Conversion Meal." *JSP* 14 (2004): 63–77.

———. "Voice and Vision: Song as a Vehicle for Ecstatic Experience in Songs of the Sabbath Sacrifice." Pages 51–58 in *Of Scribes and Sages: Early Jewish Interpretation and Transmision of Scripture*. Edited by Craig A. Evans. London: T&T Clark, 2004.

Morray-Jones, Christopher R. A. *A Transparent Illusion: The Dangerous Vision of Water in Hekhalot Mysticism: A Source-Critical and Tradition-Historical Inquiry*. JSJSup 59. Leiden: Brill, 2002.

Orlov, Andrei. *The Enoch-Metatron Tradition*. TSAJ 107. Tübingen: Mohr Siebeck, 2005.

———. "The Face as the Heavenly Counterpart of the Visionary in the Slavonic Ladder of Jacob." Pages 59–76 in volume 2 of *Of Scribes and Sages: Early*

Jewish Interpretation and Transmission of Scripture. Edited by Craig Evans. Library of Second Temple Studies. London: T&T Clark, 2004.

———. *From Apocalypticism to Merkabah Mysticism: Studies in the Slavonic Pseudepigrapha*. T&T Clark: London, 2006.

———. "Titles of Enoch-Metatron in 2 Enoch." *JSP* 18 (1998): 71–86.

Rowland, Christopher. "Apocalyptic, Mysticism and the New Testament. Pages 405–21 in *Geschichte-Tradition-Reflexion: Festschrift für Martin Hengel zum 70. Geburtstag*. Edited by Hubert Cancik, Hermann Lichtenberger, and Peter Schäfer. Tübingen: Mohr Siebeck, 1996.

Schaberg, Jane. *The Resurrection of Mary Magdalene: Legends, Apocrypha, and Christian Testament*. New York: Continuum, 2002.

Segal, Alan. *Life after Death: A History of the Afterlife in the Religions of the West*. New York: Doubleday, 2004.

Sullivan, Kevin P. *Wrestling with Angels: A Study of the Relationship between Angels and Humans in Ancient Jewish Literature and the New Testament*. AGJU 55. Leiden: Brill, 2004.

Turner, John D., and Ruth Majercik, eds. *Gnosticism and Later Platonism: Themes, Figures, and Texts*. Atlanta: Society of Biblical Literature, 2001.

This group would not have been as successful as it has been, if not for its strong leaders whose commitment to the group and yearly contributions have been truly meritorious, those who chaired the group (April DeConick, 1996–2002 [Rice University, U.S.A.]; Andrea Lieber, 2002–2005 [Dickinson College, U.S.A.]; and Kevin Sullivan, 2005– [Illinois Wesleyan University, U.S.A.) and those who have sat on the steering committee (Jim Davila, 1996– [University of St. Andrews, Scotland]; April DeConick, 1996– [Rice University, U.S.A.], Jonathan Draper, 2003– [University of KwaZulu-Natal, South Africa], Rebecca Lesses, 2004– [Ithaca College, U.S.A.], Andrea Lieber, 2001– [Dickinson College, U.S.A.], Chris Morray-Jones, 1996–2000 [independent scholar], Phil Munoa, 1996–2003 [Hope College, U.S.A.], Andrea Orlov, 2004– [Marquette University, U.S.A.], Alan Segal, 1996– [Barnard College and Columbia University, U.S.A.], and Kevin Sullivan, 2004– [Illinois Wesleyan University, U.S.A.]). The insight and wisdom of each and every one of these people has benefited the whole and, in the way of a mystery, has nurtured the heart and soul of this group.

My gracious thanks goes out to everyone who has helped to make the Early Jewish and Christian Mysticism group successful, all the presenters and leaders named above and all those who attended the sessions whose names I might not know, all those who stepped forward with excellent papers and reviews, all those who shared generously their ideas and time, all those who brought companionship and fellowship not only to a conference that can be overwhelming and impersonal but to my life as a scholar every day of the year. I would also like to thank Matthew Collins, the Society of Biblical Literature Program Committee, and the Society of Biblical Literature Executive Committee for their guidance and support of this unit. SBL Symposium Series editor Victor H. Matthews and editorial director Bob Buller have excelled throughout this process. I am very grateful to them for the hours they devoted to this manuscript, preparing it for press. Thank you also to Monika Fewell, my graduate student assistant, who collated the indexes.

The work of this group is not complete. The group has become this year (2006) a Society of Biblical Literature Section and will continue to offer a pioneering agenda. May the next ten years of the group be as successful as the first! And may there be joy in the unveiling of new mysteries.

April D. DeConick
Feast of Saint Peter, 2006

What Is Early Jewish and Christian Mysticism?

April D. DeConick

> And what mortal person is it who is able
> To ascend on high,
> To ride on wheels,
> To descend below,
> To search out the inhabited world,
> To walk on the dry land,
> To gaze at His splendor,
> To dwell with His crown,
> To be transformed by His glory,
> To recite praise,
> To combine letters,
> To recite their names,
> To have a vision of what is above,
> To have a vision of what is below,
> To know the explanation of the living,
> And to see the vision of the dead,
> To walk in rivers of fire,
> And to know the lightening?
> And who is able to explain it,
> And who is able to see it?
> —*Hekhalot Zutarti* §§349–350[1]

As a word, "mysticism" has a notorious reputation. Its polymorphic associations make precise meaning difficult to isolate, especially across cultures and eras. It is often used as an antonym for so-called "rationalism," associated with so-called "supernaturalism," in contradistinction to our contemporary scientific view of the

1. All references in this chapter to *hekhalot* texts (excluding *3 Enoch*) are to Peter Schäfer, *Synopse zur Hekhalot-Literatur* (TSAJ 2; Tübingen: Mohr Siebeck, 1981), and English translations of passages from the *hekhalot* texts (excluding *3 Enoch*) are those of idem, *The Hidden and Manifest God: Some Major Themes in Early Jewish Mysticism* (trans. A. Pomerance; Albany: State University of New York Press, 1992).

world. Broadly speaking, it has come to describe for us organized practices used to illicit direct contact with the divine.

As an "-ism," "mysticism" is not an *emic* word, a word actually used by ancient people to describe their experiences. It corresponds to no single term in the ancient literature. In fact, when the early Jews and Christians describe their mystical experiences in a single word, they do so most often by employing the term *apokalypsis*, an "apocalypse" or "revelation." In the Jewish and Christian period-literature, these religious experiences are described *emically* as waking visions, dreams, trances, and auditions that can involve spirit possession and ascent journeys.[2] Usually these experiences are garnered after certain preparations are made or rituals performed, although they can also be the result of rapture. The culmination of the experience is transformative in the sense that the Jewish and Christian mystics thought they could be invested with heavenly knowledge, join the choir of angels in worship before the throne, or be glorified in body.

So "mysticism" is an *etic* term, a modern typology, contemporary analytic vocabulary that we are imposing on the ancients in order to investigate their religiosity. It serves the modern scholar heuristically as a taxonomy aiding our engagement in historical investigation and research. It is a comparative analytic tool created and employed by outsiders to the culture and imposed on insiders. In *etic* terms, it identifies a tradition within early Judaism and Christianity centered on the belief that *a person directly, immediately, and before death can experience the divine, either as a rapture experience or as one solicited by a particular praxis.* This definition, although framed in *etic* terms, remains sensitive to the fact that the early Jews and Christians themselves neither distinguished between unsolicited rapture and solicited invasion experiences—all were "apocalypses"—nor described their experiences in terms of the *unio mystica* so central to later Christian mysticism.

1. A Dynamic Bilateral Tradition

"Early Jewish and Christian mysticism" serves to identify for us a bilateral mystical tradition flowing through Judaism and Christianity during their formative years. Since Judaism and Christianity are companion expressions of Second Temple Judaism, sibling religions that developed simultaneously within comparable historical contextures, the mystical tradition preserved in their literature is rightly characterized as manifestations of Jewish and Christian religiosity in the late Hellenistic and Roman periods. I would go as far as to suggest that the Christian mysticism of this period should be understood as essentially "Jewish," beginning to take on its own individuality only by the mid- to late second cen-

2. See particularly Frances Flannery-Dailey, *Dreamers, Scribes, and Priests: Jewish Dreams in the Hellenistic and Roman Eras* (JSJSup 90; Leiden: Brill, 2004).

tury, as can be seen, for instance, in the Alexandrian school run by Clement and then Origen.

As such, the early Jewish and Christian mystical tradition emerges in what I call, for the sake of brevity, the "period-literature," that is, in Jewish and Christian apocalyptic literature,[3] in the writings of the Jewish theologian Philo of Alexandria,[4] in the Qumran literature,[5] and possibly in the teachings of the Palestinian Jewish school of Yohanan ben Zakkai.[6] There are a growing number of scholars, myself included, who think that these early currents of mysticism form the basis for *merkabah* and *hekhalot* speculation.[7] Subsequently, these mystical traditions

---

3. Gershom Scholem, *Major Trends in Jewish Mysticism* (Jerusalem: Schocken, 1941), 40–79; idem, *Jewish Gnosticism, Merkabah Mysticism and Talmudic Tradition* (New York: Jewish Theological Seminary of America, 1960); idem, *On the Kabbalah and Its Symbolism* (trans. R. Manheim; New York: Schocken, 1965); idem, *Kabbabah* (Jerusalem: Keter, 1974), 8–21; idem, *Origins of the Kabbalah* (ed. R. J. Z. Werblowsky; trans. A. Arkush; Princeton: Princeton University Press, 1987), 18–24; idem, *On the Mystical Shape of the Godhead: Basic Concepts in the Kabbalah* (ed. J. Chipman; trans. J. Neugroschel; New York: Schoken, 1991); Ithamar Gruenwald, *Apocalyptic and Merkavah Mysticism* (AGJU 14; Leiden: Brill, 1980); Christopher R. A. Morray-Jones, "Merkabah Mysticism and Talmudic Tradition" (Ph.D. diss., Cambridge University, 1988).

4. See the classic work by Erwin R. Goodenough, *By Light, By Light* (Amsterdam: Philo, 1969). Kaufmann Kohler first determined that elements of *merkabah* mysticism can be found in Philo ("Merkabah," *JE* 8:500). Henry Chadwick ("St. Paul and Philo of Alexandria," *BJRL* 48 [1966]: 286–307) has suggested that agreements between Paul and Philo may be the result of a common background in Jewish mysticism.

5. Gruenwald, *Apocalyptic and Merkavah Mysticism*, vii; Lawrence H. Schiffman, "Merkavah Speculation at Qumran: The 4Q Serekh Shirot 'Olat ha-Shabbat," in *Mystics, Philosophers, and Politicians: Essays in Jewish Intellectual History in Honor of A. Altmann* (ed. J. Reinharz and D. Swetschinski; Durham, N.C.: Duke University Press, 1982), 15–47; Crispin H. T. Fletcher-Louis, *All the Glory of Adam: Liturgical Anthropology in the Dead Sea Scrolls* (STDJ 62; Leiden: Brill, 2002); Rachel Elior, *The Three Temples: On the Emergence of Jewish Mysticism* (trans. D. Louvish; Oxford: Littman Library of Jewish Civilization, 2004).

6. Cf. Scholem, *Major Trends in Jewish Mysticism*, 41; Ephraim E. Urbach, "Ha-Masorot 'al Torat ha-Sod bi-Tequfat ha-Tannaim," in *Studies in Mysticism and Religion: Presented to G. G. Scholem on His Seventieth Birthday* (ed. A. Altmann; Jerusalem: Magnes, 1967), 2–11; John W. Bowker, "'Merkabah' Visions and the Visions of Paul," *JJS* 16 (1971): 157–73; Jacob Neusner, *A Life of Yohanan ben Zakkai, ca. 1–80 C.E.* (2nd ed.; Leiden: Brill, 1970); Arnold Goldberg, "Der Vortrag des Ma'asse Merkawa: Eine Vermutung zur frühen Merkavamystik," *Jud* 29 (1973): 9–12; Christopher Rowland, "The Influence of the First Chapter of Ezekiel on Jewish and Early Christian Literature" (Ph.D. diss., Cambridge University, 1974); idem, *The Open Heaven: A Study of Apocalyptic In Judaism and Early Christianity* (New York: Crossroad, 1982), 282–83, 303–5; Gruenwald, *Apocalyptic and Merkavah Mysticism*, vii, 73–86; cf. Morray-Jones, "Merkabah Mysticism and Talmudic Tradition"; Jey J. Kanagaraj, *"Mysticism" in the Gospel of John: An Inquiry into Its Background* (JSNTSup 158; Sheffield: Sheffield Academic Press, 1998), 150–58.

7. On this, see now James R. Davila, *Descenders to the Chariot: The People behind the Hekhalot Literature* (JSJSup 70; Leiden: Brill, 2001); Christopher R. A. Morray-Jones, *A Transparent*

were absorbed into the Pharisaic and Tannaitic trajectory,[8] some forms of Christianity,[9] gnostic schools,[10] and later kabbalistic materials.[11]

It goes without saying, I hope, that this literature is vast and variable, representing the opinions, interpretations, and experiences of several different communities, most having no direct historical connection with or influence on the other, but all associated with Second Temple Jewish religiosity in one way or another. It is this familiarity with Second Temple Jewish religiosity, I think, that accounts for the emergence and development of a culturally and historically "unique" mystical tradition whose main features I wish to identify and describe. In this description, I do not write with any pretense or assumption that the tradition was monolithic or static. Rather, I wish to emphasize its dynamism as it erupted within different social and historical contexts. My discussion of "early Jewish and Christian mysticism" should never be taken to suggest the linear progression or "evolution" of the tradition from one historical circumstance to the next. Rather, this tradition surfaces, sometimes simultaneously, within various social contexts and historical circumstances, and the communities involved are

Illusion: The Dangerous Vision of Water in Hekhalot Mysticism: A Source-Critical and Tradition-Historical Inquiry (JSJSup 59; Leiden: Brill, 2002); Vita Daphna Arbel, *Beholders of Divine Secrets: Mysticism and Myth in the Hekhalot and Merkavah Literature* (Albany: State University of New York Press, 2003). For a contrary view, see David J. Halperin, *The Merkabah in Rabbinic Literature* (New Haven: American Oriental Society, 1980), 107–40, 179–85; Peter Schäfer, "New Testament and Hekhalot Literature: The Journey into Heaven in Paul and in Merkavah Mysticism," *JJS* 35 (1984): 19–35.

8. Cf. Schiffman, "Merkavah Speculation at Qumran," 46.

9. On Paul's familiarity with mystical Judaism, see especially now Alan F. Segal, *Paul the Convert: The Apostolate and Apostasy of Saul the Pharisee* (New Haven: Yale University Press, 1990), 34–71; Christopher R. A. Morray-Jones, "Paradise Revisited (2 Cor. 12.1–12): The Jewish Mystical Background of Paul's Apostolate. Part 1: The Jewish Sources" and "Part 2: Paul's Heavenly Ascent and Its Significance," *HTR* 86 (1993): 177–217 and 265–92; John Ashton, *The Religion of Paul the Apostle* (New Haven: Yale University Press, 2000). On Thomasine traditions, see April D. DeConick, *Seek to See Him: Ascent and Vision Mysticism in the Gospel of Thomas* (VCSup 33; Leiden: Brill, 1996); idem, *Recovering the Original Gospel of Thomas: A History of the Gospel and Its Growth* (JSNTSup 286; London: T&T Clark, 2005). On Johannine traditions, refer to April D. DeConick, *Voices of the Mystics: Early Christian Discourse in the Gospels of John and Thomas and Other Ancient Christian Literature* (JSNTSup 157; Sheffield: Sheffield Academic Press, 2001); Kanagaraj, *"Mysticism" in the Gospel of John*.

10. On this, see especially my recent articles, "Heavenly Temple Traditions and Valentinian Worship: A Case for First-Century Christology in the Second Century," in *The Jewish Roots of Christological Monotheism: Papers from the St. Andrews Conference on the Historical Origins of the Worship of Jesus* (ed. C. C. Newman, J. R. Davila, and G. S. Lewis; JSJSup 63; Leiden: Brill, 1999), 308–41; "The True Mysteries: Sacramentalism in the *Gospel of Philip*," *VC* 55 (2001): 225–61; Morray-Jones, *Transparent Illusion*.

11. Cf. Elliot R. Wolfson, *Through a Speculum That Shines: Vision and Imagination in Medieval Jewish Mysticism* (Princeton: Princeton University Press, 1994).

responsible for continually reusing and reshaping this "shared" mystical tradition for their own ends.

2. The Intersection of Hermeneutics and Experience

The persistent core of early Jewish and Christian mysticism is the belief that God or his manifestation can be experienced immediately, *not just after death or eschatologically on the last day*. This belief appears to me to be the consequence of at least two aspects of religiosity during the Second Temple period: hermeneutics and religious experience. It has been unfortunate that past academic discussions of the period-literature has been dogged by our need to treat these as antithetical. Although this attitude has encroached upon our analyses of the period-literature from the pseudepigraphical apocalypses to the Dead Sea Scrolls and the Nag Hammadi collection, it has emerged most aggressively in scholarly discussion of the *merkabah* and *hekhalot* corpus, some scholars insisting that this literature represents mainly exegetical activity,[12] others experiential.[13]

This dichotomy, of course, is a false one that has not served us well, as several studies have suggested.[14] Elliot Wolfson, in fact, thinks that it is impossible to isolate phenomenologically an experience from its literal context, a position that

12. See Halperin, *Merkabah in Rabbinic Literature*; idem, *The Faces of the Chariot* (TSAJ 16; Tübingen: Mohr Siebeck, 1988); Peter Schäfer, "Tradition and Redaction in Hekhalot Literature," *JSJ* 14 (1983): 172–81; idem, "The Aim and Purpose of Early Jewish Mysticism," in idem, ed., *Hekhalot-Studien* (TSAJ 19; Tübingen: Mohr Siebeck, 1988), 289–95; idem, "Merkavah Mysticism and Rabbinic Judaism," *JAOS* 104 (1984): 537–54.

13. Scholem, *Major Trends in Jewish Mysticism*, 45; Gruenwald, *Apocalyptic and Merkavah Mysticism*, 98; Joseph Dan, *Three Types of Jewish Mysticism* (Cincinnati: University of Cincinnati Press, 1984), 8–16; idem, "The Religious Experience of the Merkavah," in *Jewish Spirituality: From the Bible through the Middle Ages* (ed. A. Green; New York: Crossroad, 1986), 289–307; idem, *The Ancient Jewish Mysticism* (Tel Aviv: MOD Books, 1993); Rachel Elior, "The Concept of God in Hekhalot Mysticism," in *Binah, Studies in Jewish Thought II* (ed. J. Dan; New York: Praeger, 1989), 97–120; idem, "Mysticism, Magic, and Angelology," 3–53; idem, "From Earthly Temple to Heavenly Shrines," 217–67; Karl-Erich Grözinger, *Musik und Gesang in der Theologie der fruehen juedischen Literatur* (TSAJ 3; Tübingen: Mohr Siebeck, 1982); Morray-Jones, "Transformation Mysticism"; Karl-Erich Grözinger, "The Names of God and the Celestial Powers: Their Function and Meaning in the Hekhalot Literature," *Jerusalem Studies in Jewish Thought* 6 (1987): 53–69.

14. See Philip Alexander, "The Historical Setting of the Hebrew Book of Enoch," *JJS* 28 (1977): 173; Rowland, *Open Heaven*, 214–40; Wolfson, *Through a Speculum That Shines;* Arbel, *Beholders of Divine Secrets*. For complimentary views regarding mysticism generally, see Bruce Garside, "Language and Interpretation of Mystical Experience," *International Journal for the Philosophy of Religion* 3 (1972): 93–102; Peter Moore, "Mystical Experience, Mystical Doctrine, Mystical Technique," in *Mysticism and Philosophical Analysis* (ed. S. T. Katz; London: Sheldon, 1978), 101–31; Carl A. Keller, "Mystical Literature," in Katz, *Mysticism and Philosophical Analysis*, 59–67.

seems to be akin to that of Steven Katz, who has noted, I think correctly, that "*all* experience is processed through, organized by, and makes itself available to us in extremely complex epistemological ways."[15] It appears to me that this false dichotomy has been set in place because modernists have little patience for the so-called "supernatural," feeling that the "supernatural" can and should be deconstructed in the wake of God's death. But in so doing, we have forced our own demarcation between the natural world and the "supernatural" onto the ancient people we are studying, imposing as well our disposal of everything "supernatural" onto people who profoundly were invested in their "experiences" of God. The ancient Jews and Christians believed that they experienced the sacred, and they wrote about it. These people were deeply religious people whose texts are filled with feelings about and hopes for religious experience as they understood and imagined it.

In this regard, Paul's own firsthand testimony cannot be emphasized enough, because it demonstrates that the first Christian Jews believed that they were recipients of ecstatic experiences both in the form of rapture events and invasions of heaven (Gal 1:12; 1 Cor 15:8; 2 Cor 12:2–4). In the context of this latter discourse, Paul also implied that he knew of other Christian Jews, perhaps associated with the mission of the Jerusalem church, who boasted of mystical experiences (see 2 Cor 11:21–12:11). This is implied by the author of Colossians as well (2:16–18). We have a quite strong tradition that the disciples and members of Jesus' family who formed the initial church in Jerusalem had visions of Jesus following his death (1 Cor 15:5–7). To Paul's firsthand witness we must also add the waking visions of John of Patmos and the dream visions of the Pastor Hermas. Of course, the evidence for mystical experience from secondhand accounts in the early Christian literature is staggering, ranging from the transfiguration of Jesus to the postresurrection appearances to the vision of Stephen.[16]

As a historian, I am not concerned whether these ancient people "actually" experienced God. I can never know this. But this does not make its study pointless. As Bernard McGinn has aptly remarked, "Experience as such is not a part of the historical record. The only thing directly available to the historian … is the evidence, largely in the form of written records."[17] What I wish to understand and map is their belief that God had been and still could—even should—be reached, that the boundaries between earth and heaven could be crossed by engaging in certain religious activities and behaviors reflected in the stories of their primordial ancestors and great heroes.

---

15. Wolfson, *Through a Speculum That Shines,* 120; Steven T. Katz, "Language, Epistemology and Mysticism," in Katz, *Mysticism and Philosophical Analysis,* 26.

16. Mark 9:2–8; Matt 17:1–8; Luke 9:28–36; Mark 16; Matt 28; Luke 24; John 20; *Gos. Pet.* 12–14; Acts 7:55–56.

17. Bernard McGinn, *The Foundations of Mysticism* (New York: Crossroad, 1991), xiv.

It makes no difference to me whether or not we describe these narratives of the heroes as literary or experiential literature, because this distinction misses the point. The point we need to recognize is that the early Jews and Christians who were reading these texts believed that the stories were reports of actual encounters with God. The images and descriptions in these texts deeply affected the way that the early Jews and first Christians described and interpreted their own perceived experiences and the way that they framed their hopes for future experiences.

So this fundamental belief—that the sacred could be experienced—was supported by their reading and exegesis of their scriptures. In turn, it was this belief that the early Jews and Christians wrote about in new texts that they characterized as "revealed" scriptures containing heavenly *gnosis*, the *razim* or "mysteries" of God. Many of these works—from the Jewish and Christian apocalypses to the Nag Hammadi texts—freely retell the biblical narratives under the auspices of an alternative revelation from an angelic being or primeval authority. In several ways, they were providing in these works counterreadings of the old scriptures, recomposing the stories through a new hermeneutic for a contemporary audience.[18] In these new texts, the ancient Jews and Christians shared their revelation of the "things hidden" of the past, present, and future, reinterpreting and rescribing the past to serve their present experiences and future hopes.[19]

The authors of these new texts appear to me to be rebelling against the idea that the truth about the sacred can be reached through intellectual engagement, through normal epistemological routes such as traditional reading and interpre-

18. See Hindy Najman, "Interpretation as Primordial Writing. Jubilees and Its Authority Conferring Strategies," *JSJ* 30 (1999): 379–410; idem, "Torah of Moses: Pseudonymous Attribution in Second Temple Writings," in *The Interpretation of Scripture in Early Judaism and Christianity: Studies in Language and Tradition* (ed. C..A. Evans; Sheffield: Sheffield Academic Press, 2000), 202–16; idem, *Seconding Sinai: The Development of Mosaic Discourse in Second Temple Judaism* (Leiden: Brill, 2003), 41–69; idem, "The Symbolic Significance of Writing in Ancient Judaism," in *The Idea of Biblical Interpretation: Essays in Honor of James L. Kugel* (ed. H. Najman and J. E. Newman; Leiden: Brill, 2004), 139–73.

19. This is a natural function of communal memory. On this, see Maurice Halbwachs, *On Collective Memory* (trans. L. A. Coser; Chicago: University of Chicago Press, 1992), 40; Maurice Halbwach, *The Legendary Topography of the Gospels in the Holy Land* (trans. L. A, Coser; Chicago: University of Chicago Press, 1992), 7; Françoise Zonabend, *The Enduring Memory: Time and History in a French Village* (trans. A. Forster; Manchester: Manchester University Press, 1984), 203; Patrick H. Hutton, "Collective Memory and Collective Mentalities: The Halbwachs-Aries Connection," *RHist* 15 (1988): 314; John Bodnar, *Remaking America: Public Memory, Commemoration, and Patriotism in the Twentieth Century* (Princeton: Princeton University Press, 1992), 75; Iwona Irwin-Zarecka, *Frames of Remembrance: The Dynamics of Collective Memory* (New Brunswick, N.J.: Transaction, 1994), 7; Barbie Zelizer, "Reading the Past against the Grain: The Shape of Memory Studies," *Critical Studies in Mass Communication* 12 (1995): 228; Barry Swartz, *Abraham Lincoln and the Forge of National Memory* (Chicago: University of Chicago Press, 2000), 9.

tation of the scriptures. This is not to say that they shunned intellectual endeavors such as studying Torah, developing hermeneutics, or creating elaborate mythologies to explain questions of cosmogony and theodicy. In fact, in a passage from the *Hekhalot Rabbati* we are told that the mystic must prove his worthiness to enter the seventh heaven by having "read the Torah, prophets and writings, Mishnayot, Midrash, Halakhot and Haggadot," having learned "the interpretation of the Halakhot, prohibition and permission," having abided by "every prohibition that is written in the Torah," and having observed faithfully "all the warnings of the laws, statutes and instructions that were said to Moses at Sinai" (§234)!

What these Jews and Christians seem to me to be saying is that intellectual pursuit of God and "truth" can only advance a person so far spiritually. It can get the person to the gate of the highest heavenly shrine, so to speak, but no further. They insist that knowledge of the sacred itself comes only through the direct experience of God, that is, by actually meeting him face to face. It was this experiential encounter, they thought, that transformed them, that pulled them beyond the limits of their ordinary human senses and perceptions. This new godlike perspective, they believed, would lead to new understandings and revelations, allowing them to reinterpret the concealed truths and hidden histories locked within their sacred scriptures.[20] So here lies the intersection between exegesis and experience. It is at this intersection, this crossroads, that I think we should tarry, rather than running down either of these roads alone.

3. Communal Identities

Early Jewish and Christian mysticism as a tradition does not represent the imagination and opinions of isolated authors as much as those of living religious communities of people. [21] The nature of the communities, of course, varied in terms of their literature, social conventions, and historical characteristics, and any attempt to identify them must be done systematically with reference to particular texts, resisting any temptation to locate a single community responsible for the tradition. While some of the literature is more forthright with communal information, referencing rules of behavior or handbook guidelines for communal life such as those found among the Dead Sea Scrolls or in Paul's letters, most of the period-literature is very perplexing in this regard.

---

20. On this subject, see now Arbel, *Beholders of Divine Secrets;* idem, "Seal of Resemblance, Full of Wisdom and Perfect in Beauty: The Enoch/Metatron Narrative of 3 Enoch and Ezekiel 28," *HTR* 98 (2005): 130–42.

21. For a detailed account of the nature of traditions, see Edward Shils, *Tradition* (Chicago: University of Chicago Press, 1981); and my own, "The 'New' *Traditionsgeschichtliche* Approach," in *Recovering the Original Gospel of Thomas,* 3–37.

Some of the most challenging cases have been with reference to pseudepigraphical literature such as the Jewish and Christian apocalypses, the Nag Hammadi literature, and the *hekhalot* texts. Most scholars have come to think that the Jewish and Christian apocalypses, with their interest in ascension and secret teachings about the last days, can be identified with apocalyptic circles or "conventicles" of pious ascetics anxiously awaiting the imminent eschaton whose social formation could have mirrored John the Baptist's movement or the Qumran community.[22] But this opinion has been challenged recently by other scholars who have pointed to a prophetic group[23] or a collective of priests[24] as equally creditable possibilities. The Enochic corpus within the apocalyptic literature has been singled out recently by a number of scholars who think that it represents not only a socially distinct group in early Judaism but one connected to the community of Jews associated with the Dead Sea Scrolls.[25]

Identification of the "authors" of the *hekhalot* books has been hotly contested in scholarly circles, as has their historical and literary relationship to the apocalypses. According to the early opinion of G. Scholem and several scholars since him, a circle of rabbis may have been responsible for the *hekhalot* literature, literature believed to have formal connections with the Jewish and Christian apocalypses.[26] Other scholars have thought the books should be identified with either a group of people in conflict with the rabbis—people who were protesting rabbinic Judaism through the composition of the *hekhalot* literature—or a postrabbinic elite from the late talmudic period.[27] Others, such as M. Swartz and J. Davila, identify the group outside the formal rabbinic circles, with synagogue

---

22. See Morton Smith, "Palestinian Judaism in the First Century," in *Israel: Its Role in Civilization* (ed. M. Davis; New York: Jewish Theological Seminary, 1956), 69; Michael Stone, "Apocalyptic Literature," in *Jewish Writings of the Second Temple Period: Apocrypha, Pseudepigrapha, Qumran Sectarian Writings, Philo, Josephus* (ed. M. E. Stone; CRINT 2.2; Philadelphia: Fortress, 1984), 430.

23. Robert Hall, "*The Ascension of Isaiah:* Community, Situation, Date, and Place in Early Christianity," *JBL* 109 (1990): 289–306.

24. 28 Flannery-Dailey, *Dreamers, Scribes, and Priests.*

25. See George Nickelsburg, "The Apocalytpic Construction of Reality in *1 Enoch,*" in *Mysteries and Revelations: Apocalyptic Studies since the Uppsala Colloquium* (ed. J. J. Collins and J. H. Charlesworth; JSPSup 9; Sheffield: JSOT Press, 1991); John. J. Collins, *The Apocalytpic Imagination: An Introduction to the Jewish Matrix of Christianity* (New York: Crossroad, 1984), 56–63; Gabriele Boccaccini, *Beyond the Essene Hypothesis* (Grand Rapids: Eerdmanns, 1998); idem, *Enoch and Qumran Origins* (Grand Rapids: Eerdmanns, 2005).

26. Scholem, *Major Trends in Jewish Mysticism,* 41–47; idem, *Jewish Gnosticism, Merkabah Mysticism,* 7–8.

27. Halperin, *Faces of the Chariot,* 34–37, 362–62, 366–87, 429–46; Peter Schäfer, "The Aim and Purpose of Early Jewish Mysticism," in Schäfer, *Hekhalot-Studien,* 293; Schäfer, *Hidden and Manifest God,* 159.

functionaries, poets, scribes, and even shamans, practitioners of ritual power.[28] Rachel Elior has set forth the most comprehensive thesis I am aware of: that the writers of these traditions identify themselves with a disaffected priestly class of the first century C.E., particularly as expressed in the Dead Sea Scrolls and some of the Jewish apocalypses. After the destruction of the temple in 70 C.E., the priestly traditions are carried on by this disaffected class of Jews in the *hekhalot* literature in order to transport the ruined earthly cult into the heavenly spheres.[29]

Communal attribution of the Nag Hammadi collection has come up against its own problems. For years after its discovery, this collection was thought to be a library of ancient gnostic writings. This led to an indiscriminate use of the materials by scholars and the development of theories about an umbrella religion called "Gnosticism," a religion that in fact did not exist. Examination of the collection over the last decade has brought with it the recognition that the texts themselves represent the opinions of different groups of early Jews and Christians and Hermetics. In fact, there are *at least* six religious communities represented in this corpus: Sethian gnostic Christians, Valentinian gnostic Christians, Simonians, followers of Julius Cassianus, Thomasine Christians, and Hermetics. It is significant to note that the majority of Sethian gnostic and Valentinian gnostic texts from the Nag Hammadi literature were written by people who self-identified with the Christian tradition, although some of the materials they rewrote look to be originally Jewish. It appears that those who authored most of these treatises considered themselves esoteric Christians who wished to pursue advanced spiritual study in some type of seminary or Christian study circle or lodge. Consequently, scholars have shifted to speak of them in terms of "schools" rather than religious communities separate from Judaism or Christianity.

This business of identifying social groups responsible for particular texts within the period-literature has been met with varying degrees of success. Here I wish to make it clear that the early Jewish and Christian mystical tradition, in my opinion, is not the purview of a single religious community or to be located in a single community's literature. There is no claim or assumption on my part that the early Jewish and Christian mystical tradition was founded by a particular body of people or maintained by a particular body of people. What I wish to articulate fully is the opinion that we are dealing with a variety of esoteric Jews and Christians over the course of several centuries who self-identified with different religious communities. No single social group was responsible for the practice

---

28. Michael D. Swartz, *Mystical Prayer in Ancient Judaism: An Analysis of Ma'aseh Merkavah* (TSAJ 28; Tübingen: Mohr Siebeck, 1992), 211–23; James R. Davila, "The Hekhalot Literature and Shamanism," in *Society of Biblical Literature 1994 Seminar Papers* (SBLSP 33; Atlanta: Scholars Press, 1994), 767–89; idem, *Descenders to the Chariot*.

29. Elior, *The Three Temples*.

and preservation of this tradition, although there is mounting evidence that one of the main origins of the tradition was within Jewish priestly circles.

At any rate, it should be recognized that various social groups familiar with the mystical tradition employed it with different emphases and applications. This to me is one of the most the fascinating aspects about the study this tradition: how it was shaped and used within various social contexts and time periods. Future study of this tradition will need to articulate more carefully and systematically, I think, the social boundaries of various groups of esoteric Jews and Christians as well as their use and reformulation of the tradition for their own communal purposes and benefit.

4. A "Priestly" Cosmology

The early Jewish and Christian mystical tradition was supported by a distinct hermeneutic, itself based on exegesis of foundational Jewish texts, particularly but not exclusively Gen 1–3; Exod 24; 33, Ezek 1; 8; 10; 40–48, Dan 7; and Isa 6. Although the emphases and elements of this hermeneutic vary across the period-literature, several themes emerge as prominent and tend to cluster in regard to cosmology. The prominence of these themes can be tracked across the canonical and extracanonical Jewish and Christian apocalyptic literature of the Second Temple period, surging through many of the Dead Sea Scrolls and Nag Hammadi texts and flowing through the *merkabah* and *hekhalot* corpus as well as some rabbinic stories. I mention this not to suggest or capture some linear progression of ideas from old to new, as some scholars would like to do, but to underscore the insurgency of these themes in a variety of texts across many centuries and communities of believers. These themes collectively represent the "worldview" or cosmology that undergrids mystical discussions within early Judaism and Christianity, a cosmology that appears to have strong connections with older Jewish priestly traditions, as the work of Rachel Elior in particular has convinced me.[30]

4.1. The Glory of YHWH

The centerpiece of this cosmology is the belief that God has a "body," called the "Glory" or *Kavod* of YHWH.[31] This idea grew out of the study of certain Jewish scriptures, particularly sections of Ezekiel that describe his visions of an enthroned "likeness as the appearance of a Man (*'adam*)," a Man who looked like "fire" with "brightness around him." This is "the appearance of the likeness of the Glory (*kavod*) of YHWH" (Ezek 1:28). This figure is the very manifestation of the hidden YHWH, depicted in the scriptures as an anthropomorphic figure of fire

30. Ibid.

31. For complete coverage, see Jarl Fossum, "Glory," *DDD*, 348–52.

or light (see Ezek 1:27–28; 8:2; Isa 6:1–4). He presides over the created order, oftentimes seated upon his *merkabah,* a special throne consisting of two cherubim with wings spread over the *kapporet,* the lid of the ark of the covenant in the temple (see 1 Chr 28:18; 1 Kgs 6:23–28; 8:6–7; 2 Chr 3:10–11; 5:7–8).

In the period-literature of the Jews and Christians, the God who is seated on the throne in heaven is presented as YHWH's manifestation or *Kavod*. Luminous anthropomorphic descriptions of the "Hidden" God are the culmination of many of the stories of the heroes who journey to glimpse YHWH enthroned. A cluster of images are found in these descriptions. His body is enrobed in a splendid white garment with a face emitting sparks (*1 En.* 14:18–21; *2 En.* 22:1–4; 39:3–8). The *haluq,* or robe, is described as most holy, frightful, and terrible, emitting tremors, terror, and vibration. Upon the inside and outside of the garment, from the top to the bottom, the Tetragrammaton is etched; none of the angels can look directly at the enthroned deity, and the devotee heroes are usually allowed only peeks at his luminous body (*Hekh. Rab.* §102). He is exceedingly beautiful, to the extent that in the *hekhalot* literature the expression that the devotee wishes "to behold the King in his beauty" has become formulaic.[32]

This luminosity of the *Kavod* acted as a mask or screen, functioning in such a way that protected the seer from direct gaze of God's body and certain death, since it was believed that no one could directly see YHWH's face and live. So, on the one hand, it kept YHWH hidden from the direct gaze of his creatures. On the other hand, this covering of light served to reveal God indirectly, so that the presence of God would be available to the adept, usually as a quick glimpse.[33] In the later *hekhalot* literature, the negative effect of the vision is still maintained: "He who looks at him will immediately be torn. He who views his beauty will immediately be poured out like a jug."[34] At the same time, the devotee is told to report "what you have heard" and "what you have seen upon the countenance," a countenance that is revealed "three times daily in the heights" and that "no man perceives and knows" (*Hekh. Rab.* §169). Here we note the paradox of the Hidden God whose very countenance or face cannot be seen, but only the luminous mask of the Glory that simultaneously covers him and reveals him. As Rabbi Akiba relates, "He is, so to say, as we are, but he is greater than everything and his Glory consists in this, that he is concealed from us" (*Hekh. Zut.* §352).

These anthropomorphic descriptions of the Glory look to me to be very early, since such a description is present in Exod 33:18–34:8.[35] In this passage

32. See *Hekh. Rab.* §§198, 248, 259 and §§407–409, 411, 412.

33. Cf. Philo, *Mut.* 7; *Fug.* 165; *1 En.* 14; *2 En.* 22.

34. *Hekh. Rab.* §§159; 102; 104; 105; cf. *Hekh. Zut.* §356.

35. In the Priestly source, the Glory is not anthropomorphic but a phenomenon of light. It is associated with a pillar of cloud or fire that surrounded YHWH as he led the Israelites through the desert or when his presence resided in the tabernacle and then the temple (Exod 16:10; 24:16–17, 43–44; 40:34–35, 38; Num 17:7; 1 Kgs 8:10–11; Lev 9:23–24; 1 Sam 3:3; 4:21). It

Moses wishes to see God's Glory. When he asks permission, God reveals himself to Moses, but only his backside, because "man shall not see me and live." So the Lord said to Moses, "While my Glory passes by I will put you in a cleft of the rock, and I will cover you with my hand until I have passed by; then I will take away my hand and you shall see my back. But my face shall not be seen" (Exod 33:22–23).

Exegetical speculations about the *Kavod* led to the identification of the angelic figure in Dan 7, the "one like a son of man" who is described as the special angel having the "appearance of a man" in Dan 8:15 and 10:18, with the description of the *Kavod* found in Ezek 1:26, the "likeness as the appearance of a man." So in some period-literature, *Kavod*-like angels sit on heavenly thrones and act as the great Judge and God's vicegerent (*1 En.* 45:3; 55:4; 61:8; 62:2: 69:29). For example, Adam and Abel, in the *Testament of Abraham,* have thrones in heaven. Adam is described sitting on a golden throne and having "the appearance of the man" that "was fearsome, like that of the Lord" (Rec A, 11:4). Abel is the great Judge of souls, and he sits on a crystal throne that blazes. He is "a wondrous man shining like the sun, like unto a son of God" (12:5 rec. A). In the *Apocalypse of Abraham* the angel who has God's Name, Yahoel, is depicted as being "in the likeness of a man" and possessing a "golden scepter" (11:3).

Such honor is also accorded to Moses in the *Exagoge* of Ezekiel the playwright. Moses has a vision of a noble "man" seated on an enormous throne on the top of Mount Sinai. This *Kavod*-like figure gives Moses his crown and scepter, then gets up from the throne so that Moses can take his place. This fabulous scene appears to be built from Exod 24:10: "And they saw the God of Israel, and there was under his feet as it were a pavement of sapphire stone, like the very heaven for clearness." Interpretations of this passage in other literature take it to be a throne vision of the Glory or *Kavod.*[36]

Perhaps the most well-known angelic vice-regent is Metatron, the great "enthroned" angel described throughout the *hekhalot* literature.[37] Many scholars have speculated about the origins and meaning of his name, with almost a dozen suggested possibilities, none of which has emerged as the favorite.[38] He is called the "little YHWH," "youth," and "Prince of the World" and is accorded many of the characteristics of the *Kavod,* although one tradition suggests that he is whipped

---

appears that we are seeing in these texts an association of the Glory with cultic practices, since it is directly said to "fill" the tabernacle and temple (Exod 40:34–35; 1 Kgs 8:10–11), be present at the altar of sacrifice (Lev 9:23–24), and function as some sort of lamp connected with the ark (see Exod 27:20–21).

36. *Targum Onqelos*; *Targum Pseudo-Jonathan; b. Men.* 43b; *Memar Marqah* in A. E. Cowley, ed., *The Samaritan Liturgy* (Oxford: Clarendon, 1909), 25.

37. For an outstanding presentation of the materials about Metatron, see Andrei Orlov, *The Enoch-Metatron Tradition* (TSAJ 107; Tübingen: Mohr Siebeck, 2005).

38. Ibid., 92–96.

for taking a seat on his throne (*b. Hag.* 15a). The traditions of Enoch, of course, are bound up with this angel, traditions that relate Enoch's bodily transformation into this great angel. The destructive, almost infernal, transformation brings his body into conformity with the enormity of God's body, when he "was enlarged and increased in size until [he] matched the world in length and breadth. He made to grow on me 72 wings, 36 on one side and 36 on the other.... He fixed in me 365,000 eyes.... There was no sort of splendor, brilliance, brightness, or beauty in the luminaries of the world that he failed to fix in me" (*3 En.* 9).

The body of God tradition is perhaps most developed in the *Shi'ur Qomah* ("Measure of the Divine Body") material, where the dimensions and the corporeal appearance of God are enumerated in great detail. These materials describe the revelation by Metatron of the "measurement of the body" to the seers, Rabbi Akiba and Rabbi Ishmael. The materials depict anthropomorphic details of the body of God along with the mystical names of God's gigantic limbs. The enormity of the body is a theme that can be traced to earlier texts, even to some located in the New Testament.[39]

This Jewish *Kavod* doctrine had a profound impact on the development of early Christian Christologies. For instance, Paul describes Jesus as the "image" or "form" of God (2 Cor 4:4, Col 1:15; Phil 2:6). In John's Gospel Jesus is depicted as God's Glory or *Kavod* descended to earth (1:14; 2:11; 11:40; 12:23, 28, 41; 13:32; 17:1–5, 22–23). Descriptions of Jesus as the High Priest of the heavenly temple and depictions of Jesus as the Lamb all are heir to this tradition (Heb 3:1; 4:14–16; 5:1–10; Rev 5:6–14; 7:13–8:1; 14:1–5).

4.2. The Heavenly Temple

The celestial realm is understood to be a heavenly version of the Jerusalem temple. The various heavens are the *hekhalot,* shrine rooms or sanctuaries within the temple. In the approach of the highest heaven, each successive room is more holy than the last, the holy of holies where God's manifestation resides. These firmaments generally number seven. The association with the number seven appears to be a reference to the seven planetary spheres in combination with aspects of the temple that number seven: seven gates, seven steps, the seven-branched lampstand (Josephus, *Ant.* 3.6.7; *War* 5.5.5; 7.5.5), and even seven levels as enumerated by Rabbi Jose: the area within the balustrade, the court of women, the court of Israel, the court of the priests, the area between the altar and the entrance to the temple, the sanctuary, and the holy of holies.[40] As Christopher

39. See Eph 3:18–19; 4:13; Col 1:18–19; 2:9; Epiphanius, *Pan.* 30.17.6; *2 En.* 39:3–6; *Merk. Rabb.* §§688–704.

40. André Neher, "Le voyage mystique des quatre," *RHR* 140 (1951): 73–76.

Morray-Jones correctly notes, "The temple is not 'in' heaven; its seven 'sanctuaries' are the heavens."[41]

The angels associated with this heavenly temple are the temple's functionaries, its priests performing cultic activities there.[42] They are the guardians of the covenant and the heavenly temple and its gates, as well as "servants of the throne," petitioners and worshipers offering "sacrifices" and recitations to God. Prayers, praises, thanksgivings, blessings, and glorifications are sung as liturgies, filtering up through the heavens. The angelology assumed by these texts is very complex, with several grades of angels, most having names that are permutations of the divine Name or an attribute of God.

In fact, speculations about the divine Name and associations of it with various angels are quite dominant in the period-literature. Usually there is one highly exalted angel, such as the "Angel of the Lord," the "Angel of the Countenance," "Metatron," or "Christ."[43] Sometimes it is difficult to differentiate between this exalted angel and God's glorious manifestation, the *Kavod* or *Doxa,* who is enthroned on the *merkabah* seat in the holy of holies, the *devir,* the highest of the heavens. As we will see, the celestial *merkabah* is the special wheeled chariot made of four sacred creatures whose outspread wings formed the seat itself, much like the ark of the covenant in the earthly temple. The throne in some cases is exalted, personified as an object of worship and a representation of God (see *Hekh. Rab.* §§236, 257).

As the work of Rachel Elior has especially pointed out, all aspects of the celestial temple in fact correlate to an ideal aspect of the earthly temple, including associations with the liturgical calendar, the seasons, creation, the garden of Eden, life and fertility, betrothal, and sanctification. Priestly concerns such as holiness and purity are consistent, even excessive, themes. Even angels must bathe in fiery rivers flowing near the throne. Humans crossing the heavenly threshold must be

41. See pages 148–59 in this volume.

42. Elior, *The Three Temples.*

43. See Jarl E. Fossum, *The Name of God and the Angel of the Lord: Samaritan and Jewish Concepts of Intermediation and the Origins of Gnosticism* (WUNT 36; Tübingen: Mohr Siebeck, 1985), 177–91, 319–29; idem, "Jewish Christian Christology and Jewish Mysticism," *VC* 37 (1983): 260–87; Christopher Rowland, "The Vision of the Risen Christ in Rev. 1:13ff: The Debt of Early Christology to an Aspect of Jewish Angelology," *JTS* 31 (1980): 1–11; idem, *Open Heaven,* 94–113; Wesley Carr, *Angels and Principalities: The Background, Meaning, and Development of the Pauline Phrase "Hai Archai kai hai Exousai"* (SNTSMS 42; Cambridge: Cambridge University Press, 1997), 143–47; Jean Daniélou, "Trinité et angélologie dans la théologue judéo-chrétienne," *RSR* 45 (1957): 5–41; idem, *The Origins of Latin Christianity* (London: Darton, Longman & Todd, 1977): 149–52; Wolfson, *Through a Speculum That Shines,* 255–69; Gilles Quispel, "Gnosticism and the New Testament," *VC* 19 (1965): 70–85; idem, "The Origins of the Gnostic Demiurge," in *Kyriakon: Festschrift Johannes Quaesten* (ed. P. Granfield and J. A. Jungmann; Münster: Aschendorff, 1970), 1:271–76; idem, "The Demiurge in the Apocryphon of John," in *Nag Hammadi and Gnosis* (ed. R. McL. Wilson; Leiden: Brill, 1978), 1–34.

exceedingly righteous and able to endure a bodily transfiguration into a flaming being. One of the reasons that this particular cosmology appears to have developed was as a guarantee that the temple cult would not be disrupted even when the priesthood and the earthly temple in Jerusalem was threatened, contaminated, or destroyed. The continuation of a holy cultus in the heavenly temple meant that continuity of creation and life would be maintained, a standard concern of the Jewish priests since the time of ancient Israel.[44]

4.3. The *Merkabah*

The chariot-throne from Ezek 1 in the period-literature is located in the heavenly temple, in the highest and most holy heaven. A fabulous passage from *Massekhet Hekhalot* highlights its prominence:

> And the throne of Glory is high up in the air, and the appearance of his Glory is like the appearance of the *hashmal*. And a diadem of brightness is upon his head, and the crown of the explicit Name is upon his brow. One half of him is fire, and the other half is hail. On his right is life, and on his left is death. And a scepter of fire is in his hand. And the curtain is parted in two before him, and seven angels who were created in the beginning minister before him inside the curtain. (§28)

This *merkabah* is described as a chariot with wheels like the sun (*1 En.* 14:18–21). It is a crystal throne, blazing like fire, called the "Throne of Great Glory" (*T. Abr.* 8:5 rec. B; 12:5 rec. A). In the *hekhalot* tradition, the throne is not only wheeled, but hovers like a bird underneath God's splendor (*Hekh. Rab.* §98, MS Vatican). God, in fact has remained seated on his throne since its creation, and will not leave it for all eternity (*Hekh. Rab.* §119).

There is much speculation about the "faces" of the "chariot of cherubim"—the faces of the lion, the eagle, the ox, and the man.[45] One tradition even identifies the man's face with the patriarch Jacob, whose "image" was engraved on the throne.[46] Jarl Fossum has noted that the *Fragmentary Targum* on Gen 1:28 (MS Vatican) and the *editio princeps* reprinted in the London Polyglot (Venice) explicitly states that the image of Jacob was "upon" the throne, not engraved on the throne, as the other Targumim. This is highly significant when it is realized that *Tg. Ezek.* 1:26 says that some people think the Glory on the throne is the form of Jacob (MS Montefiore no. 7). So some appealed to the likeness of Jacob as the *Kavod*. The

---

44. Elior, *The Three Temples*.

45. 1 Chr 28:18 LXX; Sir 49:8; cf. *Hekh. Zut.* Sections 368–74; *Hyp. Arch.* 29; *Orig. World* 32.

46. *Targum Pseudo-Jonathan; Targum Neofiti I; Fragmentary Targum; Gen. Rab.* 68:12

angels, who long to see the Glory but cannot, descend to earth to look upon his image in the flesh![47]

In fact, in some texts the *merkabah* is anthropomorphized like God himself. The throne holds converse with God, the King, even singing glorious hymns of praise to him (*Hekh. Rab.* §§94, 99, 154, 161–162, 634, 687, 686). So glorious is the throne-chariot in these traditions that there may have been some who thought it an object worthy of veneration, if not worship. So in the *Hekhalot Rabbati* we find the statement that the throne, like God, will "reign in all generations" but that God is to be "honored beyond the throne of your Glory" and to be "appreciated more than your precious vessel" (§257).

Perhaps the most intriguing tradition about the *merkabah* is the journey that devotees thought they could make to stand before it and hymn in the presence of the Glory. In the *hekhalot* materials there is a unique development of this tradition, that the ascending devotee is a "descender to the chariot," the *yored merkabah*. What this means and how it developed has really not been adequately resolved, in my opinion, although two explanations stand out from the rest. Elliot Wolfson has made a convincing case that the phrase refers to the enthronement of the devotee during the final stage of ascent,[48] and Christopher Morray-Jones has offered in this volume an essay that suggests that the term is linked to the "downward" posture assumed by the devotee so that the "ascent" through the heavens could also be viewed as a "descent" within the "temple" of the body. The descender to the chariot is very special, very holy, because he has transcended the natural boundaries of his humanity and entered the realms of the sacred. The journey of ascent and descent is fraught with grave danger and oral examinations administered by the guardian angels (see *Hekh. Rab.* §§224–258). He must be very knowledgeable of the Torah, the Prophets, the Writings, the Mishnah, the midrashim, the halakah, the haggadah, and their interpretations and their practical observation (§234). He must show the guardians of the gates seals and know passwords (§236). If he fails, destruction or insanity result. But if he succeeds, his descent to the *merkabah* can be made.

4.4. The Heavenly Curtain

Spread in front of the *merkabah* is the secret heavenly curtain, the *pargod*. This is the heavenly counterpart of the veil, the *paroket*, which divided the holy of holies from the *hekhal* in the temple in Jerusalem (Exod 26:31; 2 Chr 3:14). Upon

47. Jarl E. Fossum *The Image of the Invisible God: Essays on the Influence of Jewish Mysticism on Early Christology* (NTOA 30; Göttingen: Vandenhoeck & Ruprecht, 1995), 135–42.

48. Elliot Wolfson, "*Yeridah la-Merkavah*: Typology of Ecstasy and Enthronement in Ancient Jewish Mysticism," in *Mystics of the Book: Themes, Topics, and Typologies* (ed. R. A. Herrera; New York: Lang, 1993), 13–44.

the heavenly curtain, the thoughts and deeds of all the human generations are recorded, including future ones. Rabbi Ishmael stresses that he saw "with his own eyes" all the deeds of Israel and the Gentiles "until the end of time" printed on the curtain (*3 En.* 45:1–6). The printed record of humanity's deeds on the curtain was for YHWH's benefit on the Day of Judgment, when one glance examines everyone's deeds and determines everyone's judgment.[49]

Ultimately, the heavenly curtain screened off the Kavod from the angels because of the destructive nature of its view (*Tg. Job* 26:9; *3 En.* 22:6 rec. B). But, as Christopher Morray-Jones has noticed, the curtain also functions as a celestial firmament, dividing the seventh heaven from the lower heavens and sanctuaries.[50]

5. An Internalized Apocalypse

Modern scholars have been slow to recognize that early Jewish and Christian mysticism is a major dimension of Jewish and Christian apocalyptic thought, even though the ancients themselves call these experiences *apokalypses*. There has been a tendency in academia to equate apocalypticism with eschatology, as if an *apokalypsis* were the last day.[51] So visions of destruction, retribution, and salvation have become associated exclusively with the study of the apocalyptic, ignoring its atemporal aspects.

This faulty understanding of apocalyptism, which concentrates almost exclusively on the revelation of end-time phenomena, is reflected in the standard definition of the term found in the well-respected *Semeia* volume on the subject: "Apocalypse is a genre of revelatory literature with a narrative framework, in which a revelation is mediated by an otherworldly being to a human recipient, disclosing a transcendent reality which is both temporal, insofar as it envisages eschatological salvation, and spatial as it involves another, supernatural world."[52] To be fair, this understanding of apocalypticism does not appear to have been only the misconception of the SBL Genres Project but has been around in the scholarly prose for a very long time.

In fact, a careful reading of the Second Temple apocalypses tells us that eschatology, the secret revelation of the imminence of the end, is only part of the discussion. The other part is the mystical, the belief in the immediate and

49. Frg. T.-S. K21.95.J, fol. 2b, lines 2–11, in Peter Schäfer, ed., *Geniza-Fragmente zur Hekhalot-Literatur* (TSAJ 6; Tübingen: Mohr Siebeck, 1984), 133.

50. Morray-Jones, *Transparent Illusion*, 153–72.

51. See David S. Russell, *The Method and Message of Jewish Apocalyptic* (Philadelphia: Westminster, 1964); Walter Schmithals, *The Apocalyptic Movement* (Nashville: Abingdon, 1975); John J. Collins, "Introduction: Towards the Morphology of a Genre," *Semeia* 14 (1979): 1–20; idem, *The Apocalyptic Imagination: An Introduction to the Jewish Matrix of Christianity* (New York: Crossroad, 1992), 1–32.

52. Collins, "Introduction," 6.

direct experience of God. This belief has to do with religious experience, the act of revelation itself, the encounter with God that results in the devotee's immediate personal transformation and the uncovering of God's mysteries.

This mystical dimension of apocalyptic thought appears to me to have been developed by esoteric Jews and Christians in response to unfulfilled redemptive promises during times when hopes for their fulfillment were being historically challenged. The redemptive myth itself was founded on what seems to have been a standard Jewish myth in the Second Temple period, that there existed a heavenly *Anthropos* who was thought to have come forth from God prior to creation.[53]

This tale was inspired by rereading Gen 1:3 in Greek. Since the word *phos* can mean both "light" (τό φῶς) and "man" (ὁ φώς), exegetes determined that a heavenly Man of Light came forth when God said, "Let there be *phos*!"[54] This luminous heavenly Man was portrayed as God's partner in creation.[55] The *Anthropos* was identified further with both the *Kavod* and the cosmic Adam and thus was perceived to be the Image of God. This Image, they thought, came into existence on the first day of creation and acted as a cosmogonic agent.[56] Later Jewish mystical traditions, in fact, explicitly call the primordial luminous Man the *Yotser Bereshith,* the "creator in the beginning."[57] In *3 Enoch* the heavenly Man and *Kavod*-like Metatron is given a crown etched with the letters of light by which "all the necessities of the world and all the orders of creation were created" (13:1–2). Christian texts, Hermetic texts, and gnostic texts, all influenced by this old Jewish mythology, also preserve reference to the demiurgic aspect of the *Anthropos*.[58]

According to this standard Jewish myth, the human being was created after the likeness of the *Anthropos*.[59] Since the first human being was created in God's image according to the Genesis story, this meant for some thinkers that

53. Fossum, *Name of God,* 266–91.

54. On this, see Gilles Quispel, "Ezekiel 1:26 in Jewish Mysticism and Gnosis," *VC* 34 (1980): 6; Fossum, *Name of God,* 280.

55. Later some rabbis reacted against this concept. See *b. Sanh.* 38b; *t. Sanh.* 8:7.

56. See especially Jarl E. Fossum, "The Adorable Adam of the Mystics and the Rebuttal of the Rabbis," in *Geschichte-Tradition-Reflexion: Festschrift für Martin Hengel zum 70. Geburtstag* (ed. H. Cancik, H. Lichtenberger, and P. Schäfer; Tübingen: Mohr Siebeck, 1996), 1:529–39.

57. On this, see Scholem, *Major Trends in Jewish Mysticism,* 65.

58. See John 1:1–5, 9–10; *Corp. herm.* 1.6–13; 13.19; *Gos. Egy.* 3.49.10–12; 4.61.8–11.

59. See Philo, *QG* 1.32; 2.62; *Opif.* 25; 69; 139; *Leg.* 3.96; *Her.* 230–231; *Fug.* 68–71; *Apoc. Abr.* 23:4–6; *T. Abr.* 11:4 rec. See also Hans-Martin Schenke, *Der Gott "Mensch" in der Gnosis: Ein religionsgeschichtlicher Beitrag zur Diskussion über die paulinische Anschauung von der Kirche als Leib Christi* (Göttingen: Vandenhoeck & Ruprecht, 1962); Fossum, *Name of God,* 266–91; Phillip B. Munoa III, *Four Powers in Heaven: The Interpretation of Daniel 7 in the Testament of Abraham* (JSPSup 28; Sheffield: Sheffield Academic Press, 1998), 85–90. The most recent article by Andrei Orlov brings together descriptions of the luminous Adam and the creation of the first human being after the Image: "'Without Measure and Without Analogy': The Tradition of the Divine Body in *2 (Slavonic) Enoch,*" *JJS* 56 (2005): 224–44.

Adam must have been a reflection of the *Kavod*. This aspect of the myth may explain some of the Adamic traditions that depict the veneration of the created Adam.[60] Be that as it may, the image of the first human being was said to have been so bright that it even surpassed the brightness of the sun.[61] His body, like the cosmic *Anthropos*, was so immense that it filled the universe from one end to the other.[62]

But this radiant image or immense body either was taken away from Adam or altered as a consequence of his fall, according to this myth.[63] Aspects of this speculation were rooted in discussion about Gen 3:21, where God made Adam and Eve "garments of skin and clothed them." It was concluded that Adam and Eve originally must have worn garments of light that were lost as a consequence of their sin.[64]

This type of exegesis brought with it the consequence that the human being was in something of a predicament. Was it possible to restore this radiant image, to return the human being to his prelapsarian glory? Most early Jews and Christians thought that piety was the key to such transformation of the soul. If the person lived his or her life in obedience to the commandments (God's and/or Jesus'), the glory that Adam had lost would be restored at death or the eschaton. This they taught by way of their doctrine of the resurrection of the dead, the restoration of the whole person as a glorious angelic-like body reflecting God's Image.[65]

---

60. See *Life Adam and Eve* 13.2–14.2; *3 Bar.* 4; *2 En.* 22; Michael Stone, "The Fall of Satan and Adam's Penance: Three Notes on the Books of Adam and Eve," in *Literature on Adam and Eve: Collected Essays* (ed. G. Anderson, M. Stone, and J. Tromp; SVTP 15; Leiden: Brill, 2000).

61. Louis Ginzberg, *The Legends of the Jew* (7 vols.; Philadelphia: Jewish Publication Society, 1928), 5:97 n. 69; Benjamin Murmelstein, "Adam, ein Beitrag zur Messiaslehre," *WZKM* 35 (1928): 255 n. 3; Willy Staerk, *Die Erlösererwartung in den östlichen Religionen* (Stuttgart: Kohlhammer, 1938), 11.

62. See *Gen. Rab.* 8:1; 21:3; 24:2; *Lev. Rab.* 14:1; 18:2; *Pirke R. El.* 11; *Chronicles of Jerahmeel* 6–12; Orlov, "Without Measure and Without Analogy."

63. See *Gen. Rab.* 11–12; *b. Mo'ed Qatan* 15b; *b. 'Aboda Zara* 8a; *Tanh. Buber Bereshit* 18; cf. *Gen. Rab.* 8.1; *b. Hag.* 12a; *Pesiq. Rab. Kah.* 1.1; Philip Alexander, "From Son of Adam to Second God: Transformation of the Biblical Enoch," in *Biblical Figures outside the Bible* (ed. M. E. Stone and T. A Bergen; Harrisburg, Pa.: Trinity Press International, 1998), 102–11.

64. See April D. DeConick and Jarl E. Fossum, "Stripped before God: A New Interpretation of Logion 37 in the Gospel of Thomas," *VC* 45 (1991): 124 n. 8. For later rabbinic reports, see Moshe Idel, "Enoch Is Metatron," *Imm* 24/25 (1990): 220–40. There is also a tradition that understands the verbs in Gen 3:21 to be pluperfects, referring to the status of Adam and Eve *before* the fall. Thus *Gen. Rab.* 20.12 states that the scroll of Rabbi Meir read אור "light" instead of עור, "skin." The Targums presuppose this wording, since they read "garments of glory (יקאר)."

65. Alan F. Segal, *Life after Death: A History of the Afterlife in the Religions of the West* (New York: Doubleday, 2004).

But it appears that some Jews and Christians felt that the lost Image could be restored, at least provisionally, *before death,* that paradise and its fruits could be had now. That this mythological paradigm was religiously operable outside the literary context is clear to me when we examine, for instance, the literature of the Dead Sea Scrolls or Philo's account of the Therapeutae or Paul's epistles. In this literature we have *firsthand accounts* of communities of believers involved in religious activities to achieve mystical transformation of the body in the here and now and the elevation of the adept to the community of angels.[66] Many of the first Christians contemplated their own ascensions into heaven and bodily transformations, believing that Jesus' exaltation and transformation had opened heaven's gate for them. Paul believed that the faithful who were possessed by Christ's spirit could start experiencing the transformation into the image of God while still on earth but that full glorification would only occur after death.[67] Others Christians promoted premortem flights into heaven and full transformation in the present as the result (*Gos. Thom.* 15, 19, 37, 50, 59, 83, 84, 108).

This shift in thought to concentrate on the fulfillment of God's promises in the present appears to me to have been largely a consequence of failed eschatological expectations. Since the mystical tradition was a "vertical" dimension of Jewish apocalyptic thought running perpendicular to the eschatological,[68] this shift would have been easy to make. It moved the eschatological encounter with God and promises of bodies glorified from the future sphere to the present, from an external cosmic apocalyptic event to an internal apocalyptic experience. This meant that the traditional rewards reserved for the last day became available to believers *now* through personal mystical encounters with the divine, encounters that were frequently described by these esoteric Jews and Christians in terms of a heavenly journey that culminated in a vision of God or his *Kavod.* This visionary experience initiated the process of the person's transfiguration whereby his or her body became "angelic" and was "glorified."[69] Since some early Christians identi-

66. See John Strugnell, "The Angelic Liturgy at Qumran—4QSerek Šîrôt 'Ôlat Haššabbāt," in *Congress Volume: Oxford, 1959* (VTSup 7; Leiden: Brill, 1960), 318–45; Lawrence H. Schiffman, "Merkavah Speculation at Qumran," in Reinharz and Swetschinski, *Mystics, Philosophers and Politicians,* 15–47; Carol Newsom, *Songs of the Sabbath Sacrifice: A Critical Edition* (HSS 27; Atlanta: Scholars Press, 1985); idem, "Merkavah Exegesis in the Qumran Sabbath Shirot," *JSJ* 38 (1987): 11–30; Morton Smith, "Two Ascended to Heaven—Jesus and the Author of 4Q491," in *Jesus and the Dead Sea Scrolls* (ed. J. H. Charlesworth; New York: Doubleday, 1992), 290–301; Fletcher-Louis, *All the Glory of Adam;* Segal, *Paul the Convert*; Morray-Jones, "Paradise Revisited."

67. Rom 7:24; 8:10, 13, 29; 2 Cor 3:18; Phil 3:21; 1 Cor 15:49; Col 3:9; 2 Cor 5:15–6:1.

68. Rowland, *Open Heaven.*

69. Regarding the rabbinic ambiguity about whether or not one can see God, refer to Gruenwald, *Apocalyptic and Merkavah Mysticism,* 93–97, who proposes that the negative opinion on seeing God in this literature rules out "the possibility of a direct visual encounter with God." Ira Chernus, "Visions of God in Merkabah Mysticism," *JSJ* 13 (1982): 123–46, outlines all of

fied Jesus with the *Kavod* or *Doxa*, they talked about visionary journeys to see Jesus as well as the Father.

The mechanism for vision *apotheosis* appears to be Greek in origin.[70] It was based on an ancient physiology that suggested that the "seen" image enters the seer through his eye and transforms his soul: "The pleasure which comes from vision enters by the eyes and makes its home in the breast; bearing with it ever the image.... it impresses it upon the mirror of the soul and leaves there its image" (Achilles Tatius, *Leuc. Clit.* 5.13). This idea is as old as Plato, who suggested that the vision of the object touched the eye and was transmitted to the soul. In fact, he uses the image of the soul as a block of wax upon which a vision received is imprinted like a stamp of a signet ring (*Theaet.* 191a–196c).

For these mystical Jews and Christians, this must have meant that a vision of the *Kavod*, the Image of God, literally resulted in the "restamping" of God's image on the soul, restoring it to its original Form and Glory. In the ancient language of their mythology, they said that they would become "glorified," "exalted," or "angelic."[71] They would be clothed in shining white garments, become "standing" angels worshiping God before his throne, be transformed into beings of fire or light, be "enthroned," regain their cosmic-sized bodies, or be invested with God's Name or Image.[72]

Ultimately, even the mind would surpass normal human limits of comprehension as it too became godlike. Enoch relates regarding his own transformation into the angel Metatron:

> The Holy One, blessed be he, revealed to me from that time onward all the mysteries of wisdom, all the depths of the perfect Torah and all the thoughts of human hearts. All mysteries of the world and all the orders of nature stand revealed before me as they stand revealed before the Creator. From that time onward, I looked and beheld deep secrets and wonderful mysteries. Before anyone thinks in secret, I see his thought. Before he acts, I see his act. There is nothing in heaven above or deep within the earth concealed from me. (*3 En.* 11:1–3)

---

the passages in mystical literature where visions of God are mentioned and concludes that the majority of mystics "did think it possible for certain individuals, both human and celestial, to see God" (141). See also Nathaniel Deutsch, *The Gnostic Imagination: Gnosticism, Mandaeism, and Merkabah Mysticism* (Brill's Series in Jewish Studies 13; Leiden: Brill, 1995), 75–79.

70. For a broader discussion, see DeConick, *Voices of the Mystics*, 34–67. On the subject of transformation, see also Morray-Jones, "Transformational Mysticism"; Martha Himmelfarb, *Ascent to Heaven in Jewish and Christian Apocalypses* (New York: Oxford University Press, 1993), 47–71.

71. See Kevin P. Sullivan, *Wrestling with Angels: A Study of the Relationship between Angels and Humans in Ancient Jewish Literature and the New Testament* (AGJU 55; Leiden: Brill, 2004).

72. See Wolfson, *Through a Speculum That Shines*, 84–85 and n. 46; idem, "*Yeridah la-Merkavah*," 13–44.

6. Communal Practices

Avenues for mystical transformation other than the visionary were also popular in Judaism and Christianity, including asceticism, imitation, washing, spirit possession, eating "divine" food or drink, anointing the body with a sacramental oil or dew, chanting permutations of God's Name, and so forth. Thus the period-literature is filled with references to practical activities associated with a mystical praxis.

The literature does not simply contain indirect references to ritual washing, anointing, studying of sacred texts, vigils, sacrifice, fasting, withdrawal, and sexual asceticism in the narratives of the heroes. The period-literature also contains pieces of actual liturgy, prayers, hymns, repetitive chants, and "magical" formulas, as well as references to periods of silence. Many of these are suggestive of communal behavior, initiation rites, and contemplative practices, although individual activity such as incubation and dream visions are also known. Some of the references point to the development of "magical" practices, at least as evidenced in the *hekhalot* handbooks,[73] and sacramental ritual behavior, particularly (but not exclusively) in the Christian tradition.

The activities appear to have varied widely, so the exploration of practices as they were developed in individual communities is essential. No single praxis can be sifted out of the period-literature, so praxis must be studied as variant practices in particular community settings whenever possible. What the community at Qumran was doing in order to participate in the angelic liturgy was different from what the Sethian gnostics were doing to ascend into the Godhead to practice the soul-journey home. What the Therapeutae were doing to become "citizens of heaven while on earth" was different from what the *hekhalot* practitioners were doing to "descend to the chariot."

What particularly has fascinated me as a scholar of Christian origins is the reformation of the mystical praxis into the sacramental rituals of the early Christian church and the "gnostic" schools. The sacraments seem to have been set in place to "democratize" the mystical, making the presence of God regularly available to believers—baptism, anointing, and the Eucharist all affecting the transformation of the soul and the integration of the Holy Spirit and the Christ into the soul. These rituals were understood to function in such a way that the person was reintegrated into the divine immediately and ontologically. Some texts even narrate this belief in terms of the ascent-journey motif! That is, the ritual is presented *as the vehicle* that elevates and transports the person into the sacred realm so that he or she can come into the very presence of God.

---

73. On this, see particularly Michael Swartz, *Scholastic Magic: Ritual and Revelation in Early Jewish Mysticism* (New Jersey: Princeton University Press, 1996); Rebecca Macy Lesses, *Ritual Practices to Gain Power: Angels, Incantations, and Revelation in Early Jewish Mysticism* (HTS 44; Harrisburg, Pa.: Trinity Press International, 1998).

Lately I have come to understand many of narratives in the apocalyptic and mystical texts to be "verbal icons," not simply "imaginative narratives" recounting the heavenly journeys and visions of the great heroes of the tradition but "verbal maps" that functioned to actually bring the devotee into the presence of God. Not unlike later Byzantine pictorial icons, meditation upon the verbal images would have expressed and made present the sacred reality. The person who contemplated these texts would have been making himself ready to receive the mysteries that would be revealed directly and immediately to him. Through verbal recitation of the narrative or mental recall of the memorized text, the devotee too would have journeyed into the heavenly spheres and the presence of God, embracing this present experience through its likeness to that which was past.[74] His ability to decipher the meaning of the words written would have provided his own journey into the heavenly world. What mattered to the devotee was not so much following the map in terms of sequential geography but rather his ability mentally to picture the "places" where the hero had gone before, seeing again what the great heroes of the Jews and Christians had themselves seen. In so doing, he would have appropriated the text, and its mysteries, for himself.

This appropriation, in my opinion, results in part from the fact that during this period the apocalypse had been internalized. The cosmic had collapsed into the personal. The period-literature indicates that some Jews and Christians hoped to achieve *in the present* the eschatological dream, the restoration God's Image *within themselves*—the resurrection and transformation of their bodies into the glorious bodies of angels and their minds into the mind of God. They developed various means to achieve this, including visionary flights to heaven, eating divine food and drinking divine drink, immersing themselves in water, anointing their bodies with sacred oil, intoning God's Name, and so on. As Alan Segal insightfully comments, "The myth suggests the goal; the mysticism gives the practical way to achieve it."[75] Although the employment of particular practices varied from community to community, all appear to me to have been vying for the glories and power of *paradise now*.

---

74. Mary Carruthers, *The Craft of Thought: Meditation, Rhetoric, and The Making of Images, 400–1200* (Cambridge: Cambridge University Press, 1998), 68–69.

75. See page 30 in this volume.

Part 1:
Hermeneutics and Experience

Religious Experience and the Construction of the Transcendent Self

Alan F. Segal

> At that time shall arise Michael, the great prince who has charge of your people. And there shall be a time of trouble, such as never has been since there was a nation till that time; but at that time your people shall be delivered, every one whose name shall be found written in the book. And many of those who sleep in the dust of the earth shall awake, some to everlasting life, and some to shame and everlasting contempt. And those who are wise shall shine like the brightness of the firmament; and those who turn many to righteousness, like the stars for ever and ever (Dan 12:1–3).

The discussion of the field of *merkabah* and *hekhalot* mysticism has been beset by the scholarly problem of whether the elaborate stories mentioned in the *hekhalot* literature could be true, whether they are the result of a kind of hallucination—a mark of disturbed minds—or represent examples of purely literary texts. I would suggest another alternative: the stories do actually reflect mystical experience, though they show the same literary developments that we expect when examining texts that are copied for many generations. To understand their connection to mystical experience, one must begin by discussing their notion of a transcendent self.

1. The Construction of the Transcendent Self in Judaism

To talk about a "transcendent self," one has to define both terms: "transcendent" and "self." For the purposes of this essay, I take the "self" as a portrait of an individual, a kind of personal narrative using culturally available terms that makes or grants definition to one's personal identity. Theories of the self in a society may be relational in that they describe the self as a member of a nation, tribe, clan, town, or other group. They may also define the self as inherently connected to the body, as in Western notions of resurrection.

Some theories of the self, particularly in the history of Western culture, have primarily attended to internal psychological states of mind. In this case, the "self" can be construed as a cultural artifact or theory that makes sense out of self-consciousness. I would define "consciousness" as the internal feeling or sense that we are aware, that the bodily "machine is on," that we are up and working, the most basic internal monitoring state. Self-consciousness, however, is formed out of cognitive reflections on that psychic fact, mediated by concepts of self available through culture. In these cases, self-consciousness is constructed by reflection on the cultural theories or vocabularies available for defining the self, a specific kind of theorizing about one's individuality in which the internal states of consciousness are given significance.

A transcendent self is that part of the self that has "ultimate meaning," which in Western traditions is usually described as surviving the death of the individual. In Western religions, the afterlife may be described as a bodily resurrection at the end of time or as continuity of consciousness in the abode of the dead. So many notions of a transcendent sense of self prescribe the ways in which the self can conquer death to survive in the afterlife. This is often described in terms of *transformation*, where the immortal part of the soul is created or realized through some mythical, ritual, or religiously altered state of consciousness. For example, for the Platonist, one's life must cleanse the soul of passions so as to warrant respite from reincarnation, a notion quite like Nirvana in Hinduism. Christians and Jews adopted Platonism but tended to deemphasize reincarnation, instead valorizing faith and the moral decisions of a single lifetime to achieve heaven or salvation.

In Judaism there are principally two different notions of transcendent self. The first is the sense of transcendent self that is created through the body. In the resurrection pattern, the body is the carrier of identity. It is revived and reconstructed by God in the end times, in consonance with the prophecies of Dan 12:1–3. The self achieves transcendency because it behaves appropriately while on earth. It stays true to the values of Judaism, even risking martyrdom to remain steadfastly faithful. The steadfast Jew, first, receives resurrection; some are even transformed into astral or angelic creatures. These are likely the martyrs and community leaders at first.

Along with this notion of the self, Jewish tradition also contains a notion of an experiential self that is particularly important to Jewish mysticism. Certainly this conception of the self receives a good deal of theoretical help from the Platonic notion of the immortal soul. The Platonic notion of self bequeathed to Judaism, Christianity, and Islam both a theory of the soul's immortality and a credible explanation for how the self could separate from the body. A self that can separate from the body in heavenly journeys is characteristic of much *merkabah* speculation. It may owe much to Persian notions of the perfected self or even stem from the ordinary Semitic notions of the *nephesh*, but it certainly received a great theoretical boost from the philosophy of Plato.

With this latter notion of self, we have many narratives of the adept journeying in trance outside of the body, traveling through the cosmos through the seven palaces (these are likely the *spherot* or heavens) to the throne of God. This is the dominant explanation of religiously altered states of consciousness in *merkabah* mysticism. Although it is hardly an innovation in Jewish life in that it occurs in Jewish apocalypticism long before it appears in *merkabah* mysticism, it does not often appear in rabbinic literature, which has a great deal of interest in the phenomenon of intention but little interest in the experiencing self. Rabbinic literature may occasionally discuss how souls come to be in bodies or arrive in heaven after death, but it does not usually relate the journey as personal experience. So these issues come together in an interesting way for rabbinic Judaism in the *merkabah* mysticism.

For example, at the beginning of *Sefer Hekhalot* (*3 En.* 3–15) there is a famous passage in which the angel Metatron reports his personal biography on earth. He recounts that he began life as the human Enoch, a primeval hero of the book of Genesis, who was magnified and exalted after having experienced a heavenly journey and was transformed into the angel Metatron (Gen 5; *1 En.* 71). Because he is the youngest of angels, it is related that he is called "youth."

But it is more likely that he is called youth (*n'r*) because he can be identified with the Prince of the World, who speaks the lines of Ps 37:25, understood together with Dan 7:9–13, "I have been young, and now am old, yet I have not seen the righteous forsaken or their children begging bread." In Dan 7:9–13 both a young divine figure and an older one appear. The "Ancient of Days" sits on the throne and cedes judgment to the "son of man." The figure Enoch-Metatron is somehow transformed into the young figure in the scene, while God himself is identified with the older figure.

This interpretation helps make sense of a very disturbing scene for a monotheistic religion. We are reminded that God is pictured sitting on his throne in other places in the Bible (see Exod 24:10) and that he has a special angel who shares his very name (Exod 23:20–21). Metatron, like the other angels sharing this role, is not only a principal angel but also likely shares God's divinity, represents the Tetragrammaton, and is another manifestation of God. In any event, the story of Enoch-Metatron is a very clear demonstration of the transformation of a human being into an angel and therefore likely the fulfillment of the prophecy in Dan 12:3: "that those who make others wise will shine like the brightness of heaven, like the stars forever."

The *Sefer Hekhalot* (*3 Enoch*) account is not the first time the theme of transformation occurs in *hekhalot* literature. In a much earlier text, *Hekhalot Rabbati*, the cosmic raiment (*haluq*) of God is described as effecting a very similar transformation. Scholem regarded this scene as a mystical reward for successful journeying and not a punishment for unsuccessful adepts, as some previous and succeeding scholars had. Scholem was undoubtedly right. Both descriptions found in *Hekhalot Rabbati* and *Sefer Hekhalot* talk about the transformation of the body into a flaming creature—eyeballs to torches of fire, flesh to flame, bones to glowing juniper embers—that can be understood either as the transformation to "stars" of Dan 12:3 or fiery angels, since "stars" and "angels" were equivalent terms in this literature. Indeed, the great god Helios Mithras, who likely moves the cosmic pole and is to be identified with the constellation Perseus, is described in rather similar terms in the so-called Mithras Liturgy, which also recounts a heavenly journey. This ensures that the images of astral transformation are not entirely Jewish or even Jewish and Christian images. They are part of the cross-cultural, religious life of late antiquity and the early medieval world.

Of course, the transformation of the adept and the angelification of Enoch are not exactly the same. Enoch is taken and appointed or, in one text, paired or partnered (*zivveg*) with a "prince," an angelic designation of special office, and finally magnified into Metatron with his enormous size and many wings and colors. In the second story we see a different transformation, started by a praxis of mystical contemplation that puts the adept into a trance.

But they have a few things in common. They both describe heavenly journeys in which the adept is transformed from being a human being into something immortal and heavenly. In one case he is proleptically transformed into his angelic, heavenly, or astral permanent immortal state while still alive; that is, he would go back to earth to finish out his natural existence. In the second he is enthroned as God's principal minister, his Prince of the Presence, at the end of his life, when he is assumed into heaven bodily, as Gen 5 relates. I would suggest that this pairing gives us the religious meaning of the story in Jewish society. The myth suggests the goal; the mysticism gives the practical way to achieve it. It is noteworthy that we also have a certain amount of evidence at Qumran that such angelic transformations not only happened but were sought in the Sabbath liturgy.

If that is true, then there is already by the first century a significant social ritual that stands behind this material. It is a myth-ritual pair that explains the prophecy of Dan 12 and shows that, through the community of faithful priests and laypersons, a transformation to an immortal form can be effected. This must have been the original understanding of resurrection and exaltation in the Jewish community. The later mystical stories appear to add to that narrative the possibility that the journey to the stars is mystically important and part of the experience that great mystics can seek. As early as Paul in 2 Cor 12 there is good evidence that such trips were sought by real people, and Paul reports that he himself has experienced the beginning of the transformation into the Christ, his "symmorphosis," as he calls it. Obviously, the mystical experience of the *merkabah* adept is far more adumbrated, but the basics can now be shown to go back to the first century within Judaism when the evidence of Paul is factored in, since Paul was a Jewish writer as well as a Christian one.

2. The Experience of Heavenly Journeys

The *hekhalot* texts themselves narrate many different kinds of heavenly journeys and contain many different genres of literature in general. There are apocalypses, magical incantations, mystical alphabetic speculations, various kinds of meditations, and various kinds of spells. But there are also accounts of how mystical trips were accomplished. The most famous one is the story of the recall of ben Hakkanah from his heavenly journey. The texts also specify that the trips may begin with the incantation of special hymns for 112 times.

This kind of heavenly journey—accomplished in trance or some other religiously interpreted state of consciousness—is entirely consistent with a number of other religious phenomena of the second and third centuries. In the Hellenistic world, we have the examples of the so-called Mithras Liturgy and the *Corpus hermeticum,* where such religious heavenly journeys are the primary mode of receiving information from the divine. In Persia we have Kartir's inscription of a heavenly journey and the story of the journey of Arda Viraf (or Arta Wiraz) in the *Arta Viraz Nama.*

Are all of these documents in non-Jewish contexts equally literary frauds or hallucinatory mental illnesses? It seems strange that so many people would have been fooled or driven crazy in such peculiar and elaborate ways, if there were no social credibility structures available to make this trip seem possible. Literary production may lie behind the transmission of these stories, and some of the descriptions are surely augmented from earlier versions. But literary production is not an adequate explanation for the phenomenon of *merkabah* mysticism. Religious truth, not entertainment, was the purpose of these texts. I submit that people did go on a "heavenly journey of the soul" in all these cultures at this time and that there are both cultural and neurological reasons why experience could be ordered in this way.

2.1. Cultural Cues and Religious Experience

In his book on Zen and brain functioning, James H. Austin relates various Zen states to perfectly normal or trainable aspects of brain activity.[1] In one interesting place he narrates a vision that came to him in Zen meditation—it was a clear vision of a red maple leaf in its full fall colors—and deeply impressed him in clarity and lucidity. He remembered that it was an image that he had actually seen in normal sight through the close-up lens of his single-lens reflex camera as he attempted to photograph the maple leaf's brilliant colors. He uses this event as a model for religiously altered states of consciousness.

Austin therefore suggests that this is an extraordinary but still natural function of the mind, even giving a quite detailed explanation of the physical processes in the brain that led to the vision. Special as this experience appeared to him, his Roshi reproved him for being distracted from the true nature of Zen meditation.

1. James H. Austin, *Zen and the Brain: Toward an Understanding of Meditation and Consciousness.* (Cambridge: MIT Press, 1998).

In other words, visions were not a state desirable for Zen meditation, so this red maple leaf vision was forcefully denigrated by his Zen Roshi.

But let us speculate about this experience in another context. If this experience had occurred in an apocalyptic context, the vision would probably have been evaluated in a much more positive way. To an apocalypticist this could have meant that Canada's destiny, symbolized by the maple leaf, was about to change, perhaps to take over world dominance.

This suggests forcefully that religious experiences are strongly influenced by the cultural context in which they occur, that the group itself through its leaders decides what is a valid or invalid experience, and that adepts learn which experiences to validate or valorize. It is not too much to suggest that in the process they learn how to generate the correct kind of physical states and extinguish those that are considered unhelpful. This means, of course, that mysticism is not a solitary experience; it is an experience that is social. It also means that it is not necessarily ineffable; the elements of mysticism can be learned and conditioned. Finally, it means that the mental qualities, the religiously interpreted and religiously altered states of consciousness that are sought in mysticism, can be learned and conditioned as well, even if there is not always a consciousness process of concentrating on mental states, as there is in Zen, for example.

2.2. Consciousness and Neurological States

The issue of consciousness and the evaluation of religiously interpreted states of consciousness is an iceberg underlying our whole discussion. So we must look at some of the consequences of religiously interpreted states of consciousness. A group of new brain imaging techniques—CAT scans, MRIs and SPECTs—have made the operation of organs in the brain evident to us in a noninvasive way so that we can ask the subjects what they are experiencing and note the correlation with brain functioning. On this basis, neuroscientists and philosophers who follow the study of the brain have agreed that what we experience as consciousness is an emergent property composed of the operations of a variety of brain organs that we normally seamlessly and unconsciously integrate into a single experience. Since it is made up of such a variety of mental and physiological operations, it is a much more varied and variable experience than we normally acknowledge, although it is made up of a finite group of components.

The fact that there are actually a series of finite, independent, and different processes that combine to yield consciousness makes the issue of consciousness and religiously interpreted consciousnesses a bit less complicated but no less miraculous. This is, of course, what keeps any physiological explanation from being reductionism. Since we normally experience consciousness as a seamless unity, the composite nature of consciousness only increases the mysterious character of our mental lives and the *emergent* or *Gestalt* nature of consciousness. The individual experience will depend both on the physiological state and the cultural training as to what the state means and expresses, a much more complicated and varied issue than the physical state itself. Religiously interpreted states of consciousness would be that part of our mental life that society or the individual categorizes as religious.

Obviously these are socially determined and differ in different societies. Some religiously interpreted states of consciousness would merely be experiencing various religious rituals and ceremonies without any necessarily extreme changes in consciousness, but we know that some religious rituals and acts have been designed to affect our consciousness. Some religiously interpreted states of consciousness would entail relatively rare and specially interpreted mental states such as prophecy or specific meditative states, which are many and must be taught to the specifications of the individual group. Obviously the category would differ in different societies, and it might as well occasion conflict in a society, as the use of glossolalia and other charismatic gifts in church services has occasioned conflict and denominational strife in the Christian religion.

There are, then, a variety of different organic states that may be labeled as religious in a specific society and trained for within the tradition. Religiously interpreted states of consciousness have been used to justify the existence of a variety of metaphysical locations—such as heaven or the underworld—as well as a variety of different mental states and a variety of different behaviors, some viewed as subversive by others, others viewed as conducive to societal health and regeneration. There is an implicit notion within these social judgments that some kinds of consciousness are appropriate while others are manifestly insane or at least abnormal. Under the circumstances, I think we should assume that even some accusations of insanity, like charges of magic and witchcraft, are importantly socially determined; actors may assert insanity or demon possession or witchcraft when they want to devalue the behavior of others. I suspect that over time we will come to see insanity as a group of specific neurological abnormalities while a wider variety of issues will become sociopathic.

2.3. Recent Neurological Evidence

Since the 1970s a great many new experiments have been done with the help of brain imaging. So there has been a lot of new research on the various neurological bases of religious and other anomalous experiences. These books demonstrate that perfectly normally functioning brains can spontaneously or by various techniques be stimulated to have anomalous and other religious experiences. These experiences are quite different from the hallucinations that produce permanent mental illness, derangement, and random acts of violence, although they are alike in that they all have an etiology in unusual functioning of our brain.

In fact, it is not necessary for us to understand all the mysteries of the mind to realize that this interaction between various mental states and our cultural expectations is a powerful tool for explaining any religious experience, including very unusual ones such as trips to heaven, and that there are transformational or transcendent experiences. Trips to heaven are really experienced then. They are self-validating experiences in the sense that people who have them have little doubt that they have them, and they learn from their peers what to expect on the trips. After all, part of our own reality testing is accomplished in the same way. If we want to verify that a table is in front of us, we can ask others if they see the same piece of furniture. In the same way, when mystics see the same things on their heavenly journeys, they validate the journeys of others as well.

It is unclear whether the myth of heavenly journey or the experience of it in trance came first, and it is not as important for understanding the phenomenon as is normally claimed. After all, humanity has always envied the birds their ability to fly, and the early myths of the ancient Near East certainly imaginatively reconstruct what the flight could have looked like. The fact that they reported sights that cannot be seen—like Adapa's perception of the world as floating in a tub—ought to alert us to the fact that no one actually did fly until technology made it possible. But the exhilaration, the feelings of ecstasy and exaltation, were available to anyone who was lucky enough by nature to produce the internal stimulus or who could train the brain to produce them. Depending on the cultural context in which the subject lives, this anomalous experience can be understood as being the feeling of heavenly journey, being at one with the universe, being one with Brahma perceiving the state of no duality. Obviously, the intellectual scheme used for expressing this state will depend on the cultural assumptions of the subject.

We have something to learn from neurobiological researchers, even when they frame their perceptions in parochial ways. As Newberg, D'Aquili, and Rause say in concluding their book *Why God Won't Go Away:*

> God, in all the personified ways humans know him, can only be a metaphor. But as C. S. Lewis' poem suggests, metaphors are not meaningless, they do not point at nothing. What gives the metaphor of God its enduring meaning is the very fact that it is rooted in something that is experienced as unconditionally real.
>
> The neurobiological roots of spiritual transcendence show that Absolute Unitary Being [their word for the feeling of unity achieved in mystical contemplation when the parietal lobe is quieted] is plausible, even probable possibility. Of all the surprises our theory has to offer—that myths are driven by biological compulsion, that rituals are intuitively shapped to trigger unitary states, that mystics are, after all, not necessarily crazy, and that all religions are branches of the same spiritual tree—the fact that this ultimate unity state can be rationally supported intrigues us the most. The realness of Absolute Unitary Being is not conclusive proof that a higher God exists, but it makes a strong case that there is more to human existence than sheer material existence. Our minds are drawn by the intuition of this deeper reality, this utter sense of oneness, where suffering vanishes and all desires are at peace. As long as our brains are arranged the way they are, as long as our minds are capable of sensing this deeper reality, spiritual-

> ity will continue to shape the human experience, and God, however we define that majestic, mysterious concept, will not go away.[2]

Their statement is culturally biased, of course. The neurological researchers seem unaware of the wider variety of religious traditions that exist in the world, limiting themselves to the "oceanic feeling" when there are in reality a number of experiences of the mystical type. However, even though they frame the question with specifically Western notions of divinity and Western unitive mystical traditions (probably they are relying virtually entirely on Christian experiences of mysticism), there is something to learn from their perception. We just have to translate their perceptions into a wider context where a great many more religious experiences can be taken into account.

Like many books that have an easy answer to a complicated question, these neurobiologists have claimed too much for a single physical factor in our brains. There are other mystical states than the experience of "Absolute Unitary Being" and other biological explanations for other kinds of religiously interpreted states of consciousness. There are other descriptions of transcendent values within human life. But, treated as provisional conclusions, their general methods of argumentation and their conclusions are significant nonetheless. Indeed, one of the most salient aspects of religiously interpreted states of consciousness is that the subject reports with absolute confidence and surety that the experience is as real as anything else in life. This is what convinces Newberg, D'Aquili, and Rause that God will not go away: the experiences themselves are valuable to humanity in that they help us confirm our worldview and therefore retain a sense of meaning and importance in our lives. Although the experiences themselves may be due to anomalous mental states, we leave with the surety that they have actually taken place. Yet they are not necessarily psychotic; instead, they are biologically adaptive for a society because they lend significance and importance to all human activity within the society.

The specific explanation of the experience will surely depend on the historically transmitted religious categories in the society. What may be experienced as unitive mystical experience of God in one culture may, for example, be experienced as Moksha in another society, although I am not propounding that these are the same phenomena at all. I am just trying to rescue Newberg, D'Aquili, and Rause's statements from their hopelessly culture-bound formulations.

Something like this must explain many contemporary near-death experiences that result in a renewed feeling of the meaning of life and comfort from the thought that our dead are lost from us. The very processes that Newberg, D'Aquili, and Rause relate are somehow involved in the self-validating experience

2. Andrew Newberg, Eugene d'Aquili, and Vince Rause, *Why God Won't Go Away: Brain Science and the Biology of Belief* (New York: Ballantine, 2001), 171–72.

of heavenly journey and soul flight, typical of the Jewish and Gentile Hellenistic world alike. They are crucially important experiences for demonstrating the novel view of heaven we find in apocalypticism in Hebrew thought and the doctrine of resurrection that is party to it. Exegesis alone would never have been sufficient for demonstrating to Hebrew society, which had eschewed views of the afterlife for so long, that God was actually promising resurrection of the body. We shall see later that it is even more clearly implicated in the demonstration of the immortality of the soul, for dissociative states were early taken as a demonstration of the separation of the "soul" from the "body."

2.4. Physiology and Culture

Some neuroscientists report that religious feelings of leaving the body correlate quite fully with quieting the proprioceptive processing areas in the parietal lobes of our brain. This center controls our feelings of where we are in space, and when that center is quiet (as determined by CAT scans, MRIs, SPECTs, and other medical diagnostic means), subjects report that they can no longer perceive their bodily location. Evidently this means that the part of our brain that tells us without conscious intervention where our bodies are in space, where our arms, legs, and other appendages are, has been "turned off," disinhibited, or deafferentated. The result is the distinct feeling that we are floating or moving through the air. Perhaps it is just an intensified form of the feeling like the one that skaters and skiers feel after a day of exercise, namely, that they are still skating even when they have removed their skates.

By most accounts, these out-of-body experiences can be very intense, especially when accompanied by shut eyes, low light, and other forms of religious meditation. Some people seem to be able to have these experiences spontaneously; others train to achieve the state in meditation; others report the state after disease or trauma or under the effects of various drugs. The drug Ketamine, known as "Special K" in the club circuit, commonly produces out-of-body experiences in its abusers. Quite often, as a matter of fact, they regard this as a disadvantage of this drug because the fun of a "Rave" is to stay in the body and dance. I suggest that the difference between this experience and a detailed ascent to heaven is due to social and cultural expectations of what a person or a soul is and what happens to that soul once it has been freed from the body. It is possibly responsible for part of the imagery in a "near-death experience." A quick check of self-help books in print will yield dozens of books that purport to teach subjects how to "astrally project" themselves or have out-of-body experiences. This suggests to me that it is not that difficult for a motivated learner to have a "heavenly journey" experience. But years of experience are required to fill in a particular heavenly landscape—whether it be Taoist heavenly ascent or Hermetic heavenly ascent or Persian heavenly ascent or *merkabah* heavenly ascent—and so use this phenomenon within any complicated cultural mystical tradition.

In her fascinating book *The Taoist Experience: An Anthology*, Livia Kohn gives us over one hundred pages of text that describe the experiences of the Taoist shamanistic journey to the stars, the techniques for attaining it, sights and visions that can be seen along the way, and its goal in immortalization of the body.[3] I am suggesting that all of this is native to the Taoist tradition and understandable only within it. In the same way, we can easily detail the practice of *merkabah* mysticism, its techniques for achieving trance and the heavenly landscape that is found along its own starry way. Now, there is no practical way to establish that these traditions are historically related to each other. We cannot hypothesize that some transmission of culture links these two vastly different but strangely similar experiences. I am suggesting that both of these traditions have similar neurological bases and that their literatures condition the novice as to what to expect along the way and provide us with the details of the heavenly architecture and landscapes.

Underneath all these traditions we should find a physiological experience that involves the quieting of the proprioceptive area of the cerebral cortex, accompanied at appropriate places by ecstasy and joy. This is quite different from other physiological states such as the dominant unitive mystical experience. I would suggest that the education of the mystic in mystical societies and conventicles is what helps fill in the specific mystical landscapes of heaven. This is exactly the same phenomenon that we find in shamanism and explains why shamanistic traditions can be so different. Though the study of shamanism continues to be an important analytical tool, there are logical limits on what shamanism among the Tungus, for example, will tell us about *merkabah* mysticism.

I would suggest instead a more neurological model for explaining the heavenly-journey motif. It seems to explain an internal, neurological event. But human beings do not look at unmediated experience. Culture intervenes and helps people come to terms with the events of their lives, giving solace and direction. Shamanism as a cultural system does spread by diffusion, but there is an underlying neurology that suggests journey into space. Shamanism therefore has two aspects: a mental state that is part of our human physiology; and a sometimes complicated cultural tradition that seeks to explain and also to produce these extraordinary experiences. The point in both cases is similar. These are real and very intense physical experiences. Those who have them need no further demonstration of the proof of the religious systems that they practice. Indeed, in many cases the accomplishment of these practices demonstrates that the adept has attained to the highest level of spiritual fulfillment that is available in earthly life and that each can expect special forms of immortality in the coming life; whether it occurs in kings or commoners, rabbis or students, it is a transforming life experience. There is no reason not to think that it was experienced by those people

3. Livia Kohn, *The Taoist Experience: An Anthology* (Albany: State University of New York Press, 1993).

who formed the core of the *hekhalot* literature where it was interpreted within the rabbinic cosmology and used to legitimate power as well as to help with the study of Torah.

In the 1970s and 1980s Huston Smith discussed the prospect that notions of the afterlife were developed out of these feelings that he experienced experimentally with LSD and psilocybin. He quotes Mary Bernard, who asks: "Which was more likely to happen first: the spontaneously generated idea of an afterlife in which the disembodied soul, liberated from the restrictions of time and space, experiences eternal bliss, or the accidental discovery of hallucinogenic plants that give a sense of euphoria, dislocate the center of consciousness, and distort time and space making them balloon outward in greatly expanded vistas?"[4]

What Mary Bernard is saying is that the internal experience seems more obviously the root of the notion of the religious doctrine of the soul's flight to heaven than the other way around. But I am not at all as confident of the order as she is. Either experience could be first. The important point is that they are deeply connected. We know that the situation is far more complicated than that, involving a complex interaction between the body and the culture's explanation of the state. Indeed, the search for explanatory origins is itself a kind of mythological privileging of causation. The resurrection pattern, in which the body is the primary carrier of the identity, is older in Jewish thought, or at least, that is what the textual evidence tells us. But both the traditions here mentioned, which feature heavenly journey, use the experience of ascent as a demonstration that immortality can be achieved, indeed experienced in anticipation of the end of life by anyone carefully enough trained in this life.

If we make allowances for the fact that a variety of different stimuli can produce similar effects in ways we are just beginning to understand, then we have not so much a justification for the afterlife as an explanation for why the afterlife came to be located at the end of a heavenly journey at the beginning of the Hellenistic period. The physical experience and the culture cooperate to produce various experiences that we find impossible to verify from the perspective our cultural norms. Nevertheless, they were real and important and quite normal for those who experienced them. Heavenly journey has a correlative in the functioning of the brain. Exaltation in the mind produces the myth of exaltation to the heavens or vice versa; the order in which the events originally took place is unimportant compared to the realization that the myths teach people what to expect when they have them and the reports of the mystical experiences confirm the myths.

Since the nineteenth century we have been aware that the concept of God is—like truth, beauty, the good, and other important values in our society—some-

4. Huston Smith, *Cleansing the Door of Perception: The Religious Significance of Entheogenic Plants and Chemicals* (New York: Penguin-Putnam, 2001), 47 note.

thing that can neither be confirmed nor disconfirmed by scientific observation. In answer to that question, a number of philosophers proposed the religious experience itself as a self-validating demonstration of the reality of God. Mystical experience, including the tours of heaven that we have been studying, are proofs of God even when reason in its technical employment is helpless to settle the issue. This approach to religious truth is even more obviously called into question by the neurological research, although the philosophical question of the existence of God still remains beyond the issue of confirmation and disconfirmation. If the issue of the afterlife is obviously partly a question of cultural tradition, so must also the issue of God's existence be partly an issue of culture as well. It may even mean that the God question is, properly speaking, an issue of meaning that may be possible to address only within any particular culture.

3. The Self and the Afterlife

In my book *Life after Death* I tried to show that the social function of resurrection in Jewish thought was born out of the necessity to add a definite view of the afterlife and to explain how God would reward those young martyrs who died to keep his laws.[5] Immortality of the soul entered Jewish life from the Greeks, where it had supported an educated leisure class by suggesting that their earthly activities of studying and teaching actually yielded supernatural rewards: it perfected the soul for its journey to its eternal reward, never to have to inhabit earth again.

Here we have a form of the immortality of the soul that is a little better suited to Jewish mystical thinking. There is not much discussion of reincarnation (none at all in the *merkabah* texts). Furthermore, there is little difficulty in Judaism in combining immortality of the soul with resurrection of the body. I say this because it bears noting that the two ideas do not mix well in Christianity. Immortality of the soul in its Greek definition is a natural property of the soul, so it erodes faith in Jesus' resurrection as the event that makes for salvation. It takes several centuries before a philosophical solution can be found to the various possible dilemmas that result from trying to hold the two beliefs simultaneously. The battle between the two beliefs is personified first of all in the battle between gnostics (who really have a notion of the immortal soul for the faithful) and the "orthodox" and then between the Arians and the orthodox.

Immortality of the soul and resurrection do not in every way synthesize in Jewish thought either. Note, for example, that unlike Hermetic thought, the dead do not necessarily follow the same path as the mystic. Exactly what becomes of them is generally obscure. This, among other things, leaves open the issue of

---

5. Alan F. Segal, *Life after Death: A History of the Afterlife in the Religions of the West* (New York: Doubleday, 2004).

whether we go to the heavens to live with God or will be resurrected upon the earth.

Do all the mystics follow in the footsteps of Enoch, who becomes Metatron in *3 Enoch*? That is possible, though it too is obscure. But the Enoch-Metatron transformation is certainly the fulfillment of the prophecy in Dan 12 that "those who are wise will shine like the brightness of the heavens, and those who turn many to righteousness, like the stars forever" (Dan 12:3). Metatron is an angel and one of those whose presence in the heavens is indicated by a star. The stars are angels, although there are other kinds of angels as well. Some of the wise will be transformed and enthroned in heaven, but the general resurrection promised by Dan 12:2 also remains intact.

That self can also make a transformation from human to the divine in the mystic anthology. This is the case of the transformation of the mystic into an angel. In this portrayal is the apotheosis of the soul. The soul can be transcendent through mystic experience. It may also become transcendent through resurrection. So there is a deep and important way in which what is valuable about the self is defined by looking into the mirror of the afterlife to find out what part of us will survive mortality. It is exactly like asking what parts of us have transcendent meaning.

Great conceptual changes in religious, social, philosophical, and artistic life—in short, culture—do affect how we understand ourselves. Self-consciousness builds on our biological consciousness by explaining the self in a socially meaningful way. The notion of the immortality of the soul had just such an effect on how we value our own self-consciousness. The notion of the soul and its immortality helps us understand who we are and why we think we are important. By positing that the soul was immortal, the Greeks were also positing that self-consciousness—or, better, memory, our learning, experiencing, and changing mind—is a transcendent and valuable phenomenon that outlasts our earthly existence. By defining the afterlife as a resurrection of the body, apocalypticists also suggested what the purpose of individual life was and also inscribed martyrdom as a fitting and sensible sacrifice to help bring about the coming of God's kingdom. Saying that, however, is saying a great deal more than we build our afterlife out of our imaginations. It is saying that we then invest those imaginative constructions with the authority of reality through a very complicated social procedure.

Visionary Experience in Ancient Judaism and Christianity

Christopher Rowland,
with Patricia Gibbons and Vicente Dobroruka

> I was in the spirit on the Lord's day, and I heard behind me a loud voice like a trumpet. (Rev 1:10)

The purpose of this essay is to put on the agenda once more the quest for visionary experience in the apocalypses, to take at face value, for example, John the seer's claim that he "was in the spirit on the Lord's day." Caution is expressed about the effects of a historical criticism that has, curiously, for all its interest in the history of religion, been less aware than it should have been about the religious experience that lies at the heart of many of the claims in the apocalypses.

Concern about the skepticism with regard to the existence of visionary experience as the motor of prophetic and apocalyptic texts goes back to the very origins of historical study of the Bible. In a famous statement, to which I have found myself returning again and again, the English poet and theologian Samuel Taylor Coleridge reproached the distinguished biblical critic J. G. Eichhorn for his reductionism in the way in which he approached what Coleridge considered to be the experiential character of prophetic texts, in this case the visions of Ezekiel:

> It perplexes me to understand how a Man of Eichhorn's sense, learning and acquaintance with psychology could form or attach belief to so cold blooded an hypothesis. That in Ezekiel's vision ideas or spiritual entities are presented in visual symbols, I never doubted; but as little can I doubt, that such symbols did present themselves to Ezekiel in visions—and by a law so closely connected with, if not contained, in that by which sensations are organized into images and mental sounds in our ordinary sleep.[1]

---

1. Samuel Taylor Coleridge, *Marginalia* (ed. George Whalley; London: Routledge, 1980), 410; Elinor S. Shaffer, *"Kubla Khan" and the Fall of Jerusalem* (Cambridge: Cambridge University Press, 1972), 89, commenting on J. G. Eichhorn, *Einleitung in das Alte Testament* (4th ed.; 5 vols.; Göttingen: Rosenbusch, 1823–24), 3:188-89.

This analytical approach to prophetic, visionary texts annoyed Coleridge. The reproach of Eichhorn for thinking that Ezekiel's vision is mere poetic decoration that needs to be explained and deciphered reflects a lack of sympathy and understanding for poetic imagination. This reflects the ways in which a prophetic text such as Ezekiel, or the Apocalypse, has been interpreted. The analytical approach, with minute attention to and exhaustive explanation of the detail of the text, contrasts with an approach in which Ezekiel's vision has in its turn inspired subsequent visionaries. In such an exercise of imagination there is the visualization in the mind, of objects, inspired by what is read in texts, or, what is in the external world, which has a close relationship with the visionary, the dreamlike, and the trance. In the latter the process is usually less deliberate than would be the case with an exercise of imagination.

Over the years of his work on *4 Ezra* Michael Stone has repeatedly pointed to the importance of a little-known compendium of texts relating to visionary experience and suggested that pseudepigraphy has too often been a reason for not taking seriously the experiential character of some of these texts. In a recent article Stone has returned to the theme of the reality of the religious experience reflected lying behind the apocalyptic texts of antiquity.[2] Likewise, Eliot Wolfson has demonstrated the importance of visualization and imagination in Jewish medieval mystical writings.[3] In a pioneering study that follows a similar methodological path to that pursued in this article, Dan Merkur uses comparative data to elucidate visionary techniques.[4] Finally, in a much-neglected book, Violet MacDermot has reminded us of the wide textual evidence there is in antiquity for this.[5]

This is a necessary, and long overdue, task, not least from the point of view of the history of religions. There is a wealth of evidence from different periods of history suggesting that visionaries or seers of various kinds felt themselves to be not just recipients but mediums of the communications that came from heavenly or distinguished "others." The notion of automatic writing, possibly prepared for by ascetic practices or other means, has a long history down to the present, and its role is not to be discounted as a way of explaining the complex problem of pseudepigraphy in writings that claim visionary authority.

---

2. Michael Stone, "A Reconsideration of Apocalyptic Visions," *HTR* 96 (2003): 167–80.

3. Eliott Wolfson, *Through a Speculum That Shines: Vision and Imagination in Medieval Jewish Mysticism* (Princeton: Princeton University Press, 1994).

4. Daniel Merkur, *Gnosis: An Esoteric Tradition of Mystical Unions* (New York: State University of New York Press, 1993).

5. Violet MacDermot, *The Cult of the Seer in the Ancient Middle East* (Berkeley and Los Angeles: University of California Press, 1971). More recently, on the religious context of the Jewish material on dreams, see Frances Flannery-Dailey, *Dreamers, Scribes, and Priests: Jewish Dreams in the Hellenistic and Roman Eras* (JSPSup 90; Leiden: Brill, 2004).

This essay sketches work done in Oxford over the last four years. The essay traverses comparative study and the psychology of experience. The approach is avowedly analogical: making full use of comparative data from other periods of history with analogous religious characteristics to the visionary claims that we find in ancient Jewish and Christian apocalyptic texts. There are contrasting emphases in the essay. On the one hand, we examine ways in which the biblical text may have been the starting point for imaginative practice; then there is a consideration of the possibility that apocalyptic seers may have thought of themselves in some sense possessed by some great figure of the past.

1. Is the Book of Revelation Reality or Fiction?

It is unclear how ancient visionaries received their revelation. Did they sit down like a poet and exercise that mixture of imagination and attention to form that is characteristic of poetry, or are visionary texts more akin to the experience of dreams. Many commentators suppose that the Apocalypse and similar visionary texts are the result of a conscious attempt to weave together scripture and contemporary challenge in a way not dissimilar to how the apostle Paul would have written his epistles. There are many signs in a book such as the Apocalypse of a dream-like quality in which the visionary not only sees but also is an active participant in the visions he sees (e.g., 1:12, 17; 5:4; 7:13; 10:9–11; 11:1; 17:3; cf. 1:10 and 21:10). There is a methodological question that arises here: Should we not interpret the text as a vision unless there are strong reasons arising from our interpretation that suggest the contrary?

Of course, in Revelation there is a close relationship with the prophetic texts such as Ezekiel and Daniel indicating a knowledge that never manifests itself in explicit quotation. John's vision draws on images that are familiar to us from elsewhere and in the history of interpretation have a fairly well-established meaning. Thus, the contribution of Dan 7 to the political symbolism of Rev 13 establishes a frame of reference that informs the sense we make of that chapter. Nevertheless, the visionary experience, while conditioned by life under Roman dominion, is not determined by it. There is also a semblance of order that does yield a coherent pattern. In this respect Revelation differs markedly from a Jewish apocalypse such as *1 Enoch*. By comparison, this is a veritable jumble of heterogeneous material.

Such conscious ordering, however, need not exclude the possibility that Revelation contains in whole or in part the visions that John saw. Such visions are familiar to us from the mystical traditions of both Judaism and Christianity. These last mentioned factors have been taken as indications that some attempt has been made to give the book shape and coherence, perhaps most particularly marked in the reflective character of the vision in 17:9–10. If Revelation is a vision, then that does affect the way in which the text is interpreted. The experience of dreams and visions, particularly when, as in the case of Revelation, it contains no interpretation from the visionary, is not susceptible to a definitive quest for the author's intention.

Scholars have highlighted the literary activity of the author of Revelation in the production of the text. Thus Jan Fekkes speaks of "John's literary and exegetical activity," his "fundamental authorial *strategy*," and his "paradigmatic *selection* of OT texts."[6] The underlying assumption of such a position seems to be that John set out to create and compose his text. According to this model, the text is the result of literary sophistication and artistry, and John is seen as an author consciously creating his work. The authority or presumption from which he works is that he is a prophet and communicates God's message in his chosen way, which on this occasion turns out to be apocalyptic. According to this model the author is self-aware of the style and shape that he has selected in order to communicate the message, so much so that the style of the book can be referred to as "His exploitation of apocalyptic device and symbol," which provides "the colour."[7] Another scholar refers to Revelation as a "work of art"[8] and yet another that Revelation is a work of "astonishingly meticulous literary artistry."[9] Behind such phrases lies the presumption that the text of Revelation is a consciously crafted piece of work and is constructed in order to achieve the author's purpose and intention. One scholar, speaking more broadly about apocalyptic literature in general (into which category Revelation has also been placed), has said "the apocalypses are literature, indeed one might even say fiction."[10]

One area of investigation concerning the origin and source of Revelation that has been neglected in recent scholarship is the suggestion that the text is a direct reflection of a visionary experience. Of course, such a position raises a host of questions, particularly in the area of cognition, mechanisms of comprehension, and memory. It is on these areas that my research has been focused.

Research undertaken by Patricia Gibbons has been to take a tool of investigation from the works of French philosopher Paul Ricoeur, particularly concerning the *a priori* conditions for human understanding, which he calls *mimesis*.[11] One

---

6. Jan Fekkes, *Isaiah and Prophetic Traditions in the Book of Revelation: Visionary Antecedents and Their Development* (JSNTSup 93; Sheffield: JSOT Press, 1994), 16 and 18.

7. Ibid., 38.

8. Steve Moyise, *The Old Testament in the Book of Revelation* (JSNTSup 115; Sheffield: Sheffield Academic Press, 1995), 18.

9. Richard Bauckham, *The Climax of Prophecy: Studies on the Book of Revelation* (Edinburgh: T&T Clark, 1993), ix.

10. Martha Himmelfarb, "Revelation and Rapture: The Transformation of the Visionary in the Ascent Apocalypses," in *Mysteries and Revelations: Apocalyptic Studies since the Uppsala Colloquium* (ed. J. J. Collins and J. H. Charlesworth; Sheffield: Sheffield Academic Press, 1991), 79–90, here 87.

11. Paul Ricoeur, *Time and Narrative* (trans. K. McLaughlin and D. Pellauer; 3 vols.; Chicago: University of Chicago Press, 1983–86). See esp. 1:55–81.

aspect of Ricoeur's work gives attention to the influences of the human environment in forming the structures of meaning and comprehension within human consciousness. His work at this point is an inquiry that explores the *a priori* conditions for human understanding.

The process of comprehension is a sophisticated set of operations whereby distinctions can be made between a number of things, such as between action as opposed to merely movement, between symbolic systems rather than literal apprehension, and in the ability to order and segment experiences, which has the effect of distending time in a conceptual way. It also involves the competence of designating appropriate lexical units to experiences, distinguishing between denotation and connotation.[12] Ricoeur's theory suggests that humans generate a cognitive ability for comprehension and narrating that becomes a precritical framework for understanding. Importantly, these processes occur at the level of the preconscious, precritical, and prelinguistic, and the human mind confers a narrativity and readability onto experience in the very process of comprehension.

The aspect of *mimesis* that Gibbons introduces into the debate on the book of Revelation is Ricoeur's insights into the *a priori* conditions for human understanding. These conditions all occur at the level of the preconscious and precritical, so that it can be said that what John encounters in his visionary experience is made sense of through the framework of understanding *already present* in his cognition. Using Ricoeur's theory, it is possible to describe the processes of comprehension of an event, in this case a visionary event, that utilizes the tools of comprehension already present at a precritical level. My work shows that language labels and conceptual categories, as well as the ability to narrate an event, are due to the abilities already present in John's preconsciousness. If a particular individual, here John, has a language reservoir that is saturated in particular language, such as biblical language, then those categories will be engaged at a preconscious level, in the very act of comprehending the visionary event.

To test out this theory, Gibbons turned to the life and writing of Anna Trapnel, a seventeenth-century English visionary.[13] Gibbons's work shows how such preconscious language categories when heavily influenced by biblical categories are engaged during *the very process* of comprehending an ecstatic experience. When Trapnel's utterances were recorded by a witness of the event, an examination of the text reveals a presence of biblical language and phraseology. Such biblical language will be taken as indicative of the precritical language reservoir already furnished in Trapnel's cognitive apparatus and engaged on a preconscious

12. Ricoeur's discussion of this is found in *La metaphor vive*, published in English as *The Rule of Metaphor: Multi-disciplinary Studies of the Creation of Meaning in Language* (trans. R. Czerny, K. McLaughlin, and J. Costello; Toronto: University of Toronto Press, 1977).

13. Anna Trapnel, *The Cry of a Stone* (ed. H. Hinds; Tempe: Arizona Center for Medieval and Renaissance Studies, 2000).

level in the process of comprehension. Thus, the presence of biblical language in the text resulting from Trapnel's vision is in no way due to conscious authorial inclusion. She suggests that the presence of biblical language in Revelation is due not to conscious authorial inclusion but rather is indicative of the very process of comprehending a visionary event utilizing John's existing cognitive apparatus that itself is saturated in biblical language and categories.

Trapnel's text was written by someone in the room transcribing what she uttered. We have no evidence to posit such a thing occurring for John of Revelation. However, Gibbons explores another area, that of memory, to show how a trained mind could retain, order, and retrieve experiences. In the premodern period, the faculty of memory was highly esteemed and highly developed by educated individuals.[14] Some present scholars consider that such memory capacity becomes a part of the individual's cognitive apparatus.[15] An exposition of the life and writings of twelfth-century mystic Hildegard of Bingen will show this to have a direct impact on the ability to retain and retrieve and later write down her visions with great accuracy. Gibbons suggests that in an analogous way John may have had a trained memory that was capable of retaining, ordering, and retrieving experiences, so that when he had his visionary experience, he could later write it down into the text that we know as the book of Revelation.

In summary, investigation into the areas of human cognition and memory capacity can be a fruitful area of research to be brought to bear on the book of Revelation, opening up the way to consider the text of Revelation as a direct reflection of a visionary experience John had, in which he was commanded to "write" what he saw.

2. Exegesis through Imagination

It seems probable that esoteric traditions associated with Ezek 1 and similar passages were inherited by some of the early Tannaim from this apocalyptic milieu. These traditions (as in apocalyptic) had both an exegetical as well as a visionary or mystical dimension. The reconstruction of the content of *merkabah* tradition in the late first century is not easy. The earliest strata of the talmudic tradition do not talk of a heavenly ascent, however, but simply of supernatural phenomena (preeminently fire) that accompanied *merkabah* exposition. Only later in connection with Rabbi Akiba do we find suggestions (in versions of the story of the four who entered *pardes;* see *b. Hag.* 14b; *y. Hag.* 77b; *t. Hag.* 2.3–4; and *Cant. Rab.* 1:4) of heavenly ascents being practiced. The paucity of information about the mystical involvement of Rabbi Yohanan ben Zakkai and his pupils Rabbi Elazar

14. Mary Carruthers, *The Book of Memory: A Study of Memory in Medieval Culture* (Cambridge: Cambridge University Press, 1990).

15. Ibid., 33.

ben Arakh, Rabbi Joshua, and Rabbi Akiba and his contemporaries Simeon ben Azzai, Simeon ben Zoma, and Elisha ben Abuyah does not allow us to reconstruct with any degree of certainty the character of this mystical interest. There are hints that visions of Ezekiel's chariot may have been involved (*t. Meg.* 4:28; *b. Meg.* 24b), though it has to be admitted that the evidence does not allow us to do any more than put this forward as a tentative suggestion.

Of course, if the practical methods were among the most closely guarded secrets of the tradition, and if some influential rabbis were hostile to them, we should expect the sources to be very reticent about them, especially when the practice was liable to cause theological and halakic deviance. Controversy concerning the status and legitimacy of the tradition is likely to have occurred during the first century, probably because of the way in which such traditions were developed in extrarabbinic circles, not least Christianity. We know Paul was influenced by apocalyptic ascent ideas (2 Cor 12:2–4). He emphasizes the importance of this visionary element as the basis of his practice (Gal 1:12 and 1:16; cf. Acts 22:17). His apocalyptic outlook enabled him to act on his mystical convictions, so that his apocalypse of Jesus Christ became the basis for his practice of admitting Gentiles to the messianic age without the practice of the law of Moses.

The interest in passages of scripture that might provide a starting point that would enable the expositor, via traditions of interpretation, to gain further information about God and the divine ways is not confined to the rabbinic tradition. In several places in apocalyptic literature there is evidence that the apocalyptists were also interested in the first chapter of Ezekiel (Dan 7:9; *1 En.* 14:20; Rev 4; 4Q405 20 ii 21–22; *Apoc. Ab.* 17–18) and the first chapter of Genesis (*L.A.B.* 28; *4 Ezra* 6:38–54; *Jub.* 2:2–16; and *2 En.* 25–26). Consideration of the use made of Ezek 1 in the apocalypses leads to the suggestion that these passages, one of which (*1 En.* 14:8–25) may go back to the beginning of the second century B.C.E., already evince an extensive speculative and visionary interest in Ezek 1. The texts from Caves 4 and 11 known as the *Songs of the Sabbath Sacrifice* have given considerable support to the view that sees the origin early in the Second Temple period of the idea of the heavenly temple, liturgy, and the existence of a complex angelology linked with speculation about God's dwelling. They are tantalizing glimpses that these fragmentary texts offer us of a speculation. The Qumran *merkabah* fragment (4Q405 20 ii 20–22) is a remarkable testimony to an extensive and sophisticated interest in the heavenly world that far exceeds the detail of all the extant apocalyptic texts and in many respects has its closest counterparts in the extensive heavenly accounts of the *hekhalot* tractates. The fragments represent an insight into the existence of an extravagant, heavenly oriented mindset of the Second Temple period that gives the lie to the notion that such speculation and interest is merely the creation of a post-Christian era.

In some forms of the interpretation of Ezek 1 the meaning of the text may have come about as the result of "seeing again" what Ezekiel saw. The visionary's own experience of what had appeared to Ezekiel becomes itself the context for a creative interpretation of the text. For John and his apocalyptic contemporaries in the first century C.E., a prophetic text such as Ezek 1 was probably not just the subject of learned debate but a catalyst for visionary experience as is found in the remarkable tradition of interpretation of Ezek 1: *ma'aseh merkabah*. In some circles this led to renewed visionary experience as expounders saw again what had appeared to the prophet, but in their own way and appropriate for their own time. In circles influenced by rabbinic Judaism, reading Ezek 1 was severely restricted because of its use by visionaries and the dangers to faith and life that visionary activity posed (*m. Meg.* 4:10, *t. Meg.* 4(3):31–34; *b. Meg.* 24a–b). Early Christians, like John the visionary of the Apocalypse (and probably also Paul), were influenced by such visionary currents. This extraordinary tradition was maintained over centuries, particularly in Judaism but also some parts of Christianity.[16] In this kind of exposition of prophetic texts, understanding of the text is discerned in the course of visionary experience. This provided the means of understanding its detail rather than it being the result of the deliberate application of exegetical methods to illuminate the ambiguities of the text.

Mysticism and *apocalypticism* are words we use as interpretative categories by which we seek to make sense for ourselves of a variety of particular characteristics within texts and in religious practice. Both relate to the understanding of and approach to the divine, which does not usually depend solely or even in the first instance on the exercise of rational modes of interpretation of sacred texts, in which the interpreter by a series of formal rites or customary practices seeks to give meaning to texts. The discovery of meaning may entail practices of relating to them in such a way that the reader or interpreter ceases to be a detached observer or expositor of the texts but is instead actively involved in a performance that allows one to be a participant and to share in that to which the text itself bears witness.

Thus, in the interpretation of Ezek 1 the meaning of the text may for some involve the explanation of its obscurities by resort to the explanatory devices familiar to us from all biblical hermeneutics, but for others (and it is this group that is most important) it involved seeing again what Ezekiel had seen. It may well have involved the resort to cross-referencing, but this contributed to a dynamic imaginative activity in which the details of Ezekiel's vision were understood by a complex interweaving of vision and textual networking. It is something akin to this that we find in Rev 4, where Ezekiel and Isaiah come together in the visionary's imagination to produce, along with images that are not always easy to explain from a biblical background, the novel vision we have in this chapter and in what follows it in Rev 5.

---

16. Michael Lieb, *The Visionary Mode: Biblical Prophecy, Hermeneutics and Cultural Change* (Ithaca, N.Y.: Cornell University Press, 1991).

Three aspects of Ezekiel's vision are often described in later interpretations of the vision: color; the meaning of the difficult word *hashmal* found in Ezek 1:4, 27 and 8:2, where it describes the figure who takes the prophet off in his vision to Jerusalem; and the human forms mentioned in the vision. It is the *hashmal* that is of particular interest. In one of the passages that discuss it there is evidence that an experiential element was involved in meditating upon the meaning of this word that could lead to damage to inexperienced individuals:

> Thus far you have permission to speak, thenceforward you do not have permission to speak, for so it is written in the Book of Ben Sira: Seek not things that are too hard for thee. ... The things that have been permitted thee, think thereupon; thou hast no business with the things that are secret. ... But may one expound [the mysteries of] *hashmal*? For behold there was once a child who expounded [the mysteries] of *hashmal*, and a fire went forth and consumed him. The case of the child is different for he had not reached the fitting age.... The rabbis taught: There was once a child who was reading at his teacher's house the Book of Ezekiel and he apprehended what *hashmal* was, whereupon a fire went forth from *hashmal* and consumed him. So they sought to suppress the Book of Ezekiel, but Hananiah said: If he was a sage, all are sages. What does the word *hashmal* mean? Rab Judah said: Living creatures speaking fire. In a baraitha it is taught [*hashmal*] means at times they are silent; at times they speak. When the utterance goes forth from the mouth of the Holy one Blessed be he, they are silent and when the utterance goes not forth from the mouth of the Holy One, they speak. (*b. Hag.* 13a [trans. Soncino]; cf. *y. Hag.* 77a)

The use of a particularly significant object as a catalyst for visionary meditation may also be ascribed to the numinous character of the *tsitsit*. In Num 15:37–39 we read: "Speak to the Israelites, and tell them to make fringes on the corners of their garments throughout their generations and to put a blue cord on the fringe of each corner. You have a fringe so that when you see it, you will remember all the commandments of the Lord and do them." The ambiguity of the Hebrew suggested to later interpreters that, by looking at the blue cord (*tekelet*), one would not look at it but at the divine world. "Rabbi Meir said: 'It does not say, And you shall look upon it, but And you shall look upon him.... those who fulfil the commandment of the tassels, it is as if they welcome the divine presence'" (*Sifre Num.* 115). So, it became the object of meditative practice, so that by looking at it one might imagine the heavenly firmament and the divine throne itself:

> It was taught: Rabbi Meir used to say, Why is the blue specified above all colours? Because blue is like the sea, the sea is like the firmament, the firmament is like the throne of glory, as it is written, Underneath his feet was the appearance of sapphire-stone and like the very heaven for clearness (Exod 24:10) and, Like the appearance of sapphire stone was the likeness of the throne. (*b. Men.* 43b)

What is hinted at in these passages is that certain forms of meditation using objects might be the means of moving beyond the physical to the spiritual, from gazing at a particular beautiful color to the process of visualizing the very environs of God.

In some examples of the interpretation of Ezek 1, therefore, the meaning of the text may have come about as the result of the interpreter's own creative and experiential appropriation of the text, a "seeing again" of what Ezekiel had seen. In this the visionary's own experience of what had appeared to Ezekiel becomes itself the context for a creative interpretation of the text. David J. Halperin has captured this aspect of *merkabah* exegesis well when he writes: "When the apocalyptic visionary 'sees' something that looks like Ezekiel's *merkabah*, we may assume that he is seeing the *merkabah* vision as he has persuaded himself it really was, as Ezekiel would have seen it, had he been inspired wholly and not in part."[17]

3. The Craft of Memory

Such meditative practices have been a key part of religion down the centuries and became the cornerstone of the religious life in the late medieval period, though the practices were rooted in a long tradition. The exercise of imagination involves the visualization in the mind of objects, inspired by what is read in texts or in the external world. It has a close relationship with the visionary and the dreamlike, therefore, though in the latter the process is usually less deliberate than would be the case with an exercise of imagination. In much of the interpretation we are not dealing with the kind of analytical exegesis that is so typical of academic discourse in which historical context and the precise meaning of words and phrases or, for that matter, the intention of the author are dealt with. Instead, it is a rather indirect relationship with the Scriptures in which the words become the catalyst for the exercise of imagination as text is taken up and infuses the imagination. Recalled texts yielded new meaning by a process of spontaneous interconnections through recall. Meditation was a regular period of deliberate thought, which may start from reading but which then opens up to a variety of subjects. The mixing of the verbal and the visual took place as, in the very process of recollection, what is retrieved is conceived of anew in meditative imagination.

Both in antiquity and also later in the medieval period we find evidence of the stimulation of an affective experience in which an encounter with divine came about through meditation. Such meditative practice might be based on books but more often was the result of a sophisticated process of memorization of scriptural texts in which the one meditating was able to recall and envision. The exercise of imagination, which might involve the visualization of objects in the mind, has

17. David J. Halperin, *Faces of the Chariot: Early Jewish Reponses to Ezekiel's Vision* (TSAJ 16; Tübingen: Mohr Siebeck, 1988), 71; Stone, "Apocalyptic Visions," 167–80.

been an important part of the reading of Scripture. Mary Carruthers has shown how in the process of memorization and the recall of memory there is a creative process of interaction of images. The medieval scholar remembers things by making a mental vision or seeing of things that are invisible from the matters in the memory, thereby embracing the present and the future through their likeness to that which is past.[18]

> The monastic practice of meditation notably involved making mental images or cognitive "pictures" for thinking and composing. The use of such pictures ... derives both from Jewish spirituality and from the compositional practices of Roman rhetoric. The emphasis upon the need for human beings to "see" their thoughts in their minds as organized schemata of images, or "pictures," and then to use these for further thinking, is a striking and continuous feature of medieval monastic rhetoric.... Medieval *memoria* was a universal thinking machine—*machina memorialis*—both the mill that ground the grain of one's experiences (including all that one read) into a mental flour with which one could make wholesome new bread, and also the hoist or windlass that every wise master-mason learned to make and to use in constructing new matters.[19]

So, ancient readers and hearers of texts could seek to "visualize" what they read (or heard), and that seeing or listening would frequently involve the creation of mental images. Such meditative practice was the result of a sophisticated process of memorization of scriptural texts, in which, in imitation of Ezekiel's and John's digestion of the scroll passages (Ezek 3 and Rev 10 are often mentioned in medieval treatises on the reading and interpretation of Scripture), the one meditating was able to recall and envision. According to Hugh of St. Victor in the *Didascalion,* meditation opened up the gateway to a network of allusions and personal context to effect a memory of Scripture that yielded an elaborate and existentially addressed meditative "*lectio*" (*Didascalion* 3:10). Recalled biblical texts yielded new meaning by a process of spontaneous interconnections, through meditative recall. This kind of imaginative activity has affinities with the kind of exegetical ingenuity that is presupposed by rabbinic legends in which fire is said to play around a Tannaitic teacher, such as Simeon ben Azzai, renowned for his skill in relating one biblical text to another (*Shir Hashirim* 1.10.2).

4. Preparation for Visions in Cross-Cultural Perspective

Vicente Dobroruka has sought to elucidate one conundrum of study of Jewish apocalyptic: whether the episodes of ecstasy and preparatory practices therein described are relics of firsthand experience. Alternatives are to suppose that they

---

18. Mary Carruthers, *The Craft of Thought: Meditation, Rhetoric, and the making of Images, 400–1200* (Cambridge: Cambridge University Press, 1998), 68–69.

19. Ibid., 3–4.

constitute a literary *topos*, with fasts, otherworldly journeys, and contemplation of secrets from the beyond just part of what is expected from a literary genre. Other arguments point to the idea that they may reflect the kind of actual experiences visionaries were having, even if they were not actually being lived by the writer of the text in question but were rather "hearsay" stories. The common assumption is that we are not dealing with texts written as evident firsthand accounts of mystical experience but with pseudepigraphy. This poses the additional difficulty that, even if the experiences described could be proven to be authentic, we would have no one to ascribe them to due to the pseudepigraphical disguise.

One possibility has been suggested by scholars since the last century: pseudepigraphy *may* indeed be in the very core of the experience; that is to say, "mechanical" writers (the people who have done the actual writing, not the portrayed characters to whom the texts are attributed) might be fully and completely identified with their mythical heroes, to a point that they might have thought they were in fact the latter.[20]

Promising as this way of investigating is, there is one additional problem: the comparative lack of parallel descriptions of ancient people being possessed and then writing automatically makes straightforward comparison within Judaism, or even toward the ancient world at large, impossible. The few examples we have are by no means conclusive: a passage in 2 Chr 21:12 to the "letter from Elijah" *may* be a reference to automatic writing, but it could be a situation similar to the finding of Deuteronomy in 2 Kgs 23:24. Lucian also provides us with a description of a contemporary editor of oracles, Alexander of Abnoteichos.[21] But in this case we are dealing with a notorious scoundrel whose religious writing was nothing but deceitful and did not involve any mystical rapture.

Another way of approaching this issue is needed, and cross-cultural analysis may lead to the use of much better documented religious practices where actual identification between mechanical and portrayed writers is the norm.

20. John J. Collins, "Inspiration or Illusion: Biblical Theology and the Book of Daniel," *ExAud* 6 (1990): 31–33; David Frankfurter, *Elijah in Upper Egypt: The Apocalypse of Elijah and Early Egyptian Christianity* (Minneapolis: Fortress, 1993), 40, 59–60, 88; Martha Himmelfarb, "From Prophecy to Apocalyptic: The *Book of the Watchers* and Tours of Heaven," in *From the Bible through the Middle Ages* (vol. 1 of *Jewish Spirituality;* ed. A. Green. New York: Crossroad, 1986), 149; Daniel Merkur, "The Visionary Practices of Jewish Apocalypticists," in *The Psychoanalytic Study of Society 14: Essays in Honor of Paul Parin* (ed. by L. B. Boyer and S. A. Grolnick; Hillsdale, N.J.: Analytic, 1989), 120–21; Christopher Rowland, *The Open Heaven: A Study of Apocalyptic in Judaism and Early Christianity* (New York: Crossroad, 1982), 234; Michael Stone, "Apocalyptic—Vision or Hallucination?" *Milla wa-Milla, The Australian Bulletin of Comparative Religion* 14 (1974): 47–56; repr. in *Selected Studies in Pseudepigrapha and Apocrypha with Special Reference to the Armenian Tradition* (ed. M. E. Stone; Leiden: Brill, 1991), 425–28.

21. A. M. Harmon, trans., *Alexander the False Prophet* (LCL; Cambridge: Harvard University Press, 1925).

In this work a variety of spiritism, Brazilian Kardecism, was chosen by Vicente Dobroruka. He did this for many reasons: its availability, due to the immense output of its main mystic, Chico Xavier (his final output of more than four hundred different titles before his death in 2002 probably qualifies him as the most prolific automatic writer ever); although Kardecist automatic writing has been little investigated in scholarly terms, the mediums themselves, and even Xavier, were quite willing to talk openly about their preparatory devices, even the self-hypnosis involved; finally, Dobroruka's firsthand knowledge of Kardecist practices made it an obvious starting point. His thesis intends to take the closest possible look at the possibility that these experiences might be pseudepigraphy itself, by using Kardecism as a heuristic device.

The passages in apocalyptic texts and Second Temple texts at large dealing with practices to get visions are not plentiful. The picture that emerges from them, however, tells us that most of the visions occur during sleep or when sleep has an important part to play in the preparation; sexual abstinence is almost absent, with the exception of the *Sibylline Oracles,* the dating of which is always problematic; the ingestion of chemical substances is numerically unimportant (appearing mostly in *4 Ezra* 9:23–29; 12:51; 14:38–48; and, possibly, in *Mart. Isa.* 2:7–11).[22] Fasting plays an important role, but, being as common as it was, we are left with a doubt whether the many fasts undergone by the visionaries in Daniel, *4 Ezra,* and *2 Baruch* are sincere experiences or just part of an expected genre. The experiences described by Chico Xavier, the main character in Kardecism and the most informative about preparations, extend much further.[23]

We should bear in mind that, even if we are dealing only with literary *topoi* in Second Temple texts (i.e., part of an expected genre), this does not in itself mean that the experiences described are false but rather that this is what the mystic was expected to see. The same pattern would apply to Kardecism: all experience, not just religious, is governed by convention.[24] We do not know, however,

---

22. The theme of chemical induction of visionary experiences in *4 Ezra* is important enough to be referred to in a separate article; see Vicente Dobroruka, "Stories about Chemical Induction of Visions in 4 Ezra in the Light of Comparative Persian Material," in *JSQ* (forthcoming).

23. The main sources for Xavier's experiences can be found in his description of his own ecstasies in *Parnaso de além-túmulo* (a book comprising poetry by famous Brazilian and Portuguese poets, from 1932), *Nosso lar* (which is in itself a kind of modern-day apocalypse, comprising a detailed newspaper-like description of the other world, 1944), and *Mecanismos da mediunidade* (1960). All were edited by the *Federação Espírita do Brasil* (originally in Rio de Janeiro, now in Brasília). It should be noted that this is a very elementary sample of Xavier's output. It is massive but not homogenous and comprises everything, ranging from commonsensical advice on piety to sophisticated poetry, emulating a vast range of deceased poets by mechanisms that are still not clear but that imply, admittedly by Xavier's spiritual guide Emmanuel, a measure of self-hypnosis.

24. Himmelfarb, "Revelation and Rapture," 153–54.

whether the apocalyptic writers regarded themselves as being channels of the wisdom of, or even "incarnating," the past heroes who then lent their names to the texts and took responsibility for them. An important element to Kardecist automatic writing (psychography) is not apparently present in the range of experiences mentioned in connection with Second Temple visionaries, namely, the manipulating of spirits. Indeed, on this issue there are interdictions (Deut 18:11), as well as confusing references in talmudic literature[25] and more precise ones in the church fathers such as Augustine, Jerome, and Origen, who reflect suspicion of it, though the references to it in their writings may indicate that there did exist this belief and practice in some circles.

5. Concluding Reflections

Where does all this leave us? First, cross-cultural comparison about the psychology of possession deserves further consideration, in order to tease out the peculiarities of the relation between human and divine and one individual and another. There is considerable scope for further study in this area. The greater body of emphasis concerning the visionary psychology of William Blake, for example, indicates that a key aspect of his experience was confusion over visionary identity. Blake was a creative, imaginative interpreter, not a detailed exegete. He took earlier texts, whether biblical or otherwise, and allowed them to become part of his mental furniture and imaginative world. For him any rereading of an authoritative text was a creative process.[26] This is exemplified in Blake's *Milton*. In this poem the living poet (Blake) takes up and reformulates the work of a deceased predecessor,[27] thereby through this second act of creativity to redeem the inadequacies of Milton's writing and life. *Milton* is in part a critique by Blake of the turn taken by the seventeenth-century poet to a religion of rules. But it is also a moment of inspired recapitulation in which the later poet redeems the earlier one's work, initiated when Blake sees Milton's spirit enter into his left foot (*Milton* 14.49).[28]

25. Cf. Claude G. Montefiore and Herbert Loewe, eds., *A Rabbinic Anthology* (London: Macmillan, 1938), with special reference to the notes between pages 660 and 666. Reincarnation plays a major part in Jewish theology, but in much later times.

26. Paul Ricoeur, "Preface to Bultmann," in *Essays on Biblical Interpretation* (ed. L. S. Mudge; London: SCM, 1981), 51.

27. William Blake, *Milton: A Poem* (ed. R. N. Essick and J. Viscomi; Blake's Illuminated Books 5; London: Blake Society/Tate Gallery, 1993), 12: "It is an existence Blake wished to overcome and replace with a more fluid and open concept of being where the gulf between self and other is bridged—indeed, annihilated."

28. There is a parallel depiction of Blake's deceased brother Robert's inspiration. Robert does not appear in the text, but his role as an inspired prophet poet alongside William is clearly

In *Milton*, there is confusion of identity between the writer and the ancient poet. The way in which the latter's artistic and personal redemption is effected has overlaps with themes in biblical texts where successors take up, take further, refine, or even alter the work of a predecessor. Blake's relationship with Milton is a tandem relationship similar to those scattered throughout the Bible, whereby the persona or charisma of one is carried on and transformed in new situations. One thinks of Elijah and Elisha, John the Baptist and Jesus, and Jesus and the Spirit-*Paraclete*. Elisha asks Elijah to give him a double portion of his spirit (2 Kgs 2:9).

Indeed, there is possibly something similar going on in Paul's relationship with Jesus. As an apostle of Jesus Christ, Paul was not merely an agent but also an embodiment of Christ as the result of the indwelling Spirit: "it is no longer I who live but Christ who lives in me" (Gal 2:20). His person is not found solely in his corporeal presence, for, as 1 Cor 5:4 indicates, Paul is able "in spirit" to be with a community assembled "in the name of the Lord Jesus." Of course, unlike Blake, Paul did not think of his apostolic vocation as a correction of the ministry of Christ (though one wonders whether the kind of freedom Paul feels able to manifest in 1 Cor 9:14, to ignore the command of Jesus, may be coming close to this). There is, however, continuation of identity, a reproduction in new circumstances of the dying Jesus, even a completion of the vicarious effects of his sufferings: "in my flesh I am completing what is lacking in Christ's afflictions for the sake of his body, that is the church" (Col 1:24). Of course, in the case of Blake and Milton, however, the successor is more important than the predecessor and corrects the work of the earlier poet. Although the separate identities of later and earlier poets are recognized, it does raise the question whether more cross-cultural study might help to elucidate the phenomenon of pseudepigraphy in some such way.

It seems plausible to go on exploring the possibility that the apocalypses of Second Temple Judaism are the form that the mystical and prophetic religion took in the Greco-Roman period. We may find in these texts examples of those moments when human experience moves beyond what is apparent to physical perception to open up perceptions of other dimensions of existence and with them other perspectives on ordinary life, different from a purely analytical or rational approach to texts or received wisdom. Such experiences may for the visionary have their origin in an approach to texts in which the pursuit of the meaning of the text is not a detached operation but may involve the interpreter as a participant in the narrative of the biblical texts (such as John's experience of realization in his own vision of what had appeared to Ezekiel in Rev 1 and 4). Thereby he (and it was probably almost always a man) becomes a recipient of insight as the text becomes the vehicle of an imaginative transport to other realms of consciousness. It contrasts with the situation when the reader seeks

---

important. Robert died in 1787, but William said that he conversed with him daily, "saw him in his imagination and wrote at his dictate" (K797).

to understand and master the intricacies of the text by comparing it with other texts or by using those techniques of interpretation by which the enigmas can be mastered, the modes of reading typical of the various midrashic methods, both ancient and modern.

There is a significant difference between such visionary appropriations and, say, the "closed" readings of *Pesher Habakkuk*, where the text has a clearly defined meaning as a result of the insight of the inspired interpreter. Although there are affinities between the apocalyptic reading and *Pesher Habakkuk* in their common belief that there is an inspired reading that leads beyond the letter to new insight, in effect the more "open-ended" approaches in the majority of the rabbinic midrashim are more akin to the visionary potential of the mystical "readings."

So, in some forms of the interpretation of Ezek 1 the meaning of the text may come about as the result of "seeing again" what Ezekiel saw. This may arise in the form of a vision (as appears to have been the case for John the visionary on Patmos), rather than by an explanation of the details of what Ezekiel saw. The visionary's own *experience* of what had appeared to Ezekiel thus becomes itself the interpretation of the text. This kind of exegesis involves the apprehension of divine wisdom that is normally beyond ordinary human perception and is dependent on a disposition that is open to the visionary or revelatory potential of the text. For the visionary who appropriates the text in this way, the earthly and the heavenly are linked and the visionary may experience the sense of being transformed into an angelic existence.

This "visionary mode" is similar to allegorical exegesis in so far as the letter of the text, because of its allusiveness and textual uncertainty, points to the need for another level of reality, whereby new dimensions of meaning may be opened up. Understanding, therefore, evokes a perception that pierces beyond the letter. This is the moment of apocalypse when the veil is removed and repentance and epistemological renewal coincide. For the ancient readers of Ezekiel, the prophet's visionary report offered a gateway for visionary perception. For Paul the words of Scripture offered a gateway to Christ, a possible though not necessary means of discerning the divine mystery, which was, in the last resort, "apart from the law." Paul is an exponent of a kind of allegorical hermeneutics in which the apocalyptic/mystical tradition, with its contrasts between above and below, appearance and reality, offers him a hermeneutical device to explain the basis of his departure from hegemonic hermeneutics. Paul inherited from the Bible the belief in revelation, but in his case it was used to subvert dominant ways of reading via a conviction that the Spirit enabled a deeper (in his case, christological) understanding of Scripture to come to the fore. The apocalypses likewise also promoted the quest for a deeper meaning in which the imagination is an interpretative space that opens up a way to eternal verities hidden with God in the heavens.

Performative Exegesis

Seth L. Sanders

Is ancient religious practice a comprehensible human activity or something fundamentally mysterious? Does it fit into the larger sweep of history, reflecting and producing cultural change? When it comes to mystical practices, such fundamental questions have often seemed unanswerable. This is at least partly because our comprehension has been suspended between the world of texts preserved for us and private experience lost to us. The texts have much to offer, permitting the tracing of influences, cataloging of features, and analysis of structures, but a gulf still separates them from private experience and the wider world of history.

To be sure, by the standards of the historian the ancient Jewish mystical and apocalyptic texts are genuinely problematic. Since we do not know who wrote them, we have been daunted by our inability to recover the "original" experiences that supposedly produced them. But this search for the "original" of the text is in many ways a dead end. Even if the author's experiences were recoverable, they would not tell us about the more historically and culturally important histories. These are the history behind the text, which made it possible and meaningful, and the history of the text's life in the world, once it left the author's hand and became subject to the interpretations and practices of the people who used it. Yet these assumptions about "original" experience have generally led scholars to interpret the pseudonymity and decontextualized quality of the Hellenistic texts as opaque surfaces interposed between the modern reader and the ancient visionary, hiding as much as they reveal. The ascents' claims of religious ecstasy resulted in ambivalence as to how to interpret the texts, whether they represent self-conscious literary activity or proof of personal experience.

The scholarly turn toward the study of performance and interpretation suggests modes of reading that lead beyond this ambivalence. Because the texts are part of a broader history of exegesis, and because exegesis is itself a form of religious practice, the history of interpretation provides links to the history of belief and practice. Focus on the religious activity attested in interpretation itself brings new perspectives to old questions of text and experience.

In integrating the perspectives of performance and interpretation, the Qumran *Self-Glorification Hymn* may serve as a privileged example. The claim of its speaker to be exalted above the angels and to have taken a throne in heaven struck its initial interpreters as outrageous,[1] but it has since been widely recognized that, however outrageous the *Hymn*'s claims may appear to us, they represent a broad-based religious phenomenon during the Hellenistic period.[2] When Morton Smith first identified the text as an independent work, he already recognized the speaker of the *Hymn* as an ideal type embodied in both the Teacher of Righteousness and Jesus Christ.

What has been less widely recognized is that the *Hymn*'s ideas and cast of characters have a documented history stretching back at least twelve hundred years. In this history, biblical texts comment on and recontextualize older Canaanite myth, as well as each other. The disparate elements of this history have an underlying unity already clearly recognized in early Jewish exegesis of the *Hymn*'s biblical proooftext. These converging historical and ritual elements provide contexts for the *Hymn* that show how its outrageous statements became not only possible but plausible.

Reading the *Hymn* in biblical, later Jewish, and earlier West Semitic discourse rewards more than antiquarian curiosity: it exposes a living political-theological controversy over the definition of the divine and the limits of the human. In this controversy, interpreters played active roles by using older traditions to alter what was considered possible, creating ideal types that would be put into practice at Qumran. Specifying the interpretive acts that led to the *Hymn* and anchoring them in history lets us specify the ritual roles and illuminate the religious life-world presented in the *Hymn:* a diachronic understanding leads to a synchronic one.

---

1. The notable exception was its first and boldest interpreter, Morton Smith, who already recognized the hymn's *typical* quality as an exemplar of Hellenistic transformational mysticism. See his "Ascent to the Heavens and Deification in 4QMa," in *Archaeology and History in the Dead Sea Scrolls* (ed. L. Schiffman; JSPSup 8; Sheffield: Sheffield University Press, 1990), 81–88.

2. A perceptive discussion of the phenomenon is found in the works of Christopher Morray-Jones. See his "Transformational Mysticism in the Apocalyptic-Merkabah Tradition," *JJS* 43 (1992): 1–31 and "The Temple Within: The Embodied Divine Image and Its Worship in the Dead Sea Scrolls and Other Early Jewish and Christian Sources," in *Society of Biblical Literature 1998 Seminar Papers* (SBLSP 37; Atlanta: Scholars Press, 1998), 400–431. Despite the avenue toward a broader cultural context this opens up, scholars have continued to search for the original author of the text. Various competing attempts to discover the true historical identity of the speaker are catalogued in the notes to Eshel's edition of the hymn; the most recent is Israel Knohl's *The Messiah before Jesus: The Suffering Servant of the Dead Sea Scrolls* (trans. D. Maisel; Berkeley and Los Angeles: University of California Press, 2000). More solid ground has been gained in the more concrete areas of literary form, producing catalogs of the types and levels of visionary enthronement in apocalyptic and mystical texts. These leave us with useful lists of features but still little agreement on how to actually understand a text such as the hymn and precisely how to interpret its extraordinary claims.

1. Ways of Reading Ascents

The relation between literary form and religious experience may be the single most vexed question in the study of early Jewish mystical and apocalyptic literature. The consensus has shifted a number of times in the past century of study, each shift driven at least as much by changes in interpretive assumptions as by new textual evidence.

An early stage, exemplified by Gershom Scholem's *Major Trends in Jewish Mysticism*, drew a distinction between the private mystical visions in which visionary ascents were experienced (now irrecoverable) and the public literary residue left behind and transmitted in textual traditions. A second stage, marked by greater caution, arrived as Scholem's scholarly dominance was receding. It identified his interpretive assumptions as merely assumptions, and in so doing put in place new ones.[3] Setting aside Scholem's cryptic, quasi-religious approach, David J. Halperin produced a comprehensive rationalist reading. In Halperin's view, it is the relative ease with which the modern scholar can provide a symbolic reading of the vision (in terms of power and sexuality) that may indicate whether a literary vision was a self-conscious literary creation or an uncontrolled hallucination—there are no other reasonable ways to understand the visionary's experience.

> Only one criterion seems to me to have the slightest validity in distinguishing consciously created fantasy from unconsciously created hallucination. It is this: Do the images used by the writer have symbolic meanings which, when deciphered, yield a more or less coherent and convincing interpretation, but which the writer gives no indication he is consciously aware of? To the degree to which the symbols of the vision are outside the writer's conscious control, we may assume that the vision itself is outside his conscious control.[4]

It should be noted here that Freud, exquisitely sensitive to the cross currents between literature and the psyche, might not have agreed with this Freudian reading of the ascent visions: "Most of the artifical dreams contrived by poets are intended for some such symbolic interpretation, for they reproduce the thought conceived by the poet in a guise not unlike the disguise which we are wont to find

3. I note in passing that other ways of assessing the visions in cultural and historical context were suggested before this time in an excellent though obscure article by Michael Stone: "Apocalyptic—Vision or Hallucination," *Milla wa-Milla, The Australian Bulletin of Comparative Religion* 14 (1974): 47–56; repr. in *Selected Studies in Pseudepigrapha and Apocrypha with Special Reference to the Armenian Tradition* (ed. M. E. Stone; Leiden: Brill, 1991), 415–28. See now idem, "A Reconsideration of Apocalyptic Visions," *HTR* 96 (2003): 167–80.

4. David J. Halperin, "Heavenly Ascension in Judaism: The Nature of the Experience," in *Society of Biblical Literature 1987 Seminar Papers* (SBLSP 26; Atlanta: Scholars Press, 1987), 226.

in our dreams."[5] This is to say that "consciously created fantasies" may indeed yield "coherent and convincing" psychological interpretations. The only criterion would then be the indications of self-consciousness in the work. This assumes that no one who has had a vision has reflected on it or been self-conscious about it, which is a problematic assumption.[6]

A more complex psychoanalytic approach was taken by the psychologist Daniel Merkur.[7] Merkur provided interpretations of the states of consciousness described by the visionaries in terms of experimental psychology and postulated a variety of possible levels of interpretation and conscious control that could be manifested in the texts. Though his discussion has not been as widely remarked as Halperin's, Merkur's phenomenological distinctions have the methodological advantage of being based on the structures of the texts themselves and therefore less dependent on one's assumptions about the experiences underlying them.

A radically contrasting view of the complex way literary texts mediate experience was provided by Martha Himmelfarb:

> it is clear that if visionary experience is reflected in the apocalypses, there are many mirrors between the experience and the text. Pseudonymity is perhaps the darkest mirror, the one we least understand. My own guess is that texts that describe a human being becoming not just an angel, but the most exalted angel of all, are more literary, and the relationship to experience is less direct, than texts that describe a somewhat more modest form of transformation.[8]

The discovery of a text in the standard Qumran liturgical collection describing a human being becoming "the most exalted angel of all" renders both Halperin's and Himmelfarb's assumptions problematic (Merkur's typology is more complex). If the most "literary" type of text, as Himmelfarb suggests, is also

5. Sigmund Freud, "The Interpretation of Dreams," in idem, *Basic Writings* (trans. A. A. Brill; New York: 1938), 189, applied to premodern literature by Constance B. Hieatt, *The Realism of Dream Visions: The Poetic Exploitation of the Dream-Experience in Chaucer and His Contemporaries* (The Hague: Mouton, 1967), 12.

6. A striking modern counterexample appears in the gnostic vision experienced by science fiction writer Philip K. Dick, which he documented in a private text he titled "The Exegesis" but reworked and published in the form of two science fiction novels, *Radio Free Albemuth* and *Valis*. See Lawrence Sutin, *Divine Invasions: A Life of Philip K. Dick* (New York: Harmony, 1989).

7. Daniel Merkur, "The Visionary Practices of Jewish Apocalyptists," in *The Psychoanalytic Study of Society 14: Essays in Honor of Paul Parin* (ed. L. B. Boyer and S. A. Grolnick; Hillsdale, N.J.: Analytic, 1989), 119–48.

8. Martha Himmelfarb, "Revelation and Rapture: The Transformation of the Visionary in the Ascent Apocalypses," in *Mysteries and Revelations: Apocalyptic Studies since the Uppsala Colloquium* (ed. J. J. Collins and J. H. Charlesworth; JSPSup 9; Sheffield: Sheffield Academic Press, 1991), 88. But why is it more realistic to become a common angel than to become a head angel?

attested in early liturgical practice, in what way is it the furthest from experience? Similarly, the fact that such transformations are described not only in late literary texts but also early liturgical materials creates difficulties for Halperin's analysis of these visions as strictly literary.[9] Whatever we assume about the experiences that went into or arose out of the *Self-Glorification Hymn* or the *Songs of the Sabbath Sacrifice*, both are, in a significant way, *practical* texts. Yet both the *Hymn* and the *Songs* are structured according to liturgical and poetic conventions, not unconscious fantasies. Most problematic is the method itself: without an explicit empirical anchor in ancient exegesis or practice, there is nothing to compel us to accept the assumptions guiding Halperin and Himmelfarb's assessments over those of their predecessors.

Alternative positions emphasizing practice and exegesis have arisen simultaneously with these strictly literary approaches. On the view of Peter Schäfer, the more practical goals of liturgical participation and magical action lie at the center of the early mystical texts.[10] A similar analysis was carried further and theorized in a monograph by Rebecca Lesses, which applies a version of the speech-act theory of the philosopher J. L. Austin to the *hekhalot* texts.[11] In this view, what matters about the texts is the fact that they were performed, and thus efficacious whatever the internal states of their practicioners may have been. This attention to performance is a crucial step forward but raises other theoretical issues. In assuming that performance, in general, implies effect, it begs the questions of specific contexts, performers, and performances: Who performed the texts, to what effect? It is on precisely this point—the way performance is always a part of history, with all the dependence on context and contingency that entails—that Austin's theory has been repeatedly criticized.[12] Yet the criticism has served to

---

9. There are larger problems with these interpretative assumptions. See Elliot Wolfson's thoughtful treatment of Halperin's presuppositions in Wolfson's *Through a Speculum That Shines: Visions and Imagination in Medieval Jewish Mysticism* (Princeton: Princeton University Press 1994), 112–15.

10. Peter Schäfer, "The Aim and Purpose of Early Jewish Mysticism," in idem, ed., *Hekhalot-Studien* (TSAJ 19; Tübingen: Mohr Siebeck, 1988), 289–95.

11. Rebecca Macy Lesses, *Ritual Practices to Gain Power: Angels, Incantations, and Revelation in Early Jewish Mysticism* (HTS 44; Harrisburg, Pa.: Trinity Press International, 1998).

12. Catharine Bell, in her extensive study of ritual theory, pointed out how an emphasis on performance has been used to bracket earlier problems in the interpretation of ritual. See her *Ritual Theory, Ritual Practice* (Oxford: Oxford University Press, 1992). Michael Silverstein demonstrated that the very notion of the speech act is the result of reading grammatical features of English and other modern European languages as universal features of social action. See Silverstein's "Language Structure and Linguistic Ideology," in *The Elements: A Parasession on Linguistic Units and Levels* (ed. P. R. Clyne, W. F. Hanks, and C. L. Hofbauer; Chicago: Chicago Linguistic Society, 1979), 193–247. Austin's energetic and pointed deconstruction of his own categories, which occupies the last third of his book, is routinely (ritually?) ignored by scholars who apply his work. The bibliography of criticism is large but vital to the question of whether speech-act

nuance and broaden the theory. Likewise with its application to ancient texts: while we cannot document specific performances of the *Hymn*, we can place its actions, roles, and performers in a historical and cultural context. A major step forward in understanding this context is Naomi Janowitz's work on the rabbinic theories of language underlying *hekhalot* texts.[13] This sort of careful attention to ancient concepts of performance are our best hope for understanding what ancient performances meant and what they were thought to accomplish.

The second part of this trend is part of a general return to exegesis in biblical studies.[14] Unifying the earlier positions of the philosopher of religion Steven Katz and the scholar of apocalyptic Christopher Rowland, Christopher Morray-Jones and Elliot Wolfson have argued that the dichotomy proposed between primary experience and secondary interpretation is false.[15]

> Study should not be reduced to mere exegesis devoid of any experiential component; on the contrary, *one must assume* that the visions and revelatory experiences recorded in the apocalypses are not simply literary forms but reflect actual experiences deriving from divine inspiration. *It can be assumed, therefore*, that at least some of the apocalyptic visions arose from reflection on scripture: exegesis of recorded visions leads to revelation of God.[16]

---

theory actually works—even in our own culture. A good, short bibliography on speech acts in other cultures appears in Kathryn A. Woolard's "Introduction: Language Ideology as a Field of Inquiry," in *Language Ideologies: Practice and Theory* (ed. B. B. Schieffelin, K. A. Woolard, and P. V. Kroskrity; New York: Oxford University Press, 1998), 14–15. Two excellent theoretical treatments are those of Stanley Cavell, "What Did Derrida Want of Austin?" in idem, *Philosophical Passages: Wittgenstein, Emerson, Austin, Derrida* (Cambridge: Blackwell, 1995); and Judith Butler, *Excitable Speech: A Politics of the Performative* (New York: Routledge, 1997). I provide an overview of performative utterances and theories of religious language in ancient Semitic in "Performative Utterances and Divine Language in Ugaritic," *JNES* 63 (2004): 161–81.

13. Naomi Janowitz, *The Poetics of Ascent: Theories of Language in a Rabbinic Ascent Text* (Albany: State University of New York Press, 1989), an approach broadened in her *Icons of Power: Ritual Practices in Late Antiquity* (University Park: Pennsylvania State University Press, 2002).

14. Michael Fishbane's foundational *Biblical Interpretation in Ancient Israel* (Oxford: Clarendon, 1985) brought sweep and rigor to the subject, and the trend has enriched biblical criticism through the work of his students, exemplified by Benjamin Sommer's *A Prophet Reads Scripture: Allusion in Isaiah 40–66* (Stanford, Calif.: Stanford University Press, 1998) and William Schniedewind's *Society and the Promise to David: The Reception History of 2 Samuel 7:1–17* (New York: Oxford University Press, 1999).

15. Christopher Rowland, *The Open Heaven: A Study of Apocalyptic in Judaism and Early Christianity* (New York: Crossroad, 1982). Katz has edited a number of volumes exploring this position; a recent example is Steven Katz, ed., *Mysticism and Language* (New York: Oxford University Press, 1992). Morray-Jones's arguments, presented in a lecture at the 2000 SBL meeting, appear in this volume. For Wolfson's, see below.

16. Wolfson, *Through a Speculum That Shines*, 124, emphasis added. He goes on to distinguish between "theoretical-exgetical" and "practical-ecstatic" approaches. For a vivid explication

Religious experiences are always culturally structured and thus always "interpretation" of preexisting cultural material. Further, experience is never raw and unmediated but itself constructed using available concepts and forms. The exegetical elements in mystical and apocalyptic texts are thus not a sign of self-conscious literariness detached from experience. Instead, they may themselves be part of the religious experience.

This turn toward interpretation has liberated scholarship to focus intensely on how texts were brought to life in ancient contexts. Yet when it comes to the fundamental problems of the field, old tautologies remain. Because an interpretation can produce a religious experience, do we know in any given case that it actually did? If all experience is somehow exegetical and all exegesis is somehow experiential, are all interpretations of visions themselves divinely inspired? If not, how does one draw meaningful distinctions between them? In the absence of explicit native testimony as to the nature of a given religious practice and the status of a specific experience, the new emphasis on exegesis risks ending up another a priori assumption.[17] But this difficulty is not inherent in the approach. Indeed, since interpretation is also practice, placing texts into new life contexts, this tendency toward context and history can be followed through, bringing its questions together with the pragmatic emphasis of Schäfer, Janowitz, and Lesses.

Performative and exegetical analysis meet when we place texts in specific histories. We unify them when we ask how a performance role developed over time through interpretive practices that applied the characters and themes of a text to new contexts. In our case, what is the historical relationship between the texts in which the myth of ascent to heaven appeared in the ancient Levant and the personal roles those texts made available for reading and performance? Answering this question requires tracing a kind of map of the routes by which ascent to heaven was created as a culturally available goal in the Hellenistic period. Posed in philological terms, it does not require us to rely on a priori assumptions about the nature of religious texts and human experience. Instead, we can track how the texts were used by detailing the history (rather than the "historical background")[18] of the mythical themes in an ascent text, as they were applied and

of the former category, see Michael Fishbane, "The Book of Zohar and Exegetical Spirituality," in idem, *The Exegetical Imagination: On Jewish Thought and Theology* (Cambridge: Harvard University Press, 1998), 105–22.

17. Especially subsceptible to the circularity problem is the *nature* of the evidence one might draw upon to bolster the assumption of pneumatic exegesis, since it is by nature intertextual—the exact same type of evidence that was earlier used to demonstrate literariness!

18. Too often material from non-Jewish cultures has been used in a foreshortened and ahistorical manner to bolster arguments about Judaism and Christianity. Mesopotamian or Canaanite culture is taken as a frozen, static "background" to a rich and developing Israelite or Western culture. For bibliography and critique of this quasi-Orientalist practice, see "The Problem of a Babylonian Background for Apocalyptic Literature" in my 1999 Johns Hopkins

reinterpreted and their authority invoked and changed over time. We can then examine how these myths staked their claims in life by looking for features in the texts that provided ritual roles for people.

An ideal type only enters actual human experience when it is taken on as a performable role or influences existing roles. The pathway we will explore from visions of God's face to human adoption of a divine role is through the divine persona.[19] This ends up in a set of Qumran texts that would appear far removed from the myths: calendrical documents, astronomical texts, physiognomies, and medical texts. But in these practical documents about the year, the body, and the cosmos, certain recurrent mythic concerns are played out. These will in turn suggest a cosmological difference we should take seriously: an ancient Jewish culture's modes of classifying mythic entities as corporeal and material helps explain how an angelic persona on earth could be at once interpreted, experienced and enacted.

2. A Mask of Light

To understand how the human adoption of a superhuman role evolved as a ritual practice in early Judaism, it is necessary to look at the earlier interpretive practices that led to it, making the role believable and even traditional. Two biblical texts about the human adoption of divinely illuminated personae that were important to Hellenistic Jewish belief play central roles in our story. The first is the old crux in Exodus of Moses' shining face. Though it has never been pointed out before, there is a well-attested Near Eastern interpretation of light as a material object that was continued at Qumran. Moses' transfiguration into a semidivine being provided not only a literary inspiration but a specific cultural precedent for the physical transfiguration of the visionary into a being of light known from apocalyptic literature and Qumran ritual. The second text is the description of the "sages" in the final vision of the book of Daniel. The innerbiblical interpretation of Isaiah's "Suffering Servant" in Dan 11–12 envisioned an ideal type, the sage (*maśkîl*), which was adopted as the name of Qumran's religious leaders and thus

Ph.D. dissertation, "Writing, Ritual and Apocalypse," 22–54, to be published by Brill as *Myths of Revelation: The Practice of Ascent to Heaven in Israel and the Ancient Near East*.

19. As the sociologist Marcel Mauss long ago demonstrated, the dramatic—and eventually political and legal—metaphor for this role in Western tradition is the persona. The *persona* was originally a dramatic mask worn in Roman theater that acquired a broader sense describing the legal and social role of a human being that underlies the modern concept and word "person." This *persona* also surfaces literally in one of our texts, evoking the ancient range of senses: a physical mask, the role one plays using the mask, one's role in life, and finally one's physical person. For a collection incorporating Mauss's essay and valuable critiques, see Michael Carrithers et al., eds., *The Category of the Person: Anthropology, Philosophy, History* (New York: Cambridge University Press, 1985).

brought from interpretation to a role in real-life institutions. These two exegetical histories of originally unrelated texts meet at Qumran, where inhabitable roles were created through the invocation and convergence of these earlier texts.

We begin with a myth about Moses' persona.[20] As Elliot Wolfson has emphasized, biblical denials of God's corporeality and bans on his depiction coexist uneasily with a God who *appears:* in Exod 33, Moses is denied a vision of God's face but allowed to see his back, an affirmation that there *was* in fact a body to see—a foundational paradox, since this denial of God's body resorts to physical means.[21] Directly after this vision, Moses's own face undergoes a transformation. He is coming down from Mount Sinai, where he has spent forty days and nights reinscribing the Ten Commandments. During this time he has not eaten or drunk. Thus Exod 34:29:

> ויהי ברדת משה מהר סיני ושני לחת העדת ביד־משה ברדתו מן־ההר
> ומשה לא־ידע כי קרן עור פניו בדברו אתו׃

> As Moses came down from Mount Sinai—the two tablets of the testimony in Moses' hand as he came down from the mountain—then Moses did not know that the skin of his face *radiated* from speaking with him.

Moses' appearance terrifies the Israelites: upon seeing him they withdraw, refusing to approach until he calls out and reassures them with his voice.[22] But what did they see that frightened them? The crux, since Jerome, has been in separating the verb קרן, which appears three times in this passage in the *qal* describing the skin of Moses' face (34:29, 30, 35), from either the sense of radiating light or the sense of bearing horns (the meaning of the verb the one other

---

20. I have published a closely related version of this argument in a different context as "Old Light on Moses' Shining Face," *VT* 52 (2002): 400–407.

21. See the first chapter of Wolfson's *Through a Speculum That Shines,* "Israel: The One Who Sees God."

22. The sequence of verbs in 34:30 emphasizes and perhaps plays on the words for seeing and fearing: וייראו ... ויראו מגשת אליו. "And they *saw* … and they *were afraid* to approach him." This sequence of seeing and fearing is identical to that found in the other Exodus text describing the people of Israel seeing a divine visage, where Exod 20:18 reads וַיַּרְא הָעָם "the people saw," and Moses responds אל־תיראו "Do not be afraid" in Exod 20:20. While Exod 20:18's vocalization of וירא, entailing a mass vision of God at Sinai, is not attested in the other ancient versions (which all reflect a reading וַיִּירְאוּ "the people *were afraid*"), it is implied in the ancient tradition according to which the entire people saw God during the exodus (early examples are found in *Mekhilta di Rabbi Ishmael*, tractates *Beshalah* and *Bahodesh*) and explicit in the later compilation *Mekhilta di Shimom bar Yohai*. For further discussion see Wolfson, *Through a Speculum That Shines*, 40.

place it appears, in the *hip'il* [Ps 69:32]).[23] Something divine has changed the way Moses looks, but we are faced with a problem of visualizing it: no matter which side we come down on, whether as metaphor or literal description, something is left over. Our visualization is faced with an inescapable remainder.

Interestingly, other people in the ancient Near East had the same problem, and it will help to examine their solution. Babylonian astronomy exegetically equated the celestial bodies with gods, and the pragmatic nature of this exegesis is clear in the way the observation and interpretation of celestial omens directly affected government policy. The visualization of divine radiance was a daily activity for the astronomer, who was faced with a problem of both physical and cosmic interpretation when he saw the moon eclipse the sun, throwing the entire sky into darkness.

Thus, in the Babylonian astronomical series *Enūma Anu Enlil,* found in the library of Assurbanipal, the astronomer is advised:

> *šumma ūmu* si-*šu imqut-ma Sîn adir mītūti ibaššû ina barārīti Sîn atalâ išakkan-ma* si=*qarnu* si=*šarūru*....[24]
> If the sun's horn (***si***) fades and the moon is dark, there will be deaths. (*explanation:*) in the evening watch, the moon is having an eclipse (and in this context,) ***si*** means "horn," ***si*** means "shine." ...

The text's exegesis moves from raw visual experience to lexicography, providing a model for the reader to interpret both what he sees and reads. It explains that what he sees is an eclipse and that when he reads the Sumerian word ***si*** in the base text, "***si*** means 'horn,'[25] and ***si*** also means 'shining.'" After reading the commentary, the person who sees the thin shining rim of the sun should interpret both visual and written signs as simultaneiously horn and light. A second commentary adds that the lemma means "'to daze,' ***si*** means 'to mask,' ***si*** means 'shining,' ***si*** means 'radiance,' ***si*** means 'light.'"[26]

Here the range of associations is extended to the affective—the word translated "be dazed" can also mean "be numb with terror"—and the physical: light can mask, cover over, and block things like a fog.[27] The phenomenon unifies astronomy, myth, and politics. This spectrum of associations is embodied in

23. An insightful discussion is provided by Thomas Dozeman in "Masking Moses and Mosaic Authority in Torah," *JBL* 119 (2000): 21–45.

24. Charles Virolleaud, *L'astrologie chaldéenne* (Paris: Geuthner, 1905–12), Adad 33:21. I thank Wayne Horowitz for discussing the text with me.

25. Note that the Akkadian here is *qarnu*, cognate with Hebrew *qeren*.

26. Babylonian Astronomical Commentary CT 26 43 viii 5–10, cited after *CAD*, s.v. *šarūru*, lexical section, which contains an abundance of further examples.

27. The Mesopotamian view of the sheer *physicality* of light is beautifully illustrated by the description of the sun's radiance in the Great Shamash Hymn: "Shamash, you are binding like a cord, you are choking like a mist; Your broad canopy is overreaching the lands." See Wilfred

the Mesopotamian mythological object called the *melammu*, a blinding mask of light.[28] The *melammu* is the property of gods and monsters, as well as the sun, and one is conferred by the gods on the king at his coronation. This mask of light is thus cosmic, physical, and political at once, a somatic mark of divine rulership, and it is external to the body, even alienable, as the theft of Mummu's *melammu* in *Enuma Elish* (I 68) shows. A *melammu* can be stolen, but it can also be conferred on someone who has not previously possessed one.

This mythic pattern provides the most compelling model for understanding what happened to Moses' face: it is not the face itself but its surface, the skin, that radiated. Mose's physical proximity to the source of revelation added a new layer to his appearance, a physical mark of inhumanity. The Israelites feared contact with Moses because of his divine persona. The Exodus passage introduces the religious problem of how divine radiance might be visualized and incorporated into the body. It also makes a political point: Moses' radiance is unique, a historical singularity connected to his unique and exclusive contact with God and transmission of divine revelation, embodied in the Torah and reinforcing its authority.

There is a subversive possibility in this account of Moses' uniqueness. This is the fact that his radiance is *derived* and thus inherently secondary, pale fire from a divine sun. In Mesopotamian versions of this mythic pattern, the divinized being is not absolutely unique; he is merely the incumbent of a role. If Moses becomes godlike by reflecting God, could others reflect that light from Moses or God? Interest in precisely this point is manifest in the New Testament. The most obvious point of contact is the Synoptic Gospels' account of the transfiguration of Jesus. All three Synoptics (Matt 17:1–8; Mark 9:2–8; Luke 9:28–36) describe Jesus as transfigured on a mountain, while speaking with Moses and Elijah, just as Moses himself was transfigured while speaking with God. Even closer connections are found in Matthew, where Jesus' face shines (17:2), and Luke (9:29), where his face is simply changed.[29] Each Synoptic account gives a different description of the visual change in Jesus alongside a consistent parallel description of Jesus' garments, rendered pure white. There are already multiple exegetical layers to this invocation of Sinaitic revelation and Mosaic transfiguration: Jesus' disciples witness a theophany in which God covers the mountain in the form of a cloud, evoking the cloud theophany of Exod 19–20, and Moses is accompanied

G. Lambert, *Babylonian Wisdom Literature* (Oxford: Oxford University Press, 1960), 128, lines 39–40.

28. On which see A. Leo Oppenheim, "Akkadian *pul(u)h(t)u* and *melammu*," *JAOS* 63 (1943): 31–34; and Elena Cassin, *La splendeur divine: Introduction à l'étude de la mentalité mésopotamienne* (Paris: Mouton, 1968).

29. Compare the summary in 2 Pet 1:16–18, where God's glory is given to Jesus.

by Elijah, himself Jesus' predecessor as a second Moses through 1 Kings' inner-biblical revision of the Sinaitic revelation on Horeb.[30]

If the Gospels' Jesus literally reflects his biblical antecedents, the process of spiritual and physical reflection is not supposed to stop at Jesus but continue through his followers.[31] Christ's role as an adoptable model encouraged the early Christians to think of the Scriptures and their own lives as forming a veritable hall of mirrors. In this context, the mystical phenomenon of transformation of one's own face through seeing the face of God is prominent. Thus in 2 Corinthians, after two explicit invocations (3:7, 13–14) of the episode of Moses' shining face applied to present day behavior, Paul writes: "And we, with unveiled faces reflecting like mirrors the brightness of the Lord, all grow brighter and brighter as we are turned into the image that we reflect."[32] The model of transfiguration through seeing God was not just recommended but thought by early Christians to be enactable, at least by martyrs. In the story of Stephen, during his trial his face becomes like that of an angel (Acts 6:15), and he gazes directly into heaven, seeing God with Christ at his right hand (Acts 7:55).

The second biblical locus where knowledge of God results in a shining body represents a turning point in the history we are tracing. For the first time it is not a historically unique person (Moses) whose face shines but a *type* of person who can exist in the present. This moment in the history of the divine persona occurs in the final revelation in the book of Daniel. Drawing on the "Suffering Servant" language of Second Isaiah, this text provided a script for the Qumran community's dominant personae, the sages or *maśkîlîm*, exegetically read out of Isaiah into Daniel and then into the constitutive documents of the Qumran community.

The Qumran use of the terminology of the sages, as well as their constituency, "the many," rises out of an close interpretive relationship with both the final revelation of Daniel and the prophecy of Second Isaiah that Daniel's vision interprets. The influences of Isa 52–53 on the rhetoric of Daniel's final vision are apparent in its vocabulary and have long been recognized.[33] These include the echo of the verbal root *śkl* from Isa 52:13 in the participial form *maśkîl*, the adoption of the common noun *rabbîm* with the special sense of "the many" from Isa 53:11–12, and the incorporation of these two forms with the *hip'il* of *ṣdq* found in

30. See 1 Kgs 19:8–18, which invokes and applies two key moments of Moses' ritual transformation and experience of God: in 1 Kgs 19:8 Elijah fasts for forty days and nights (Exod 34:28), and in 1 Kgs 19:11 the Lord "crosses" before him (Exod 33:19–23). I thank Elisha Fishbane for pointing this out to me in conversation.

31. See Bernard McGinn, *The Foundations of Mysticism* (New York: Crossroad, 1991), 66–67 with references there.

32. 2 Cor 3:18, in the translation of ibid., 7.

33. For summary and references, see Fishbane, *Biblical Interpretation in Ancient Israel*, 493 and n. 88.

Isa 53:11, all found together in Dan 12:3. In both of the latter loci God's servant makes the many righteous.[34]

But a mere list of lexical connections does not grasp the depth of change being wrought. The density and intensity of scriptural allusion in this Danielic oracle represents a more profound kind of recognition. It was H. L. Ginsberg who first described the identification of the religious roles and actors that the Daniel text was performing: "[T]he author of Dan xi–xii has simply identified the Servant of Isa lii 13–liii 12 with the Maskilim (Enlightened or Enlighteners) of his day, and the Many of the said passage with the Many of Dan xi 33, 34, etc."[35]

Daniel's identification of Isaiah's servant with the *maśkîlîm* goes beyond the literary and religious: it legitimates an institution. The Danielic oracle transforms Isaiah's prophecy about the unique life of a singular figure into a script. Scripture provides roles for multiple actors to live out the role of the originally singular enlightened servant, a process we have already seen with Moses' shining face in early Christianity. A more detailed picture of how Isaiah's ideal type is pluralized in Daniel and then enacted at Qumran is gained when we note the pointed way in which Isaiah's vocabulary is grammatically changed. In the Isaianic source text, the roots *śkl* and *ṣdq* occur in third masculine singular prefix forms of the *hipʿil*: "he shall prosper" and "he shall make righteous/vindicate," respectively. They describe acts that, while they may occur repeatedly or over a duration of time, represent unique accomplishments by a single individual, the divinely chosen protagonist of the prophecy. The object of *ṣdq* in Isa 53:11 is *rabbîm*, "many," understood as a generic term.

The Danielic oracle in 12:3 transforms these verbs, together with their Isaianic objects, by inflecting both together as participles, nouns reflecting human roles: the ones who enlighten and the ones who make righteous. Now, seen out of context and in isolation the participle form of the *hipʿil* of *śkl* is not uncommon in the Bible; it is found frequently in Proverbs (e.g., 14:35) and typically describes a wise or prudent person. But while the semantics of the term are retained in the four places it appears in Daniel (11:33, 35; 12:3, 10), it unmistakably draws on the language of Second Isaiah, evoking the unique cluster of terms found there. In two of the four places that *maśkîl* appears in Daniel, it retains the verbal sense of its prooftext. In Dan 11:33 this is obvious because it takes the people (*ʿām*) as an object, parallel with the many (*rabbîm*), parallelling Isa 53:11. Similarly in 12:3

---

34. In Isaiah we probably have to do with a juridical, not simply a moral-pedagogical, activity. In the context of the Suffering Servant's vindication, the text's edge is sharpened with the irony that the servant was judged while "acquitting others," as the *hipʿil* of *ṣdq* often bears a delocutive sense, as Delbert R. Hillers, following Benveniste, terms it: "to pronounce righteous," hence "to acquit." See Hillers, "Delocutive Verbs in Biblical Hebrew," *JBL* 86 (1967): 320–24.

35. H. L. Ginsberg, "The Oldest Interpretation of the Suffering Servant," *VT* 3 (1953): 400–404.

the phrase parallels the key terms from Isa 53:11, *ṣdq* in the *hip'il* with *rabbîm* as an object.

The changes in grammatical form entail changes in participant roles. In Dan 11–12 the *maśkîlîm* appear as the central actors in an eschatological drama, teaching ("The ones who enlighten the people *(maśkîlê ʿām)* will make the many [*rabbîm*] understand" [11:33]), suffering ("Some of the *maśkîlîm* will fall, that they may be refined and purged and whitened until the time of the end" [11:35]), and, in the first and only biblical reference to the concept, achieving a heavenly afterlife ("And the *maśkîlîm* will shine like the brightness of the firmament, those who make the many righteous, like the stars for all eternity" [12:3]).

If in its evocation of the ideal type of the sages Dan 11–12 creates potential roles through nominalization into participles, these roles are then inhabited at Qumran. What is especially striking about the fit between the Qumran and Danielic usages of the term *maśkîlîm* is the way the Qumran personae are modeled on and act out the apocalyptic text of Daniel. The *Community Rule* not only designates the figure of the *maśkîl* in the same role—(literally?) enlightened teacher—that we find in Daniel's vision, but the inner circle of the community is designated with the same term used in Daniel for the students of the *maśkîlîm*: the many.[36]

If one compares the extensive exegetical use of Moses' shining face in the New Testament with the exegetical enactment of the role of *maśkîl* at Qumran, it becomes clear that the inhabitance of a previously unique biblical role is not an isolated occurrence in the Hellenistic period. Indeed, the reverse may be true, as we will see in the following discussion of a surprising claim to inhabit another uninhabitable, previously taboo biblical role, one that again will draw us into exegesis of both biblical and ancient Near Eastern myth.

3. Lucifer's Ascent to Heaven

The second persona is the opposite of the first. Rather than receiving illumination by being allowed to approach God, the second figure is already illuminated, a light-bearing being who attempts to approach God illegimitately by seizing his throne. For convenience he may be referred to etymologically as Lucifer, "light-bringing."[37] The argument, played out over more than a thousand years, is over

---

36. The term is very widely attested at Qumran: for an illustrative example, see 4Q258 II 5; for further attestations, see the index to Philip Alexander and Geza Vermes, eds., *Qumran Cave 4.XIX: 4QSerekh Ha-Yaḥad and Two Related Texts* (DJD 26; Oxford: Clarendon, 1998), *q.v.*, and 1QS *passim.*

37. It was Jerome who first applied this Latin epithet for the dawn star to the villain of Isa 14. For an insightful characterization of this myth and its politics to which the present study is indebted, see David J. Halperin's "Ascension or Invasion: Implications of the Heavenly Journey in Ancient Judaism," *Religion* 18 (1988): 47–67.

who was capable of ascending to the divine realm and sitting in the throne of a god. Over the course of the controversy, the myth of an illegitimate usurper in the past is transformed into a ritual of legitimate possibility in the present.

The earliest example known to us in Canaanite myth is found in the Ugaritic Epic of Baal, in the dispute over who will be Baal's successor. Thus, KTU 1.6 I.56–65:

> Thereupon Athtar the Terrible (*ʿrẓ*)
> ascends (*yʿl*) the heights of Zaphon,
> sits (*yṯb*) on Mighty Baal's seat.
> (But) his feet do not reach the footstool,
> his head does not reach the top (of the seat).
> (To this) Athtar the Terrible responds:
> "I will not reign (*mlk*) on the heights of Zaphon!"
> Athtar the Terrible descends (*yrd*),
> he descends from the seat of Mighty Baal,
> and reigns (*mlk*) over the earth, god of it all.[38]

The text is classic myth, a third-person poetic narrative about gods, and contains no application to the present. The plot was clarified by Jonas Greenfield, who explained that the previous contestant was rejected because he was too weak: he "could not run (with Baal); with Baal could not handle the lance."[39] By contrast, Athtar's epithet *ʿrẓ*, , cognate with the biblical Hebrew root *ʿrṣ*, "be terrible, mighty," makes clear that he did indeed resemble Baal on this count. What he lacked was Baal's gigantic physical size (like that ascribed to Marduk in *Enuma Elish*), a somatic sign of his rulership and superiority. Ultimately, no one can gain Baal's exalted throne because they all remain *incomparable* to him.

The *māšāl* ("similitude, parable") of Isa 14 invokes this mythic pattern. Not only thematic but lexical continuities with the Ugaritic text make it clear that a similar form of the Canaanite myth was inherited by Isaiah.

---

38. For detailed notes, compare the translation of Dennis Pardee in *COS* 1.86:269. Note that the first candidate for Baal's replacement, *yd ʿylḥn*, is characterized in his epithet by *knowing* (whatever the real force of his second name may be) but is not mighty enough. Might is something Athtar the Terrible possesses in abundance, according to his name. It is also by virtue of his military might that Isaiah's pretender to the divine throne, "who shook the earth, who made realms tremble, who made the world like a waste and wrecked its towns" (16b–17a) tried to equal God, while Ezekiel's false god attempts to rival God in wisdom

39. Jonas Greenfield, "Ba'al's Throne and Isa. 6:1," in *Mélanges bibliques et orientaux en l'honneur de M. Mathias Delcor* (ed. A. Caquot, S. Légasse, and M. Tardieu; AOAT 215; Neukirchen-Vluyn: Neukirchener, 1985), 193–98.

12 How are you fallen from heaven, O Shining One, son of Dawn!	איך נפלת משמים הילל בן־שחר
How are you felled to earth, O vanquisher of nations!	נגדעת לארץ חולש על־גוים:
13 Once you thought in your heart, “I will climb to the sky;	ואתה אמרת בלבבך השמים אעלה
Higher than the stars of God I will set my throne.	ממעל לכוכבי־אל ארים כסאי
I will sit in the mount of assembly, On the summit of Zaphon:	ואשב בהר־מועד בירכתי צפון:
14 I will mount the back of a cloud—I will match the Most High.”	אעלה על־במתי עב אדמה לעליון:

Isaiah’s prophetic taunt is phrased not like a narrative but in the second person, formally addressed to a present listener. It takes up our Canaanite Lucifer myth, as we see from the core of shared motifs and words: a pretender to the divine throne attempts to *resemble* the dominant god by *ascending* (Hebrew and Ugaritic *ʿlh*) the heights of Mount Zaphon (the term is identical in Hebrew and Ugaritic) and *sitting* (Hebrew *yšb,* Ugaritic cognate *yṯb*) on the throne there in order to rule as supreme god. Further proof of a shared mythic background is the image of mounting a cloud. This evokes an epithet common to both Ba’al (who is *rkb ʿrpt* “the cloud-rider” in KTU 1.2 iv 8) and YHWH (*rkb bʿrbwt* “the cloud-rider” in Ps 68:5; compare the cloud-theopanies book-ending the Sinai revelation in Exod 19 and 24). The same theme appears again in biblical prophecy in Ezekiel’s attack on the prince of Tyre, whom he accuses of attempting to gain a divine throne and being cast off a sacred mountain (Ezek 28:2) against the prince of Tyre:

ותאמר אל אני מושב אלהים ישבתי בלב ימים ... ותתן לבך כלב אלהים

> and [you] have said, “I am a god; I sit enthroned like a god in the heart of the seas” … You deemed your mind equal to a god’s.

Again we witness the failed attempt to sieze the throne atop a sacred mountain. The two prophetic texts add God’s punishment: asserting against the would-be divinity the most basic taxonomic indicator of mortality, death.

Despite their shared mythic pattern, these Israelite prophetic texts are crucially different from the earlier Ugaritic example: they are not poetic narratives, phrased in the third person, but parables or taunts, phrased in the second person to a listener in the here and now. But this second-person transgressor is both mythic and apostrophized: the texts may have originally been taunts against Babylonian or Phoenician kings, but as soon as they entered the stream of written transmission the invocation became rhetorical. What the texts continued to do was invoke and reactivate a common myth of hubris in the form of a figure who attempts to resemble the ruling god. He ascends, tries to take the throne, and falls.

4. Resembling God

A look at the interpretive life of the Lucifer myth reveals the problem at its heart, as the myth is merged in remarkable ways with biblical texts. In theological issues of this magnitude, rhetoric is always more than rhetoric because when the wording of such central texts is inverted, new possibilities open up between the lines. We begin with a thematically related text that will demonstrate this point. The Song at the Sea, Exod 15:1–19, is a famous case of a song embedded in narrative. In particular, 15:11 becomes the most famous Jewish prayer about resembling God.

Who is like you among the gods, O Lord?	מי־כמכה באלם יהוה
Who is like you, majestic in holiness?	מי כמכה נאדר בקדש
Awesomely praised, doing wonders?	נורא תהלת עשה פלא

It is represented as being sung by Moses and the people of Israel after God drowned the Egyptians. The song's differences in details of language and plot from its narrative context suggest its preexistence as an old liturgical piece incorporated into the exodus story. In fact, Exodus itself immediately depicts the Song of the Sea being taken up in ritual: after being sung by the leader and men, Moses and the Israelites, it is then cited by incipit as being sung by Miriam the prophetess in a dance performed by the women of Israel (Exod 15:20–21). The earliest appearance of the Song of the Sea already provides a model of its own reuse.

Already recontextualized within its own original narrative framework, the Song of the Sea continues to be invoked in early Jewish exegesis. The earliest extended rabbinic discussion of the Song of the Sea, tractate *Shirta* of the early midrashic compilation *Mekhilta de Rabbi Ishmael,* is a virtual catalogue of heavenly ascents, uniting Exod 15:11 with precisely the texts we have just examined, Isa 14 and Ezek 28. This fact is significant because it demonstrates that ancient Jewish exegetes themselves connected the rhetorical question of resemblance to God, מי כמכה, "who is like you?" with the Lucifer myth, which calls that question to account. What happens when ritual rhetoric about divine uniqueness is brought together with its opposite number, a myth that dares to really ask if someone who is not God might become like God?

We find someone who dared to ask this question in the ritual texts from Qumran. Among the liturgical matrials, the text definitively published by Esti Eshel in DJD 29 as "4QSelf-Glorification Hymn" existed in at least two basic versions and four manuscript copies at Qumran. The texts are paleographically dated to the second half of the first century B.C.E., and in the three manuscripts that preserve an extended context for the hymn it is integrated into public liturgical material (including the *Hodayot* manuscript 1QHa). In these contexts we find plural imperative forms of verbs of praising indicating that they were designated for use in public prayer. The best preserved version is 4Q491 fragment 11, which I translate here based on Eshel's edition:

> ... He established his truth of old, and the secrets of his devising in al[l... hea]ven and the counsel of the humble as an eternal council [...] forever a mighty throne in the divine council. None of the Kedemite kings[40] shall sit in it, nor shall their nobles [...] shall not resemble my glory, and none shall be exalted save me, nor approach me, for I have taken my seat in [the council] of heaven and none [...] I shall be reckoned with angels, and my station in the council of the Holy Ones. I do not desire like mortals; everything precious to me is in the glory [...] in the holy dw[elling. Wh]o has been denigrated on my account, yet who can resemble my glory? Who [...] who bear[s all s]ufferings like me and who [end]ures evil—did it resemble mine? I have been taught, and there is no teaching that is like [my teaching]. Who can stop me when I op[en my mouth,] and the flow of my speech—who can measure it? Who can arraign me or compare to my justice? [...Fo]r I am rec[koned] with angels, [and my g]lory with the sons of the King. Not [with] gold or precious gold of Ophir.[41]

The claim of "a mighty throne in the divine council" in which kings cannot sit, the impossibility of *resembling* the speaker's glory, the statement that "none shall be exalted save me, nor approach me, for I have taken my seat in [the council] of heaven," and the speaker's insistence, repeated twice, that he is reckoned with angels—all are worthy of note. But the final and most disconcerting statement comes from the variant version of the text found in 4Q471b and 4Q427: מי כמוני בעלים, "Who is like *me* among the angels?"

Our old Canaanite myth is back. As in the Baal epic, Isa 14, and Ezek 28, we find talk of assuming a divine throne and of resembling gods. But this time the myth is invoked with a further significant gramatical change in the phrase from Exod 15. If our myth was first attested in third-person Ugaritic narrative poetry and invoked in the second person by Isaiah and Ezekiel, we see here a reenuncia-

40. Figures of proverbial wisdom in Isa 19:11 and 1 Kgs 5:10

41. For her edition of 4Q491 frag. 11, see Esther Eshel, "4Q471b: A Self-Glorification Hymn," *RevQ* 17 (1996): 184. My citation begins in the middle of Eshel's line 3. I have produced a more detailed treatment of the manuscripts of the most controversial passage in Sanders, *Writing, Ritual and Apocalypse*, 274–75.

tion of the words of Exodus by the usurper of Isaiah and Ezekiel, with the person shifted from the second to the first and thus from the praise of God to the self-predication of the speaker. By speaking as the enthroned ascendant, the speaker of the text makes himself the new protagonist of an old myth.

But who is the speaker, and what kind of text are we reading now? First, the contents of our passage make clear he is human: it is not plausible for an angel to boast that he is considered an angel. More decisively, the text is integrated into larger liturgical compositions, and there is no break in speaker marked at the beginning of this text. Here we reach a point that has not been sufficiently emphasized, though the phenomenon has been seriously explored by Crispin Fletcher-Lewis and Christopher Morray-Jones.[42] This is that the speaker of the *Hymn,* whoever he may have been in the author's mind, is, in practice, the speaker of other Qumran prayers. Specifically, examination of the physical features, paleography, and language show that in two of the manuscripts the *Hymn* was part of the well-known Qumran *Thanksgiving Hymns* or *Hodayot*. Scholars tend to believe that these hymns were authored by the founder of the Qumran community, the Righteous Teacher. But if he did indeed write them for other people's liturgical use—as it seems clear he did—then the issue of his authorship loses relevance, because the purpose of the text was for it to be reused in ritual.[43] We may have found the author, with his original religious experiences, but our more important discovery is the audience, the very reason why the author's experience does not matter as much as what his text does. The words are taken over by the sectarian worshiper: in Qumran practice, the "I" of the text was the reader himself.[44]

---

42. In a pair of papers read at the 1998 SBL meeting. Crispin Fletcher-Lewis, "Heavenly Ascent or Incarnational Presence? A Revisionist Reading of the Songs of the Sabbath Sacrifice," and Christopher Morray-Jones, "The Temple Within: The Embodied Divine Image and Its Worship in the Dead Sea Scrolls and Other Early Jewish and Christian Sources," both in *Society of Biblical Literature 1998 Seminar Papers* (SBLSP 37; Atlanta: Scholars Press, 1998), 367–99 and 400–31, respectively. See now Fletcher-Lewis's *All the Glory of Adam: Liturgical Anthropology in the Dead Sea Scrolls* (STDJ 42; Leiden: Brill, 2002).

43. This is not to say that it would not matter if there were explicit evidence that the users of the text kept such a unique author in mind. It is to say that the lack of this evidence is the sort of thing that created the quest for the original author in the first place.

44. As Andrea Lieber showed in a 2000 SBL paper delivered alongside this one (now published as "Voice and Vision: Song as a Vehicle for Ecstatic Experience in Songs of the Sabbath Sacrifice," in *Of Scribes and Sages: Early Jewish Interpretation and Transmision of Scripture* [ed. C. A. Evans; London: T&T Clark, 2004], 51–58), the ecstatic performance of Exod 15 as liturgy is also attested in Philo's astonishing description of the Therapeutae (*Contempl.* 85–89). If the Qumran and Philonic evidence does indeed suggest a Hellenistic Jewish practice of using Exod 15 as a model of achieved religious experience, it is surely intimately related to the early exegetical tradition of a vision of God at the Red Sea discussed here.

We have seen that the biblical passages from Isaiah and Ezekiel that inform the Qumran *Self-Glorification Hymn* are themselves active reinterpretations of a preexisting corpus of myth. The theme of this mythic corpus is the comparison of human and divine in terms of both proximity (how physically close one can come to God's throne) and resemblance (how much one one can resemble God). Thus when the *Hymn* reinterprets this old mythic debate about how close one can get to God, it places itself in a complex historical trajectory. This trajectory has two major directions, one in which divine or semidivine competitors to the high god are dismissed as incomparable, and a second one in which humans are elevated to semidivine status, bridging the gap of incomparability. In the last case we examined, older prooftexts were recruited to provide previously unprecedented levels of human participation in divine activity: As the materials of the corpus were invoked and reworked, they shifted from a rhetoric of impossibility to one of possibility. This rhetoric reflects and, I would argue, helped create a larger religious shift in the Hellenistic period: from the locative to the utopian, and from an anthropology of human limits to one of unbounded possibility.[45] If Jewish apocalyptic is the first example of this shift, Jewish and Christian mysticism is its most enduring legacy.

5. A Body of Light

What place did this exalted new position that the reader could inhabit in prayer have in the larger world of sectarian practice? The role was not performed in a vacuum. As our next selection of Qumran texts shows, the notion of achieving a pure body of light was a deep-seated part of sectarian cosmology. A wide range of texts worked to both reflect and help build a worldview that existed in practice as well as theory.

A major Qumran liturgical text, the *Songs of the Sabbath Sacrifice*, lets us fit this hymn into a larger picture of how the sectarians imagined themselves. The *Songs of the Sabbath Sacrifice* are both speculative, giving a detailed visual and auditory description of angelic praise in each of the seven layers of heaven, and ritual, keyed liturgically to the first thirteen Sabbaths of the year. The texts directly address our old questions of comparison to the divine and corporeality. In the song for the first Sabbath, it is stated that the angelic company is of incomparable ritual purity, that there is nothing unclean in their midst (4Q400 1 14). In the second Sabbath, the logical consequence of this intolerance of impurity is followed: the speaker asks, "How shall we be reckoned among [the]m, and

45. For the first dimension of this shift see Jonathan Z. Smith's *Map Is Not Territory* (Leiden: Brill, 1978), esp. 101; for the second dimension, see Ithamar Gruenwald's "Two Essential Qualities of Jewish Apocalyptic," in idem, *Apocalyptic and Merkavah Mysticism* (AGJU 14; Leiden: Brill, 1980), 3–28.

our priesthood, how (shall it be considered) in their dwellings?" (4Q400 2 6). The question follows: "What is the offering of our tongue of dust compared with angelic knowledge?" (4Q400 2 7).

The texts here stress the gap between human and divine, conjuring the inarticulate and unknowing nature of the sectarians in comparison to the might and eloquence of the angels. But the *Songs* continue, proceeding to describe deeper and deeper layers of heaven. It appears that the very *asking* of the question has initiated the bridging of the gap through the sectarians' ritual purity and enactment of the heavenly secret embodied in the singing of the Sabbath songs themselves: knowledge of angelic praise. The fact that the sectarians also sing the songs the angels sing constitutes proof that they are indeed *comparable* to the angels. The validity of this proof is based on the way that the criteria for success are defined within the text itself, as it models and then achieves the thing that makes humans like angels: divine praise. The songs create and fulfill their own terms of success through performance as an act of divine resemblance.[46]

The comparison, in fact, goes beyond words. Scholars have long remarked on the profound dualism of the Qumran worldview: the sectarians are the people of light, and they oppose the people of darkness. Generally this dualism has been perceived in literary texts as an abstract and moralistic phenomenon. But as Devorah Dimant argued in a brilliantly incisive article, this approach misses "the concrete, material aspects of this dualism and fail[s] to recognize its links to other facets of the Qumran community social world and literary product."[47] As an all-embracing principle divinely preordained, the dualistic configuration underlies the physical world, which is the real arena of the dualistic struggle. It has long been known that one of the main issues that separated the Qumran community from other Jewish groups was their unswerving adherence to the 364-day solar calendar. This calendar is the subject of a number of polemics at Qumran, and it separated them completely from the liturgical practice of the Jerusalem temple, which used a 360-day lunar year, because the sectarian Sabbaths and holidays no longer fell on the same days as those of the temple.

By showing why the solar calendar had both material and cosmological significance, Dimant provides a context for the performed exegesis of the Lucifer myth. She first considers 4Q503, a record of daily evening and morning prayers. As its editor, Maurice Baillet, was the first to recognize, the text conforms to the solar calendar of 364 days and arranges the morning prayers according to the

46. The process by which a mystical text can model its own performance was most powerfully theorized by Janowitz in *The Poetics of Ascent,* drawing on the approaches of anthropologists such as Silverstein and Parmentier.

47. "Dualism at Qumran: New Perspectives" in *Caves of Enlightenment: Proceedings of the ASOR Dead Sea Scrolls Jubilee Symposium* (ed. J. H. Charlesworth; N. Richland Hills, Tex.: Bibal, 1998), 55–73, here 59.

position of the sun each day, marked by the number of gates of light through which the sun enters.[48] The evening prayers refer to the proportion of darkness, apparently based on the visibilty of the moon. This description of the solar course, synchronized to the lunar cycle, is strikingly similar to the lunisolar synchronism revealed to Enoch in the course of his heavenly journey in the Book of the Luminaries, probably the oldest apocalyptic ascent text and known in four copies at Qumran. *Calendrical Documents A* and *B* (4Q320 and 4Q321) fill out this picture, linking the Qumran festivals to longer days and brighter nights, which were seen as auspicuous; the moon, by contrast, was a source of the dark days of evil. As Dimant notes, such a link is meaningful only if the light is perceived as the material emanation of good. A further calendar, *Calendrical Document C* (4Q322), inserts historical events into a special chronology correlated with the 364-day year. These lists, as well as other interpretive texts such as *Pesher on the Periods* (4Q180, 181), calculate periods of good and evil in history itself in a manner similar to that of the apocalypses.

The dualism is extended to the body itself in 4Q186, an astrological physiogomy that descibes the physical qualities of persons born under particular zodiac signs. Based on the features of their bodies, every individual's spiritual features may be ranked on a nine-point scale, divided between portions in the house of light and the pit of darkness. This ratio decides their place in the community hierarchy, according to the *Damascus Document* (13:12, preserved in 4Q267 9 iv 9). Qumran medical beliefs and practices likewise operate on the principle of the physical presence of evil in the world. Qumran versions of the *Damascus Document* connect the corporeality of spirits (4Q266 6 i) with the notion of sickness as a punishment for sin (as lepers are categorized as transgressors in 4Q270 2 ii 12). *Jubilees,* present in fifteen copies at Qumran, provides a similar demonic etiology of disease: people who sin are vulnerable to bodily attack by the descendants of fallen angels (10:1–8), but a book of heavenly antidotes was transmitted to Noah's line at the hands of angels (10:13). The Qumran healing practices attested in our texts exorcise demons by means of songs of divine praise, suggesting that the heavenly antitodes, given by Noah to Shem, were also thought to be materially present in the Qumran library and liturgical traditions.

These texts order time, the body, and the cosmos on a single opposition: between light and darkness. For the sectarians, the discovery of a single organizing principle behind all three allows the possibility of putting them in synch, coordinating microcosm and macrocosm. The presence of this principle in such practical documents as calendrical, physiognomic, and medical texts allowed them to practice their dualism in a material way.

---

48. Maurice Baillet, *Qumrân grotte 4.III (4Q482–4Q520)* (DJD 7; Oxford: Clarendon, 1982), 105–36.

We are now in a position to trace the history of process by which ascent to heaven became a cultural fact. In this process not just interpretations but life roles were exegetically read out of texts. This interweaving of interpretation and practice did not place the texts at the center of its cultural universe so much as fit them into a bricolage by which that universe was pieced together. In the Torah, Moses is uniquely allowed to approach God's divinity, but the divine persona is a mask, external to his body. This persona is conferred in a single historical event by God and connected to the unique authority of the prophet and his books. In Isaiah and Exekiel, the divine or semidivine Lucifer is a figure of hubris, cast down to earth and death. At Qumran, Lucifer's sense of hubris is totally neutralized: Isaiah's villain or victim, dethroned and humiliated, was authorized as a hero; assumption of the promised heavenly throne is cited as a model by the sectarians in their liturgy. There are both liturgical and material models for this change. While the *Songs of the Sabbath Sacrifice* define and activate the ways men can resemble angels, the sectarians' cosmology made the divine persona simultaneously less literal and more physical than Moses'. The element of light already present in both the cosmos and each one of the sectarians' bodies is already divine; it only needs to be realized through religious practice. A Qumran text for new members (4Q298) whose purpose is to reveal wisdom about the cosmic order addresses the initiates as people of dawn. Initiation reclassified them both cognitively and physically, letting the new sectarians dawn into beings of light.

We have traced the history of a language, a set of ideas and practices that provides a context for the *Self-Glorification Hymn* and the divine personae of Qumran ritual. In it we encounter a process that is quintessentially exegetical, yet turns the stereotypical relationship of exegete to text inside-out. Rather than reading elements of life into a sacred text, elements of preexisting texts are used to forge new roles in ritual and thus lay the foundation for new experiences in life. Each sectarian is able to resemble God not just because of the texts they read but because the way they imagine their bodies and perform their rituals places them in systematic relation with God based on their analysis of the cosmos into light and dark. The historically unique precedents—Moses, Isaiah's Suffering Servant, and Isaiah and Ezekiel's Lucifer—are radically revised: the new identities constructed through ritual enlightenment are no longer unique, one-time affairs but replicable, accessible to the sectarians through initiation.

Thus did the inextricable intertwining of interpretation and performance generate a new religious possibility. The history we have traced leads us past unanswerable questions of inner life into answerable questions of cultural change. The interpretation of texts is a way of changing history; in this case, it was one of the key mechanisms by which divine revelation was democratized in the Hellenistic period. The evidence presented here traces the pathway to transformative religious experience that performative exegesis laid.

Part 2: Communal Identities

The Emergence of the Mystical Traditions of the *Merkabah*

Rachel Elior

The cherubim fall before him and bless.
They give blessing as they raise themselves.
The sound of divine stillness [is heard].
[ ] and there is a tumult of jubilation as they lift their wings.
A sound of divine stillness.
The pattern of the chariot-throne they bless
Above the firmament of the cherubim.
The splendor of the luminous firmament do they sing
Beneath his glorious seat (4Q405 20-21-22).

Gershom Scholem initiated the scholarly discussion on the history of Jewish mystics in his groundbreaking book *Major Trends in Jewish Mysticism* in 1941. The historical survey of the subject was inaugurated with a chapter entitled "Merkabah Mysticism and Jewish Gnosticism."[1] This chapter pertains to "the oldest organized movement of Jewish mysticism in late talmudic and posttalmudic times, that is, the period from which the most illuminating documents have come down to us."[2] Scholem is referring to the pseudepigraphic or anonymous authors of the *hekhalot* and *merkabah* literature, who were pursuing heavenly knowledge and visionary experience described as *razei merkabah* (mysteries of the chariot), which he entitled "Jewish Gnosticism." These mystics were defined by Scholem as those "who were the *first* to make an attempt ... to invest Judaism with the glory of mystical splendor."[3]

1. Gershom Scholem, *Major Trends in Jewish Mysticism* (New York: Schocken, 1941), 40–79. The word *merkabah* referring to the divine chariot of the cherubim shown to seers and prophets and to its ritual representation in the tabernacle and in the temple (Exod 25; Ezek 1; 1 Chr 28:18) can be transcribed in English as *merkabah* and *merkavah*. See below.

2. Ibid., 41.

3. Ibid.

Many of the contentions in this chapter regarding the date, provenance, and identity of the writers were studied in depth and reconsidered by Scholem himself in a book devoted to the subject appearing twenty years later, entitled *Jewish Gnosticism, Merkabah Mysticism and Talmudic Tradition*.[4] His work on the relation between *merkabah* literature and the rabbinic tradition maintained that Jewish mysticism was a central, though esoteric, aspect of early rabbinic Judaism.

His position was further elaborated by students of Jewish mysticism and rabbinic tradition, and while some debate particular aspects of this conception,[5] most agreed upon his initial assumption. For most historians of Jewish mysticism in the second half of the twentieth century, the starting point of the discussion concerning the history of Jewish mysticism was the otherworldly descriptions appearing in the *hekhalot* literature, which were composed in the Mishnaic and the talmudic era or in the Roman-Byzantine period in the land of Israel.

In the sixty-five years that have passed since the publication of *Major Trends in Jewish Mysticism,* we have learned that the first chapter in the history of Jewish mysticism in the postbiblical period started a number of centuries earlier, in the period during which the extensive priestly library known as the Dead Sea Scrolls was written. Scholem could not have known this chronological-bibliographical data, since the Dead Sea Scrolls were revealed only in 1947, six years after *Major Trends in Jewish Mysticism* was first published. The editorial work on the remnants of the nine hundred scrolls required many years of research, and the complete publication through thirty-nine volumes has been accomplished only in 2002, thanks to the cooperative efforts of many scholars from all over the world.[6]

1. The Mystical Traditions of the *Merkabah*

In my work on *hekhalot* literature and the *merkabah* tradition of the mishnaic and talmudic period,[7] as well as on the *merkabah* tradition appearing in the

4. Gershom Scholem, *Jewish Gnosticism, Merkabah Mysticism and Talmudic Tradition* (New York: Jewish Theological Seminary of America, 1960).

5. See a survey on the developments in this field in the section devoted to *merkabah* mysticism and Jewish Gnosticism in in *Gershom Scholem's* Major Trends in Jewish Mysticism *Fifty Years After: Proceedings of the Sixth International Conference on the History of Jewish Mysticism* (ed. P. Schäfer and J. Dan; Tübingen: Mohr Siebeck, 1993), 25–86. See n. 52 below.

6. DJD 1–39 (Oxford: Clarendon 1965–2002); note the introduction of Emanuel Tov in idem, ed., *The Text from the Judaean Desert: Indices and an Introduction to the* Discoveries in the Judaean Desert *Series* (DJD 39; Oxford: Clarendon, 2002).

7. Rachel Elior, "From Earthly Temple to Heavenly Shrines: Prayer and Sacred Song in the *Hekhalot* Literature and Its Relation to Temple Traditions," *JSQ* 4 (1997): 217–67.

Dead Sea Scrolls in the last few centuries B.C.E.,[8] I argue that, while both these mystical traditions of the *merkabah* (written over the span of hundreds of years between the last few centuries B.C.E. and the first half of the first millennium C.E.) are clearly distant in time and style and exhibit obviously unique and variegated aspects that derive from separate times and provenance, different writers, and a changing sociohistorical context, they also share significant common denominators. Both traditions reveal exceptional interests in celestial sanctuaries and holy angels that establish a heavenly pattern for the priestly perceptions of holy time, holy place, and holy ritual. Both traditions focus their attention on the heavenly domain known as the world of the *merkabah* as was revealed to seers and mystics (Sir 49:8; *1 En.* 14:8–25), who, in the mystical tradition, ascended to the heavenly sanctuaries in different periods and described what they had seen and heard in poetical-visionary writings. Both traditions are profoundly interested in mystical descriptions of the *holy space* in heaven (seven *merkabot;* seven *hekhalot*; *pardes*–paradise; garden of righteousness) and in the sacred ritual performed by the angelic watches in the celestial realm in eternal cycles.[9] Both literary traditions express a profound interest in *holy angels* as guardians of *holy time* in sevenfold divisions within the *seven heavenly sanctuaries.*

Both textual traditions focus on various aspects of angelic knowledge, angelic writings, and divine liturgy, and both demonstrate a singular interest in the person of Enoch son of Jared (Gen 5:21–24). Enoch is the seventh of the prediluvium patriarchs, who is alleged to have brought the holy calendar of 364 days and fifty-two Sabbaths/weeks from heaven. He is the one who was chosen among human beings to be the first person to learn from the angels reading, writing, and counting and various means of historical memory and ritual commemoration. Enoch is also revered as the first scribe, the messenger of heavenly knowledge concerning time and space, the founder of the ritual incense sacrifice, and the founder of the priestly written tradition based on angelic knowledge and divine vision (*1 En.* 14:8–25; *Jub.* 4:17–21; Sir 44:16; *2 En.* [J] 40:1–6).[10] Enoch son of

8. Rachel Elior, *The Three Temples: On the Emergence of Jewish Mysticism* (trans. D. Louvish; Oxford: Littman Library of Jewish Civilization, 2004).

9. See Carol Newsom, *Songs of the Sabbath Sacrifice: A Critical Edition* (HSS 27; Atlanta: Scholars Press, 1985), 23–58; Elior, *The Three Temples*, 165–200; Johann Maier, "Šire Olat Haššabbat: Some Observation on Their Calendric Implications and on Their Style," in *The Madrid Qumran Congress* (ed. J. Trebola-Barrera and L. Vegas-Montaner; 2 vols.; Leiden: Brill 1992), 2:543–60; James Davila, "The Macrocosmic Temple, Scriptural Exegesis and the Songs of the Sabbath Sacrifice," *DSD* 9 (2002): 1–19.

10. On Enoch son of Jared, see Jonas C. Greenfield and Michael E. Stone, "The Books of Enoch and the Traditions of Enoch," *Numen* 26 (1979): 89–103; Michael A. Knibb, *The Ethiopic Book of Enoch: A New Edition in the Light of the Aramaic Dead Sea Fragments* (2 vols.; Oxford: Clarendon, 1978); Matthew Black, *The Book of Enoch or 1 Enoch* (SVTP 7; Leiden: Brill, 1985); George W. E. Nickelsburg, *1 Enoch 1: A Commentary on the Book of 1 Enoch, Chapters 1–36;*

Jared, the protagonist of the priestly tradition before the Common Era, was transformed into the angelic entity of Enoch-Metatron in the centuries that followed the destruction of the temple. His exceptional figure incorporates both a human priestly dimension and the angelic eternal tradition united into one entity.

I have maintained in various articles and books over the last two decades that these striking similarities in the mystical conception of holy time, holy place, and holy ritual, which all focus on priestly angelic figures, divine knowledge, and angelic liturgy, could be better understood in light of the fact that the two traditions reflected in the Dead Sea Scrolls and in the *hekhalot* and *merkabah* literature were written by those priestly circles who were deposed from their holy service in the Jerusalem temple. The authors of *hekhalot* literature were writing after the destruction of the Second Temple by the Romans in the year 70 C.E. The *hekhalot* literature was consolidated within various factions associated with the priestly circles over the following centuries and clearly demonstrates by means of a unique poetical language and prose written in Hebrew, under mystical inspiration, their ceaseless effort to transform the lost priestly ritual of the Jerusalem temple worship into a celestial eternal worship. All the cardinal dimensions and sacred objects required for temple worship were founded upon divine paradigms as appearing in their inception in the biblical period (Exod 25:18–22) and could have been transformed after the destruction into their ancient celestial patterns with new adaptations within the *hekhalot* literature.

The new authors of the *hekhalot* attempted to transform the liturgical tradition of the lost temple cult into an eternal angelic service as performed in the seven heavenly temples. According to this literature, the ministering angels (*malakhei hasharet*) within these sanctuaries eternally serve and worship before the divine chariot, or "the radiance of the *merkabah*" (4Q385, 4:5–6),[11] in a similar manner to the priests who served the earthly image that once stood in the holy of holies of the earthly temple (Exod 40:1–3, 20–21; 1 Kgs 7–8; 1 Chr 28:18).[12] All expressions of the celestial world of the *merkabah* are connected to the vision

---

81–108 (Hermeneia; Minneapolis: Fortress 2001); James C. VanderKam, *Enoch: A Man for All Generations* (Columbia: University of South Carolina Press, 1995); Rachel Elior, "Enoch Son of Jared and the Solar Calendar," in Elior, *The Three Temples*, 88–110; Andrei Orlov, *The Enoch-Metatron Tradition* (TSAJ 107; Tübingen: Mohr Siebeck, 2005). On Enoch's role in the *hekhalot* literature, see Philip Alexander, "3 (Hebrew Apocalypse of) Enoch," *OTP* 1:223–316; David J. Halperin, *The Faces of the Chariot: Early Jewish Responses to Ezekiel's Vision* (TSAJ 16; Tübingen, Mohr Siebeck, 1988); Peter Schäfer, *The Hidden and Manifest God: Some Major Themes in Early Jewish Mysticism* (Albany: State University of New York Press, 1992).

11. Devorah Dimant and John Strugnell, eds. *Qumran Cave 4.XXI: Parabiblical Texts, Part 4: Pseudo-Prophetic Texts* (DJD 30; Oxford: Clarendon, 2001), 42.

12. Elior, "From Earthly Temple to Heavenly Shrines."

of the chariot that is described by the exiled priest Ezekiel.[13] Ra'anan Boustan summed up this contention: "Ezekiel established a paradigm of the priestly figure grappling with the loss of the cult in creative new ways."[14]

The identity of the mystical authors who endorsed the vision of Ezekiel and immensely elaborated its visionary contents, as well as their relation to the contemporary rabbinic tradition, is an enigma and a subject of an ongoing scholarly debate. The intentions of some members of the rabbinical circles attempting to censor Ezekiel from the biblical canon (*b. Šabb.* 25a) and certain reports concerning the prohibition to read aloud the vision of the chariot (*b. Meg.* 13a) indicate an opposing opinion in regards to the tradition of the chariot. The two contradictory though affiliated traditions knew each other well. The protagonists of the *hekhalot* tradition, Rabbis Akiva and Ishmael, are likewise most prominent figures within the rabbinic tradition. The rabbinic tradition retains portions of the *hekhalot* narratives concerning the ascent to the heavenly world and the mystical sanctuary, while also retaining prohibitions concerning the study of the chariot tradition (*m. Hagigah; b. Megillah; b. Hag.* 14a–15a; *b. Ber.* 7a).

Despite these affinities, the two traditions are profoundly conflicting. The *hekhalot* liturgical tradition focuses upon the heavenly world, and its authors write the ineffable name of God in four letters according to the biblical tradition, while the diversified legal rabbinic traditions focuses on all aspects of worldly existence in a hermeneutical-conversation manner, exegesis, midrash, or legal discussion, and always refrain from writing the four letters of the divine name. In general, the rabbinic tradition avoids discussing sacred names, holy angels and heavenly sanctuaries, mystical ascents or angelic liturgy—all the subjects that are richly discussed in the contemporaneous *hekhalot* literature, ascribed to prominent rabbinic figures. The historical and social contextualization of the *hekhalot* and *merkabah* literatures, as well as their relation to rabbinic Judaism, is far from being completely understood or agreed upon; however, the mystical identity of the authors of the *hekhalot* and *merkabah* traditions and their inclination to poetical modes of expression and mystical inspiration as well as their obvious interest in angelic ritual and heavenly sanctuaries is agreed on by all scholars.

The *Songs of the Sabbath Sacrifice* (*Shirot 'Olat Hashabat*) and the *Blessings* (*Berakhot*) may be introduced as the missing link between the priest-prophet Ezekiel and the foundation of the biblical chariot tradition, on the one side, and the *hekhalot* literature chariot tradition, on the other side. The *Songs of the Sabbath Sacrifice*, written on parchment scrolls in the last few centuries B.C.E.,

13. 4Q385, 4:5–6: Dimant and Strugnell, *Qumran Cave 4.XXI,* 42; Ezek 1:10. Compare Halperin, *Faces of the Chariot,* and Rachel Elior, "Merkabah Mysticism; A Critical Review [D. J. Halperin, *Faces of the Chariot* Tübingen 1988]," *Numen* 37 (1990): 233–49.

14. Ra'anan Boustan, response to Rachel Elior's "The Three Temples" (paper presented at the Society of Biblical Literature Annual Meeting, San Antonio, 22 November 2004).

were found in 1947–1956 in caves of the Judean Desert in Qumran and Masada, among many other ancient Hebrew and Aramaic texts, all of which are sacred texts, written on parchment, and stored in clay jars. The discovery of the *Songs* marked a fundamental change in the history of the study of Jewish mysticism and in the contextualization of its development. The *Songs of the Sabbath Sacrifice*, previously unknown, was part of an ancient priestly library that revealed the mystical-liturgical-angelic foundations of the *merkabah* tradition and illuminated its links to Ezekiel vision and to priestly-angelic ritual.

The importance of this find was immediately apparent to John Strugnell and Gershom Scholem from the very inception of the preliminary publication of the *Songs*. John Strugnell designated the texts in 1959/60 as "The Angelic Liturgy at Qumran—4QSerek Šîrôt 'Ôlat Haššabbāt."[15] Twenty-five years later Carol Newsom entitled the texts *Songs of the Sabbath Sacrifice* in the first critical edition of the angelic liturgy.[16] Scholem stated immediately upon reading the first texts in 1960: "These fragments [of *Songs of the Sabbath Sacrifice*] leave no doubt that there is a connection between the oldest Hebrew Merkabah texts preserved in Qumran and the subsequent development of Merkabah mysticism as preserved in the Hekhalot texts."[17] Notably, Scholem in this short, seminal sentence did not elaborate on the identity of the writers or on their provenance but related only to the writings and the inherent historical/literary context.

Now, forty years later after that remark was published, with the publication of the entire library of those finds from the Judean Desert and since a more comprehensive context of these writings is available, I would like to reflect on the historical consequences of this remark. Further, I will attempt to elaborate on the connection between the earliest *merkabah* traditions and the angelic liturgy that were set down before the Common Era, as found in Qumran and Masada, and the later *merkabah* tradition and angelic hymns that were deemed to form the early stages of Jewish mysticism after the Common Era.

The most striking common denominator that can be formulated between the four Hebrew concepts pertaining to the early stages of Jewish mystical writings mentioned above—that is, *merkabah* (chariot of the cherubim),[18] *hekhalot*

15. John Strugnell, "The Angelic Liturgy at Qumran—4QSerek Šîrôt 'Ôlat Haššabbāt," in *Congress Volume: Oxford, 1959* (VTSup 7; Leiden: Brill, 1960), 318–45.

16. Newsom, *Songs of the Sabbath Sacrifice*.

17. Gershom Scholem, *Jewish Gnosticism, Merkabah Mysticism and Talmudic Tradition* (2nd ed.; New York: Jewish Theological Seminary, 1965), 128.

18. See 1 Chr 28:18; cf. Exod 25:18–20; 37:7–8; 1 Kgs 6:23–28; 8:7; 1 Chr 6:24–27; 2 Chr 3:10–14; 5:7–8; Ezek 10:2–19. On the transformation of the biblical concept in *hekhalot* literature, see Scholem, *Major Trends in Jewish Mysticism*, 40–79; Johann Maier, *Vom Kultus zur Gnosis* (Kairos 1; Salzburg: Müller, 1964); Halperin, *Faces of the Chariot*; Schäfer, *Hidden and Manifest God*, 193 and index entry "Merkavah"; Elior, "From Earthly Temple to Heavenly Shrines," 217–67; idem, *The Three Temples*, index entry "Merkavah."

(heavenly sanctuaries),[19] Sabbath sacrifice (*'olat hashabbat*),[20] and songs (*shir-shirot*)[21]—concerns their appearance in biblical literature, where all are connected to sacred space and to the cycles of the sacred ritual: to the tabernacle (Lev 25:18–27); to the temple, *hekhal*, where the cherubim stood (1 Kgs 6:24–27; 1 Chr 28:18); to the heavenly paradigms of the cherubim in the earthly sanctuary known as *merkabah* or *merkebet hakrubim* (Exod 25:9, 17–22, 40; 1 Chr 28:18–19); to their mystical transformation (Ezek 1; 10); and to the cycles of divine worship and sacred song that were performed in the temple by priests and Levites (Ps 92:1; 1 Chr 6:17; 2 Chr 7:6). Notably, the majority of the references to these concepts in biblical literature are to be found in priestly sources and in those chapters that refer directly to temple worship or to the mystical prophetic memory of the First Temple after its destruction (Ezek 1:10).

The transformations of *hekhal, merkabah, cherubim, shir,* and *shirot* into the mystical tradition *after* the destruction of the Second Temple have been discussed in different perspectives in regard to the *hekhalot* literature,[22] but their conceptual origins in the mystical literature written in the last centuries *before* the Common Era and the overwhelming concern with angelic priests, angelic liturgy and heav-

---

19. See in the singular form of the holy sanctuary, *hekhal*, as the common name of the Jerusalem temple: 1 Sam 3:3; 1 Kgs 6:5, 33; 7:50; Isa 6:1; Jer 7:4; Ezek 41:1, 20, 25; Zech 8:9; Neh 6:10; Ezra 4:1; Pss 5:8; 11:4; 138:2; 144:12; 2 Chr 4:22; Dan 5:2–3; Ezra 5:14. The English transliteration of the biblical word in singular and plural forms could *be hekhal/hekhalot* or *heikhal/heikhalot*. On its mystical transformation in the plural form, see Peter Schäfer, *Synopse zur Hekhalot-Literatur* (TSAJ 2; Tübingen: Mohr Siebeck, 1981); idem, ed., *Konkordanz zur Hekhalot-Literatur* (TSAJ 12–13; 2 vols.; Tübingen: Mohr Siebeck, 1986–88), entries "heikhal" and "Hekhalot"; cf. Elior, "From Earthly Temple to Heavenly Shrines."

20. *'Ola* is translated as holocaust or sacrifice offered in the temple in permanent daily weekly and festive cycle; see Num 28:10; 2 Chr 31:3. On the mystical transformation of the Sabbath sacrifice, see Newsom, *Songs of the Sabbath Sacrifice*, 23–58; idem, "He Has Established for Himself Priests: Human and Angelic Priesthood in the Qumran Sabbath Shirot," in *Archeology and History in the Dead Sea Scrolls* (ed. L. H. Schiffman; JSPSup 8; Sheffield: Sheffield Academic Press, 1990), 100–120; Maier, "Shire Olat hash-Shabbat," 543–60; Davila, " Macrocosmic Temple," 1–19.

21. Pss 30:1; 46:1; 68:1; 92:1; 1 Chr 6:16; 25:6; 2 Chr 23:13. On the mystical transformation of the songs, see Newsom, *Songs of the Sabbath Sacrifice*, 23–39; Elior, "From Earthly Temple to Heavenly Shrines"; Carol Newsom, "Merkabah Exegesis in the Qumran Sabbath Shirot," *JJS* 38 (1987): 11–30; Devorah Dimant, "Men as Angels: The Self -Image of the Qumran Community," in *Religion and Politics in the Ancient Near East* (ed. A. Berlin; Potomac: University Press of Maryland, 1996), 93–103.

22. Ithamar Gruenwald, "The Place of Priestly Traditions in Consolidating Merkavah Mysticism" (Hebrew), *Jerusalem Studies in Jewish Thought* 6 (1987): 65–119; Rachel Elior, "The Priestly Nature of the Mystical Heritage in Heykalot Literature," in *Expérience et écriture mystiques dans les religions du livre: Actes d'un colloque international tenu par le Centre d'études juives, Université de Paris IV-Sorbonne 1994* (ed. R. B. Fenton and R. Goetschel; EJM 22; Leiden: Brill, 2000), 41–54.

enly sanctuaries, divine chariot, and ritual calendar associated with Enoch son of Jared and with the ritual cycles in the temple were not sufficiently recognized.

As we shall see, the mystical priestly literature before the Common Era was written as part of the bitter dispute that took place in the second century B.C.E., in the period of the Hellenized high priests Jason, Menelaus, and Alkimos (175–159 B.C.E.) and throughout the Hasmonean period (152–37 B.C.E.), concerning the legitimate priestly hierarchy and the conduct of the temple service. The dispute between the "deprived" and "deposed" "sons of light," on the one side, and the "usurpers" and "sons of darkness" who became the new hegemony for 115 years, which generated a good deal of the mystical literature found in the Dead Sea Scrolls, is the dispute between deposed priests from the house of Zadok (those who had served exclusively in the temple until 175 B.C.E., according to biblical historiography and Sir 51:29) and the illegitimate priests (the Hellenized priests and the Hasmonean dynasty) who took their place.

This struggle between the powerless and the powerful is of primal importance among the factors that generated the writing of the *merkabah* literature that was found in Qumran. This literature is composed from mystical priestly writings concerned with the eternally pure heavenly sanctuaries and the eternally sanctified cycles of holy time, guarded by cycles of angelic ritual. This priestly mystical literature of the last few centuries before the Common Era that was composed by exiled/deposed priests, concerned with an eternal angelic order pertaining to ritual calendar, and concentrated on undisturbed eternal time cycles preserved by angelic liturgy in seven sacred unharmed heavenly sanctuaries did not cease to exist in the last century B.C.E.. This mystical literature of the *merkabah* that constructed sevenfold divisions of holy time, holy place, and holy ritual and elaborated on the eternal fourfold world of the divine chariot, revealed to the exiled priest Ezekiel, affected later stages of early Jewish mysticism, composed after the destruction of the Second Temple, that which became known as the tradition of *hekhalot* and *merkabah*.

2. Characteristics of the *Merkabah*

Merkabah texts that were preserved in Qumran in *Songs of the Sabbath Sacrifice* and in the *Blessings*[23] are marked by three distinct characteristics. First, the significant place of texts that relate to the heavenly *chariot of the cherubim* known

23. See Esther Eshel et al., eds., *Qumran Cave 4.VI: Poetical and Liturgical Texts, Part 1* (DJD 11; Oxford: Clarendon, 1998); *Blessings* appears on pages 1–73, *Songs of the Sabbath Sacrifice* on 173–399; cf. Florentino García Martínez and Eibert J. C. Tigchelaar, eds., *The Dead Sea Scrolls Study Edition* (2 vols.; Leiden; Brill, 1997), 644–71, 804–36, 1016–30, 1212–18. Other *merkabah* texts are spread in DJD 1–39 (Oxford: Clarendon 1964–2002) and are now indexed in vol. 39.

from the vision of Ezekiel is immediately apparent.[24] The different components of the priestly-prophetic vision that were defined in the Septuagint translation of Ezekiel in the middle of the third or second century B.C.E. as "the vision of the chariot" (Ezek 43:3) and described by the priest Yehoshua ben Sira as "vision of the chariot" in his book written in the beginning of the second century B.C.E. are all present.[25] The Qumran text of the vision of Ezekiel (1:4) relates a version that reads *nogah merkabah*[26] ("the radiance of the chariot"), whereas the traditional biblical reading has only *nogah* ("the radiance"), omitting the priestly keyword *chariot* that connects it to the cherubim in the temple (1 Chr 28:18).

Second, the *merkabah* texts are replete with angels and cherubim who are depicted as primarily fulfilling a liturgical role reserved to biblical priests and Levites in the heavenly sanctuaries. The angels are blessing, singing, counting, and serving in the seven heavenly sanctuaries in a perpetual ritual manner that evokes the priestly ritual responsibilities and liturgical tasks in the temple.[27] An example from the *Songs of the Sabbath Sacrifice* mentioning in detail the priestly-Levitical service (verbs pertaining to the temple service are marked with italics) and the different components of the divine chariot (pattern of the chariot-throne, cherubim, *ʾopannim*, holy angels, spirits of the holy of holies, godlike beings) may illustrate the angelic-priestly ritual in the heavenly sanctuary:

> By the *maskil* (the instructor): Song of the *sacrifice* of the twelfth Sabbath
> [on the twenty-first of the third month.
> *Praise* the God of…] wondrous [appointed times?] and exalt him … the Glory
> in the tabernacle of the God of knowledge.
> The cherubim fall before him and *bless*.
> They *give blessing* as they raise themselves:
> The sound of divine stillness [is heard].
> [ ] and there is a *tumult of jubilation* as they lift their wings.
> A sound of divine stillness.
> The pattern of the chariot-throne do they *bless*
> Above the firmament of the cherubim.
> The splendor of the luminous firmament do they *sing*
> Beneath his glorious seat.
> When the *ʾopannim* (wheels) go, the angels of the holy place return
> The spirits of the holy of holies go forth
> Like appearance of fire
> From beneath his glorious wheels […]

---

24. See especially Ezek 1; 10; 43:3; see Halperin, *Faces of the Chariot,* 38–60.

25. On the Septuagint version for Ezek 43:3, see ibid., 56–57. On Sir 49:11, see Moshe Zvi Segal, *Sefer ben Sira ha-Shalem* (*The Complete Book of Ben Sira*) (2nd ed.; Jerusalem: Bialik Institute, 1958); Halperin, *Faces of the Chariot,* 48.

26. 4Q385, frag. 4:5–6; Dimant and Strugnell, *Qumran Cave 4.XXI,* 42.

27. Newsom, *Songs of the Sabbath Sacrifice,* 23–39; Elior, *The Three Temples,* 165–200.

The spirits of the living God that walks about perpetually
With the Glory of the wondrous chariots
There is a still sound of *blessing* in the tumult of their movement
And they *praise* the holy place as they turn back.
When they raise themselves, they raise wondrously
And when they return they stand still.
The joyful sound of *singing* falls silent,
And there is a stillness of divine *blessing*
In all the camps of godlike beings
And the sound of *praises* ... from between all their divisions on the[ir] si[des
And all their mastered troops *rejoice,*
Each o[n]e in [his] stat[ion].[28]

Like the priestly courses who were serving as a living calendar of changing weeks in a precalculated pattern of fifty-two Sabbaths/weeks[29] and who were in charge of guarding the cosmic cycles of time and the corresponding liturgical cycles in the holy of holies in the temple, where the chariot of the cherubim stood, the angelic watches are responsible for guarding and preserving all the eternal cosmic cycles and divisions of time in the heavenly sanctuaries and the world of the chariot, where the cherubim are eternal beings.

Third, the *merkabah* texts possess a marked chronological structure: each one of the thirteen Sabbath songs found in the Dead Sea Scrolls was designated to be sung on one of the thirteen Sabbaths that fall upon undeviating dates and position within one of the four seasons according to the established priestly annual calendar of fifty-two Sabbaths.[30] The priestly solar calendar of 364 days that was brought from heaven by Enoch son of Jared, founder of the priesthood according

28. 4Q405 20–21–22, lines 6–14; see Newsom, *Song of the Sabbath Sacrifices,* 303–21 for the Hebrew text, discussion, and translation. I consulted the translations of Halperin, *Faces of the Chariot*, 52, 524–25, as well as the translation of J. Strugnell (n. 15 above) and Lawrence H Schiffman, "Merkavah Speculation at Qumran: The 4QSerekh Shirot Olat Ha-Shabat," in *Mystics, Philosophers and Politics: Essays in Jewish Intellectual History in Honor of Alexander Altmann* (ed. J. Reinharz and D. Swetschinski; Durham, N.C.: Duke University Press, 1982), 15–47, and amended the translation. The unique poetic Hebrew syntax and mystical content makes this text particularly hard for translation; thus, it could be rendered in more than one form.

29. The traditions on the calendar are reflected in *1 En.* 72–82; *Jub.* 6; Eshel et al., *Qumran Cave 4.VI,* 4Q287 2:7–80. The Scroll of Priestly Watches in DJD 21 (see n. 35 below) and the opening of each one of the *Songs of the Sabbath Sacrifice* offer many examples for this contention.

30. On the central role of the 364-day calendar that is attested in the angelic liturgy, see Maier, "Shire Olat hash-Shabbat," 543–60; Newsom, *Songs of the Sabbath Sacrifice,* 1–21. On this priestly calendar, see James C. Vanderkam, "The Origin, Character and Early History of the 364 Day Calendar: A Reassessment of Jaubert's Hypotheses," *CBQ* 41 (1979): 390–411; Shemaryahu Talmon, *The World of Qumran from Within: Collected Studies* (Jerusalem: Magnes, 1989), 147–50, 273–300; Elior, *The Three Temples*, 44–62, 82–110.

to the books of *1 Enoch*, *2 Enoch*, and *Jubilees*, was divided symmetrically into a year of four seasons, each possessing ninety-one days. These were divided into thirteen Sabbaths each season.

This calendar of fourfold and sevenfold divisions (91 x 4 = 364; 13 x 7 x 4 = 364; 364 ÷ 7 = 52) is described in detail through various documents found among the Dead Sea Scrolls; while some had been known previously within the pseudepigraphic literature, their priestly context went unrecognized. The details of the annually recurring fourfold divisions of the seasons known as *merkabot hashameim* "heavenly chariots" (*1 En.* 75:3) and sevenfold calculations of the Sabbaths known as *moadei dror* (appointed times of freedom)[31] are detailed and explained in seven different texts found among the Dead Sea Scrolls. Some of these texts were known previously and appeared in the pseudepigraphic literature, while some are unique to the Qumran collection. The calendar is explained in *1 En.* 72–82, in *Jub.* 6, in the *Temple Scroll*, in the *Scroll of the Priestly Watches*, at the conclusion of the *Psalm Scroll* found in Qumran, in the Qumran version of Noah and the flood story, and in the calendar appearing in the opening verses of the priestly epistle *Miqsat Ma'ase Ha-Torah* (4QMMT).[32]

3. The Priestly Solar Calendar

The priestly solar calendar was founded on the assumption that time is holy and its sacred eternal divisions had been decreed in heaven. Its heavenly seasonal divisions (four) and weekly Sabbath divisions (fifty-two) were eternal, predetermined, precalculated, and preserved by angelic watches (*Jub.* 2:17–29; 6). These divisions and calculations were considered to have been conferred from heaven by the angels to Enoch son of Jared (*Jub.* 4:17–19). Enoch, the seventh antediluvian patriarch (Gen 5:21–24), is considered in this literature as the founder of the

31. 4Q286 frag. 1 ii 8–12; Eshel et al., *Qumran Cave 4.VI*, 12.

32. For *1 En.* 72–82, see *OTP* 1:50–61. The versions of the book of Enoch in Qumran 4Q208–209 are in Stephen J. Pfann, *Qumran Cave 4.XXVI: Cryptic Texts;* Philip S. Alexander et al., *Miscellanea, Part 1* (DJD 36; Oxford: Clarendon, 2000), 3–191. For *Jub.* 6, see James C. VanderKam, *The Book of Jubilees* (2 vols.; CSCO 510–511; Scriptores Aethiopici 87–88; Leuven: Peeters, 1989), ch. 6; *OTP* 2:67–69. For the *Temple Scroll*, see Yigael Yadin, *The Temple Scroll* (3 vols. and supplement; Jerusalem: Israel Exploration Society, 1977–83). For the *Scroll of the Priestly Watches*, see Shemaryahu Talmon, Jonathan Ben-Dov, and Uwe Glessmer, eds., *Qumran Cave 4.XVI: Calendrical Texts* (DJD 21; Oxford: Clarendon, 2001). For the conclusion of the *Psalms Scroll*, see James A. Sanders, ed., *The Psalms Scroll of Qumran Cave 11 (11QPs)* (DJD 4; Oxford: Clarendon, 1965), 48. For the Noah and the flood story, see 4Q252, col. II frags. 1, 3:1–5; 3: 1–3; George Brooke et al., eds., *Qumran Cave 4.XVII: Parabiblical Texts, Part 3* (DJD 22; Oxford: Clarendon, 1996), 198, 235. For *Miqsat Ma'ase Ha-Torah*, see Elisha Qimron and John Strugnell, eds., *Qumran Cave 4.V: Miqsat Maase Ha-Torah* (DJD 10; Oxford: Clarendon, 1994), 6–7.

priestly dynasty[33] who brought the calendar after his sojourn in heaven.[34] The calendar was taught again after the course of forty-nine Jubilees (after forty-nine reoccurrences of the passage of forty-nine years) to Moses, son of Amram from the tribe of Levi, who was instructed in all the details of its calculations on Mount Sinai along forty days, by the Angel of the Presence.[35] The calendar was taught to Moses as *Torah veteu'da* (angelic testimony on the calendar) after he had received the *Torah vehamitzva* (divine testimony on the law).[36]

The holy annual divisions of the calendar to units of seven days and seven appointed times, four seasons, and twelve months,[37] as well as its seven-year divisions between the fallow year (*shemitah*), formed the very foundation of temple worship, according to the priestly-mystical perception revealed in the Dead Sea Scrolls. Its cycles were kept eternally in heaven by the angels and were maintained on earth in the temple by the priests and the high priests from the tribe of Levi and the family of Zadok.[38]

The heavenly time integrated a fourfold annual division based on solar observations and seasonal changes pertaining to the vernal and autumnal equinoxes, the summer and winter solstices (four seasons *tekufot*), all of which were called in *1 En.* 75 "the heavenly chariots" (*merkabot hashamayim*). Heavenly time was further divided into a sevenfold division of the appointed times specified by the deity (*moadim:* the seven appointed holidays of the Lord; Lev 23), fifty-two

---

33. On Enoch's priestly role, see *Jub.* 4:25; *1 En.* 108:1; *2 En.* 13–14; 16; 18; 19–23 (*OTP* 1:91–222).

34. On Enoch son of Jared, see Greenfield and Stone, "Books of Enoch," 89–103; Knibb, *Ethiopic Book of Enoch;* Black, *Book of Enoch;* VanderKam, *Enoch;* Elior, *The Three Temples*, 82–110.

35. James C. Vanderkam, "The Angel of the Presence in the Book of Jubilees" *DSD* 7 (2000): 378–93.

36. The revelation to Moses is described in the opening of *Jubilees;* see VanderKam, *Book of Jubilees*, introduction); *OTP* 2:35–53.

37. See Sanders, *Psalms Scroll of Qumran Cave 11*, 48; Elior, *The Three Temples*, 34–62.

38. According to priestly historiography, the divine worship was directed by one priestly dynasty for more than a thousand years. Aaron and his direct descendants, Eleazar, Phinehas, Abishua, served in the desert tabernacle. Their descendant was Zadok the high priest, who officiated in the days of David and Solomon in the time of the foundation of the First Temple. His direct descendants the "sons of Zadok" served until the destruction of the First Temple in the beginning of the sixth century B.C.E., and members of his direct dynasty served until the year 175 B.C.E. in the middle of Second Temple period. One may argue about the precision of the historical fact as far as chronology and genealogy are concerned; however, one cannot deny the importance and centrality of the consciousness of continuity of the dynasty of the high priesthood in the Bible and in the Scrolls. For a critical appraisal, see Cana Werman, "The Sons of Zadok," in *The Dead Sea Scrolls: Fifty Years after their Discovery* (ed. L. W. Schiffman, E. Tov, and J. C. VanderKam; Jerusalem: Israel Exploration Society, 2000), 623–30; cf. Elior, *The Three Temples*, 24–29, 165–200.

Sabbaths as well as the seventh year *shemitah* (year of fallow) and the seventh of seven of years (or Jubilee).

According to this calendar, as noted above, each year possessed an unchanging and fixed number of days: 364; the year was divided into four parallel seasons of ninety-one days; each one of the seasons included thirteen Sabbaths spread over three months that were calculated mathematically as counting consecutively thirty, thirty, and thirty-one days, starting respectively always on Wednesday, Friday, or Sunday according to their order. Each one of the thirteen Sabbaths in a quarter fell on a predetermined date, the first being the fourth day of the first month (a month that starts always on Wednesday 1/1), the second Sabbath the eleventh, the third eighteenth, and the last one, the thirteenth Sabbath, always on the twenty-eighth day of the third month (a month that will start always on Sunday and will end on Tuesday 3/31).

The synchronization of the dates between the four seasons (4 x 91), the twelve months (12 x 30 + 4), and the fifty-two Sabbaths (4 x 13 x 7) in cycles of seven years, six years of service and one Sabbatical year (*shemitah*), was vested in the hands of the twenty-four priestly courses (1 Chr 24) that served in the temple in weekly cycles of watches known as *mishmeret hakodesh* (holy watches). In a period of six years, each course would serve thirteen times, as is demonstrated in the scrolls of the priestly courses found in Qumran.[39]

This eternal divine calendar, which was in the center of religious life for the anonymous writers of the Scrolls, formed the background and structure for the priestly service in the temple and was maintained by the twenty-four priestly watches as recorded in the historiography and mystical literature found in Qumran, ascribed by its authors to "the priests, the sons of Zadok, and their allies."[40]

4. The Priestly Dynasty

The biblical tradition and its recensions in the Dead Sea Scrolls reserved the rights of the high priesthood for the children of Moses' brother, Aaron (Lev 10:12–13; 1 Chr 23:13), and his descendents were the sole members of the twenty-four

39. See Talmon, Ben-Dov, and Glessmer, *Qumran Cave 4.XVI;* Talmon, *World of Qumran from Within*, 147–50, 273–300; Shemaryahu Talmon and Israel Knohl, "A Calendrical Scroll from a Qumran Cave," in *Pomegranates and Golden Bells: Studies in Biblical, Jewish, and Near Eastern Ritual, Law, and Literature in Honor of Jacob Milgrom* (ed. D. P. Wright, D. N. Freedman, and A. Hurvitz; Winona Lake, Ind.: Eisenbrauns, 1995), 267–302; Elior, *The Three Temples*, 42–43.

40. On the priests as sons of Zadok in the Scrolls, see *Community Rule* 5:2, 9 (Geza Vermes, *The Complete Dead Sea Scrolls in English* [London: Penguin, 1997], 103–4); *Messianic Rule* (1Q28a) 1:23–5 (Vermes, *Complete Dead Sea Scrolls*, 158); *Damascus Document* III, 21–IV, 1; IV, 3–4 (Vermes, *Complete Dead Sea Scrolls*, 130); *Florilegium* (4Q174 I 16–18; Vermes, *Complete Dead Sea Scrolls*, 404).

priestly courses responsible for the order of the eternal calendar of divine worship. The priestly dynasty passed from Aaron to his son Eleazar, from Eleazar to his son Phinehas, from Phinehas to Abishua, then continued, consecrated by divine decree, from father to son throughout the course of the biblical collection.[41] The consecrated dynastic continuity relates to the genealogy of the high priesthood, which was limited to one branch of the priestly dynasty, the direct descendents of Aaron. Since the days of David and Solomon, Zadok son of Ahitub, a direct descendent of Aaron, was the high priest, and his children, generation after generation, were described and identified as sons of Zadok who served as high priests in the temple.[42]

This dynastic line of priests, the sons of Zadok, served exclusively until the year 175 B.C.E., when Antiochus IV, the Selucid emperor, conquered the land of Israel and imposed a new calendar on his empire, the Selucid lunar calendar.[43] Onias III, serving as high priest at this time (2 Macc 3:1), rejected the royal imposition, while his brother Jason conceded, deposed Onias, purchased the high priesthood from Antiochus (1 Macc 1:11–15; 2 Macc 4:7–14), and instituted a new royal-priestly order. From this moment, the biblical order and the priestly solar calendar of fifty-two Sabbaths ceased to exist, and various differing calendars were imposed and accepted by the Hellenized priests Alkimos and Menelaus and the later Hasmonian priests Jonathan, Simon, and John Hyrcanus in the course of the second century B.C.E. and by Alexander Janneus and his descendents in the first century B.C.E.

5. The Priestly Library at Qumran

The former ruling priestly circles of the sons of Zadok, those who perceived themselves as keepers of the holy written heritage and the sacred ritual and liturgy, were deposed and persecuted as emerging from *Pesher Habakuk* and 4QMMT. They abandoned the Jerusalem temple, apparently taking with them the temple library. Its remains were found in Qumran as the nine hundred Dead Sea Scrolls that include 250 copies of biblical scrolls; numerous liturgical scrolls and traditions concerning angels, priests, rituals, and sacred history that remained for the most part forgotten and unknown; and polemic scrolls against those who had unlawfully deposed them that were entirely unknown until 1947.[44]

41. Exod 28–30; 40:13–16; Lev 8:21–22; Num 17–18; 25; 1 Chr 6:34–38; 23:13, 28–32; 24:1–5.

42. On the priests as sons of Zadok, see 1 Kgs 1:32, 35, 38–39; 2:35; 1 Chr 5:27–41; 9:11; 24:3–6; 29:22; Ezra 7:2–5; Neh 11:11.

43. Dan 7:25; 1 Macc 1:41–47; 2 Macc 6:6–7. See Otto Morkholm, *Antiochus IV of Syria* (Copenhagen: Gyldidal, 1966).

44. See Tov, *Text from the Judaean Desert*, on the entire scrolls library.

The deposed priests concentrated on intensive writing and copying, as all their sacred legitimacy was attested according to a divine decree that was similarly preserved in sacred writings. They wrote *legal* literature addressed to the new ruling priesthood urging the reinstitution of the old priestly order and the ancient divine calendar (4QMMT; the *Temple Scroll;* scrolls of priestly courses). They also copied and composed *mystical* literature in order to demonstrate the divine paradigm of the priestly calendar (*1 Enoch; Jubilees;* the Qumran *Psalm Scroll; Blessings*) or copied in many versions the angelic paradigm of the divine worship according to this calendar (*Songs of the Sabbath Sacrifice; Blessings*).

The angelic world where the solar calendar is kept eternally through holy liturgical cycles was described in close relation to the ancient priestly calendar and its liturgical divisions. These priestly circles wrote further scrolls aggressively attacking those who dethroned them from their position; those new priests who changed the calendar into a lunar calendar were identified as "sons of darkness" and "sons of evil," as against the Zadokite priests, the keepers of the solar-angelic calendar and the chariot tradition of holy time and holy space, who are called "sons of light" and "sons of justice" (*Rule of the Community; War Scroll; Pesher Habakuk*).[45]

These mystical traditions were written by different writers in different periods and various places, but they always elaborate upon these items:

- the *sacred numbers of the solar calendar* (seven days and thirteen Sabbaths in each one of the four quarters; further divided into twelve months of thirty days and four additional days separating the four seasons);
- *their divine source and angelic framework* (Enoch the seventh patriarch learned the calendar of four seasons, twelve months, and fifty-two Sabbaths combining visual time and audible time from the Angel of the Presence and learned the duties of the angels in regard to its preservation);
- its *liturgical cycles* (thirteen Sabbath songs, sung on exactly the same dates four times a year); and
- its *ritual cyclical preservation* (twenty-four priestly courses monitored the sevenfold divisions of time *shabatot, shivaa moadim, shemitot, yovlim*; Sabbath, seven appointed times of the Lord, fallow years, Jubilees) alongside the angels in their *seven heavenly sanctuaries* in the world of the chariot.

45. See Vermes, *Complete Dead Sea Scrolls,* for English translation to all these writings. See details on their new translations in the respective volumes of DJD detailed in vol. 39 of the series.

This priestly mystical literature relating to holy time was concerned both with the seven heavenly sanctuaries that were associated as spatial dimensions with the sevenfold divisions of time (Lev 23) as well as with the four spatial dimensions of the heavenly chariot that pertained to the fourfold division of the seasons and cosmic directions. This mystical literature, which delineated holy time and holy place in relation to the priestly solar calendar of fifty-two Sabbaths and fixed number of days, was constrained by the sages who after the destruction of the temple held to the lunar calendar and its unknown changing number of days. The sages defined the priestly writings on holy time and holy place as "books that should remain outside of the canonical literature" (*m. Sanh.* 10:1), books that became known in different periods as *separim hitsonim,* pseudepigraphical literature, Apocrypha, or Dead Sea Scrolls. The sages constrained and prohibited "expounding on the deeds of the chariot" (*m. Hag.* 2:1; *b. Hag.* 13b–14b) without explaining the background of this ruling and its connection to ancient priestly perceptions of holy time and holy place, angelic liturgy, priestly ritual, and heavenly chariots.

6. Enoch

As noted above, the protagonist of the priestly literature found in the Judean desert, and the angelic hero of significant parts of the later mystical tradition known as *hekhalot* literature, is Enoch son of Jared (Gen 5:21–24), who had brought the calendar from heaven to earth and who is considered the founder of the priestly ritual and the source of the priestly dynasty of written knowledge derived from an angelic source. Enoch was the first human being who learned from the angels to read, to write, and to calculate heavenly divisions of *holy time* (*Jub.* 4; *1 En.* 72–82). He was the first one who had seen the vision of the heavenly *holy place,* the vision of the chariot of the cherubim (*1 En.* 14:8–25; 71:1–9). This heavenly paradigm of the holy place seen in the seventh generation would later be depicted in the holy of holies in the tabernacle and in the temple (Exod 40:20; 1 Chr 28:18). Enoch, the founder of the priestly heritage, who is described in Qumran liturgy in the line "You have chosen Enoch from among human beings,"[46] was the first man to be taught the complexities of the astronomic divisions of the calendar, known as *merkabot hashamayim* (heavenly chariots; *1 En.* 75:3). He is described as enjoying direct contact with the heavenly retinue, notably with the angel Uriel (angel of light) or with the Angel of the Presence,

46. See Menahem Kister, "5Q13 and the *Avodah*: A Historical Survey and Its Significance," *DSD* 8 (2001): 137; Rachel Elior, "You Have Chosen Enoch from among Human Beings," in *Creation and Re-creation in Jewish Thought: Festschrift in Honor of Joseph Dan on the Occasion of His Seventieth Birthday* (ed. P. Schäfer and R. Elior; Tübingen: Mohr Siebeck, 2005), 15–65 (Hebrew section).

who revealed the heavenly knowledge on holy place and holy time, as well as the knowledge of writing and counting, both to him and later to Moses on Mount Sinai (*Jub.* 1; 8:19).

The unique role of Enoch is described in detail in the Aramaic book of *Enoch* that was found in Qumran[47] and in its Ethiopic translations and various versions that were known in the pseudepigraphical literature before their original Aramaic and Hebrew versions were found in Qumran.[48] Enoch's heavenly position as a dweller of paradise is described in *Genesis Apocryphon*, in the *Book of Giants*, and in chapters of *Jubilees* found among the Dead Sea Scrolls.[49] A significant part of the later *hekhalot* tradition retells Enoch's exceptional history during a period in which his identity was a matter of dispute and not only a matter of reverence.[50] Enoch, who is described as a heavenly scribe dwelling in paradise after he brought the calendar and as a witness to the angelic liturgy and the divine chariot that he saw and heard in heaven, is also described in *2 Enoch*, a Slavonic translation of a version from the first century, as well as in other ancient sources.[51] Enoch's mystical ascents, the heavenly knowledge acquired in relation to calendar and chariot, the priestly role assumed, as well as the cardinal role of angels in regard to priestly worship, priestly calendar, and priestly chariot tradition in this literature cannot be overly emphasized.

During the long period while the "illegitimate" priestly dynasty served in the temple and functioned under a spurious calendar from 175 B.C.E. onward, the deposed priests, the sons of Zadok, continued to write and contend regarding the establishment of the priestly legitimacy and about the sanctity of the priestly solar calendar. Enoch's heavenly knowledge of holy time and holy place, the angelic source of knowledge and paradigm for divine worship, calendars of 364 days and fifty-two Sabbaths as the foundation for holy time, and the heavenly chariot of the cherubim as the origin for holy place were central in their writings. The heavenly sevenfold divisions (Sabbath; seven *hekhalot*) and fourfold divisions (four seasons; fourfold *merkabah;* fourfold division of the Zodiac) pertaining to holy time and holy place, as well as sevenfold groups of angels and fourfold divisions of the living creatures of the *merkabah*, were elaborated in diverse ways in their written tradition.

---

47. See Jozef T. Milik, ed., *The Books of Enoch: Aramaic Fragments of Qumrân Cave 4* (with the collaboration of Matthew Black; Oxford: Clarendon, 1976); and Pfann, *Qumran Cave 4.XXVI*, 3–191.

48. *1 Enoch* in *OTP* 1:5–90.

49. For the Genesis Apocryphon, see Nahman Avigad and Yigael Yadin, *A Genesis Apocryphon: A Scroll from the Wilderness of Judaea* (Jerusalem: Magnes, 1956). For the *Book of Giants*, see Pfann, *Qumran Cave 4.XXVI*, 8–94. See *Jubilees* in Harold Attridge, *Qumran Cave 4.VIII: Parabiblical Texts, Part 1* (DJD 13; Oxford: Clarendon, 1994).

50. See n. 52 below and Elior "You Have Chosen Enoch."

51. On *2 (Slavonic) Enoch*, see *OTP* 1:91–222; Orlov, *Enoch-Metatron Tradition*.

7. The Mystical Traditions of the *Hekhalot*

The angels hold a central position as well in the *merkabah* literature that appeared centuries later, after the destruction of the Second Temple, that which came to be known as the *hekhalot* and *merkabah* literature, or the seven sanctuaries and divine chariot mystical tradition. Here too Enoch is a major protagonist appearing in some of its traditions, although he is renamed Enoch-Metatron (most likely in relation to the number four, *tetra* in Greek, a number of central significance in the chariot tradition relating to the fourfold cosmic division). The sevenfold division of the heavenly world to seven *hekhalot* is a noticeable characteristic of *hekhalot* literature, as well as the fourfold structure of the chariot, and the sevenfold angelic liturgy is a distinct feature of the *hekhalot* and *merkabah* tradition written in the centuries that followed the destruction.[52]

No direct connection may be ascertained between traditions that were written in the last few centuries before the Common Era and those emerging in the early centuries of the Common Era; however, it is interesting to note that the ancient priestly mystical traditions were revived through confirmation and struggle. Enoch the hero of the priestly literature of the calendar and the chariot, also described as an eternal scribe residing forever in paradise, before the Common Era, is the angelic hero of *3 Enoch*, known as *Sefer Hekhalot*. In this book written in the talmudic period, the number of the days of a solar year, 365, is mentioned time and again (as in *2 Enoch*), as well as the seven heavenly sanctuaries, the angelic retinue, and the fourfold divisions of the seasons and the *merkabah*.[53]

Of great interest as well, Enoch-Metatron, the mystical hero of the priestly calendar, appears in the rabbinic literature as a subject of punishment and an object for denunciation. Enoch, who is depicted in the Bible as a unique individual, one who was taken *alive* unto heaven (Gen 5:24), is described by the sages

52. See Scholem, *Major Trends in Jewish Mysticisn*, ch. 2; Scholem, *Jewish Gnosticism, Merkabah Mysticism;* David J. Halperin, *The Merkabah in Rabbinic Literature* (New Haven: American Oriental Society, 1980); idem, *Faces of the Chariot;* James R. Davila, *Descenders to the Chariot: The People behind the Hekhalot Literature* (JSJSup 70; Leiden: Brill, 2001); Joseph Dan, *The Ancient Jewish Mysticism* (Tel-Aviv: MOD Books, 1993); idem, *Jewish Mysticism: Late Antiquity* (2 vols.; Northvale, N.J.: Aronson, 1998); Nathaniel Deutsch, *Guardians of the Gate: Angelic Vice Regency in Late Antiquity* (Brill's Series in Jewish Studies 22; Leiden: Brill, 1999); Ira Chernus, *Mysticism in Rabbinic Judaism* (Studia Judaica 11; Berlin: de Gruyter, 1982); Peter Schäfer, *Übersetzung der Hekhalot-Literatur* (4 vols; TSAJ 17, 22, 29, 46; Tübingen, Mohr Siebeck, 1987–95); Rachel Elior, *Sifrut haHekhalot uMasoret haMerkavah* (Tel Aviv: Miskal 2004); Vita Daphna Arbel, *Beholders of Divine Secrets: Mysticism and Myth in the Hekhalot and Merkavah Literature* (Albany: State University of New York Press, 2003); Rebecca Macy Lesses, *Ritual Practices to Gain Power: Angels, Incantations, and Revelation in Early Jewish Mysticism* (HTS 44; Harrisburg, Pa.: Trinity Press International, 1998).

53. Philip Alexander, "3 (Hebrew Apocalypse of) Enoch," *OTP* 1:223–316; on *3 Enoch*, see Halperin, *Faces of the Chariot*; Schäfer, *Hidden and Manifest God.*

in the Aramaic translation of this verse as a person who was *executed* by heavenly decree. Noticeably, in the older Enoch tradition it is related that he was taken to heaven by divine decree while still alive for an eternal life in paradise, on the first day of the biblical reckoning of the year, the *beginning of the solar priestly calendar* (the first day of the Nisan month, according to Exod 12:2–3),[54] the same day that the tabernacle was set forth (Exod 40:1) and the day that Levi, the father of the priesthood, was born.[55] In opposition to this priestly tradition, the rabbinic alternative tradition relates that Enoch was *executed* on the first day of the seventh month (Tishri), the day chosen to be nominated as Rosh Hashanah—the celebration of the New Year—according to the *new rabbinic calendar*, a date that has no substantiation in the biblical narrative of the holidays, although this date does appear as a day of memorial in the seventh month.[56]

Many of the principal features of the *hekhalot* mystical literature of the first five centuries of the Common Era show significant precedents from the priestly literature that was written before the Common Era in historical circumstances marked by dispute and despair, when ancient perceptions of holy place and holy time, divine chariot, and angelic calendar were challenged, the ancient priestly order was changed, when sons of Zadok were replaced by sons of Hasmonai, and written law was gradually replaced by oral law.

The historical processes that took place under the Selucid-Greek rule that imposed the Greek lunar calendar on the empire (175–66 B.C.E.) and the Roman rule that imposed a new solar calendar on the Roman Empire (from 45 B.C.E.) generated complicated spiritual responses that were reflected in the mystical "war of the sons of light against the sons of darkness" (sons of Zadok against sons of Hasmonai), a war of the solar calendar against the lunar calendar in the first stage (175–37 B.C.E.) that is well reflected in the Dead Sea Scrolls and in the later dispute between Sadducees (*tzdokim*, sons of Zadok), who held to the ancient angelic-priestly solar calendar of 364 days, relating to a year commencing in Nisan according to the biblical calendar (Exod 12:2–3), and the Pharisees (*prushim;* the sages), who chose the lunar calendar, based on human observation, of a variable number of days (a year could be 354–358 or 384 days), a year that starts in Tishri, the seventh month, and that required the addition of a leap year, an action that has no foundation in the Bible. This dispute between priests (364 days in early traditions or 365 in later tradition) and sages (354 + 30 in leap years) is well reflected in the different instances in the Mishnah whenever a dispute over the dates of the holidays confronts Sadducees with Pharisees.

---

54. *2 En.* 19:2 Hebrew version; see F. I. Andersen, "2 (Slavonic Apocalypse of) Enoch," *OTP* 1:196 (*2 En.* 68:1).

55. *Jub.* 28:14; see *OTP* 2:110.

56. Lev 23:23–25; see *Jub.* 6:23; *OTP* 2:68.

Those who held to the lunar calendar and the new leap year wrote negative and derogatory accounts concerning the messenger of the priestly solar calendar, Enoch (*Gen. Rab.* 25). These new rabbinic stories told by those who had changed the calendar into a lunar calendar after the destruction of the temple distorted the priestly traditions concerning Enoch's ascent to heaven as well as his instruction from the angels regarding the details of this priestly-solar calendar. The new calendar postulates a changing, unpredicted, uncalculated system based on every person's observation though decided by a rabbinical court that must then intercalate in order to settle the differences between a lunar year of twelve months (354 days) and a solar year of four seasons (365.4 days).

All the details of holy time and priestly calendar associated with the chariot tradition that were written in books such as *Enoch*, *Jubilees*, and *Songs of the Sabbath Sacrifice* as well as the *Temple Scroll*, *Psalms Scroll*, *Miqsat Ma'ase Ha-Torah* (MMT), and in traditions such as the flood calendar 4Q252 and the scroll of the priestly watches were suppressed, censored, and marginalized by the proponents of the new lunar calendar based on human observation. Notably, the priestly calendrical traditions written before the Common Era were forbidden for study by the leader of the sages, Rabbi Akiva, who labeled them "external books" (*m. Sanh.* 10:1). Akiva took a central part in shaping the alternative rabbinical order based on new perception of lunar time and human observation (*m. Roš. Haš.* 2:9). The new hegemony further replaced the narrative of heavenly ascent and angelic knowledge that were associated with the priestly solar calendar with stories relating to Enoch's humiliation, punishment, and death (*b. Hag.* 15a; *Tg. Onq.* on Gen 5:21–24; *Gen. Rab.* 25). These supporters of the lunar calendar also replaced the priestly orientation of the stories relating to the origin of the solar calendar with an alternative story connecting Enoch with the greatest calendric prohibition, changing the number of days in a year (*Jub.* 6:30–38) required by *sod haibur* (the secret of the leap year required by lunar calendar; *Pirqe R. El.* 8).

The fact that these pro-Enoch and anti-Enoch traditions were being debated centuries after the temple was destroyed and the priestly calendar or priestly service abolished generates interesting speculations concerning our historical perspective and the role of mystical memory. Mystical literature reflects much more than heavenly perspectives and transcendental spiritual yearning; it also reveals very interesting historical and social dimensions often biased by earthly disputes and human competing interests.

In light of all the above, I suggest that we reconsider those various mystical traditions centered on Enoch, the priestly solar calendar, the fourfold and sevenfold cycles of the angelic ritual, the chariot vision, the heavenly chariot, the "heavenly chariots" of cosmic time divisions and seven chariots of sacred ritual, and the sevenfold angelic liturgy that were written before the Common Era, as the first chapter of Jewish mysticism, while considering the *hekhalot* and *merkabah* literature written after the destruction of the temple, incorporating similar topics, as the second chapter that reflects the dialectical continuity with its priestly sources.

Many questions still remain unanswered, a central one of which is the identity of the authors who chose Rabbi Akiva to be the central hero of the mystical priestly-heavenly tradition collected in *hekhalot* literature. He is the central earthly hero of the sages tradition who took a major part in instituting the new lunar calendar (*m. Roš Haššanah*) and who considered the priestly literature labeled *separim hitsonim* (apocryphal books) to be forbidden reading (*m. Sanh.* 10:1).[57]

I would like to conclude by explaining that in the above discussion I intended to contribute to the history of the marginal voices of those deposed and the ousted who wrote mystical treaties to define the core of their identity and its sacred foundations, as well as to offer a mystical perspective to the history of bitter dispute around the idea of the sacred, especially as pertaining to the sources of divine authority and changing human hegemony.

57. The common denominator appearing throughout the majority of these apocryphal texts relates to the priestly solar calendar of 364 days and to the mythical descriptions of the priestly dynasty that is associated with this reckoning (Enoch, Melchizedek, Levi, Kehat, Amram, Zadok) along its angelic-priestly counterparts, the angels of the presence officiating in the heavenly sanctuaries and the serving angels who were in charge on the seasons and the cosmic cycles (*1 En.* 72–82).

The Ancient Jewish Apocalypses and the *Hekhalot* Literature

James R. Davila

> When the Holy One, blessed be he, took me to serve the throne of glory, the wheels of the chariot and the needs of the Shekinah, at once my flesh turned to flame, my sinews to blazing fire, my bones to juniper coals, my eyelashes to lightning flashes, my eyeballs to fiery torches, the hairs of my head to hot flames, all my limbs to wings of burning fire, and the substance of my body to blazing fire. (*3 En.* 15:1–2)

This essay explores the relationship between the *hekhalot* literature—the pre-kabbalistic corpus of mystical texts that give instructions on how to ascend (or "descend") to the celestial "palaces" or the "*merkabah*," God's heavenly throne-chariot, and the Jewish apocalypses that survive from the early centuries C.E. and earlier.[1] Elements of the *hekhalot* literature can be shown to be as early as the fifth to seventh centuries C.E., although the surviving manuscripts were copied and extensively edited in the Middle Ages. Since the *hekhalot* literature and the Jewish apocalypses share an interest in revelations from the heavenly realm, it seems worthwhile to compare them in order to learn whether and to what degree

1. For the *hekhalot* literature, see Peter Schäfer, *The Hidden and Manifest God: Some Major Themes in Early Jewish Mysticism* (Albany: State University of New York Press, 1992); Michael D. Swartz, *Scholastic Magic: Ritual and Revelation in Early Jewish Mysticism* (Princeton: Princeton University Press, 1996); Rebecca Macy Lesses, *Ritual Practices to Gain Power: Angels, Incantations, and Revelation in Early Jewish Mysticism* (HTS 44; Harrisburg, Pa.: Trinity Press International, 1998); James R. Davila, *Descenders to the Chariot: The People behind the Hekhalot Literature* (JSJSup 70; Leiden: Brill, 2001). Seven important manuscripts are published in transcription by Peter Schäfer, Margaret Schlüter, and Hans George von Mutius, *Synopse zur Hekhalot Literatur* (TSAJ 2; Tübingen: Mohr Siebeck, 1981). The genre "apocalypse" involves an account of divine revelations given to a human being (usually a pseudonymous scriptural or ancient worthy) by a divine being such as an angel. See especially John J. Collins, ed., *Apocalypse: the Morphology of a Genre*, *Semeia* 14 (1979); and Adela Yarbro Collins, ed., *Early Christian Apocalypticism: Genre and Social Setting*, *Semeia* 36 (1986).

these early Jewish texts anticipate patterns of ideas in the later *hekhalot* texts. This is the objective of this essay.

1. Initial Considerations

Important methodological issues arise in the study of both the *hekhalot* texts and the Jewish apocalypses, as well as in any attempt to compare them. The *hekhalot* literature is a large mass of Hebrew and Aramaic traditions about Tannaitic rabbis and the techniques they supposedly used either to "descend to the chariot" in order to experience the realm of the heavenly throne room or to summon the angelic "Prince of Torah" in order to compel him to give them instantaneous knowledge of Torah. Other angels are sometimes summoned for other purposes as well.

There is still much debate about the date, provenance, social context, and purpose of the *hekhalot* texts, so we must be quite clear initially about what in them we are comparing to the Jewish apocalypses. It is an important principle that, when comparing texts with other texts, it is crucial to concentrate on patterns of parallels rather than individual, unrelated parallels, so in this essay I will use the global pattern for which I argued in my book *Descenders to the Chariot:* the *hekhalot* adept as a magico-religious practitioner with striking similarities to the cross-cultural practitioner known as the "shaman/healer."

This pattern is supported mainly from the internal evidence of the *hekhalot* texts themselves but also some external evidence from Mesopotamian incantation bowls and incantation texts from the Cairo Genizah. It involves six elements:

(1) a *shamanic call* in which the practitioner is normally chosen by the spirits on the basis of distinctive physiognomic traits or ancestry. Ancestry is a factor in the *hekhalot* and related traditions, and physiognomic criteria are hinted at. Other types of shamanic calls, such as initiatory illness and summons to shamanhood by spirits in dreams or visions, are not found in the *hekhalot* literature.

(2) the use of *shamanic ascetic techniques*, including fasting, dietary restrictions, temporary celibacy, purification rites, isolation and sensory deprivation, and songs and words of power (recitation of numinous hymns and repetition of *nomina barbara* and divine names).

(3) *initiatory disintegration and reintegration:* the experience of being torn apart and incinerated before the throne of God, with the apparent objective of being temporarily transformed into a fiery angel suited to survive in such an environment.

(4) an *otherworldly journey* to the seven-tiered celestial realm of the *merkabah*, which culminates in a visit to God's throne room and is also seen to be identified with the archetypal paradise. The journey is fraught with tests and dangers and is undertaken to gain divine revelations or dispen-

sations and to join with the angels in the singing of the heavenly liturgy. The cosmography of the otherworld in the *hekhalot* texts corresponds well to typical shamanic cosmology, which involves travel through a multitiered universe whose levels include the underworld, the earth, and the heavens; a "world tree" or other cosmic axis that connects them; and the further subdivision of the heavens and the underworld, often into seven or nine levels.

(5) the *control of the spirits*, almost always angels in human form (indeed, Metatron may even function as an ancestral spirit) for various purposes, including the wresting of knowledge of Torah from the Prince of Torah; the commandeering of angels as guides on the otherworldly journey; the gaining of raw theurgic power from the Prince of Torah; and protection from misfortune and demons.

(6) *service to the human community*, mainly as healers and exorcists, diviners and dream interpreters, mediators of social conflicts, and perhaps also as psychopomps (that is, those who lead the dead to their proper rest).[2]

One can, of course, debate whether one or another of these points is a central component of the experience of the descenders to the chariot, but I have argued in my book that this pattern is at the very least heuristically useful for understanding the material, and I adopt it here since it was developed for another purpose and cannot be accused of being created to get a particular result in the inquiry that is taken up in this essay. The question, then, is to what degree, if at all, this pattern appears in surviving Jewish apocalypses of the early centuries C.E. and earlier.

Elsewhere I have discussed fully the problem of isolating Jewish pseudepigrapha among Old Testament pseudepigrapha that have been transmitted primarily or only by Christians.[3] Suffice to say here that I have defended Robert Kraft's view

2. It is true that "shamans" in the Siberian context that originated the term are associated with hunting cultures and therefore cannot readily be compared either with the descenders to the chariot or with ancient Jewish apocalyptists. Nevertheless, there is good evidence that such practitioners continue to survive in sedentary agricultural communities (and, for that matter, sometimes even in modern urban ones). Following Michael Winkelman, I refer to such practitioners in agricultural societies as "shaman/healers." The societal context of shaman/healers is comparable to those of both the descenders to the chariot and the ancient Jewish apocalyptists. For discussion, see my *Descenders to the Chariot*, 49–51, 292–305.

3. James R. Davila, *The Provenance of the Pseudepigrapha: Jewish, Christian, or Other?* (JSJSup 105; Leiden: Brill, 2005); idem, "The Old Testament Pseudepigrapha as Background to the New Testament," *ExpTim* 117 (2005): 53–57. See also Robert A. Kraft, "The Pseudepigrapha in Christianity," in *Tracing the Threads: Studies in the Vitality of Jewish Pseudepigrapha* (ed. J. C. Reeves; SBLEJL 6; Atlanta: Scholars Press, 1994), 55–86; idem, "The Pseudepigrapha and

that in analyzing pseudepigrapha we should begin with the earliest manuscripts of a given work and try to understand it in that social and linguistic context, moving backward to earlier contexts only as required by positive evidence.

On the basis of external evidence (fragments of the Aramaic or Hebrew originals from the Qumran library) I have concluded that the Book of the Watchers, the Astronomical Book, the Book of Dreams, and the Epistle of Enoch (all component parts of *1 Enoch*) are all Jewish apocalypses that existed by the first century B.C.E., some earlier. On the basis of internal evidence I have argued that *2 Baruch*, *4 Ezra*, and the Similitudes of Enoch (*1 En.* 37–71) are Jewish apocalypses, the first two being composed by the early second century C.E. and the last within the first few centuries C.E., if not a little earlier. I regard all of these texts to be Jewish compositions beyond reasonable doubt. The book of Daniel is an apocalypse that survives in its original Hebrew and Aramaic in something close to its putative original form. Internal evidence indicates that it was composed during the Maccabean revolt, very ancient fragments of it survive in the Qumran library, and it has been transmitted by Jews throughout its history. Its Jewish origin is rightly undisputed.[4]

It is important to note that the genre apocalypse is different in fundamental ways from the *hekhalot* literature. Although the *hekhalot* literature does include a number of fictional episodes, its basic orientation is one of instruction. Much of the material (the exception is *3 Enoch*, which is an apocalypse) amounts to straightforward instruction manuals for achieving altered states of consciousness that allow the descender to the chariot to pursue goals in the supernatural world. These include instructions for rituals, accounts of paradigmatic otherworldly journeys, and the texts of magical spells and numinous hymns to be used by the practitioner. The ancient apocalypses under consideration here, on the contrary, consist of fictional accounts of scriptural or other events. At times they deal with matters parallel to those in the *hekhalot* texts, but they present the material as stories rather than instructions.

This difference in orientation leaves us less than certain in any given case whether the text is describing a real ritual that might actually have been used rather than an entirely imaginary ritual conceived by the author, as well as a vision or audition actually experienced by the author while in an altered state of consciousness (perhaps "channeling" the Old Testament visionary to whom the vision is attributed) as opposed to a vision simply imagined for a fictional Old Testament setting. It also compels us to try to infer the nature and details of the rituals from the fictional accounts of their use rather than relying on actual instructions for them. I have suggested in an article on ritual in the Old Testament

Christianity Revisited: Setting the Stage and Framing Some Central Questions," *JSJ* 32 (2001): 371–95.

4. John J. Collins, *Daniel* (Hermeneia; Minneapolis: Fortress, 1993), 1–38.

pseudepigrapha that we should concentrate on rituals prescribed for the readers of the works and on accounts of ritual acts not found in biblical stories and that we should think of ritual in terms of explicit descriptions of physical actions in a specified ritual-related social context.[5] I follow these methodological guidelines here as well, although none of the rituals discussed below are prescribed for the reader, and the Hebrew Bible has very little to say about such rituals at all.

2. The Texts

The apocalypses fall naturally into two groups, those now collected in the Ethiopic book of *1 Enoch*, and those that have always circulated separately (Daniel, *4 Ezra*, and *2 Baruch*). I will begin by considering each Enochic book individually, then discuss how our evidence indicates that combinations of these books have been read together during their transmission and how this transmission may affect our reading of them alongside the *hekhalot* literature.[6] I will then turn to Daniel, *4 Ezra*, and *2 Baruch*, in that order, the likely chronological order of their composition.

2.1. The Book of the Watchers

In the Book of the Watchers (*1 En.* 1–36, perhaps with 81:1–4), Enoch is presented as a magico-religious practitioner who displays a number of similarities to the much later descenders to the chariot. There is no explicit call to shamanhood or any indication why Enoch was chosen. There is also no explicit reference to an initiatory disintegration and reintegration, but, at the same time, in the background of the story is the assumption that Enoch was taken to heaven never to return and therefore must have undergone some transformation from mortal to immortal status.[7]

---

5. James R. Davila, "Ritual in the Jewish Pseudepigrapha," in *Anthropology and Biblical Studies: Avenues of Approach* (ed. L. J. Lawrence and M. I. Aguilar; Leiden: Deo, 2004), 158–83, esp. 161–63. In this article I propose eight methodological guidelines for studying ritual in the pseudepigrapha, but the rest are not relevant here.

6. The major critical commentaries on *1 Enoch* are Matthew Black in consultation with James C. VanderKam, *The Book of Enoch or I Enoch* (SVTP 7; Leiden: Brill, 1985); Patrick A. Tiller, *A Commentary on the Animal Apocalypse of* I Enoch (SBLEJL 4; Atlanta: Scholars Press, 1993); George W. E. Nickelsburg, *1 Enoch 1: A Commentary on the Book of 1 Enoch, Chapters 1–36; 81–108* (Hermeneia; Minneapolis: Fortress, 2001). The standard English translation is George W. E. Nickelsburg and James C. VanderKam, *1 Enoch: A New Translation* (Minneapolis: Fortress, 2004).

7. We are told in *1 En.* 14:19–15:1 that neither angels nor humans can look God in the face, and it appears that Enoch did not look directly at God on the throne. This basic understanding of the dangers of the divine throne room is shared with the *hekhalot* texts, although in them

Enoch does engage in shamanic ascetic techniques. According to 13:7, in response to the request of the Watchers that he intercede for them, he goes to an isolated area at "the Waters of Dan" near Mount Hermon. There he reads over the prayers that the Watchers had written out for him until he goes to sleep (evidently, an incubation ritual). As a result, he has inauspicious dreams that he recounts to the repentant Watchers when he awakes. These dreams are given in detail in 14:1–16:4. The interesting point here is that Enoch actively seeks out a revelation using ritual means rather than the revelation coming to him unsolicited, as was normal with the biblical prophets.[8]

Unlike the shamanic cosmology, there is no seven-tiered celestial realm connected by a world ladder or world tree. (This is an idealized model, and many shamanic systems have different cosmologies.[9]) But as in the *hekhalot* literature, the heavenly realm is construed as a fiery macrocosmic temple in which the deity sits enthroned and surrounded by angelic attendants (*1 En.* 14–15). The vision has two purposes: to carry out the prophetic initiation of Enoch and to send back to earth a negative divine response to the request of the Watchers for mercy. Enoch does not seek to join the celestial liturgy or to gain the granting of a wish, although he does receive a divine revelation about the Watchers.

The control of spirits is not a major theme in the Book of the Watchers but it is nevertheless present. A number of angels take Enoch on his tour of the universe in chapters 17–36/81:1–4, and they seem to be obligated to answer whatever questions Enoch asks and to respond to his comments (see *1 En.* 21:4–5; 22:3, 6; 23:2–4; 24:5–25:3; 27:1–2; 32:5–6; 33:2–4). These roles correspond to the roles of angels in the *hekhalot* literature as guides on the otherworldly journey and revealers of esoteric knowledge (although the knowledge revealed in the *hekhalot* texts generally has more to do with Torah than secrets about the natural world).

As for service to the community, Enoch does not engage in healing, exorcism,[10] divination, or psychopompy, but he does receive a revelation by means of a dream, and this provides a resolution to an earthly (if not, strictly speak-

---

at least some of the descenders to the chariot do look at God and suffer the consequences. See chapter 5 of Davila, *Descenders to the Chariot.*

8. Enoch has at least three other unsolicited visionary experiences in the Book of the Watchers: he has a vision that is described in 1:2–9; God sends an angel to him with a revelation in 10:1; and he is taken up onto his (final?) tour of the universe in 17:1, continuing through 36:4 and perhaps 81:1–4.

9. For example, the Native American Lakota Sioux cosmology pictures a heavenly realm centered around the vertical axis of the world tree and divided into quadrants corresponding to the four winds, which quadrants are each assigned to a "grandfather" spirit. These spirits are collectively under the authority of the Great Spirit. See Davila, *Descenders to the Chariot*, 159–65, 167–69.

10. The revelatory material in 15:8–16:3 explains the origins of demonic spirits and may have been intended as background information for exorcists.

ing, "human") request for mediation. It is also perhaps worth highlighting 33:2–4, in which Enoch seems to receive a revelation about calendrical matters (matters taken up in much greater detail in the Astronomical Book; see below). The proper observance of the Jewish calendar was a major issue for the people who collected the Qumran library and also for the people who produced some of the Enochic literature.[11] The author and intended readers of the Book of the Watchers may well have taken this passage to refer to revelations of immediate relevance both to Enoch's earthly community and to themselves. Likewise, if we follow George Nickelsburg in positing that 81:1–4 represents a fragment from the lost conclusion of the Book of the Watchers (see below), Enoch is given access to the heavenly tablets, which tell the entire history of the human race. Presumably this information too would be regarded as intended for the benefit of his earthly community.

2.2. The Astronomical Book

The Astronomical Book (*1 En.* 72–82, perhaps minus 81:1–82:4ab) presents Enoch being given a tour of the cosmos by the angel Uriel (72:1), with the specific purpose of revealing which calendar corresponds directly to physical reality. In this book, Uriel reveals the details of the celestial mechanics to Enoch (*1 En.* 74:2; 75:3–4; 78:10; 79:2–3), although, unlike in the Book of the Watchers, Enoch acts as a passive recipient of the revelations and never asks any questions. Uriel also reveals the names of the angels in charge of the various celestial phenomena in 82:7–20. Enoch, in turn, passes the revelations on to his son Methuselah (76:14; 79:1).

Thus Enoch engages in an otherworldly journey that does not involve a shamanic cosmology, but he has no explicit call to shamanhood, engages in no shamanic ascetic techniques, experiences no initiatory disintegration and reintegration, and exhibits no control over spirits or angels. There is no healing, exorcism, divination, dream interpretation, or psychopompy, but by implication the revelations about the solar calendar are intended to benefit Enoch's human community (as well as the actual audience of the Astronomical Book). These revelations correct errors in calendrical observance (82:5–6) that have profound effects on the well-being of humanity (80:1–8).

2.3. The Book of Dreams

The Book of Dreams (*1 En.* 83–90) consists of two dream visions revealed to Enoch and passed on to his son Methuselah. The second dream (chs. 85–90)

11. James C. VanderKam, *Calendars in the Dead Sea Scrolls: Measuring Time* (Literature of the Dead Sea Scrolls; London: Routledge, 1998).

forms a discrete work, the Animal Apocalypse, to which the opening episode (chs. 83–84) has been added. There is no shamanic call, no report of the use of ascetic techniques, no initiatory disintegration and reintegration, no otherworldly journey,[12] and Enoch does not exercise control over any spirits or angels.

He does, however, serve the human community by means of his intermediation. In the first episode his dream is interpreted by his grandfather Mahalalel, and then Enoch successfully intercedes with God on behalf of humanity so that a remnant survives the flood. In the second episode Enoch's dream vision reviews the history of the world from the creation of humanity to what appears to be the author's present at the time of the Maccabean revolt, with the eschaton and final judgment expected immediately thereafter. Although presented as an esoteric revelation to an antediluvian audience, its actual audience would have found the account of the ongoing Maccabean revolt (90:6–19) to be of considerable practical interest. It presents the revolt in a highly positive light, promising that Judah the Maccabee (the sheep with the one great horn) would receive angelic aid and achieve victory.[13] This call to arms is a rather different message than the roughly contemporary call to passive resistance and martyrdom in the book of Daniel, and we may take it that there were conflicting views among Jewish apocalyptists about how to react to the revolt.[14]

2.4. The Epistle of Enoch

The Epistle of Enoch may have originated in a short recension (91:1–94:5 and 104:7–105:2), known in Aramaic in the Qumran manuscripts, which was expanded with 94:6–104:6 into the longer recension known from the Greek and Ethiopic versions.[15] In addition, the Epistle now incorporates the Apocalypse of Weeks, a short work that likely once circulated independently but now survives only in the Ethiopic version in disordered form (93:1–10 + 91:11–17) and in an Aramaic manuscript from Qumran in the correct order.[16] I will consider the final form of the Epistle here, along with the fragments of Enochiana appended at the end of *1 Enoch* (106–108).

12. Enoch's ascent to the celestial Temple appears to be noted in 87:3, but it does not play a significant part in the narrative. See Nickelsburg, *1 Enoch 1*, 374.

13. Ibid., 396–401. The material on the Maccabean revolt may be an interpolation that updates the original oracle but, even if so, my point remains the same.

14. See James R. Davila, "The Animal Apocalypse and Daniel," in *Enoch and Qumran Origins: New Light on a Forgotten Connection* (ed. G. Boccaccini; Grand Rapids: Eerdmans, 2005), 35–38, esp. 38.

15. Gabriele Boccaccini, *Beyond the Essene Hypothesis: The Parting of the Ways between Qumran and Enochic Judaism* (Grand Rapids: Eerdmans, 1998), 104–13, 131–38.

16. Jozef T. Milik, ed., *The Books of Enoch: Aramaic Fragments of Qumrân Cave 4* (with the collaboration of Matthew Black; Oxford: Clarendon, 1976), 48, 265–67.

The Epistle of Enoch proper does not include a shamanic call, the use of ascetic techniques, an initiatory experience, an otherworldly journey, or control of spirits or angels. Although Enoch does not heal, exorcise demons, interpret dreams, or engage in divination, he does serve the human community with prophetic revelations about the time of the end (especially in his revelations to his son Methuselah in 91 and in the revelations in the Apocalypse of Weeks) and, in the bulk of the book, about the postmortem rewards and judgments of the righteous and the wicked and the sort of lives that lead a person to one fate or the other.

The latter revelations could be taken to have a psychopompic component, inasmuch as they involve guidance for the living concerning the state of the dead, but no actual leading of the dead to their proper place in the afterlife is involved. The précis of Enoch's role in 93:11–14 does have a shamanic ring to it, although it summarizes elements that are found only elsewhere in the Enochic literature (see below).[17] According to chapters 106–107, after Enoch's final ascent to heaven Methuselah contacted him as a kind of shamanic ancestral mentor to learn the truth about the paternity of his son Noah. The final chapter of *1 Enoch*, 108, calls itself "Another Book" of Enoch and presents to Methuselah a vivid account of the final judgment.

2.5. The Similitudes of Enoch

The Similitudes of Enoch (*1 En*. 37–71) is a Jewish apocalypse that is usually understood to have been composed in the first century B.C.E. or first century C.E., although a somewhat later date cannot be ruled out entirely.[18] Unlike the other works in *1 Enoch*, no fragments of the Similitudes are preserved in the Qumran library or even in a Greek manuscript. The text survives only in the Ethiopic version, although it is generally agreed that the original language was Aramaic or Hebrew and that the Ethiopic is translated from a Greek version. It is possible that most of chapter 70 and all of chapter 71 are a secondary addition and that the original work did not envisage Enoch as the messianic Son of Man, but this is debated.

The Similitudes include no shamanic call of Enoch, but in chapter 65 Noah travels to the ends of the earth to consult his translated grandfather Enoch about the fate of the earth and Enoch answers his questions, an interchange that may present Enoch as a kind of shamanic ancestor mentor. In 67:1 Noah receives

17. Specifically, the passage describes a practitioner who can hear the words of God without fear, view the works of heaven, see souls and spirits, and ascend and receive revelations and learn cosmic secrets.

18. For a recent discussion of critical issues pertaining to the Similitudes, see Davila, *Provenance of the Pseudepigrapha*, 132–37.

what looks to be a prophetic call from God, but this comes after his interchange with Enoch and may be predicated upon it. No ascetic techniques are used in the Similitudes.

There is no initiatory experience per se, although in the only surviving form of the work Enoch is translated into the messianic Son of Man after his final ascent to heaven (ch. 71, especially vv. 11, 14). The otherworldly journey features prominently in this text, with Enoch ascending to heaven in chapters 39, 52, and 70–71.[19] In the first vision (39:4–8) Enoch reports that he longed to join in with the celestial liturgy of the angels and the righteous dead, much like the later descenders to the chariot. In the second (52:1–2) he tells us that he saw the secrets of heaven and of the future. The celestial cosmography of chapter 71 follows Daniel and the Book of the Watchers in presenting the heavenly throne room as the fiery macrocosmic temple with the deity enthroned therein and surrounded by angelic attendants.

Control of the spirits—once again, angels—figures prominently in the Similitudes. In his journeys through space and time Enoch is guided by angels. Sometimes they provide him with unasked-for information (e.g., 60:11), but more often he asks specific questions and is answered (40:2, 8–10; 43:3–4; 46:2–3; 52:3–9; 53:4–7; 54:4–6; 56:2–8; 60:9–10). The revelations he receives include heavenly secrets (41:1) and natural and calendrical secrets (41:3–9; 43:1–2; 44:1; 59:1–3; 60:11–23). In heaven Enoch encounters a fountain of righteousness surrounded by fountains of wisdom from which the thirsty could drink and be filled with wisdom (48:1–2), anticipating aspects of the *Sar Torah* revelations in the *hekhalot* literature. In chapter 66 Noah is shown the angels who will bring the flood, and in chapter 69 he is given the names and roles of the Watchers who corrupted humanity and he is told about (or given?) the oath of creation that exercises control over the physical world.

Service to the human community is not emphasized in the Similitudes. The revelations therein are aimed in 37:2–3 at both Enoch's generation and the people in the last days (i.e., the contemporary audience of the actual author), but there is no practical service (healing, exorcism, etc.) offered to either audience. It is conceivable that the author meant to imply that knowledge of the oath of creation gave Noah and potentially others the ability to provide such services, but this is not made explicit.

2.6. Larger Units in the Enochic Literature

Having examined the component works in *1 Enoch* individually, we can also consider them as aggregated in larger units in which they also circulated. Nickelsburg

19. Other visions of Enoch are noted in chapters 57 and 60, but these are not presented as otherworldly journeys.

argues on the basis of the Qumran manuscripts that the Book of the Watchers, the Book of Dreams, and the Epistle of Enoch circulated as a unit, with chapters 81–82 containing part of the otherwise lost ending of the Book of the Watchers, as well as transitional material added secondarily.[20] This configuration is of special interest, since it survives in a verifiably Jewish manuscript and must have been read as a unit by the users of the Qumran library.

No shamanic call is included, although Enoch may act as a shamanic ancestral mentor to Methuselah; Enoch engages in an incubation rite in order to interpret dreams; he goes on otherworldly journeys involving realms with a cosmology that anticipates important elements of that found in the *hekhalot* texts; he controls spirits who guide him on his second otherworldly journey and answer his questions during this tour of the universe. His service to the earthly (although not exclusively human) community includes mediating between God and the Watchers, interceding with God to preserve a remnant of humanity after the flood, advising the readers of the Animal Apocalypse how to react to the persecution by Antiochus Epiphanes and the Maccabean revolt, and offering instruction on calendrical matters and on the fate and state of the dead. The last element could be regarded as containing an element of psychopompy.

We do not know whether the entire book of Ethiopic *1 Enoch* ever circulated as a unit in its original Aramaic (and Hebrew?) form in Jewish circles, but as an aggregate it does give us a range of ancient Jewish material on Enoch, and it is worth considering the entire collection together from this perspective. Doing so adds relatively little new data but reinforces what we have learned from the Qumran collection. It addition to the material attested in the threefold Enochic work found at Qumran, the Astronomical Book underscores the

---

20. Nickelsburg, *1 Enoch 1*, 21–26, 334–38. This text seems to have been contained in 4QEn[c] (Milik, *Books of Enoch*, 182). 4QEn[d] and 4QEn[e] also contain material from the Book of the Watchers and the Book of Dreams, and Milik takes them to have had the same contents as 4QEn[c] (*Books of Enoch*, 217, 227). 4QEn[a] and 4QEn[b] contain material from the Book of the Watchers, 4QEn[f] survives in a single fragment of the Book of Dreams, and 4QEn[g] contains material from the Epistle of Enoch. These manuscripts are very fragmentary, and their full original extent is unknown.

The Book of Giants was also found in 4QEn[a], 4QEn[c], and perhaps 4QEn[e], its place in these manuscripts being uncertain. This work is also known from a number of other Qumran manuscripts. It is very poorly preserved, both in the Qumran Aramaic manuscripts and in later recensions in other languages. It covered much of the same ground as the Book of the Watchers and involved dreams, dream interpretation by Enoch, and visions, but little more can be said about it usefully in this context. See Milik, *Books of Enoch*, 298–339; John C. Reeves, *Jewish Lore in Manichaean Cosmogony: Studies in the* Book of Giants *Traditions* (HUCM 14; Cincinnati: Hebrew Union College Press, 1992); Loren T. Stuckenbruck, *The Book of Giants from Qumran* (TSAJ 63; Tübingen: Mohr Siebeck, 1997); Émile Puech, ed., *Qumrân Grotte 4.XXII: Textes araméens, première partie: 4Q529–549* (DJD 31; Oxford: Clarendon, 2001), 9–115 (*Livre des Géants*, 4Q530–533, 4Q203 1).

cosmic importance for humanity of the calendrical revelations given to Enoch by an angel. The Similitudes too seems to present Enoch as an ancestral shamanic mentor, in this case to Noah. The translation of Enoch into the messianic Son of Man is similar to the later initiatory transformation of the descenders to the chariot. And there are spirit-guided otherworldly journeys, including one to the celestial throne room, in which Enoch interrogates the angels and they reply to his questions.

2.7. Daniel

The book of Daniel, the only canonical apocalypse to be discussed here, has been shown on internal grounds to have been composed during the Maccabean revolt (ca. 167–165 B.C.E.), although it made use of some earlier material. It survives in its original Hebrew and Aramaic, although the Old Greek version may have been translated from a somewhat variant Semitic original. In chapters 1–6 the book tells stories about Daniel and his three friends in the Babylonian royal court during the exile. Chapters 7–12 are written in the first person in the name of Daniel and present apocalyptic revelations given to him.

There is no specific shamanic call for the practitioners in the book of Daniel, but they do make use of shamanic ascetic techniques. In 2:17–19, 28 Daniel and his three friends elicit a divine revelation through prayer and receive knowledge of the king's dream and its interpretation. To learn the esoteric meaning of a difficult passage in the book of Jeremiah, Daniel engages in an unspecified period of fasting in sackcloth and ashes (9:1–3) and prayer (9:4–21a), with the result that the angel Gabriel comes and answers his questions (9:21b–27). A few years later, according to the author's chronology, Daniel engages in a three-week program of self-denial in which he eats no delicacies, meat, or wine and refrains from anointing himself (10:2–3). In response, an angel appears (10:4–11) and grants him eschatological revelations (10:12–12:13).[21]

The visionaries of the book do not experience an explicit initiatory disintegration and reintegration, but the story of the golden idol in Dan 3 does seem to describe their temporary transformation into angelic beings of fire. When Shadrach, Meshach, and Abednego have been bound and cast into the superheated fiery furnace, the king marvels at seeing them unbound and walking around unharmed in the fire in the company of a divine being (3:24–27). The

21. We are also told in 1:11–16 that Daniel and his friends followed an ascetic diet. This dietary regime is not tied explicitly to any revelatory experience, although it may be assumed as part of the background of the revelations in Dan 2. In addition, in 8:15a Daniel informs us that when he saw the vision of 8:1–4 he "sought understanding," with the result that the angel Gabriel was ordered by a divine voice to give him the interpretation of the vision (8:15b–26). It is possible that we are meant to assume the use of ritual techniques here, as elsewhere in the book.

implication is that only their bonds were destroyed by the fire and they themselves were changed into beings like the one that accompanied them, although when they left the furnace their humanity was restored.

This is strikingly similar to the experience of the descenders to the chariot during their visionary experiences: Rabbi Ishmael's body was transformed into fire, and Rabbi Akiva ascended to heaven in a chariot of fire. The descender to the chariot is described as someone "who walks in rivers of fire and knows the lightning." According to *3 Enoch*, Enoch was permanently transformed into the fiery angel Metatron.[22] It is true that Daniel's friends overcome earthly fire and the descenders to the chariot overcome heavenly fire, but both seem to be transformed temporarily into fiery divine beings.

Although the book of Daniel does not include a tour of the universe as in the Enochic literature, it does present Daniel in chapter 7 as going on an otherworldly journey in a dream vision. Daniel sees the vision of the four monsters in 7:1–8, 11–12 but seems himself to be present in the vision of the enthroned deity surrounded by angelic attendants (7:9–10, 13–14), inasmuch as Daniel approaches one of these angels and asks for an interpretation (7:16). The scene of the divine throne room is also prototypical of the *merkabah* scene in the *hekhalot* literature, although, again, no cosmology of seven heavens appears.

Most of the incidents in which Daniel exercises control over angels have been noted above. The angel gives him the requested interpretation of the vision in chapter 7 (7:16–28). When Daniel seeks understanding of the vision of chapter 8, Gabriel is ordered by a divine voice to provide it, and he does so. In response to Daniel's ascetic regime in chapter 9, Gabriel comes once again to answer his question. Likewise, a different ascetic regime in chapter 10 summons an angel who gives the practitioner eschatological revelations.

Daniel also provides service to his community, although this consists mostly of service to the king. He and his friends interpret Nebuchadnezzar's dream in chapter 2 using prayer as a ritual technique. Daniel interprets another dream of Nebuchadnezzar in chapter 4 without any ritual acts being mentioned, although the interpretation comes at the practitioner's initiative. Daniel interprets the writing on the wall for King Belshazzar in chapter 5, again without any explicit ritual techniques but also at his own initiative. It appears also that the visionary material in the book of Daniel is intended to tell the author's actual audience how to respond to the persecutions during the Maccabean revolt. The author promotes passive resistance that will lead to martyrdom but also to a heavenly reward in the imminent eschaton (see especially 11:32–35 and 12:1–4).

---

22. Davila, *Descenders to the Chariot*, ch. 5. The specific references are as follows. The first three appear in the *Hekhalot Zutarti*: R. Ishmael's immolation (*Synopse*, §420); R. Akiva's chariot of fire (*Synopse*, §366); and the reference to walking in rivers of fire (*Synopse*, §349//§361). Enoch's transformation into Metatron is in *3 En.* 1–16.

2.8. *4 Ezra*

The book of *4 Ezra* (2 Esd 3–14) is generally dated to around the end of the first century C.E. and is preserved in Latin and Syriac versions (as well as translations into other languages based on these). A Greek version also existed but is almost entirely lost now. The Greek is generally assumed to be the text from which the Latin and Syriac were translated, and it is possible, although by no means certain, that the Greek was translated from a Semitic (probably Hebrew) original. The book claims to present an account of Ezra wrestling with issues of theodicy arising from the exile, in visionary dialogue with the angel Uriel and perhaps also with God himself.[23]

There is no mention of Ezra's call to become an intermediary, but we are given comparatively abundant information about ascetic techniques used by Ezra to generate visionary experiences. The book opens with a nighttime prayer of Ezra (3:1–36) that may have an incubatory function, since it results in the angel Uriel being sent to him to address his concerns. It is unclear whether this encounter with Uriel is meant to be a dream or a vision or both. Ezra falls at the angel's feet in 4:11, so the experience is visual, not just auditory. According to 5:14–15 Ezra awakens (evidently from a dream) but is so disturbed that he promptly faints. Yet the angel strengthens him and helps him up, which implies that he is still there when Ezra is awake.

Uriel repeatedly gives Ezra instructions for generating each subsequent visionary encounter. He tells Ezra in 5:13 to carry out a seven-day fast while praying and weeping. Ezra does so (5:20–30), and Uriel is sent to him again to debate theodicy and grant him eschatological revelations (5:31). In 6:31–32 Uriel instructs him to pray and fast again for seven days, and Ezra weeps and fasts for this period (6:35) and then prays at length (6:36–59), after which Uriel is sent to him again (7:1–2) with more revelations about theodicy and eschatology. In 9:23–25 Uriel instructs Ezra to go to a field of flowers away from human habitation for seven more days, praying and subsisting only on flowers. Ezra does so (9:26) and then prays at the end of the period (9:27–37), after which he receives the vision of the woman who represents an idealized or heavenly Jerusalem (9:38–10:28). Uriel then makes an appearance, strengthens the exhausted Ezra, and interprets the vision (9:29–57).

In 10:58–59 Uriel tells him to sleep overnight in the field, after which he has the dream of the eagle that arose from the sea (11:1–12:3a). Ezra then awakes and prays for an interpretation (12:3b–9), which is provided, evidently by Uriel rather than by God, although this is not made explicit (12:10–38). This speaker commands Ezra to spend seven more days in the field (12:39), which he does

23. Michael E. Stone, *Fourth Ezra* (Hermeneia; Minneapolis: Fortress, 1990), 1–51; Davila, *Provenance of the Pseudepigrapha*, 137–41.

after meeting with the people (12:51). After the seven days he has the nocturnal dream about the man from the sea (13:1–13a). Ezra awakes and prays to God for an interpretation (13:13b–20a), and "he" (Uriel? God?) provides one by audition (13:20b–55). Then the speaker promises more revelations in three days, so Ezra remains in the field for that period (13:56–58), after which a divine audition informs him of his coming translation and arranges for him first to reconstruct the lost exoteric and esoteric scriptures.

Not every one of Ezra's prayers and previsionary night's sleeps need be taken as ritual preparation, but by the same token some of these clusters of actions can hardly be anything but ascetic techniques for generating an altered state of consciousness. Elsewhere I have called his seven-day rite of isolation, fasting, mourning, and prayer a "vision quest."[24] It has striking similarities both to shamanic vision-quest rituals that result in altered states of consciousness and visionary experiences, as well as to rites described in the *hekhalot* texts for generating visions and revelations. The latter include long periods of fasting (from seven to forty days); prolonged isolation; and the reciting of prayers, songs, words of power, and divine names.[25]

There is no initiatory disintegration and reintegration in *4 Ezra*, but the book does conclude with Ezra's translation to heaven (14:48+ in all versions but the Latin), the permanent state evidently enjoyed temporarily in this life only by shamans, practitioners like Daniel's three friends, and the descenders to the chariot. The work also contains no otherworldly journey, although the cosmology of the celestial throne room is epitomized in 8:20–22. Some control of Uriel may be implied, in that Ezra's original prayer summoned him and he seems to have been bound to address Ezra's questions and to provide Ezra with instructions for the ritual that would summon him again. But perhaps not too much should be made of this, inasmuch as in *2 Baruch* God also engages in dialogue with Baruch, answers his questions, and instructs him on what ritual to undertake to generate the next revelation (see below). Since presumably God should not be regarded as under the control of Baruch, it may be that we should not regard Ezra as controlling Uriel.[26]

The theology of the writer of *4 Ezra* may have precluded presenting Ezra as providing much service to the human community, inasmuch as the writer seems to have believed that the vast majority of humanity, including Jews and presumably virtually the entirety of Ezra's community, were eternally damned and

---

24. Davila, "Ritual in the Jewish Pseudepigrapha," 164–66, 178.

25. See Davila, *Descenders to the Chariot*, ch. 4. For a Lakota vision-quest ritual, see pp. 81–83. Notable examples in the *hekhalot* literature covered in this chapter include the fasting regimes in *Sar Torah* §§299–303; *Hekh. Zut.* §§422–424; *Ma'aseh Merkavah* §§560–565; and *Merkabah Rabbah* §§681–684.

26. At times it is unclear whether Ezra is speaking with Uriel or God (e.g., 5:31–56 and the cases noted above).

beyond help.[27] But Ezra does solve one problem for the community when with God's help he reconstructs the exoteric scriptures for the larger community and the esoteric scriptures for the elect.

2.9. *2 Baruch*

The book of *2 Baruch* is generally agreed to have been composed in the late first or early second century C.E. and to be dependent on *4 Ezra*. It survives now in a Syriac version and in two Arabic translations of the Syriac. Fragments of a Greek text survive, and it is likely that the Syriac was translated from a Greek version. It has been suggested that the Greek is in turn a translation from Hebrew or Aramaic, but this is speculative. In Baruch's name the book narrates the destruction of Jerusalem, describing a series of divine revelations he was granted about the destruction and its theological implications.[28]

There is no reference to any specific call experience for Baruch. The book opens in 1:1–2 with a typical (that is, unsolicited) prophetic oracle being revealed to him. But thereafter he consistently initiates the revelations he receives by the use of rituals and ascetic techniques. In 5:5–7 Baruch takes a group of leaders to the Kidron Valley, where they lament and fast until evening. The result is a vision of the angelic deliverance of the holy vessels from the Jerusalem temple the next day (6:4–7:1).

Two episodes in the book can be interpreted to involve incubation rituals that lead to dreams, of which Baruch prays for and receives an interpretation. In 34:1–36:1 Baruch goes to the holy of holies at the site of the destroyed temple, where he weeps and prays until he falls asleep. The result is a dream vision of the apocalypse of the forest (36:2–37:1). When he awakes, he prays for an interpretation of the vision (38:1–4). God then explains its meaning in an audition (39:1–40:4), and he and Baruch engage in a dialogue about those who have fallen away (41:1–43:2). Then in Hebron, following another revelation (see below), Baruch falls asleep (52:7) and has a dream vision of the apocalypse of the clouds (53). Again, Baruch prays for an interpretation (54), and the angel Ramiel is sent to give him an extended explanation of the dream (55–76).

Several revelations are generated by vision-quest rituals similar to those found in *4 Ezra*. These involve a seven-day fast, prayer, and isolation. In 9:2 Baruch and Jeremiah tear their clothing, weep, mourn, and fast for seven days, after which they receive an audition from God (10:1–3). In 12:5 Baruch undertakes a seven-day fast, after which God engages him in a dialogue about theodicy

27. Bruce W. Longenecker, *Eschatology and the Covenant: A Comparison of 4 Ezra and Romans 1–11* (JSNTSup 57; Sheffield: JSOT Press, 1991), 113–32.

28. Pierre Bogaert, *Apocalypse de Baruch* (2 vols; SC 144–145; Paris: Cerf, 1969); Davila, *Provenance of the Pseudepigrapha*, 126–31.

(13–20) while Baruch stands on Mount Zion. At the end of this dialogue God gives Baruch instructions for the rituals in his next vision quest (20:5–6).

Following these, Baruch goes to the Kidron Valley, where he isolates himself in a cave and fasts from both food and water for seven days (21:1–3).[29] On the seventh he recites a prayer that has some similarities to the *merkabah* hymns of the *hekhalot* literature (21:4–26, esp. vv. 4–10[30]). God then replies and engages him in another dialogue pertaining to theodicy and eschatological revelations (22–25), after which Baruch is granted a vision of the apocalypse of the twelve calamities (26–30). Then in 43:3 God commands Baruch to depart from Jerusalem and to fast for another seven days. Baruch goes to Hebron and does so (47:1–2), afterward offering another prayer, again with some similarities to *merkabah* hymns (48:1–25). Once again, God then engages in a dialogue with him, this time on the fate of the righteous and the wicked (48:26–52:6).

No experience of shamanic initiatory disintegration and reintegration is described in *2 Baruch*, but the eschatological transformation of the righteous is anticipated in 51:3 and, more important, we are told repeatedly that Baruch himself is to be translated to heaven without death (13:3; 46:7; 48:30; 76:2–4), just as we have seen happen to Enoch and Ezra in other works.

Baruch himself does not go on an otherworldly journey, but one such journey seems to be reported in *2 Baruch*. In the revelatory discourse of the angel Ramiel, we read in 59:3–12 of God taking Moses, showing him the macrocosmic temple and the celestial paradise (cf. 4:5–7), and taking him on a tour of the universe very similar to the experiences of Enoch in *1 En.* 14–36.

The book of *2 Baruch* shows very little interest in control of the spirits. The best example is the summoning of the angel Ramiel through Baruch's prayer (54–76), although, unlike the angels associated with Enoch and Baruch, Ramiel does not answer any specific questions when he interprets Baruch's dream.

Baruch has an active relationship with his community, addressing and instructing them in chapters 31–34, 44–47, and 77–78. He addresses their specific concerns but does not engage in healing, exorcism, divination, or psychopompy. The only dreams he interprets are his own, but they presumably were meant to be useful for his followers and the readers of the book.

---

29. This feat is virtually physically impossible and suggests that any genuine rituals reflected in this work are colored by fantasy.

30. Compare, for example, the *merkabah* hymns I have translated in *Descenders to the Chariot*, 118–22, which share with this passage the themes of God's enthronement in heaven, his power over the angels surrounding his throne and over creation, and his sustaining of the righteous. Likewise, *2 Bar.* 48:1–25 (see below) shares with them the themes of God's power over creation and the angels; his knowledge of the secrets of the universe and the eschatological future; Israel's supplication to him; and his solicitude for fragile, righteous human beings. Many more *merkabah* hymns with significant parallels could be cited.

3. Concluding Remarks

The Jewish apocalypses from a few centuries on either side of the Common Era present intermediary figures who have a number of traits that are untypical of earlier prophetic literature but are also characteristic of the much later quasi-shamanic magico-religious practitioners known as the descenders to the chariot. If we take the six components of the shamanic model applied to the latter, we find the following six conclusions.

First, the apocalyptic visionaries are usually not presented as experiencing a *shamanic call,* although Enoch, the paradigmatic apocalyptic practitioner, can perhaps be interpreted to be acting as an ancestral shamanic mentor to Methuselah and Noah.

Second, the relative lack of *ritual and ascetic techniques* in the biblical prophetic literature can be contrasted with its comparative abundance in the apocalypses. We find incubation rites used by Enoch, Ezra, and Baruch. Ezra and Baruch engage in seven-day vision-quest rituals that involve fasting (or consuming unusual foodstuffs), self-isolation, and prayer. Daniel's rites of prolonged fasting and prayer, in Dan 9 and 10, look to be variants of the vision-quest ritual genre. Shorter periods of prayer and/or fasting are also used to generate revelations.

Third, the shamanic process of *initiatory disintegration and reintegration* does not appear as such in the apocalypses, but there are some suggestive features that may be connected, even ancestral, to it. First, most of the apocalyptic visionaries (Enoch, Ezra, and Baruch) are translated directly to heaven without experiencing death. For Enoch in the Similitudes, this is explicitly a transformation into an angelic being in the fiery realm of the divine throne room (*1 En.* 71:1–14). Daniel does not undergo such a translation, although he is by implication included among the wise who shall shine like stars in the eschaton (Dan 12:3, 13). It looks very much as though Daniel's three friends are understood to undergo a temporary assumption into this state when they are joined by an angel in the fiery furnace and rendered impervious to its flames. The experience of intermediation described by the descenders to the chariot seems to have included an (also temporary) proleptic spiritual transformation into a fiery divine being as part of the process of reaching the divine throne and joining the angelic choir. It is tempting to posit some connection between the translation of the ancient apocalyptic visionaries and the experience of the later mystics, although its nature is debatable. It may be that the stories in the apocalypses objectified an otherwise unmentioned personal spiritual experience of the apocalyptic visionaries—one known also to the later descenders to the chariot—but it is also possible that the descenders to the chariot interpreted their own initiatory experience in terms borrowed from the physical translations reported of the legendary ancient visionaries.

Fourth, *otherworldly journeys* are undertaken by Enoch, Daniel, and (according to *2 Bar.* 59) Moses. These journeys do not present a shamanic cosmology per se, but they do present the experience as an ascent to the fiery throne room of

God where the deity sits surrounded by angels. This pattern is adopted and developed in terms of the shamanic cosmology by the descenders to the chariot.

Fifth, some level of *control of spirits* (angels) is found in the Book of the Watchers, the Similitudes, Daniel, and *4 Ezra*. Angels are required to lead Enoch on tours of the universe and to answer his questions. They also provide interpretations of visions for Daniel and Ezra, and one engages in a series of dialogues about theodicy with Ezra. Presumably the angels are required, often in the context of ritual summonses, to cooperate with the visionaries, at least to the point of dialoguing with them. Nevertheless, the picture in the *hekhalot* texts is quantitatively if not qualitatively rather different, with highly detailed rituals being prescribed to control angels during the descent to the chariot, to compel the Prince of Torah to reveal knowledge of the Torah, and to gain open-ended theurgic power over the Prince of the Presence.[31]

Sixth, the apocalyptic visionaries provide a number of *services to their community*. Dream interpretation is included, and some revelations may serve as background to exorcistic and psychopompic concerns. The visionaries help solve conflicts in their own communities, such as when Daniel interprets the writing on the wall, Ezra is granted the ability to reconstruct all lost scriptures, and Baruch instructs the people of Jerusalem in various ways. The revelations promoted in the apocalypses also aim to minister to their actual readers, for example, by providing them instruction on the proper calendar to use and how to respond to the persecutions of Antiochus during the Maccabean revolt.

What are the implications for the historical origins of *merkabah* mysticism as presented in the *hekhalot* literature? The figure of Enoch in the various books in *1 Enoch* (especially the Book of the Watchers and the Similitudes) anticipates much of the quasi-shamanic template we find much later in the *hekhalot* texts. Since one of these texts, the book of *3 Enoch*, has some more or less direct relationship (whether literary or based on oral tradition) with the Similitudes, and since Metatron, the angel who in later centuries was identified with Enoch, plays an important role in the *hekhalot* literature as a whole, a genetic relationship of some sort between the descenders to the chariot and the ancient Enochic traditions and practitioners seems likely.[32] But the figures of Daniel, Ezra, and Baruch also display much of the same template, including incubations, vision quests, acquaintance with proleptic and eschatological disintegration and reintegration, otherworldly journeys, limited control of angels, and service to their own communities.

---

31. For the descent to the chariot, see, e.g., *Hekh. Rab.* §§198–237 (Davila, *Descenders to the Chariot*, 123–24, 169–72, 265–68). For the Prince of Torah, see *Sar Torah* §§299–306 (Davila, ibid., 93–95, 269–77). For the Prince of the Presence, see *Sar Panim* §§623–639 (Davila, ibid., 104–105, 209–210) and Rebecca Lesses, "The Adjuration of the Prince of the Presence: Performative Utterance in a Jewish Ritual," in *Ancient Magic and Ritual Power* (ed. M. Meyer and P. Mirecki; Religions in the Greco-Roman World 129; Leiden: Brill, 1995), 185–206.

32. Davila, *Provenance of the Pseudepigrapha*, 132–33 and n. 26.

Taken as an aggregate, the visionaries described in the ancient Jewish apocalypses thus display a fairly high density of key elements associated with the much later descenders to the chariot, when we categorize the latter according to the shamanic/healer model of magico-religious practitioner. That said, there are also many important differences, although these have limited relevance for the model. The apocalypses describe fictional experiences of scriptural prophets and scribes, whereas the *hekhalot* literature gives ritual instructions illustrated by accounts of fictional experiences of Tannaitic rabbis. In both cases the existence of actual practitioners in the time the works were written is a matter of inference, but the inferential case is considerably stronger for the *hekhalot* practitioners.

A multitude of *nomina barbara* and divine names appear in the *hekhalot* literature but are not found in the apocalypses, although Uriel reveals angelic names to Enoch in the Astronomical Book (*1 En.* 82:9–20). Most of the apocalypses have a strong eschatological interest, but such interest is very muted in the *hekhalot* texts. And the apocalypses deal with revelations granted by God at the initiative of either God or the visionary, generally through angelic mediation, whereas the *hekhalot* literature focuses on the means for human practitioners to elicit revelatory experiences and gain power to compel angels to do their will.

In addition, there is a great chronological, social, and geographical distance between the apocalyptic visionaries and the descenders to the chariot. The visionaries are attested mostly in Palestinian contexts between the late Persian/early Hellenistic periods and the early centuries C.E., whereas the earliest securely established social context for the descenders to the chariot is Babylonia in the fifth to seventh centuries C.E.[33]

Nevertheless, at least in the case of the Enochic literature, a historical link does seem plausible. It is possible that the Palestinian Jewish apocalyptic visionaries transmitted their lore and ritual techniques to a line of disciples who over time developed into the descenders to the chariot. But it is also possible that many of the parallels between the two groups can be explained not by any historical connection but by independent developments of techniques that exploit innate human neurophysiological and psychological traits to generate altered states of consciousness, along with independent exegesis of scriptural and noncanonical traditions that showed interest in such altered states. These possibilities are not mutually exclusive.

Christopher R. A. Morray-Jones has argued persuasively that some of the *hekhalot* traditions go back at least to the Tannaitic period and that many concepts and ideas in this material go back even to the New Testament period.[34] I

33. See Davila, *Descenders to the Chariot*, ch. 8.

34. Christopher R. A. Morray-Jones, "Paradise Revisited (*2 Cor* 12:1–2): The Jewish Mystical Background of Paul's Apostolate, Part 1: The Jewish Sources" and idem, "Paradise Revisited (*2 Cor* 12:1–2): The Jewish Mystical Background of Paul's Apostolate, Part 2: Paul's Heavenly

have also shown that some of these ideas and concepts can be found already as early as the Dead Sea Scrolls.[35] All in all, there is a good case that elements of the magico-religious ritual traditions and experiences presented in the ancient Jewish apocalypses were ancestral to the ritual practices and experiences described in the *hekhalot* literature. But the exact nature of the relationship between the apocalyptic visionaries and the descenders to the chariot remains to be determined, and we can only hope that someday we recover more direct evidence about such magico-religious practitioners in the intervening centuries.

Ascent and Its Significance," *HTR* 86 (1993): 177–217, 265–92; idem, *A Transparent Illusion: The Dangerous Vision of Water in Hekhalot Mysticism: A Source-Critical and Tradition-Historical Inquiry* (JSJSup 59; Leiden: Brill, 2002).

35. James R. Davila, "The Hodayot Hymnist and the Four Who Entered Paradise," *RevQ* 17/65–68 (1996): 457–78; idem, "The Dead Sea Scrolls and Merkavah Mysticism," in *The Dead Sea Scrolls in Their Historical Context* (ed. T. H. Lim et al.; Edinburgh: T&T Clark, 2000), 249–64; idem, *Liturgical Works* (Eerdmans Commentaries on the Dead Sea Scrolls 6; Grand Rapids: Eerdmans, 2000), 41–167.

Rabbi Ishmael's Priestly Genealogy in *Hekhalot* Literature

Ra'anan S. Boustan

> "He [Rabbi Ishmael] is of the nation of Israel, whom the Holy One, blessed be He, chose from the seventy nations to be his people. He is of the tribe of Levi, (which presents) the priestly offering to His name. He is from the seed of Aaron, whom the Holy One, blessed be He, chose to be his servant and on whom the Holy One, blessed be He, placed the priestly crown at Sinai." At once they [i.e., the angelic host] began to say: "This one is certainly worthy to behold the chariot-throne, as it is written, *Happy the people who have it so*; [*happy the people whose God is the Lord*] (Ps 144:15)." (*3 En.* 2:3–4).

Hekhalot literature, the earliest systematic collection of Jewish "mystical" and "magical" writings, juxtaposes and combines a bewildering variety of motifs, themes, and genres.[1] How scholars of early Jewish mysticism ought to make use of this textual data has long divided the field of early Jewish mysticism—and continues to do so. It has now been more almost three decades since Peter Schäfer began to challenge the fundamental methodological assumption that *hekhalot* literature, as it has been transmitted to us in the medieval manuscript tradition and the surviving fragments from the Cairo Genizah, reflects a unified and internally consistent religious system.[2] Schäfer has instead argued that the various compositions that make up this corpus represent shifting assemblages of smaller or larger

* I delivered an earlier version of this paper in the Early Jewish and Mysticism Group at the Society of Biblical Literature Annual Meeting in Denver, November 2001. I would like to thank the members of the group for their feedback in the early stages of this project. I have analyzed many of these same sources at considerably greater length and in a different context in Ra'anan S. Boustan, *From Martyr to Mystic: Rabbinic Martyrology and the Making of Merkavah Mysticism* (TSAJ 112; Tübingen: Mohr Siebeck, 2005), 245–88.

1. All citations of *hekhalot* literature refer to Peter Schäfer, Margaret Schlüter, and Hans George von Mutius, eds., *Synopse zur Hekhalot-Literatur* (TSAJ 2; Tübingen: Mohr Siebeck, 1981). All translations of *hekhalot* literature are mine unless otherwise noted.

2. See especially the studies collected in Peter Schäfer, ed., *Hekhalot-Studien* (TSAJ 19; Tübingen: Mohr Siebeck, 1988).

literary units. Schäfer has, therefore, argued that a firm textual foundation must serve as the starting point for understanding *hekhalot* texts as socially and culturally meaningful documents.

Schäfer's project has been understood by some as an out and out rejection of the possibility of exploring the "lived" dimension of early Jewish mysticism. Certainly his paradigm places high value on careful study of textual data. Yet in my view the conviction that research on *hekhalot* literature must begin from the minutiae of textual archaeology need not imply a narrow research agenda restricted to empirical description of its transmission and reception histories. Indeed, only finely tuned attention to compositional history, rhetorical texture, and narrative structure can ultimately illuminate how religious authority and experience are represented in and thus constructed by *hekhalot* literature. Problems of language and textuality are not obstacles to be overcome but opportunities to analyze early Jewish mysticism in ways that do not reduce its richness and specificity to teleological evolutionary schema or overly facile transcultural categories.

In this paper I survey the highly variable and even contradictory attitudes expressed in the different parts of the corpus toward one of its central characters, Rabbi Ishmael ben Elisha the High Priest. While some sources present R. Ishmael's priestly status as an unimpeachable source of power and authority, others treat this potential claim to special privilege with considerable suspicion. I argue that a positive appraisal of R. Ishmael's priestly genealogy is particularly characteristic of—but not confined to—those *hekhalot* compositions that most closely conform to the conventions of the apocalyptic genre, such as the frame narrative of *3 Enoch* (*Synopse,* §§1–3). By contrast, those *hekhalot* compositions that present ritual technique taught and performed within a community of initiates as the primary means for approaching the divine—either through heavenly ascent or angelic adjuration—tend to downplay or, in some cases, reject outright the genealogical principle. In particular, the extensive collection of ascent traditions found at the heart of *Hekhalot Rabbati* (*Synopse,* §§198–268) challenges the notion that R. Ishmael's singular genealogy confers upon him superior—and fundamentally inimitable—powers, subordinating priestly status to learning transmitted from master to disciple. This passage advocates what I call an "egalitarian" orientation toward heavenly ascent: the visionary's ability to undertake successfully a heavenly journey depends on proper mastery of esoteric knowledge and practice rather than being conferred upon him automatically by birth.

The diversity of representations of R. Ishmael in *hekhalot* literature serves an index of the heterogeneous character of this fluid corpus of materials. In my view, therefore, any reconstruction of the socioreligious context that produced the constituent components of *hekhalot* literature must take into account the full range of ideological perspectives encompassed within it. The radically divergent attitudes toward the Levitical priesthood that are articulated in *hekhalot* texts should caution against drawing general conclusions about the ideological orientation of the corpus without first considering the shifting literary contexts of the individual composition units.

1. Interpreting the Priestly Traditions in *Hekhalot* Literature

The recent interest in the priestly or cultic background of early Jewish mysticism makes a focused appraisal of the attitude(s) toward R. Ishmael's priestly status in *hekhalot* literature particularly relevant. Indeed, a number of scholars have argued that "*merkabah* mysticism" was profoundly shaped by cultic traditions associated with the Jerusalem temple. The greatest proponent of this position, Rachel Elior, has written that "it was in reaction to the destruction of the earthly temple that the creators of the tradition of the 'descent to the Merkavah' and the 'ascent to the *hekhalot*' conceived the heavenly shrines as depicted in the *hekhalot* literature."[3] Elior views the imaginative depictions of the heavenly temple that fill *hekhalot* literature as intentional attempts to compensate for the deprivation of postdestruction reality. In her most recent formulations she develops this argument even further, suggesting that these literary representations of the heavenly temple and its ritual-liturgical drama reflect the religious orientation and social identity of actual priestly groups that played an active and influential role within the Jewish community of Byzantine Palestine.[4]

Interestingly enough, Ithamar Gruenwald, who was the first to study the attitude of *hekhalot* literature toward cultic and priestly traditions in a systematic fashion, offers a diametrically opposed interpretation of the evidence.[5] Gruenwald asserts that the *hekhalot* corpus is in fact aligned with the antipriestly attitudes that characterized the "Pharisaic-rabbinic" movement. This argument is most likely designed to substantiate Gershom Scholem's general thesis that *merkabah* mysticism arose in the heart of the rabbinic movement. Gruenwald does acknowledge that the Aaronide priesthood is often mentioned favorably in

3. Rachel Elior, "From Earthly Temple to Heavenly Shrines," *JSQ* 4 (1997): 217–67, here 223. See also idem, "The Merkavah Tradition and the Emergence of Jewish Mysticism," in *Sino-Judaica: Jews and Christians in Historical Dialogue* (ed. A. Oppenheimer; Tel Aviv: Tel Aviv University, 1998), 101–58; idem, "From Earthly Temple to Heavenly Shrines: Prayer and Sacred Liturgy in the Hekhalot Literature and Its Relations to Temple Traditions" (Hebrew), *Tarbiz* 64 (1995): 421–80.

4. Rachel Elior, "*Hekhalot* and *Merkavah* Literature: Its Relation to the Temple, the Heavenly Temple, and the 'Diminished Temple'" [Hebrew], in *Continuity and Renewal: Jews and Judaism in Byzantine-Christian Palestine* (ed. L. I. Levine; Jerusalem: Yad Ben-Zvi, 2004), 107–42; idem, *The Three Temples: On the Emergence of Jewish Mysticism* (trans. D. Louvish; Oxford: Littman Library of Jewish Civilization, 2004), esp. 201–65.

5. See especially Ithamar Gruenwald, "The Place of Priestly Traditions in the Writings of Merkavah Mysticism and the *Shi'ur Qomah*" (Hebrew), *Jerusalem Studies in Jewish Thought* 1 (1981–82): 65–120.

hekhalot texts. But he accounts for this phenomenon with the rather speculative claim that the "rabbinic" mystics of *hekhalot* literature were apparently willing to express their admiration for the institution of the priesthood because it no longer posed a challenge to their authority.

Although Elior and Gruenwald have come to opposite conclusions concerning the significance of the cultic motifs in *hekhalot* literature, I think they share several problematic assumptions. First, both scholars approach *hekhalot* literature as if it were a unified body of texts reflecting a single sociohistorical and ideological perspective. This tendency causes them to overlook the protracted and complex literary development of the corpus as well as the diversity of its contents. Second, both offer a stereotyped and overly general picture of the priesthood; they tend to speak of it as if it were a politically and ideologically cohesive social class. But as we know, in the literature of the Second Temple period indictments of the purity and legitimacy of the priesthood are most often to be found in works that were produced in priestly circles and are concerned largely with cultic practice.[6] It has come to be widely acknowledged that critique of specific cultic practices ought not to be confused with rejection of cultic practice as such. Consideration of the internal rivalries that often plagued the priesthood must necessarily complicate analysis of these "antipriestly" polemics. Finally, both appear to treat the sociological categories that were operative in the Second Temple as if they continued to be salient for understanding the social context from which *hekhalot* literature emerged.

Recently a number of Jewish historians and scholars of Hebrew liturgical poetry have suggested that priestly lineage did in fact continue to exert a certain degree of concrete social effect on social status and identity in Jewish communities throughout late antiquity.[7] Yet, in my view, the stylized portrait of the priesthood in *hekhalot* literature and its highly local rhetorical functions should give us pause before we jump to connect literary trope with social reality. It is, therefore, necessary to distinguish carefully between real people who viewed themselves and were viewed by others as enjoying priestly privilege, on the one hand, and texts that found it productive to "think with" priests to advance their agenda, on the other. Especially because *hekhalot* literature encompasses such contradictory attitudes toward the Levitical priesthood, each case must be analyzed within its local literary context before we can decide how—and even whether—R. Ishmael's

6. For analysis of innerpriestly polemic in the Second Temple period, see especially Martha Himmelfarb, "Levi, Phinehas, and the Problem of Intermarriage at the Time of the Maccabean Revolt," *JSQ* 6 (1999): 1–24. For further discussion, see also idem, "Sexual Relations and Purity in the Temple Scroll and the Book of *Jubilees*," *DSD* 6 (1999): 11–36.

7. See especially Oded Irshai, "The Priesthood in Jewish Society in Late Antiquity" (Hebrew), in Levine, *Continuity and Renewal*, 67–106; Joseph Yahalom, *Poetry and Society in Jewish Galilee of Late Antiquity* (Hebrew) (Tel Aviv: Hakibbutz Hameuchad, 1999), 107–36.

priestly identity can contribute to our understanding of the social profile of the creators of *hekhalot* literature.

2. The Crown of the Priesthood as a Source of Ritual Power

Perhaps most noteworthy among the passages in the *hekhalot* corpus that specifically thematize priestly lineage as a positive criterion for enabling a person to better negotiate the dangerous business of heavenly ascent is the literary frame of *3 Enoch* (*Synopse*, §§1–3).[8] This text describes R. Ishmael's ascent to heaven and his reception by the angel Metatron, who in turn recounts to the visionary his human origins as the patriarch Enoch before his elevation to heaven.[9] This introductory passage thus supplies the narrative setting for Metatron's revelations concerning both his own past and a wide variety of heavenly secrets.[10] Upon ascending to the seventh palace, R. Ishmael's first action is to utter a prayer to God:

> "Master of the Universe, I beg of you that the merit of Aaron ben Amram (זכות אהרן בן עמרם), lover of peace and pursuer of peace, who received the crown of priesthood (כתר כהונה) on Mount Sinai in the presence of your glory, may avail for me now, so that Prince Qatspi'el and the angels with him may not prevail over me and cast me from heaven."[11]

In response to R. Ishmael's plea, God summons Metatron to protect him from the rest of the angelic host. Even more provocatively, when the angels do subsequently threaten R. Ishmael, God himself chastises them: "My servants, my *serapim*, my *kerubim*, my *ʾopannim*, cover your eyes from Ishmael My beloved son, My favored, and My glory, so that he not shrink and tremble" (§2 = 1:8).

---

8. In the *Synopse*, this passage is found both at §§1–3 (MS V228) and at §§882–884 (MS M40). A different version of the first two units of the passage (§§1–2) is also found in G8/2a:2–16 (Peter Schäfer, ed., *Geniza-Fragmente zur Hekhalot-Literatur* [TSAJ 6; Tübingen: Mohr Siebeck, 1984], 135–39). I use MS V228 as the primary basis for my discussion.

9. Among the numerous studies of Enoch's angelification as Metatron, see especially Nathaniel Deutsch, *Guardians of the Gate: Angelic Vice Regency in Late Antiquity* (Leiden: Brill, 1999), 27–77; Elliot R. Wolfson, *Through a Speculum That Shines: Vision and Imagination in Medieval Jewish Mysticism* (Princeton: Princeton University Press, 1994), 82–85; Christopher R. A. Morray-Jones, "Transformational Mysticism in the Apocalyptic-Merkabah Tradition," *JJS* 43 (1992): 1–31.

10. On the redactional function of this passage, see Annelies Kuyt, *The "Descent" to the Chariot: Towards a Description of the Terminology, Place, Function, and Nature of the Yeridah in Hekhalot Literature* (TSAJ 45; Tübingen: Mohr Siebeck, 1995), 342–68, esp. 367; Ithamar Gruenwald, *Apocalyptic and Merkavah Mysticism* (AGJU 14; Leiden: Brill, 1980), 192.

11. *Synopse*, §1 = Alexander 1:3. I have largely followed the translation in Philip S. Alexander, "3 (Hebrew Apocalypse of) Enoch," *OTP* 1: 255–57 (1:1–2:4 in his edition).

God's assertion of his special relationship with R. Ishmael is reminiscent of the depiction of the sage in *The Story of the Ten Martyrs*, although, unlike the martyrology, this passage does not explicitly attribute the sage's elevated status to his miraculous conception and his resulting resemblance to Metatron.[12] Nevertheless, both sources link R. Ishmael's ability to ascend to heaven successfully to his priestly lineage.

The emphasis on R. Ishmael's priestly lineage is heightened further in the subsequent unit of the text, where the angels challenge the visionary's right to be in heaven:

> Then the eagles of the chariot, the flaming *ʾopannim*, and the *kerubim* of devouring fire asked Metatron, "Youth, why have you allowed one born of women to come in and behold the chariot? From what nation is he? From what tribe is he? What is his character (מה טיבו של זה)?'"[13]

The interrogatory formula *mah tib-* (-מה טיב) at the end of the angels' challenge serves to highlight the fundamental incompatibility of the human and divine spheres.[14] In response, Metatron defends R. Ishmael's right to be in heaven:

> "He (R. Ishmael) is of the nation of Israel, whom the Holy One, blessed be He, chose from the seventy nations to be his people. He is of the tribe of Levi (משבט לוי הוא), (which presents) the priestly offering to His name.[15] He is from the seed of Aaron (מזרע אהרן הוא), whom the Holy One, blessed be He, chose to be his servant and on whom the Holy One, blessed be He, placed the priestly crown at Sinai." At once they [i.e., the angelic host] began to say: "This one is certainly

---

12. On the conception narrative as the basis of R. Ishmael's special powers in the post-talmudic martyrology *The Story of the Ten Martyrs*, see Raʿanan Abusch, "Rabbi Ishmael's Miraculous Conception: Jewish Salvation History in Anti-Christian Polemic," in *The Ways That Never Parted: Jews and Christians in Late Antiquity and the Middle Ages* (ed. A. H. Becker and A. Y. Reed; TSAJ 95; Tübingen: Mohr Siebeck, 2003), 307–43.

13. *Synopse*, §3 = Alexander 2:2. It should be noted that §3 does not appear in all versions of the text, making it difficult to judge whether it is integral to this introductory frame or a later redactional addition. See Peter Schäfer, "Ein neues Fragment zur Metoposkopie und Chiromantik," in idem, *Hekhalot-Studien*, 84–95; also idem, *The Hidden and Manifest God: Some Major Themes in Early Jewish Mysticism* (trans. A. Pomerance; Albany: State University of New York Press, 1992), 137–38.

14. On this phrase, see also Abusch, "Rabbi Ishmael's Miraculous Conception," 329–32; Christopher R. A. Morray-Jones, *A Transparent Illusion: The Dangerous Vision of Water in Hekhalot Mysticism* (JSJSup 59; Leiden: Brill, 2002), 118–23.

15. The syntax of this phrase in MS V228 is problematic, since it lacks a verb and the juxtaposition between "tribe" and "offering" is unclear. Alexander translates according to Munich 40, which contains the verb "to offer up, present" (מרים), as does MS Florence 44.13. On the difficulty of this phrase and the contradictory manuscript evidence, see Alexander, "3 Enoch," 1:257 n. e.

> worthy to behold the chariot-throne, as it is written, *Happy* (אשרי) *the people who have it so*; [*happy the people whose God is the Lord*] (Ps 144:15).[16]

This unit returns to the motif of "the crown of priesthood" (כתר כהונה), which is found in R. Ishmael's prayer at the beginning of the narrative in §1, thereby forming a kind of *inclusio*. Here, however, Metatron explicitly links R. Ishmael's wish that he be protected by the "merit of Aaron" to his genealogical ties to the Levitical line. His successful ascent is thus directly attributed to his priestly lineage.

Martha Himmelfarb has convincingly argued that *3 Enoch* represents a hybrid form that integrates an eclectic arrangement of motifs originating in *hekhalot* literature into the type of ascent account that is characteristic of apocalyptic literature.[17] Indeed, similar appeals to the efficacy of R. Ishmael's priestly lineage are most often found in the Hebrew apocalyptic compositions that circulated alongside (but rarely within) the *hekhalot* corpus, such as the "Messiah-Aggadah."[18] Here the angel Metatron informs R. Ishmael that he is worthy of having the events and chronology of the coming of the Messiah revealed to him because "his glory is equal to that of Aaron the priest" (*Synopse*, §140). These apocalyptic sources do not describe or advocate ritual techniques as a source of special power or hidden knowledge but instead emphasize the visionary's priestly genealogy as the determining factor in his capacity to gain entrance to the heavenly realm. The introductory framework of *3 Enoch* cannot be taken as a direct reflection of the priestly interests or identities of the *hekhalot* authors in general. Rather, this reflex belongs to a limited current within *hekhalot* literature that is largely governed by the specific conventions of the subgenre of *hekhalot* apocalypses.

3. Priestly Lineage and Ritual Praxis

In contrast to the frame narrative of *3 Enoch*, with its strong emphasis on R. Ishmael's priestly lineage, other passages from *hekhalot* literature present priestly lineage and ritual practice as complementary explanations for R. Ishmael's ability

---

16. *Synopse*, §3 = Alexander 2:3–4.

17. On the "mixed" form of *3 Enoch*, see Martha Himmelfarb, "Heavenly Ascent and the Relationship of the Apocalypses and the Hekhalot Literature," *HUCA* 59 (1988): 73–100, esp. 98. On the relationship of *3 Enoch* to the other *hekhalot* apocalypses, see also Peter Schäfer, ed., *Übersetzung der Hekhalot-Literature* (4 vols.; TSAJ 17, 22, 29, 46; Tübingen: Mohr Siebeck, 1995), 1:l–lv; Kuyt, *The "Descent" to the Chariot*, 161–63; Alexander, "3 Enoch," 1:223–53.

18. This passage, which is printed in the *Synopse* at §§140–145, has been inserted into *Hekhalot Rabbati* in only one manuscript, the idiosyncratic New York 8128, where it is found in a cluster of apocalyptic sources (§§122–145). These sources are more often found independent of the *hekhalot* corpus (e.g., MSS New York JTS ENA 3021, 1a–b and Jerusalem 80 5226, 16b–17b, both of which contain this passage).

to ascend to heaven or to summon angels to him on earth. An adjurational text found in the macroform *Merkabah Rabbah* (§§680–681) provides what is perhaps the clearest example of a practitioner's priestly identity setting him apart from—and above—his nonpriestly colleagues.[19] Adjurations directed to the *Sar Torah* (the Prince of the Torah), like the one found here, claim to confer upon the practitioner unfailing ability to acquire and retain knowledge of the Torah.[20] According to the narrative, after R. Ishmael has gotten a first taste of the enormous power of the *Sar Torah* ritual, his colleague Rabbi Akiva advises him that he still must learn to control and harness this technique. Rabbi Neḥunya ben ha-Qanah then proceeds to teach his star pupil the method for making use of a praxis that the text explicitly notes is intended for "every disciple of a sage":

> "Go return to R. Neḥunya ben ha-Qanah your teacher and ask your teacher that he tell and say and specify for you this praxis (מידה) in detail—how one makes use of it, how one adjures by it—lest you err and make use of it incorrectly, and act inappropriately, and they harm you as was the case with so-and-so, whom they harmed, and their bile dissolved within them, so that it became like water, because they heard it incorrectly and acted improperly." And when I asked this question before R. Neḥunya ben ha-Qanah, he said to me: "My student! What R. Akiva said to you I will also say: if it were not for the covenant (ברית) that was made for Aaron and the branch from which you came, they would already have harmed you and obliterated you from the world."[21]

The technique, described in the subsequent unit (§§682–684), is exacting and elaborate, though highly conventional within *hekhalot* literature.[22] It is noteworthy, however, that the passage above juxtaposes adjurational technique with the authority of the priestly covenant and line. Thus, although R. Ishmael's identity as a priest apparently protects him from the violence of the *Sar Torah*, it is more a stop-gap measure than a primary strategy. R. Ishmael, like all other practitioners, is advised to undergo the processes of purification and abstention that are required of all practitioners (§683). It seems, then, that proper preparation is a prerequisite for interacting with the divine, even if one is from the branch of Aaron.

The motif of priestly lineage also appears in a short unit (§§583–585) that is embedded in an extended ascent account in the macroform *Ma'aseh Merkabah*

---

19. This unit is found in an almost identical form at §§278–280 (*Hekhalot Rabbati*); a parallel passage is found at §§307–314. For detailed analysis of these two versions of this material, see Michael D. Swartz, *Scholastic Magic: Ritual and Revelation in Early Jewish Mysticism* (Princeton: Princeton University Press, 1996), 63–74.

20. Of course, "Torah" in this context includes mastery of all aspects of biblical and rabbinic learning.

21. *Synopse*, §681. I have slightly adapted the translation in Swartz, *Scholastic Magic*, 83, which follows MS O1531, supplemented by N8128. The unit is also found in MS M40.

22. The ritual instructions begin with a unit that is also found at §310 in MS V228.

(§§579–591).[23] According to the passage, immediately following R. Ishmael's vivid description of the heavenly liturgy being carried out before the throne of God, Zevudi'el, the Angel of the Presence, reprimands the visionary for his careless performance of the ritual techniques that he has learned (although exactly what his error is we are not told): "Son of the exalted (בן גאים), what merit do your father and mother have (מה זכות לאביך ולאמך) that you have deserved to endure this mystery (שזכית לעמוד על רז זה)?"[24] The sage has apparently survived precisely because of his lineage, although here again this special attribute serves only as a measure of last resort.[25] The angel warns him not to exalt himself above his colleagues (אל תתגאה מכל חביריך), nor to say "only I was privileged among the others (אני זכיתי מכולם)" (§584). Indeed, according to the angel, "all human beings who possess (this mystery) and recite it every morning in prayer" can visit the heavenly throne-world just like R. Ishmael (§584).

The portrait of R. Ishmael in this passage is thus highly ambivalent: it casts him in a critical light for presuming to be superior to his colleagues, while at the same time suggesting that his priestly status does in fact confer certain advantages on him. The title "son of the exalted" takes on an almost contemptuous tone here: in §583 and §584 the root גאה, meaning "proud," appears both in his title and in the charge against him.[26] He must defend himself against the allegation that he considers his elevated rank to set him apart from his colleagues. It is instructive that the *hitpa'el* form of this word is also found in a comparable phrase elsewhere in *hekhalot* literature in a hymn praising God as "the exalted one who exalts himself over the exalted [i.e., the angels] (גאה ומתגאה על גאים)."[27] It seems that R. Ishmael has wrongfully adopted a superior attitude toward his colleagues, perhaps in a manner suitable only for God. Even when *hekhalot* authors might accord R. Ishmael a comparative advantage over his peers because of his Levitical identity,

---

23. I follow the division of the text proposed in Swartz, *Mystical Prayer in Ancient Judaism: An Analysis of Ma'aseh Merkavah* (TSAJ 28; Tübingen: Mohr Siebeck, 1992), 91–100. This macroform encompasses *Synopse*, §§544–596. Aside from Swartz's detailed treatment of the macroform's literary history, see also Kuyt, *The "Descent" to the Chariot*, 269–303; Schäfer, *Hidden and Manifest God*, 77–95; N. Janowitz, *Poetics of Ascent: Theories of Language in Rabbinic Ascent* (Albany: State University of New York Press, 1989); Gruenwald, *Apocalyptic and Merkavah Mysticism*, 181–87.

24. *Synopse*, §583. I follow the translation of this passage in Swartz, *Mystical Prayer in Ancient Judaism*, 242, which follows MS O1531, supplemented by MSS N8128, M40, and D436.

25. But compare *Synopse*, §304, in which the "merit" (זכות) and "righteousness" (צדקת) of a person's parents help him make effective use of a magical seal and crown (זכות אבותיו מסייעתו וצדקת יולדיו עומדת לו). The practitioner is said to use the seal and crown in "exaltation" (בגיאות).

26. This same title is used repeatedly throughout the *ḥavurah* material (e.g., *Synopse*, §§200–201, §225, and §239; cf. §§402–403).

27. The term גאים is regularly applied in *hekhalot* literature to the angels (e.g., *Synopse*, §1, §98).

they were often troubled by the possibility that he would thus be set apart from the rest of Israel.

4. The "Egalitarian" Impulse in *Hekhalot Rabbati*

I have argued thus far that the shifting representations of R. Ishmael in *hekhalot* literature reflect competing conceptions of his power and authority. In some sources this central protagonist of *hekhalot* literature embodies—simply by virtue of his priestly lineage—the attributes necessary for a favorable reception in heaven. At the same time, another strand within the corpus presents R. Ishmael's priestly identity in a critical light. I believe that his latter concern is most fully articulated in the often analyzed ascent material in *Hekh. Rab.* §§198–268.[28] This passage roundly censures him for lording this advantage over other aspiring initiates. Indeed, the polemic against priestly privilege in this passage is intended to bolster its conviction that any *properly trained Jewish man* can ascend to heaven by means of esoteric instruction and ritual practice. The egalitarian rhetoric in this passage should not be mistaken for the democratization of religious practice in early Jewish mysticism. It should be emphasized that I do not use the notion of egalitarianism in the modern, democratic sense; Jewish women and all non-Jews are implicitly and, in some cases, explicitly barred from membership in the "mystical" fellowship and prohibited from undertaking a heavenly journey or otherwise interacting with the divine realm. Instead, in what follows I focus on the discursive function of the various models of ascent practice and ritual power put forward in *hekhalot* literature—and contrast these with the representations of heavenly ascent in related texts.

Sections 238–240 directly addresses the central preoccupation of the larger complex of ascent material in *Hekh. Rab.* §§198–268, namely, what criteria, if any, should determine whether a person is worthy to undertake a heavenly journey. The narrative opens as follows:[29]

---

28. Numerous studies have been dedicated to analyzing the sources and structure of all or part of this passage, most notably: Kuyt, *The "Descent" to the Chariot,* 60–124; Peter Schäfer, "Ein neues *Hekhalot Rabbati*-Fragment," in idem, *Hekhalot Studien,* 96–103; Joseph Dan, "The Gate to the Sixth Palace" (Hebrew), *Jerusalem Studies in Jewish Thought* 6 (1987): 197–220; Margarete Schlüter, "Die Erzählung von der Rückholung des R. Nehunya ben Haqana aus der *Merkava*-Schau in ihrem redaktionellen Rahmen," *FJB* 10 (1982): 65–109; Lawrence H. Schiffman, "The Recall of Rabbi Nehuniah Ben Ha-Qanah from Ecstasy in Hekhalot Rabbati," *AJS Review* 1 (1976): 269–81; Arnold Goldberg, "Einige Bemerkungen zu den Quellen und der Redaktionellen Einheiten der grossen Hekhalot," *FJB* 1 (1973): 1–49; repr. in *Mystik und Theologie des rabbinischen Judentums: Gesammelte Studien* (ed. M. Schlüter and P. Schäfer; TSAJ 61; Tübingen: Mohr Siebeck, 1997), 49–77.

29. For *Synopse,* §§238–240, I follow the version in MS V228, unless otherwise indicated. I note only significant textual variation. This passage is also found in the Genizah fragment T.-S.

> R. Ishmael said: Rabban Simeon ben Gamaliel was angry with me and said to me: "ZHPNWRY'Y almost chastised us and crushed us like bran. Why? You committed a conscious error against us, in that you consider Yonatan ben Uziel to be an insignificant man in Israel (אדם קטן בישראל). What if he were to ascend [lit. descend] somewhat haphazardly (מה אם ירד סתם), and come and stand at the entrance to the seventh palace[30] [without a seal? What would have happened to him then? He would just barely have enough time to lower his eyes before the guardians at the entrance to the seventh palace brought total destruction upon him.]"[31]

The Patriarch Rabban Simeon ben Gamaliel has accused R. Ishmael the High Priest of having failed to provide the knowledge required for entering the seventh palace safely. The tension captured in this text between one idealized figure who is associated with the Davidic monarchy and one linked to the Levitical priesthood is an obvious reflex of a deeply entrenched ideological conflict with deep roots in both ancient Israel and Second Temple Judaism.[32] *Hekhalot Rabbati* builds on this long-standing motif. Rabban Simeon ben Gamaliel claims that, if Yonatan ben Uziel had mistakenly or carelessly attempted to ascend without having mastered the full technique, he would only just barely have escaped with his life.[33] The Patriarch attributes R. Ishmael's negligent disregard to his lowly opinion of Yonatan, whom he is accused of considering "an insignificant man in Israel."[34] Indeed, the Patriarch seems to imply that R. Ishmael has omitted this final bit of information *intentionally*.[35]

AS 142.94 (G5 in Schäfer, *Geniza-Fragmente*, 76–81). For comparison of the versions, see the *partiturtext* at Schäfer, *Geniza-Fragmente*, 78–79.

30. The unit ends here in MSS V228, N8128, O1531, M40, D436, and Florence 44.13. Some manuscripts (e.g., M22, B238, Leiden 4730, and G5/1a:15–1b:2) contain a long recension of the unit, which extends through the bracketed material. For the bracketed section, I follow M22.

31. *Synopse*, §238. In my view, the material in brackets, which appears only in the long recension of this unit, is a secondary addition to the text. Cf. Kuyt, *The "Descent" to the Chariot*, 105 n. 170.

32. David Goodblatt, *The Monarchic Principle: Studies in Jewish Self-Government in Antiquity* (TSAJ 38; Tübingen: Mohr Siebeck, 1994), 57–76. On the conflict between patriarchal and priestly authority in rabbinic literature, see Reuven Kimelman, "The Conflict between the Priestly Oligarchy and the Sages in the Talmudic Period (PT *Shabbat* 2:3, 13c = *Horayot* 3:5, 48c)" (Hebrew), *Zion* 48 (1983): 135–48.

33. The specific connotation of the word סתם (*stam*), which I have rendered "somewhat haphazardly," is not certain. Nevertheless, the phrase as a whole plainly refers to the fact that Yonatan is not prepared for the dangers posed by the guardians of the "seventh palace."

34. Cf. *Synopse*, §305; G8/ 2a:12–23 and 2b: 21–24 (Schäfer, *Geniza-Fragmente*, 103–5). I discuss these passages and their relationship to the *ḥavurah* material below, pp. 138–40.

35. It is worth noting that the relevant phrase "a conscious error" (*shegagat zadon*) is virtually an oxymoron: whereas the first term typically denotes an *unintentional* sin, the second term refers to an *intentional* transgression.

Whether or not R. Ishmael had intended to harm his colleague, he does not contest the legitimacy of the Patriarch's charges. Instead, he seeks out his teacher R. Neḥunya ben ha-Qanah in great distress (§§239–240). Rabbi Neḥunya acknowledges to his pupil that the key to completing the heavenly journey successfully remains to be taught. He seems to imply that he has waited to reveal the names of the guardians of the seventh palace because their similarity to the divine name renders them especially potent. But now that R. Ishmael has explicitly demanded access to this as-yet-undisclosed information, the master agrees to reconvene his disciples so that it can be transmitted to the whole fellowship (*ḥavurah*)—and even recorded for posterity.

The background of the passage is obscure. In earlier rabbinic literature Yonatan ben Uziel is said himself to have been chastised by God for having revealed to human beings the secrets of the Torah through his Aramaic translation (Targum) of the prophetic books. The charge against him implies that he has undertaken to do so specifically for the purpose of self-glorification. In the version of this tradition found in the Babylonian Talmud, Yonatan defends himself to God, saying: "It is surely known to You that I did this neither for my own honor nor for the honor of my father's house (לא לכבודי עשיתי ולא לכבוד בית אבא), but for I did it for Your honor (אלא לכבודך עשיתי), so that disputes will not proliferate in Israel" (*b. Meg.* 3a). More interesting still, the formulation of his denial is echoed closely elsewhere in *hekhalot* literature in a passage that critiques R. Ishmael's motives for revealing the secret names of the angels who guard the heavenly palace: "Not for my own glorification did I do it (לא לקילוס עצמי עשיתי), but for the praise of the King of the World (אלא לשבח מלכו של עולם)" (*Synopse*, §586). Apparently, for the author of this unit the figure of Yonatan ben Uziel represented a suitable foil for R. Ishmael. The irony could hardly have been lost on an educated reader. The text is clearly suggesting that in withholding divine secrets from his colleagues, R. Ishmael has acted in an even more self-aggrandizing fashion than did Yonatan ben Uziel when he made his translation of the prophets available to the public. Within the context of *Hekhalot Rabbati* §§238–240, the figure of Yonatan ben Uziel thus functions as an emblematic example of the universal efficacy of ritual practice.[36]

The controversy concerning Yonatan ben Uziel establishes the thematic framework for the remainder of the ascent account in *Hekhalot Rabbati*, which consists of esoteric instructions that must be mastered by the visionary before he embarks on his journey. This theme is most poignantly encapsulated in the "water vision" episode that is placed at the culmination of the instructional material (§§258–259), in which the visionary must demonstrate his worthiness to enter the sixth palace by passing two separate tests. First he must wait at the gate

36. Comparable passages, which emphasize the universal efficacy of *hekhalot* ascent practices, can also be found at *Synopse*, §305; G8/2b: 21–24 (Schäfer, *Geniza-Fragmente*, 105).

to the palace until the angels have invited him to enter *twice;* if he enters at their first summons, they "throw iron bars at him," and he perishes. Second, he must refrain from asking the angels concerning the nature of the waves of water that he sees rushing at him. I cite the description of this "water test" in full:

> Because the guardians of the entrance to the sixth palace throw and cast thousands upon thousands of waves of water upon him—although there is not even a single drop there—if he says: "What is the nature of this water?" they immediately run after him in order to stone him, saying: "Good-for-nothing, perhaps you are from the seed of those who kissed the calf, so that you are not worthy to see the king and his throne?" If that is the case, a heavenly voice goes forth from the *'aravot raqia'* and says: "You have spoken well! He is from the seed of those who kissed the calf and is not worthy to see the king and his throne!" He does not move from there until they throw thousands upon thousands of iron bars upon him.[37] (*Synopse*, §259)

This puzzling test appears in a number of different forms in the *hekhalot* corpus.[38] It is not my intention here to enter into the enormously complicated question of the interrelationship of these sources or to analyze the rich symbolic background of the image of heavenly water in *hekhalot* literature—questions to which many studies have been dedicated.[39] Rather, I wish to set the "water test" in the context of the notion of worthiness in *Hekhalot Rabbati.*

Joseph Dan has subjected this unit to meticulous analysis in his treatment of the traditions in *hekhalot* literature concerning the dangers encountered by the visionary during his ascent to heaven.[40] Dan has argued that, at the earliest stage of its development, the danger motif is used to characterize the behavior of the guardians of the sixth palace as arbitrary and absurd but that over time this irrational impulse was suppressed by later editors. In his view, this sense of randomness explains why in *Hekh. Rab.* §224 the angels inexplicably destroy

---

37. I translate according to Vatican 228. The unit is also translated at Kuyt, *The "Descent" to the Chariot,* 112.

38. In addition to §§258–259, also §§407–408 (*Hekhalot Zutarti*), §345 (*Hekhalot Zutarti,* only in MS N8128); §§672 (*Merkavah Rabbah,* only in MS N8128); cf. §§224–228 (*Hekhalot Rabbati*). The motif also appears in the version of the "Four who entered the *pardes*" at *b. Hag.* 14b.

39. See now the lengthy *Forschungsgeschichte* at Morray-Jones, *Transparent Illusion,* 34–53. On the interrelationship of these sources and their specific redactional functions, see especially Morray-Jones, *Transparent Illusion,* 54–82; Kuyt, *The "Descent" to the Chariot,* 110–13. In this sweeping tradition-historical treatment Morray-Jones largely revives Scholem's contention that this image has authentic visionary experience as its generative source. However, he also builds on David J. Halperin's valuable insight that the waters symbolize the cosmic forces of chaos that have been tamed by God at creation (*Faces of the Chariot* [TSAJ 16; Tübingen: Mohr Siebeck, 1988], 199–249). For critique of Halperin's eclectic approach, however, see Ronen Reichman, "Die 'Wasser-Episode' in der Hekhalot-Literatur," *FJB* 17 (1989): 67–100, esp. 78–79.

40. Dan, "Gate to the Sixth Palace," 197–220.

those visionaries who are worthy of ascending to heaven while sparing those who are unworthy. Moreover, Dan argues that the "water test," which distinguishes between those who are "from the seed of those who kissed the calf" and those who are not, is aimed squarely at the descendents of Aaron the high priest, who was responsible for the sin of the golden calf (Exod 32).[41] Accordingly, he considers the test itself to be wholly superfluous. The ability of an aspiring visionary to enter the sixth palace depends entirely on his lineage; no one of priestly stock will be allowed to pass.

While I accept most of Dan's argument, I part ways with him on this final point. In my view, the "water test"—at least within the specific context of *Hekhalot Rabbati*—is designed to make a rather different point, namely, that prior knowledge of the nature of the dangers associated with the entrance to the sixth palace enables the visionary to enter heaven. There is no indication in the text that a priestly figure such as R. Ishmael cannot learn to answer properly.

Ronen Reichman has similarly concluded that the fate of the visionary depends entirely on his own actions.[42] Reichman, however, understands the text in strictly typological terms: those who fail the tests are *like* those who worshiped the golden calf but not actually related to them genealogically. But this purely symbolic reading threatens to isolate the passage from its larger discursive context. I would submit instead that claims to priestly lineage posed serious problems for the ideology of ritual practice advocated by the creators of *Hekhalot Rabbati*. It is difficult, if not impossible, to know whether such claims reflected the interests of actual priestly groups. What is certain, however, is that the notion of priestly identity was deployed as part of a sophisticated rhetorical strategy that characterizes some *hekhalot* texts to legitimate their particular brand of ritual practice.

The antipriestly polemic of the "water test" represents the direct counterpart to the positive conception of Levitical lineage that we have seen animates various other strands of the *hekhalot* corpus. At the same time, numerous *hekhalot* texts—*Hekhalot Rabbati* most prominent among them—adopt the opposite stance. Subjecting R. Ishmael's comportment and behavior to careful scrutiny, these passages explicitly link both his ethical shortcomings and his ritual failures to the superior attitude he has adopted concerning his priestly status. Ironically, however, in critiquing R. Ishmael's special status, *Hekhalot Rabbati* succeeds in transforming him into the quintessential mystical initiate. The dominant claim of *Hekhalot Rabbati* turns on the notion that anyone at all can attain the exalted

41. Ibid., 199–200. As we have seen earlier, the term "seed" is used elsewhere in *hekhalot* literature to refer to the perquisites of Aaronide lineage (esp. §3 of *3 Enoch*). But compare Morray-Jones, *Transparent Illusion*, 192–99, which argues that the phrase "those who kissed the golden calf" in fact refers to all of Israel *except* the Levites, the one tribe that refrained from worshiping the calf.

42. Reichman, "Wasser-Episode," 80–82.

status of R. Ishmael merely by imitating the ritual practices that he helped transmit to his colleagues in the "mystical" fellowship.

5. Concluding Remarks

This essay has explored the methodological implications that the essentially heterogeneous nature of *hekhalot* literature has for the study of its literary history and religious significance. From this one test case—the highly particular representation of R. Ishmael in the ascent material in *Hekhalot Rabbati*—I would suggest that attention to the variety of ways in which various themes, motifs, and figures are deployed in different components of the corpus is essential to a proper reading of this literature. Our increasing awareness of the continuing diversity of Jewish culture well into the posttalmudic period (600–1000 C.E.) complicates the task of mapping the heterogeneous strands of *hekhalot* literature, each with its own distinct conception of religious authority, onto the equally heterogeneous landscape of Jewish society. *Hekhalot* literature encodes a range of conflicting and evolving points of view about the purpose of the various ritual techniques that it advocates and, in particular, about who may legitimately engage in these practices. Such variation should not be viewed merely as "noise" that conceals an underlying unity of religious sensibility or experience. In fact, it is precisely the fluidity and diversity of *hekhalot* literature that enables us to trace its literary development, thereby shedding light on the history and nature of early Jewish mysticism. We miss a great deal if, for the sake of an appealing coherence, we generalize about the literary function, ideological valance, or sociohistorical background of R. Ishmael in *hekhalot* literature.

Part 3:
Cosmology

The Temple Within

Christopher R. A. Morray-Jones

The celestial temple is a central motif of Jewish apocalyptic literature and of the "*merkabah* mystical" traditions preserved in the *hekhalot* ("palaces" or "temples") writings of the rabbinic and immediately postrabbinic periods.[1] In these sources, the ascent into heaven is envisaged as a journey through the courts of a cosmic temple to the innermost sanctuary where God appears in the form of a vast manlike figure of fire or light, called the "Power" (δύναμις/גבורה) or "Glory" (δόξα/כבוד), seated upon the throne of glory (כסא הכבוד), also called the "chariot" (מרכבה). This imagery is deeply rooted in the Hebrew biblical tradition.[2] The term *merkabah* is derived from 1 Chr 28:18, where it refers to "the chariot of

---

* This chapter will also appear in Christopher C. Rowland and Christopher R. A. Morray-Jones, *The Mystery of God: Jewish Mystical Traditions in the New Testament* (CRINT; Assen: Van Gorcum, forthcoming). An earlier version was published in *Society of Biblical Literature 1998 Seminar Papers* (SBLSP 37; Atlanta: Scholars Press, 1998), 400–31.

1. See further Johann Maier, "Das Gefährdungsmotiv bei der Himmelsreise in der jüdischen Apokalyptic und 'Gnosis,'" *Kairos* 5 (1963): 18–40; idem, *Vom Kultus zur Gnosis* (Salzburg: Müller, 1964); R. G. Hamerton-Kelly, "The Temple and the Origins of Jewish Apocalyptic," *VT* 20 (1970): 1–15; Martha Himmelfarb, "Apocalyptic Ascent and the Heavenly Temple," in *Society of Biblical Literature 1987 Seminar Papers* (SBLSP 26; Atlanta: Scholars Press, 1987), 210–17; idem, *Ascent to Heaven in Jewish and Christian Apocalypses* (New York: Oxford University Press, 1993); Allan J. McNicol, "The Heavenly Sanctuary in Judaism: A Model for Tracing the Origin of the Apocalypse," *JRelS* 13 (1987): 66–94; Craig R. Koester, *The Dwelling of God: The Tabernacle in the Old Testament, Intertestamental Jewish Literature and the New Testament* (CBQMS 22; Washington, D.C.: Catholic Biblical Association of America, 1989); Rachel Elior, "Mysticism, Magic, and Angelology—The Perception of Angels in Hekhalot Literature," *JSQ* 1 (1993/94): 3–53, esp. 43–51; idem, "From Earthly Temple to Heavenly Shrines: Prayer and Sacred Song in the Hekhalot Literature and Its Relation to Temple Traditions," *JSQ* 4 (1997): 217–67; idem, "The *Merkavah* Tradition and the Emergence of Jewish Mysticism," in *Sino-Judaica: Jews and Chinese in Historical Dialogue: An International Colloquium, Nanjing, 11–19 October, 1996* (ed. A. Oppenheimer; Tel Aviv: Tel Aviv University, 1999), 101–58.

2. See, above all, Jon D. Levenson, "The Temple and the World," *JR* 64 (1984): 275–98; and idem, *Sinai and Zion: An Entry into the Jewish Bible* (Minneapolis: Winston, 1985). See also E. Theodore Mullen Jr., *The Divine Council in Canaanite and Early Hebrew Literature* (HSM 24;

the cherubim" that carried the ark of the covenant in the holy of holies. In Isa 6, a central text of the later mystical tradition, the prophet encounters the enthroned deity in the holy of holies of the temple. The seraphim that Isaiah sees above the throne evidently correspond to the cherubim of 1 Chr 28:18, whose wings were outstretched above the ark. God's throne is, therefore, already identified with the chariot by which the ark was carried, as it is in the later esoteric sources.[3]

Several commentators have maintained that there is a fundamental difference between the visions of the biblical prophets and the heavenly ascents described by the later apocalyptic writers. The prophets, it is argued, did not claim to have ascended to heaven but experienced their visions while remaining on the earth.[4] Thus Isaiah's vision is said to have occurred in the earthly temple and not, as in the later apocalypses, its heavenly counterpart.[5] This distinction may be somewhat overstated. Although it is true that detailed accounts of heavenly ascents are not found in the prophetic writings, the vision of the heavenly council provides the context for the commissioning of the prophet, who therefore experiences himself as present at the scene.[6] Geo Widengren, moreover, has shown that the forms of these commissioning narratives originated in prebiblical Mesopotamian enthronement ceremonies in which the king, having ritually entered the heavenly palace of the god, is awarded the status of a "sent one."[7] Like Enoch, Daniel, and other ascending heroes of the apocalypses, Isaiah is a participant in the action. His mouth is purified by an angel with a coal from the altar (Isa 6:6–7), after

---

Chico, Calif.: Scholars Press, 1980), 147–69; and Margaret Barker, *The Gate of Heaven: The History and Symbolism of the Temple in Jerusalem* (London: SPCK, 1991), esp. 151–52.

3. See further Gershom G. Scholem, *Jewish Gnosticism, Merkabah Mysticism, and Talmudic Tradition* (2nd ed.; New York: Jewish Theological Seminary of America, 1965), 20–30.

4. See, e.g., Maier, *Vom Kultus zur Gnosis*, 14–15 and 106–28; Ithamar Gruenwald, "Knowledge and Vision: Towards a Clarification of Two 'Gnostic" Concepts in Light of Their Alleged Origins," *Israel Oriental Studies* 3 (1973): 257–77, reprinted in idem, *From Apocalyptic to Gnosticism* (BEATAJ 14; Frankfurt am Main: Lang, 1988), 69–70 and 98–115; idem, *Apocalyptic and Merkavah Mysticism* (AGJU 14; Leiden: Brill, 1980), 32; idem, "Priests, Prophets, Apocalyptic Visionaries, and Mystics," in idem, *From Apocalyptic to Gnosticism*, 125–44; George W. E. Nickelsburg, "Enoch, Levi, and Peter: Recipients of Revelation in Upper Galilee," *JBL* 100 (1981): 576–82; David J. Halperin, *The Faces of the Chariot: Early Jewish Responses to Ezekiel's Vision* (TSAJ 16; Tübingen: Mohr Siebeck, 1988), 63–74; Himmelfarb, *Ascent to Heaven*, 9–28.

5. See, for example, Ivan Engell, *The Call of Isaiah: An Exegetical and Comparative Study* (Uppsala Universitets Årsskrift 1949:4; Uppsala: A.-B. Lundequistska Bokhandeln, 1949), 27–28; and compare Himmelfarb, *Ascent to Heaven*, 11.

6. See further: Frank Moore Cross, "The Council of Yahweh in Second Isaiah, *JNES* 12 (1953): 274–77; idem, *Canaanite Myth and Hebrew Epic: Essays in the History of the Religion of Israel* (Cambridge, MA: Harvard University Press, 1973), 187; and Mullen, *The Divine Council*, 205–26.

7. Geo Widengren, *The Ascension of the Apostle and the Heavenly Book* (Uppsala Universitets Årsskrift 1950:7; Uppsala: Lundequistska, 1950), 30–35.

which he engages in a dialogue with God, volunteering his services and receiving his instructions (Isa 6:8–13).

Similar considerations apply to the commissioning scene in Ezek 1–3, which appears to take place not on earth but above the firmament, where the throne is said to be located (Ezek 1:26). Having fallen on his face (Ezek 1:28), the prophet gets up and interacts with the figure on the throne, eating the scroll that he offers him and receiving his commission (Ezek 2:1–3:11). Following this, he is returned to earth by a wind (רוח), which appears to be generated by the wings of the living creatures (Ezek 3:12–14) and, perhaps, to be identical with the רוח החיה (conventionally translated "spirit of the living creatures") of Ezek 1:20–21. Although Ezekiel is a priest, his vision does not occur in the earthly sanctuary but in Babylonia. Isaiah is not said to be a priest and so is not permitted to enter the sanctuary on earth. He must, therefore, have been relocated in his vision. Whether the "house" into which he has been transported is the earthly temple or its celestial counterpart is nowhere specified, and it is perhaps doubtful whether this distinction would have been very meaningful to the author, for whom the ritual identification of the one with the other was not merely a dramatic metaphor. As observed by Levenson: "Isaiah is privileged to see the difference between the earthly antitype and the heavenly archetype disappear: iconography becomes the reality it symbolizes."[8] The ritual identification of the earthly sanctuary with the heavenly throne room was, then, a central theme of the preexilic cult tradition, as expressed, for example, in the poetic parallelism of Ps 11:4: יהוה בהיכל קדשו יהוה בשמים כסאו "The LORD (is) in the temple of his holiness; the LORD, in the heavens (is) his throne."

1. VISIONS OF THE ENTHRONED GLORY

Under the conditions of the exile, access to the divine throne via the physical temple in Jerusalem was, of course, no longer possible. Ezekiel's visions of the enthroned "Glory of the LORD" (כבוד־יהוה), drawn on awesome wheels (אופנים) by mysterious "living creatures" (חיות) who are identified in Ezek 10:14–15 with the temple cherubim, occurred in response to this situation and provided an assurance that the heavenly reality was still accessible by other means. When the prophet is transported to and conducted around the temple of the future (Ezek 40–48), what he sees is, presumably, a celestial archetype, since it does yet not exist on earth.

Perhaps the earliest occurrence of the term *merkabah* in connection with Ezekiel's vision is in Sir 49:8: "It was Ezekiel who saw the vision of the Glory,

8. Jon D. Levenson, "The Jerusalem Temple in Devotional and Visionary Experience," in *From the Bible through the Middle Ages* (vol. 1 of *Jewish Spirituality;* ed. A. Green; New York: Crossroad, 1986), 54.

which was shown to him upon a chariot of cherubim (Ιεζεκιηλ ὃς εἶδεν ὅρασιν δόξης, ἣν ὑπέδειξεν αὐτῷ ἐπὶ ἅρματος χερουβιν)."[9] The earliest detailed account of an ascent into heaven, however, occurs in *1 En.* 14:8–25.[10] Here Enoch's journey to heaven leads him into a temple whose threefold structure, consisting of two concentric houses surrounded by a wall, corresponds closely to that of the earthly sanctuary in Jerusalem.[11] The two "houses" correspond to the sanctuary building (היכל) and the holy of holies (דביר). The wall (v. 9, according to the Ethiopic text) of white marble corresponds either to the wall surrounding the inner courts of the temple or, perhaps, to the balustrade (סורג) beyond which no Gentile was allowed to pass.[12] The wheels of God's throne (v. 18) identify it as Ezekiel's *merkabah,* and the cherubim mentioned in the same verse are clearly identical with Ezekiel's living creatures. The structure of this celestial temple involves a curious reversal of normality: the inner of the two "houses" is larger than the outer (vv. 15–16).

I have argued elsewhere that the threefold structure of the temple in *1 En.* 14 reflects a cosmology of three heavens, which is also attested in other parts of the early Enoch literature.[13] According to the majority of commentators, an early form of the *Testament of Levi* employed a similar three-tier cosmology, although the number of heavens was increased to seven in later versions.[14] Here again the

---

9. Hebrew: יחזקאל ראה מראה ויגד זני מרכבה ("Ezekiel saw a vision and declared varieties [?] of chariot"); see further C. R. A. Morray-Jones, *A Transparent Illusion: The Dangerous Vision of Water in Hekhalot Mysticism: A Source-Critical and Tradition-Historical Inquiry* (JSJSup 59; Leiden: Brill, 2002), 180–91.

10. *1 En.* 14:8–17. Greek text in Matthew Black, ed., *Apocalypsis Henochi Graece* (PVTG 3:1; Leiden: Brill, 1970), 28–29. The Aramaic text preserved at Qumran, 4QEnoch^{c} vi.20–25, is very fragmentary (see Jozef T. Milik, ed., *The Books of Enoch: Aramaic Fragments from Qumrân Cave 4* [with the collaboration of Matthew Black; Oxford: Clarendon, 1976], 194–99). See further, Morray-Jones, *Transparent Illusion,* 105–9.

11. See Maier, "Gefährdungsmotiv bei der Himmelsreise," 22–23; idem, *Vom Kultus zur Gnosis*, 127; Nickelsburg, "Enoch, Levi, and Peter," 580; idem, *Jewish Literature between the Bible and the Mishnah* (Philadelphia: Fortress, 1981), 53; Christopher Rowland, *The Open Heaven: A Study of Apocalyptic in Judaism and Early Christianity* (New York: Crossroad, 1982), 83–84; Barker, *Gate of Heaven*, 158.

12. See *m. Mid.* 2:3; *b.Yoma* 16a; Josephus, *War* 5.193. Alternatively, Himmelfarb (*Ascent to Heaven*, 14) suggests that the first stage of the vision corresponds to the temple vestibule (אולם), but her statement that the Greek text of *1 En.* 14:9 reads "building" for "wall" is inaccurate and appears to be derived from Milik's speculative reconstruction of the text (see Milik, *Books of Enoch*, 195; refuted by Black, *Books of Enoch*, 146–47).

13. See Christopher Morray-Jones, "Paradise Revisited (2 Cor 12:1–12): The Jewish Mystical Background of Paul's Apostolate. Part 1: The Jewish Sources," *HTR* 86 (1993): 203–5; idem, *Transparent Illusion*, 29–33. Himmelfarb (*Ascent to Heaven*, 9–28 and 31) assumes that the passage refers to a single heaven only. For attestations of a three-tiered heaven in other parts of the early Enoch literature, see Milik, *Books of Enoch*, 40–41 and 231–36.

14. See, e.g., R. H. Charles, *APOT* 2:304; idem, *The Greek Versions of the Testaments of the Twelve Patriarchs* (1908; repr., Oxford: Oxford University Press; Hildesheim: Olms, 1960),

highest heaven, the dwelling place of "the Great Glory" (ἡ δόξα ἡ μεγάλη), is called "the holy of holies." As observed by Himmelfarb,[15] in the extended version of the text the chambers of the temple are identical with the higher celestial levels.

In the later apocalypses, the three-tier cosmology is largely displaced by a more complex model of seven heavens. As Himmelfarb has shown, the idea that the universe is a temple, corresponding in structure to the temple in Jerusalem (or at least to the ideal form thereof), continues to pervade this literature.[16] A similar idea is expressed by Philo: "The whole universe must be regarded as the highest and, in truth, the holy temple of God. As sanctuary it has the heaven, the most holy part of the substance of existing things; as votive offerings it has stars; as priests it has angels, ministers of His powers."[17]

2. The *Merkabah* at Qumran

The Qumran sectarians,[18] who believed the temple in Jerusalem to have been defiled and its cult perverted by a corrupt and illegitimate priesthood, evidently

xxviii; Howard Clark Kee, "Testaments of the Twelve Patriarchs," *OTP*, 1:775–80 and 788–89 nn. 2d and 3a; Rowland, *Open Heaven*, 81; Adela Yarbro Collins, "The Seven Heavens in Jewish and Christian Apocalypses," in *Death, Ecstasy and Other Worldly Journeys* (ed. J. J. Collins and M. Fishbane; Albany: State University of New York Press, 1995), 62–66. Himmelfarb maintains that "no form of the text with three heavens ever existed" (*Ascent to Heaven*, 126–27 n. 7), but this assertion appears to be based on a misunderstanding of the analysis of Marinus de Jonge ("Notes on Testament of Levi II-VII," in idem, *Studies on the Testaments of the Twelve Patriarchs* [SVTP 3; Leiden: Brill, 1975], 247–60). De Jonge comments that the relevant fragment of the Aramaic Levi document from Qumran (4Q213, 1.ii.15–18) "does not necessarily presuppose more than one heaven" (ibid, 253), but this observation does not apply to the developed recensions of *Testament of Levi*. The "non-α" Greek and Armenian recensions, which refer twice to an arrangement of three plus four heavens, are believed by de Jonge to have priority over the "α" recensions, which have three only. Nonetheless, he states that the extra four heavens in the "non-α" recensions are "clearly redactional" (ibid, 259), implying that a three-heaven version of the text did, in fact, precede the seven-heaven version.

15. Himmelfarb, *Ascent to Heaven*, 33.

16. Ibid., *passim*.

17. Philo, *Spec.* 1.66, trans. C. T. R. Hayward, *The Jewish Temple: A Non-biblical Sourcebook* (London: Routledge, 1996), 109. Compare *Somn.* 1.215 and see further Hayward, ibid, 108–12.

18. I use the terms "sect" and "sectarians" to refer to the organized group represented by the *Community Rule*, the *Damascus Rule*, and associated texts. The sectarian or nonsectarian provenance of individual documents will be discussed briefly below. On this subject, see especially Carol Newsom, "'Sectually Explicit' Literature from Qumran," in *The Hebrew Bible and Its Interpreters* (ed. W. H. Propp, B. Halpern, and D. N. Freedman; Biblical and Judaic Studies from the University of California, San Diego 1; Winona Lake, Ind.: Eisenbrauns, 1990), 167–87, esp. 168–71. I assume that the site at Qumran was the primary center of the sect, but not that all members resided there. See further, e.g., Shemaryahu Talmon, "The Community of the Renewed

attached great significance to the prophecies of Ezekiel.[19] It is perhaps possible that the site of the community settlement was chosen on the basis of Ezek 47:1–12, which states that in the last days a river will flow eastward from beneath the Jerusalem temple and revitalize the waters of the Dead Sea.[20] In the *Damascus Rule* (CD 1:16), the foundation of the Sect is dated to 390 years after the exile, on the basis of Ezek 4:4–5. In the same document, the leaders of the sect are identified with the "sons of Zadok," who, according to Ezek 44:15, are to serve as priests in the restored and purified temple of the coming age (CD 3:12–4:4). According to this text, Ezekiel's eschatological temple already exists as a metaphysical reality. It is closely associated with the "glory of Adam," and, for the community that "holds fast" to it, it is the means of access to eternal life.

Aside from Sir 49:8, the earliest instances of the term *merkabah* in connection with the vision of the heavenly throne are found in writings that were either produced by this sectarian group or at least held in its possession. In 1988, John Strugnell and Devorah Dimant published some fragments from Cave 4 of several copies of an extended paraphrase of Ezekiel, which they designated *Second Ezekiel*.[21] In 1990 they published a further fragment of the same text (4Q385, frag.

Covenant: Between Judaism and Christianity," in *The Community of the Renewed Covenant: The Notre Dame Symposium on the Dead Sea Scrolls* (ed. E. Ulrich and J. C. VanderKam; Christianity and Judaism in Antiquity Series 10; Notre Dame: University of Notre Dame Press, 1994), 1–24; James C. VanderKam, *The Dead Sea Scrolls Today* (Grand Rapids: Eerdmans; London: SPCK, 1995), 12–27 and 71–119; Florentino García Martinez and Julio Trebolle Barrera, *The People of the Dead Sea Scrolls: Their Writings, Beliefs and Practices* (Leiden: Brill, 1995), 3–91; John J. Collins, *The Scepter and the Star: The Messiahs of the Dead Sea Scrolls and Other Ancient Literary* (ABRL; New York: Doubleday, 1995), 4–11.

19. See further Matthew Black, *The Scrolls and Christian Origins: Studies in the Jewish Background of the New Testament* (New York: Scribner, 1961), 109; Barbara Thiering, "The Biblical Source of Qumran Asceticism," *JBL* 93 (1974): 429–44; William H. Brownlee, "The Scroll of Ezekiel from the Eleventh Qumran Cave," *RevQ* 4 (1963/64): 11–28; Johan Lust, "Ezekiel Manuscripts in Qumran," in *Ezekiel and His Book: Textual and Literary Criticism and Their Interrelation* (ed. Johan Lust et al.; BETL 74; Leuven: Leuven University Press, 1986), 100; Halperin, *Faces of the Chariot*, 49; E. Gothenet, "Influence d'Ézéchiel sur la spiritualité de Qumrân," *RevQ* 13 (1988): 431–39; Florentino García Martínez, "L'interprétation de la Torah d'Ézéchiel dans les ms. de Qumrân," *RevQ* 13 (1988): 441–52; Ben Zion Wacholder, "Ezekiel and Ezekielianism as Progenitors of Essenianism," in *The Dead Sea Scrolls: Forty Years of Research* (ed. D. Dimant and Uriel R.; STDJ 10; Leiden: Brill; Jerusalem: Magnes, 1992), 186–96.

20. Cf. Joel 3:19; Zech 14:8; Rev 22:1–2; and see Wacholder, "Ezekiel and Ezekelianism," 195. This suggestion is in no way incompatible with the widely held view that the sect's withdrawal into the desert was partly inspired by Isa 40:3, as indicated in the *Rule of the Community* (1QS 8:12–16) (see, e.g., VanderKam, *Dead Sea Scrolls Today*, 104–5; Florentino García Martinez, "The Men of the Dead Sea," in García Martinez and Trebolle Barrera, *People of the Dead Sea Scrolls*, 32–35.

21. John Strugnell and Devorah Dimant, "4Q Second Ezekiel (*4Q385*)," *RevQ* 13 (1988): 45–58.

4) which includes a summarized version of Ezek 1.[22] The fragment consists of fourteen legible lines from what seems to be the fourth column of the scroll, with the right margin more or less intact.[23]

1 and my people shall be [....]
2 with contented heart and with wi[lling soul ....]
3 and conceal thyself for a little while [....]
4 and cleaving [....]
5 the vision which Ezek[iel] saw [....]
6 a radiance (נגה) of a chariot (מרכבה), and four living creatures; a living creature[... and while walking they would not turn ....]
7 backwards; upon two each living creature was walking, and [its] two le[gs ....]
8 [le]g[ ]$_{\circ}$[....] was spiritual and their faces were joined to the oth[er. And the shape of the ....]
9 fac[es, one of a lion, and on]e of an eagle, and one of a calf, and one of a man, and each [one had a hand of ....]
10 man joined (דבקה) from the backs of the living creatures and attached to [their wings] and the whe[els ....]
11 wheel joined (חובר) to wheel as they went, and from the two sides of the whe[els were streams of fire ....]
12 and there was in the midst (בתוך) of the coals living creatures, like coals of fire[, like torches in the midst of ....]
13 the whe[e]ls and the living creatures and the wheels; and there wa[s over their heads a firmament like ....]
14 the terri[ble] ice. [And there w]as a sound[from above the firmament ....]

The appearance of the chariot (מרכבה) in line 6 is a departure from the order of the biblical chapter, where the throne appears only at the end of the vision, after the description of the living creatures and the wheels, at the point where this fragment ends. The word נגה (radiance) does, however, occur in Ezek 1:4. It may be that the term *merkabah* is being applied in an extended sense to the vision as a whole, as is sometimes the case in rabbinic sources.

The rest of the fragment follows the biblical sequence with only very minor variations but, despite being much shorter than the biblical text, adds several interpretative details. In lines 6–7, Dimant and Strugnell detect the influence of Isa 6:2, concerning the wings of the seraphim, "two covering his face, two covering his feet, and two with which he flew." In lines 10–12 the relationship between the terminology of the fragment and that of the biblical account becomes somewhat confusing. In line 10, the term דבקה (joining), which does not occur in the

22. Devorah Dimant and John Strugnell, "The Merkabah Vision in *Second Ezekiel* (*4Q385* 4)," *RevQ* 14 (1990): 331–48.

23. Following translation by Dimant and Strugnell, "Merkabah Vision," 333–36.

biblical text, is derived from 2 Chr 3:12, where it applies to the wings of the cherubim in the sanctuary. In Ezek 1:9 the wings of the living creatures are likewise said to be joined to each other, but here the verb used is חבר. In the fragment, this verb is applied to the wheels (line 11). In the biblical version, we read "a wheel within (בתוך) a wheel" (1:16). In the fragment, בתוך occurs on the next line: "in the midst of the coals, living creatures"; Ezek 1:13, however, states simply that the appearance of the living creatures *was like* coals of fire. In short, it seems that the author is using the terminology of Ezek 1 but that the various terms have been displaced by the additional word דבקה, borrowed from 2 Chr 3:12:

4Q385.4	**Ezekiel 1 (MT)**	**Other**
lines 6–7: the living creatures have (?) six legs.		Isa 6:2: the seraphim (= the cherubim of 1 Chr 28:18) have six wings. Ezek 10:14–15: the living creatures = the cherubim (cf. Sir 49:8 and *1 En.* 14:18).
line 10: the hands of the living creatures are joined (דבקה).	1:9: the wings of the living creatures are joined (חברת).	2 Chr 3:12: the wings of the cherubim above the ark are joined (דבקה).
line 11: a wheel joined (חובר) to a wheel.	1:16: a wheel within (בתוך) a wheel.	
line 12: the living creatures are in the midst of (בתוך) the coals.		

It appears, then, that the author is interpreting Ezekiel's *merkabah* vision in the light of other scriptural passages (2 Chr 3; Isa 6; and Ezek 10) that describe the interior of the holy of holies and the angelic beings who draw the chariot of the ark. Dimant and Strugnell draw attention to the fact that the author does not explicitly identify the living creatures with the cherubim of Ezek 10, although the identification is clearly implied by the allusion to 2 Chr 3:12.[24] The nonoccurrence of the term *cherubim* may, in their opinion, imply that the writer was unwilling to endorse this identification.[25] It is, however, so strongly implicit in the text that it seems more probable that the equation living creatures = cherubim =

24. Ibid., 346.

25. Dimant and Strugnell (ibid.) further observe that the *Songs of the Sabbath Sacrifice* (see further below) "refer only to the Cherubim but pass in silence over the living Creatures."

seraphim was something that he simply took for granted. This is consistent with the evidence surveyed above, which indicates that in biblical literature they are all terms for the fiery heavenly beings who guard and bear the throne or ark in the heavenly sanctuary.[26] It contrasts, however, with the usage encountered in Jewish literature of the Second Temple period and later, including many of the pseudepigrapha, the rabbinic literature, and the *hekhalot* writings, where the three terms represent distinct categories of angels. The author of *Second Ezekiel* seems, then, to have observed the older usage encountered in scripture and not to have been influenced by the tendency toward differentiation and proliferation of angelic species, a tendency that is very characteristic of literature produced during the later Second Temple period.[27] These observations may perhaps be indicative of an early date of composition of *Second Ezekiel*, which, if so, is "presectarian." This may then be the earliest known instance of the term *merkabah* in the context of Ezekiel's vision, antedating even Sir 49:8.

The most significant locus of *merkabah* material at Qumran occurs in the thirteen *Songs of the Sabbath Sacrifice* (שירות עולת השבת), which form a liturgical cycle intended for performance on the thirteen Sabbaths of the first quarter of the year according to the fixed solar calendar observed by the community. It is unknown whether or not the cycle was repeated during the second, third, and fourth quarters of the year.[28] This is certainly possible, but we shall find that its integration with the first quarter of the cultic calendar was especially significant. Fragments of ten copies of the text have survived: eight from Cave 4 (4Q400–407), one from Cave 11 (11QShirShabb), and one from the Zealot stronghold of Masada (Masada ShirShabb).[29]

---

26. As will be seen below, the role of the cherubim as the guardians of Eden (Gen 3:24) is consistent with this observation.

27. On this subject, see especially Saul M. Olyan, *A Thousand Thousands Served Him: Exegesis and the Naming of Angels in Ancient Judaism* (TSAJ 36; Tübingen: Mohr Siebeck, 1993), reviewed in detail by Morray-Jones, *JSS* 42 (1997): 154–59.

28. This is inferred by Elior, "The *Merkavah* Tradition," 119, who observes: "The months of the year are specified by numbers, not by names, so that the liturgical order of the thirteen Sabbaths may be repeated in each of the four seasons, whose dates coincide in the 364–day calendar." On the fourfold repeating structure of the solar year, see James C. VanderKam, *Calendars in the Dead Sea Scrolls: Measuring Time* (London: Routledge, 1998), especially 52–90 and the sources cited there.

29. Carol Newsom, *Songs of the Sabbath Sacrifice: A Critical Edition* (HSS 27; Atlanta: Scholars Press, 1985). Studies of this material include J. Carmignac, "Règle des Chants pour l'Holocauste du Sabbat: Quelques détails de lecture," *RevQ* 4 (1964): 563–66; John Strugnell, "The Angelic Liturgy at Qumran—4QSerek Šîrôt 'Ôlat Haššabbāt," in *Congress Volume: Oxford, 1959* (VTSup 7; Leiden: Brill, 1960), 318–45; Lawrence H. Schiffman, "*Merkavah* Speculation at Qumran: The 4Q Serekh Shirot 'Olat ha-Shabbat," in *Mystics, Philosophers and Politicians: Essays in Jewish Intellectual History in Honor of Alexander Altmann* (ed. J. Reinharz and D. Swetschinski; Durham, N.C.: Duke University Press, 1982), 15–47; Carol Newsom, "Merkabah

In her original study of this material, Carol Newsom believed the text to be a sectarian composition.[30] She has subsequently reconsidered this opinion and concluded that it is probably of extrasectarian, even presectarian, provenance.[31] She acknowledges, however, that the evidence is not at all conclusive. Three points are held to weigh against the probability of sectarian authorship: the absence in this text of explicitly sectarian polemic; the discovery of a copy at Masada; and the frequent occurrence of the word אלהים, deviating from the convention of avoidance of this term that is observed in texts the sectarian origin of which is largely undisputed. Newsom rightly regards the first of these three points as indecisive, on the grounds that "a religious sect may have other needs as a community that do not have to do explicitly with defining the boundaries between itself and the larger religious community from which it has separated."[32] With regard to the second point, a variety of theories are able to account for the presence of a sectarian document at Masada. If discovery outside Qumran were held to be proof of nonsectarian authorship, the unambiguously sectarian *Damascus Rule* would likewise be excluded. The remaining objection, deviant use of the term אלהים, carries greater weight, although the term also occurs in the *Songs of the Maskil* (4Q510–511). This text appears to be very closely related to the *Sabbath Songs*, but Newsom nonetheless believes it to be a sectarian composition "composed under the strong influence both of the Hodayot and the Sabbath Songs."[33] In this case, she explains the anomalous occurrence of אלהים on the grounds that "the Songs of the Maśkil are conceived of as words of power. In such a context the use of a normally restricted divine name is readily explicable."[34] This point, however, applies equally to the *Songs of the Sabbath Sacrifice,* which involves the summoning or adjuration of angelic companies to assist in the performance of the worship of the heavenly temple and, if the interpretation advanced below is correct, in the ritual construction of that temple. The fact that the *Sabbath Songs* also seems to be related to the explicitly sectarian 4QBerakhot (see further below) further strengthens the case for its sectarian origin, as does the formulaic use of the

---

Exegesis in the Qumran Sabbath Shirot," *JJS* 38 (1987): 11–30; Joseph M. Baumgarten, "The Qumran Sabbath Shirot and Rabbinic Merkabah Traditions," *RevQ* 13 (1988): 199–213; Stanislav Segert, "Observations on Poetic Structures in the Songs of the Sabbath Sacrifice," *RevQ* 13 (1988): 215–23; and Bilhah Nitzan, *Qumran Prayer and Religious Poetry* (STDJ 12; Leiden: Brill, 1994), 273–311; Elior, "The *Merkavah* Tradition," especially 113–15, 125–28, and 139–42; James R. Davila, *Liturgical Works* (Eerdmans Commentaries on the Dead Sea Scrolls; Grand Rapids: Eerdmans, 2000), 83–167; and Crispin H. T. Fletcher-Louis, *All the Glory of Adam: Liturgical Anthropology in the Dead Sea Scrolls* (STDJ 42; Leiden: Brill, 2002), 252–394.

30. Newsom, *Songs of the Sabbath Sacrifice*, 1–5.

31. Newsom, "Sectually Explicit," 179–85.

32. Ibid., 180.

33. Ibid., 184.

34. Ibid., 185.

expression למשכיל as part of the heading of each song.[35] Nonetheless, Newsom concludes that:

> The most plausible explanation seems to be that the Sabbath Songs alone originated outside of and probably prior to the emergence of the Qumran community. Appropriated by the Qumran sect, this document became an important text in the community.... At some point, probably during the first century B.C.E., the Songs of the Maśkil were composed, under the strong influence of both the Hodayot and the Sabbath Songs.[36]

Arguably, the theory that the *Sabbath Songs* is a sectarian composition has the advantage of economy over Newsom's rather tentative hypothesis. As she herself remarks, the text clearly implies the existence of a highly organized worshiping community.[37] To deny its sectarian provenance thus requires us to postulate the existence of another, unknown religious group. Even if she is right, moreover, the influence exerted by the *Sabbath Songs* indicates that the sectarians attributed a high importance to it. This inference is confirmed by the existence of multiple copies of the *Sabbath Songs* at Qumran. Thus, whether or not they are sectarian in origin, they provide us with valuable evidence of the sect's beliefs and practices. Newsom is therefore right to observe that, even if the actual composition text is ascribed to nonsectarian sources, it nonetheless "functioned as an adopted or naturalized text within the sectarian perspective of the Qumran community."[38]

Each song begins with a summons to praise God, addressed to the angels, and goes on to describe the performance of the angelic liturgy. The heavenly temple is divided into seven sanctuaries (דבירים or, in two instances, היכלים[39]), also called paths (נתיבות), each under the presidency of an angelic Prince. The first five songs of the cycle deal with the angelic priestly councils of the lower *debirim* and create the framework of a ritual journey through the courts of the temple toward the sacred center. As observed by Newsom, the language of songs 6–8, at the heart of the cycle, is characterized by a repetitious and hypnotic quality, suggestive of an increase in intensity of devotion.[40] In these songs especially, the number seven occupies a major role (cf. Masada ShirShabb ii.16–22; song 6).[41]

If the sixth song marks a transition, corresponding to entry from the outer courts of the temple into the sanctuary proper, the seventh song, at the heart of

35. E.g., 4Q403 1.i.30: למשכיל שיר עולת השביעית בשש עשר לחודש. See further Newsom, *Songs of the Sabbath Sacrifice*, 3.

36. Newsom, "Sectually Explicit," 184.

37. Ibid., 184 n. 13.

38. Ibid., 185.

39. 4Q400.1.i.13: בהיכלי מלך; 11QShirShabb 2-1-9.7: להיכלי כבודו.

40. Newsom, *Songs of the Sabbath Sacrifice*, 15. See further below.

41. Ibid., 13–14.

the cycle, takes us into the holy of holies. Here, instead of a single call to the angels to worship God, we find a series of seven such calls. These are almost certainly addressed to the angelic councils of the seven *debirim*. The temple itself is portrayed as an animate structure, and its architectural features and appointments as angelic entities who participate in the praise of God:

> Sing praises to the mighty God with the choicest spiritual portion, *that there may be* [*melod*]*y* together with divine joy, and (*let there be*) a celebration with all the holy ones, that there may be wondrous songs together with *e*[*ternal*] joy.
>
> With these let all the *f*[*oundations of the hol*]*y of* holies praise, the uplifting pillars of the supremely lofty abode, and all the corners of its structure.
>
> Sin[g praise] to Go[d who is *Dr*]*eadful* in power, [*all you spirits of* knowledge and light] in order to [exa]lt together the splendidly shining firmament of [His] holy sanctuary.
>
> [*Give praise to Hi*]*m*, O you god[like] spirits, *in order to pr*[*aise* for ever and e]ver the firmament of the uppermost heaven, all [*its beams*] and its walls, a[l]l its [*for*]*m*, the work of [its] struc[ture.[42]

It is important to observe that, according to this passage, the innermost sanctuary of the heavenly temple is also the highest heaven. This is indicated by the parallel expressions "firmament of His holy sanctuary" and "firmament of the uppermost heaven." "The uppermost heaven," moreover, is said to have beams and walls. As in *1 Enoch* and *Testament of Levi*, the courts and chambers of the temple are, in fact, the celestial levels. The temple is not "in" heaven; its seven "sanctuaries" are the heavens. At the end of the song, we encounter a plurality of *merkabot*. These too are angelic entities who participate in the temple's worship:

> And all the crafted furnishings of the debir hasten (to join) with wondrous psalms in the debi[r ...] of wonder, debir to debir with the sound of holy multitudes. And all their crafted furnishings [...]
>
> And the chariots (מרכבות) of His debir give praise together, and their cherubim and thei[r] ophanim bless wondrously [...] the chiefs of the divine *structure*. And they praise Him in His holy debir.[43]

The fact that the cherubim are associated with *ʾopannim* (wheels) clearly identifies them as Ezekiel's living creatures.[44] The plural chariots, also encountered in songs 11 and 12 (see further below), are apparently angelic entities.[45] Newsom observes that the praise of these multiple *merkavot* may well be related to the

42. 4Q403.1, i.30–ii.16 (song 7), trans. Newsom, *Songs of the Sabbath Sacrifice*, 211–13.

43. 4Q403.1, i.30–ii.16 (song 7), trans. Newsom, *Songs of the Sabbath Sacrifice*, 211–13. Cf. 4Q405 20-21-22.ii.1–5 (song 11, end), trans. Newsom, *Songs of the Sabbath Sacrifice*, 306).

44. See n. 25 above.

45. Compare, perhaps, Isa 66:15, where the *merkabot* accompany God in the execution of his final judgment.

expression "*debir* to *debir* with the sound of holy multitudes," in which case the *merkabot* are involved in the process of "relaying" the praise of God from the lower *debirim* to the higher ones. This might mean that there are seven *merkabot*, one in each sanctuary or heaven. The image of a throne or *merkabah* in each of seven heavens is found, for example in *The Ascension of Isaiah*, in a *merkabah* midrash entitled *The Visions of Ezekiel*,[46] and in *Hekhalot Zutarti* (§§413–419).[47] On the other hand, MT Ps 68:18 states that "the chariots of God are twenty thousand and two thousand" (רכב אלהים רבתים אלפי שנאן[48]), and a midrashic tradition attributed to rabbis of the third and fourth centuries, and to a mysterious "band that came up from Babylonia," takes this to mean that "twenty-two thousand chariots of ministering angels (מרכבות של מלאכי השרת) descended with the Holy One, blessed be he, at Sinai."[49] MT Ps 68:18 is the first of a pair of verses,[50] the Hebrew syntax of which is, in places, unclear:

18 רכב אלהים רבתים אלפי שנאן אדני בם סיני בקש:
19 עלית למרום שבית שבי לקחת מתנות באדם

18 The chariots of God are twenty thousand and two thousand;
the Lord among them; Sinai in holiness;
19 You ascended to the height; you led captives in captivity;
you received gifts among mankind.

46. See Halperin, *Faces of the Chariot*, 263–89, 356–58, and 500–504.

47. Translation forthcoming in Rowland and Morray-Jones, *The Mystery of God*.

48. According to William F. Albright ("A Catalogue of Early Hebrew Lyric Poems [Psalm LXVIII]," *HUCA* 23 [1950–51]: 24–25), followed by Cross (*Canaanite Myth and Hebrew Epic*, 102) and Mullen (*Divine Council*, 193), the hapax שִׁנְאָן is derived from a Ugaritic word meaning "warrior" or "bowman." Knowledge of this meaning seems, however, to have been lost at an early stage of the Jewish exegetical tradition, in which the word is invariably understood to carry the meaning of "doubling" or "repetition." See further below.

49. *Pesiq. Rab Kah.* 12.22 (Bernard Mandelbaum, *Pesikta de-Rav Kahana* [2 vols.; New York: Jewish Theological Seminary of America, 1962], 1:219–21); *Tanh. Buber, Yitro*, §14 (Salomon Buber, *Midrasch Tanchuma: Ein Agadischer Commentar zum Pentateuch von Rabbi Tanchuma ben Rabbi Abba* [3 vols.; Wilna: Wittwe & Gebrüder, 1885], 3:38b–39a); *Tanh. zaw* §12 (Enoch Zondel ben Joseph, *Midraš Tanhuma'* [2 vols.; Jerusalem: Eshkol, 1990], 2:9a); *Tanh. Buber, waw* §15 (Buber, 4.10b). See further Halperin, *Faces of the Chariot*, 141–44. The puzzling attribution, "some (members) of a party that came up from Babylonia said…" (מכת שעלה מבבל אמרו) occurs only in *Pesiqta de Rab Kahana*. Suggested emendations of מכת have included מסכת ("a text") and במסורת ("in a tradition"). See further Saul Lieberman, "Mišnat Šir ha-Širim," apendix D of Scholem, *Jewish Gnosticism, Merkabah Mysticism*, 122 n. 20; William G. Braude and Israel J. Kapstein, trans., *Pěsiḳta dě-Rab Kahăna: R. Kahana's Compilations of Discourses for Sabbaths and Festal Days* (London: Routledge & Kegan Paul, 1975), 243 n. 58; Jacob Neusner, trans., *Pesiqta deRab Kahana: An Analytical Translation* (2 vols.; BJS 122–123; Atlanta: Scholars Press, 1987), 1:211; see also note below.

50. MT Ps 68:18–19 = LXX Ps 67:18–19 = RSV Ps 68:17–18 (cited here and below in accordance with MT).

David Halperin has shown that this couplet performs an important function in exegetical traditions associated with the festival of Shavuot (Pentecost), which commemorates the Sinai revelation.[51] In some rabbinic circles the prescribed Torah portion and prophetic reading (*haftara*) for this festival were, respectively, Exod 19 and Ezek 1 (*t. Meg* 3[4]:5; *b. Meg.* 31a). Psalm 68:18 provided a natural connection between these two passages, while the following verse contributed to the widespread tradition of Moses' ascent from the summit of Sinai to the heavenly throne. Further evidence of the existence of this tradition in third-century Palestine is provided by Origen, who interprets "the heavens were opened" (Ezek 1:1) in the light of Eph 4:8–12, which quotes Ps 68:19.[52] Origen also quotes Ps 68:19 in connection with the "opening of the heavens" at Jesus' baptism and with the gift of the Spirit to the apostles at Pentecost.[53] Halperin concludes:

> Origen knows the Jewish stories of Moses' ascension; he knows that their germ and nucleus is Psalm 68:19, and he knows that they are connected, through this verse, to Ezekiel's *merkabah*. By replacing the ascension *haggadot* with Ephesians 4:10–12, he lets Jesus take the place of Moses as the hero who invades heaven and brings back *gifts for humanity*, including the institutions of a new covenant and the help of the angels.[54]

It should be observed, however, that Origen's claim concerning Christ's status did not originate with him, since it is already implicit in Eph 4:8–12, where the spiritual gifts given to humans by the ascended Christ are the Pentecostal commissioning gifts of the Holy Spirit. This observation in turn suggests that the Shavuot stories of Moses' heavenly ascent are much earlier than the third century C.E.[55]

Halperin detects a connection between Sinai and Ezekiel's *merkabah* in *Apoc. Abr.* 15–18 and notes that, according to a rabbinic tradition, Abraham saw Sinai in the vision described in Gen 15:17 (see *Apoc. Abr.* 15:1), while *Jub.* 14:8–20 states that the same vision occurred at Shavuot.[56] A further indication of the early date of the connection between Sinai and the *merkabah*, via Ps 68:18, is

51. David Halperin, *The Merkabah in Rabbinic Literature* (AOS 62; New Haven: American Oriental Society, 1980), 132–33; idem, "Merkabah Midrash in the Septuagint," *JBL* 101 (1982): 351–63; idem, "Origen, Ezekiel's Merkabah and the Ascension of Moses," *CH* 50 (1981): 261–75; idem, *Faces of the Chariot*, 57–58, 141–49, 316–17, and 331–45.

52. Origen, *Hom. Ezech.* 1.6–8. See Halperin, *Faces of the Chariot*, 331–33.

53. Origen, *Hom. Luc.* 27.5; and *Com. Jo.* 6.287–294. See Halperin, *Faces of the Chariot*, 340–42.

54. Halperin, *Faces of the Chariot*, 336.

55. See further Wayne Meeks, "Moses as God and King," in *Religions in Antiquity: E. R. Goodenough Memorial Volume* (ed. J. Neusner; Numen Supplements 14; Leiden: Brill, 1968), 354–71; idem, *The Prophet-King: Moses Traditions and the Johannine Christology* (NovTSup 14; Leiden: Brill, 1967).

56. Halperin, *Faces of the Chariot*, 105–10 (for the rabbinic sources, see 109).

provided by the LXX version of Ezek 43:2: καὶ φωνὴ τῆς παρεμβολῆς, ὡς φωνὴ διπλασιαζόντων πολλῶν, "the voice of the camp was like the voice of many repeaters."[57] Halperin points out that "the voice of the camp" must be derived from Ezek 1:24 ("like the sound of many waters ... like the sound of a camp"). The strange word διπλασιαζόντων ("repeaters"), he suggests, reflects the equally puzzling שנאן of Ps 68:18:[58]

> The translator of Ezekiel 43:2—or, more likely, the tradition that he followed—deduced from this etymology that the *shin'an* are the "repeaters" of God's praise, who were present with God's chariotry (*rekheb*) at Sinai, and who therefore were part of Ezekiel's chariot vision. He aptly translated their title into Greek as *diplasiazontōn* (Greek *diplos*, "double," corresponds to Hebrew *shanah*).[59]

The presence of this "midrash" in the LXX leads Halperin to conclude that the origins of the *merkabah*/Sinai exegetical complex, including the use of Ps 68:18–19 as a link between the two, goes back to a pre-Christian Alexandrian Jewish community.[60] Subsequent research has, however, demonstrated that these traditions also played an important role in the cultic cycle at Qumran. Bilhah Nitzan has published a preliminary study of two fragments of a collection of ceremonial blessings and curses from Cave 4 (4QBerakhot), dating from the early first century C.E.[61] The text includes a reference to "the council of the community" (עצת היחד), and is therefore almost certainly a sectarian composition.[62] Nitzan's study confirms Milik's identification of the text as part of an expanded version of the liturgy for the annual ceremony of the renewal of the community's covenant, which occurred on the fifteenth day of the third month, at Shavuot.[63] The first fragment begins as follows:

---

57. MT: וקולו כקול מים רבים ("and his voice was like the sound of great waters").

58. See n. 48 above.

59. Halperin, *Faces of the Chariot*, 58.

60. See especially Halperin, "Merkabah Midrash."

61. Bilhah Nitzan, "4QBerakhot (4Q286–290): A Preliminary Report," in *New Qumran Texts and Studies: Proceedings of the First Meeting of the International Organization for Qumran Studies, Paris 1992* (ed. G. J. Brooke with F. García Martínez; STDJ 15; Leiden: Brill, 1994), 53–71; see also Davila, *Liturgical Texts*, 41–82.

62. 4Q286 10.ii.1. See Newsom, *Songs of the Sabbath Sacrifice*, 2; idem, "Sectually Explicit," 181.

63. Jozef T. Milik, "Milkî-ṣedeq et Milkî-reša' dans les anciens écrits juifs et chrétiens," *JJS* 23 (1972): 135–37; idem, *Ten Years of Discovery in the Wilderness of Judaea* (SBT 26; Naperville, Ill.: Allenson, 1959), 117–18; see also Elior, "The *Merkavah* Tradition," 131–36. Milik arrives at the date of the ceremony by combining the evidence of "our oldest manuscript of the *Damascus Document*," which places it in the third month, with that of *Jubilees* (6:17–22; 14:18–20; 22:1–7; 29:7; 44:5–8), which places the festival of Shavuot on the fifteenth of that month (*Ten Years of Discovery*, 117). Given the covenantal significance of Shavuot in *Jubilees*, Milik's argument is compelling. A simpler form of the same blessings and curses occurs in the *Community Rule*

1 מושב יקרכה והדומי רגלי כבודכה ב[מ]רומי מומדכה ומדר[ך
2 קודשכה ומרכבות כבודכה כרוביהמה ואופניהמה וכול סודיהמה

1 The seat of Thy glory and the footstools of Thy honour in the [h]eights of Thy standing and trea[ding]-place of
2 Thy holiness; and the chariots of Thy glory, their cherubim and their ophanim (wheels) with all [their] councils.[64]

The language of the text as a whole is very similar to that of the *Sabbath Songs*, and the reference to a plurality of *merkabot* should be noted.[65] Nitzan identifies allusions to the *merkabah* descriptions of Dan 7:9, *1 En.* 14, and, indirectly, Ezek 1:26–27 and 8:2. There are detailed allusions to biblical lists of divine attributes occurring in contexts associated with renewal of the Sinai covenant (Exod 34:6–7; Deut 10:17, 21) and to descriptions of the Sinai theophany in Moses' final blessing (Deut 33:2–5, 26–27). Allusions to Ps 68 are also evident, especially in the second fragment.[66]

In the solar calendar observed at Qumran, the fifteenth day of the third month fell on the day following the eleventh Sabbath of the sect's cultic year.[67] It is, therefore, almost certainly significant that one of the two or three surviving fragments of the eleventh *Sabbath Song*, like 4QBerakhot, makes reference to a multitude of angelic *merkavot*, which are mentioned not once but several times:

(1QS 2:2–17), in the context of the ceremony of admission to the sectarian covenant community.

N.B.: Milik initially identified the Qumran manuscript as "4Q D[b]" (*Ten Years of Discovery*, 58) but subsequently corrected this to "4QD[a] (4Q266) 3 X 16 fin-21 début, le manuscrit qui date du premier tiers du Ier siècle avant J.-C.," which he published with lacunae supplied from "4QD[e] (4Q270) 6 X, qui est tracé en alphabet hérodien classique" ("Milkî-ṣedeq et Milkî-reša'," 135). The two fragments appear to correspond, respectively, to "4QDamascus Document[b] (4Q267 [4QD[b]]), *Frag.* 18 *col.* v, 17–20," and "4QDamascus Document[e] (4Q270 [4QD[e]]), *Frag.* 11 *col.* ii (= 4QD[b] 18 v, 16–20)," in Florentino García Martínez, *The Dead Sea Scrolls Translated* (Leiden: Brill, 1994), 57 and 67.

64. 4QBer[a] 1.ii (Nitzan, "4QBerakhot," 56 [text] and 57 [translation]).

65. Thus also Newsom, *Songs of the Sabbath Sacrifice*, 2; and idem, "Sectually Explicit," 180.

66. See Nitzan, "4QBerakhot," 63–71. In the light of this material, I am tempted to entertain the speculation that the unique expression in *Pesiq. Rab Kah.* 12.22, "a party that came up from Babylonia" (see n. 49 above), may be a garbled reference to a long-forgotten sectarian group that preserved the traditions represented at Qumran.

67. According to the sectarian calendar as reconstructed on the basis of 1 *En.* 72–82 and *Jubilees* by Milik (*Ten Years of Discovery*, 107), the eleventh Sabbath falls on the fourteenth day of the third month; see also Annie Jaubert, *The Date of the Last Supper* (Statten Island, N.Y.: Alba House, 1965), 26–29. Elior ("The *Merkavah* Tradition," 108) observes that, according to the solar calendar, "the festivals fell on fixed days of the week and in fixed seasons of the year; no festival could fall on a Sabbath, and every festival stood in a seven-fold relationship to other festivals."

1. [*They do not delay when they arise ... the deb*]*irim* of all the priests of the inner sanctum [...]
2. By [strict ordinance they] are steadfast in the ser[vice of...] a seat like His royal throne (משב ככסא מלכותו) in [His glorious debirim. *They* do not sit ...]
3. His glorious chariot(s) (מרכבות כבודו) [...] holy cherubim, luminous ophanim *in the de*[*bir* ... spirits of godlike beings ... purity ...]
4. of holiness, *the construction of* [*its*] *cor*[*ners* ...] royal [...] the glorious seats of the chariot th[rones (למכרבות מושבי כבוד) ... wings of knowledge ... wondrous powers ...]
5. truth and righteousness, eternal [...] His glorious chariots as they move (מרכבות כבודו בלכתמה) [...*they do not turn to any side ... they go straight*...][68]

A passage in the later *hekhalot* literature tells of vast numbers of angelic *merkabot* who, with their accompanying "flames" (שלהביות), relay God's praises from the lowest sanctuary to the highest.[69]

> In the first *hekhal*, the fiery chariot-thrones say: "Holy! Holy! Holy is the LORD of Hosts! The whole earth is full of His Glory!" And the fiery flames disperse and reassemble in the second hekhal, saying: "Holy! Holy! Holy is the LORD of Hosts! The whole earth is full of His Glory!"
>
> In the second *hekhal*, the fiery chariot-thrones say: "Blessed be the Glory of the LORD from His place!" And again the fiery flames disperse and reassemble in the third hekhal, saying: "Blessed be the Glory of the LORD from His place!" [The process continues through *hekahalot* three to six.]
>
> In the seventh *hekhal*, the fiery chariot-thrones say: "Blessed be the King of the kings of kings, the LORD, the Lord of every power! Who is like God, who lives and endures? His praise is in the highest heavens! His holy kingdom is in the most exalted and highest heavens! His Power is in the innermost chambers! Sanctification from here, and sanctification from there!" And they pour forth song unceasingly, and commemorate the Name of גהוריאל the LORD God of Israel, saying: "Blessed be the name of His glorious kingdom for ever and ever from the place of the House of His Indwelling!"

These angelic *merkabot* are distinctly reminiscent of the "repeaters" of God's praise of God encountered in LXX Ezek 43:2 (cf. Ps 68:18–19),[70] and it may well be that the expression "*debir* to *debir* with the sound of holy multitudes" in the seventh song of the Qumran cycle refers to a scenario very much like that

68. 4Q405 20-21-22.ii.1–5 (trans. Newsom, *Songs of the Sabbath Sacrifice*, 306).

69. *Ma'aseh Merkabah* §6 (Scholem, *Jewish Gnosticism, Merkabah Mysticism*, 106–7; Schäfer, §§544–45; all translations of the *hekhalot* literature are my own). The numbers vary considerably between the manuscripts. Majority readings are followed where possible above.

70. See pp. 157–58 above.

described in this *hekhalot* passage. The formulaic style of the *hekhalot* passage is quite similar to what we find in the *Sabbath Songs*. The image of praise being relayed and repeated by the angels, which is reflected in the antiphonal structure of the *Songs* themselves, may also be associated with the calling of the seraphim "one to another" as they recite the Kedusha (Isa 6:3).[71]

As observed above, the seventh song, marking the entrance to the holy of holies, brings the first half of the ritual cycle to its climax. The eighth song is only fragmentarily preserved but appears to be closely parallel to song 6. Songs 9–11 describe in detail the vestibules, courts, and furnishings of the temple. There are numerous references to celestial life-forms whose images are carved on the interior walls. These correspond to the carvings of cherubim, trees, and flowers in both Solomon's temple and Ezekiel's ideal form (1 Kgs 6:18–36; 2 Chr 3:5–6; Ezek 40:31–34; 41:17–26). As in the previous songs, they are animate beings and participate in the praise of God.

Newsom regards the seventh song as the climax of the *Sabbath Songs* cycle as a whole, forming the apex of a liturgical pyramid structure.[72] I suggest that this analysis requires modification and that the seventh song is, in fact, no more than a preliminary crescendo. In my opinion, it is the twelfth song, falling on the Sabbath following the covenant-renewal ceremony of 4QBerakhot, that forms the true climax of the liturgical cycle as a whole.[73] This song describes the manifestation of the Glory upon the *merkabah:*

> By the Instr[uctor. Song of the Sacrifice of] the twelfth [Sa]bbath [on the twenty-first of the third month.
> Praise the God of ...] wondrous [...] and exalt him, ... the Glory in the tabern[acle of the God of] knowledge.
> The cherubim fall before him and bless. When they rise, the sound of divine silence (קול דממת אלוהים) [is heard], then a tumult of jubilation as their wings are raised.
> In the sound of divine silence, they bless the image of the chariot-throne (תבנית כסא מרכבה) above the firmament of the cherubim, [and] they sing of [the splendo]r of the radiant firmament beneath the seat of his Glory (מושב כדזבו).
> And when the wheels (אופנים) go, the holy angels return. From between the [w]heels of his Glory (גלגלי כדזבו), like the appearance of fire, go forth the holy spirits. Round about is the appearance of streams of fire.

71. See Nitzan, *Qumran Prayer*, 276–82 and 315–16.

72. Newsom, *Songs of the Sabbath Sacrifice*, 5–21.

73. Neither Newsom (*Songs of the Sabbath Sacrifice*, 55–56) nor Nitzan (*Qumran Prayer*, 313–14) seem fully to appreciate the significance of this song, but Davila (*Liturgical Texts*, 87–90) concurs with my opinion.

> Like חשמל,[74] a radiant substance of glorious colors, wondrously hued and purely blended, are the spirits of the living *elohim* that move continuously with the glory of the wondrous chariots (כבוד מרכבות פלא).
> There is a sound of silent blessing in the tumult of their movement, and they praise his holiness while returning on their paths.
> When they rise up, they rise marvelously, and when they settle, they stand still.
> The sound of joyful praise falls silent, and there is a silence of divine blessing in all the camps of the *elohim*.
> And the sound of their praises [...] from among all their divisions [...] and all the numbered ones praise, each in his turn.[75]

The second half of the *Sabbath Songs* cycle is evidently based on the description of the ideal temple in Ezek 40–48, and Newsom is clearly right to connect the passage shown above with the vision described in Ezek 43:1–5, where the Glory on the *merkabah* returns to the holy of holies:

> 1 Then he brought me to the gate that faces eastward, 2 and behold, the Glory of the God of Israel coming from the east! His voice was like the sound of many waters, and the earth was illuminated by his Glory. 3 And the vision that I saw was like the vision that I had seen when he came to destroy the city, and like the vision that I had seen by the River Khebar, and I fell upon my face. 4 And the Glory of the LORD came into the house by way of the gate that faced eastward. 5 Then the Spirit lifted me up and brought me to the inner court, and the Glory of the LORD filled the house.

Newsom comments: "I would suggest that the author of the Shirot, still following the outline of Ezek 40–48, first described the structure of the heavenly temple and then gave an account of the entry of the divine chariot throne into the temple and the appearance of its glory there, an account modelled after Ezek 43:1–5 but enriched with details from Ezek 1 and 10."[76] Halperin suggests that the "sound of divine silence" in the twelfth song is derived from the account of God's appearance to Elijah in 1 Kgs 19:11,[77] but, given the fact that this liturgical composition is clearly based on an idealized form of the temple-cult tradition,[78] the reference is more likely to Hab 2:20: "But the LORD is in his holy temple; let all the earth keep silence before him!"and/or to Zech 2:17 (2:1): "Be silent, all flesh,

74. Cf. Ezek 1:4; 1:27. See further below.

75. 4Q405 20-21-22.ii.6–11 (song 12), Newsom, *Songs of the Sabbath Sacrifice*, 303. The above translation is my own; cf. Newsom, *Songs of the Sabbath Sacrifice*, 306–7.

76. Newsom, *Songs of the Sabbath Sacrifice*, 55.

77. Halperin, *Faces of the Chariot*, 51.

78. Compare *Aristeas* 92, 95, on which see Hayward, *Jewish Temple*, 32–34. See now Israel Knohl, "Between Voice and Silence: The Relationship between Prayer and Temple Cult," *JBL* 115 (1996): 17–30.

before the Lord; for he has roused himself from his holy dwelling." The *hekhalot* texts likewise speak of a moment of awesome stillness at the climax of the heavenly liturgy, when the tumultuous sound of the angelic worship falls silent and the divine Glory descends upon the *merkabah*. A striking example occurs in the *Shi'ur Qomah* section of the *Siddur Rabbah diBereshit*, where the angelic high priest, here called "the Youth" (הנער) enters beneath the throne and summons the divine Glory to appear:

> And the angels who are with him [the Youth] come and encircle the Throne of Glory. They are on one side, the Living Creatures are on the other side, and the *Shekhina* is in the center. And one living creature rises above the Throne of Glory and draws near to the Seraphim, then alights upon the tabernacle of the Youth and says in a loud voice, a voice of silence: "The Throne alone shall I exalt above him!" At once, the Wheels are silent, the Seraphim are still, the troops of Watchers and Holy Ones are thrust into the River Dinur, the Living Creatures turn their faces to the ground, and the Youth brings fire of deafness and puts it in their ears, so that they do not hear the voice that is spoken, and so that he alone remains. And the Youth calls Him the Great, Mighty, Awesome, Majestic, Strong, Powerful, Pure, Holy, Stalwart, Precious, Honoured, Clean, Guiltless, Beloved, Wonderful, Exalted, Uplifted and Glorified God![79]

There are several points of contact between this passage and the twelfth song from Qumran. In both we find the same dynamic quality and the same paradoxical combination of sound and silence. The prostration of the living creatures parallels that of the cherubim in the song. In the song, the cherubim "rise up" and "settle," as does the living creature in the *Shi'ur Qomah* piece. Both texts are describing the same climactic moment in the celestial liturgy. It should be observed that the *Shi'ur Qomah* passage is, like the *Sabbath Songs*, a liturgical text and designed for recitation.

The thirteenth and final song of the Qumran cycle describes the sacrifices performed before the divine throne by the angelic priests and, epecially, their ritual vestments. Fletcher-Louis considers these figures to be identical with the senior priests of the community, who are held to be the embodiments of the divine Glory itself.[80] He concludes, therefore, that the climax of the cycle is located in neither the seventh song (as advocated by Newsom) nor the twelfth (as proposed by me) but in the thirteenth: "It is here, in the XIIIth, that the liturgy truly reaches its climax with a vision of the community's priesthood taking the place of the occupant of the throne-chariot.... It is in the XIIIth Song that the human form seated on God's throne in Ezek 1 first comes into view. The human

79. *Siddur Rabbah diBereshit*, lines 40–46, in Martin Samuel Cohen, ed. *The Shi'ur Qomah: Texts and Recensions* (TSAJ 9; Tübingen: Mohr Siebeck, 1985).

80. See Fletcher-Louis, *All the Glory of Adam*, 356–94.

high priesthood here makes manifest the anthropomorphic appearance of the Glory of the Lord."[81]

This conclusion follows from Fletcher-Louis's very detailed and insightful exegesis of the cycle as a whole, in which he demonstrates that a relationship of "functional synchronicity" and "spatial overlap" exists between the priestly community on earth and the angelic denizens of the heavenly temple.[82] It is undoubtedly true that the Qumran sectarians considered themselves to be in fellowship with the celestial hosts and attributed to themselves, (quasi-) angelic status.[83] Moreover, the glory of the celestial Adam (or Logos) was ritually embodied in the person of the high priest, and that his vestments were symbolic of that glory is, as Fletcher-Louis shows, by no means unique to the Qumran literature.[84] His suggestion that at Qumran the chief priests of the holy community were considered in their liturgical function to be visible manifestations of the divine *Kabod* is not merely plausible but probable almost to the point of certainty.[85] The role of this "glorified" human priesthood is to represent and mediate the divine *Kabod* to the community of worshipers, which is thereby incorporated into the celestial hierarchy of glory.

Fletcher-Louis seems, however, to imply that the celestial Glory has no other mode of visible appearance than in the person(s) of the priest(s), and in this he overstates his case. The clothing of the priests with glory in the thirteenth song—if this is indeed what is happening—is an expression of their mystical communion with the divine *Kabod,* which in turn facilitates the union between the community's worship and the liturgy of the angels. It does not mean that the cosmic function of the manifest Glory has wholly usurped by the person(s) of the priest(s). Thus, while the glorification of the priests in song 13 may legitimately be regarded as, in a sense, climactic, it flows as a consequence from the descent of the *Kabod* to the sanctuary, as described in song 12. This descent, which, as we have seen, was preceded by the covenant-renewal ceremony of Shavuot, seems, therefore, to form a more fitting climax to the cycle as a whole. It may further be noted that, according to Hayutin, the lunar date of Ezekiel's *merkabah* vision, "in the fourth month, on the fifth day of the month" (Ezek 1:1), corresponds in the solar calendar to either the fourteenth or the fifteenth day of the third month,

81. Ibid., 375 and 386, emphasis original.

82. Ibid., 252–355, here 355.

83. On the angelic status of priests and *merkabah* practitioners, see further Morray-Jones, *Transparent Illusion,* 192–205.

84. This motif is encountered in a variety of Jewish sources. See Fletcher-Louis, *All the Glory of Adam,* 56–87; see further Hayward, *Jewish Temple,* 38–84, 108–18, and the sources cited there.

85. It should be noted in passing that Fletcher-Louis (*All the Glory of Adam,* 248–51) traces the origin of the term "Essene" to the breastplate (חשן) worn by the high priest (Exod 25:7, etc.).

that is, to the eleventh Sabbath or, as is perhaps more likely, to the festival of Shavuot itself.[86]

Newsom describes the purpose of the *Sabbath Songs* cycle as "something like the praxis of a communal mysticism,"[87] which aimed to produce an intense experience of being present in the heavenly temple and participating in the worship of the angels.[88] She comments:

> During the course of this thirteen week cycle, the community which recites the compositions is led through a lengthy preparation. The mysteries of the angelic priesthood are recounted, a hypnotic celebration of the sabbatical number seven produces an anticipatory climax at the center of the work, and the community is then gradually led through the spiritually animate temple until the worshippers experience the holiness of the merkabah and of the Sabbath sacrifice as it is conducted by the high priests of the angels.[89]

These songs, then, enabled the community to gain access to the heavenly temple and to join with the angelic hierarchy in its worship before the throne. By performing the liturgical cycle, the worshipers undertake a "ritual journey," which involves an "ascent" through the seven *debirim* (songs 1–7), followed by a detailed tour of the celestial temple, moving inwards toward the center, where the Glory manifests upon the throne. Another, perhaps better, way to understand this liturgy is to regard it as a process of "ritual construction." The performance of these songs, presumably combined with intensive visualization of the images described, will have had the effect of "building" the celestial temple in the personal and collective imagination of the participants. The imperative formulae of the early hymns indicates that they are calling on the angels to participate with them in this ritual "temple-building" project. The process of construction culminates in song 11, which was performed immediately before the renewal of the community's covenant at the feast of Shavuot. On the two Sabbaths following this act of rededication, in songs 12 and 13, the divine Glory is called upon to indwell the temple that has been constructed by the now reconsecrated community, to clothe

86. See Michael Hayutin, *Milhamat luhot ha-šanah bi-tequfat bayit šeni* (Tel Aviv: Modan, 1993), 75; cf. Elior, "The *Merkavah* Tradition," 134–35.

87. Newsom, *Songs of the Sabbath Sacrifice*, 19

88. Elliot R. Wolfson ("Mysticism and the Poetic-Liturgical Compositions from Qumran: A Response to Bilhah Nitzan," *JQR* 85 [1994]: 185–202) questions the application by Newsom and Nitzan of the adjective "mystical" to this material, preferring to limit the term to the practice of the heavenly ascent. Since, however, religious ritual has the capacity to embody both mystical meaning and mystical experience, this arbitrary semantic restriction seems unjustified. In any case, the ritual cycle of the *Sabbath Songs* is, according to the above analysis, very closely related to the ascent tradition and therefore contains a "mystical" dimension even if Wolfson's narrow definition were to be accepted.

89. Newsom, *Songs of the Sabbath Sacrifice*, 19.

its priests with glory, and to receive its offerings. As observed above, it is the descent of the divine Glory in the holy of holies, described in song 12, that forms the true climax of the cycle. The sacred structure within which this manifestation occurs has been constructed by means of this extended ritual performance. The worship of the holy community and its celestial, angelic counterpart is, so to speak, the substance of which the temple is composed.

The idea that this spiritual temple is ritually constructed in and through the act of worship may perhaps be inherent in the very language and terminology of this remarkable liturgy. In addition to the emphasis on song and music that pervades the text, we have observed that, especially in the latter part of the cycle, this music is produced not only by the angels and the human worshipers but by the architectural components of the temple itself, which appears to be a living structure. The term דביר, used of the seven courts or chambers of the temple, applies in Scripture to the holy of holies (1 Kgs 6:5–31; 7:49; 8:6–8; 2 Chr 3:16; 4:20; 8:6–8; Ps 28:2) and is probably derived from a common root with the Arabic word for "back" or "part behind."[90] The King James Bible, however, renders the term by "oracle," a mistranslation that goes back via the Vulgate (*oraculum*) to Aquila (χρηματιστηριον) and that is based on the midrashic assumption that this word is derived from the root דבר "to speak." It seems not impossible that the author of the *Sabbath Songs* may have made the same verbal association and interpreted the word דביר as indicative, in addition to its straightforward meaning, of "speech" or "utterance." If so, the phrase: "*debir* to *debir* with the sound of holy multitudes" implies that the courts or sanctuaries of the temple are formed by the "utterances" of the angels and the worshiping community and that the heavenly temple is conceived of as a structure composed of living sound.[91]

Elsewhere in the Scrolls, as is now widely recognized, the community itself is identified with the temple.

> When these are in Israel, the Council of the Community shall be established in truth. It shall be an Everlasting Plantation, a House of Holiness for Israel, an Assembly of Supreme Holiness for Aaron.... It shall be that tried wall, that *precious corner stone,* whose foundations shall neither rock nor sway in their place (Isa. xxviii, 16). It shall be a Most Holy Dwelling for Aaron, with everlasting knowledge of the Covenant of justice, and shall offer up sweet fragrance. It shall be a House of Perfection and Truth in Israel that they may establish a Covenant according to the everlasting precepts. (1QS 8:4–9)[92]

90. See BDB (1977) 184a–b.

91. I am indebted to Mr. W. G. Davies for this interesting suggestion.

92. Translation by Vermes, *Dead Sea Scrolls,* 72–73. Compare 1QpHab xii.3–4, on which see further Vermes, "The Religious Ideas of the Community," ibid., 50–51.

The hierarchically ordered community thus embodies the living structure of the cosmic temple, and its members are incorporated into that celestial reality.

> He has joined their assembly to the Sons of Heaven
> to be a Council of the Community,
> a foundation of the Building of Holiness,
> and eternal Plantation throughout all ages to come. (1QS 11:8–9)[93]

The expression "an eternal plantation" reflects an ancient tradition according to which the temple, and especially the interior of the sanctuary building (corresponding to the sixth and seventh *debirim* of the Qumran model), is identified with the primordial garden of Eden, which was also the future paradise of the righteous.[94] Incorporation into the structure of the temple confers "advance membership" of the world to come and is, at the same time, a return to humanity's original state of angelic purity. Thus, those who are admitted to this spiritual community "are destined to live for ever, and all the glory of Adam shall be theirs."[95]

The same tradition occurs in a variety of rabbinic sources, where the righteous in the world to come are divided into seven hierarchical classes[96] and where the garden of Eden is described as a series of seven concentric celestial chambers, built of gold, silver, and precious stones.[97] This imagery appears to be derived at least in part from the language of Ezekiel's prophecy against the king of Tyre (Ezek 28:12–14). It has long been recognized that behind this passage lies a ver-

93. Translation by Vermes, *Dead Sea Scrolls*, 79.

94. See further Levenson, "Temple and the World" 297–98; idem, *Sinai and Zion*, 127–33; Barker, *The Older Testament: The Survival of Themes from the Ancient Royal Cult in Sectarian Judaism and Early Christianity* (London: SPCK, 1987), 233–45; idem, *The Gate of Heaven*, 57–103; Himmelfarb, "The Temple and the Garden of Eden in Ezekiel, the Book of the Watchers, and the Wisdom of ben Sira," in *Sacred Places and Profane Spaces: Essays in the Geographics of Judaism, Christianity, and Islam* (ed. J. Scott and P. Simpson-Housley; Contributions to the Study of Religion 30; New York: Greenwood, 1991), 63–78; Mullen, *Divine Council*, 147–54; Morray-Jones, "Paradise Revisited. Part 1," 204–8; Jacques van Ruiten, "The Garden of Eden and Jubilees 3:1–31," *Bijdr* 57 (1996): 305–17, esp. 310–12; Hayward, *Jewish Temple*, 88–93, 111–12.

95. CD 3:20. On the notion that the ministry of the high priest in the temple sanctuary reflects that of Adam in Eden and that the high priestly vestments are symbolic of the pre-fallen Adam's glory, see Hayward, *Jewish Temple*, 44–46 and 70–71 (on Sir 49:15–50:26). See also van Ruiten, "Garden of Eden," 315–16.

96. See, e.g., *y. Hagigah; Lev. Rab.* 30:2; *Midr. Teh.* to Ps 11:6.77a; cf. *4 Ezra* 7:92–98.

97. See *Yalqut Shimoni Bereshit* 1:20 (Arthur B. Hyman, Isaac Nathan Lerer, and Isaac Shilon, eds., *Yalqut Šim'oni* [5 vols. in 9; Jerusalem: Mossad haRab Quq, 1973–91], 1:68–71); and *Seder Gan-Eden*, recension B (Adolf Jellinek, ed., *Bet ha-Midrasch: Sammlung kleiner Midraschim und vermichster Abhandlungen aus der ältern jüdischen Literatur* [6 vols.; 1853–77; repr., Jerusalem: Bamberger & Wahrmann, 1938], 3:131–40), where the garden of Eden and the temple are closely associated (note that Jellinek's recension A [2:52–53] is identical with *Yalqut Shimoni Bereshit* 1:20).

sion of the primordial paradise tradition that is independent of, and possibly older than, that preserved in Gen 2–3.[98] The description, then, referred originally to the primordial Adam, who is the embodiment of the Divine Image or "seal of perfect proportion" and is here identified with the golden, bejewelled cherub whose outstretched wings overshadowed the ark in the holy of holies of the temple. That the rabbis were aware of this meaning of the passage is confirmed by several sources.[99]

By about the first century C.E., the seven-level cosmology had largely displaced the three-tier model, although Paul in 2 Cor 12 equates paradise (i.e., the holy of holies) with the third heaven.[100] The sevenfold model is most commonly found in rabbinic sources, although alternative traditions that enumerate two or three heavens are also sometimes mentioned.[101] A correspondence between the cosmos and the structure of the temple is implied in *m. Kelim* 1:6–9, which lists ten areas of increasing holiness in Jerusalem, three outside the temple and seven within. Differing opinions are expressed about the precise divisions between these areas, but all agree that there were seven levels of holiness in the temple. According to Rabbi Yose, these levels were as follows: (1) the area within the balustrade (סורג), from which Gentiles were excluded; (2) the court of women; (3) the court of Israel; (4) the court of the priests; (5) the area between the altar

98. See further Hermann Gunkel, *Genesis übersetzt und underklart* (Göttingen: Vandenhoeck & Ruprecht, 1922), 25–40; G. A. Cooke, "The Paradise Story of Ezekiel 28," in *Old Testament Essays* (London: Charles Griffin, 1927), 37–45; idem, *A Critical and Exegetical Commentary on the Book of Ezekiel* (2 vols.; ICC; New York: Scribner, 1937), 2:313–24; Widengren, *Ascension of the Apostle,* 94–97; idem, "Early Hebrew Myths and their Interpretations," in *Myth, Ritual and Kingship: Essays on the Theory and Practice of Kingship in the Ancient Near East and in Israel* (ed. S. Hooke; Oxford: Clarendon, 1958), 165–69; Walther Eichrodt, *Ezekiel* (OTL; Philadelphia: Westminster, 1970), 392; Walther Zimmerli, *Ezekiel* (2 vols.; Hermeneia; Philadelphia: Fortress, 1983), 2:81–95.

99. *Pesiq. Rab Kah.* 4.4 and 26.3 (ed. Mandelbaum, *Pesikta de-Rav Kahana,* 1:66–67; 2:389 = William G. Braude and Israel J. Kapstein, trans., *Pĕsikta dĕ-Rab Kahăna: R. Kahana's Compilations of Discourses for Sabbaths and Festal Days* [London: Routledge & Kegan Paul, 1975], 72–73); *Tanh. Buber, 'Aharei-Mot,* §3 (= Hans Bietenhard, trans., *Midrasch Tanhuma B: R. Tanhuma über die Tora, genannt Midrasch Jelammedenu* [2 vols.; Judaica et Christiana 5–6; Bern: Lang, 1980–82], 2:89). See further Philip Munoa, *Four Powers in Heaven: The Interpretation of Daniel 7 in the Testament of Abraham* (JSPSup 28; Sheffield: Sheffield Academic Press, 1998), 85–87. The destruction and rebuilding of the temple are linked to humanity's loss and recovery of the divine image in a fragment from the Cairo Genizah, on which see Alon Goshen-Gottstein, "The Body as Image of God in Rabbinic literature," *HTR* 87 (1994): 185–86 and the sources cited there.

100. See Christopher Morray-Jones, "Paradise Revisited. Part 2: Paul's Heavenly Ascent and Its Significance," *HTR* 86 (1993): 265–92.

101. For the former, see, e.g., *Lev. Rab.* 29:11; *'Abot. R. Nat.* (A) 37; *Pesiq. Rab.* 20.4; *Midrash HaGadol* to Exod 7:1. For the latter, see, e.g., *b. Hag.* 12b; *Midr. Teh.* to Ps 114:2; and *Deut. Rab.* 2:32 (to 6:4).

and the entrance to the sanctuary; (6) the sanctuary building; and (7) the holy of holies.[102]

This sevenfold conceptual structure doubtless reflects the seven planetary spheres of Greek cosmology and/or the seven heavens encountered in Sumerian and Babylonian magical texts.[103] Since the sacred space of the temple is conceptually arranged in concentric "areas of holiness" around the ark or chariot on which God's Glory is enthroned, it may be that the sevenfold structure also embodies "the appearance of the likeness of the Glory of the LORD," as described in Ezek 1:28: "As the appearance of the bow that is in the cloud on the day of rain, so was the appearance of the radiance that surrounded him." In other words, the seven heavens or courts of the temple may correspond to the bands of the rainbow-colored aura that surrounds the Glory on the throne. This hypothesis perhaps helps to explain an image encountered above, in song 12 of the Qumran cycle: "Like חשמל, a radiant substance of glorious colors, wondrously hued and purely blended, are the spirits of the living *'lohim* that move continuously with the glory of the wondrous chariots."[104] A similar description of the *hashmal* is encountered in *Hekhalot Zutarti*: "It is *like the appearance of fire* (Ezek 1:27), but it is not fire. Rather, it is like fiery flames of all kinds of colors mixed together, and the eye cannot master their likenesses."[105]

3. Descenders to the Merkavah

The *hekhalot* writings represent the continuation and adaptation of these traditions within rabbinic Judaism. They are so called because they describe, and give instructions regarding, a visionary journey through seven concentric "palaces" or "temples" (*hekhalot*, corresponding to the *debirim* of the *Sabbath Songs*) to the celestial holy of holies, where the Glory appears on the *merkabah*.[106] The

102. See André Neher, "Le voyage mystique des quatre," *RHR* 140 (1951): 73–76.

103. See Yarbro Collins, "Seven Heavens," 81–87.

104. 4Q405 20-21-22.ii.6, Newsom, *Songs of the Sabbath Sacrifice*, 303.

105. Schäfer, *Synopse*, §371 = Rachel Elior, ed., *Hekhalot Zutarti, Ms. New York 8218 (828)* [Jerusalem Studies in Jewish Thought Supplement Series 1; Jerusalem: Magnes, 1982], lines 261–66. The passage is discussed in detail in Morray-Jones, *Transparent Illusion*, 174–91 and 213–14.

106. This is only a partial description of the contents of this literature, emphasizing the elements that are significant for the purposes of this study, not a comprehensive definition of the genre. For a range of viewpoints, see Gershom Scholem, *Major Trends in Jewish Mysticism* (3d ed.; 1954; repr., New York: Schocken, 1961), 40–79; Ithamar Gruenwald, *Apocalyptic and Merkavah Mysticism* (AGJU 14; Leiden: Brill, 1980), 98–234; Peter Schäfer, *Gershom Scholem Reconsidered: The Aim and Purpose of Early Jewish Mysticism* (12th Sacks Lecture; Oxford: Oxford Centre for Postgraduate Hebrew Studies, 1986); repr. as "The Aim and Purpose of early Jewish Mysticism" in idem, *Hekhalot-Studien* [TSAJ 19; Tübingen: Mohr Siebeck, 1988], 277–95); idem, *The Hidden and Manifest God* (Albany: State University of New York Press, 1992);

methods employed by the "*merkabah* mystics" included the recitation of hymns and prayers that are very similar in content and tone to those found in the *Sabbath Songs*, though often with the addition of long strings of *nomina barbara*. These hymns, some of which are said to have been revealed to Rabbi Aqiba by the angels,[107] must be known and recited correctly by the adept if one is to make the ascent in safety. One must also know the names of the angelic gatekeepers of the *hekhalot* and show them the correct magic seals, on which are inscribed the secret names of God. As in the apocalypses and the *Sabbath Songs*, the chambers of the temple (the seven *hekhalot*) are identical with the celestial levels.[108]

In one important respect, however, the temple and the cosmos are structural opposites. The temple's areas of holiness are concentric upon the holy of holies. "Ascent" of the levels is therefore conceptualized as a journey "inward," to the center. The ascent into heaven, on the other hand, proceeds outward, away from the earth, so that the sphere of greatest holiness is assigned to the periphery. This "dimensional shift" may perhaps help to explain why in *1 En.* 14 the "inner" house is greater than the "outer."

A similar apparent confusion of dimensional relationships is encountered in the *hekhalot* literature. The journey through the *hekhalot* to the *merkabah* is described both as an "ascent" (employing the verb עלה) and, somewhat disconcertingly, as a "descent" (employing the verb ירד). These two terminologies appear to be virtually interchangeable, but the mystics themselves are always called "descenders to the chariot" (יורדי מרכבה), even where the narrative verb is "to ascend." Various explanations of this puzzling terminology have been offered.[109] Here mention should be made of Alan F. Segal's suggestion that the

Halperin, *Faces of the Chariot*, 359–446; Joseph Dan, *The Ancient Jewish Mysticism* (Tel-Aviv: MOD Books, 1993).

107. *Hekh. Rab.* 4:3 (Schäfer, *Synopse*, §106).

108. According to *3 En.* 18.3 (Schäfer, *Synopse*, §24) and *Massekhet Hekhalot* §4, all seven *hekhalot* are located in the highest heaven, but these texts are not typical of the corpus as a whole. See further Morray-Jones, "Paradise Revisited. Part 1," 179–80 n. 6; idem, *Transparent Illusion*, 31–32.

109. Scholem (*Jewish Gnosticism, Merkabah Mysticism*, 20 n. 1) suggests that the language of "descent" may be derived from the rabbinic expression יורד לפני התבה, referring to the cantor in the synagogue who "goes down before the ark." Dan (*Three Types of Ancient Jewish Mysticism* [Seventh Annual Rabbi Louis Feinberg Memorial Lecture; Cincinnati: University of Cincinnati Press, 1984], 34 n. 29; idem, *The Ancient Jewish Mysticism*, 79–80) believes it to be derived from Song 6:11 ("I went down into the nut garden"). Halperin (*Faces of the Chariot*, 226–27) relates it to midrashic traditions about the "descent" of the Israelites to the Red Sea. Guy G. Stroumsa (*Hidden Wisdom: Esoteric Traditions and the Roots of Christian Mysticism* [NumenSup 70; Leiden: Brill, 1996], 169–83] submits that it may been borrowed from the Greek and Hellenistic tradition of descent (καταβασις) into the underworld. Wolfson ("*Yeridah la-Merkavah*: Typology of Ecstasy and Enthronement in Ancient Jewish Mysticism," in *Mystics of the Book: Themes, Topics, and Typologies* [ed. R. A. Herrera; New York: Lang, 1993], 13–44;

conception of the journey as a "descent" may be associated with the "fetal" position that, according to Hai Gaon of Pumbeditha (writing in the eleventh century C.E.), was adopted by the *hekhalot* practitioners:

> You may be aware that many sages were of the belief that an individual possessing certain explicitly defined qualities who wishes to behold the Merkabah and the palaces of the heavenly angels has methods of achieving this. He must sit in fast for a certain number of days and lay his head between his knees and whisper to the ground many hymns and songs whose words are known from tradition. He then gazes into the inner rooms and chambers as if he were seeing the seven palaces with his own eyes, and beholds as if he were journeying from one palace to another and seeing what is there.[110]

The posture described by Hai corresponds to that of Elijah on Mount Carmel in 1 Kgs 18:42. Rabbinic sources state in passing that the first-century miracle worker Hanina ben Dosa adopted the same position when praying for the life of Yohanan ben Zakkai's son (*b. Ber.* 34b; *b. ʿAbod. Zar.* 17a). Gershom Scholem found an intriguing parallel in a nineteenth-century account of a Chinese trance-somnabulist.[111]

The idea that the Jerusalem temple embodies or reflects the structure of the universe is widely documented in rabbinic sources and in Josephus.[112] The

---

idem, *Through a Speculum That Shines: Vision and Imagination in Medieval Jewish Mysticism* [Princeton: Princeton University Press, 1994], 82–85) argues that the expression ירידה למרכבה refers primarily to the final stage of the heavenly ascent, i.e., the entrance of the mystic into the heavenly throne-room, and to his personal enthronement, not to the visionary journey as a whole. Annelies Kuyt ("Once Again: Yarad in Hekhalot Literature," *FJB* 18 [1990]: 45–69; idem, *The "Descent" to the Chariot: Towards a Description of the Terminology, Place, Function and Nature of the Yeridah in Hekhalot Literature* [TSAJ 45; Tübingen: Mohr Siebeck, 1995]) offers a very detailed analysis of all the "descent" passages in the *hekhalot* corpus in which she attempts, with limited success, to define the range of phenomena covered by the terms ירד, ירידה, etc. but makes no attempt to explain what this strange terminology may have meant.

110. Bernard Lewin, ed., *Tractate Jom-Tow, Chagiga and Maschkin* (vol. 4 of *Otzar ha-Geonim;* Haifa: Hebrew University Press Association, 1931), part 2, 13–15. See Alan F. Segal, *Paul the Convert: The Apostolate and Apostasy of Saul the Pharisee* (New Haven: Yale University Press, 1990), 322 n. 77.

111. Scholem, *Major Trends in Jewish Mysticism*, 49–50. Scholem seems to be referring to N. B. Dennys, *The Folklore of China and Its Affinities with That of the Aryan and Semitic Races* (London: Trubner, 1876; repr., Detroit: Tower, 1971), 60–61.

112. E.g., *t. Yoma* 4:6; *b. Yoma* 54b; *Gen. Rab.* 1:4; *Tanh. Qed.* 10. See further Louis Ginzberg, *The Legends of the Jews* (7 vols.; Philadelphia: Jewish Publication Society of America, 1911–38), 1:12–13; Avigdor Aptowitzer, "Bet hamMiqdaš šel Maʿalah ʿal Pi haʾAggadah," *Tarbiz* 2 (1931): 137–53 and 257–77; Raphael Patai, *Man and Temple in Ancient Jewish Myth and Ritual* (2nd ed.; New York: Ktav, 1967), 105–39; Levenson, *Sinai and Zion*, 115–25 and 142–15. See also Josephus, *Ant.* 3.179–187; *War* 5.217–218. See Patai, *Man and Temple*, 112–13.

אבן השתיה, or foundation stone, beneath the altar posesses the attributes of an *omphalos* or "world-navel." Just as the holy of holies is said to be the source of the light that shone forth on the first day of creation, so the foundation stone, immediately outside the sanctuary, is identified with the primordial mound that emerged in the midst of the waters of chaos on day three.[113] Josephus, moreover, tells us that the curtain at the entrance to the sanctuary represented the firmament that was created on day two.[114] Several midrashic sources add a further dimension to this model:

> In the hour when the Holy One, blessed be He, said to Moses: *And make me a sanctuary* (Exod 25:8), Moses said: How shall I know how to make it?
>
> The Holy One, blessed be He, said: Do not be afraid. Just as I created the world and your body, so shall you make the tabernacle.
>
> Whence do we know that this is so? You find in the tabernacle that the frames were fixed into the bases, and in the body the ribs are fixed into the vertebrae, and so in the world the mountains are fixed to the foundations of the earth. In the tabernacle, the frames were covered with gold, and in the body the ribs are covered with flesh, and in the world the mountains are covered and coated with earth. In the tabernacle there were bolts in the frames to keep them upright and in the body limbs and sinews are extended to keep a man upright, and in the world trees and plants are extended in the earth. In the tabernacle there were curtains covering its top and both its sides, and in the body a man's skin covers his limbs and his ribs on both his sides, and in the world the heavens cover the earth on both its sides. In the tabernacle there was the veil dividing the sanctuary from the holy of holies, and in the body the diaphragm divides the heart from the stomach, and in the world it is the firmament that divides the upper waters from the lower waters, as it is said: "… and let it divide the waters from the waters" (Gen 1:6).[115]

As Raphael Patai has demonstrated, this three-way correspondence between the world, the temple, and the human body is well-documented in the midrashic literature. More succinctly, *Midrash Tanhuma* states: "The temple corresponds to the whole world and to the creation of man who is a small world (המשכן שקול כנגד כל העולם וכנגד האדם שהוא עולם קטן)."[116] All this seems strongly to

113. *Gen. Rab.* 3:4 (Julius Theodor and Chanoch Albeck, eds., *Bereschit Rabba mit kritischem Apparat und Kommentar* [2nd ed.; 3 vols.; Jerusalem: Wahrmann, 1965], 1:20); *Tanh. Buber, Bereshit* 112; *Pesiq. Rab Kah.* 21 (ed. Solomon Buber, *Pesiqta de-Rav Kahana* [Lvov: Meqitzei Nirdamim, 1868], 145b); Jellinek, *Bet ha-Midrasch*, 5:63; *Pirqe R. El.* 35. See further Patai, *Man and Temple*, 84–85.

114. Josephus, *War*, 5.212–214. See Morray-Jones, *Transparent Illusion*, 169.

115. Enoch Albeck, ed., *Midraš Berešit Rabbati ex Libro R. Mosis hadDaršan* (1940; repr., Jerusalem: Mĕqiẓei-Nirdamim, 1966/67) 32, lines 8–18 (and see Albeck's notes *ad loc.*). See further Patai, *Man and Temple*, 113–17.

116. *Midr. Tanh., Pequde* §3 (Enoch Zondel ben Joseph, *Midraš Tanhuma'*, 132b).

suggest that the יורד־מרכבה, in making the "ascent" through the levels of the heavenly temple to ערבות־רקיע, the highest firmament, could also be conceptualized (at least in some circles) as "descending" within the temple of his own body to the holy of holies within, where, as in the outer temple, the divine Glory (or Image of God) was believed to dwell. If Segal is right to associate this posture with the "downward" direction of the *merkabah* practice, this would suggest that the "ascent" through the heavens could also sometimes be understood to be a "descent" within the "temple" of the body.

The body of the Glory is the subject of the *Shi'ur Qomah* liturgies of the *hekhalot* tradition, which involve the recitation of the secret names and vast measurements of the limbs and measurements of that body.[117]

> From the soles of His feet to His ankles is one thousand myriad and five hundred *parasangs:* the name of His right ankle is אטרקם, and the name of the left is אוא טרקם.
>
> From His ankles to His knees is nineteen thousand myriad parasangs: the name of His right calf is קנגי and the name of the left is מהריה.
>
> From His knees to His thighs is twelve thousand myriad *parasangs.*[118]

In the following passage of the text, we learn that these measurements are not in human *parasangs* (or Persian miles) but divine ones, each being 120,000 times the length of the universe. The key to this apparently absurd material, which is obviously not intended to be taken literally, is a three-way pun on the Hebrew word גדולה, which is taken to mean (1) majesty, (2) praise and (3) giant size. The underlying idea seems to be that the praise of the created universe, the angels, the community of Israel, and the mystic himself is actually the "substance" of the glorious form in which God manifests himself upon his throne. In other words, the worship of creation is what makes God visible, and by "magnifying" God the mystic causes him to appear in his Glory.

As Peter Schäfer has emphasized, participation in the angelic liturgy was a primary goal of the *hekhalot* practitioners: "The Merkavah mystic represents in his person the participation of Israel in the heavenly liturgy and simultaneously confirms for the earthly congregation that it stands in direct contact with God in its synagogue liturgy."[119] The mystical practice of ascent to the heavenly temple thus maintains the connection between God and his people that had formerly been provided by the earthly temple in Jerusalem. The *merkabah* practitioner in

---

117. See further, Morray-Jones, "The Body of the Glory: Shi'ur Koma Mysticism in Judaism, Gnosticism, and the Epistle to the Ephesians," in Rowland and Morray-Jones, *The Mystery of God.*

118. *Sefer Haqqomah* (ed. Cohen, *Texts and Recensions*), lines 55–59.

119. Schäfer, *Gershom Scholem Reconsidered,* 11 (= idem, *Hekhalot-Studien*, 288).

the innermost *hekhal,* who worships before the throne, performs the mediatorial function of the high priest in the holy of holies.

Recent research has drawn attention to the theme of transformation in the apocalyptic and *merkabah* traditions.[120] There are numerous references in the apocalypses, the *hekhalot* writings, and the midrashic traditions of the heavenly ascent, to the metamorphosis of the mystic's body into a purified angelic or supra-angelic form of fire or light that embodies or reflects the Image of the divine Glory and, like that Glory, expands to fill the universe.[121] This is frequently associated with the idea that the mystic "assumes" or "is clothed with" the divine Name.[122] This transformation was held to be extremely dangerous, should the mystic prove unworthy, but it seems to have been a central goal of the mystical endeavor. This motif is found in several gnostic sources and is surely the background of the language of "glorification" that is encountered in the letters of Paul and other early Christian writings. It seems that the vision of the Glory entailed the transformation of the visionary into an angelic likeness of that Divine Image.

As we have seen, the interior of the temple was identified with the garden of Eden or paradise. One who enters this garden, therefore, recovers "the Glory of Adam" and is conformed to the Image of God.[123] According to rabbinic tradition, the unfallen Adam's body was, like the manifest Glory of the *Shi'ur Qomah,* so great that it filled the universe.[124] This explains the expansion of the visionary's body when he enters the temple and worships before the throne.

The body of the Glory, which both fills and contains the universe, is therefore greater than the temple in which it dwells: "But will God in truth dwell with mortals on earth? Behold, heaven and the heaven of heavens cannot contain you! How much less this house that I have built!" (2 Chr 6:18). If it is true that the "descent to the *merkabah*" was sometimes conceptualized as a journey within or into the "temple" of the practitioner's own body, then the Divine Image or "Glory of Adam" enthroned at the center must likewise be much greater than the outer "house."

The last three chapters of *Hekhalot Rabbati*, at the climax of the mystical ascent, contain a series of hymns that are said to be uttered by the throne of Glory in the presence of God each day and that the mystic himself is instructed to recite.[125] This implies that he is identifying himself with the *merkabah* and asking

---

120. Segal, *Paul the Convert*, 34–71; Himmelfarb, *Ascent to Heaven*; Morray-Jones, "Transformational Mysticism in the Apocalyptic-Merkabah Tradition," *JJS* 43 (1992): 1–31; Wolfson, "*Yeridah la-Merkavah*"; idem, *Through a Speculum That Shines*, 82–85.

121. See especially the account of Enoch's transfomation in *3 En.* 9–15.

122. See Morray-Jones, "Transformational Mysticism," 18–19 and 26–31.

123. See n. 94 above.

124. See, e.g., *b. Sanh.* 38b; *Gen. Rab.* 8:1; 21:3.

125. Schäfer, *Synopse*, §§251–77.

God to be enthroned upon or within him. In other words, he is offering himself as a bodily "vehicle" for the manifestation of the Divine Image or Glory.

I suggest that the "descent within" and the "ascent without" may best be understood as two aspects or dimensions of a single transformational process, not mutually exclusive conceptual alternatives. The one who enters the holy of holies gains access to the highest heaven, since the courts of the temple are in symbolic reality the levels of the cosmos. Since this same structure obtains within the "temple" of the human body, the process of the heavenly journey may be enacted both "within" and "outside of" the body of the practitioner, who may thus be said both to "descend" and to "ascend." These observations may perhaps help to explain the cryptic utterance of Paul, when he states twice that he ascended into paradise (i.e., the heavenly holy of holies), "whether in the body or outside of the body, I do not know: God knows" (2 Cor 12:2–3).

The image of the body as a temple occurs several times in the New Testament. In John 2:19–21 (and, probably, parallels: Matt 26:61; 27:40; Mark 14:58; 15:29), Jesus' body is compared with the Jerusalem temple. In 1 Cor 6:19, Paul calls the body of the individual Christian "a temple (ναός) of the Holy Spirit." Elsewhere he makes the same statement of the church (1 Cor 3:9–17; 2 Cor 6:16), which is also very frequently called Christ's body. We recall that at Qumran the community regarded itself as the embodiment of the celestial temple.

The same theme occurs in Eph 2:14–16. Here the church is a both a new creation and a resurrected body. Christ has abolished "the law (תורה) of the commandments (מצוות) in ordinances (הלכות)," which formerly divided one section of the body of humanity from the rest. This is also expressed in temple imagery ("the middle wall of the partition").[126] Thus, the Gentiles are no longer excluded from the worship of the holy community. This metaphor, which is developed in some detail in the following verses, reflects the structural imagery of the *merkabah* tradition: "body" and "temple" are complementary expressions of the same paradoxical reality. The Glory of the Lord, the Divine Image, is enthroned at the center "within" but at the same time comprehends all things within himself (2:21–22). This interweaving of body and temple imagery appears to be deeply indebted to the traditions that we have been considering. Finally, consider Eph 4:7–13:

> [7] But to each one of us was given grace according to the measure (κατὰ τὸ μέτρον) of the gift of Christ, [8] wherefore it is said: Having ascended to the height, he led captivity captive; he gave gifts to men (Ps 68:19). [9] Now what does "ascended" mean, except that he also [first] descended into the lower [regions] of the earth (τὸ δὲ Ἀνέβη τί ἐστιν, εἰ μὴ ὅτι καὶ [πρῶτον] κατέβη εἰς τὰ κατώτερα [μέρη] τῆς γῆς[127])? [10] The one who has descended is himself the one who has

126. See Michael D. Goulder, "The Visionaries of Laodicea," *JSNT* 43 (1991): 29–31.

127. The two words given in brackets are found only in some manuscripts.

ascended far above the heavens, so that he might fill all things. [11] And he gave some to be apostles, and some to be prophets, and some to be evangelists, and some to be shepherds, and some to be teachers, [12] for the equipping of the holy ones for the work of ministry, for the building up of the body of Christ, [13] until we all arrive at the unity of the faith and the full knowledge of the Son of God, at a man of complete maturity, at the measure of the stature of the fullness of Christ (εἰς μέτρον ἡλικίας τοῦ πληρώματος τοῦ Χριστοῦ).

Here Christ is identified with the Divine Glory that fills the universe (cf. Isa 6:3). The members of his church participate in that spiritual-bodily transformation, which is described in terms that are highly reminiscent of the *Shi'ur Qomah* (vv. 7 and 12). The (misquoted) citation of Ps 68:19 links this passage to the Shavuot-*merkabah* cycle discussed above and to the traditions about Moses' heavenly ascent. The language of "ascent" and "descent" in verses 6 and 9–10 is ambiguous and puzzling. This is remarkably similar to the characteristic language of the *merkabah* tradition. Christ, his church, and its individual members have become the body of God's Glory. In this new and "glorified" creation, the former distinction between "sacred" and "profane" is abrogated, and the purity laws associated with the temple cult are therefore rendered meaningless (cf. Heb 10:1–13). Since the very structure of the temple, with its ascending degrees of purity and danger, is conceived as both a barrier and a means of approach between the holy and the unholy, it is rendered obsolete by the convergence of heaven and earth in one spiritually transformed "body," made mystically one with the fullness of the everlasting Glory (cf. Rev 21).

4. Concluding Remarks

According to the Hebrew Bible, the earthly temple is the embodiment of a celestial archetype: the heavenly palace and throne room of the Lord. In Isaiah's vision, the distinction between these two levels of reality seems to disappear. In the literature of the Second Temple period, this symbolic correspondence acquires cosmological significance. The cosmos itself is now conceptualized as a temple, and the earthly temple reflects this structure. Its seven (or three) courts and chambers, centered on the holy of holies, correspond to the celestial levels. In the apocalyptic-*merkabah* tradition, the visionary ascends to heaven by entering a temple whose interior is greater than its exterior, an image that expresses the opposing dimensional structures of the temple courts and the (three or) seven heavens, which are nonetheless considered to be identical. There he participates in the angelic worship of the "Great Glory," enthroned in the central chamber, and is himself transformed into an angelic likeness of that Glory. There is some evidence in the later sources to suggest that this "ascent to heaven" may also sometimes have been conceptualized as a "descent" within the "temple" of the visionary's own body. The fourfold correspondence of temple, cosmos, community and body is represented in figure 1 on page 178.

Many of these ideas are encountered in the *Songs of the Sabbath Sacrifice*, a liturgical text the performance of which may be interpreted as the ritual construction by the worshiping community, in association with the angelic hosts, of a seven-tiered temple, which is identified with that of Ezekiel. This temple not merely reflects but actually embodies the structure of the cosmos, for its seven sanctuaries are the seven heavens. The construction of this imaginary temple is completed on the eleventh Sabbath, which falls on the day before the annual ceremony of the renewal of the sect's covenant at Shavuot, partially preserved in 4QBerakhot. On the Sabbaths following this ceremony of rededication, the Divine Glory descends on the *merkabah* to indwell the temple that has been constructed and to receive the pure sacrifices that are offered in it (songs 12–13). If this analysis is correct, a unified liturgical framework links the *Sabbath Songs* to 4QBerakhot. It is perhaps legitimate to suspect that the *Songs of the Maskil* may also belong within this framework.

Despite repeated references to the recovery of Adam's lost glory, the theme of correspondence between the temple and the body is not developed in the Qumran sources. Instead, we find an emphasis on the embodiment of the temple archetype in the structure of the community as a whole. The rabbinic writings, in contrast, posit a three-way correspondence between cosmos, temple, and body but make no reference to the correspondence between temple and community. All of these themes, however, are taken up and developed in combination by the Christian writers, who regarded their Savior-Messiah as "a great high priest who has gone through the heavens" (Heb 4:14) and for whom the image of the holy community as both body and temple was of central importance in the formulation of their faith.

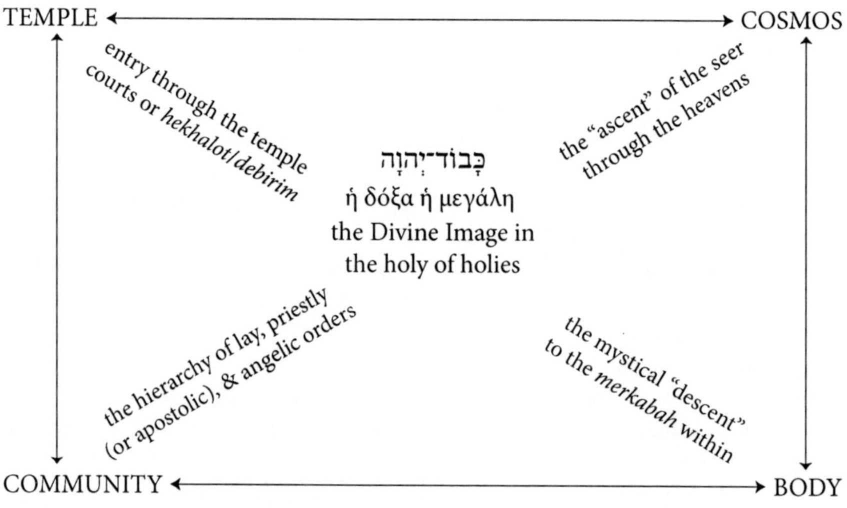

Figure 1. Approaches to the Glory

God's Face in the Enochic Tradition

Andrei A. Orlov

> Moses said, "Show me your glory, I pray." And he said, "I will make all my goodness pass before you, and will proclaim before you the name, YHWH, and I will be gracious to whom I will be gracious, and will show mercy on whom I will show mercy. But," he said, "you cannot see my face; for no one shall see me and live." And the LORD continued, "See, there is a place by me where you shall stand on the rock. And while my glory passes by I will put you in a cleft of the rock, and I will cover you with my hand until I have passed by. Then I will take away my hand, and you shall see my back; but my face shall not be seen." (Exod 33:18–23)

Exodus 33:18–23 depicts Moses asking the Lord to show him his glory. Instead, the Lord agrees to proclaim his name before Moses, telling him that it is impossible for a human being to see God's face.

In recent scholarship this prominent motif of Moses' story has become a stumbling block for students of the Hebrew Bible. Currently most biblical scholars agree upon apparent difficulties in the literary-critical analysis of this section of Exodus. Martin Noth comments that "a literary-critical analysis of Exod 33 is probably impossible."[1] Bervard Childs confirms that there are several fundamental exegetical problems with Exod 33:18–23 and that "the most difficult one is to determine the role of this passage in its larger context."[2]

The internal logic of the passage about the divine face is also problematic. The whole narrative about God's פנים in Exod 33 is quite perplexing. Exodus 33:11 informs a reader that God would speak to Moses face to face (פנים אל פנים) as a person speaks with a friend. A few verses later, in 33:14–15, God promises Moses that his face will go (פני ילכו) with him. In the context of these promises and early

* The first draft of this paper was presented in 2000 to the Early Jewish and Christian Mysticism Group at the Annual Meeting of the Society of Biblical Literature and appeared in the *Society of Biblical Literature 2000 Seminar Papers* (SBLSP39; Atlanta: Scholars Press, 2000), 130–47.

1. Martin Noth, *History of Pentateuchal Traditions* (trans. B. A. Anderson; Englewood Cliffs, N.J.: Prentice-Hall, 1972), 31 n. 114.

2. Brevard S. Childs, *The Book of Exodus: A Critical, Theological Commentary* (Philadelphia: Westminster, 1974), 595.

testimonies about "face-to-face" relationships, it comes as a surprise that in 33:20 the Lord suddenly rejects Moses' request to see his face (לא תוכל לראת את־פני).

It is clear that the anthropomorphic tradition about the divine face in Exod 33 has a fragmentary character.[3] It may well contain polemics between the anthropomorphic position of the J source and the Deuteronomic theology of the divine name: instead of seeing of God's face, the Lord offers Moses to hear his name.[4] Noth observes that Exod 33 can be seen as "a conglomeration of secondary accretions."[5]

The apparent difficulties one encounters in clarifying the concept of the divine face within the context of the known sources of the Pentateuch call for an investigation of the broader biblical and extrabiblical traditions where this motif could be possibly preserved in its extended form. Implicitly linked to the "original" Exodus motif, these later "interpretations" might provide some additional insights that may help us better understand the fragmentary tradition preserved in Exod 33. This essay will focus on one of the possible echoes of Exod 33: the theophanic tradition of the divine countenance preserved in the corpus of the Enochic writings.

---

3. Antony F. Campbell and Mark A. O'Brien (*Sources of the Pentateuch: Texts, Introductions, Annotations* [Minneapolis: Fortress, 1993], 263) placed Exod 33 within the nonsource texts.

4. The Old Testament materials reveal complicated polemics for and against an anthropomorphic understanding of God. Scholars agree that the anthropomorphic imagery of the Hebrew Bible was "crystallized" in the tradition known to us as the Priestly source (Moshe Weinfeld, *Deuteronomy and the Deuteronomic School* [Oxford: Clarendon, 1972], 191). Theological developments of the Priestly tradition demonstrate that the anthropomorphism of the Priestly source is intimately connected with the place of divine habitation. In this tradition, "in which the Divinity is personalized and depicted in the most tangible corporeal similitudes," God, who possesses a human form, has a need for a house or tabernacle (ibid.). Weinfeld rightly observes that this anthropomorphic position was not entirely an invention of the Priestly source but derived from early sacral conceptions found in the early sourses. In these traditions the Deity was sitting in his house ensconced between the two cherubim, and at his feet rested the ark, his footstool. In spite of the active promulgation of anthropomorphic concepts in some Old Testament materials, such as J, P, and Ezekelian sources, the Hebrew Bible also contains polemics against God's corporeality. Scholars note the sharp opposition of the book of Deuteronomy and the Deuteronomic school to the anthropomorphism of the Priestly source and early anthropomorphic traditions. In their opinion, the Deuteronomic school "first initiated the polemic against the anthropomorphic and corporeal conceptions of the Deity and … it was afterwards taken up by the prophets Jeremiah and Deutero-Isaiah" (ibid., 198). In contrast to the anthropomorphic imagery of J and P, the Deuteronomic school promulgated an anticorporeal theology of "divine name" with its conception of sanctuary (tabernacle) as the place where only God's name dwells. On Deuteronomic antianthropomorphism, see T. N. D. Mettinger, *The Dethronement of Sabaoth: Studies in the Shem and Kabod Theologies* (ConBOT 18; Lund: Wallin & Dalholm, 1982); Weinfeld, *Deuteronomy and the Deuteronomic School*, 191–209.

5. Noth, *History of Pentateuchal Traditions*, 31 n. 114.

1. The Face of the Lord

The *Slavonic Apocalypse of Enoch*, a Jewish text apparently written in the first century C.E., [6] contains two striking theophanic descriptions involving the motif of

6. On *2 Enoch*, see Iosif D. Amusin, *Kumranskaja Obshchina* (Moscow: Nauka, 1983); Francis Andersen, "2 (Slavonic Apocalypse of) Enoch," *OTP* 1:91–221; G. Nathanael Bonwetsch, *Das slavische Henochbuch* (AGWG, 1; Berlin: Weidmannsche Buchhandlung, 1896); idem, *Die Bücher der Geheimnisse Henochs: Das sogenannte slavische Henochbuch* (TU 44; Leipzig: Hinrichs, 1922); Christfried Böttrich, *Weltweisheit, Menschheitsethik, Urkult: Studien zum slavischen Henochbuch* (WUNT 2.50; Tübingen: Mohr Siebeck, 1992); idem, *Das slavische Henochbuch* (Gütersloh: Gütersloher Verlaghaus, 1995); idem, *Adam als Mikrokosmos: Eine Untersuchung zum slavischen Henochbuch* (Frankfurt am Main: Lang, 1995); R. H. Charles and William Richard Morfill, *The Book of the Secrets of Enoch* (Oxford: Clarendon, 1896); James H. Charlesworth, "The SNTS Pseudepigrapha Seminars at Tübingen and Paris on the Books of Enoch (Seminar Report)," *NTS* 25 (1979): 315–23; idem, *The Old Testament Pseudepigrapha and the New Testament: Prolegomena for the Study of Christian Origins* (SNTSMS 54; Cambridge: Cambridge University Press, 1985); John J. Collins, "The Genre of Apocalypse in Hellenistic Judaism," in *Apocalypticism in the Mediterranean World and the Near East* (ed. D. Hellholm; Tübingen: Mohr Siebeck, 1983); Léon Gry, "Quelques noms d'anges ou d'êtres mystérieux en II Hénoch," *RB* 49 (1940): 195–203; Ulrich Fischer, *Eschatologie und Jenseitserwartung im hellenistischen Diasporajudentum* (BZNW 44; Berlin: de Gruyter, 1978); Annie S. D. Maunder, "The Date and Place of Writing of the *Slavonic Book of Enoch*," *The Observatory* 41 (1918): 309–16; Nikita Meshcherskij, "Sledy pamjatnikov Kumrana v staroslavjanskoj i drevnerusskoj literature (K izucheniju slavjanskih versij knigi Enoha)," *Trudy otdela drevnerusskoj literatury* 19 (1963): 130–47; idem, "K voprosu ob istochnikah slavjanskoj knigi Enoha," *Kratkie soobshchenija Instituta narodov Azii* 86 (1965): 72–78; Jozef T. Milik, ed., *The Books of Enoch: Aramaic Fragments of Qumrân Cave 4* (with the collaboration of Matthew Black; Oxford: Clarendon, 1976); Hugo Odeberg, *3 Enoch or the Hebrew Book of Enoch* (New York: Ktav, 1973); Andrei Orlov, "Titles of Enoch-Metatron in *2 Enoch*," *JSP* 18 (1998): 71–86; idem, "Melchizedek Legend of 2 (Slavonic) Enoch," *JSP* 32 (2000) 23–38; Shlomo Pines, "Eschatology and the Concept of Time in the *Slavonic Book of Enoch*," in *Types of Redemption* (ed. R. J. Zwi Werblowsky; SHR 18; Leiden: Brill, 1970): 72–87; Arie Rubinstein, "Observations on the *Slavonic Book of Enoch*," *JJS* 15 (1962): 1–21; Paolo Sacchi, *Jewish Apocalyptic and Its History* (JSPSup 20; Sheffield: Sheffield Academic Press, 1996); Aurelio de Santos Otero, "Libro de los secretos de Henoc (Henoc eslavo)," in *Apócrifos del Antiguo Testamento* (ed. A. Díez Macho; Madrid: Cristiandad, 1984), 4:147–202; Gershom Scholem, *Jewish Gnosticism, Merkabah Mysticism and Talmudic Tradition* (New York: Jewish Theological Seminary of America, 1965); M. I. Sokolov, "Materialy i zametki po starinnoj slavjanskoj literature: Vypusk tretij, VII. Slavjanskaja Kniga Enoha Pravednogo. Teksty, latinskij perevod i izsledovanie. Posmertnyj trud avtora prigotovil k izdaniju M. Speranskij," *Chtenija v Obshchestve Istorii i Drevnostej Rossijskih* 4 (1910); Michael E. Stone, "Apocalyptic Literature," in *Jewish Writings of the Second Temple Period: Apocrypha, Pseudepigrapha, Qumran Sectarian Writings, Philo, Josephus.* (ed. M. E. Stone; CRINT 2.2; Philadelphia: Fortress, 1984), 406–8; André Vaillant, *Le livre des secrets d'Hénoch: Texte slave et traduction française* (Paris: Institut d'Études Slaves, 1952); James C. VanderKam, *Enoch: A Man for All Generations* (Columbia: University of South Carolina Press, 1995).

the divine face. The first one occurs in *2 En.* 22,[7] which portrays Enoch's encounter with the Lord in the celestial realm. Enoch recounts:

> I saw the view of the face of the Lord, like iron made burning hot in a fire and brought out, and it emits sparks and is incandescent. Thus even I saw the face of the Lord. But the face of the Lord is not to be talked about, it is so very marvelous and supremely awesome and supremely frightening. And who am I to give an account of the incomprehensible being of the Lord, and of his face, so extremely strange and indescribable? And how many are his commands, and his multiple voice, and the Lord's throne, supremely great and not made by hands, and the choir stalls all around him, the cherubim and the seraphim armies, and their never-silent singing. Who can give an account of his beautiful appearance, never changing and indescribable, and his great glory? And I fell down flat and did obeisance to the Lord. (*2 En.* 22:1–4, the longer recension)[8]

In chapter 39 Enoch reports this theophanic experience to his sons during his short visit to the earth, adding some new details. Although both portrayals demonstrate a number of terminological affinities, the second account explicitly connects the divine face with the Lord's anthropomorphic "extent." The following account is drawn from the shorter recension of *2 Enoch:*

> And now, my children it is not from my lips that I am reporting to you today, but from the lips of the Lord who has sent me to you. As for you, you hear my words, out of my lips, a human being created equal to yourselves; but I have heard the words from the fiery lips of the Lord. For the lips of the Lord are a furnace of fire, and his words are the fiery flames which come out. You, my children, you see my face, a human being created just like yourselves; I am one who has seen the face of the Lord,[9] like iron made burning hot by a fire, emitting sparks. For you gaze into my eyes, a human being created just like yourselves;

---

7. In this paper I have used Andersen's ("2 [Slavonic Apocalypse of] Enoch,") English translation of *2 Enoch* and follow his division in chapters.

8. Ibid., 136. The shorter recension of the Slavonic text gives a less elaborate description of the Lord's appearance: "I saw the Lord. His face was strong and very glorious and terrible. Who (is) to give an account of the dimensions of the being of the face of the Lord, strong and very terrible? Or his many-eyed ones and many-voiced ones, and the supremely great throne of the Lord, not made by hands, or those who are in attendance all around him, the cherubim and the seraphim armies, or how unvarying and indescribable and never-silent and glorious is his service. And I fell down flat and did obeisance to the Lord" (see ibid., 137). Andersen observes that the absence of the comparison with hot iron in manuscripts of the shorter recension shows the embarrassment of scribes over this attempt to describe the Lord's appearance.

9. Slavonic: lice Gospodne. See André Vaillant, *Le livre des secrets d'Hénoch: Texte slave et traduction française* (Paris: Institut D'Études Slaves, 1952), 38. Unless noted otherwise, this and the subsequent Slavonic citations are drawn from Vaillant's edition.

> but I have gazed into the eyes of the Lord, like the rays of the shining sun[10] and terrifying the eyes of a human being. You, my children, you see my right hand beckoning you, a human being created identical to yourselves; but I have seen the right hand of the Lord, beckoning me, who fills heaven. You see the extent of my body, the same as your own; but I have seen the extent of the Lord,[11] without measure and without analogy, who has no end.... To stand before the King, who will be able to endure the infinite terror of the great burning. (*2 En.* 39:3–8)[12]

In both theophanic descriptions the notion of the Lord's "face" plays a crucial role. It is not a coincidence that in both of them the "face" is associated with light and fire. In biblical theophanies smoke and fire often serve as a divine envelope that protects mortals from the sight of the divine form. Radiant luminosity emitted by the Deity fulfills the same function, signaling the danger of the direct vision of the divine form. Luminosity also represents the screen that protects the Deity from the necessity of revealing its true form. Scholars note that in some theophanic traditions God's form remains hidden behind his light.[13] The hidden כבוד is revealed through this light, which serves as the luminous screen, "the face" of this anthropomorphic extent. The theophanies of *2 Enoch* that use the metaphors of light and fire may well be connected with such traditions where the divine "extent" is hidden behind the incandescent "face" that covers and protects the sovereignty of the Lord.

In *2 En.* 39:3–6 the "face" is closely associated with the divine "extent" and seems to be understood not simply as a part of the Lord's body (face) but as a radiant *façade* of his anthropomorphic "form."[14] This identification between the

---

10. The important detail of this description is solar symbolism, which plays an important role in *2 Enoch*. The text often uses solar metaphors in various descriptions of angelic beings, e.g., in *2 En.* 1, where Enoch meets two angels with "faces like the shining sun." Later, during his heavenly journey, Enoch sees "a group of seven angels, brilliant and very glorious with faces more radiant than the radiance of the sun." The images of fire and light are often involved in these solar descriptions of angelic hosts. The text pictures "glorious and shining and many-eyed stations of the Lord's servants ... and of the ranks of powerful fireborn heavenly armies." Andersen rightly observes that "fire and light are fundamental elements in the physics of *2 Enoch*" (Andersen, "2 [Slavonic Apocalypse of] Enoch," 104).

11. Slavonic: objatie Gospodne. Vaillant, *Le livre des secrets d'Hénoch*, 38.

12. Manuscripts of the longer recension do not demonstrate substantial differences with this description.

13. April DeConick's (*Seek to See Him: Ascent and Vision Mysticism in the Gospel of Thomas* [SVC 33; Leiden: Brill, 1996], 104–5) pioneering research shows that in Enochic traditions God's form remains hidden behind his light.

14. Gershom Scholem's research on the presence of the שיעור קומה traditions in *2 En.* 39 helps to clarify the "anthropomorphic" character of the Lord's "extent" in *2 Enoch*. See his lecture "The Age of *Shiur Qomah* Speculation and a Passage in Origen" in idem, *Jewish Gnosticism, Merkabah Mysticism.*

Lord's face and the Lord's "form" is reinforced by an additional parallel pair in which Enoch's face is identified with Enoch's "form":

> You, my children, you see my face, a human being created just like yourselves; but I am one who has seen the face of the Lord, like iron made burning hot by a fire, emitting sparks.... And you see the form of my body, the same as your own: but I have seen the form (extent) of the Lord, without measure and without analogy, who has no end. (*2 En.* 39:3–6)

The association between the divine face and divine form in *2 En.* 39:3–6 alludes to the biblical tradition from Exod 33:18–23 where the divine *panim* is mentioned in connection with his glorious divine form: God's *kavod*:[15]

> Then Moses said, "Now show me your glory (כבדך)." And the Lord said, " I will cause all my goodness to pass in front of you, and I will proclaim my name, the Lord, in your presence ... but," he said, "you cannot see my face (פני), for no one may see me and live."

It is clear that in the biblical passage the impossibility of seeing the Lord's face is understood not simply as the impossibility of seeing the particular part of the Lord but rather as the impossibility of seeing the complete range of his glorious "body." The logic of the whole passage, which employs such terms as God's "face" and God's "back," suggests that the term *panim* refers to the "forefront" of the divine extent. The imagery of the divine face found in Psalms[16] also favors this motif of the identity between the Lord's face and his anthropomorphic "form." For example, in Ps 17:15 the Lord's face is closely associated with his form or likeness (תמונה): "As for me, I shall behold your face (פניך)[17] in righteousness;

---

15. The term כבוד can be translated as "substance," "body," "mass," "power," "might," "honor," "glory," and "splendor." In its meaning as "glory" כבוד usually refers to God, his sanctuary, his city, or sacred paraphernalia. The Priestly tradition uses the term in connection with God's appearances in the tabernacle. P and Ezekiel describe כבוד as a blazing fire surrounded by radiance and a great cloud. See Moshe Weinfeld, "כבוד," *TDOT* 7:22–38.

16. On the face of God in the Psalms, see Samuel Balentine, *The Hidden God: The Hiding of the Face of God in the Old Testament* (Oxford: Oxford University Press, 1983), 49–65; Walther Eichrodt, *Theology of the Old Testament* (2 vols; Philadelphia: Westminster, 1967), 2:35–39; Michael Fishbane, "Form and Reformulation of the Biblical Priestly Blessing," *JAOS* 103 (1983): 115–21; Joseph Reindl, *Das Angesicht Gottes im Sprachgebrauch des Alten Testaments* (ETS 25; Leipzig: St. Benno, 1970), 236–37; Mark S. Smith, "Seeing God in the Psalms: The Background to the Beatific Vision in the Hebrew Bible," *CBQ* 50 (1988): 171–83.

17. Note also that the poetic rhyme תמונתך/פניך further reinforces the correspondence between the face and the form of God in this passage.

when I awake, I shall be satisfied with beholding your form (תמונתך)."[18] It is evident that all three accounts, Exod 33:18–23, Ps 17:15, and *2 En.* 39:3–6, represent a single tradition in which the divine face serves as the *terminus technicus* for the designation of the Lord's anthropomorphic extent.

Apparently all these accounts deal with the specific anthropomorphic manifestation known as God's *kavod*.[19] The possibility of such identification is already hinted in Exod 33, where Moses, who asks the Lord to show Moses the Lord's *kavod*, receives the answer that it is impossible for him to see the Lord's "face." The correlation of the divine face with "likeness"(תמונה) in Ps 17:15 can be also an allusion to *kavod*, which in Ezek 1:28 is described as "the likeness of the glory of the Lord (דמות כבוד־יהוה)."

There is another early Mosaic account that correlates the Sinai encounter with *kavod*. This important tradition, found in the fragments of the drama *Exodus* written by Ezekiel the Dramatist, depicts Moses' experience at Sinai as the vision of God's anthropomorphic *kavod*.[20]

> I dreamt there was on the summit of mount Sinai
> A certain great throne (θρόνον μέγαν) extending up to heaven's cleft,
> On which there sat a certain noble man
> Wearing a crown and holding a great scepter in his left hand.[21]

Wayne Meeks observes that this passage may be safely taken as a witness to traditions of the second century B.C.E., since it was quoted by Alexander Polyhistor, who lived around 80–40 B.C.E.[22] It means that by the second century B.C.E. Moses' association with the divine *kavod*, hinted in Exod 33, was already surrounded by an elaborate imagery, in which the throne of glory played a crucial role.

This theophanic pattern in which the encounter with the divine face is understood as the vision of God's throne is further strengthened in *2 En.* 22, which provides various pieces of evidences that prove that the anthropomorphic

---

18. Although the passage uses a different terminology, namely, the term תמונה, the identification still has a strong anthropomorphic flavor. The term תמונה can be translated as "form," "likeness," "semblance," or representation."

19. Contra Walther Eichrodt, who insists that the *panim* had no connection with the *kavod*. He argues that the two concepts derive from different roots, and were never combined with one another (Eichrodt, *Theology of the Old Testament*, 2:38).

20. Pieter W. van der Horst ("Moses' Throne Vision in Ezekiel the Dramatist," *JJS* 34 [1983]: 24) observes that Ezekiel the Dramatist's vision of God in human shape seated on the throne is based on the first chapter of the biblical Ezekiel.

21. Carl R. Holladay, *Fragments from Hellenistic Jewish Authors* (4 vols.; SBLTT 20, 30, 39–40; Atlanta: Scholars Press, 1989), 2:363.

22. Wayne Meeks, *The Prophet-King: Moses Traditions and the Johannine Christology* (NovTSup 14; Leiden: Brill, 1967), 149. See also Holladay, *Fragments from Hellenistic Jewish Authors*, 2:308–12.

"extent," identified with the divine face, indeed represents the divine *kavod*. The theophany of the divine countenance in the Slavonic apocalypse is surrounded by a peculiar *kavod* imagery, which plays a prominent role in the Ezekelian account. There are several noteworthy parallels.

First, the theophany of the divine face took place in the highest of the heaven.[23] The highest of the heaven is a traditional place of God's throne, the abode of his Glory. A later account found in *3 Enoch* states that "in 'Arabot there are 660 thousands of myriads of glorious angels, hewn out of flaming fire, standing opposite the throne of glory. The glorious King covers his face, otherwise the heaven of 'Arabot would burst open in the middle, because of the glorious brilliance."[24] Second, the theophanic description in *2 En.* 22 refers to "his many-eyed ones,"[25] alluding to האופנים, the wheels, the special class of the angels of the throne who in Ezek 1:18 are described as the angelic beings "full of eyes (מלאת עינים)." Third, a reference to the "many-voiced ones" probably alludes to choirs of angelic hosts surrounding the throne. Fourth, in *2 En.* 22 there is a direct reference to the throne of the Lord, which occupies a central place in the theophanic description and is pictured as "supremely great and not made by hands."[26] The throne of glory is surrounded by the armies of the angelic hosts, cherubim, and seraphim, with "their never-silent singing."[27]

2. Moses' Face

Previous research shows that the correlation between God's face and his luminous form (his glorious *kavod*) was already implicitly articulated in Exod 33. The Enochic theophany found in *2 Enoch* further strengthens this connection, giving a theophanic description of the Lord's face as his terrifying "extent" that emits light and fire.

The important detail of these two accounts is the "danger motif": the warnings about the peril of seeing the Deity. Both of them contain specific references to the harmful effect this theophanic experience has on the mortals who dare to behold the divine face. In Exod 33:20 the Lord warns Moses about the danger of seeing his face: "You cannot see my face, for no one may see me and live." The motif of peril is further reinforced by the Lord's instructions in 33:22, where he commands Moses to hide himself in a cleft in the rock and promises to protect the prophet with his hands.

---

23. Andersen, "2 (Slavonic Apocalypse of) Enoch," 136–37.
24. Philip Alexander, "3 (Hebrew Apocalypse of) Enoch," *OTP* 1:305.
25. Andersen, "2 (Slavonic Apocalypse of) Enoch," 137.
26. Ibid.
27. Ibid.

The danger motif also looms large in *2 Enoch*. In *2 En.* 39, immediately after his description of the theophany of the face, Enoch gives a warning to his children about the danger of this theophanic experience:

> Frightening and dangerous it is to stand before the face of an earthly king, terrifying and very dangerous it is, because the will of the king is death and the will of the king is life. How much more terrifying [and dangerous] it is to stand before the face of the King of earthly kings and of the heavenly armies, [the regulator of the living and of the dead]. Who can endure that endless misery? (*2 En.* 39:8)[28]

The "danger motif" in Exod 33 and in *2 Enoch* implicitly suggests that both of these accounts support the idea that the human being actually can see the face of God. Moshe Weinfeld argues that the warning about the danger of seeing the Deity usually affirms the possibility of such an experience. In his observations about antianthropomorphic tendencies of Deuteronomy, Deutero-Isaiah, and Jeremiah, Weinfeld points to the fact that these texts demonstrate a lack of usual warnings about the danger of seeing the Deity found in pre-Deuteronomic books. He concludes that it happened because the Deuteronomic school could not conceive of the possibility of seeing the Deity.[29]

The possibility of theophany hinted in *2 Enoch* and Exod 33 might suggest that the Exodus account implicitly asserts that Moses could see the divine form.[30] The distinctive details in the depiction of Moses' face in Exod 34 may further support this conclusion. But before we explore this motif, let us again return to the narrative of *2 Enoch*.

From this Enochic account we learn that the vision of the divine face has dramatic consequences for Enoch's appearance. His body endures radical changes as it becomes covered with the divine light. The important detail here is that the luminous transformation of Enoch takes place in front of the radiant "face" of the Lord. In 22:6 Enoch reports that he was lifted up and brought before the Lord's face by the archangel Michael. The Lord decides to appoint Enoch as שר הפנים, the prince of the divine presence: "Let Enoch come up and stand in front of my face forever."[31] Further, the Lord commands the archangel Michael to remove Enoch from earthly clothing, anoint him with the delightful oil, and put him into the clothes of the Lord's glory (22:8–9).[32] The text describes the actions of

28. Ibid., 164.

29. Weinfeld, *Deuteronomy and the Deuteronomic School*, 207.

30. Another "Mosaic" account, attributed to J, openly articulates this possibility: "With him (Moses) I speak mouth to mouth (פה אל־פה), clearly and not in riddles; he sees the form (ותמנת) of the Lord" (Num 12:8).

31. Andersen, "2 (Slavonic Apocalypse of) Enoch," 139.

32. Ibid.

Michael, who anoints Enoch with the delightful oil and clothes him. The symbolism of light permeates the whole scene; the oil emanates the rays of the glittering sun "greater than the greatest light."[33] At the end of this procedure, Enoch "had become like one of the glorious ones, and there was no observable difference." [34]

In Enoch's radiant metamorphosis before the divine face an important detail can be found that links Enoch's transformation with the account in Exodus. In *2 En.* 37 we learn about the unusual procedure performed on Enoch's face during the final stage of his encounter with the Lord: the Lord called one of his senior angels to chill the face of Enoch. The text says that the angel appeared frigid; he was as white as snow, and his hands were as cold as ice. The text further depicts the angel chilling Enoch's face, who could not endure the terror of the Lord, "just as it is not possible to endure the fire of a stove and the heat of the sun." Right after this "chilling procedure," the Lord informs Enoch that, if his face had not been chilled, no human being would be able to look at his face.[35] This reference to the radiance of Enoch's face after his encounter with the Lord is an apparent parallel to the incandescent face of Moses after the Sinai experience in Exod 34.[36]

References to the shining countenance of a visionary found in *2 Enoch* return us again to the Exodus story, where 34:29–35 portrays Moses after his encounter with the Lord.[37] The passage tells that "when Moses came down from Mount Sinai … he was not aware that his face was radiant, because he had spoken with the Lord." The strange logic of the last sentence, which points to an ambiguous connection between the speech of the Lord as a cause of Moses' glowing face, can be explained by the Enochic theophanic account, where "the lips of the Lord are a furnace of fire, and his words are the fiery flames which come out."[38]

---

33. Ibid., 138. Jarl Fossum (*The Image of the Invisible God: Essays on the Influence of Jewish Mysticism on Early Christology* [NTOA 30; Göttingen: Vandenhoeck & Ruprecht, 1995], 84) provides a number of allusions to the theme of "shining oil" in *2 Enoch*.

34. Andersen ("2 [Slavonic Apocalypse of] Enoch," 139) observes that "this motif [Enoch's transformation into the glorious angel] seems to have been influenced by the legend of Moses, whose shining face was a reflection of God's magnificent glory."

35. Ibid., 160.

36. About the possible Mesopotamian provenance of this motif, see Menahem Haran, "The Shining of Moses's Face: A Case Study in Biblical and Ancient Near Eastern Iconography [Ex 34:29–35; Ps 69:32; Hab 3:4]," in *In the Shelter of Elyon* (JSOTSup 31; Sheffield: JSOT Press, 1984), 159–73; William Propp, "The Skin of Moses' Face—Transfigured or Disfigured?" *CBQ* 49 (1987): 375–86.

37. On Moses traditions, see R. Bloch, "Die Gestalt des Moses in der rabbinischen Tradition," in *Moses in Schrift und Überlieferung* (Düsseldorf: Patmos, 1963): 95–171; George W. Coats, *Moses: Heroic Man, Man of God* (JSOTSup 57; Sheffield: Sheffield Academic Press, 1988); Scott Hafemann, "Moses in the Apocrypha and Pseudepigrapha: A Survey," *JSP* 7 (1990): 79–104; Meeks, *Prophet-King;* Robert Polzin, *Moses and the Deuteronomist: A Literary Study of the Deuteronomic History* (New York: Seabury, 1980).

38. Andersen, "2 (Slavonic Apocalypse of) Enoch," 163.

These parallels between the later Enochic text and the biblical Mosaic account are not inappropriate. As will be demonstrated later, the connection between the Enochic and Mosaic accounts has quite ancient roots. Evidences of the early link between Enoch and Moses includes the already mentioned drama of Ezekiel the Dramatist, which was apparently written during the second century B.C.E.[39]

Wayne Meeks and Pieter van der Horst observe that the depiction of Moses in the drama of Ezekiel the Dramatist bears some similarities to Enoch's figure in the Enochic traditions.[40] They note a number of remarkable allusions in the drama to the Enochic motifs and themes. First, Moses' account is depicted as his dream vision in a fashion similar to Enoch's dreams in *1* and *2 Enoch*. Second, in the text Moses is "elevated" by God, who gives him the throne, the royal diadem,[41] and the scepter. Third, God appoints Moses as an eschatological judge of humankind able to see "things present, past and future,"[42] the traditional role of Enoch found already in early Enochic booklets. Fourth, Moses is an "expert" in "a variety of things," including cosmological and astronomical information:

> I beheld the entire circled earth
> Both beneath the earth and above the heaven,
> And a host of stars fell on its knees before me;
> I numbered them all,
> They passed before me like a squadron of soldiers.[43]

This preoccupation with various meteorological, astronomical, and eschatological "secrets" are typical duties of the elevated Enoch that are here transferred to Moses, apparently for the first time.[44]

Finally, the motif of assigning the seat/throne is a peculiar feature of Enochic literature where Enoch-Metatron is depicted as a scribe[45] who has a seat (later

39. Holladay, *Fragments from Hellenistic Jewish Authors*, 2:312.

40. Meeks, *Prophet-King*, 147; van der Horst, "Moses' Throne Vision," 21–29.

41. The crowning of Enoch-Metatron became a prominent *leitmotif* in later Enochic tradition, especially, in *3 Enoch*. Meeks observes that the enthronement of Enoch-Metatron in *3 Enoch* "betrays interesting similarities to Moses' traditions" (Meeks, *Prophet-King*, 207). See also van der Horst, who observes that "like Moses, Enoch is assigned a cosmic and divine function that involves the wearing of regalia" ("Moses' Throne Vision," 25).

42. Holladay, *Fragments from Hellenistic Jewish Authors*, 2:367.

43. Ibid., 2:365.

44. R. H. Charles argued that this transition of Enoch's function to Moses first was made in *2 Apocalypse of Baruch*, where God shows Moses "the measures of the fire, also the depths of the abyss, and the weight of the winds, and the number of the drops of rain" (*APOT* 2:514).

45. In *1 En.* 74:2 Enoch writes the instructions of the angel Uriel regarding the secrets of heavenly bodies and their movements. See Michael Knibb, *The Ethiopic Book of Enoch: A New Edition in the Light of the Aramaic Dead Sea Fragments* (2 vols; Oxford: Clarendon, 1978), 2:173. Qumran Enochic fragments (4QEnGiants 14; 4QEn 92:1) picture Enoch as "the scribe of

a throne) in the heavenly realm.[46] For example, in *2 En.* 23:4 the angel Vereveil commands Enoch to sit down:[47] "You sit down; write everything...." Enoch reports, "And I sat down for a second period of 30 days and 30 nights, and I wrote accurately" (23:6).[48] The theme of Enoch-Metatron's seat became a prominent motif in rabbinic tradition, where according to *b.* Hag. 15a the privilege of "sitting" beside God was accorded solely to Metatron by virtue of his character as a "scribe," for he was granted permission as a scribe to sit and write down the merits of Israel.

The tacit links between Enoch and Moses found in the early Enochic theophanic tradition later becomes openly articulated in rabbinic literature. In this later enunciation, as in the initial encounters, the familiar theophanic motif from the Exodus story again plays a crucial role. From *3 Enoch* we learn that it is Enoch-Metatron, whose face once was transformed into fire,[49] who is now the one who tells Moses about his shining visage: "At once Metatron, Prince of the Divine Presence, said to Moses, Son of Amram, fear not! for already God favors you. Ask what you will with confidence and boldness, for light shines from the skin of your face from one end of the world to the other." [50]

distinction" ספר פרשא (Milik, *Books of Enoch*, 261–62 and 305). In *Jubilees* Enoch is attested as "the first of mankind ... who learned (the art of) writing, instruction, and wisdom and who wrote down in a book the signs of the sky" (James C. VanderKam, *The Book of Jubilees* [2 vols.; CSCO 510–511, Scriptores Aethiopici 87–88; Leuven: Peeters, 1989], 2:25–6).

46. Van der Horst ("Moses' Throne Vision," 25) also stresses unique features of Moses' enthronement in Ezekiel the Dramatist, which depart from Enochic and *merkabah* imagery. He observes that "in Moses' vision, there is only one throne, God's. And Moses is requested to be seated on it, not at God's side but all alone. God leaves his throne. This scene is unique in early Jewish literature and certainly implies a deification of Moses."

47. Slavonic: Sjadi. See Vaillant, *Le livre des secrets d'Hénoch,* 26.

48. Andersen, "2 (Slavonic Apocalypse of) Enoch," 141.

49. *3 En.* 15:1 depicts this radiant metamorphosis of Enoch-Metatron: "When the Holy One, blessed be he, took me to serve the throne of glory, the wheels of the chariot and all the needs of the Schekinah, at once my flesh turned to flame, my sinews to blazing fire, my bones to juniper coals, my eyelashes to lightning flashes, my eyeballs to fiery torches, the hairs of my head to hot flames, all my limbs to wings of burning fire, and the substance of my body to blazing fire" (Philip Alexander, "3 (Hebrew Apocalypse of) Enoch," *OTP* 1:267).

50. *3 En.* 15B:5. See ibid., 304. Scholars observes that in *merkabah* tradition Metatron is explicitly identified with the face of God. See April DeConick, "Heavenly Temple Traditions and Valentinian Worship: A Case for First-Century Christology in the Second Century," in *The Jewish Roots of Christological Monotheism* (ed. C. C. Newman, J. R. Davila, and G. S. Lewis; JSJSup 63; Brill: Leiden, 1999), 329; David J. Halperin, *The Faces of the Chariot* (TSAJ 16; Tübingen: Mohr Siebeck, 1988), 424–25.

3. Concluding Remarks

The foregoing research has examined some extrabiblical materials related to the motif of the divine face found in Exod 33. The investigation has shown that the evolution of this motif in later traditions is dependent on Enoch-Moses *gestalt*, which plays a prominent role in Enochic theophanies of the divine face. This research, however, would not be complete without mentioning another important source also related to the traditions about the patriarch Enoch and the prophet Moses. This source is the Priestly editor of the Pentateuch.

Much attention has been devoted to the peculiar interest of the Priestly editor in anthropomorphic descriptions of the Deity.[51] Weinfeld and Mettinger show that the Priestly source played a crucial role in promoting biblical theophanic traditions. In these traditions Moses' figure has occupied an important place.[52]

The Priestly source also was the locus where the enigmatic figure of Enoch for the first time appeared in its esoteric complexity,[53] indicating that the priestly author was cognizant of the broader Enochic developments. Some scholars believe that perhaps it is "to some such developed Enoch tradition that the author of Genesis is making reference when he emits his cryptic statements about Enoch in Genesis 5:22–24."[54] Students of the Enochic tradition are now aware that the Priestly editor was familiar with the peculiar Mesopotamian traditions that constituted a conceptual framework for Enoch's figure.[55]

---

51. On the issue of Old Testament's anthropomorphism, see James Barr, "Theophany and Anthropomorphism in the Old Testament," in *Congress Volume: Oxford, 1959* (VTSup 7; Leiden: Brill, 1960), 31–38; Johannes Hempel, "Die Grenzen des Anthropomorphismus Jahwes im Alten Testament," *ZAW* 57 (1939): 75–85; Frank Michaeli, *Dieu à l'image de l'homme: Étude de la notion anthropomorphique de Dieu dans l'Ancien Testament* (Neuchâtel: Delachaux, 1950); Edmond Jacob, *Théologie de l'Ancien Testament* (Neuchâtel: Delachaux, 1955), 30ff.; Marjo C. A. Korpel, *A Rift in the Clouds: Ugaritic and Hebrew Descriptions of the Divine* (Münster: Ugarit-Verlag, 1990), 87–590; Mettinger, *Dethronement of Sabaoth*.

52. Mettinger, *Dethronement of Sabaoth;* Weinfeld, *Deuteronomy and the Deuteronomic School*, 191–209.

53. The traditions about Enoch are different in J and P. For the discussion of the differences, see James C. VanderKam, *Enoch and the Growth of an Apocalyptic Tradition* (CBQMS 16; Washington, D.C.: Catholic Biblical Association of America, 1984), 23–51; Helge S. Kvanvig, *Roots of Apocalyptic: The Mesopotamian Background of the Enoch Figure and of the Son of Man* (WMANT 61; Neukirchen-Vluyn: Neukirchener, 1988), 40–53.

54. Michael E. Stone, "Enoch, Aramaic Levi and Sectarian Origins," *JSJ* 19 (1988): 162.

55. On the Mesopotamian traditions behind the Enoch's figure, see Heinrich Zimmern, "Urkönige und Uroffenbarung," in *Die Keilinschriften und das Alte Testament* (ed. E. Schrader; 2 vols.; Berlin: Reuther & Reichard, 1903), 2:530–43; Herman L. Jansen, *Die Henochgestalt: Eine vergleichende religionsgeschichtliche Untersuchung* (Norske Videnskaps-Akademi i Oslo II. Hist.-Filos. Klasse 1; Oslo: Dybwad, 1939); Pierre Grelot, "La légende d'Hénoch dans les apocryphes et dans la Bible: Origine et signification," *RSR* 46 (1958): 5–26, 181–210; VanderKam, *Enoch and the Growth;* Helge S. Kvanvig, *Roots of Apocalyptic*. Important witnesses to these traditions

In these Mesopotamian traditions a prototype of Enoch, Enmeduranki, is portrayed as a "translated" figure, the one "who sat in the presence (*maḫar*) of Shamash and Adad, the divine adjudicators."[56] This reference to Enmeduranki's access to the glorious presence/face of the solar deity[57] indicates that the later role of Enoch as *sar hapanim*, the prince of the divine presence or the prince of the face, was already present in its rudimentary form in the Mesopotamian traditions known to the Priestly editor.[58]

---

include the various versions of the so-called Sumerian antediluvian king list, the materials that dated from 1500 to 165 B.C.E. The list demonstrates a number of similarities with the genealogy of Gen 5. One of its interesting details is that Mesopotamian kings, as well as patriarchs from the Genesis account, had extraordinary long reigns, ranging from 3,600 to 72,000 years. A second important parallel is that two versions of the list give ten kings, the last of whom is designated as the hero of the flood. It demonstrates a close resemblance to the role of Noah, who occupies the tenth place in the list of Gen 5. VanderKam notes that "in the literature on Genesis 5 there is a well established tradition which holds that P modeled his pre-flood genealogy on a Mesopotamian list of antediluvian kings, the so-called Sumerian King List" (VanderKam, *Enoch and the Growth*, 26). An important character in the Sumerian King list is Enmeduranki (Enmeduranna), the king of Sippar, the city of the sun-god Shamash. In three copies of the list he occupies the seventh place, which in the Genesis genealogy belongs to Enoch. Moreover, in other Mesopotamian sources Enmeduranki appears in many roles and situations that demonstrate remarkable similarities with Enoch's story. VanderKam's research shows that the priestly author was aware of these broader Mesopotamian traditions that served as a prototype for Enoch's figure, whose symbolical age of 365 years reflects the link between the patriarch and the solar cult of Shamash. VanderKam concludes that "the biblical image of Enoch is based on the Mesopotamian picture of Enmeduranki" (ibid., 50).

56. Wilfred G. Lambert, "Enmeduranki and Related Matters," *JCS* 21 (1967): 128 and 130. In another text about Enmeduranki the same motif of the divine presence can be found: "he may approach the presence (*maḫar*) of Shamash and Adad" (ibid., 132).

57. On Mesopotamian solar symbolism and its influence on biblical concepts, including the concept of the divine *panim*, see André Caquot, "La Divinité Solaire Ougaritique," *Syria* 36 (1959): 90–101; Bernd Janowski, *Rettungsgewissheit und Epiphanie des Heils* (WMANT 59; Neukirchen-Vluyn, Neukirchener, 1989), 1:105ff.; Birgit Lang, *Gott als "Licht" in Israel und Mesopotamien: Eine Studie zu Jes. 60:1–3.19f* (OBS 7; Klosterneuburg: Österreichisches Katholische Bibelwerk, 1989); Willem Smelik, "On Mystical Transformation of the Righteous into Light in Judaism," *JSJ* 26 (1995): 122–44; Mark S. Smith, *The Early History of God: Yahweh and the Other Deities in Ancient Israel* (San Francisco: Harper & Row, 1990); idem, "The Near Eastern Background of Solar Language for Yahweh," *JBL* 109 (1990): 29–39; Hans-Peter Stähli, *Solare Elemente im Jahweglauben des Alten Testaments* (OBO 66; Fribourg: Universitätsverlag; Göttingen: Vandenhoeck & Ruprecht, 1985).

58. Some scholars argue that the biblical concept of the divine face also has Mesopotamian roots. Michael Fishbane ("Form and Reformulation," 115–21) and Mark S. Smith ("'Seeing God' in the Psalms," 171–83) show that the language of the Lord's shining face was part of Israel's inheritance from ancient Near Eastern culture. Fishbane stresses that "the various and abundant use of such imagery in ancient Near Eastern literature, particularly from Mesopotamia where it recurs in a wide range of genres, suggests that ancient Israel absorbed such imagery as part and parcel of its rich patrimony" ("Form and Reformulation," 116).

In the light of these observations, the idea that Exod 33 could actually contain the original Enochic motif is not inappropriate. The implicit link between the Enochic account of the divine presence and the Mosaic account of the divine *panim* may well reflect the conceptual world of the Priestly editor, who often "has expressed his acquaintance with a fairly broad range of Mesopotamian traditions in remarkably few words."[59]

59. VanderKam, *Enoch and the Growth*, 50.

Wheels of Time in the Apocalypse of Jesus Christ

Cameron C. Afzal

> At once I was in the spirit, and there in heaven stood a throne, with one seated on the throne! And the one seated there looks like jasper and carnelian, and around the throne is a rainbow that looks like an emerald. Around the throne are twenty-four thrones, and seated on the thrones are twenty-four elders, dressed in white robes, with golden crowns on their heads. Coming from the throne are flashes of lightning, and rumblings and peals of thunder, and in front of the throne burn seven flaming torches, which are the seven spirits of God. And in front of the throne there is something like a sea of glass, like crystal. (Rev 4:2–6)

The *merkabah* vision of Rev 4 announces the majesty of God, introduces the drama of the heavenly court, and provides the transition from the prophetic letters beginning the book to the visionary cycles in which are proclaimed a Christian understanding of the true workings of the cosmos. A significant aspect of this message involves the author's perception of a melding of the heavenly and earthly realities over which God has control. The book proclaims a working out on earth of God's will as the author "sees" it being accomplished in the heavenly realm. In a sense the visions of the Apocalypse portray realizations of the petition in the Lord's prayer, "Your will be done on earth as it is in heaven."

This study involves an examination of some of the presuppositions needed to understand a revelation of God's activity on behalf of his people as presented by the early Christian prophet, John of Patmos, in his work the Apocalypse of Jesus Christ. Although New Testament scholars have long noted the use of Ezekiel in the throne vision of Rev 4–5,[1] it was not until the work of Ithmar Gruenwald,

1. Among the more prominent commentators, see R. H. Charles, *A Critical and Exegetical Commentary on the Revelation of St. John* (ICC; 2 vols.; Edinburgh: T&T Clark, 1920), 1:119; George Bradford Caird, *The Revelation of St. John the Divine* (HNTC; New York: Harper & Row, 1966), 63–64; Henry Barclay Swete, *The Apocalypse of John* (3rd ed.; London: Macmillan, 1909), 69–70; Pierre Prigent, *L'Apocalypse de Saint Jean* (CNT; Paris: Delachaux & Niestlé, 1981), 82–83. On John's use of Ezekiel in general throughout Revelation, see also Jean-Pierre Ruiz, *Ezekiel in the Apocalypse: The Transformation of Prophetic Language in Revelation 16,17–19,10* (European University Studies Theology Series 23; Frankfurt: Lang, 1989).

Apocalyptic and Merkavah Mysticism, that this vision was set clearly in the context of an emerging Jewish *merkabah* mysticism.[2]

The work of David J. Halperin, *The Faces of the Chariot*, places this segment of the Apocalypse in the context of a continuing stream of what he has come to call *merkabah* exegesis.[3] *Ma'aseh merkabah* represented a form of piety that in first-century Jewish Palestine was considered productive and indeed praiseworthy. However, by the time of the Mishnah, *merkabah* speculation became feared in mainstream rabbinic circles, who warned the casual speculator away from this pursuit. The vision in the Apocalypse remains perhaps our fullest first-century artifact of this form of Jewish piety. Though the Revelation is clearly the work of a Christian Jew (that is a Jew who believes Jesus is the Messiah of Israel whom God has raised from the dead), this need not distract us from the fact that his work represents unique evidence of the kind of *merkabah* exegesis only hinted at or referred to obliquely in later rabbinic materials. The Apocalypse of John is therefore an important part of the puzzle, not only of the bridge between Palestinian and Gentile Christianity but between apocalyptic forms of intertestamental Judaism and non-Christian Jewish mystical speculation.

The purpose of this study is to examine John's use of sources in creating and presenting his own version of the *merkabah* and how he puts it at the disposal of his Christian prophetic message to the churches of Asia Minor. Specifically, I wonder what governs John's choice in his use of sources. My essay supports and develops the position that the *merkabah* as portrayed in this book is dependent on an ongoing tradition of *merkabah* exegesis. The vision of the Apocalypse is a snapshot, so to speak, of a continuing stream of *merkabah* exegesis and as such develops and manipulates a communal icon of the *merkabah*, that is, a set of images already a part of pious discourse so that the *merkabah* as portrayed in Revelation represents the cosmos, or the created order, upon which the Creator sits and directs the course of history.

One of the ways in which human beings inherit complex ideas from previous generations or exchange them among different groups over time involves what I have come to call "communal icons."[4] Communal icons are a cognitive-social appropriation of an image by a community. They represent an integration of ele-

2. Ithamar Gruenwald, *Apocalyptic and Merkavah Mysticism* (AGJU 14; Leiden: Brill, 1980). Prigent (*L'Apocalypse de Saint Jean*, 82) notes that Gershom Scholem had already begun to recognize that traditions residing at the root of some forms of Jewish mysticism may be found refelected herein. See Christopher Rowland, "The Visions of God in Apocalyptic Literature," *JSJ* 10 (1979): 145–50; James C. VanderKam, *Enoch and the Growth of Apocalyptic Tradition* (CBQMS 16; Washington, D.C.: Catholic Biblical Association of America, 1984), 134.

3. David J. Halperin, *The Faces of the Chariot: Early Jewish Reponses to Ezekiel's Vision* (TSAJ 16; Tübingen: Mohr Siebeck, 1988).

4. Cameron Afzal, "The Communal Icon: Complex Cultural Schemas, Elements of the Social Imagination (Matthew 10:32//Luke 12:8 and Revelation 3:5, A Case Study," in *Putting*

ments of the communal imagination that participants in a given community can assume they possess in common. The pattern of thoughts involved can therefore be taught, edited, commented upon, satirized, or simply referred to in the communal effort involving communication. Borrowing from progress made in the field of cognitive anthropology regarding *schema theory*, I understand that the communal icon functions at the level of the communal imagination analogous to the way in which schemas function in the interpretive process of the individual human mind.[5] As such, charismatic individuals can invoke these icons in their work in order to interpret, reshape, or manipulate the experience of reality apprehended in them.

By the first century the *merkabah* represents one such communal icon, and texts such as the Apocalypse represent not so much a representation of the *merkabah* itself, whatever that may be, nor simply commentary on Ezekiel, but a "reading" of the communal icon *merkabah* as it has grown and developed since the work of Ezekiel was first circulated. To say it differently, texts such as *1 En.* 14 and Rev 4 represent not so much different versions of the *merkabah* nor formal examples of an exegesis of the Ezekiel text but attempts on the part of the authors at innovation either through manipulation, interpretation, or revision of the community's apprehension of the *merkabah*. Let us explore this possibility in Rev 4.

1. The Author and His Book

The Apocalypse begins with an introduction of the book and of its "author" John, or more precisely with the book's "authors," (1:1); the first few verses involve some play with the sense of who the author is. The book is titled Ἀποκάλυψις Ἰησοῦ Χριστοῦ (Apocalypse of Jesus Christ).[6] The contents of the book, the revelation, we are told has been given to Jesus Christ by God to communicate to his servants. Verse 4, however, begins Ἰωάννης ταῖς ἑπτὰ ἐκκλησίαις ταῖς ἐν τῇ Ἀσίᾳ, employing an epistolary form, and the text explicitly names John as author. We are subsequently told that John has seen visions that he must write down in a book (1:11).[7] The reader, or in its original setting the hearer, is being prepared for the implica-

---

Body and Soul Together: Essays in Honor of Robin Scroggs (ed. V. Wiles, A. Brown, and G. F. Snyder; Valley Forge, Pa.: Trinity Press International, 1997), 58–80.

5. For a good introduction to schema theory, see Roy D'Andrade, *The Development of Cognitive Anthropology* (Cambridge: Cambridge University Press, 1995), 122–49.

6. The title Ἀποκάλυψις Ἰωάννου is found in the two best manuscripts ℵ and A, but these both stem from the third century. It is reasonable to assume that the first few words were considered the title by the author, as was the custom in late antiquity.

7. At first glance, one could perhaps assert that John is the author while God is the authority, since it is a revelation given by God to be written down by John. Yet, this introduction is followed by the so called epistolary section (1:17c–3:22) which is an extended quotation from the mouth of the "one like a Son of Man." This change in person carries the implication that the

tion of divine authorship regarding the content of the visions reported by John in what follows. John himself is written into the text as a character and narrator, with God as the implied author. The hearer is invited to perceive reality as inscribed by God, as has John, and so the vision begins with a depiction of the true source of an authoritative "reading" of the world, the Creator of the universe.[8]

The epistolary portion of the work consists of a prophetic critique of the real-life situation of the seven named churches in Asia Minor. The letters exhibit elements that indicate the author was indeed familiar with circumstances in the seven named cities,[9] yet these churches also function as a set representing the Christian church as a whole.[10] The visions that follow are therefore meant to address the Christian situation in general and not simply the circumstances of the seven named churches. To this end, after exhorting, chiding, and comforting the churches, the main part of the book presents their social circumstances as they really are, that is from a divine perspective. John's vision intends a "God's-eye view" of the Christian plight at the end of the first century.[11]

The portrayal of the true state of the world as contained in the apocalypse of Jesus Christ is introduced in Rev 4:1–11 with a *merkabah* vision, a vision of YHWH's throne-chariot. The vision is a complex and multiform icon constructed of elements or ideas taken from a variety of sources. Among these there is a general consensus regarding the use of imagery from Isaiah (1:6; 66:1) Ezek (1:1–2:7); Dan 7; *1 En.* 18; 39; *2 En.* 20–22, as well as elements taken from the iconography of Iranian and Greco-Roman royal courts.[12] Gruenwald has already noted that

author of the seven letters is indeed really the resurrected Jesus (ἐγώ εἰμι ὁ πρῶτος καὶ ὁ ἔσχατος καὶ ὁ ζῶν, καὶ ἐγενόμην νεκρὸς καὶ ἰδοὺ ζῶν εἰμι εἰς τοὺς αἰῶνας τῶν αἰώνων [1:17c–18a]).

8. On the function of the apocalyptic narrative to interpret reality, see Cameron Afzal, "Time Revealed: The Eschatology of Revelation Chapters 6–7" (Ph.D diss., Columbia University, 1993), 66–77; cf. Leonard L. Thompson, *The Book of Revelation: Apocalypse and Empire* (New York: Oxford University Press, 1990); and Wayne A. Meeks, "Social Functions of Apocalyptic Language in Pauline Christianity" in *Apocalypticism in the Mediterranean World and the Near East* (2nd ed.; ed. D. Hellholm; Tübingen: Mohr Siebeck, 1989), 687–706.

9. I.e., he knows of local lore, history, and details about the civic life in each of these cities. See the classic work by William M. Ramsey, *The Letters to the Seven Churches in Asia Minor and Their Place in the Plan of the Apocalypse* (London: Hodder & Stoughton, 1904), which has been vindicated and greatly enhanced in the erudite study of Colin J. Hemer, *The Letters to the Seven Churches of Asia in Their Local Setting* (JSNTSup 11; Sheffield: Sheffield Academic Press, 1986).

10. The language addressed to the churches is stylized. Each church is singled out for one problem and one compliment except two, Philadelphia and Sardis, each of which is basically good and bad, respectively. This schema is artificial and intended to highlight the symbolic function of the issues enumerated in the specific churches.

11. See Thompson, *Book of Revelation*, and more recently Thomas B. Slater, "On the Social Setting of the Revelation to John," *NTS* 44 (1998): 232–56.

12. Most commentaries (e.g., Charles, Caird, Swete) note the uses of the Jewish material. On the Hellenistic court imagery, see David E. Aune, "The Influence of Roman Law Court

these various combinations of elements from the theophanic throne and chariot-throne visions in 2 Kings, Isaiah, Ezekiel, and Daniel are common components in the mystical visions in Jewish apocalyptic texts, Revelation, and the *merkabah* visions of the *hekhalot* literature.[13]

Important progress has been made by Halperin in John's use of sources. He has persuasively argued for the existence of a tradition of *merkabah* exegesis, originating with Ezek 10:9–17, which he calls the hymnic tradition.[14] This tradition, evident in the "Angelic Liturgy" of Qumran and in the Targum of Ezekiel, is also evident in Revelation.[15] He notes the close ties between Revelation's use of Ezekiel and the tradition of the Palestinian Targums, which preserve "Scripture exegesis that accompanied synagogue worship."[16] In doing so, he provides further evidence of John's association with first-century synagogues. My purpose is not so much as to establish a "direct link" between Revelation and the rabbinic *ma'aseh merkabah* materiel[17] but rather to examine *the way* in which John stands in the midst of an ongoing interpretive process involving the *merkabah*.[18] As such, this study supports and builds upon Halperin's thesis.

2. God as Creator

It is clear that the *merkabah* vision and the accompanying throne-room scene sets up all that is to come. Most commentators agree that in some sense we have here

Ceremonial on the Apocalypse of John," *BR* 18 (1983): 5–26; Elisabeth Schüssler Fiorenza, *Revelation: Vision of a Just World* (Proclamation Commentaries; Minneapolis: Fortress, 1991), 59.

13. Gruenwald, *Apocalyptic and Merkavah Mysticism*, 31.

14. Halperin, *Faces of the Chariot*, 46, 51–54, 59–61, 85–92.

15. Ibid., 90.

16. Ibid., 87, who builds on the work of Martin McNamara, *The New Testament and the Palestinian Targum to the Pentateuch* (AnBib 27; Rome: Pontifical Biblical Institute, 1966), 97–125, 189–237.

17. See the criticism of Gruenwald leveled by Florentino García Martínez (*Qumran and Apocalyptic* [STDJ 9; Leiden: Brill, 1992] 72 n. 83), who argues that the roots of the kind of *merkabah* mysticism can indeed be seen in the Book of the Watchers, yet no direct link can be established.

18. My position therefore supports the view that in John we have a Jewish writer well versed in Jewish tradition. I do expressly disavow the view that this portion of the Revelation is somehow not "Christian." Views like those expressed by Ford (J. Massyngberde Ford, *Revelation: Introduction, Translation, and Commentary* [AB 38; Garden City, N.Y.: Doubleday, 1975], 79: "There does not appear to be any specifically Christian element in this chapter and the present writer has not been able to find one example of a throne or *merkabah* vision in Christian literature") or Rowland ("Visions of God," 145: "This chapter shows no evidence of Christian influence whatsoever") impose a distinction between Jew and Christian that had not yet clearly emerged.

a vision of the heavenly court that guides the history of the world.[19] Schüssler Fiorenza, in agreement with Aune, drawing attention to the references to "Oriental" court imagery, states the current consensus that there is an intentional parody of the Roman court and that the scene is meant to depict God, not Caesar, as the true ruler of the world.[20] This view dovetails with that of Gruenwald that sees in the proto-*merkabah* material a conflation of the imagery from the throne-chariot with that of the temple in Jerusalem.[21]

I concur with the view that John intends to portray God as the true ruler of the world, yet I want to push it further. The throne vision is not simply a parody, though I agree that this can become one of its various effects. John uses apocalyptic language to depict God as creator and hence ruler. It is a point made explicit by the acclamation in Rev 4:11:

> Ἄξιος εἶ, ὁ κύριος καὶ ὁ θεὸς ἡμῶν, λαβεῖν τὴν δόξαν καὶ τὴν τιμὴν καὶ τὴν δύναμιν, ὅτι σὺ ἔκτισας τὰ πάντα καὶ διὰ τὸ θέλημά σου ἦσαν καὶ ἐκτίσθησαν.
>
> You are worthy, our Lord and God, to receive glory and honor and power, for you created all things, and by your will they existed and were created.

God rules the created order because God has created it to be what it is; God guides its movements and is ultimately responsible for everything embodied within it.[22] A prayer formula involving an epithet for God coming into frequent use by the end of the first century in Aramaic- (or Hebrew-) speaking circles captures the thought behind this image precisely: Rev 4–5 depicts the God of Israel as מלך העולם.

19. See, e.g., Caird, *Revelation of St. John*, 60–69; M. Eugene Boring, *Revelation* (IBC; Louisville: John Knox, 1989), 102–4: the image means that the "universe is not a chaos nor is it ruled by blind faith."

20. See Allen A. Boesak, *Comfort and Protest: Reflections on the Apocalypse of John of Patmos* (Philadelphia: Westminster, 1987), 52–53.

21. Gruenwald (*Apocalyptic and Merkavah Mysticism*, 29–31) notes, for example, that *merkabah* visions in Jewish intertestamental literature display characteristic features derived from a common set of Old Testament sources, mainly 1 Kgs 22:19; Isa 6:1–3; Ezek 1–3; and Dan 7.

22. This emphasis is echoed yet again in rabbinic traditions that reflect an interest in Genesis; see Rowland, "Visions of God," 148. Boring (*Revelation*, 107–8) also stresses the God as Creator aspect of the throne image, yet he does so differently than what is being proposed here. For Boring, the four living beings are meant to symbolize all creatures, each being representing a segment of the animal kingdom. I think this is stretching it, since only mammals and a bird are depicted; I think if the symbol were to function as Boring would have it, there would be an insect or creeping thing, a fish, a beast or mammal, and a human, following the pattern in Gen 1. See Rachel Elior, *The Three Temples: On the Emergence of Jewish Mysticism* (Oxford: Littman Library of Jewish Civilization, 2004), which explores the cosmological symbolism of Ezekiel's *merkabah* vision and its role in the subsequent development of Jewish mystical tradition.

The meaning of עולם has, of course, a dual aspect in Hebrew, that of "world" or "creation" and that of "age" or "eternity."[23] Both meanings come into play in John's depiction of God: he is depicted as ruler of creation and is acclaimed as ὁ ἦν καὶ ὁ ὢν καὶ ὁ ἐρχόμενος (Rev 4:8), a temporal epithet. Though the epithet מלך העולם for YHWH is biblical (Jer 10:10), it does not seem to become an important one until the Hellenistic period. According to Joseph Heinemann, the rabbis did not include the formula in the Eighteen Benedictions, which "underwent their final editing" at Yavneh in 70. He writes,

> It is seems ... reasonable to assume that the introduction of the formula *mäläk ha'ôlam* did not take place before the beginning of the second century C.E. (approximately). I tend to agree with those scholars who have claimed the mention of God's Kingship was introduced as a protest against Roman emperor-worship.[24]

The icon behind the formula does, however, seem to play an important role in the theology of some Jewish circles well before the end of the first century, notably among those groups who have left us some apocalyptic literature. We find a Greek form of the epithet βασιλεὺς τῶν αἰώνων in Tob 13:7 and in *1 En.* 9:4.[25] Among the Qumran Scrolls we find that 1QapGen 2:4 and 7 contain במלך כול ע[למים, while 20:12–13 and 21:2 have the variant forms מרי לכול עלמים and מרה עלמיא, respectively. One should also note *Jub.* 31:13 and Josephus, *Ant.* 14.24 (βασιλεὺς τῶν ὅλων). In Christian texts the epithet is found in 1 Tim 1:17 and *1 Clem.* 61:2, as well as in a variant reading of Rev 15:3 (P^{47} $\aleph^{*2}$ C 1006 *pc*). Heinemann's observation that the epithet may be linked to a reaction on the part of Jews to dominant Gentile powers coincides nicely with the view being put forth here and accurately reflects John's stance vis-à-vis Caesar.[26]

---

23. BDB, 761

24. Joseph Heinemann, *Prayer in the Talmud: Forms and Patterns* (Berlin: de Gruyter, 1977), 94.

25. This is the preferred reading in Matthew Black, ed, *Apocalypsis Henochi Graece* (PVTG; Leiden: Brill, 1970), 23: Καὶ εἶπα[ν] τῷ κυρίῳ Σὺ εἶ κύριος τῶν κυρίων καὶ ὁ θεὸς τῶν θεῶν καὶ βασιλεὺς τῶν αἰώνων. In addition, Henry Barclay Swete's edition of *1 Enoch* (*The Old Testament in Greek* [4th ed.; 3 vols.; Cambridge: Cambridge University Press, 1930]) presents the epithet as the preferred reading, following Codex Panopolitanus. The English edition of *1 Enoch* by Matthew Black (*The Book of Enoch or 1 Enoch* [SVTP 7; Leiden: Brill, 1985]) reads "King of the ages" as the preferred reading (cf. note on 130); also 12:3; 25:3–7; 27:3; 58:4; 81:10.

26. See Heinemann, "Once Again melekh ha-'olam," *JJS* 15 (1964): 149–54; Ephraim Jehudah Wiesenberg, "The Liturgical Term melekh ha-'olam," *JJS* 15 (1964): 1–56; and idem, "Gleanings of the Liturgical Term Melekh Ha-'olam," *JJS* 17 (1966): 47–72. See also Alan F. Segal, "Ruler of This World: Attitudes about Mediator Figures and the Importance of Sociology for Self-Definition," in *Aspects of Judaism in the Greco-Roman Period* (vol. 2 of *Jewish and Christian Self-Definition*; ed. E. P. Sanders; Philadelphia: Fortress, 1981), 245–68, who argues that this and

The vision presented throughout Rev 4–5 supports this position. The images invoke God as Creator and Ruler, preparing the listener familiar with Jewish apocalyptic tradition for visions that will reveal something of the hidden mystery of God's activity regarding his creation. The presence of the *merkabah* in the text is a pointer that John has invoked traditions typically concerned with mysteries involving the nature of the created order and the mystery of the role of evil in God's redemptive plan.

3. The Visions in Revelation 4–5

Reading Rev 4:2–6 in this way involves the recognition of several components. First, John's image involves a conflation of two separate features found in Isaiah, the heavenly court scene of 6:1–8 and the exclamation in 66:1: השמים כסאי והארץ הדם רגלי (heaven is my throne and earth my footstool). The latter verses are of course preserved as part of an oracle responding to the destruction of the First Temple. It is not for nothing that the court imagery is here combined with elements associated with the temple in Jerusalem. The image of seven burning torches and the sea of glass (Rev 4:5–6) is reminiscent of the items set around the altar in the temple of Yhwh. The θάλασσα ὑαλίνη ὁμοία κρυστάλλῳ (a sea of glass, like crystal) recalls the lavers of 1 Kgs 7:38[27] or more probably the "molten sea" (הים מוצק) of 1 Kgs 7:23.[28] The lampstand with seven branches (one of the items taken to Rome by Titus after the war is depicted on his triumphal arch; see Josephus, *War* 7.149) is recalled by the seven flaming torches.[29] Images from a temple, now destroyed for the second time, are transposed to God's true court in heaven, the true seat of his power. This image undergirds the belief that no earthly temple is the true place of God' ruling power.

Whereas one could argue that in Isa 66:1 "heaven" is technically the throne, earth only the footstool, the force of the image is to place God "above" the created order with the earth as its lowest point. The footstool is still part of the throne in ancient royal courts; it is simply a lowly part. That the use of the image was alive and well in Christian circles is made evident from Matt 5:34 ("But I say to you, Do not swear at all, either by heaven, for it is the throne of God…"). The passage in Isa 66:1 questions the hubris of those who think any earthly temple could truly delimit the Lord of all creation, and the use of this image in Revelation follows

---

similar epithets were also a feature in the polemic between emerging Christianity and greater Judaism by the end of the first century.

27. Austin Farrer, *The Revelation of St. John the Divine* (Oxford: Clarendon, 1964), 90.

28. Caird, *Revelation of St. John*, 65.

29. It is interesting to note that, according to Gruenwald (*Apocalyptic and Merkavah Mysticism*, 72), it is only in some Christian examples of a *merkabah* vision, i.e., in Revelation and in the *Apocalypse of Paul*, that elements associated with the temple are combined with elements associated with the throne of God.

iconographically the sentiment expressed in Isa 40:22–23: "It is he who sits above the circle of the earth, and its inhabitants are like grasshoppers; who stretches out the heavens like a curtain, and spreads them like a tent to live in; who brings princes to naught, and makes the rulers of the earth as nothing."

A second feature of importance involves the τέσσαρα ζῷα of 4:6, living beings. Ezekiel's *hayyot* are identified with the seraphim from Isa 6:1.[30] This conflation is perhaps not original with John, as it is found albeit in a very indirect manner in another *merkabah*-related text. In *Second Ezekiel* (4Q385), an "exegetical abridgment" of Ezek 1, lines 6–7 the influence of Isa 6:2 is observed by Dimant and Strugnell with regard to the description of the wings of the seraphim.[31] Significantly, John's living beings are depicted as a part of the throne. The problematic phrase, Καὶ ἐν μέσῳ τοῦ θρόνου καὶ κύκλῳ τοῦ θρόνου τέσσαρα ζῷα γέμοντα ὀφθαλμῶν ἔμπροσθεν καὶ ὄπισθεν, as we shall see, highlights directly the particular reading of the *merkabah* being put forth by John.[32] Moreover, the *hayyot* are tied to the imagery for the heavenly temple/court by singing the Sanctus from Isa 6:3.[33] A third but very important feature of the conflation of images in Revelation involves the subtle identification of the Ezekiel's *ʾopannim* (wheels) with the *hayyot* (living beings) and thus the seraphim implied in the text.[34] Although the wheels are never mentioned in the text of Revelation, their presence is implied; that is, the text is written with the assumption that "every-

30. Halperin, *Faces of the Chariot*, 91.

31. Devorah Dimant and John Strugnell, "The Merkbah Vision in Second Ezekiel (4Q385 4)," *RevQ* 14 (1990): 346. Cf. Christopher R. A. Morray-Jones, "The Temple Within: The Embodied Divine Image and Its Worship in the Dead Sea Scrolls and Other Early Jewish and Christian Sources," *SBLSP* (1998): 408, and more recently *A Transparent Illusion: The Dangerous Vision of Water in Hekhalot Mysticism* (Leiden: Brill, 2002).

32. See Robert G. Hall, "Living Creatures in the Midst of the Throne: Another Look at Revelation 4,6," *NTS* 36 (1990): 609–13, who argues that Charles incorrectly dismisses the reading Καὶ ἐν μέσῳ τοῦ θρόνου καὶ κύκλῳ τοῦ θρόνου τέσσαρα ζῷα γέμοντα ὀφθαλμῶν ἔμπροσθεν καὶ ὄπισθεν in 4:6 found in all extant manuscripts. The beings are imagined as constituting "within the space taken up by" the throne, i.e., like "the feet arms and back surround a chair (612)." On the problematic history of translation, see Raymond R. Brewer, "Revelation 4.6 and Translations Thereof" *JBL* 71 (1952): 227–31. See also Gruenwald, *Apocalyptic and Merkavah Mysticism*, 67–68; Halperin, *Faces of the Chariot*, 92.

33. According to Charles (*Commentary on the Revelation*, 1:123), this connection was first made by Heinrich Zimmern and Hugo von Winckler in Eberhard Schrader, ed., *Die Keilinschriften und das alte Testament* (2 vols.; Berlin: Reuther & Reichard, 1903), 63ff., who identified the living beings as the four winds of heaven and therefore the four constellations. See also Halperin, *Faces of the Chariot*, 91.

34. As Halperin points out, this identification may not have been original with John. He states, "the author of the Enochian Book of Parables, who stands in the hymnic tradition, attributes a threefold 'holy' to his angelic triad of 'Cherubin, Seraphin, and Ophannin,' as well as a second formula ('Blessed be though and blessed be the name of the Lord for ever and ever') reminiscent of the doxology in Revelation 7:12" (*Faces of the Chariot*, 91).

one knows the throne chariot has wheels." It is this unspoken identification that points to the communal icon of the *merkabah* presupposed by John in his vision. He is subtly working with images already known to his audience to reshape it for his own purposes.

We are now ready to examine the implications of associating the *hayyot* with the wheels in Revelation. As we shall see, the conflation of symbols has the effect of invoking cosmological speculation associated with the *merkabah* visions that preceded John's and with the association of the throne/temple of God with the created order, the cosmos.[35] In order to tease out this set of meanings, let us examine the cosmological associations invoked by the association of the *hayyot* and the wheels more closely.

We begin by looking at one of Revelation's apocalyptic predecessors, *1 Enoch*, which, according to Milik, John "had first hand knowledge of ... probably a Greek translation."[36] It is here we find some interesting clues for the interpretation of the *merkabah* in Rev 4. First we may note that the four winds at the foundation of the world are said in *1 En.* 18:4 to move the stars in the heavens in their delicately patterned movements.[37] Then, in the vision of *1 En.* 14, the way of ascension (by the seer) is through a house of "crystals," or "hailstones." The proper translation of this phrase has proven a bit of a puzzle.[38] The Aramaic reconstruction of 4QEn[c] 14:9 by Milik reads באבני ברד but is rendered by the Greek translators as λίθοις χαλάζης.[39] Milik, Black, and García Martínez[40] translate the phrase quite literally

35. Gruenwald (*Apocalyptic and Merkavah Mysticism*, 8–16) asserts that one of the "essential qualities" of Jewish apocalyptic that is found continued in the *merkabah* tradition is the interest in cosmological speculation, the study of the revealed knowledge about the secrets of nature.

36. Jozef T. Milik, ed., *The Books of Enoch: Aramaic Fragments of Qumrân Cave 4* (with the collaboration of Matthew Black; Oxford: Clarendon, 1976), 199.

37. ἴδον ἀνέμους τῶν οὐρανῶν στρέφοντας καὶ διανύοντας τὸν τροχὸν τοῦ ἡλίου, καὶ πὰντας τοὺς ἀστέρας. Quotation is from Swete's edition of the Greek text, here following Codex Panopolitanus. Astronomical speculation is a significant feature of the *1 Enoch* corpus. In fact, according to Black (building on the work of Milik) the so-called astronomical chapters seem to represent an edited text abridged out of a significantly larger mass of Aramaic astronomical and calendrical speculation (see Black, *The Book of Enoch*, 10, 18–19 and translation and notes by O. Neugebauer (appendix A, 386–419). Fragments of this portion of *1 Enoch* are represented among the Qumran fragments. It seems that this kind of calendrical speculation was still a significant feature of Jewish apocalypticism into the common era.

38. Halperin, *Faces of the Chariot*, 80–81, esp. nn. 14–16.

39. Milik's (*Books of Enoch*, 194) reconstruction of line 21 is: לעלא ואובלוני ואע[לו]ני ב[סמיא ועלת בהון עד די אדבקת לסורי בניאן מתבנא אבני ברד]—"upwards and brought me up and made me enter into [heaven. And I entered it until I drew near to the walls of a building built with hailstones]...." Only the smallest portion of this verse remains in the Aramaic, not including the relevant phrase.

40. Florentino Garcia Martinez, ed, *The Dead Sea Scrolls Translated: The Qumran Texts in English* (Leiden; Brill, 1994), 252.

"hailstones." I prefer Charles's (*APOT*) translation of the Ethiopic "crystals," which Isaac renders "white marble" because this brings out the force of the conjunction "like": "like rock-crystal or rock-ice," that is, hailstones. The floor and walls of the house are ὡς λιθόπλακες, according to the ancient Greek translator, rendered from the Ethiopic as "tessellated crystal" (Charles) or "mosaic" (Isaacs). Here the Aramaic reconstruction of 14:10 by Milik, כותלי ביתא דן הוו כלוחת אבנין, is translated by Black, "tessalated paving stones," by Milik as "stone slabs," and by García Martínez as "stone planks." In my view, Charles's translation, "tessalated crystals," correctly associates the image of the walls with the previous description of the house in general as being made of crystals. Be that as it may, the whole is clearly described in the text as being *like snow*.[41]

The description of the ceiling is the more problematic. Again the Aramaic reconstruction of the phrase וטלליא כזקין וכברקין (4QEn^{c} 14:11) is translated by Black as "fireballs and lightenings" and by Milik as "like lightning-flashes and like thunders," but it is rendered by the ancient Greek translator as αἱ στέγαι ὡς διαδρομαὶ ἀστέρων καὶ ἀστραπαί.[42] The Ethiopic follows this latter reading,[43] so that we have the phrase "like the paths of the stars" in both Charles's and Isaac's rendering. If the Aramaic reconstruction is accurate, it seems, admittedly, that the Greek translator has interpreted the Hebrew or Aramaic phrase for his readers, but I think he has done so correctly.[44] The ceiling of the house, made of "fireballs and lightings," would then be interpreted as being a reference to the path of the stars. Again, these references to "ice-rocks," "patterns of crystal," and floors and ceiling "like snow" all point in the same basic iconographic direction. One is to visualize *white dots* sprayed and arrayed in patterns; the image is intended to render poetically a gaze into the heavens, the night sky, with the seer being transported up through the stars before the throne of God. From the perspective of earth, as the seer looks up into heaven he perceives the throne-chariot of God ascending first through the vault of heaven with its myriads of stars.

Modern readers of Revelation have in turn already noted the association of the four beings to the four elements, to the cherub wind, and to the four winds at the foundation of the world and as a result stellar constellations.[45] The latter are,

---

41. The Greek reads καὶ πᾶσαι ἦσαν ἐκ χιόνος, καὶ ἐδράφη χιονικά, while the Aramaic is reconstructed as [די תלג ומבנא ד]י תלג אס[נ. Note that the word "snow" is the only clearly extant description in the text.

42. The reconstructed line 24 reads: [די תלג ומבנא ד]ט תלג אס[נ ותלליא כזקין וכברקין ובינתהון כרובין די נור וסמיהון די מין] (Milik, *Books of Enoch*, 194).

43. Michael A. Knibb, *The Ethiopic Book of Enoch* (2 vols.; Oxford: Clarendon, 1978), 2:98.

44. See Rowland, "Visions of God," 148, where he discusses the association of "crystal" with the firmament of Gen 1 that separates the heavens from the waters below, a subject of mystical speculation in "early rabbinic meditation on creation (*ma'seh bereshith*)."

45. See n. 33 above.

moreover, associated specifically with the pivotal constellations of the zodiac.[46] Austin Farrer's presentation of the zodiac interpretation is one of the clearest by those who hold this view, so I reproduce it here:

> The four faces according to Ezekiel 1 have the order Man, Lion, Bull, Eagle.... We know that current Jewish symbolism associated them with the four quarters of heaven; St. John identifies them with the middle signs in the four quarters of the Zodiac, and is going presently to associate them with the four winds blowing from the four quarters (chs vi and vii). The Eagle, indeed, is not a Zodiacal sign, but is also a constellation; and does duty for the scorpion, a sign of ill omen; for their helical risings were equivalent. That is to say, when the sun rose in Scorpion, and so the Scorpion rose too, the Eagle came over the horizon at the same moment. St. John makes the minimum change in Ezekiel's order which will allow the four signs to read straight round the Zodiacal ring. Lion (summer), Bull (spring), Man, the Waterer (winter) and Eagle, for Scorpion (autumn).[47]

Caird argues that the four beings are indeed related to the cherub-wind (2 Sam 22:11; Ps 18:10) and would also be identified as the four winds at the foundation of the world. He cautions against seeing a simple reference to the zodiac here, since this kind of symbolism is not developed in the rest of the book.[48] Indeed, these four winds are said to be the source of the movement of the constellations in *1 Enoch*. Moreover, if I am correct in arguing for the existence of a communal icon behind this passage, we are justified in asking if there are other common uses of zodiacal imagery in first-century Judaism and if they relate to perceptions of God as Creator. If so, I would argue that the use of a zodiacal imagery here would not mean that John would have to be primarily concerned with astrological speculation as such[49] but that here in Rev 4 this image is invoked in order to express a specific theological point, that God is the Creator of the universe and thus all worldly powers are each given their due in their own time.

---

46. Farrer, *Revelation of St. John the Divine*, 91–92. See also Charles (*Commentary on the Revelation*, 1:121–22); Ernst Lohmeyer, *Die Offenbarung des Johannes* (2nd ed.; HNT 16; Tübingen: Mohr Siebeck, 1953), 48–49, who, following Zimmern and Gunkel on the Ezekiel vision of the beings, bring out the zodiac reference; Heinrich Kraft, *Die Offenbarung des Johannes* (HNT 16a; Tübingen: Mohr Siebeck, 1974), 99; and Charles Homer Giblin, *The Book of Revelation: The Open Book of Prophecy* (Good News Studies; Collegeville, Minn.: Liturgical Press, 1991), 72, who ties in the zodiac idea with that of the four elements. See also Prigent, *L'Apocalypse de Saint Jean*, 86 n. 29. Most recently Bruce J. Malina (*On the Genre and Message of Revelation: Star Visions and Sky Journeys* [Peabody, Mass.: Hendrickson, 1995]) has interpreted the whole book as an example of what he calls "astral-prophecy." In doing so he too interprets the *hayyot* as references to the zodiac (97–104) and thereby in the context of Hellenistic astral speculation. I cannot claim to understand completely Malina's star-only reading of Revelation.

47. Farrer, *Revelation of St. John the Divine*, 91–92.

48. Caird, *Revelation of St. John*, 64.

49. *Pace* Malina, *On the Genre and Message*.

One has only to acknowledge the popularity of zodiacal symbolism in Judaism of Hellenistic times to argue that John could assume that the imagery was familiar to his Jewish audience and that he therefore intended to use the seasonal associations of that symbolism to accomplish his own purposes. Reference to the signs of the zodiac as a way of emphasizing YHWH's mastery of all creation is not simply tied to Jewish apocalyptic thought. Josephus (*War* 5.210) tells us that the sanctuary of the temple in Jerusalem contained three works of art: a seven-branched lampstand; a table with twelve loaves representing "the circle of the zodiac and the year"; and an altar of incense.[50] Philo in *Mos.* 2.123–126 describes the ephod, one of the high priest's vestments, as a symbol of heaven insofar as its decorative stones were interpreted in terms of the signs of the zodiac.

Similarly, we know that a zodiac mosaic was a common feature of ancient Palestinian synagogues.[51] Joseph Yahalom even conjectures that the *Sitz im Leben* of early liturgical poetry included a kind of litany listing of the signs of the zodiac and probably involved recitation, with the community "gathered on the floor standing around a zodiac mosaic" (though he makes this conjecture in order to provide a possible social context for the recitation of the poetry of Yannai in the early seventh century).[52] We may observe here that use of the imagery associated with the zodiac does not represent assimilation to Hellenistic culture but may in fact reflect an earlier cultural inheritance. This would be an instance where Palestinian Judaism shared an inherited prehistory with the dominant Hellenistic society in which it found itself.

There was, however, some tension between a pervasive and common association of the zodiac with the mysteries of the universe as derived from Babylonian speculation and Jewish monotheism. Josephus, when describing the veil of the Jerusalem temple, notes it was a "Babylonian tapestry" in which the "mixture of material" had its mystical meaning as the image of the cosmos (εἰκόνα τῶν ὅλον, *War* 5.213). He adds, "On this tapestry was portrayed a panorama of the heavens, the signs of the Zodiac excepted" (5.214). However, more important for our purposes is a comment made by Philo in *Quis rerum divinarum heres sit.* He contrasts the Babylonian worldview, which identifies the universe with the divine, and that of Judaism, which understands God as its Creator. He states:

50. See also *2 En.* 21 [the longer recension] in a throne-vision where the zodiac plays a role in the seventh heaven.

51. Wolfgang Hübner, *Zodiacus Christianus: Jüdisch-christliche Adaptationen des Tierkreises von der Antike bis zur Gegenwart* [Königstein: Hain, 1983], 23); see the zodiac mosaic floors of the Hammath Tiberias synagogue and the Beth Alpha synagogue pictured, e.g., in Lee I. Levine, *The Rabbinic Class of Roman Palestine in Late Antiquity* (Jerusalem: Yad Izhak Ben-Zvi, 1989).

52. "The *Piyyuṭim* as Poetry," in *The Synagogue in Late Antiquity* (ed. L. I. Levine; Philadelphia: American Schools of Oriental Research, 1987), 111–26, here 120.

> those whose views are of the Chaldaean type have put their trust in heaven, while he who has migrated from his home [i.e., Abraham] has given his trust to Him who rides on the heaven and *guides the chariot of the whole world*, even God.
> τοὺς μὲν γὰρ τὰς γνώμας χαλδαΐζοντας οὐρανοῷ πεπιστευκέναι, τὸν δ᾽ ἐθένδε μεταναστάντα τῷ ἐπόχῳ τοῦ οὐρανοῦ καὶ ἡνιόχῳ τοῦ παντὸς κόσμου, Θεῷ. (*Her.* 99, LCL, emphasis added)

Philo expressly contrasts Babylonian astrological speculation with that of a Judaism that interprets the cosmos as the divine chariot controlled by but not identified as God. Perhaps a conclusion can be drawn as a result of these observations and the association of Revelation with the hymnic tradition of *merkabah* exegesis in the Hellenistic synagogue. Perhaps it is in just such settings, replete with zodiacal iconography, that the *merkabah* began to be associated with cosmological speculation.

Returning to Revelation, let us focus on the wheels of this chariot. We recall that each face symbolizes each of the four quarters of heaven and that each is experienced on earth in terms of the changing four seasons. They are described as having six wings (Rev 4:8), clearly associating them with the seraphim of Isa 6.[53] As noted above, missing is any literal reference in Revelation to the wheels of the Ezekiel vision. The *ʾopannim* of the Ezekiel vision have in fact been conflated with the *hayyot*, which are associated in the hymnic tradition with the seraphim, as they are here. The image of the wheels is invoked with the reference to "the eyes." The living beings in Rev 4:8 are described as κυκλόθεν καὶ ἔσωθεν γέμουσιν ὀφθαλμῶν (full of eyes all around and inside), a phrase that in Ezek 1:18 is applied only to the wheels.

The wheels are thus referred to by memory and association in the reception of the text, that is, through apprehension of the communal icon of the *merkabah* that John presupposes on the part of his community. Charles asserts that John has misapplied the image in Revelation, since, unlike wheels, which are circular, "such an expression could not be easily used of a living creature which had a definite face such as a man, or ox, or lion, or eagle, with their eyes in front."[54] This problem is resolved, however, if by associating these creatures with the turning of the heavenly constellations we see how they have been identified with the wheels. The "eyes all around" refer to the stars,[55] which the seer envisions revolving in the heavens. This peculiar conflation of the imagery is the very effect intended by the Christian prophet. The stars contemplated, having been perceived in patterns, are

53. The cherubim of Ezek 1 have four wings.

54. Charles, *Commentary on the Revelation*, 1:124.

55. Ibid., 123; and Malina, *On the Genre and Message*, 98–99, on the association of eyes with stars in the ancient world.

imagined as the spinning spheres of heaven, marking the passing of the time and the seasons.

The image of the four living beings therefore is intended to invoke all the things discussed above. We have here a multivalent symbol referring to the dynamic, hence "living," aspect of the created order, the "movement" of time as it is represented in the heavens. In Rev 4 the cherubim/seraphim, covered in stars, "move" the *merkabah* forward. The living beings, who are invoked by John from Ezekiel's wheels within wheels, are here portrayed as constellations representing the cyclical/calendrical experience of time. Days within weeks within months within years, ever in motion—they are the four seasons moving God's creation forward in time.

In sum, in Rev 4 the Lord of creation is enthroned upon his handiwork; before him are the seven spirits, the sevenfold holy spirit, aflame with the life of the world,[56] and the abyss into which all things fall that do not return to God.[57] The throne is creation itself, the four living beings, representing the motion of the stars symbolize the movement of the four seasons. The throne of God, creation, "moves" through time. Having invoked the communal icon *merkabah,* John conflates the living beings with the wheels within wheels and as such associates the circular implication of the wheels with the motion of God's creation in calendrical cycles. The vision of *merkabah* authenticates Revelation by establishing John as one who has seen the creator in his role as the director of history. John's vision proclaims, in the image of the living beings, God's majesty as Lord of ages or Lord of time. In the passing of the seasons, all creation cries out, Ἅγιος ἅγιος ἅγιος κύριος ὁ θεὸς ὁ παντοκράτωρ, ὁ ἦν καὶ ὁ ὢν καὶ ὁ ἐρχόμενος (Rev 4:8), glorifying the Creator, מלך העולם, as the eternal one.

56. Sweet (*Apocalypse of John,* 119) also invokes the image from Zech 4:2, 10, wherein the seven lamps are the eyes of God that "range through the whole earth." It is the sevenfold spirit of prophecy alight in the world among Christian communities. The torches are in a sense a counterpart to the image of the seven lamp stands identified as the seven churches in Rev 1:20.

57. The symbolism of θάλασσα ὑαλίνη ὁμοία κρυστάλλῳ as a reference to the cosmic sea, the abyss, is brought out by Caird, *Revelation of St. John,* 65–66; see also Charles, *Commentary on the Revelation,* 1:118. But see Rowland, "Visions of God," 145, who associates "the crystal sea" with the firmament of Gen 1.

Sexuality and Gender of Angels

Kevin Sullivan

> When people began to multiply on the face of the ground, and daughters were born to them, the sons of God saw that they were fair, and they took wives for themselves of all that they chose.... The giants were on the earth in those days—and also afterwards—when the sons of God went in to the daughters of humans, who bore children to them. (Gen 6:1–2, 4)

Angels have as their primary function the delivery of God's message to human beings.[1] They typically reside in the heavens, but they do travel to earth. They are able to alter their physical appearance, and in particular they are able to take on human form. Angels are not bound by the same limitations as humans, such as the passage of time, hunger, and death. Nor are they bound by sexual desire or the need to procreate.

1. Sexuality of Angels

What can be known about beliefs concerning the sexual nature of angels? Why were these beliefs held? How may these beliefs have influenced the practices of the early Jewish and Christian mystics? Part of the reason that these questions have not been discussed by scholars is that there are relatively few texts from the late Second Temple period that explicitly discuss the issue of the sexual activity of angels. However, there are two important traditions to consider. The first tradition suggests that in their natural state angels were not sexually active; the other suggests that some angels may have become sexually active with humans on earth.

1.1. The Gospels: Like Angels in Heaven

In Mark 12:18–27 (par. Matt 22:23–33; Luke 20:27–40) the Sadducees, who appear to have rejected the idea of resurrection (Matt 22:23; Mark 12:18; Luke

1. Kevin Sullivan, *Wrestling with Angels: A Study of the Relationship between Angels and Humans in Ancient Jewish Literature and the New Testament* (Leiden: Brill, 2004), 27–35.

20:27; Acts 4:1–2; 23:8–9; Josephus, *War* 2.165; *Ant.* 18.16), challenge Jesus on the nature of the afterlife. They ask Jesus whose wife a woman would be in the resurrection, if in keeping with Torah a series of seven brothers had all wed the same woman but had died without male issue (12:19–23).[2] Jesus responds, "For when they rise from the dead, they neither marry nor are given in marriage, but are like angels in heaven (εἰσὶν ὡς ἄγγελοι ἐν τοῖς οὐρανοῖς)"; the Lukan versions reads "equal to the angels (ἰσάγγελοι)."[3] Jesus' answer covers the situation of both the brothers, who do not marry (γαμοῦσιν), and the woman, who is not given in marriage (γαμίζονται).

What belief about angels, sex, and marriage underlies Jesus' statement? It seems to be that, like many Jews from this period, Jesus closely linked sexual intercourse with marriage (Gen 1:28; 2:24). The command to "be fruitful and multiply" necessarily assumes sexual intercourse for the purposes of procreation. Jesus' statement, however, suggests that in the resurrected state there is a return to the prelapsarian state: human beings would be immortal beings without sin, much like the angels. As such, they will no longer need to have sex for reproduction, so as death is transcended, so too is sexuality.

Contrary to this interpretation, Ben Witherington argues that while this Gospel passage does suggest the cessation of the act of marrying, it does not mean "the dissolution of all marriages … or that mankind will live a sexless, genderless existence in that age."[4] However, his interpretation is quite literal. Jesus' statement, especially in the Lukan form, seems to suggest more than the disregard of the institution of marriage, but also the lack of need for the primary purpose of the union, namely, procreation. Witherington's interpretation notwithstanding, the emphasis on the fact that the angels live in an unwed, sexless (and apparently genderless) state seems fairly clear. It does not appear, however, that all contemporary Jews necessarily had a positive attitude about sexuality simply because it had been divinely ordained. Recent scholarship has suggested that Jewish attitudes toward

---

2. The Sadducean argument is based on the marriage prescription of Deut 25:5–10; cf. Gen 38:8; Ruth 4:1–10; *m. Yebam.* 3:9.

3. Turid Karlsen Seim argues that Luke modified the Markan form to support his community's rejection of marriage as a means to angelic existence; see *The Double Message: Patterns of Gender in Luke-Acts* (Edinburgh: T&T Clark, 1994). See also Crispin Fletcher-Louis, *Luke-Acts: Angels, Christology and Soteriology* (Tübingen: Mohr Siebeck, 1997), 86–88; and David E. Aune, "Luke 20:34–36: A Gnosticized Logion of Jesus?" in *Geschichte-Tradition-Reflexion: Festschrift für Martin Hengel zum 70. Geburtstag* (ed. H. Cancik, H. Lichtenberger, and P. Schäfer; Tübingen: Mohr Siebeck, 1996), 187–202, who sees this teaching passage as being (1) stripped from its original narrative, (2) reformulated in an encratite baptismal context, and (3) inserted into the Gospel of Luke.

4. Ben Witherington, *Women in the Ministry of Jesus: A Study of Jesus' Attitudes to Women and Their Roles as Reflected in His Earthly Life* (Cambridge: Cambridge University Press, 1980), 35.

sexuality were mixed.[5] In fact, as we will see, it seems a number of early Jewish and Christian mystics came to eschew sexual intercourse, particularly in light of our next text in which the sexuality of angels becomes very dangerous.

1.2. Genesis 6:1–4 and Interpretations: The Fallen Angels

The other important tradition to consider regarding angelic sexuality begins in the Hebrew Bible. Genesis 6:1–4 is an esoteric passage that in the Hebrew (MT) does not contain the word for angel (מלאך), but the context strongly suggests angels, because the beings are referred to as "the sons of God." In the story, the sons of God descend to the earth and procreate with human females. The product of their union is a race of angel-human hybrids.

A number of texts from the late Second Temple period, such as *1 En.* 6–11, *Jub.* 5:1–2, the *Book of Giants*, and the *Genesis Apocryphon*, seem to have expanded upon these four short verses from Genesis, dedicating entire texts to the story.[6] These traditions go as far as to suggest that the angelic copulation with women was the cause of sin and evil in the world. Both within the Genesis passage itself and even more so in its later interpretations it is clear that the union of angels and humans (divine and human) was thought to be dangerous. The belief seems to have been that sexual intercourse between angels and humans represented a serious transgression of the established boundaries of creation and resulted in hybrid beings that were never meant to exist: the giants (נפלים).[7] That God was displeased by the giants is clear in the Genesis story, since the giants were wiped out in the flood.

What, then, can we say about beliefs concerning the sexuality of angels in late Second Temple literature? It seems from the texts examined that angels were created by God and were immortal, thus having no need to procreate; therefore, angels did not need to have sex with one another. This does not appear to have meant, however, that angels were thought to be *incapable* of sexual intercourse. It appears that good angels, who maintained their proper place in the celestial order, were nonsexual (Mark 12:25 and parallels) but that bad angels, those who went down to earth (Gen 6:1–4 and parallels), became sexually active. When angels did become sexually active with humans, there was successful mating in that viable, human-angel giants were born. Most interpreters believed that this serious transgression led to the eventual destruction of the giants and to the origin of sin in

5. See April DeConick, *Rediscovering the Original Gospel of Thomas: A History of the Gospel and Its Growth* (London: T&T Clark, 2005), 176–82.

6. For more on the fallen angels, see Christopher Auffarth and Loren Stuckenbruck, eds., *The Fall of the Angels* (Leiden: Brill, 2004); and Sullivan, *Wrestling with Angels*, 197–225.

7. Gigantism is a characteristic often attributed to divine beings (esp. angels) in late Second Temple texts (e.g., *Joseph and Aseneth*, *Ezekiel the Tragedian*, *Gospel of Peter*). On this topic, see Fletcher-Louis, *Luke-Acts*, 143 and 232.

this world. Angelic intercourse with humans seems to have represented a "fall," much like the sin of Adam and Eve, a sin that actually led to human need to have sex and to procreate.

2. Gender and Angels

2.1. Angels and Men

Even though it is apparent in the passage discussed above (Gen 6:1–4), it is prudent to begin this discussion of the gender of angels by highlighting the fact that it is the "*sons* of God" who are understood as "angels" and then have sex with human *women*. This suggests that, from an early period, there was in the minds of ancient authors the belief that divine beings were *male*. This understanding is in some sense reinforced by the preceding material in Genesis. In one version of the creation story, Eve is created out of the protoplast Adam (Gen 2:18–23); this story subordinates Eve to Adam. In Gen 3 she is then seen as the cause of Adam's sin. Childbirth is Eve's punishment for this failure (3:16), thus Eve (and all women) through childbirth and mortality (and the need for procreation) are inextricably linked to her sin.

Virtually all of the ancient evidence suggests that angels were understood to be male. Angels are regularly portrayed as men in the Hebrew Bible and are often called "men" (אדם) in the Hebrew text (as opposed to "angels" (מלאך) only to be interpreted as angels (ἄγγελος) in the LXX (e.g., Gen 18–19; Josh 5:13–15; Tob 5) as well as in other interpolations (e.g., Philo, *Jubilees*). It makes some sense that angels would be envisioned as male in their role as messengers for God, since the equivalent role in the ancient world—that of messenger for a king or noble—would most likely have been fulfilled by a man. Additionally, within the Greco-Roman pantheon, the prototype for the messenger was the god Hermes, who is often called ἄγγελος.[8]

In an interesting development in some late Second Temple literature, angels begin to be referred to as "young men." An excellent example of this apparent shift can be seen in the varied empty tomb narratives from the Gospels. Each of the four canonical Gospels and also the *Gospel of Peter* contain a tradition about the empty tomb of Jesus, and each of these traditions makes mention of beings who are either explicitly called or seem by context to be angels. It is worthwhile to note in light of the present topic that all the accounts have *women* coming to Jesus' tomb and receiving the announcement from the angels.

First, in Mark 16:5 we read, "And entering the tomb, they [the three women] saw a young man (νεανίσκον) sitting on the right side, dressed in a white robe;

8. See Simon Hornblower and Antony Spanforth, *The Oxford Classical Dictionary* (New York: Oxford University Press, 1996), 89.

and they were amazed." This "young man" is privy to some crucial information, telling them, "Do not be amazed; you seek Jesus of Nazareth, who was crucified. He has risen, he is not here; see the place where they laid him. But go, tell his disciples and Peter that he is going before you to Galilee; there you will see him, as he told you" (Mark 16:6–7). The white robe is a signal of angelic status, a characteristic of numerous angelophanies (e.g., Dan 10:5–6; Acts 1:10; Rev 1:14; 6:11). So it would appear that this being is an *angel*—a messenger who delivers God's plan—but he is called a "young man (νεανίσκον)."

Matthew's version of the empty tomb narrative differs from Mark's.

> And behold, there was a great earthquake; for an angel of the Lord (ἄγγελος κυρίου) descended from heaven and came and rolled back the stone and sat upon it. His appearance was like lightning, and his raiment white as snow. And for fear of him the guards trembled and became like dead men. But the angel said to the women, "Do not be afraid; for I know that you seek Jesus who was crucified. He is not here; for he has risen, as he said. Come, see the place where he lay. Then go quickly and tell his disciples that he has risen from the dead, and behold, he is going before you to Galilee; there you will see him. Lo, I have told you." (Matt 28:2–7)

Like the Markan passage, *women* approach the tomb, but as they do, there is an earthquake and the Angel of the Lord (Gen 16; 22; Exod 4; Num 22; Judg 6; 13) comes to move the stone that blocks the entrance to the tomb. The commands of the young man in Mark and of the Angel of the Lord in Matthew are strikingly similar. The close literary connection between the command to see the place where Jesus' body had lain and to go out and tell the disciples that Jesus had risen suggest that there is literary dependence between the Markan and Matthean versions. If there is dependence, then Matthew has made some significant changes to the scene, making it clear that an angel is present. This could mean that Matthew understood Mark's "young man" as an angel but saw it as somewhat ambiguous and so bolstered the appearance to make it obvious.

Luke 24:4–5 says, "While they [the women] were perplexed about this, behold, two men (ἄνδρες δύο) stood by them in dazzling apparel;[9] and as they were frightened and bowed their faces to the ground, the men said to them, 'Why do you seek the living among the dead?'" Here there are two beings at the tomb. They are not referred to as young men but simply as men. They do have dazzling clothing and announce to the women that Jesus is not in the tomb but has gone before his disciples to Galilee.[10]

---

9. Cf. the divine appearance of Jesus in the transfiguration narratives in Mark 9:2–10; Matt 17:1–9; and Luke 9:28–36.

10. Similarly in Acts 1:10–11, Luke describes two men in heaven, "And while they were gazing into heaven as he went, behold, two men (ἄνδρες δύο) stood by them in white robes

John 20:12 records that Mary Magdalene "saw two angels (δύο ἀγγέλους) in white, sitting where the body of Jesus had lain, one at the head and one at the feet." These angels ask Mary, "Why are you weeping?" She replies, "Because they have taken away my Lord, and I do not know where they have laid him." The angels have no more part in the story, since Jesus then appears to Mary in verse 14.

Lastly, the *Gospel of Peter* is known in a fragment discovered in the late nineteenth century.[11] At verses 35–37 it also includes a narrative about the empty tomb:

> Now in the night in which the Lord's day dawned, when the soldiers were keeping guard, two by two in each watch, there was a loud voice in heaven and they saw the heavens open and two men (δύο ἄνδρας) come down from there in a great brightness and draw near the sepulchre. That stone which had been laid against the entrance to the sepulchre started of itself to roll and move sideways, and the sepulchre was opened and both young men [οἱ νεανίκοι] entered.[12]

"Men" from heaven who appear with a great brightness seems to suggest that these beings are angels, but, as seen in other cases, these angels are referred to as "young men." It is very possible that the author of *Gospel of Peter* knew of and drew upon the (canonical) Gospel traditions in creating this narrative, but it is still valuable to consider in terms of seeing the development of the belief about angels as young men.

It seems that the announcement to the women at the tomb was delivered by angels. The description of the beings in each of the four Gospels is quite different, however. Matthew is the most explicit, saying it is the Angel of the Lord who arrives with imagery typical of angels. John says there are two angels in white.[13] Mark says the being was a "young man." Referring to angels as "young men" seems to have become commonplace by the late Second Temple period. Luke calls the beings two "men," but they also appear with "dazzling apparel," suggesting they are something special. The Gospel of Peter seems to have synthesized the picture from the canonical Gospels, calling them "two men" from heaven who are then revealed to be "angels." There does not seem to be any indication from any of the texts that these beings are not angels, whatever their appearance. They have

---

(ἐν ἐσθήσεσι λευκαῖς), and said, 'Men of Galilee, why do you stand looking into heaven? This Jesus, who was taken up from you into heaven, will come in the same way as you saw him go into heaven.'"

11. James K. Elliott (*The Apocryphal New Testament* [Oxford: Oxford University Press, 1999], 150) suggests that the *Gospel of Peter* likely dates to the mid- to late second century C.E.

12. Greek text from Maria Grazia Mara, *Évangile de Pierre: Introduction, text critique, traduction, commentaire et index* (Paris: Cerf, 1973), 56.

13. The appearance of angels in white occurs regularly in the late second Temple period, likely stemming from the visions in Ezek 1 and Dan 7–12.

specific knowledge of Jesus' whereabouts and sometimes appear with imagery commonly associated with angels, even if their physical form is of human beings.

The portrayal of angels as "young men" extends well beyond the New Testament. One example that parallels the Gospels from the *Shepherd of Hermas* will demonstrate the ongoing transition.[14] First, *Herm. Vis.* 3.1.6 states, "And she [the ancient lady] came with six young men (νεανίσκων), whom I [Hermas] had seen on the former occasion, and stood by me, and listened to me praying and confessing my sins to the Lord." These young men appear again in 3.1.7–8. Eventually Hermas enquires as to the identity of these young men (*Vis.* 3.4.1):

> I answered and said to her: "Lady, great and wonderful is this thing. But, Lady, who are the six young men (νεανίσκοι) who are building?" "These are the holy angels of God (οἱ ἅγιοι ἄγγελοι τοῦ θεοῦ), who were first created, to whom the Lord delivered all his creation to make it increase, and to build it up, and to rule the whole creation.

Carolyn Osiek believes that the six young men (= angels) may represent along with the angel Michael (who appears in *Herm. Sim.* 8.3.3; 9.6.1) the seven primary archangels (cf. *1 En.* 90:21, *T. Levi* 8:1).[15] This is certainly possible, since the archangels are seen in groups of seven (Tob 12:15; *2 En.* 19:1), but they also appear in groups of four in the literature of the period.[16] Whether angels or archangels, the identification between angels and young men is explicit.

The significant amount of evidence supporting the idea that angels were understood as young men has led Crispin Fletcher-Louis to contend that "youthfulness was also assumed of angels, to the point that a reference to 'youth' could be considered a euphemism for an angel."[17] There is certainly significant diversity in the sources that demonstrate angels being portrayed as youthful men in the first century C.E. and onward. This may have been some accommodation or adaptation to the Greco-Roman images of the gods and demigods in statues and iconography. "Young men" in the prime of their life would most closely approximate the ideals seen in Greek statues of the gods.[18] The tradition about angels and "youth" seems to have influenced Jewish circles also, and we see it well into the rabbinic period. In addition, the angel Metatron is called "youth" in *2 Enoch.*[19]

---

14. Other possible examples of "young men" as angels may appear in 2 Macc 3:26; *4 Ezra* 2:43; and Tob 5:5 (Sinaiticus).

15. Carolyn Osiek, *Shepherd of Hermas: A Commentary* (Hermeneia; Minneapolis: Fortress, 1999), 69.

16. Groupings of four appear in 1QM 9:14–16; *1 En.* 9:1; 40:9; 54:6; 71:8; *Apoc. Mos.* 40:2.

17. Fletcher-Louis, *Luke-Acts*, 131 n. 135. See also Michael Mach, *Entwicklungsstadien des judischen Engelglaubens in vorrabinischer Zeit* (Tübingen: Mohr Siebeck, 1992), 307 n. 81.

18. On the accommodation to Hellenistic ideas, see Fletcher-Louis, *Luke-Acts*, 80–81.

19. On "youth" and the angel Metatron, see Andrei Orlov, *The Enoch-Metatron Tradition* (Tübingen: Mohr Seibeck, 2005), 133–36. See also Alan Segal, *Two Powers in Heaven: Early*

Overall this suggests that in some circles the human ideal was extended back into the heavens, where the archetypal or divine/angelic form is a youthful male. All of these beliefs served to separate women from the divine and thus also from angels, but we now turn to those few occasions where the texts say something about angels and women.

2.2. Angels and Women

In most instances in the Hebrew Bible and New Testament when angels interact with women the focus is around birth (or the announcement of an impending birth).[20] This seems to be an outgrowth of the belief that women are closely linked with sexuality and childbirth/procreation (Gen 1–3; 6). Moreover, in the androcentric culture in which these texts arose, the primary social role for women would have been childrearing, so such beliefs served also to reinforce social roles of women as divinely ordained.

In the Hebrew Bible, God and two angels visit Sarah and Abraham in Gen 18–19 to announce Sarah's pregnancy. The Angel of the Lord appears to the wife of Manoah in Judg 13 to announce to her that she will bear a son, Samson. Interestingly, the text says "the Angel of the Lord," but in her description to Manoah, his wife calls the angel "a man from God" (13:6). These announcements likely acted as a model for the annunciations in the infancy narrative in the Gospel of Luke.

Angels appear to humans on three occasions in the Lukan infancy narrative: to Zechariah (1:11–24); to Mary (1:26–38); and to the shepherds (2:9–15, 21).[21] In the first occurrence, an angel of the Lord (ἄγγελος κυρίου) appears to Zechariah to announce the birth of a son (John the Baptist) to Zechariah's wife Elizabeth. The angel Gabriel is sent to Mary (1:26) to announce to her the miraculous birth of Jesus (1:31–33)—this is the only announcement directly to a woman (cf. Judg 13). Because she is unwed (1:34), Mary is dubious, but Gabriel tells her that the Holy Spirit will enter her and she will conceive.[22]

Rabbinic Reports about Christianity and Gnosticism (Leiden: Brill, 1977), 67 n. 24, where he discusses youth and old age regarding God in rabbinic texts.

20. However, above I have just noted an important exception, the women at the empty tomb in the Gospels.

21. In the Matthean infancy narrative the Angel of the Lord is said to appear to Joseph (1:20; 2:13, 19) "in a dream," telling him God's plan in order to protect the life of Jesus. In the New Testament apocryphon *Gospel of Pseudo-Matthew* 13, a "young man in shining garments" appears to Mary (trans. Elliott, *Apocryphal New Testament*, 94).

22. While not specifically about the angels, it is worthwhile in a discussion of gender to note that in Christian literature of the second century onward the Holy Spirit was often conceived of as female. Some examples of this are Origen, *Comm. Jo.* 2.12.87; and Hippolytus, *Elench.* 9.13. On this, see Sebastian Brock, "The Holy Spirit as Feminine in Early Syriac Lit-

There is one other important passage concerning women and angels in the New Testament that does not concern a birth or impending birth: 1 Cor 11:10. Therein Paul makes the enigmatic statement, "That is why a woman ought to have [ἐξουσίαν (lit. "authority," although most translate as "veil" as a symbol of authority)] on her head, because of the angels [διὰ τοὺς ἀγγέλους]."[23] Many interpreters suggest that the "authority" (ἐξουσία) on her head is a mark of subordination in keeping with Paul's statement in 11:3. Others have suggested that it is simply a veil that is meant to maintain the correct social mores in keeping with 11:5; that is, a woman's bare head is like having a shorn head—it is not socially acceptable. However, neither of these interpretations explains why Paul then includes the phrase διὰ τοὺς ἀγγέλους.

It has been suggested that the sense of the phrase "because of the angels" may be that, without some sort of covering for their heads as a prophylactic, the women of the Corinthian congregation were vulnerable to evil angels such as the "sons of God" who lusted after women (Gen 6:1–4).[24] This interpretation has on the whole been disregarded because it does not make sense in the context of Paul's discussion. Paul has said nothing to suggest these angels would represent any problem.[25] Other interpreters have suggested that the angelic presence may be "good" angels interested in the maintenance of the order of creation and proper worship.[26] In such a case, the women must be veiled because they might cause the angels to sin (*T. Reu.* 5:5–6).

Jospeh Fitzmyer points out that Paul's statement reflects the idea seen in some of the texts from the Dead Sea community that angels dwell among the actual human members of the congregation. In this case the concern of Paul and the Corinthians is something akin to what is seen in the *War Scroll* (cf. Deut 32), where purity is an issue for angelic presence. The women need to have a "veil" because an uncovered head represents the equivalent to a "bodily defect." Fitzmyer summarizes his insights from the Qumran evidence, "We are invited by the evidence from Qumran to understand that the unveiled head of a woman is like a bodily defect which should be excluded from the assembly, 'because holy

erature," in *After Eve: Women, Theology and the Christian Tradition* (ed. J. M. Soskice; London: Collins, 1990), 73–88; and Susan Ashbrook Harvey, "Feminine Imagery for the Divine: The Holy Spirit, the Odes of Solomon, and Early Syriac Tradition," *SVTQ* 37 (1993): 111–40.

23. The word κάλυμμα "veil" appears in several manuscripts and patristic sources (Irenaeus, Jerome). It appears to be a gloss meant to explain the difficult term ἐξουσίαν. See also Tertullian, *Virg.* 7:2.

24. Bo Ivar Reicke, *The Disobedient Spirits and Christian Baptism* (Copenhagen: Munksgaard, 1946).

25. Morna Hooker, "Authority on Her Head: An Examination of I Cor XI.10" *NTS* 10 (1964): 412.

26. Ibid., 412–13.

angels are present in the congregation.'"[27] However, we should recall that the evidence from Qumran demonstrates an equal concern for infirm and impure men as it is does for women. Thus, the concern is for the purity of the liturgical space. If the space is made pure, angels may be present during the liturgy. The Corinthian community mentioned above may not have been the only early Christian community to have had beliefs about angelic presence during the liturgy.[28]

Besides these few biblical references there are three other relevant passages from outside the New Testament that relate to angels and women.[29] *Life of Adam and Eve* 21 expands upon the story of Adam and Eve after their expulsion from the garden.[30] This text is another relating to women and childbirth. Eve is in the throngs of childbirth when we read in chapter 21:

> And behold, twelve angels and two excellencies (*virtutes*) came and stood to the right and to the left of Eve. And Michael stood to the right and touched her from her face to the breast and said to Eve, "Blessed are you, Eve, because of Adam. Since his prayers and utterances are many, I am sent to you that you might receive our help. Now rise and make ready to give birth." And she bore a son, and he was lustrous. And at once the infant rose, ran, and brought in his hands a reed and gave it to his mother. And his name was called Cain.[31]

Eve is flanked by twelve angels and two archangels. The Latin term *virtutes* has a strong masculine component.[32] Similar to the Hebrew Bible texts mentioned above, Eve is told that she is with child; she then gives birth to a son—not an ordinary son, however, but a son who is "lustrous." Luminosity is an angelomorphic

---

27. Joseph Fitzmyer, "A Feature of Qumran Angelology and the Angels of 1 Cor 11:10," in *Paul and Qumran* (ed. J. Murphy-O'Connor; London: Chapman, 1968), 31–47, here 43. See also Henry J. Cadbury, "A Qumran Parallel to Paul" *HTR* 51 (1958): 1–2.

28. See Col 2:18. Christopher Rowland ("Apocalyptic Visions and the Exaltation of Christ in the Letter to the Colossians" *JSNT* 19 [1983]: 73–83) argues persuasively for taking τῶν ἀγγέλων in Col 2:18 as a subjective genitive. See also Fred Francis, "Humility and Angelic Veneration in Col 2:18," in *Conflict at Colossae* (ed. F. Francis and W. Meeks; SBLSBS 4; Missoula, Mont.: Scholars Press, 1975), 163–95. Two recent studies show that scholarship is moving in this direction of understanding the Colossians text as referring to a concern for the worship of the angels in heaven: James Dunn, *The Epistles to the Colossians and to Philemon* (Grand Rapids: Eerdmans, 1996), 177–85; and C. Marvin Pate, *Communities of the Last Days: The Dead Sea Scrolls, the New Testament, and the Story of Israel* (Leicester: Apollos, 2000), 179–95.

29. Some of these texts relating to women and angels are also briefly discussed by Ross Shepard Kraemer, *When Aseneth Met Joseph: A Late Antique Tale of the Biblical Patriarch and His Egyptian Wife Reconsidered* (New York: Oxford University Press, 1998), 210–11.

30. M. D. Johnson ("Life of Adam and Eve," *OTP* 2:252) suggests a date range for this text of ca. 100 B.C.E. to 200 C.E., with a strong probability of a late first century C.E. date.

31. Ibid., 2:264.

32. "Manliness," "manhood," and "virility" are among the primary definitions of the term in *The New College Latin English Dictionary* (New York: Bantam, 1995), 446.

characteristic.[33] A particularly good example of this is the description of Noah at his birth in the *Genesis Apocryphon*.[34] Eve is not an angel herself, but she is visited by angels at the moment of birth and gives birth to a child with angelomorphic characteristics. It seems that the presence of the angels (presumably male angels) perfects Eve's birthing experience, making her son Cain wondrous.

A second text concerning angels and women is *Jos. Asen.* 18. In the preceding chapters (14–17) "a man from heaven" appears to Aseneth. The "man" is said to be very similar to Joseph in his garb, but his face and extremities are brilliant. Ross Shepard Kraemer has noted that what is special about the case of Aseneth's encounter with the angel is that Aseneth calls down the angel to herself. Moreover, Kraemer argues that Aseneth was herself transformed into an angel.[35] Kraemer cites *Jos. Asen.* 18:9–10 as important to her understanding of Aseneth's angelic transformation:

> And she brought her pure water from the spring and poured it into the basin. And Aseneth leaned (over) to wash her face and saw her face in the water. And it was like the sun and her eyes (were) like a rising morning star, and her cheeks like fields of the Most High, and on her cheeks (there was) red (color) like a son of man's blood, and her lips (were) like a rose of life coming out of its foliage, and her teeth like fighting men lined up for a fight, and the hair of her head (was) like a vine in the paradise of God prospering in its fruits, and her neck like an all-variegated cypress, and her breasts (were) like the mountains of the Most High God. And when Aseneth saw herself in the water, she was amazed at the sight and rejoiced with great joy, and did not wash her face, for she said, "Perhaps I (will) wash off this great beauty."

It is not clear how far this passage can be taken in terms of Aseneth's actual transformation into an angel, but it is suggestive. Her beauty is dramatically increased, and the hyperbolic language suggests her appearance is more than human. It may be that this transformation is meant to be understood as a lasting one, but it is not clear from the text. More important, however, Kramer has shown quite clearly that Aseneth has an actual hand in summoning the angel with whom she interacts. Aseneth spends time with the angel and even partakes of his special food. This is intimate interaction between a woman and an angel, and if Kraemer is correct, then Aseneth initiates the contact with the angel, making this text quite unique.

Lastly, we consider excerpts from the *T. Job* 48:1; 49:1; 50:1. Like other writings in the testament genre, the work purports to record the words of Job near

33. Sullivan, *Wrestling with Angels*, 30–32.

34. Ibid., 93–96.

35. Kraemer, *When Aseneth Met Joseph*, 104–5.

the end of his life.[36] The three daughters of Job receive and put on garments that seem to bring about an angelomorphic transformation:

> [48:1] Thus, when the one called Hermera arose, she wrapped around her own string just as her father had said. [2] And she took on another heart—no longer minded toward earthly things—but she spoke ecstatically in the angelic dialect (τῇ ἀγγελικῇ διαλέκτῳ), sending up a hymn to God in accord with the hymnic style of the angels (τὴν τῶν ἀγγέλων ὑμνολογίαν). And as she spoke ecstatically, she allowed, "The Spirit" (τό πνεῦμα) to be inscribed on her garment.
>
> [49:1] Then Kasia bound hers on and had her heart changed so that she no longer regarded worldly things. [2] And her mouth took on the dialect of the archons (τῶν ἀρχῶν) and she praised God for the creation of the heights. [3] So, if anyone wishes to know "The Creation of the Heavens," he will be able to find it in "The Hymns of Kasia."
>
> [50:1] Then the other one also, named Amaltheia's Horn, bound on her cord. And her mouth spoke ecstatically in the dialect of those on high, [2] since her heart also was changed, keeping aloof from worldly thing. For she spoke in the dialect of the cherubim, glorifying the Master of virtues by exhibiting their splendor. [3] And finally whoever wishes to grasp a trace of "The Paternal Splendor" will find it written down in "The Prayers of Amaltheia's Horn."[37]

It seems clear that the daughters of Job were transformed by putting on their garments. One of the important transformations mentioned for each is the internal "change of heart." They no longer were concerned with things of mortal life but were more focused on the worship of God. Most important, their worship took the form of speaking (ecstatically) in the melodic form of the angels (cf. Luke 2:13–14; 1 Cor 13:1). Van der Horst suggests the women undergo "a radical and lasting change; in fact they become virtually heavenly beings."[38] However, it is not clear that their change is a permanent one or if it is specifically related to their putting on of garments. What is particularly fascinating about this passage is that it is the *daughters* of Job who are the ones who become angelomorphic.

What, then, can be said about women and angels? There are several instances where angels interact with human females, but far fewer than those in which angels interact with men. It is often the case that this interaction involves birth or the announcement of an impending birth, but it is not exclusive to this, as in the empty tomb narratives. Virtually no texts present angels as female. Only in the

---

36. Russell P. Spittler ("Testament of Job," *OTP* 1:833–34) dates the work to about the end of the first century B.C.E.

37. Translations from *OTP* 1:865–66; Greek text taken from Sebastian Brock, *Testamentum Iobi* (Leiden: Brill, 1967), 56–57.

38. Pieter Willem van der Horst, "Images of Women in the Testament of Job" in *Studies on the Testament of Job* (ed. M. Knibb and P. van der Horst; Cambridge: Cambridge University Press, 1989), 104.

Testament of Job is there a hint that human females might achieve angelic status, but even in that text the permanence of their transformation is not certain.

It is important in this context also to mention briefly the Holy Spirit. While very rarely referred to as an angel specifically, it nevertheless has a number of angelic characteristics and, importantly in later Christian literature, is sometimes understood as female.[39] A feminine aspect within the Godhead would not represent a Christian innovation, however. First, the word for "spirit" in Hebrew (רוח) is feminine.[40] This spirit/wind is present in creation (Gen 1:2), and the spirit of the Lord is mentioned numerous times in the Hebrew Bible (e.g., Judg 6:34; 1 Sam 16:14; Job 27:3). Also, Wisdom (חכמה) appears as an independent, female entity that participates in creation (Prov 8:22–31), is understood to have acted in history as the Angel of the Lord (Wis 10), and has a place in the heavens (*1 En.* 42:1–2).[41]

Thus, a cue taken from Hebrew grammar, namely, that both *spirit* and *wisdom* are feminine, might have suggested a gender for the Holy Spirit to some early Christian writers. Indeed, the Holy Spirit was conceived of as female in a number of texts (*Gos. Phil.* 55:23–6; *Gos. Heb.* frag. 3; Irenaeus, *Haer.* 1.29–30; Origen, *Comm. Jo.* 2.12.87; Hippolytus, *Elench.* 9.13; and Epiphanius, *Pan.* 53.1.9 report that Elchesai claimed the Holy Spirit to be the sister of Christ).[42] The Holy Spirit appears to have some angelic qualities, such as independent being, ability to act in the world, convey God's will, and the like, and it was sometimes likened to an angel (e.g., *Ascen. Isa.* 11:32; *Herm. Mand.* 11.9), perhaps most clearly by Elchesai, as reported in Hippolytus, *Ref.* 13.2–3, where Jesus Christ and the Holy Spirit seem to be male and female angels, respectively.[43] In Theophilus of Antioch, *Autol* 1.7; 2.15, 18, and Irenaeus, *Demon.* 5, 10, the third person of the Trinity is not called "Holy Spirit" but instead "Wisdom," which suggests some sort of identification between them. Lastly, Sophia, is portrayed in many so-called gnostic texts as a feminine, angelic being often identified with Wisdom from the Hebrew Bible and sometimes with activities often associated the Holy Spirit (e.g.,

---

39. On "spirits" and "the spirit" as angels, see Charles A. Gieschen, *Angelomorphic Christology: Antecedents and Early Evidence* (AGJU 42; Leiden: Brill, 1998), 114–19.

40. For discussion of the "spirit" in Judaism, see John R. Levison, *The Spirit in First Century Judaism* (Leiden: Brill, 1997); and Arthur Everett Sekki, *The Meaning of Ruaḥ at Qumran* (SBLDS 110; Atlanta: Scholars Press, 1989).

41. On Wisdom as a hypostatic being or angel, see Gieschen, *Angelomorphic Christology*, 89–103.

42. On this, see Sebastian Brock, "The Holy Spirit as Feminine in Early Syriac Literature," in Soskice, *After Eve*, 73–88; and Harvey, "Feminine Imagery for the Divine," *SVTQ* 37 (1993): 111–40.

43. For a discussion of this passage, see Gerard P. Luttikhuizen, *The Revelation of Elchasai* (Tübingen: Mohr Siebeck, 1985), 123, 196–99; and Guy G. Strousma, "Le couple de l'ange et de l'esprit: Traditions juives et chrétiennes," *RB* 88 (1981): 42–61.

Apocryphon of John, Eugnostos, Sophia of Jesus Christ, On the Origin of the World, A Valentinian Exposition).[44]

It is not entirely clear why such a gender bias should necessarily exist in the discussion of angels. Some of the bias against woman may stem from a belief in women as being ritually impure during menstruation (Lev 12:1–8; 15:25–30; see also *m. Kelim* 1:8), thus excluded from holy places such as the inner parts of the Jerusalem temple. This may have been extended by analogy to the heavens. That is, women could be ritually impure and therefore would not be able to occupy sacred space. Such beliefs were created and perpetuated in a male-dominated culture. What stands out even more from these texts is that the issues of sexuality, gender, and sin seem to be integrally bound up in the role of women in many of these texts. From the human females who copulate with the "sons of God" in Gen 6 to the women in the Corinthian church to the daughters of Job, these texts from an androcentric culture portray women as flawed and sinful and in need of male (divine) assistance for perfection. Clearly, this mindset was pervasive into the first Christian centuries, as we will see below, so consideration will be given to the ways in which it appears that these beliefs about the sexual nature of angels may have influenced the practice of early Jewish and Christian mystics.

3. Angels and Mystics

Robin Lane Fox writes that "in the single most influential text (Luke 20:35–36), he [Jesus] stated that Christians who are worthy of the next life 'neither marry nor give in marriage, neither can they die any longer.' … It needed only a slight shift of emphasis to refer the absence of marriage to this world, not the next."[45] What Lane Fox is suggesting is that this Gospel saying was absolutely central to the early Christian appropriation of ascetic practices.[46] Why would the early Christians take on a abstinent lifestyle? I want to suggest that, based on their belief that angels, who resided in heaven with God, did not marry or have sex for procreation, the early mystics, who sought to commune with God, chose to imitate the angels. Other New Testament passages such as Paul's saying in Gal 3:28 ("There is neither Jew nor Greek, there is neither slave nor free, *there is neither male nor female;* for you are all one in Christ Jesus") and 1 Cor 7:8 ("To the unmarried and the widows I say that it is well for them to remain single as I do") likely only added fuel to their desire to put this belief about sexual abstinence into practice.

---

44. On this see also Simone Pétrement, *A Separate God: The Origins and Teachings of Gnosticism* (New York: HarperCollins, 1990), 75–100; and esp. see George W. MacRae, "The Jewish Background of the Gnostic Sophia Myth," *NovT* 12 (1970): 86–101.

45. Robin Lane Fox, *Pagans and Christians* (New York: Penguin, 1986), 363.

46. On this see also Karl Frank Suso, *Angelikos Bios: Begriffsanalytische und begriffsgeschichtliche Untersuchung zum 'engelgliechen Leben' im frühen Mönchtum* (Beiträge zur Geschichte des alten Mönchtums und des Benediktinerordens 26; Münster: Aschendorff, 1964).

The imitation of the angelic ideal may have served two purposes (which are not mutually exclusive). First, this may have been seen as a preparation for a future reality; that is, the ascetics believed that their practices on earth would make them better able to be received into the heavenly realm after their death. Second, the ascetics may have believed that they were already participating in the angelic life while on earth, and it seems that this was the case at least as some traditions developed. Those same beliefs also meant that females were at a distinct disadvantage in terms of their ability to commune with God. Their gender separated them from the divine and even perhaps from even achieving the divine throne room. In a well-known passage from the *Gospel of Thomas* (114) we see a hint as to what at least one community felt about the readiness of women to enter into the kingdom

> Simon Peter said to them, "Let Mary leave us, for women are not worthy of life." Jesus said, "I myself shall lead her in order to make her male, so that she too may become a living spirit resembling you males. For every woman who will make herself male will enter the kingdom of Heaven."

DeConick sees this logion as coming into the Thomasine tradition at the accretion stage (ca. 80–120 C.E.).[47] This means the attitudes in logion 114 likely reflect the attitudes of one strand of some late first-century Christians and could represent ideas that circulated even earlier. Thus, women had to make themselves male, through ascetic practice, in order to enter the kingdom of God.[48]

This seems to have been the beginning of the trajectories that led to celibate clergy and also virgins for Christ in the second century C.E. and onward. Thus Susanna Elm writes,

> If the ascetic life transforms humans into angels … then the symbiosis of male and female ascetics represents the highest form of ascetic perfection. If through asceticism a woman achieves "male" virtue (*aretē*), and is thereby transformed into a "manly woman", then she has not only achieved true equality with her male counterparts, but has been transformed into an ideal, complete human being.[49]

Here, then, we see the irony in the imaging of the sexual nature of angels. The image of angels as celibate (or nonsexually active) males, and even specifically as young males, was likely a reflection of the patriarchal society in which those beliefs

---

47. April DeConick, *Rediscovering the Original Gospel of Thomas*, 187–88.

48. DeConick has also discussed the importance of the human-angel analogous spiritual marriage in Valentinianism, see April DeConick, "The Great Mystery of Marriage: Sex and Conception in Ancient Valentinian Traditions," *VC* 57 (2003): 307–42.

49. See also Susanna Elm, *Virgins of God: The Making of Asceticism in Late Antiquity* (Oxford: Clarendon, 1994), ix.

arose; however, that very same ideal, now understood as a heavenly archetype, was thus re-enforced as the ideal that even women should strive to achieve through celibacy. Thus belief about the gender and sexual nature of angels seems to have had a significant impact upon the practice of some early Christian mystics.

The idea of the celibate lifestyle is not without some parallels in Jewish circles, however. Two groups merit consideration: the Theraputae and the Qumran community. Philo discusses the Theraputae in his treatise *De vita contemplativa* (esp. 2–3, 10–40, 64–90).[50] Philo says that among the Theraputae were both men and women and that the women "spurned the pleasures of the body and desire no mortal offspring but those immortal children which only the soul that is dear to God can bring to birth" (*Contempl.* 68). Philo adds the Theraputae exemplify a community focussed on contemplation and mystical attainment:

> The Theraputae, a people always taught from the first to use their sight, should desire the vision of the Existent and soar above the sun and our senses and never leave their place in this company which carries them on to perfect happiness ... but carried away by a heaven-sent passion of love, remain rapt and possessed like bacchanals or corybants until they see the object of their yearning. Then such is their longing for the deathless and blessed life that thinking their mortal life already ended they abandon their property to their sons and daughters or to other kinsfolk, thus voluntarily advancing the time of their inheritance. (11–13)

Philo ends his discussion by calling the Theraputae those who have "lived in the soul alone, citizens of Heaven and the world" (90). There is no explicit mention of angels in *De vita contemplativa*. So, if Philo's portrayal is of an actual community, then it seems their choice to eschew sexual practice seems to be directly linked with the hope of attainment to the divine.[51]

Lastly, we must discuss briefly the Qumran community, whom most scholars equate with the Essenes mentioned by Philo and Josephus. Some of the texts record that this community had members who were celibate. Qimron and Baumgarten have argued that *Damascus Document* 6:11–7:8 is demonstrative of the reports of Josephus (*War* 2.119–121, 160–161), who records that there were

---

50. Francis H. Colson and George W. Whitaker, trans., *Philo* (10 vols.; LCL. Cambridge: Harvard University Press, 1932–62), 9:119, 121.

51. Brian McNeil ("The Narration of Zosimus," *JSJ* 9 [1978]: 68–82) has argued that the text known as the *History of the Rechabites* (= *The Narration of Zosimus*) is a writing of the Theraputae. However, in considering the Theraputae, McNeil himself notes, "Also significant is the lack of a single mention of angels—we are not even told that the Theraputae believe in angels—whereas the Rechabites are 'brethren of angels'" (77). So while his is an interesting assertion, the connection between the Theraputae and Rechabites cannot be proven. On the Rechabites, see Jer 35:2, 3, 5, 18.

two types of Essenes: some who were married and others who were celibate.[52] The results of Qimron's and Baumgarten's work suggest that the primary reason for the celibate strand of Essenes/Qumranites was the belief that celibacy was necessary for angelic life.[53] Other texts from the Dead Sea Scrolls, such as the *Songs of the Sabbath Sacrifice,* also seem to evince a concern for angelic presence, especially at liturgy.[54]

One final issue with regard to angels and Qumran is the priesthood. The recent work of Rachel Elior is of particular relevance here.[55] Elior argues for a strong correspondence between the secessionist priests and the angels. She notes that "the angels, the immortal counterparts of the priests, provide a source of heavenly validity, role model or reference group.... the angels are the heavenly witnesses to the Covenant, in parallel to the priests, who fulfil that function on earth."[56] Thus the priesthood was likely a specific social circle in which beliefs about the gender of angels (as males) reinforced social realities, namely, that priests should be male.

In sum, if the goal of these mystics was communion with God, it would necessarily mean transcending the human condition.[57] The mystics certainly had role models to whom they could aspire (e.g., Enoch, Jacob, Moses).[58] These individuals had transcended their human nature and had been transformed into divine beings and now resided with God. These righteous individuals, however, were just that, exceptionally righteous individuals chosen by God to a special status.

What hope was there for the individual mystic? I suggest that the texts considered here offer us an important clue. The mystics sought to understand the nature of heavenly existence in order to commune with God. Angels were the

52. Joseph Baumgarten, "The Qumran-Essene Restraints on Marriage," in *Archaeology and History in the Dead Sea Scrolls* (ed. L. Schiffman; Sheffield: Sheffield Academic Press, 1990), 13–24; Elisha Qimron, "Celibacy in the Dead Sea Scrolls and the Two Kinds of Sectarians," in *The Madrid Qumran Congress: Proceedings of the International Congress on the Dead Sea Scrolls* (ed. J. Trebolle Barrera and L. Vegas Montaner; 2 vols.; Leiden: Brill, 1992), 1:287–94.

53. That the Essenes or Qumran community might also be the descendants of the biblical Rechabites has been suggested by some scholars. This has on the whole been rejected. See Chris H. Knights, "The Rechabites of Jeremiah 35: Forerunners of the Essenes?" *JSP* 10 (1992): 81–87.

54. For much more on this subject, see Crispin Fletcher-Louis, *All the Glory of Adam: Liturgical Anthropology in the Dead Sea Scrolls* (Leiden: Brill, 2002).

55. Rachel Elior, *The Three Temples: On the Emergence of Jewish Mysticism* (Oxford: Littman Library of Jewish Civilization, 2004), 165–200.

56. Ibid., 180.

57. On the overall outlook and goals of the early Jewish and Christian mystics, see April DeConick, ed., "Early Jewish and Christian Mysticism: A Collage of Working Definitions," in *Society of Biblical Literature 2001 Seminar Papers* (SBLSP 40; Atlanta: Society of Biblical Literature, 2001), 278–304.

58. Sullivan, *Wrestling with Angels*, 235–36.

perfect intermediary for their contemplation. The mystics knew from their own traditions that angels traveled between heaven and earth. They knew also that angels were in God's presence in the divine throne room. Lastly, they knew some specific human beings had achieved angelic status.

These beliefs could have convinced the early mystics that they themselves could have access to God through imitation of the angels. The individuals who had reached heaven and been transformed, though, were all *males*. Moreover, maleness seems to have been closely linked to the divine—both God and angels were believed to be male. I suggest that beliefs about the nonsexual nature of angels, and their strong maleness (even youthful maleness), especially influenced the early Christians who lived the ascetic life and wrote texts such as the *Gospel of Thomas,* promoting both asexuality and maleness as means to becoming closer to God. Such beliefs were, of course, socially conditioned and also functioned to maintain roles of power already extant in society, but they were empowering insomuch as they sought to transcend human mortality for both males and females. In a close analogy, some early Jewish mystical predecessors, such as the Therapeutae and the Essenes, also seem to have believed that the nature of the angelic life and the angelic proximity to the divine made their life one worth imitating. Whether in Jewish or Christian circles, the belief that angels were male and nonsexual seems to have influenced the encratic practices of some early ascetics and mystics.

Part 4:
Apocalypticism

Lessons on Early Jewish Apocalypticism and Mysticism from Dream Literature

Frances Flannery-Dailey

> And I gazed at all of myself, and I had become like one of the glorious ones, and there was no observable difference. (*2 En.* 22:10)

Hellenistic Jewish authors showed a marked interest in relating dream narratives, some of which they borrowed from the Hebrew Bible and expanded and some of which they seem to have invented whole cloth. Sheer numbers are one indication of this interest. While there are less than thirty dreams in the whole Hebrew Bible and only five or six in the New Testament, there are easily over a hundred narrated dream episodes in early Jewish extracanonical literature, including the apocryphal and pseudepigraphal works, Josephus, Dead Sea Scrolls, and Philo.[1] More important, these dreams are *much* more complex and well- developed than are biblical dreams.

1. Using form-critical methods based on ancient Near Eastern dream patterns established by A. Leo Oppenheim, I identify the following episodes as dreams in the Hebrew Bible containing narrative content: Gen 15:12–21; 20:3–7; 26:24; 29:10–22; 31:10–13; 31:24; 37:5–7; 37:9; 40:9–15; 40:16–19; 41:1–4; 41:5–8; 46:2–4; Num 22:9–13, 20–21; Judg 7:13–14; 1 Sam 3:2–5, 5b–6, 6b–15; 1 Kgs 3:5–15; 19:5–7; Zech 1:8–4:2; Job 4:12–21; Dan 2:31–35; 4:4–18; 7:1–28; Jer 30:1–31:26. See A. Leo Oppenheim, *Interpretation of Dreams in the Ancient Near East: With a Translation of an Assyrian Dream-Book* (TAPA 46.3; Philadelphia: American Philosophical Society, 1956). Also see Robert Gnuse, *The Dream Theophany of Samuel: Its Structure in Relation to Ancient Near Eastern Dreams and Its Theological Significance* (Lanham, Md.: University Press of America, 1984). New Testament dreams include Matt 1:20, 2:13, 2:19; Acts 12:6, 16:9 and probably 23:11. One or more dreams appear in each of the following Jewish texts from the third century B.C.E. to the second century C.E.: *1 En.* 1–36; 83–90; Daniel; *Jubilees*; 2 Maccabees; Additions to Esther; *Liber antiquitatum biblicarum; Testament of Abraham; Testament of Naphtali; Testament of Joseph; Testament of Job;* Josephus's *War, Jewish Antiquities, Life,* and *Against Apion;* 1QapGen; 11QtgJob; 4QEn; 4QBook of Giants; 4QApocryJac; 4QAramLevi; 4QVisions of Amram; 4QPrayerNab; 4QVisSam; 4QPsalms; 11QPs; perhaps 4QElect of God; and Philo, *Somn.* and *Migr.* Dreams also occur in *2 Enoch, Testament of Levi,* Ezekiel the Tragedian, and *Ladder of Jacob,* which are arguably Jewish and early in their original versions.

Although early Jewish dreams share much with contemporary and antecedent dreams of other traditions, a number of unique developments and emphases arose as Hellenistic Jewish authors creatively reinvented standard literary conventions of divinely sent dreams. Many of the changes boldly envision a suspension of the conventional limits placed on human reality, as pseudepigraphic dreamers transcend space, time, and bodily constraints. I contend that the "dream logic" employed by these authors sheds significant light on ancient apocalyptic and mystical worldviews, with implications for current scholarly approaches used in researching early Jewish apocalypticism and mysticism.

1. The Context for Dreams in Antiquity

Any investigation of ancient dreams should begin with the question: What is a dream? Post-Freudian audiences assume that a dream is an imaginary set of scenes stemming from the subconscious brain that occurs only when the dreamer sleeps, while a vision is akin to an imaginary perception that occurs in a waking state.[2] Although materially unreal, dreams are thus valuable for discerning a dreamer's past or present psychology. None of these assumptions can be applied to ancient dreams.

Because ancient and modern conceptions of dreams differ markedly, form criticism is an important tool for identifying which narrative episodes are construed *by ancient peoples* as dreams, in terms of stylized formal patterns bearing some relation to the nightly act of actual dreaming. I maintain that this initial formal identification is essential if we are to avoid imposing our modern conceptions on ancient dreams.[3] In the case of ancient Near Eastern and Mediterranean dreams, a dream setting is usually present in which someone lies down in a bed at night, goes to sleep, and dreams, after which he or she wakes up and relates the deep impression the dream has made.

However, the "sleep" that ancient texts describe seems to be a kind of hypnagogic waking sleep, in which the dreamer is capable of *seeing* things that he or she cannot withstand or perceive during a normal waking state. The etymology of many cultures' vocabulary for dreaming stresses the act of seeing; for example, the Egyptian word for dream, *rswt,* is written with the determinative of an open eye, and the most common Hebrew word for dream, *ḥalom,* probably stems from the Ugaritic root meaning "to see" and is often used interchangeably with *ra'ah*

---

2. Sigmund Freud, *The Interpretation of Dreams* (8th ed.; trans. J. Strachey, New York: Basic Books, 1965).

3. Although dreams and visions are closely intertwined, for the sake of manageability I have chosen to concentrate my attention on revelatory episodes in antiquity clearly articulated form-critically or linguistically as dreams; additional studies on visions would be helpful and most welcome.

"to see" and *ḥazon* "vision."[4] Thus a narrative dream frame usually connotes the idea that a person has been able to see or understand something extraordinary in a semiwaking state.

Ancient people knew of "psychological status" dreams thought to be induced by the dreamer's state of mind, health, or what one had for dinner, which is somewhat consonant with our view of things.[5] Most recorded dreams, however, were considered to be objectively real visits or messages by deities. Oppenheim's "message dream" and "symbolic dream" types are remarkably consistent for thousands of years across cultures of the ancient Near East and Mediterranean in both literature and cult, suggesting that the actual dreams of people in cultic situations were articulated through these stylized patterns.[6]

In message dreams, a deity or representative of the deity "stands" next to a dreamer and relates a message, although sometimes only a voice is heard in an "auditory message dream." Although the text typically concludes by saying "Then I awoke," the visit is deemed to be entirely real, so that sometimes an object from the dream persists or, in a *Wecktraum,* the dream visitor remains in the room upon awakening.[7] In symbolic dreams, messages are relayed from deities in strange, cryptic symbols that must be decoded by other deities in dreams or, upon awakening, by professional dream interpreters.[8] In both literature and cult, dreams in antiquity had three main functions: the revelation of extraordinary knowledge, usually about the future; the sanction or punishment of the dreamer; and healing or the reverse.

Obviously, the dream traditions from antiquity that have the most bearing on early Jewish dreams are biblical dreams. Twenty-eight dreams are present in the Hebrew Bible, and all of Oppenheim's dream patterns from the ancient Near

4. See Frances Flannery-Dailey, *Dreamers, Scribes and Priests: Jewish Dreams in the Hellenistic and Roman Eras* (JSJSup ; Leiden: Brill, 2004), 24–26, 46–47, 62, 88.

5. Even this situation is not strictly comparable to modern notions, since Oppenheim argues that peoples of the ancient Near East understood the psychological status and health of a person to be a general expression of the person's cultic standing or "the extent to which [the person was] endowed with the protective deities who safeguard the life, success, and happiness of the individual" (*Interpretation of Dreams,* 232). Ancient dream books such as that of Artemidorus served to interpret such ordinary dreams, which were nevertheless important to interpret and act upon in a manner consonant with the will of the gods.

6. For Oppenheim's types, see ibid., 186–90, 206–8. See further Flannery-Dailey, *Dreamers, Scribes and Priests,* 57–99.

7. Oppenheim, *Interpretation of Dreams,* 189–90.

8. E.g. ibid., 220–22; Serge Sauneron "Les songes et leur interprétation dans l'Égypte ancienne," in *Les songes et leur interprétation* (ed. S. Sauneron; Sources orientales 2; Paris: Seuil, 1959), 32–35; Marcel Leibovici, "Les songes et leur interprétation à Babylone," in Sauneron, *Les songes,* 70–72; Maurice Vieyra, "Les songes et leur interprétation chez les Hittites," in Sauneron, *Les songes,* 89; Aksel D. F. Volten, *Demotische Traumdeutung* (Analecta Aegyptiaca 3; Kopenhagen: Munksgaard, 1942).

East are found: the message dream, the auditory message dream, the *Wecktraum*, and the symbolic dream.[9] There are a few differences between biblical dreams and other dream traditions, but the similarities generally outweigh the differences.[10]

The messenger in dreams is most often YHWH himself or his voice (Gen 15:12–21; 20:3–7; 28:10–22; 31:24; Num 22:9–13; 1 Sam 3:2–15; 1 Kgs 3:5–15). Much as in the ancient Near East, no humans—living or dead—appear in biblical dreams except in symbolic form.[11] Also, although angels serve as messengers of YHWH throughout the Hebrew Bible, they do not typically do so in dreams.[12] The idea that God cannot be seen might lead us to presume that the Tetragrammaton is somehow shorthand for "angel of YHWH," but this is actually our importation into the text, which often simply states "YHWH stood" (יהוה נצב; e.g. Gen 28:10–22), just as do other dream deities, such as Ishtar, Asclepius, or Isis.[13]

Biblical dreams share two of the functions of dreams in surrounding cultures: conferring extraordinary knowledge of the future (less often of the present) and especially bestowing divine sanction. Covenants are made with the three patriarchs through dreams (Gen 15:12–21; 26:24; 28:10–22). One difference is that in biblical dreams the dreamers are not healed physically.[14]

Finally, the phenomenon of soul travel that occurs in scattered dream accounts in the ancient Near East, Greece, and Rome appears to be absent in biblical dreams. Most ancient Near Eastern netherworld journeys of humans occur in dreams or visions, as in the case of Enkidu's dream in the Epic of Gilgamesh

---

9. For a classification of each dream type, which are relatively straightforward for biblical dreams except for Gen 28, see Flannery-Dailey, *Dreamers, Scribes and Priests*, 42–44.

10. One important difference between biblical dreams and cognate literature concerns gender. Ancient Near Eastern dream literature records a few dreams by women, and the number steadily increases in Greek and Roman dreams, yet there are no dreams by females in the Hebrew Bible. Women are also renowned as dream interpreters in the ancient Near East, Greece, and Rome, but the famous dream interpreters of the Bible are men: Joseph and Daniel. See Vieyra, "Les songes et leur interprétation," 92–94; *ARM* X 50, 100; Jack Sasson, "Mari Dreams," *JAOS* 103 (1983): 283–93; Abraham Malamat, "A Forerunner of Biblical Prophecy: The Mari Documents," in *Ancient Israelite Religion: Essays in Honor of Frank Moore Cross* (eds. P. D. Miller, P. D. Hanson, and S. D. McBride; Philadelphia: Fortress, 1987), 33–52; Oppenheim, *Interpretation of Dreams*, 190, 220–22.

11. Dreams of dead and living persons rarely if ever appear in the ancient Near East, except in a few Hittite dreams featuring the voices of living persons and, once, of a deceased person (Oppenheim, *Interpretation of Dreams*, 193). Humans, living and dead, abound in Greek and Roman dreams, e.g., Euripides, *El.* 410–425; *Hec.* 1–97; *Orest.* 618–620; *Alc.* 349–356; Aeschylus, *Eum.* 94–104; Virgil, *Aen.* 1.341–372; 2.264–294; 4.326–360; 5.705–739; cf. the *catabasis* of book 6.

12. Cf. the appearance of an angel in a dream to Joseph in Matthew (1:20; 2:13, 19), which becomes well known and influential in the iconography of early and medieval Christianity.

13. Oppenheim, *Interpretation of Dreams*, 189.

14. An exception might be argued in the case of 1 Kgs 19:5–7, which may be a *Wecktraum* wherein an angel provides Elijah with strengthening food and drink.

in which he sees Ereshkigal, Queen of the Netherworld, seated on her throne. Closely related to this idea is the theme in both ancient Near Eastern and Greco-Roman dreams that the underworld is the source of dreams.[15] This motif is related in complex ways to much later dream-tours of heaven, such as Cicero's "Dream of Scipio" (ca. 50 B.C.E.).[16] Thus, it is striking that in the Hebrew Bible no such soul journey occurs in a dream, whether "up" or "down." Rather, Ezekiel's visionary tour, which possesses none of the formal characteristics of dreams, appears to serve as the carrier of this tradition between ancient Near Eastern and Hellenistic Jewish literature.

2. Hellenistic Jewish Dreams

Against this background the unique contours of Hellenistic Jewish dreams become apparent. As both cultural horizons and the perceived cosmos broadened dramatically, Hellenistic peoples reacted by practicing various methods of gaining intimacy with remote gods who suddenly seemed even more transcendent. Interest in mystery cults, oracles, and divinatory arts soared, as did the practice of dream incubation, or the purposeful provoking of a dream from a deity. For example, Asclepius, the most popular divine patron of dreams, had over four hundred temple sites throughout the Mediterranean and Near East in the Hellenistic period, including in ancient Israel/Palestine.[17]

Jews in particular found that Hellenism brought a variety of conceptual and material crises from the fourth century B.C.E. to the second century C.E., including the Diadochoi wars that wreaked havoc over Palestine; the threat of Hellenistic syncretism and changing lifestyles; Antiochus IV Epiphanes' proscription of Torah in 168 B.C.E.; rule by Macedonian Greeks, Ptolemies, Seleucids, and Romans; numerous desecrations of the Jerusalem temple by Gentiles and illegitimate Jewish priests; competing interpretations of Torah and temple among Jews; the destruction of the Second Temple by the Romans in 70 C.E.; and the Jewish-Roman wars of 68–72 and 132–135 C.E., culminating in the expulsion of Jews from Jerusalem. Out of this crucible of crisis came the most creative innovations in dream traditions that the ancient world had ever seen.

---

15. Flannery-Dailey, *Dreamers, Scribes and Priests*, 66; Alan Segal, *Life after Death: A History of the Afterlife in the Religions of the West* (New York: Doubleday, 2004), 77–78, 85; cf. 186, 196–97.

16. Segal, *Life after Death*, 222, 240–44. Ralph Feen ("Nedyia [*sic*] as Apocalypse: A Study of Cicero's *Dream of Scipio*," *JRS* 9 [1981]: 28–34) has drawn parallels between Cicero's "Dream of Scipio" and the Jewish apocalyptic literature, without positing dependence.

17. Emma Jeannette Edelstein and Ludwig Edelstein, *Asclepius: A Collection and Interpretation of the Testimonies* (2 vols.; Baltimore: Johns Hopkins University Press, 1945; repr., New York: Garland, 1975), 1:370–441.

As compared with biblical dreams, early Jewish dreams soar in both number and complexity. The typical patterns established by Oppenheim—message dreams, auditory message dreams, symbolic dreams and *Weckträumen*—still obtain. However, several new emphases appear, and overall there is a shift in worldview vis-à-vis biblical dreams that both constructs and radically deconstructs symbolic orderings of the world along three axes: spatial, temporal, and ontological orderings.[18] On the one hand, early Jewish authors presupposed a *construction* of the world that generally follows the viewpoint of many later biblical texts.[19] Spatially, heaven is perceived as a temple/palace (the *hekhal*) from which God rules on high, seated on a throne; the mercy seat in the Jerusalem temple is the main point of connection between God's presence and earth (Isa 6; cf. Ezek 10:18–19). Temporally, humans recognize that we live in the present with some knowledge of the past, but knowledge of the far-removed past and of the future is known only to God (e.g., Job 38:4–11). Even when God promises assurances to prophets that present crises will pass, one readily senses that only God fully knows the details (e.g., Isa 65:16–25; Jer 50:31–32; cf. Ezek 39:23, 29). Ontologically, humans are confronted with limited life in a broken world where the validity of the reward and punishment system of the covenant is often called into question (Job; Eccl 9:1–11), and we mortal humans are generally barred from the kind of access to the divine that angels enjoy (e.g., Josh 5:13–15; Zech 1:13–14; Eccl 3:19–20; cf. Isa 6).

On the other hand, early Jewish authors then proceed to use dream narratives and, to some degree, vision narratives, to *deconstruct* all of these barriers in a radical fashion. As anyone who has ever dreamed knows, dreams erase normal spatial, temporal, and ontological lines of reality. Hellenistic Jewish dream narratives exploit this dream logic to the fullest, far beyond their ancient Near Eastern and Greco-Roman counterparts. Spatially, dreamers such as Enoch and Levi fly around the remote edges of the earth or even shoot up to the heavenly temple, previously the domain of only the angels and God (*1 En.* 14–36; *T. Levi* 5–7).

---

18. Many early Jewish innovations to the standard dream traditions demonstrate the influence of Greco-Roman traditions. In early Jewish dreams, both living humans (Josephus, *Ant.* 11.333–335) and dead humans appear as dream messengers (2 Macc 15; Josephus, *War* 2.114–116; *Ant.* 17.349–353), which is consonant with Greco-Roman dream culture but extremely rare in the ancient Near East and abhorrent to the Bible. As in Greece and Rome, but unlike in the Bible, a few women are given dreams (*L.A.B.* 9.10; *Jub.* 35:6; Josephus, *War* 2.114–116; *Ant.* 17.349–353; *Ap.* 1.206–207; Matt 27:19). Finally, in numerous early Jewish dreams we see a remarkable, Roman-like fascination with death intertwined with dreaming in all sorts of ways, from deathbed testaments relating dreams to the Angel of Death drawing out Abraham's soul "as in a dream." See further, Flannery-Dailey, *Dreamers, Scribes and Priests,* 120, 125, 201–8, 228–43, 267–69.

19. Many, but not all. Clearly, Zech 1–7 presents similar scenarios of bridging heavenly and earthly realms; a few other texts might be included.

This is possible ontologically in that they are transformed into angelic beings themselves, as Enoch says in *2 Enoch:* "And I gazed at all of myself, and I had become like one of the glorious ones, and there was no observable difference" (*2 En.* 22:8–10; see also *T. Levi* 8:1–19).[20] Temporally, early Jewish dreams erase the boundaries between past, present, and future. Dreamers (and hence readers) are privy to secrets about primordial events (e.g., *1 En.* 1–36; 83–84; *2 Bar.* 56) or more commonly about eschatological resolutions to come, addressing a variety of areas of concern. Daniel witnesses the future judgment of the Seleucid kingdom, Ezra learns of national judgment as well as the death and resurrection of all of humankind, and Baruch sees the whole span of cosmic time symbolically portrayed in periodic shifts culminating with God's victory (Dan 7:9–28; *4 Ezra* 11–13; *2 Bar.* 56–74). The precise contents of each revelation differ, but the overall premise is that a dreamer learns extraordinary knowledge that connotes divine sanction and favor on him as well as on his descendents, who constitute the immediate readership of the texts.

Thus, through dreams pseudepigraphic characters from Israel's history leave the earth, see places of punishment and reward of the dead, mix freely with angels, become angels themselves, glimpse the primordial past or eschatological future, and even enter the holy of holies in heaven. By means of a dizzying array of literary formulas, the fictional seers completely overcome all spatial, temporal, and bodily constraints.

Another important development is that angels are active participants in message dreams, in sharp contradistinction to dreams in the Hebrew Bible. Angels deliver spoken messages to dreamers (*L.A.B.* 9:10; *T. Job* 4:1; Josephus, *Life* 208–210; *2 En.* 1:3–10) or act as interpreters of messages that are relayed by the voice of YHWH or that appear in symbolic form (Dan 7:16–28; 8:15–26; *Jub.* 32:22; *4 Ezra* 4:1; 5:31; 7:1; 10:29; *Lad. Jac.* 3:4–7:35; *2 Bar.* 55:3; *T. Levi* 2:7–5:6; *1 En.* 19–32). Some angels even have dream interpretation as their primary role (Sariel in *Lad. Jac.* 3:3, Ramael in *2 Bar.* 55:3). Angels may also act as tour guides, escorting dreamers around strange places, whether in heaven or hell or in the farthest reaches of the earth (*1 En.* 14–36; *T. Levi* 2–5; 4QEn [4Q206] frag. 3; *2 En.* 33:6), or they themselves might act as transportation for the dreamer (e.g., *2 En.* 72:3–10; *T. Napht.* 5:7). A frequent motif is the angel who appears in a dream and remains as the dreamer transitions to a waking state (e.g., *4 Ezra* 5:15; Dan 9:21; *Lad. Jac.* 3:2–3; *2 En.* 1:6). Also, many angels act as healers in dreams—a function that was largely or entirely absent in dreams in the

20. Crispin Fletcher-Louis (*All the Glory of Adam: Liturgical Anthropology in the Dead Sea Scrolls* [Leiden: Brill, 2002]) has convincingly demonstrated that the Qumran community believed themselves to partake in such "angelomorphism" or transformation into angels during collective liturgical practice.

Bible—in that they touch and strengthen dreamers who are overcome by their responses to revelation.[21]

It is often noted that angelology develops markedly in this period of Judaism out of concerns for access to heaven and divinity.[22] What I wish to add is that the intimate interaction between humans and angels is often accomplished through dreams, which facilitate an overcoming of normal perceptual barriers. The latter is made clear by Jacob's statement in the *Ladder of Jacob:* "And Sariel the archangel came to me and I saw, and his appearance was very beautiful and awesome. But I was not astonished by his appearance, for the vision which I had seen in my dream was more terrible than he" (*Lad. Jac.* 3:4–5). Moreover, the ontological barriers between humans and angels may even be overcome in dreams through human transformation into an angelic state (*2 En.* 22; *T. Levi* 8) as well as by more subtle progressions of dreamers along a human-angelic ontological continuum, as signified by a growing ability to receive revelation and by access to interior regions of the heavenly *hekhal.*[23]

3. Hellenistic Jewish Dreams and Apocalyptic Literature

The identification of these developments in early Jewish dream traditions has consequences for the study of apocalyptic literature. Almost all of the commonly identified early Jewish apocalypses[24] contain either a dream or a vision, and around half contain a dream (*1 En.* 1–36; 85–90; Dan 7–12; *2 Baruch; 4 Ezra; 2 Enoch; T. Levi* 2–5; *Testament of Abraham;* and *Ladder of Jacob*). Several of the dream episodes are conspicuously predominant in length vis-à-vis the text as a whole (*1 En.* 14–36; *4 Ezra; Ladder of Jacob*), or they are arguably pivotal in each

---

21. Angels do not heal within biblical dreams other than in Dan 8; the early Jewish model seems to follow the iconography of Hellenistic dream-gods such as Asclepius, who stands near the dreamer and reaches out and touches him/her in order to heal.

22. Carol Newsom, "Angels: Second Temple Period," *ABD* 1:251–53.

23. For example, Uriel's exclamation to Ezra to "stand up like a man" at the conclusion of a dream may have deep implications. "Standing" is the typical action of deities in ancient dreams, but the dreamer almost never stands, except in early Jewish dreams, where the action typically signifies a gaining of physical, perceptual, and spiritual strength. When a dreamer such as Ezra stands and is able to converse with an angel, he may be progressing along a human-angelic continuum of ontological evolution that subsequently allows him access into the heavenly *hekhal* (*4 Ezra* 10:33ff.). This sense of angel or perhaps of glorified Adam may be captured by the term "man" (*vir*) in the Latin (but not Syriac) of *4 Ezra* 10:33. See Flannery-Dailey, *Dreamers, Scribes and Priests,* 212–20; for a parallel case in the Dead Sea Scrolls, see Fletcher-Louis, *All the Glory of Adam,* esp. 91–103.

24. John J. Collins, "Introduction: Towards the Morphology of a Genre," *Semeia* 14 (1979): 1–20. The exception is *Jub.* 23, but the whole of *Jubilees* contains twelve dreams.

plotline. Thus, the relationship of dreams and apocalypses must be examined carefully.

The SBL Genres Project published a definition of apocalypse in *Semeia* 14 that has by now become standard: "Apocalypse is a genre of revelatory literature with a narrative framework, in which a revelation is mediated by an otherworldly being to a human recipient, disclosing a transcendent reality which is both temporal, insofar as it envisages eschatological salvation, and spatial insofar as it involves another, supernatural world."[25] The definition deals not with the social ideology of "apocalypticism" but rather with a literary genre in which revelation from an otherworldly figure to a human occurs within a narrative. The world that is evoked is two-tiered, comprising heaven and earth, and a future end time is sharply differentiated from the present. Some scholars who follow this definition proceed to divide apocalypses into two major subtypes: "otherworldly journeys" such as *1 Enoch*, which emphasize the spatial elements of the worldview while not excluding temporal elements, and "historical apocalypses" such as Daniel, which emphasize the eschatological unfolding of temporal elements more than they do spatial elements.[26]

The mountain of scholarship generated by the *Semeia* definition attests to its value in clarifying constitutive elements of a body of coherent texts. What remains problematic is that all too often the use of the *succinct definition* itself has become axiomatic and hence limiting,[27] without regard to nuances that are apparent in the rest of *Semeia* 14 as well as to developments made in the subsequent scholarship of the contributors to the original project of *Semeia* 14. The insights gained from studying the dream texts can both refresh our thinking about the language involved in the *Semeia* definition and challenge our concomitant assumptions.

The succinct version of the *Semeia* definition itself gives no direct attention to the mode of revelation.[28] However, the fuller "master-paradigm" explored in the same article does address the "manner of revelation" by breaking down the "medium" as follows:

1.	*Medium* by which the revelation is communicated.
1.1	*Visual* revelation may be either in the form of
1.1.1	*Visions*, where the content of the revelation is seen, or
1.1.2	*Epiphanies*, where the apparition of the mediator is described.

25. Ibid., 9.

26. See ibid., 14–15.

27. Based on other grounds, the standard *Semeia* approach is currently being called into question by Crispin Fletcher-Louis, who favors a new approach that draws heavily on the approaches of Christopher Rowland. See Crispin Fletcher-Louis, "Apocalypticism," *The Handbook of the Study of the Historical Jesus* (ed. S. E. Porter and T. Holmén; 4 vols.; Leiden: Brill, forthcoming).

28. Collins, "Introduction," 9.

1.2 *Auditory* revelation usually clarifies the visual. Epiphanies are always followed by auditory revelation. They may be either in the form of

1.2.1 *Discourse*, uninterrupted speech by the mediator, or

1.2.2 *Dialogue*, where there is conversation between the mediator and recipient, often in the form of question and answer.[29]

It therefore appears that the intention of Collins and other contributors to the original *Semeia* 14 project was to stimulate a focus on the medium as well as on the content of revelation. Lamentably, since the "medium of revelation" is not specifically addressed in the definition, which has taken on a life of its own, too much of the scholarship on apocalypses gives scant attention to the mode in which revelation is received.

Recognition of the near ubiquity of *dreams* and visions in the Jewish apocalypses only intensifies this problem, which is not solved by the paradigm as quoted above, since dreams can only be fitted rather clumsily into the skeletal outline. While the paradigm recognizes that visual and auditory elements are complementary, there is a certain messiness that ensues in using it to describe dreams in apocalypses, since dreams may include both visual and auditory elements—only the former in the case of certain symbolic dreams; only the latter in the case of auditory message dreams—and/or the senses of touch and taste. Also, some early Jewish dreams blur "visions" and "epiphanies" as delineated above, such as when an angelic dream messenger interprets visual symbols imparted within the same dream (e.g., Dan 7:17; 8:16).

Perceptively, Christopher Rowland specifically suggested that *dreams* and visions are integral to apocalyptic literature, stating "apocalyptic, therefore, is a type of religion whose distinguishing feature is a belief in direct revelation of the things of God which was mediated through *dream, vision or divine intermediary*."[30] Collins likewise has discussed "the symbolic dream vision" as an important medium of revelation and has noted the dreamlike character of apocalyptic symbolism.[31] I concur with their insights and suggest that, at the very least, "the

29. Ibid., 6.

30. Christopher Rowland, *The Open Heaven: A Study of Apocalyptic in Judaism and Early Christianity* (New York: Crossroad, 1982), 9, 16, 17, 21. Similarly, Jean Carmignac ("Description du phénomène de l'Apocalyptique dans l'Ancien Testament," in *Apocalypticism in the Mediterranean World and the Near East* [ed. D. Hellholm; Tübingen: Mohr Siebeck, 1983], 163–70) postulated that the origin of apocalyptic literature in the Hebrew Bible lay in dreams, but the suggestion garnered little support.

31. John J. Collins, *Daniel with an Introduction to Apocalyptic Literature* (FOTL 20; Grand Rapids: Eerdmans, 1984), 6–7; idem, *Daniel* (Hermeneia; Minneapolis: Fortress, 1993), 54–55, 323, 402; idem, "Apocalyptic Literature," *The Blackwell Companion to the Hebrew Bible* (ed. L. Perdue; Malden, Mass.: Blackwell, 2001), 432–47, here 436.

medium of revelation" needs to be addressed squarely in definitions and studies of apocalypses, with dreams receiving clear attention.

Even more important, the lens of early Jewish dream texts brings into sharper focus an important concern of apocalypses, namely, the transcendence of human limitations on experiencing reality. Rowland astutely maintains that "the key … is that God reveals his *mysteries* directly to man and thereby gives them knowledge of *the true nature of reality so that they may organize their lives accordingly*."[32] Here as elsewhere Rowland stresses that the central characteristic of apocalypses is the reorientation that occurs as a divine view of reality becomes accessible to humans. Repeatedly he states that "to speak of apocalyptic is to concentrate on the theme of the direct *communication of the heavenly mysteries* in all their diversity."[33] I contend that Rowland's emphasis on "the true nature of reality" and "heavenly mysteries" is vital to understanding a core aspect of apocalypses, namely, that dreams and visions allow humans to suspend normal spatial, temporal, and ontological constraints, thereby to *experience reality from a divine-like perspective*, to varying degrees. Put simply, God is not constrained by space, time, or a physical body; through dreams and visions, the pseudepigraphic seers in apocalypses are also able to apprehend divine "mysteries" through an experience in which space, time, and ontological restraints are overcome.[34]

In this sense, the *Semeia* definition is valuable in illuminating the spatial and temporal constructions of reality present in the commonly identified apocalypses, but subsequent conclusions that apocalypses are marked by dualism, which are too commonplace to enumerate, skew the situation if they end there.[35] The *emphasis* is not on two stratified tiers of spatial reality, on "now" versus "then," or on "human" versus "angel." The constructed spatial, temporal, and ontological dualisms function in the worldview of the early Jewish apocalypses as obstacles to be overcome, deconstructed, and ultimately erased by means of dreams and visions. By privileging this worldview, the accent is properly placed on the dreamer or visionary achieving a *divine-like access to reality on multiple planes.*

In this context it is clear that much current scholarly language used in the study of apocalypses may be problematic without constant reminders of the complexity of that language. Dreamers can be both "here" and "there," and spatial

32. Rowland, *Open Heaven*, 11. Note from the previous quote that Rowland's use of "direct" and "directly" seems to connote a powerful experiential dimension and does not preclude revelation mediated by angels, dreams, and visions.

33. Ibid., 14; see also 70. Rowland does not distinguish neatly between the genre of "apocalypse" and a social ideology of "apocalypticism" and instead refers to a general, thematically coherent outlook called "apocalyptic"; cf. Collins, "Introduction," 2–3.

34. Moreover, although the dream or vision is temporary, the experience or its influence may be enduring, particularly if ontological transformation into an angel is operative.

35. Note Rowland's attempts to mitigate too great an emphasis on dualism in apocalypses in *Open Heaven*, 92, 436–39.

boundaries can collapse through perceptual shifts as well as through soul/body travel, rendering the language of "ascent" and "otherworldly journeys" misleading if spatial travel is assumed. Temporal knowledge may include not only eschatology but primordial secrets as well, and all of this can be mixed with cosmological secrets in the same revelation,[36] which calls for careful appraisals of the importance of eschatology in the apocalyptic worldview. Also, given that in the dream corpus humans may exist along a gradient of ontological purity culminating in angelic status, language about "human recipients" may be misleading if interpreters assume that the recipients of revelation are fully "humans," just as interpreters must not think only of nonhuman angels as "otherworldly mediators."[37]

In addition, the categories of "historical apocalypse" and "otherworldly journey"[38] may prohibit us from seeing the complex interactions between the temporal, spatial, and ontological axes of reality, the latter of which is largely absent in the standard *Semeia* definition of apocalypse. For instance, when Daniel dreams and sees the Ancient of Days on his throne, usually locatable in the heavenly holy of holies (Dan 7:9–14), he not only glimpses eschatological realities but also has access to heavenly holy space although he is seemingly not an angel (or even a high priest). In complex ways, the dream thereby erases the human limitations on experiencing reality, defying our categories of "here" and "there," "now" and "then," "impure" and "pure." To label Daniel's dream a "Historical Apocalypse with No Otherworldly Journey"[39] privileges the eschatological material in a way that, in my view, overly minimizes the unusual spatiality and ontological transformation involved in his access to these events. The question then arises as to whether the genre "apocalypse" is a useful one.

---

36. Related is von Rad's thesis that the origins of apocalypticism originate from the wisdom tradition rather than the prophetic tradition. See Gerhard von Rad, *Theologie des Alten Testaments* (4th ed.; Munich: Kaiser, 1965), 2:315–30; and idem, *Wisdom in Israel* (Nashville: Abingdon, 1972), 263–83. Though refuted, his idea called attention to noneschatological sapiential elements in apocalypses, a point echoed in the work of Michael E. Stone, "Lists of Revealed Things in the Apocalyptic Literature," in *Magnalia Dei: The Mighty Acts of God* (ed. F. M. Cross, W. E. Lemke, and P. D. Miller Jr.; Garden City, N.Y.: Doubleday, 1976), 414–52; this focus has subsequently been developed in the Wisdom and Apocalypticism in Early Judaism and Early Christianity Section of the Society of Biblical Literature. For a list of criticisms of von Rad's thesis, see Collins, "Apocalyptic Literature," in *Early Judaism and Its Modern Interpreters* (ed. R. A. Kraft and G. W. E. Nickelsburg; SBLBMI 2; Atlanta: Scholars Press, 1986), 355–56; cf. Rowland, *Open Heaven*, 203–4.

37. For instance, the high priest Jaddus, who may be angelic, appears as an otherworldly mediator in an early Jewish dream (Josephus, *Ant.* 11.333–335); see Flannery-Dailey, *Dreamers, Scribes and Priests*, 207–8.

38. Collins rightly rejects treating historical apocalypses and apocalypses containing otherworldly journeys as two separate genres ("Introduction," 16).

39. Collins, "Introduction," 14, 17; idem, "The Jewish Apocalypses," *Semeia* 14 (1979): 30–34.

I find that dreams in "apocalypses" are indeed distinguishable from those in "nonapocalypses" by their inclusion of eschatology, although they share many other features in common.[40] Whereas dreams in the commonly defined apocalypses (*1 En.* 1–36; 85–90; Dan 7–12; *2 Baruch; 4 Ezra; Testament of Levi*) relate eschatological secrets, dreams in nonapocalypses (e.g., *Liber antiquitatum biblicarum;* 2 Maccabees; Josephus) are noneschatological in content, even when they feature future temporal elements in the life of the dreamer or Israel.[41]

Another factor adds to the coherence of the commonly identified apocalypses, although it is not part of the standard *Semeia* definition, namely, that in those texts the dreamers and visionaries *as well as the readers* gain knowledge by learning details of the eschatological future and/or the cosmos. In Ezekiel the Tragedian, which is not usually classified as an apocalypse, Moses learns of otherworldly spheres (heaven, earth, and the underworld) and probably learns eschatological secrets as well (past, present, and future), but the reader is not made privy to the content of these revelations.[42] By contrast, those texts that are commonly labeled apocalypses readily impart knowledge to both the dreamers and the readers regarding eschatology, but not to the exclusion of other kinds of cosmic secrets.[43] What is crucial is that scholars not allow the label "apocalypse,"[44] which denotes a certain kind of revelatory literature, to obscure the relation of this subgroup of eschatological texts to the larger corpus of revelatory texts featuring dreams and visions that facilitate access to divine perspectives of reality.

To conclude, I contend that the development of the Hellenistic Jewish dream traditions made possible the articulation of the apocalyptic worldview in its nar-

---

40. Neither dream types, complexity, nor the presence of priestly and scribal themes distinguish dreams in early Jewish apocalypses from non-apocalypses. See Flannery-Dailey, *Dreamers, Scribes and Priests,* 274 n. 83.

41. In the cases of the apocalypses *2 Enoch* and *Testament of Abraham,* the dream episodes are noneschatological yet closely tied to eschatology, since they foreshadow or trigger ascents to heaven that in turn serve to transmit both eschatological and cosmological knowledge of the workings of the universe.

42. However, caution must be exercised, since *Exagoge* is only preserved as quotations in Eusebius, Clement of Alexandria, and Pseudo-Eustathius. See R. G. Robertson, "Ezekiel the Tragedian," *OTP* 2:803.

43. As George W. E. Nickelsburg ("The Apocalyptic Construction of Reality in *1 Enoch,*" in *Mysteries and Revelations: Apocalyptic Studies since the Uppsala Colloquium* [ed. J. J. Collins and J. H. Charlesworth; Sheffield: JSOT Press, 1991], 50–64) has noted of Enoch's tours, "Cosmology undergirds eschatology," since the sites he *and* the reader see—such as Eden and the places of punishment of the damned—have eschatological as well as cosmological implications (*1 En.* 12–36; cf. *T. Levi* 2–5; 8–10).

44. Rowland (*Open Heaven,* esp. 28) wishes to minimize eschatology as constitutive of "apocalyptic literature," while Collins obviously draws the boundaries in terms of the inclusion of eschatology as well as other elements. See also Jean Carmignac, "Les Dangers de l'Eschatologie," *NTS* 17 (1981): 365–90.

rative form. Form goes hand in hand with function, and it is the freedom of the dream form itself that catalyzed the articulation of the imaginative construction and deconstruction of reality that is constitutive of apocalyptic literature. Taking seriously Rowland's suggestions that purported and perhaps actual religious experiences lay at the core of the apocalypses, attention to the rituals present in early dream and vision texts, particularly in connection their cultic and priestly settings,[45] may even shed light on the origins of apocalypticism.

4. Hellenistic Jewish Dreams and Mystical Literature

Just as the assumptions surrounding the study of apocalypses and apocalypticism must be reassessed, so too must those of early Jewish mystical texts and mysticism. Scholem and especially Gruenwald argued early on that the roots of early Jewish mysticism reach well back into the pseudepigraphic literature, beginning with *1 En.* 1–36, with Gruenwald labeling Enoch's dream report "the oldest Merkavah vision we know of from the literature outside of the canonical Scriptures."[46] Others posit no direct trajectory between the Hellenistic Jewish dreams texts and *hekhalot* texts[47] and/or maintain that the study of the mystical literature does not bear on the practice of mysticism.[48]

In part, the issue turns on the fact that most interpreters work with the extant late, redacted corpus of *hekhalot* and *merkabah* texts and attempt to trace influence backwards chronologically, landing upon selected texts, depending on which features are highlighted.[49] Scholars who emphasize ascent as the core attribute of the mystical corpus thus tend to make connections to those representatives of the apocalyptic material that contain clear ascent to heaven, particularly *1 En.* 14.[50] The argument is convincing, since, unlike the visions of Ezekiel that influ-

45. Rowland, *Open Heaven,* 214–47. For further discussion of priestly themes in Jewish dreams, see Flannery-Dailey, *Dreamers, Scribes and Priests,* 147–52, 201–11, 256–64.

46. Ithamar Gruenwald, *Apocalyptic and Merkavah Mysticism* (AGJU 14; Leiden: Brill, 1980), 36.

47. Martha Himmelfarb, *Ascent to Heaven in Jewish and Christian Apocalypses* (New York: Oxford Unviersity Press, 1993), 7.

48. Peter Schäfer, *Hidden and Manifest God: Some Major Themes in Early Jewish Mysticism* (trans. A. Pomerance; Albany: State University of New York Press 1992), 150–55; David J. Halperin, *Faces of the Chariot: Early Jewish Reponses to Ezekiel's Vision* (Tübingen: Mohr Siebeck, 1988), 359–63; Himmelfarb, *Ascent to Heaven,* 106–14.

49. Rachel Elior's recent work is an exception, beginning with Ezekiel and the Dead Sea Scrolls and working forward; see Rachel Elior, *The Three Temples: On the Emergence of Jewish Mysticism* (trans. D. Louvish; Oxford: Littman Library of Jewish Civilization, 2004).

50. See especially Gershom Scholem, *Major Trends in Jewish Mysticism* (New York: Schocken, 1941; repr., 1995), ch. 2; Gruenwald, *Apocalyptic and Merkavah;* Elior, *The Three Temples;* Christopher R. A. Morray-Jones, "Paradise Revisited (2 Cor 12:1–12): The Jewish Mystical Background of Paul's Apostolate, Part 2: Paul's Heavenly Ascent and Its Significance," *HTR* 86

ence them, the *hekhalot* texts and *1 En.* 14 depict a dreamer gaining access to the heavenly temple,[51] culminating in a vision of the Glory of God on the throne.[52] Recently Lesses and Davila have greatly expanded the conversation by arguing that the adjuration of angels is *a,* if not *the,* central theme of the mystical literature, which leads them to make connections with magical texts at Qumran and from late antiquity and with the angelic passages in the Enochic corpus.[53] Finally, Elior has shown that a priestly-angelic milieu pervades the mystical texts, which she traces back most convincingly to the Qumran community and less firmly to the priesthood of the First Temple.[54]

Indeed, thematic connections between earlier dream texts (including the apocalypses) and later mystical texts abound, as may be illustrated by the earliest Hellenistic Jewish dream text, *1 En.* 13–14. Enoch sits and chants in a position characteristic of *merkabah* mystics, reminiscent of the lengthy trance-inducing recitations of hymns and prayers of the *hekhalot* texts[55]; he does so by a river, which recalls the water divination some posit behind *merkabah* mysticism[56]; *1 Enoch's* descriptions of stone walls as white as snow and a heaven made of water find a parallel in *hekhalot* traditions that describe the white marble stones of the *hekhal* flashing like "thousands upon thousands of waves of water" (*Hekhalot Zutarti* and *Hekhalot Rabbati*); *1 En.* 14:9–12 develops specific images from Ezekiel in the same way as do later *hekhalot* texts, juxtaposing cherubim, hailstones, building stones, fire and water, and rivers of fire (14:19) in essentially the same order as does *Hekhalot Zutarti,* over and against the original in Ezekiel.[57]

Although such lists are convincing and may be multiplied, I think such parallelomania still misses the main point. Working forward from the worldview of the early Jewish dream (and vision) narratives provides the conceptual means for transcending multiple constraints on human reality through a variety of formulas, including heavenly ascent to the *hekhal,* theurgic descent of the *hekhal,* the adjuration of angels, and ontological transformation of humans into angels. All of

---

(1993): 265–92; idem, "Transformational Mysticism in the Apocalyptic-Merkabah Tradition," *JJS* 43 (1992): 1–31.

51. Gruenwald, *Apocalyptic and Merkavah,* 36–37; George W. E. Nickelsburg, *1 Enoch 1: A Commentary on the Book of 1 Enoch, Chapters 1–36; 81–108* (Hermeneia; Minneapolis: Fortress 2001), 257–75.

52. See *1 En.* 14:15, 18–20, 21, 24; Schäfer, *Hidden and Manifest God,* 12, 124.

53. Rebecca Macy Lesses, *Ritual Practices to Gain Power: Angels, Incantations, and Revelation in Early Jewish Mysticism* (HTS 44; Harrisburg, Pa.: Trinity Press International, 1998), 16–20, 130–31; James R. Davila, *Descenders to the Chariot: The People behind the Hekhalot Literature* (JSJSup 70; Leiden: Brill, 2000), 32–33, 150–51.

54. Elior, *The Three Temples.*

55. *Hekh. Zut.* §424; cf. 1 Kgs 18:42; the Ethiopic but not Greek of *1 En.* 13–14; Scholem, *Major Trends in Jewish Mysticism,* 57–63.

56. So Gruenwald and Idel in Halperin, *Faces of the Chariot,* 231–32.

57. *Hekh. Zut.* §356; cf. Halperin, *Faces of the Chariot,* 83–84.

these themes are present in the mystical *worldview* of the *hekhalot* and *merkabah* texts, as has been convincingly and artfully described by Arbel:

> the ultimate goal of the seekers' spiritual journey is to "behold the king in his beauty" and to "gaze at the visions of the Merkavah." These goals seem to express a mystical aspiration *to encounter God and to perceive the nature of concealed divine reality....* adepts undergo a complex process of an ethical, spiritual, and mental metamorphoses. *They expand their perception beyond its ordinary limits and in so doing gain a new awareness.*[58]

According to Arbel, the mystical encounters have at their core the correspondence of human perception and divine reality for a short time, during which humans can "share the divine perspective."[59] The importance of Arbel's insights on the mystical literature and Rowland's earlier and similar points about the apocalyptic literature should not be overlooked. This focus on attaining a divine perspective on reality directly illuminates the larger context for the many thematic emphases scholars identify in the mystical and apocalyptic corpuses.

If we posit the dream and visionary texts as a broader context for investigating both apocalypticism and mysticism (such that we transgress the established scholarly limits of the mystical literature [*hekhalot*, *merkabah*, *Shi'ur Qomah,* and Genizah texts] and also reconsider the apocalypses as a subgroup of dream and vision texts), the appropriate question becomes: Which texts in the dream/visionary corpus of early Judaism are "mystical" in themes, ritual, worldview, and goal? My hunch is that we will find that the "mystical" corpus interpenetrates but exceeds the "apocalyptic" one. Thus, we should strive to avoid approaches and scholarly language leading to the unnecessary bifurcation of the two investigations.

Finally, given archaeological information on the cultic practice of dream incubation in antiquity, and given that the stylized patterns of cultic dreams nevertheless reflect some aspects of the actual dreams of real people, this avenue of research might clarify not only the relationship of the dream, apocalyptic, and mystical corpuses but also the practices delineated therein. In other words, the dream materials might illuminate activities associated with the social ideology of early Jewish apocalypticism and the practice of Jewish mysticism. With all due caution as befits evidence from a literary text, future investigations might then attend to literary relationships between dreaming and visionary activity; descriptions of rituals in the dream and visionary materials; the social realities of the temple as a locus of dream incubation and of priests as dream interpreters in

58. Vita Daphna Arbel, *Beholders of Divine Secrets: Mysticism and Myth in the Hekhalot and Merkavah Literature* (Albany: State University of New York Press, 2003), 23.

59. Arbel, 24. Her holistic view avoids many of the common pitfalls in scholarly vocabulary, leading her for instance to speak of the "Inner-Otherworldly Journey" that is not *only* an ascent, 75–76.

Israel (as they were elsewhere); and the articulations of subjective religious experience of the (fictional) characters in early Jewish texts as a possible refraction of actual practice.

What I propose is a new door and a new key. The door is the dream and visionary literature of Second Temple Judaism. The key is a worldview that envisions many ways of accessing various planes of divine reality: spatial, temporal, and ontological (and probably ethical as well). It becomes impossible, in my view, to separate the apocalyptic and mystical worldviews cleanly from one another, since both so permeate the Hellenistic Jewish dream and visionary traditions.

Situating the Afterlife

Kelley Coblentz Bautch

> And taking me, they led me away to a certain place, where those who are there become like burning fire.... they led me away to a dark place and to a mountain whose summit reached into the heavens.... beyond this chasm, I saw a place where (there was) neither firmament of heaven above nor below it well-founded earth, neither water was under it nor bird, but an empty and fearful place. There I saw seven stars like great burning mountains. (*1 En.* 17:1–2, 18:12–13)

Localizing the realm of the dead, places of punishment, and utopian space was a primary concern of one of the earliest apocalypses with an otherworldly journey, the Book of the Watchers. The second half in particular (*1 En.* 17–36) of this third-century B.C.E. text that recounts the cosmic tours of the patriarch Enoch takes special interest in sites related to afterlife. It is illuminating that the Book of the Watchers presents sites associated with afterlife and the eschaton especially on a worldly plane, although such space is portrayed as largely inaccessible and intelligible only in reference to eschatological effects.

In order to demonstrate this trend, the following study describes the cosmology of the Book of the Watchers and goes on to make note of redactional issues that might frustrate study of spatial or geographical features in the text. Thereafter, the "this-worldly" eschatology of the Enochic booklet is explored with an eye to the location of places associated with postmortem conditions and judgment. I consider here the extent to which these geographical traditions or arrangement of space would have been comprehensible to ancient audiences (Could a map be reconstructed from the imagery?) and ask whether the narrative in this Enochic booklet suggests an actual visionary experience.

The fragmentary Aramaic of the Book of the Watchers, attested from the scrolls found at Qumran, serves as a primary base for the study, since it provides the earliest extant traditions associated with this section of *1 Enoch*. We also consider the Greek, preserved in a fourth–fifth century C.E. manuscript referred to as Panopolitanus and multiple Ge'ez versions to help us in our reading of the text. While the Ge'ez manuscripts are of a much later date, many, some perhaps from the twelfth century, could contain quite early traditions and superior readings.

Both the Greek and Ge'ez manuscripts are valuable for the variant readings they provide concerning the geographical traditions in question.

1. Cosmology and the Book of the Watchers

We begin with some initial observations about the cosmology reflected in the Book of the Watchers. The Book of the Watchers is hardly the only text in Second Temple period Judaism or early Christianity to take up extraordinary places that occupied the religious imagination. The Book of the Watchers is, however, one of the earliest texts to address in some detail sacred space, especially those sites relegated to the edges of the *oikoumene* (the inhabited world). While Ezek 40–48 proved influential for visionary journeys described in many Second Temple period texts,[1] the Enochic literature takes discussion of sacred space beyond Ezekiel's primary points of reference, the Temple Mount and Jerusalem. One observes that Jerusalem, including the Temple Mount, *and* sites of the Upper Galilee figure prominently in the Book of the Watchers. Jerusalem, the very center of the world (*1 En.* 26:1), becomes the locus for eschatological reward; in the shadow of the temple (a renewed temple perhaps) the righteous dwell for an unspecified period following God's return (*1 En.* 25:5–6). Places such as Hermon, the site of the Watchers' descent and Enoch's ascent (*1 En.* 6:6; 14:8) and Dan, where Enoch petitions on behalf of the watchers (*1 En.* 13:7), provide the setting for the narrative and perhaps provide clues as to the author or community's provenance.[2]

Even so, in the second half of the Book of the Watchers the seer is led primarily to places that exist at the edge of the known world, and it is unarguable that the text draws attention to places inaccessible to humankind or to the living (see *1 En.* 19:3).[3] In this respect the tours in the Book of the Watchers are reminiscent of the journeys of Gilgamesh (in the Epic of Gilgamesh 9–11) or the geography of the Babylonian Mappa Mundi (the sixth-century tablet designated BM 92687) and interests of Greek ethnography in that they too demonstrate a fascination with remote locations and peripheral sites.[4] The interest of the tours in sites and

1. This observation has been made especially by Martha Himmelfarb. See *Tours of Hell: An Apocalyptic Form in Jewish and Christian Literature* (Philadelphia: University of Pennsylvania Press, 1983), 50–67.

2. See, e.g., George W. E. Nickelsburg, "Enoch, Levi, and Peter: Recipients of Revelation in Upper Galilee," *JBL* 100 (1981): 575–600; esp. 586; idem, *1 Enoch 1: A Commentary on the Book of 1 Enoch, Chapters 1–36; 81–108* (Hermeneia; Minneapolis: Fortress 2001), 65, 238–47; and David Suter, "Why Galilee? Galilean Regionalism in the Interpretation of *1 Enoch*," *Hen* 25 (2003): 167–212, esp. 178–79, 186–201.

3. So also Richard Bauckham, *The Fate of the Dead: Studies on the Jewish and Christian Apocalypses* (NovTSup 93; Leiden: Brill, 1998), 84.

4. See my *A Study of the Geography of 1 Enoch 17–19: "No One Has Seen What I Have Seen"* (JSJSup 81; Leiden: Brill, 2003), 231–57.

phenomena inaccessible to humankind recalls also the musings of wisdom literature, such as Job 28 and 38, where aspects of the cosmos are depicted as beyond the ken of humankind.[5]

Further, the cosmology assumed by this third-century B.C.E. text is distinctive vis-à-vis the traditions that would follow it in describing sites pertaining to the afterlife. Unlike the Enochic Parables or the *Apocalypse of Paul,* texts that suggest a multiheaven schema, the Book of the Watchers reflects a view of the cosmos that is tripartite. According to this model, which was prominent in the ancient Near East and echoed in the writings of the Hebrew Bible, the cosmos consists of three levels: the netherworld (or chthonic realm), the earth, and the heavens.[6] The ascent narrative of *1 En.* 6–16 suggests that there is above the earth only a single heaven populated by God and his agents, the angels. Likewise, *1 En.* 17–36 presupposes that the world is flat. As J. Edward Wright observes, *1 En.* 17–36 allows one to travel only so far before reaching the ends of the earth; beyond the surface of the flat earth and the numinous zone that surrounds it there is a chasm (cf. *1 En.* 18:11–12), a cosmological model also familiar from the ancient Near East.[7]

A curious feature of the cosmology, however, is that the Book of the Watchers does not present the realm of the dead below the earth disk (the traditional setting of Sheol), as one might expect from ancient Near Eastern or the biblical tripartite models. The realm of the dead in the Book of the Watchers is located, rather, beyond the inhabited world and along a horizontal plane (*1 En.* 22), a matter I shall revisit. Interestingly, Greek traditions such as Homer's *Odyssey* from the archaic period also feature a modified view of the tripartite model that is comparable to that in the Book of the Watchers; there the netherworld and then Tartarus were located also at the ends of the earth.[8] Thus, when the Enochic booklet is placed on a spectrum, it approximates a long-standing view of the cosmos, the tripartite cosmology favored by biblical authors who based their own models predominantly on those from the ancient Near East, because it largely ignored the cosmologies of Greek and Roman contemporaries who envisaged multiple heavens. The Enochic text does seem acquainted, however, with views of afterlife that circulated widely throughout the Hellenistic world.[9]

---

5. Ibid., 223–27; and Michael Knibb, "The Use of Scripture in *1 Enoch* 17–19," in *Jerusalem, Alexandria, Rome: Studies in Ancient Cultural Interaction in Honour of A. Hilhorst* (ed. F. García Martínez and G. P. Luttikhuizen; JSJSup 82; Leiden: Brill, 2003), 165–78, esp. 171–73.

6. See J. Edward Wright, *The Early History of Heaven* (New York: Oxford University Press, 2000), 30–37, 53–58, 117–23. On the Jewish (and subsequent Christian) adoption of the multiple-heaven schema that became prominent in the Greco-Roman period, see 139–84.

7. Ibid., 121.

8. See also ibid., 110.

9. Coblentz Bautch, *Study of the Geography,* 82–90, 238–53.

2. Textual History of the Book of the Watchers

We see as many as five distinctive sections in the Book of the Watchers, each the product of a particular provenance.[10] Chapters 17–36 have a rather complicated textual history, as redactional activity is quite characteristic of the second half of the book.[11] Repetitions (the concerns of *1 En.* 18 and 19 are taken up again in chs. 21 and 24), telltale seams (e.g., *1 En.* 19:3 clearly brings to a close a distinct section), and abrupt shifts in focus (such as the discussion of the archangels in *1 En.* 20 or interests in the gates of heavens through which winds pass in *1 En.* 33–34) communicate something of the development of these traditions that concern Enoch's extraordinary journeys. From these discrepancies we see that the text is made up of originally independent units; most scholars affirm that an editor is to be credited with their amalgamation "into a passable literary unity."[12]

Indeed, the second half of the Book of the Watchers does appear coherent and is distinguished from the first half of the booklet by its horizontal orientation. Whereas chapters 6–16 are especially concerned with the Watchers, their immoral conduct and subsequent punishment from God as well as Enoch's intercession and ascent to the Divine, chapters 17–36 concentrate on the tours Enoch makes accompanied by angels. Chapters 6–16 do not contain the elaborate travelogue or cosmological speculation of the sort found in *1 En.* 17–36. For example, while one learns about sites in the Upper Galilee in *1 En.* 13 and the heavenly temple in 14:8–23, many of the sites mentioned in the latter half of the Book of the Watchers concern natural phenomena and topography and are to be found at the ends of the earth.[13] This leads Matthew Black, for one, to maintain that chap-

10. Nickelsburg has argued, as have R. H. Charles (*The Book of Enoch or 1 Enoch* [Oxford: Clarendon, 1912], xlvii–xlviii) and James C. VanderKam (*Enoch and the Growth of an Apocalyptic Tradition* [CBQMS 16; Washington, D.C.: Catholic Biblical Association of America, 1984], 110), that the Book of the Watchers consists of five major divisions: an oracular introduction (*1 En.* 1–5); the story of the evil Watchers (*1 En.* 6–11); Enoch's ascent to heaven (*1 En.* 12–16); a first cosmic journey (*1 En.* 17–19); and a discussion of seven archangels along with a second tour of the cosmos (*1 En.* 20–36). See George W. E. Nickelsburg, *Jewish Literature between the Bible and the Mishnah* (Philadelphia: Fortress, 1981), 48–55; and idem, *1 Enoch 1*, 25.

11. When focusing on the second half of the Book of the Watchers, Eibert Tigchelaar (*Prophets of Old and the Day of the End: Zechariah, the Book of the Watchers and Apocalyptic* [OtSt 35; Leiden: Brill, 1996], 152–64) observes further evidence of redactional activity. Tigchelaar maintains that *1 En.* 17:1–18:5; 18:6–16; 19:1–3; 20:1–32:6; and 33:1–36:4 spring from various hands.

12. VanderKam, *Enoch and the Growth*, 110.

13. Pieter Venter expresses the difference in terms of spatial concerns thus: the first journey (*1 En.* 12–16) takes up geopolitical space (towns) and architectural space (like the temple), whereas topographical space (sea or desert) is used in the journeys in chapters 17–36. See "Spatiality in Enoch's Journeys (*1 Enoch* 12–36)," in *Wisdom and Apocalypticism in the Dead Sea*

ters 17–36 "form quite a new and separate apocalypse," while "the so-called '*Book of the Watchers*'... ends at 16:4."[14]

In spite of the fact that Book of the Watchers in general and chapters 17–36 in particular indicate redactional activity, the views of the cosmos and of sacred sites that the units presuppose are fairly consistent. Nickelsburg dates the completion of the booklet to the middle of the third century B.C.E.[15] My reflections, therefore, on the localization of the realm of the dead, the postmortem places of punishment, and various paradises depicted in *1 En.* 17–36 concern the work in its entirety, a product of the mid-third century.

3. The This-Worldly Eschatology of *1 Enoch*

Interest in places related to the afterlife and judgment as well as the text's selective approach to cosmology serve well the text's eschatology (or apocalyptic eschatology), a consistent thread throughout the booklet and much of the Enochic corpus.[16] Sites related to God's majesty are juxtaposed with places of death, judgment, and punishment. The booklet also makes reference to sites that will be central to the renewed earth once the former world has been cleansed of all wickedness by God at his return; these places are associated with the chosen and pious. Though such locales seem to resemble the heavenly paradises envisioned by later Jewish and Christian writings, the Enochic sites merely presage the later ideals.

In fact, Nickelsburg, reflecting on the eschatology of *1 Enoch,* observes that the literature is primarily "this-worldly" in its focus. His assessment is meant to convey that, while the end times are presented in the Enochic writings as part of a transformative period, the place of eschatological blessing is a new or renewed

Scrolls and the Biblical Tradition (ed. F. García Martínez; BETL 168; Leuven: Peeters, 2003), 211–30, esp. 211–14.

14. Matthew Black, *The Book of Enoch or 1 Enoch: A New English Edition with Commentary and Textual Notes* (SVTP 7; Leiden: Brill, 1985), 10.

15. Nickelsburg, *1 Enoch 1*, 7.

16. For the purposes of this study, I understand eschatology (literally "study of the last things") as "a form of radical orientation to the future, which may involve a sort of social and/or cosmic arrangement fundamentally different from that which currently exists" (David L. Petersen, "Eschatology, Old Testament," *ABD* 2:576). The Book of the Watchers does not suggest, in my opinion, a cataclysmic end to the world or to human history. See John J. Collins, "Apocalyptic Eschatology as Transcendence of Death," *CBQ* 36 (1974): 21–43, esp. 26. The booklet envisions, rather, the end of a world corrupted by the wicked and impious (principally the fallen angels and their offspring) and the beginning of God's reign on earth (see esp. *1 En.* 1; 5; 10; 25). This transformation of the old order and forward-looking nature constitute the eschatology of the Book of the Watchers. Inasmuch as the great day of judgment described by the Book of the Watchers concerns the fate of individuals, one might argue that personal eschatology is a concern of this work as well; see *1 En.* 22.

earth.[17] The notion is especially prevalent in the Book of the Watchers. The authors of this early Enochic text indicate that they awaited an earth cleansed of evil and pollution (*1 En.* 10:1–11:2) that would coincide with a final judgment; thereafter the righteous and chosen would remain in the environs of the temple and feast on the tree of life. They would enjoy a bodily existence of a length comparable to that of the early patriarchs without incurring pain or suffering (25:6). As Nickelsburg observes, there is no clear indication in the Book of the Watchers as to what the Enochic authors anticipated for this generation following a protracted life span.[18] While no final or permanent postmortem state is described for the righteous, the text offers further reflections on intermediate postmortem locales. Although the temple and Jerusalem, described as holy and blessed places, are found in the very center of the earth (25:5–6; 26:1), the intermediate resting places, in contrast, are truly liminal, relegated to the periphery of the earth disk.

We begin with sites related to the afterlife and judgment. The Book of the Watchers is striking in its thoroughgoing interest in repositories or holding cells for all manner of creature.[19] Celestial beings, whether angels or stars, and humans alike are subject to definitive judgment, but prior to this judgment they remain confined. We read of the chasm where the spirits of the fallen angels are kept and of the "chaotic place" where seven stars are held. Both are to be found along the edge of the inhabited earth or beyond the earth disk altogether. The prison for the angels, an abyss containing fiery pillars (*1 En.* 18:10–11; 19:1–2 || 21:7–10) is situated at the "end of the great earth" (πέρας τῆς μεγάλης γῆς), according to the Greek, or "beyond the great earth" (māʿdotu la-ʿabiy medr), following the Ethiopic.

The site offers a terminus of some sort; it is here, apparently, where the heavens meet the earth. As best expressed by Panopolitanus's reading, the site is more reflective of earth because at this point the heavens have come to their end.[20] Like-

17. George Nickelsburg, "Where Is the Place of Eschatological Blessing?" in *Things Revealed: Studies in Early Jewish and Christian Literature in Honor of Michael E. Stone* (ed. E. G. Chazon, D. Satran, and R. A. Clements; JSJSup 89; Leiden: Brill, 2004), 53–71, esp. 53.

18. Nickelburg, "Where Is the Place," 55.

19. One might think also of the descriptions of Tartarus found in Hesiod's *Theogony* and in Homer's *Odyssey* and of the Isaianic apocalypse. Within the latter, Isa 24:21–23 describes the hosts of the heavens and the kings of the earth gathered together like prisoners in a pit; comparable to the function of the repositories in the Book of the Watchers, the offending parties will remain in their dungeon for "many days" and then be punished.

20. Black (*Book of Enoch*, 36, 159–60) considers this expression "great earth" to be highly unusual. He suggests that a misreading of the Aramaic has occurred and offers instead "beyond the ends of the earth" (לעבר בריתא דארעא), a phrase familiar from *Tg. Prov.* 30:4. While the expression "great earth" seems rather awkward, Nickelsburg (*1 Enoch 1*, 286) observes a verbal parallel with Hesiod (*Theogony*), who locates Tartarus, the prison of the Titans, at "the ends of the huge earth" (πελώρης ἔσχατα γαίης). We learn, then, in *1 En.* 18:10 that at this site the heavens are finished or gathered together ותמן אשת]יציו שמיא; συντελεσθήσονται οἱ οὐρανοί;

wise, seven disobedient stars[21] who did not emerge at their appointed time are bound at the end of heaven and earth (τὸ τέλος τοῦ οὐρανοῦ καὶ γῆς; tafṣāmētu la-samāy wa-la-medr; *1 En.* 18:14). According to the Greek gloss of *1 En.* 18:15, they are kept beyond the heavens (ὅτι τόπος ἔξω τοῦ οὐρανοῦ κενός ἐστιν), envisaging a cosmos like that depicted in Gen 1 of the tripartite schema including the firmament.

While it is clear that these otherworldly prisons exist outside the *oikoumene*, the text provides little to indicate where, in terms of geography, these prisons exist. Comparable Near Eastern traditions may suggest, nonetheless, that such places were located to the east. The Book of the Watchers (*1 En.* 10:4) locates the angels' prison in the desert in Dudael (Gr^{Pan} = Δαδουήλ; Gr^{Syn} = Δουδαήλ; Eth. = Dudā'ēl); the location and even the identity of Dudael are here utterly enigmatic.[22]

---

yetgābe'u samāyāt). For Charles and Black, this latter expression conveys that the site is where the heavens come to an end or are completed (so *1 En.* 18:5; 33:2; Charles, *Book of Enoch*, 42; and Black, *Book of Enoch*, 160). Black (*Book of Enoch*, 160) calls the future tense of the Greek inappropriate and assigns to the work of a later translator. Some Ethiopic manuscripts (Abb 35 and Abb 55) read instead: "there the waters (māyāt) were gathered together." August Dillmann (*Das Buch Henoch Übersetzt und Erklärt* [Leipzig: Vogel, 1853], 118), Adolphe Lods (*Le Livre D'Hénoch: Fragments Grecs, Découverts à Akhmîm [Haute-Égypte] Publiés Avec Les Variantes du Texte Éthiopien* [Paris: Leroux, 1892], 161), and Siegbert Uhlig (*Das äthiopische Henochbuch* [Jüdische Schriften aus hellenistisch-römischer Zeit 5; Gütersloh: Mohn, 1984], 549) prefer this variant. Dillmann (*Das Buch Henoch*, 118) describes the site as the place where waters are collected, the same as the encircling Okeanos of *1 En.* 17:7–8; for Lods (*Le Livre D'Hénoch*, 161) this is an ocean located at the extremities of the earth that Enoch comes upon anew. Curiously, though, there is nothing in the context of *1 En.* 18 and 19 to suggest that Enoch is near an ocean or any body of water. In fact, *1 En.* 18:12 explicitly states that there is no water in the region (see below). The Greek and fragmentary Aramaic, as well as the majority of Ethiopic manuscripts, supply the correct reading: Enoch has traveled to the perimeters of the earth, where the heavens come to an end. Though Dillmann is inclined to locate the site in the vicinity of the seven mountains, to the south, there is nothing in the text to indicate that Enoch remains in that region (*Das Buch Henoch*, 118).

21. ἑπτὰ ἀστέρας ὡς ὄρη μεγάλα καιόμενα; sab'ata kawākebta kama 'abayt 'adbār za-yenadded.

22. Though the origin of "Dudael" is unknown, its etymology has been explained variously. One frequently cited proposal is that Dudael is the Beth Hadure (בית הדורי, from הֲדוּרָא or הַדְּרָא) mentioned in *Targum Pseudo-Jonathan* in connection with the place where the goat for Azazel is led in Lev 16:21. This hypothesis was proposed originally by M. Geiger ("Einige Worte über das Buch Henoch," *Jüdische Zeitschrift für Wissenschaft und Leben* 3 [1864/65]: 196–204); then promulgated by Charles, *Book of Enoch*, 22–23. Cf. Milik, "The Dead Sea Scrolls Fragment of the Book of Enoch," *Bib* 32 (1951): 393–400, esp. 395. The place, alternatively named Beth Ḥadudu (בית חדודו), is described as a precipitous or rocky wilderness, located in the vicinity of Jerusalem, according to *m. Yoma* 6:8 (Charles, *Book of Enoch*, 22–23). Since חדד refers to that which is sharp or pointed, one can detect perhaps some wordplay as Azazel is to be tossed upon rough and jagged rocks in *1 En.* 10:5. See Michael A. Knibb, *The Ethiopic Book of Enoch: A New Edition in the Light of the Aramaic Dead Sea Fragments* (2 vols.; Oxford: Clarendon, 1978), 87.

Dudael appears again in the later Parables as Dendayn; there we learn that it is located to the east of the garden for the chosen and righteous (*1 En.* 60:8). Jozef T. Milik has argued that Dudael of the Book of the Watchers and Dendayn of the Parables reflect the Babylonian notion of Mount Mašu, the mountain with twin peaks that oversee the setting and rising of the sun.[23] The idea of seven stars bound also recalls Near Eastern traditions concerning the Pleiades. In this context, the Pleiades were associated with the binding of the Sibettu demons, of which there are seven.[24] At night the demon sons are seen in the Pleiades in the eastern sky. Further, the Maqlû or "burning" ceremony as described in Akkadian magical series prescribes that witches, capable of travels from the netherworld to the celestial realm, be confined in the eastern horizon.[25]

Unambiguous, though, is that the human dead remain in the west, where they await judgment. Held in pits, the place of their confinement, the spirits of the souls of the dead tarry in a mountain located to the west (δυσμὰς; meʿrāb). As Marie-Theres Wacker has observed in her thorough study of *1 En.* 22, mountains play prominent roles in the topography of the afterlife in Mediterranean, Egyptian, and Mesopotamian traditions.[26] Though perhaps subject to some revision, the text of *1 En.* 22 as we now know it calls attention to four caverns or pits that are home to the spirits of the dead. The four hollow places serve various types of patrons: those who are righteous; those who were sinners and godless; those

---

23. See Jozef T. Milik, ed., *The Books of Enoch: Aramaic Fragments of Qumrân Cave 4* (with the collaboration of Matthew Black; Oxford: Clarendon, 1976), 15, 30. See also Helge Kvanvig, *Roots of Apocalyptic: The Mesopotamian Background of the Enoch Figure and of the Son of Man* (WMANT 61; Neukirchen-Vluyn: Neukirchener, 1988), 247; contra Kvanvig's location of Mašu, see Wayne Horowitz, *Mesopotamian Cosmic Geography* (Winona Lake, Ind.: Eisenbrauns, 1998), 96–98, esp. 266 and 332. Against Kvanvig's interpretation of geography described in the Epic of Gilgamesh, see Wolfgang Heimpel, "The Sun at Night and the Doors of Heaven," *JCS* 38 (1986): 127–51.

24. Alasdair Livingstone, *Court Poetry and Literary Miscellanea* (SAA 3; Helskini: Helsinki University Press, 1989), 103, lines 5, 21; Frans Wiggermann, "Mythological Foundation of Nature," in *Natural Phenomena: Their Meaning, Depiction and Description in the Ancient Near East* (Amsterdam: Royal Netherlands Academy of Arts and Sciences, 1992), 279–306, esp. 287–88. See also E. Douglas Van Buren, "The Seven Dots in Mesopotamian Art and their Meaning," *AfO* 13 (1939–41): 277–89; and H. W. F. Saggs, *The Encounter with the Divine in Mesopotamia and Israel* (London: University of London, Athlone Press, 1978), 97–102, on the complex of traditions associated with Enmešara and his sons.

25. See Gerhard Meier, "Studien zur Beschwörungssammlung Maqlû," *AfO* 21 (1966): 70–81; Tzvi Abusch, "Maqlû," *RlA* 7:346–51; idem, "Mesopotamian Anti-Witchcraft Literature: Texts and Studies. Part I: The Nature of *Maqlû*: Its Character, Divisions, and Calendrical Setting," *JNES* 33 (1974): 251–62; idem, "Ascent to the Stars in a Mesopotamian Ritual: Social Metaphor and Religious Experience," in *Death, Ecstasy, and Other Worldly Journeys* (ed. J. J. Collins and M. Fishbane; Albany: State University of New York Press, 1995), 15–39, esp. 18.

26. Marie-Theres Wacker, *Weltordnung und Gericht: Studien zu I Henoch 22* (Würzburg: Echter, 1982), 151–60.

sinners who were not brought to justice in their lifetime; and those who were murdered and cry out against their murderers.[27] This separation of the "righteous and various groups of non-righteous from one another," as Nickelsburg describes, anticipates end time retribution.[28] The righteous, for example, enjoy something like a bright fountain of water, as they wait a final judgment. Since *1 En.* 22:13 specifies that certain of the dead will not be raised, the reader is to presume, as Nickelsburg suggests, that the others will be resurrected.[29]

As so much of the second half of Enoch's journey in *1 En.* 21–36 mirrors and elaborates upon the concise formulation of the patriarch's travels in *1 En.* 17–19, we find a parallel tradition of the realm of the dead represented sparsely in *1 En.* 17:6.[30] There Enoch encounters the great darkness where no human walks (μέχρι τοῦ μεγάλου σκότους κατήντησα καὶ ἀπῆλθον ὅπου πᾶσα σὰρξ οὐ περιπατεῖ; wa-ʾeska ʿabiy ṣelmat wa-ḥorku xaba kʷellu šegā yānsosu). The declaration in *1 En.* 17:6 that no human (specifically "flesh" [σάρξ/šegā], that is, the body or that which is carnal as opposed to spiritual)[31] may travel to this place confirms the association of the dark realm with Hades. The Greek translation necessitates an interpretation to the effect that humans set aside flesh at the time of death and that the psyche alone passes to the realm of the dead.[32] If the Geʿez translation "where all flesh goes" is original and the difference in the Greek manuscript is due to the preference of a translator, the notion conveyed by *1 En.* 17:6 would be that all humanity possessing creatureliness is subject to death and, hence, eventually comes to Hades, the dark realm.[33] The Greek and Ethiopic variants both facilitate the notion that Enoch approaches the realm of the dead.[34]

The author does not linger on the description of the realm of the dead and does not speak to its inhabitants, which seems curious until one recognizes that

---

27. For more on the classification of souls in these depositories, see Nickelsburg, *1 Enoch 1*, 300–309.

28. Nickelsburg, "Where Is the Place," 55.

29. Ibid.

30. Coblentz Bautch, *Study of the Geography*, 20. So also Dillmann, *Das Buch Henoch*, 121.

31. See Eduard Schweizer, "σάρξ," *TDNT*, 7:98–151, esp. 120; and Wolf Leslau, *Concise Dictionary of Geʿez (Classical Ethiopic)* (Wiesbaden: Harrassowitz, 1989), 54–55; idem, *Comparative Dictionary of Geʿez* (Wiesbaden: Harrassowitz, 1991), 526.

32. Schweizer, "σάρξ," 7:120. See also *1 En.* 22:3 and 102:5.

33. So Schweizer, "σάρξ," 7:120.

34. Black (*Book of Enoch*, 157) emphasizes that the Greek describes a place inaccessible to ordinary persons and that the translator has in mind Hades as the place where no flesh goes. Similarly, Lods (*Le Livre D'Hénoch*, 156) maintains that the Ethiopic version, "where all flesh walks," is a clear allusion to Hades. The great darkness where no flesh walks, a realm that is inaccessible to living persons, seems an apt description for Sheol or Hades. If one accepts the Ethiopic "where all flesh walks" as original to *1 En.* 17:6, the great darkness must refer to Hades, the realm of the dead to which eventually all persons go. Otherwise, the reference is nonsensical: To what great darkness do all people travel?

chapter 17 addresses only in the briefest manner the sites located on the extremities of the earth; the author of this particular unit of the booklet has another focus: the places of punishment for celestial beings in *1 En.* 18 and 19 that also lie outside the *oikoumene*. Immediately prior to this, Enoch journeys to the fire of the west that provides sunsets, to a river of fire flowing into the great sea of the west, and then to various rivers. The enigmatic bodies of water recall the Pyriphlegethon and the infernal rivers (the Styx, Cocytus, and Acheron) of Homer's *Odyssey* and Plato's *Phaedo*. The text makes explicit the western provenance of these phenomena.

This second version of Enoch's journey to the realm of the dead underscores that the authors of this literature understand that the western region served as a necropolis. The association made between the west and the realm of the dead is an ancient one, an association not limited to the Enochic authors. One recalls, for example, that the Greek ζόφος not only represented the realm of the dead but also indicated the west. The relationship of the realm of darkness to the west is clear; the sun sets in the west, so the west is void of light. Many cultures, especially in the ancient Mediterranean environs and the Near East, understood the realm of the dead to be in the west, the place of darkness where the sun sets.

Situating *1 En.* 22 in its ancient context, Wacker surveys Egyptian, Ugaritic, Babylonian, and Greek texts that all locate the realm of the dead in the west, relating the netherworld to the course of the sun. Wacker maintains that preexilic Israel would certainly have known such a trend that was prevalent in its environs but that rigorous Yahwism suppressed the motif so intimately connected to cults of the sun.[35] Nonetheless, *1 En.* 17:4–8 and *1 En.* 22 preserve this very typical association between the realm of the dead and the west, the region of the setting sun.

While the Enochic *Weltanschauung* posits temporary repositories for human and celestial beings, places that have some association with eschatological blessings are also located on the periphery of the earth. These places do not serve as the ultimate loci for end-time events but, as with the holding cells for humankind and the Watchers, are provisional homes, in this case for phenomena associated with future rewards or gifts for the pious. The Book of the Watchers calls attention to two places, both comparable in some respects to Eden of Gen 2–3. Neither proves a resting place for the righteous dead in this Enochic tradition, but both marry protology with eschatology through what seem to be allusions to the exceptional trees of Eden.

The first of these places is identified by seven distinctive mountains consisting of different gemstones; one mountain in particular is said to serve as the throne of God (*1 En.* 18:6–9 || 24:2–25:4). Here among fragrant trees exists an extraordinary tree that is to be transplanted in Jerusalem; the tree enables the righteous

35. Wacker, *Weltordnung und Gericht*, 151.

to enjoy extended lives free from suffering of any kind. The Enochic authors situate the mountain throne and tree of life at the bounds of the *oikoumene* as well. The seven mountains are located, according to *1 En.* 18:6, in a place "that burns day and night." The mountain-throne of God whose top is lapis lazuli and associated with burning fire is reminiscent of Sinai as it is presented in the theophany of Exodus. Further, the Geʿez of *1 En.* 18:6 locates these same mountains to the south or southwest (mangala ʾazēb; see above). While the parallel tradition in *1 En.* 24–25 is ambiguous with regard to the location of the mountain range, the unusual configuration and characteristics of these mountains suggest that they lie at the ends of the earth, much like the bejeweled woodland Gilgamesh encounters in his journeys to Utnapishtim (see Epic of Gilgamesh 9).[36] While this particular tradition with allusion to a tree of life might bring to mind first the garden in

---

36. There exists also in the Greek and Ethiopic of *1 En.* 32 a tradition concerning seven mountains surrounded by fragrant trees. While the expression "seven mountains" occurs in Gr^{Pan} and Ethiopic manuscripts, the earliest extant tradition from $4QEn^{e}$ 1 xxvi shows instead that *1 En.* 32:1 speaks only of "other mountains," without reference to a specific number (Milik, *Books of Enoch*, 232, 234). These mountains are understood to lie in the north or northeast (see *1 En.* 30:1 and 32:1). Charles also looks to the Astronomical Book for insight into the location of the mysterious mountain range of *1 En.* 18:6. Reference is made in *1 En.* 77:4 to seven mountains that are higher than all other mountains on earth. Although the Ethiopic of the preceding verse features a description of the north as a region divided into three parts, the Aramaic text recovered for *1 En.* 77 demonstrates that the Ethiopic reading is an abridgment. The Aramaic tells of a fourth quarter in the north but then returns to a description of the eastern quarter. Following the description of the east, the Aramaic of 77:3 recounts the three divisions of the entire earth. This, in turn, is followed by a mention of seven mountains in 77:4 (see Milik, *Books of Enoch*, 289–90). We find ourselves again with a motif of seven mountains but no mention of the location of these mountains to prove useful to the task of interpreting 18:6. When one examines the tradition of the seven mountains as they occur in *1 En.* 24; 32; and 77, it becomes clear that the mountains function as part of a motif, but one that is not fixed. The mountains of *1 En.* 32 (seven in number only in the Greek and Ethiopic manuscripts and not in the more ancient Aramaic), which are before the garden of righteousness in the east, do not include a mountain that reaches to heaven like the throne of God. No orientation of any sort is provided for the seven mountains of 77:4, nor is there mention of a "mountain of God," a paradise, or a life-giving tree. The tradition that most closely approximates that of 18:6 is the description of the seven mountains in *1 En.* 24, mountains of precious stones arranged similarly with three mountains to the east and three to the south. Chapters 32 and 77 do not shed light on the seven mountains of 18:6, nor do they hint at their location. Against the claim that the mountains are located in the northwest, Dillmann (*Das Buch Henoch*, 117), Lods (*Le Livre D'Hénoch*, 158), and more recently Daniel Olson (*Enoch: A New Translation: The Ethiopic Book of Enoch, or 1 Enoch, Translated with Annotations and Cross-References* [North Richland Hills, Tex.: BIBAL Press, 2004], 266–68) affirm the variant reading of the Ethiopic for 18:6 (ḥalafku mangala ʾazēb z(w)a-yenadded), which indicates that the seven mountains must be located in the south as well. The fire mountains that burn day and night, Dillmann (*Das Buch Henoch*, 117) suggests, might best be understood as rooted in traditions concerning the hot south (Africa).

Eden of Genesis, the Enochic authors also seem to have in mind Sinai traditions from Exodus.[37]

In *1 En.* 32 we also read of an exceptional garden, one referred to as the paradise of righteousness. From the use of פרדס, one observes that the Persian loanword is used "as if it were a technical term," rather than the expected גנתא (the Aramaic equivalent of גן).[38] This garden, which the text indicates is located to the east (though perhaps we are to infer a northeasterly direction), also is home to all manner of trees, including one known as the tree of wisdom.[39] Its fruit confers to the holy ones who eat of it, we read, great wisdom. According to the angelic guide of Enoch, this tree of wisdom (meant to recall the tree of the knowledge of good and evil from Gen 2–3) was the very one that Adam and Eve enjoyed. Once they ate of it, they gained wisdom and were expelled from the garden (*1 En.* 32:6).[40] Again, this leg of the journey takes Enoch eastward or northeasterly, a tradition that recalls the biblical setting of Eden to the east (Gen 2:8).[41] Yet to reach the garden paradise, Enoch must travel beyond the Red Sea

---

37. Coblentz Bautch, *Study of the Geography*, 221–23.

38. See Nickelsburg, *1 Enoch 1*, 327.

39. Pierre Grelot ("La géographie mythique d'Hénoch et ses sources orientales," *RB* 65 [1958]: 33–69, esp. 43) explains this garden, the site where Adam and Eve dwelled and from which they were expelled, as a second garden of justice, the Eden of Gen 2:8. The author of *1 Enoch* distinguishes two gardens of justice in his cosmology, suggests Grelot, in order to harmonize the garden of Eden in the east from Gen 2, the divine mountain in the north of Isa 14, and the mountain identified as Eden in Ezek 28. For the author, he suggests, the traditions could be resolved thus: "Dieu réside au paradis sur la montagne du N.-O. Avant de créer l'homme, il a planté un «jardin de justice» au N.-E.; c'était une réplique du «jardin de justice» du paradis. Il y a temporairement transporté l'arbre de vie; mais après la chute il l'a ramené au paradis du N.-O. C'est dans ce paradis qu'il a transféré Hénoch, pour l'y mettre en réserve en attendant le jour du jugement" ("La géographie mythique d'Hénoch," 43). Hence in some sense Grelot understands an exegetical problem stemming from multiple depictions of paradise in the Hebrew Bible to have contributed to a view of the world in which there exist paradises located in the east and in the west.

40. Of this tradition, James C. VanderKam (*Enoch: A Man for All Generations* [Studies on Personalities of the Old Testament; Columbia: University of South Carolina Press, 1995], 59) remarks that the Eden language is unmistakable and explicit. The tree of wisdom, he suggests, is obviously the tree of knowledge of good and evil (Gen 2:9); that the garden lies in the east also reflects the geography of the biblical paradise (Gen 2:8). VanderKam thinks that the Enochic author echoes Genesis by suggesting that the first couple's partaking from the tree of knowledge resulted in knowledge for the first couple (Gen 3:7, 22: "See, the man has become like one of us, knowing good and evil").

41. VanderKam (*Enoch,* 59) views the Enochic tradition of an eastern paradise with a tree of wisdom as reflecting an oriental location of paradise in the east and thinks the western paradise with a tree of life to reflect the Hellenistic tradition of placing Elysium in the west. See also Black, *Book of Enoch*, 179.

and past a realm of darkness that apparently separates the inhabited land from this numinous space.

Thus, Enoch's journeys as described in chapters 17–36 focus on what is outside the *oikoumene* and inaccessible for humankind. Two notable exceptions with regard to localization of eschatological events are to be found, however, among these tours of Enoch in the Book of the Watchers. Both *1 En.* 24:5–25:6 and 27:14 envision Jerusalem and its surroundings as the setting for the great judgment and new era. The end of the former era will be marked by God's return, when, in the words of 25:3, the Holy One descends to visit the earth in goodness. The righteous will enjoy the fruit of what appears to be a tree of life (cf. 24:4–6) that is transplanted by the temple (called "the holy place" and "the house of God"; later referred to as the "sanctuary"; 25:5–6). Allusions to the topography of Jerusalem then lead to a cursed valley, where those who blaspheme will be gathered together; the text alludes to the Valley of Hinnom (Gehenna), which will serve as the final resting place for at least one particular group within the damned (27:1–4). In this respect, the Enochic view of the eschaton is quite comparable to Zech 14 and to some extent Isa 27; in these texts also Jerusalem may serve as both the setting for judgment against the enemies of God and as a home to the pious, who go to the temple to worship once the dust of the eschatological skirmish settles.

With regard to geography and places associated with the afterlife or postmortem judgment, the righteous can content themselves with the knowledge that the universe confirms their views about the eschaton. Though judgment is imminent, space has been allotted in the cosmos to serve as temporary homes for the deceased and as prisons for the especially wicked. The work communicates expectation for a coming time of judgment in which God, in the guise of the divine warrior (*1 En.* 1:4; 19:1; 22:11; 25:3–4; 27:3), returns to earth; meanwhile, all manner of creature are assigned to particular temporary locations where they await that day. Though the Book of the Watchers underscores the existence of places such as the realm of the dead and the prison abyss for the evil angels, the sites are not accessible to the audience of the work (19:3). Also on the periphery are unique phenomena associated with wisdom and longevity, the tree of life and the tree of wisdom, reserved for the pious or for the community that has preserved such literature.

4. The Visionary's Worldview

It does seem that the authors, assuming redaction, provide the reader with just enough information that one can discern a general geography or mental map for places associated with the numinous. The narrative hints that the realm of the dead is situated to the west, that celestial beings are bound in the east, that a paradise of righteousness (though not a postmortem dwelling of any kind) is located in the east, and that a tree of life next to the mountain throne of God exists to the south.

Is a reader of the text to locate these seemingly otherworldly places? It seems to me that that is not the case. The message one receives from the Book of the Watchers is that these extraordinary places exist beyond the inhabited world; given the very opaque description of the geography, one is not meant to re-create this particular journey of Enoch. To paraphrase *1 En.* 19:3, Enoch alone is the recipient of these visionary journeys, and no others have seen what he has seen. Some would maintain that the biblical description of Eden's location is similar. Edward Noort suggests that the precise setting of the garden is rendered obscure; the narrator wants to present a "mystified location for paradise."[42] According to Noort, by means of references to familiar rivers in Gen 2:10–14 suggesting known geography, the author demonstrates the reality of paradise. Yet the narrator is portraying paradise as inaccessible and does not want the audience to locate the garden of Eden; for this reason, the geography is only discussed in a very general way.

Such is the case with the realm of the dead, the prisons for the wayward angels and stars, and the location of the tree of life and tree of wisdom in the Book of the Watchers: the reader is offered a guarantee that these places really exist (Enoch has seen them!) but no clues as to how one might encounter these sites beyond the inhabited world. On the other hand, chapters 26–27 do mean for the audience to identify sites associated with Jerusalem. Both the Temple Mount and the Valley of Hinnom are indicated by the text, but with regard to their eschatological import, their time to serve in this capacity has not yet come.

Study of these geographical traditions provides some clues as to the background of the Enochic authors. In locating the realm of the dead to the west, prisons for the angels and stars to the east, the tree of wisdom to the east or northeast, and tree of life to the south at a place reminiscent of Sinai, the Book of the Watchers replicates or alludes to traditions familiar from the Hebrew Bible.[43] At

---

42. Edward Noort, "Gan-Eden in the Context of the Mythology of the Hebrew Bible," in *Paradise Interpreted: Representations of Biblical Paradise in Judaism and Christianity* (ed. G. P. Luttikhuizen; Leiden: Brill, 1999), 21–36, esp. 22. Many attempts have been made to locate the paradise of Gen 2–3. See, e.g., E. A. Speiser, *Genesis* (AB 1; Garden City, N.Y.: Doubleday; 1964), 20; and William F. Albright, "The Location of the Garden of Eden," *AJSL* 38 (1922): 15–31. Noort evaluates many of the theories concerning the garden of Eden's location and ultimately deems the attempts unsuccessful, since the geography is insoluble. In his estimation, the text does not mean for the garden to be locatable ("Gan-Eden in the Context," 28–33). See also Gordon J. Wenham, *Genesis 1–15* (WBC 1; Waco, Tex.: Word, 1987), 66–67.

43. Grelot ("La géographie mythique d'Hénoch") understands the descriptions of the location of paradise, the divine mountain, and the throne of God in *1 En.* 17–36 to be largely informed by Gen 2; Isa 14; and Ezek 28. Grelot (esp. 38–41) hypothesizes that *1 En.* 17–36 presents two paradises, possibly the result of an attempt to harmonize the traditions of Gen 2, where Eden is located in the east; Isa 14, where the mountain of the divine abode is located to the north; and Ezek 28, where Eden, the "garden of God," is equated with the "mountain of God." Milik (*Books of Enoch*, 39–40) similarly traces the depiction of the "mountain of God" in the north and a pit beneath reserved for rebels to Isa 14:12–15 and Ezek 28:16–18.

the same time, the Enochic authors demonstrate familiarity with the geographical sensibilities, sacred sites, and cosmology of Near Eastern, Egyptian, and Greek traditions as well.[44]

Do these chapters reflect actual visionary experiences? Perhaps. Acknowledging that the second half of the Book of the Watchers exhibits signs of redaction and the work of more than one author, one might examine the individual units for evidence of religious experience. We find elsewhere in the Book of the Watchers, for example, the dream incubation of Enoch prior to his ascent (*1 En.* 13:4–7); this account may provide a description of the sort of ascetical practices undertaken by seers in the Second Temple period in order to obtain a vision.[45] The journeys of Enoch in the second half of this booklet could also reflect material obtained from a trance or dream. We observe that the sites described in the journeys exhibit awareness or familiarity with both biblical and nonIsraelite traditions. Daniel Merkur, following Christopher Rowland, suggests that the content of the visions may have been produced by discursive meditations on older texts or traditions that determine in advance the contents of the revelation.[46] According to this hypothesis, the sites that are referred to in the journeys would have been known to the author prior to the visionary experience and would thus have informed the experience.

On the other hand, the visionary journeys of Enoch in the second half of the Book of the Watchers are distinguished from the ascent of the patriarch to the divine throne room that is described in chapters 13–14 and perhaps from certain *merkabah* accounts of ascent in one important respect. I do not observe any transformative experience of the seer in *1 En.* 17–36 that is comparable to what has been described as "a quasi-deifying vision" or angelification.[47] Even while we can argue that Enoch's heavenly ascent in chapter 14 anticipates the later traditions of angelification of the seer, the second half of the Book of the Watchers, certainly the work of a different hand, does not portray transformative

---

44. Coblentz Bautch, *Study of the Geography*, 231–57.

45. See Frances Flannery-Dailey, *Dreamers, Scribes, and Priests: Jewish Dreams in the Hellenistic and Roman Eras* (JSJSup 90; Leiden: Brill, 2004).

46. Daniel Merkur, "The Visionary Practices of Jewish Apocalyptists," in *The Psychoanalytic Study of Society 14: Essays in Honor of Paul Parin* (ed. L. B. Boyer and S. A. Grolnick; Hillsdale, N.J.: Analytic, 1989), 119–48, esp. 140–41. See also Christopher Rowland, *The Open Heaven: A Study of Apocalyptic in Judaism and Christianity* (New York: Crossroad, 1982), 215–28. Says Merkur of the visionary's technique: "The seers rehearsed what they knew in order to encourage their psychic states to manifest further and unknown matters on the same topics" (141). See also Alan Segal, "Apocalypticism and Life after Death," *PIBA* 22 (1999): 41–63, esp. 43–46 and 54–61.

47. See Nathaniel Deutsch, *The Gnostic Imagination: Gnosticism, Mandaeism and Merkabah Mysticism* (Leiden: Brill, 1995); and Elliot R. Wolfson, *Through a Speculum That Shines: Vision and Imagination in Medieval Jewish Mysticism* (Princeton: Princeton University Press, 1994), 84 n. 46.

experiences. There are no suggestions of enthronement of the seer or of investiture. We are reminded of the fact that there is no ascent in *1 En.* 17–36; rather, the journeys to the realm of the dead and places associated with postmortem judgment as well as future paradises suggest that such locations are *this-worldly*.

Eschatological Sorrow, Divine Weeping, and God's Right Arm

Rebecca Lesses

> Those—dying then,
> Knew where they went -
> They went to God's Right Hand -
> That Hand is amputated now
> And God cannot be found.
> (Emily Dickinson)

In *Sefer Hekhalot* (*3 Enoch*), Metatron, the prince of the divine presence (*sar hapanim*), reveals to Rabbi Ishmael the secrets of the heavenly world, the fate of the human soul before birth and after death, the course of ultimate redemption, and the coming of the Messiah.[1] The souls of the righteous fly above the throne of Glory in the presence of God, and the "fathers of the world" (Abraham, Isaac, and Jacob) and the other righteous dead intercede on behalf of the suffering people of Israel on earth (*3 En.* 43:2). They ask God why he has not saved his people and why his right hand, by which he stretched out the heavens, is still set behind him (44:7). As part of his heavenly journey, Rabbi Ishmael is shown the vision of God's right hand, "which has been banished behind him because of the destruction of the temple" (48:1). In a striking image, the five fingers of God's hand weep in sorrow, and five tears fall into the great sea that make the whole world quake (48:4). The souls of the righteous beseech God's hand three times a day with the prayer, "Awake! Awake! Clothe yourself in strength, arm of the Lord" (48:3, quoting Isa 51:9). Only when God realizes that there are no righteous people on earth will he deliver his right hand and bring the final redemption (*3 En.* 48:8).

In this essay I explore several themes that emerge from *Sefer Hekhalot:* the role of the righteous dead in protesting God's judgment and their ritual cry to

1. Unless otherwise specified, all translations from *Sefer Hekhalot* (*3 Enoch*) are from Philip Alexander, ed. and trans., "3 (Hebrew Apocalypse of) Enoch," *OTP* 1:223–315.

awaken God's arm; the hypostasis of God's strength in the figure of his right arm set behind him and of his sorrow in the image of the weeping fingers of his right hand; and the theurgical intertwining of the fate of the people of Israel and God's strength. This essay discusses the ways in which *Sefer Hekhalot* transforms theological conceptions found in earlier midrashic and talmudic literature that are then taken up by the later kabbalistic and Hasidic traditions.[2]

Across different historical contexts, the passages discussed in here engage in a theological effort to understand the destruction of the temple and the exile of the Jewish people and call for an end to Jewish suffering through divine redemption. They range from the fifth-century C.E. *Lamentations Rabbah,*[3] edited in Byzantine Palestine during a time of increasing imperial and ecclesiastical limitations on Jewish life, to the fifth or sixth century *Sefer Hekhalot,* probably redacted in Sasanian Babylonia but containing traditions of Palestinian Jews,[4] to the late thirteenth-century *Zohar,* written during the Reconquista in Spain, when educated Jews were faced with a choice between the attractions of the courtly ethos and an attachment to traditional Judaism,[5] and finally to the *Esh Kodesh,* homilies spoken and written during the Nazi occupation of Poland. In all these circumstances the motif of divine suffering together with the people of Israel has proven to be a powerful image for those seeking to understand Jewish suffering and persecution at the hands of non-Jews.

---

2. See, e.g., *Lam. Rab.* proem 24, *b. Hag.* 5b, the *Zohar* (thirteenth-century Spain), and the teachings of Rabbi Kalonymus Kalman Shapira in his homiletical work, the *Esh Kodesh* (Nehemiah Polen, *The Holy Fire: The Teachings of Rabbi Kalonymus Kalman Shapira, the Rebbe of the Warsaw Ghetto* [Northvale, NJ: Aronson, 1994]).

3. For the dating, see Hermann L. Strack and Günther Stemberger, *Introduction to the Talmud and Midrash* (trans. and ed. M. Bockmuehl; Minneapolis: Fortress, 1992), 286.

4. Alexander ("3 Enoch," 1:229), dates the redaction of the text to the fifth or sixth century C.E. He points out that "the work draw draws extensively on Palestinian apocalyptic traditions about Enoch, and some of its distinctive ideas can be paralleled in Palestinian sources," but that "there are also close parallels to 3 Enoch in terms of Babylonian provenance." He comes to the conclusion that the final redaction is Babylonian. The connections that I trace here between *3 Enoch* and *Lamentations Rabbah* would tend to support the notion that some of *3 Enoch*'s traditions are Palestinian in origin.

5. For this dating, see Gershom Scholem, *Major Trends in Jewish Mysticism* (New York: Schocken, 1941), 156–204. Scholem argues that "Moses de Leon wrote the Zohar in order to stem the growth of the radical rationalistic mood which was widespread among his educated contemporaries" (203). See also the discussion in Isaiah Tishby, *The Wisdom of the Zohar* (trans. D. Goldstein; 3 vols.; Oxford: Littman Library, 1989), 1:87–96; and Yehuda Liebes, "How the Zohar Was Written," in *Studies in the Zohar* (trans. S. Nakache; Albany: State University of New York Press, 1993), 85–138.

1. Divine Weakness

In *Sefer Hekhalot*, the crucial image is of God's right arm, which he has placed behind himself "because of (*mipne*) the destruction of the temple" (*3 En.* 48:1). This hand, which once "stretched out and spread the heavens, the earth, and the heaven of heavens" (44:7), is now useless. It can only weep from its five fingers when entreated by the souls of the righteous (48:3–4) This hypostasis of God's arm builds on a complex web of midrashic allusions, traced eloquently by Michael Fishbane, centering on Lam 2:3 ("He has withdrawn his right hand in the presence of [*mipne*] the foe"), Isa 51:9 ("Arise, arise! Put on strength, arm of the Lord!), and other biblical passages that mention God's arm as a sign of divine strength.[6] In Lam 2:3, as in other parts of Lamentations, God directly punishes the people of Israel for their sins: "In blazing anger he has cut down all the might of Israel;/ he has withdrawn his right hand in the presence of the foe;/ he has ravaged Jacob like flaming fire, consuming on all sides." There is no hint here that God himself has become weakened; on the contrary, he uses his strength against his people: "He bent his bow like an enemy, poised his right hand like a foe;/ he slew all who delighted the eye./ He poured out his wrath like fire in the tent of fair Zion" (Lam 2:4).

In *Lam. Rab.* proem 24, God's arm is the protection that must be removed in order for enemies to enter and destroy the temple:

> At the time that the Holy One, blessed be he, sought to destroy the temple, he said, "As long as I am within it, the nations of the world will not touch it, but I will hide my eyes from it, and I swear that I will not be attached to it until the time of the end, and the enemies will enter and destroy it." Immediately the Holy One, blessed be he, swore by his right hand and placed it behind him, as it is written, "he has drawn back his right hand from before the enemy" (Lam 2:3). At that time the enemies entered the temple and set it afire.[7]

This midrash assumes that God's presence in the temple affords it protection from enemies (the Babylonians, initially, or, for the rabbis, the Romans) and that God removes his protection because of the sins of Israel. As Fishbane points out, "the

6. Michael Fishbane, "Arm of the Lord: Biblical Myth, Rabbinic Midrash, and the Mystery of History," in *Language, Theology, and the Bible: Essays in Honour of James Barr* (ed. S. E. Balentine and J. Barton; Oxford: Clarendon, 1994): 271–92. See also the discussion in Michael Fishbane, *Biblical Myth and Rabbinic Mythmaking* (Oxford: Oxford University Press, 2003), 37–57, 66, 98–99, 146–59; and Yehuda Liebes, "*De Natura Dei*: On the Development of the Jewish Myth," in *Studies in Jewish Myth and Jewish Messianism* (trans. B. Stein; Albany: State University of New York Press, 1993), 1–64.

7. The quotation is my translation of Solomon Buber, ed., *Midrash Eikhah Rabbah* (Vilna: Romm, 1899), 13a.

biblical metaphor of withdrawn protection has been literalized and mythicized."[8] In contrast to this interpretation of God's withdrawn arm, in *Pesiq. Rab Kah.* 17.5 God places his arm behind him in an act of "sympathetic identification" with the bound warriors of Israel:[9]

> R. Azariah and R. Abbahu said in the name of Resh Laqish: You find that when Israel's sins brought it about that enemies invaded Jerusalem, the enemies seized Israel's warriors and bound their hands behind their backs.
>
> [Thereupon] the Holy One, blessed be He, said, "It is written in Scripture [of Me], 'I will be with him in times of trouble' (Ps 91:15); [and now that] My children are mired in trouble, can I remain at ease?"
>
> [Thus] if one may say so, "[God] put his right hand behind (*'aḥor*) Him before (*mipne*) the enemy" (Lam 2:3)....[10]

This midrashic rereading of Lam 2:3 follows another line of thinking, in which God voluntarily permits himself to suffer along with his people. Proem 34 in *Lamentations Rabbah* continues this theme with a comment on Jer 40:1:

> "The word which came to Jeremiah from the Lord, after Nebuzaradan, the captain of the guard, had let him go from Ramah, when he had taken him being bound in chains among all the captives of Jerusalem and Judah that were carried away captive unto Babylon." R. Aḥa commented, "If one could possibly say so, both He [God] and he [Jeremiah] were bound in chains."[11]

As Jakob Petuchowski comments, "What R. Aḥa is saying is that the phrase, 'him being bound in chains,' refers as much to God as it does to Jeremiah."[12] This meaning is far from God's wrathful destruction in Lam 2. Here God himself is enslaved.[13] The midrash in *Pesiqta de-Rab Kahana* goes further to link the fate of Israel with the fate of God's bound right arm:

---

8. Michael Fishbane, "'The Holy One Sits and Roars': Mythopoesis and the Midrashic Imagination," in *The Midrashic Imagination: Jewish Exegesis, Thought, and History* (ed. M. Fishbane; Albany: State University of New York Press, 1993), 70.

9. Fishbane, "Arm of the Lord," 283; see also Fishbane, *Biblical Myth and Rabbinic Mythmaking*, 147–50.

10. Fishbane, "Arm of the Lord," 275–76.

11. Buber, *Midrash Eikhah Rabbah*, 19b; translation and interpretation from Jakob J. Petuchowski, *Theology and Poetry: Studies in the Medieval Piyyut* (London: Routledge & Kegan Paul, 1978), 86.

12. Buber, *Midrash Eikhah Rabbah*, 19b; from Petuchowski, *Theology and Poetry*, 86.

13. The notion that God's power could be limited in any way, expressed in such an anthropomorphic fashion, drew the ire of both Muslims and Karaite Jews. The Qur'an seems to know (and harshly criticize) this notion of the binding of God's right arm and hence God's voluntary weakness. In Surah 5 (The Feast), 64: "The Jews say, 'Bound are the hands of God.' Tied be their own hands and damned may they be for saying what they say! In fact, both His hands are open

> The Holy One said, "I have set an end for My right arm's being enslaved. As long as My children are bound in slavery, My right arm shall be enslaved with them; [but] when I redeem My children, I shall [also] redeem My right arm."[14]

This midrashic reading comes closer to the hypostasis of God's arm in *Sefer Hekhalot*. There also God will free his people when he frees his right arm:

> "My own arm brought me salvation" (Isa 63:5): The Holy One, blessed be He, will say then, "How long shall I expect the children of men to work salvation for my arm by their righteousness? For my own sake, for the sake of my own merit and righteousness, I shall deliver my arm, and by it save my sons from among the gentiles." (*3 En.* 48A:8)

Is God's weakness a choice, or has something else weakened God? In both *Sefer Hekhalot* and *Lamentations Rabbah* God laments that he is helpless to save because of Israel's sins.[15] In *Lam. Rab.* proem 24, God says, "I caused my Presence (*Shekhinah*) to dwell below for the sake of Israel, and now that they have sinned I have returned to my former abode!" Because of the sins of Israel God has been forced to leave the earth and return to his heavenly place. In *Sefer Hekhalot*, God says,

> Since these wicked ones have sinned thus and thus, and have transgressed thus and thus before me, how can I deliver my sons from among the nations of the world, reveal my kingdom in the world before the eyes of the gentiles and deliver my great right hand, which has been brought low by them? (*3 En.* 44:8–9)

---

wide: He spends of His bounty in any way He please" (Ahmed Ali, trans., *Al-Qur'an: A Contemporary Translation* [Princeton: Princeton University Press, 1988], 106). On this point, see Reuven Firestone, "Jewish Culture in the Formative Period of Islam" in *Cultures of the Jews* (ed. D. Biale; New York: Schocken, 2002), 281; David J. Halperin, *Faces of the Chariot: Early Jewish Reponses to Ezekiel's Vision* (TSAJ 16. Tübingen: Mohr Siebeck, 1988), 467–68; and Fishbane, *Biblical Myth*, 149. The Karaite writer al-Qirqisani (in Leon Nemoy, "Al-Qirqisani's Account of the Jewish Sects and Christianity," *HUCA* 7 [1930]: 355), writing in about the year 937 in his work *Book of Lights and Watch-Towers*, criticizes a Yom Kippur *piyyut* by Elazar Qallir for referring to God's hand being bound: "And the exalted hand bound in the chain." Al-Qirqisani speculates that this may be the source of the Qur'anic statement, "The Jews say: God's hand is chained up" (on this point, see Jacob Mann, "An Early Theologico-Polemical Work," *HUCA* 12–13 [1937–38]: 414–15 n. 8). On Karaite, Muslim, and Christian denunciations of anthropomorphic passages in rabbinic literature, see further, Fishbane, *Biblical Myth and Rabbinic Mythmaking*, 254.

14. Fishbane, "Arm of the Lord," 276.

15. Buber, *Midrash Eikhah Rabbah*, 13a. My translation adapts that found in Harry Freedman and Maurice Simon, eds., *Midrash Rabbah: Lamentations* (trans. A. Cohen; London: Soncino, 1939), 41.

The sins of Israel prevent God from bringing salvation and delivering his own right arm.

Moshe Idel's category of "augmentation theurgy," which he analyzes both in ancient midrashic sources and in medieval kabbalistic texts, sheds additional light on the interrelationship that this passage assumes between the actions of Israel and God's power.[16] He cites a passage from *Pesiqta de-Rab Kahana:*

> R. Azariah said in the name of R. Yehudah bar Simon, so long as the righteous act according to the will of heaven, they add power to the *Dynamis* (*mosifim koaḥ ba-gevurah*), as it is written, "And now, I pray thee, let the power (*koaḥ*) of my Lord be great" (Num 14:17). And if they do not, it is as if (*kivyakhol*): "you have weakened [the power of] the Rock that formed thee" (Deut 32:18).[17]

As Idel says, "this passage assumes a direct dependence of the power of the divine *Dynamis* upon human activity; the way to increase it is to fulfill the divine will, which is presumably tantamount to performing the commandments."[18] *Kivyakhol*, "as it were," is a frequent midrashic phrase used when making a daring anthropomorphic statement about God.[19] This passage from *Pesiqta de-Rab Kahana* does not say that when people do not fulfill God's will they actually weaken God (such is the force here of the phrase *kivyakhol*), but other midrashic passages do, as Idel points out. A passage from *Leviticus Rabbah* interprets Deut 32:18 as "you have diminished the power of the Creator."[20] Idel comments, "in the last quotation, the phrase 'as if' or 'so to say' (*kivyakhol*) does not occur, allowing a more literal interpretation of the text—sin actually diminishes the strength of the supernal *Dynamis*.... Sin thus counteracts divine activity, causing divine hesitation and weakness."[21] In the same way, in *Sefer Hekhalot* the sins of Israel weaken God and prevent him from delivering his people.

Yet in the end of days, when there are no righteous people, and the pleas of the righteous dead have not moved God, God will choose to save "for the sake of my own merit and righteousness," which suggests that, despite the sins of Israel, God will still retain the ultimate power to bring salvation. The mystery is why he

---

16. Moshe Idel, *Kabbalah: New Perspectives* (New Haven: Yale University Press, 1988), 157–66.

17. Solomon Buber, ed., *Pesiqta de-Rav Kahana* (Lvov: Meqitzei Nirdamim, 1868), *piska* 26, 166a–b. English translation is from Idel, *Kabbalah*, 158.

18. Idel, *Kabbalah*, 158–59.

19. See the nuanced discussion by Fishbane, "The Term *Kivyakhol* and Its Uses," in *Biblical Myth and Rabbinic Mythmaking*, 325–30. He says: "Almost universally, the term is found in the context of theological and homiletical teachings, and evincing a strong anthropomorphic and anthropopathic character in the framework of midrashic exegesis found in the great midrashic and Talmudic compendia (or extracts derived therefrom)" (325).

20. Idel, *Kabbalah*, 159, quoting *Lev. Rab.* 23:12.

21. Idel, *Kabbalah*, 159, quoting *Lev. Rab.* 23:12.

has still not chosen to do so. The theme of weeping, especially divine weeping, will bring us deeper into this question of divine suffering and weakness.

2. Human and Divine Weeping

In *Sefer Hekhalot*, God, the angels, and the souls of the righteous all weep over the sins of Israel and the subsequent destruction of the temple. The "fathers of the world" (Abraham, Isaac, and Jacob) say that God sits on his throne "as a mourner sits in the days of his mourning" (*3 En.* 44:7). When God informs them that he cannot deliver his people because of their sins, each of the patriarchs begins to weep (44:10). Even Michael, the Prince of Israel, shouts and weeps, saying, "Lord, why do you stand aside?" (44:10, quoting Ps 10:1). When the souls of the righteous stand beside God's glorious right arm and three times a day praise it and urge it, "Awake! Awake! Clothe yourself in strength, arm of the Lord," then God's right hand weeps, and rivers of tears fall from its five fingers and make the whole earth quake (*3 En.* 48:4, quoting Isa 51:9).

Lamenting and mourning come about both as a spontaneous reaction to the deeds and fate of Israel and as part of ritualized, liturgical acts, as Michael Fishbane points out: God sits on his throne like a mourner, and his hand weeps three times a day in response to the beseeching of the righteous souls.[22] This thrice-daily ritual acts as a parallel to the prayers of Israel on earth and also correlates to the recitation of the Qedushah in heaven by the angels. There is performative power in the words of the righteous souls: their call to God's right hand ultimately causes the earth to quake, but their prayers do not bring the final redemption.

Moshe Idel's notion of "theurgical weeping" may shed some light on the processes described in *Sefer Hekhalot*. According to him, theurgical weeping "was intended to induce 'weeping' above—internal processes within the Divine triggered by the shedding of human tears.... the focus of this technique was the supernal processes, the Kabbalist being the instrument and not the goal of this activity."[23] In *Sefer Hekhalot*, the righteous souls play this theurgical role: their praise and entreaties (but not their weeping!) cause five rivers of tears to fall from the five fingers of God's right hand. As we will see below, this notion of theurgical weeping may also illuminate proem 24 of *Lamentations Rabbah*, where the weeping of the righteous dead ("Rachel our Mother") finally roused God's compassion so that he promised to return his people to their land.

The motifs of divine, human, and angelic weeping in *Sefer Hekhalot* also build on midrashic allusions, some of which are found in the same passages that I have already noted in reference to God's right arm. Already in the midrashim the locus of divine weeping is in heaven (and not just on earth), a precursor of

---

22. Fishbane, "The Holy One Sits and Roars," 71.
23. Idel, *Kabbalah*, 76.

the heavenly scene of sorrow described in *Sefer Hekhalot* chapters 44 and 48A. In several places *Lam. Rab.* proem 24 describes God's weeping after the destruction of the temple and his gathering together of others, both humans and angels, to weep with him. At first God weeps alone and does not want any angel, even Metatron, to weep instead of him:

> At that time the Holy One, blessed be He, wept and said, "Woe is me! What have I done? I caused my Presence (*Shekhinah*) to dwell below for the sake of Israel, and now that they have sinned I have returned to my former abode! Heaven forfend that I become a mockery to the nations and a sport to human beings." At that time Metatron came and fell on his face and said before him, "Master of the Universe, Let me weep, and may you not weep."[24] He said to him, "If you do not permit me to weep, I will enter now into a place where you have no permission to go, and I will weep," as it is written, "For if you will not heed it, my soul will weep in secret places because of pride.[25] [My eye must stream and flow with copious tears, because the flock of the Lord is taken captive]" (Jer 13:17).[26]

This midrash transforms the words of Jeremiah, "If you will not heed it," which were originally addressed to the concrete people of Judah as a warning to change their ways, lest they be destroyed, into a divine rebuke of Metatron, the highest angel (and transformed human being). God has a secret place to which he will retire to weep, if Metatron does not allow him to weep openly. Into this place not even Metatron is permitted to enter—God's innermost being is a divine secret from him, perhaps because he is a transformed human being. This evocative

---

24. Liebes ("*De Natura Dei*," 36) interprets Metatron's actions as his attempt to protect God's honor: "wishing to protect God's honor, the angel offers to weep in His place and God refuses, threatening to weep in secret. In the rest of this chapter, it is again God who wishes to forego His honor because of Israel's grief." I am not sure that Liebes is correct, because Metatron seems to want to take on the divine sorrow in God's place and prevent him from grieving.

25. Compare the NJPS translation of Jer 13:17: "For if you will not give heed, my inmost self must weep, because of your arrogance."

26. Buber, *Midrash Eikhah Rabbah*, 13a, my translation, adapted from the translation of Cohen, *Lamentations*, 41. Compare also the version of the story in Buber, *Midrash Eikhah Rabbah*, 32b, which is almost identical. Another reference to divine weeping occurs in a midrash from *b. Ber.* 59b, discussing the meaning of the word *zevaot*. "What is *zevaot*? Rav Qaṭina said: *guha* (earthquake). Rav Qaṭina was walking on the way when he came to the door of a necromancer over bones (*'ova ṭamya*). An earthquake rumbled. He asked, 'Does the necromancer over bones know what this earthquake is"? He called after him, 'Qaṭina, Qaṭina, why should I not know? At the time when the Holy One, blessed by He, remembers his children who are engulfed in trouble among the nations of the world, he lets fall two tears into the great sea, and the sound is heard from one end of the earth to the other—hence the earthquake.'" For a more extended discussion of this midrash, see Fishbane, *Biblical Myth and Rabbinic Mythmaking*, 98–99.

notion is further elaborated in *b. Hag.* 5b, where divine weeping is reserved for the "secret place," while praise of God is to be found in the outer chambers.

> "For if you do not heed it, my soul will weep in secret places (*mistarim*) because of pride" (Jer 13:17). Rav Samuel bar Inya said in the name of Rav: "The Holy One, blessed be He, has a place (*maqom*), and 'secret places' (*mistarim*) is its name."[27] What does it mean "because of pride"? Rav Samuel bar Isaac said, "Because of the pride of Israel which was taken from them and given to star-worshippers." Rabbi Samuel bar Nahmani said, "Because of the pride of the kingdom of heaven."[28] But is there weeping before the Holy One, blessed be He? Didn't Rav Pappa say, "There is no sadness before the Holy One, blessed be He, as it is said, 'glory and majesty are before Him, strength and splendor *ḥedva* are in His Place (*maqom*)'"? (Ps 96:6). There is no problem. One is in the inner chambers [that is, in the "secret places" there is weeping]. The other is in the outer chambers ["honor and majesty before him"—there is no weeping]. And [there is no weeping] in the outer chambers? Isn't it written, "My Lord God of Hosts called on that day to weeping and lamenting, to baldness and girding with sackcloth" (Isa 22:12)? The destruction of the temple is different, for even the angels of peace wept, as it is said, "Hark! The Arielites cry outside; the angels of peace bitterly wept" (Isa 33:7).

In this midrash God explicitly has a special place called "secret places" (*mistarim*) where he goes to weep. Rav Pappa objects, based on Ps 96:6: Is there sadness before God? The interpretive problem is solved by making a distinction between the "inner chambers" (the "secret places") where God may weep and the "outer chambers," where the angels praise God without weeping. This distinction, however, is dissolved on the day the temple is destroyed, when there is weeping in both the inner and outer chambers and both God and the "angels of peace" weep. This motif of a place that is kept secret from the angels is echoed in *Sefer Hekhalot*, where the seraphim and *'opannim* are not permitted to look on God's splendid

---

27. Al-Qirqisani (Nemoy, "Al-Qirqisani's Account," 352–53) denounces this midrash with these words, "They say in the Talmud that God has a place called 'Secret places,' where He weeps; as it is said [Jer 13:17]: 'My soul shall weep in secret places.' They say in the same passage that He says: 'Woe unto Me, for I have destroyed My house and exiled My people.' They say that the angels weep with Him, and that ever since His house was destroyed His stature is bent down. They say that He plucked out some of His hair with His own hands, and that up to this day no one has been allowed to see Him. All this contradicts the saying of the Scripture [Job 26:14]: 'How little a portion is heard of Him!'"

28. Liebes ("*De Natura Dei*," 36) says that God is not concealing his grief from the angels by weeping in secret but in order to protect the "pride of the Kingdom of Heaven." "Public weeping would hurt God's pride and, for this reason, He cries in 'Secret'; namely 'inwardly' and not 'outwardly' as do the angels."

right arm, which weeps every day when the righteous praise and entreat it (*3 En.* 48A 1–4).[29]

In proem 24 of *Lamentations Rabbah*, the motif of divine and human weeping continues until the end of the text. Just after the previously quoted passage from *Lamentations Rabbah*, God says to the ministering angels, "Come, let us go together and see what the enemy has done in my house." Then God and the ministering angels go together, led by the prophet Jeremiah. When God sees the ruined temple, he weeps and says, "Woe is me for my house! My children, where are you? My priests, where are you? My lovers, where are you? What shall I do with you, seeing that I warned you but you did not repent?"[30] God then sends Jeremiah to raise the patriarchs and Moses from their graves to weep with him. When Moses and the patriarchs learn why they have been awakened,

> They immediately also rent their garments, placed their hands upon their heads, and cried out and wept until they arrived at the gates of the Temple. When the Holy One, blessed be He, saw them, immediately, "In that day did the Lord, the God of hosts, call to weeping, and to lamentation, and to baldness, and to girding with sackcloth" (Isa 22:12). Were it not explicitly stated in Scripture, it would be impossible to say such a thing, but they went weeping from one gate to another like a man whose dead is lying before him, and the Holy One, blessed be He, lamented saying, "Woe to the King Who succeeded in His youth but failed in His old age!"[31]

---

29. The *Zohar* (my translation of Reuven Margaliot, ed., *Sefer ha-Zohar* [3 vols.; Jerusalem: Mossad ha-Rav Kook, 1984], 2.17b) also refers to the notion of God's weeping in secret in relation to the interpretation of Jer 13:17. The "secret place" is defined as the ten *sefirot*, the kabbalistic potencies, confirming the idea that the angels exist outside the *sefirot* and that God's sorrow is a matter of intradivine concern.

"Rabbi Hama bar Guria said, 'When Israel sighs under the rule of the nations He sits and roars and cries, as it is written, "My soul weeps in secret places" (Jer 13:17).' Rabbi Yosi said, 'Exactly (*davka*), in secret places.' Rabbi Judah came to Rabbi Eleazar. He found that he was sitting with his hands on his mouth, and he was sad. He said to him: 'What is the master engaged in?' He said to him, 'As it is written (Prov 16:15), "The king's smile means life." If the master is sad, since it is said that he roars and cries, what do his servants do? It is written (Isa 33:7): "Hark, the Arielites cry outside." Why "outside"? Their Master is inside, and they are outside. Their Master is in the inner chambers, and they are in the outer chambers.' The inner chambers, what are they? Rabbi Isaac said, 'They are from the ten crowns of the king.'"

30. Cohen, *Lamentations*, 42.

31. Buber, *Midrash Eikhah Rabbah*, 13a–b; translation is Cohen, *Lamentations*, 42–43. Al-Qirqisani (in Nemoy, "Al-Qirqisani's Account," 352), also denounces this midrash: "But they [the Rabbanites] say in the 'Order of the Gehenna' and 'Repentance (?) of Ahab' that this mourning, weeping, plucking out of the hair, and coarse clothing were instituted by the Creator for Himself only? Will God ever make Himself truly known to people who assert that he weeps and mourns and covers Himself with sackcloth?"

Abraham then accuses God: "Why have I become different from every people and language that I came to such shame and disgrace?" The ministering angels follow Abraham with accusations against God. God answers them by saying to Abraham that "your children sinned and transgressed against all the Torah."[32] This section also mentions God calling upon all of the letters in the Torah to testify against the people of Israel that they have sinned and thus deserve the punishment they have received. When each letter appears, Abraham rebukes it and argues that his children have obeyed the Torah, whereupon they stand aside and refuse to continue testifying. This section is obviously related to *3 En.* 44:9, where Rabbi Ishmael reads in the heavenly books that Israel has transgressed the Torah "from *'aleph* to *tav.*"[33]

Moses decides he wants to see what has happened to his people in Babylon, so Jeremiah says to him, "It is impossible to walk on that way because of the slain." Moses replies, "Despite everything [I still want to see]." Then Moses goes with Jeremiah before him, until they come to the rivers of Babylon. When the exiles see Moses, they say to each other, "the son of Amram has come from his grave to save us from the hand of our enemy." Then a heavenly voice sounds and says, "It is a decree before Me." Moses says to the people, "It is impossible, my children, for me to return you, because the decree has already been decreed." The exiles then cry out until their cry ascends to heaven. Moses then returns to the patriarchs and tells them what he had seen, and they weep and cry. Moses cries out and says, "May the sun be cursed! Why did you not go dark when the enemy entered the temple?" The sun replies that it had to shine or else it would be lashed with sixty lashes of fire. Moses' arguments end with this plea and rebuke of God, "You wrote in your Torah, 'An ox or a ram, do not slaughter it on the same day as its young' (Lev 22:28). Have they not killed many many children and their mothers and you remain silent?"[34]

At the end of this long and complex proem, Rachel appears before God and describes how she conquered her jealousy of her sister Leah (when Jacob married her first) and argues that God should also conquer his jealousy of the idols of the other nations and free his people. She states:

> "I had mercy on her, and I was not jealous of her, and I did not shame her. Just as I, made of flesh and blood, dust and ashes, was not jealous of my co-wife and did not cause her embarrassment and shame, so you, who are the eternal and merciful king, why should you be jealous of idolatry that has no substance and exile my children, who are slain by the sword, and enemies do with them what they wish?" Immediately the mercy of the Holy One, blessed be He, was aroused, and he said, "Because of you, Rachel, I will return Israel to their place,"

32. Buber, *Midrash Eikhah Rabbah*, 13b, my translation.
33. Noted also by Alexander ("3 Enoch," 1:296) in note w to *3 En.* 44:9.
34. Buber, *Midrash Eikhah Rabbah*, 14a–b, my translation.

> as it is written, "Thus said the Lord: 'A cry is heard in Ramah—wailing, bitter weeping—Rachel weeping for her children. She refuses to be comforted for her children who are gone'" (Jer 31:15), and it is written, "Thus said the Lord: 'Restrain your voice from weeping, your eyes from shedding tears; For there is a reward for your labor' [—declares the Lord: 'They shall return from the enemy's land'"] (Jer 31:16), and it is written, "There is hope for your future—declares the Lord: 'Your children shall return to their country'" (Jer 31:17).[35]

The weeping of Rachel and the force of her argument ultimately convince God to save his people and return them to their land, thus reversing the oath he made at the beginning when he withdrew his protection from the temple and placed his right hand helplessly behind him. In the end, the weeping of the righteous dead, of "Rachel our Mother" (as she is classically referred to), causes God to relent and promise that the people of Israel will return to their land. The proem thus ends on a note of salvation brought by Rachel.

In contrast, in *Sefer Hekhalot*, there is nothing that human beings, whether the righteous dead or those still living, can do to bring salvation. Salvation will come in a time of great evil when there is no one left to beseech God. When God sees that

> there is none righteous in that generation, none pious on the earth, no righteousness in men's hands, no one like Moses, no intercessor like Samuel ... then the Holy One, blessed be He, will at once remember his own righteousness, merit, mercy, and grace, and for his own sake, will deliver his great arm, and his own righteousness will support him. (*3 En.* 48A:5–6)

When God delivers his right arm, "by it [he will] save [his] children from among the gentiles." God's salvation is thus inextricably linked to the salvation of the people of Israel. God will "reveal his great arm in the world, and show it to the gentiles.... At once Israel shall be saved from among the gentiles and the Messiah shall appear to them and bring them up to Jerusalem with great joy" (*3 En.* 48A:5–10).

If we compare proem 24 and *Sefer Hekhalot* in terms of the type of theurgical action discussed by Idel, it seems that in the end *Lamentations Rabbah* maintains the theurgical or performative power of human weeping—because Rachel's weeping brings salvation, while in *Sefer Hekhalot* human weeping and remonstration with God can go only so far. As we will see next, these ideas about divine weeping and the possible theurgical power of human weeping are taken up in medieval kabbalah and eastern European Hasidism also to great effect.

35. Buber, *Midrash Eikhah Rabbah*, 14b, my translation.

3. God's Weeping and the Exile of the *Shekhinah*

In medieval kabbalah, the idea that God's Presence (*Shekhinah*) was exiled by the destruction of the temple was elaborately reworked in accordance with kabbalistic concepts. While in *Lamentations Rabbah* the term *Shekhinah* is merely a name for God in his dealings with human beings, in the kabbalah *Shekhinah* is a female hypostasis separate from the male aspect of God, the Holy One, blessed be He, who is identified as the *sefirah* Tiferet.[36] *Shekhinah* represents the tenth *sefirah*, through which blessing flows to the world from the upper *sefirot*. Ideally *Shekhinah* should be eternally united with her male consort, Tiferet, but the destruction of the temple and the exile of the Jewish people effected a separation between the male and female divine potencies.[37] These medieval kabbalistic notions build directly upon rabbinic midrashim that maintain that, when Israel was exiled, God's Presence went with them. For example:

> Come and see how beloved Israel are to the Holy One, blessed be He, for wherever they are exiled the *Shekhinah* is with them ... and when they are redeemed in the future the *Shekhinah* will again be with them, as it is written, "Then the Lord your God will return [*ve-shav*] your captivity" (Deut. 30:3). *Ve-heshiv* [He will cause to return] is not said, but rather *shav* [He will return]. This teaches that the Holy One, blessed be He will return from among the exiles.[38]

As Isaiah Tishby says, "In kabbalistic literature, and especially in the Zohar, this idea is equated with the new mystical and mythical concept of the *Shekhinah* as the female force in the Godhead, and as the supernal mother of Israel."[39] One passage from the Zohar illustrates this new idea of the *Shekhinah* and her relationship to the Holy One, blessed be He, at the time the temple was destroyed.

> When the Temple was destroyed the *Shekhinah* came and went up to all those places where she used to dwell at first, and she would weep for her home and for Israel, who had gone into exile, and for all the righteous and the pious ones who used to be there and had perished. How do we know this? Because it is written, "Thus says the Lord: A voice is heard in Ramah, lamentation and bitter weeping, Rachel weeping for her children" (Jer 31:15).

---

36. For a concise explanation of these kabbalistic concepts, see Arthur Green, *A Guide to the Zohar* (Stanford, Calif.: Stanford University Press, 2004).

37. Or, as Michael Fishbane (*Biblical Myth and Rabbinic Mythmaking*, 293–94) points out, one Zoharic passage posits that a rupture in the Godhead occurs *before* the destruction of the temple and the exile of the *Shekhinah*.

38. *b. Meg.* 29a, as quoted in Tishby, *Wisdom of the Zohar*, 1:382.

39. Ibid.

> And it has already been explained that at that time, the Holy One, blessed be He, questioned the *Shekhinah* and said to her, "What ails you now, that you have gone up entirely to the roofs?" … And she said to Him—"My children are in exile, and the Temple is burnt, and so why should I remain here? And yet You have said: 'You are that are full of uproar, a tumultuous city, a joyous town, your slain are not slain with the sword, or dead in battle' (Isa 22:2); "Therefore I said: Look away from me, I will weep bitterly…" (ibid., 4).[40]

In this Zoharic passage "the mother-*Shekhinah* goes into exile quite willingly, out of love and pity for her exiled children. She cannot forsake them in their time of trouble, and she tries to bear the burden of defeat and subjection with them, in order to strengthen and protect them, and to hasten their final redemption."[41] We can well compare this passage from the Zohar with proem 24, where God weeps for his destroyed house and his exiled people. In the midrash Rachel is the personified nation whose weeping finally causes God to show pity, but in this Zoharic passage Rachel is a name for the *Shekhinah,* and her weeping aligns with God's weeping in proem 24.[42]

Another passage from the Zohar directly reworks the passage from proem 24, as follows:

> Come and see. When the Temple was destroyed and the sins [of Israel] began to take effect, and Israel were exiled from the land, the Holy One, blessed be He, departed to the higher realms, and He did not look upon the destruction of the Temple, or upon His people who had gone into exile. And the *Shekhinah* went into exile with them.[43]

Here it is the Holy One, blessed be He (the *sefirah* Tiferet), who leaves earth because of Israel's sins and the destruction of the temple, while the *Shekhinah* goes into exile with Israel. The one divine figure in *Lamentations Rabbah* is split into two hypostases, one who leaves Israel and one who remains with them. Then, the Holy One, blessed be He, descends again.

> When He came down, He looked upon His house that had been burned; He looked for His people, and they had gone into exile; He inquired for the consort [*Shekhinah*] and she had been sent away. Immediately, "In that day the Lord, the God of hosts, proclaimed weeping, and lamentation, and baldness, and girding with sackcloth" (Isa 22:12).[44]

---

40. Tishby, *Wisdom of the Zohar,* 1:406–7 (Margaliot, *Sefer ha-Zohar,* 1:202b–203a).
41. Tishby, *Wisdom of the Zohar,* 1:382.
42. Ibid.
43. Ibid., 1:409; cf. *b. Meg.* 29a.
44. Tishby, *Wisdom of the Zohar,* 1:409 (Margaliot, *Sefer ha-Zohar,* 1:210a–b).

The Holy One, blessed be He, proclaims weeping because of the destruction of the temple and the exile of his people and his consort, the *Shekhinah,* while, as it says about the *Shekhinah:*

> And of her also, what is written? "Lament like a virgin girded with sackcloth for the husband of her youth" (Joel 1:8), as it is said, "because he is not" (Jer 31:15), for he had left her, and there was a separation [between them].... And all the upper and lower realms wept for her, and went into mourning. Why was this? Because "the other side" had control of her, because it had control of the holy land.[45]

The daring idea of *Lamentations Rabbah* and *Sefer Hekhalot* that God himself weeps for the sufferings of Israel seems to be displaced upon the *Shekhinah,* while Tiferet, as one of the higher *sefirot,* is further removed from suffering. And what is more, the *Shekhinah* does not just go into exile with the people, but she is given over to the sovereignty of others, just as the people are. As Nehemiah Polen says, "But as one climbed the rungs of the sefirotic ladder, one eventually left the pathos of earthly affections behind. At the upper reaches of the sefirotic tree, the kabbalists teach, there is no pain, no division, no opposition and no conflict—only unity and delight."[46] This is unlike *Lamentations Rabbah* and *b. Hagigah,* where God weeps in the inner chambers—in his innermost self, closed off from the angels, even Metatron.

In an eloquent discussion Michael Fishbane explores how another Zoharic passage sharply expresses the separation between the exiled *Shekhinah* and her divine husband.[47] She weeps for him in the three watches of the night, and in one particularly poignant cry she says, "O My husband, My husband! Where have You gone? This is the time I would seek You and see You everywhere; but You are not (here). Where may I seek You, that I not beseech You?! This is Your place, at this time, to come to Me. Truly, I am ready here; (but) truly You have forgotten Me."[48] She cries out all night for him, but only at the morning does he come. As Fishbane notes, "This inner splitting of the Godhead starkly personalizes the difference between the abandoned wife and caring mother down below, and the removed husband and unresponsive father on high."[49] With this Zoharic passage,

45. Tishby, *Wisdom of the Zohar,* 1:409 (Margaliot, *Sefer ha-Zohar,* 1:210a–b). "The other side" is the forces of evil, identified with Lilith, the evil counterpart of *Shekhinah,* and Lilith's consort, Samael.

46. Polen, *The Holy Fire,* 142.

47. Fishbane, *Biblical Myth and Rabbinic Mythmaking,* 296–300. Like the passage explored above, this one also plays elaborately with previous midrashic themes, in particular with one that elaborates the three watches of the night when God cries out over his people's exile, in *b. Ber.* 3a.

48. Fishbane, *Biblical Myth and Rabbinic Mythmaking,* 323.

49. Ibid., 299.

"We are thus readers of a great myth of a Mater Dolorosa, of a mother of sorrows who is abandoned by her Lord and entreats Him on behalf of her absent children."[50] The separation between the Holy One, blessed be He, and the *Shekhinah* mirrors the separation between the people of Israel and God.

4. In the Inner Chamber

The daring notion of divine weeping in the inner chambers is explored to great effect by Rabbi Kalonymous Kalman Shapira in several *drashot* (homilies) given to his Hasidim in the Warsaw Ghetto.[51] Rabbi Shapira was one of the luminaries of prewar Polish Hasidism, who established a yeshiva in Warsaw and developed innovative pedagogical techniques to try to bring rapidly secularizing Jewish youth back to orthodox Judaism.[52] When the Nazis invaded Poland in 1939, his son and daughter-in-law were killed almost immediately, but he remained in Warsaw with his Hasidim.[53] When the Ghetto was enclosed in December 1940, he continued actively to lead his own Hasidic community as well as taking part in the "spiritual leadership of the Jews in the Ghetto."[54] Part of that spiritual leadership were the *drashot* that he gave on Shabbat afternoons, from September 1939 to 18 July 1942 (just before the mass of Warsaw's Jews were deported to Treblinka).[55] Rabbi Shapira did not survive the Nazi occupation, but his writings did; the homilies are found in a work called *Esh Kodesh*, which he bundled together and hid just before the destruction of the Ghetto.[56]

As Nehemiah Polen has described in *The Holy Fire*, Rabbi Shapira's first attempts to understand and explain the suffering endured by the Jews at the hands of the Nazis utilized traditional Jewish notions that suffering is caused by sin.[57] We have already seen this idea expressed in the midrashim and *Sefer Hekhalot:* the temple was destroyed and the people went into exile because of their sins. By December 1941, however, he had become aware that "the march of events was making talk of sin and chastisement simply inappropriate, incommensurate with the magnitude of the ongoing crisis and its attendant pain."[58] Instead, he

50. Ibid., 300.

51. Polen, *The Holy Fire*, 106–21. See also his earlier discussion in Nehemiah Polen, "Divine Weeping: Rabbi Kalonymos Shapiro's Theology of Catastrophe in the Warsaw Ghetto," *Modern Judaism* (1987): 253–69.

52. Polen, *The Holy Fire*, 1–6.

53. Ibid., 8–12.

54. Ibid., 12.

55. Ibid., 15.

56. Ibid., 150.

57. PolenIbid., 106–110.

58. Ibid., 111.

began to talk of divine suffering, in particular the idea of God's weeping in the inner chambers. In a *derashah* from 11 February 1942, he states,[59]

> Now the Jew who is tormented by his afflictions thinks that he alone suffers, as if all his personal afflictions and those of all Israel do not affect [God] above, God forbid. Scripture states, however, "In all their troubles He was troubled" (Isa 63:9), and the Talmud states: When a person suffers, what does the *Shekhinah* say? "My head is too heavy for me, My arm is too heavy for Me." Our sacred literature tells us that when a Jew is afflicted, God blessed be He, suffers as it were much more than the person does. It may be that since He, blessed be He, is not subject to any limitation—for which reason no conception of Him is possible in the world—therefore His suffering from Israel's troubles is also boundless.

Rabbi Shapira here reasserts the traditional idea that God is with Israel, and with the individual Jew, in suffering. He goes beyond this notion to assert that God's suffering is much more than the person's, because God is without any limitation. As Polen says, "Precisely because God is infinite, His suffering is infinite and beyond human conception."[60]

But the world does not know of God's suffering, because if God's suffering "penetrated the world," it could not remain standing. God weeps in his inner chamber so that his suffering will not destroy the world. "Now since His suffering, as it were, is boundless and vaster than all the world—for which reason it has never penetrated the world and the world does not shudder from it—therefore the angel said, 'Let me weep so that You won't need to weep.'"[61] Unlike *Sefer Hekhalot,* where the streams of tears from God's right hand cause earthquakes every day, God's suffering remains entirely interior. In Rabbi Shapira's novel formulation, the angel (Metatron) wanted "the divine weeping to be manifested in the world; the angel wanted to transmit the weeping into the world. For then God would no longer need to weep; once the sound of divine weeping would be heard in the world, the world would hear it and explode. A spark of His suffering, as it were, would penetrate the world and would consume all His enemies."[62] The angel is thus trying to hasten the end, but God does not want the world to explode, since "God wanted to atone for Israel's sins, and that time was not yet a time of salvation, He answered [the angel], 'I will go to a place where you have no permission to enter and weep there.'"[63] God's suffering in the inner chambers is for the purpose of the atonement of Israel. Rabbi Shapira goes on to say that God's suffering "is so great that the world cannot contain it.... He causes His

59. Ibid., 116.
60. Ibid., 117.
61. Ibid.
62. Ibid., 117–118.
63. Ibid., 118.

suffering and pain to expand, as it were, still more so that they would be too sublime even for the angel, so that even the angel would not see."[64] The reason Metatron cannot enter his chamber is because even he could not bear the divine suffering that atones for Israel's sins. Unlike the Zohar and medieval kabbalistic writings, God's suffering is to be found in his innermost and secret places; it is not reserved for his lower manifestation in the *Shekhinah.*

Although the angel cannot enter into the inner chamber with God, it is possible for a human being to suffer together with God there, to study Torah with him and to weep with him. Rabbi Shapira says,

> There are occasions when, at a time of [divine] concealment [*hester*]—meaning, when He, blessed be He, conceals Himself in His inner chambers—the Jewish person communes with Him there, each individual in accord with his situation, and [new aspects of] Torah and divine service are revealed to him there.... God, blessed be He, is to be found in His inner chambers weeping, so that one who pushes in and comes close to Him by means of studying Torah, weeps together with God, and studies Torah with Him. Just this makes the difference: the weeping, the pain which a person undergoes by himself, alone, may have the effect of breaking him, of bringing him down, so that he is incapable of doing anything. But the weeping which the person does together with God—that strengthens him. He weeps—and is strengthened; he is broken—but finds courage to study and teach.[65]

A person who endures the conditions of the Warsaw Ghetto, having seen his family and close followers murdered, who daily sees people dying in the streets of hunger and disease, can still commune with God through his suffering, because God is not distant, is not transcendent and above human suffering. Even in his inner chambers, God is close to the person who seeks him through the study of Torah and weeping. In the end, it is God's very suffering on behalf of the people of Israel and the individual Jew that makes it possible for the bond to be preserved.

In a very personal way, Rabbi Shapira's *derashah* gives a profound meaning to the midrashic and *hekhalot* passages that also speak of divine weeping and weakness. I believe that his remarks reveal some of the personal feelings that underlie these more impersonal literary forms. In *Sefer Hekhalot* and *Lamentations Rabbah,* the righteous dead express the feelings of the authors of those times: they ask God why he has not yet redeemed his people; they entreat him to unleash his power (his right arm) and save them. They weep together with God as they go from one gate to another of the ruined temple. Abraham, Isaac, Jacob, and the ministering angels all reproach God for permitting his people to be slain and sent into exile. God, in a sense, is put on the defensive by their accusations

64. Ibid.

65. Ibid., 119, homily of 14 March 1942.

and, at least in *Lamentations Rabbah,* is finally moved by the weeping of Rachel. In the Warsaw Ghetto, Rabbi Shapira never lost his hope for divine redemption, but his *derashot,* finally, do not reveal either the divine mercy that comes because of Israel's weeping or the redemption that God's right arm brings when there are no righteous people left to beseech him. The authors of *Lamentations Rabbah* and *Sefer Hekhalot* also did not see the final redemption, but, like Rabbi Shapira, the bond with God is preserved for them by the communion of divine suffering.

Part 5:
Practices

The Therapeutae, Text Work, Ritual, and Mystical Experience

Celia Deutsch

> I will say what is fitting about those who have embraced the life of contemplation....They read the holy scriptures and study their ancestral philosophy, interpreting it allegorically.... Every seventh day they come together as for a general assembly.... Then the person most senior, best versed in the teachings, gives a well-reasoned and wise discourse. (Philo, *Contempl.* 28, 30–31)[1]

In first-century Alexandria, a time and place where the overwhelming majority were illiterate, Philo gives his readers a treatise, *On the Contemplative Life or the Suppliants, the Fourth Part about the Virtues.* There he describes a Jewish community given over to ascetical practice, study, and contemplation.

Philo's implied readers include a wide swath of Alexandrine elites immersed in the social, political, and economic concerns of upper-class life. Jew and non-Jew alike have been educated in the classical Greek curriculum that prevails in the Hellenistic world. They are confronted by the attraction exercised by Sophistic rhetoric. Philo's readers have access to the mysteries, and they live in Egypt, a land with its own ancient traditions and whose priesthoods possess their own scribal class. Jewish readers represent, in addition, a variety of positions toward their own tradition.

De Vita Contemplativa serves an apologetic function in relation to a varied audience, and it well may serve as a way for Philo to reflect on his own experience as philosopher and text worker. One of the strategies Philo employs in this trea-

This essay is based on a paper given for the Early Jewish and Christian Mysticism Group at the Annual Meeting of the American Academy of Religion/Society of Biblical Literature, Toronto, Canada, 24 November 2002. I am grateful to Elizabeth Castelli (Barnard College/Columbia University) for her many helpful suggestions.

1. Unless otherwise indicated, all translations are my own.

tise, an encomium,[2] is to relate text work to ritual and mystical experience. This is the focus of our study.

With Catherine Bell, I understand ritual as a "matter of various culturally specific strategies for setting some activities off from others, for creating and privileging a qualitative distinction between the 'sacred' and the 'profane,' and for ascribing such distinctions to realities thought to transcend the powers of human actors."[3] Differentiation, distinctions, marking off the sacred from the profane—these are ways in which to think about the function of study and text interpretation in *De vita contemplativa*. Ritual employs a variety of strategies:

> a delineated and structured space to which access is restricted; a special periodicity for the occurrence and internal orchestration of the activities; restricted codes of communication to heighten the formality of movement and speech; distinct and specialized personnel; objects, texts, and dress designated for use in these activities alone; verbal and gestural combinations that evoke or purport to be the way things have always been done; preparations that demand particular physical or mental states; and the involvement of a particular constituency not necessarily assembled for any other activities.[4]

All these elements are "framing" strategies that mark off boundaries around a given activity, indicating which elements are "within the environment of the activity" and which are outside it.[5]

A careful reading of the *De vita contemplativa* demonstrates how Philo uses a variety of framing strategies to signal text work, including activities such as study, interpretation, and transmission, as a site of mystical experience. In other words, such a reading discloses text work as situated in a context of "delineated and structured space," "a special periodicity," and so forth. And it shows how Philo describes text work both as result of and vehicle for mystical experience.

1. Ritual Language

In *De vita contemplativa* Philo presents a group of people, male and female, who have embraced the life of contemplation (θεωρία).[6] Philo praises the Lake Mareot

---

2. See Manuel Alexandre Jr., "The Eloquent Philosopher in Philo's *De uita contemplatiua*," *Euphrosyne* 29 (2001): 319.

3. Catherine Bell, *Ritual Theory, Ritual Practice* (New York: Oxford University Press, 1992), 74. See also Bell's *Ritual: Perspectives and Dimensions* (New York: Oxford University Press, 1997), 80–83. Bell prefers the term "ritualization," although she uses "ritual" as well.

4. Bell, *Ritual Theory, Ritual Practice*, 204–5.

5. Bruce Kapferer, "The Ritual Process and the Problem of Reflexivity in Sinhalese Demon Exorcisms," in *Rite, Drama, Festival, Spectacle: Rehearsals Toward a Theory of Cultural Performance* (ed. J. J. MacAloon; Philadelphia: Institute for the Study of Human Issues, 1984), 189.

6. The status of *De vita contemplativa* as a work of fiction or an account of an actual group is a matter of debate. See Baruch M. Bokser, "Philo's Description of Jewish Practices," in idem,

community, implying that they are models for his audience. He describes the members' way of life in ritual terms, calling them "therapeutae" (θεραπευταὶ) and "therapeutrides" (θεραπευτρίδες). With this and other terms Philo uses the vocabulary of Greek and Egyptian cult, including mysteries, as well as that of Jewish ritual.[7]

The verb θεραπεύω and its cognates have a range of meanings, including "to heal," "to attend or serve," and "to worship."[8] Philo plays on the word, noting its reference to healing and worship (*Contempl.* 2).[9] He contrasts the community's members with others who are "incurable" (ἀθεράπευτοι) and sightless (*Contempl.* 10). Philo leaves behind the connotation of healing later in the *De vita contemplativa*, but in the early paragraphs he uses healing and "therapeutae" as correlatives of sight and vision. In associating language of ritual and vision, he suggests the ritual quality of contemplative experience: "But let the Therapeutic household, always taught beforehand to see, fix their minds on the vision of the Existent and ascend beyond the sense-perceptible sun" (*Contempl.* 11).[10]

"Therapeutae" is actually a designation from Greek and Egyptian cult, including the mysteries, for "those who serve the gods."[11] Philo's association

Philo's Description of Jewish Practices (Center for Hermeneutical Studies in Hellenistic and Modern Culture, Colloquy 30; Berkeley and Los Angeles: Graduate Theological Union; University of California Press, 1977), 1; Troels Engberg-Pedersen, "Philo's *De Vita Contemplativa* as a Philosopher's Dream," *JSJ* 30 (1999): 40–64. Certainly the document is part of a tradition presenting idealized descriptions of philosophical schools, but, with most scholars, I believe that the document, while highly stylized, depicts a group whom Philo knew personally. See Marcel Simon, "L'ascétisme dans les sectes juives," in *Tradizione dell'enkrateia: Motivazioni ontologiche e protologiche, atti del Colloquio Internazionale Milano, 20–23 aprile 1982* (ed. U. Bianchi; Rome: Edizioni dell'Ateneo, 1985): 395, 416–17; Joan E. Taylor and Philip R. Davies, "The So-Called Therapeutae of *De Vita Contemplativa*: Identity and Character," *HTR* 91 (1998): 18–19.

7. Taylor and Davies point out that θεραπευταὶ is a word associated with Egyptian cults and that Philo also uses it of the Essenes. They believe that it may be a general cultic term and not a specific title ("So-Called Therapeutae," 7). Taylor and Davies discuss the term in Greek and Egyptian cultic usage. On use of this term in the mysteries, see Walter Burkert, *Ancient Mystery Cults* (Cambridge: Harvard University Press, 1987), 39.

8. For the meaning "to heal," see, e.g., Philo, *Cher.* 15; *Sacr.* 121, 123; *Det.* 43; *Ios.* 33; *Prob.* 58; *Prov.* 2.17; *Legat.* 17. For the meaning "to attend or serve," see, e.g., *Sacr.* 58; *Ios.* 98, 251; *Mos.* 1.20, 147; *Contempl.* 70. For the meaning "to worship, see, e.g., *Sacr.* 87, 118–119; *Plant.* 38; *Ebr.* 144; *Conf.* 94; *Fug.* 42.

9. See Joan E. Taylor, *Jewish Women Philosophers: Philo's 'Therapeutae' Reconsidered* (Oxford: Oxford University Press, 2003), 57. In view of the fact of the significance of the cult of Asclepius in the Hellenistic world and the use of temples of Asclepius as places of healing, healing itself may have ritual associations in Philo's usage here in *De vita contemplativa.*

10. The use of the imperative (ἐφιέσθω, ὑπερβαινέτω) is curious here. It suggests that Philo is in relation to the community, either directly or through his spiritual and intellectual identification with them.

11. Taylor and Davies, "So-Called Therapeutae," 6–7.

of θεραπεύω with the mysteries is perhaps most evident in *Mos*. 2.149, where Philo speaks of the "rites" (τελετή) into which "servants and ministers of God ... were to be initiated" (θεραπευταῖς καὶ λειτουργοῖς θεοῦ τελετὰς ἔμελλον ἱεροφαντεῖσθαι; trans. LCL). While the reference is to the consecration of Aaron and his sons as priests, the language is that of the mysteries, as signaled by τελετὰς and ἱεροφαντεῖσθαι.[12]

In the title of the book, Philo also calls the group ἱκέται, or suppliants. The term occurs only here in *De vita contemplativa*,[13] but elsewhere Philo sometimes uses the word to refer to the Levites (cf. *Her*. 124; *Somn*. 2.273; *Ebr*. 94). Ἱκέται and θεραπεύω, or their cognates, frequently occur together in Philo's work (e.g., *Det*. 160; *Deus* 116; *Congr*. 105; *Spec*. 1.309, 312; *Virt*. 185, 221). At one place he uses ἱκέται with θεράποντες specifically of the Levites who have guardianship of the sacred things pertaining to the tabernacle (*Det*. 62–63).[14] At another point, referring to Num 3:12–13, he says that the Levites are "appointed to the service of Him who alone is worthy of service" (θεραπευτὰς τοῦ μόνου ἀξίου θεραπεύεσθαι). The Levites are God's suppliants (ἱκέτης αὐτοῦ), and their service to God symbolizes the "fountain of ... devout contemplation" (θεωρίας δὲ τῆς τοῦ μόνου σοφοῦ ... πηγὴ τὸ θεραπευτικῶς; *Sacr*. 118–120, LCL). Philo's language thus reflects not only that of the mysteries but that of the cultic language of the Septuagint and its interpretation, designating the members of the Lake Mareot community as initiates and/or priests whose contemplation is a cultic act.

The designation of the group as θεραπευταὶ/θεραπευτρίδες and ἱκέται, as well as the use of mystery terminology, suggest at the outset of *De vita contemplativa* that Philo is signaling the community's ritual nature. Philo gives us other indications, both literal and metaphorical. For example, their hours of prayer parallel those of the Levites' temple services (*Contempl*. 27).[15] Their white robes

---

12. See Exod 29:1–34; Lev 8:1–9:24. On these terms as belonging to the language of the mysteries, see Walter Burkert, *Greek Religion: Archaic and Classical* (trans. J. Raffan; London: Blackwell, 1985), 98, 242, 291–92.

13. The full title is usually given in the manuscripts as *On the Contemplative Life or the Suppliants, the Fourth Part about the Virtues* (ΠΕΡΙ ΒΙΟΥ ΘΕΩΡΗΤΙΚΟΥ Η ΙΚΕΤΩΝ, ΠΕΡΙ ΑΡΕΤΩΝ ΤΟ ΤΕΤΑΡΤΟΝ). Eusebius gives a shorter form of the title, omitting the phrase "the Fourth Part about the Virtues"; see *Hist. eccl*. 2.17.3; 2.18.7; Taylor, *Jewish Women Philosophers*, 34.

14. See Jean Riaud, "Les Thérapeutes d'Alexandrie et l'idéal Lévitique," in *The Teacher of Righteousness: Literary Studies* (part 2 of *Mogilany 1989: Papers on the Dead Sea Scrolls Offered in Memory of Jean Carmignac*; ed. Z. J. Kapera; Cracow: Enigma, 1993), 227–40.

15. 1 Chr 23:30; see Pierre Geoltrain, "Le traité de la Vie Contemplative de Philon d'Alexandrie; introduction, traduction et notes," *Sem* 10 (1960): 54; Valentin Nikiprowetzky, "Le 'De Vita Contemplativa' revisité," in *Sagesse et Religion; Colloque de Strasbourg, 1976* (Paris: Presses Universitaires de France, 1979), 113.

recall those of the High Priest (66).[16] The bread of the feast evokes the memory of the bread of the presence in the holy of holies (73, 81).[17] The biblical prohibition against the high priest drinking wine or other fermented drink before entering the tent of meeting is extended to include the whole of the members' lives—they drink only water, whether in the sanctuary of their individual dwelling or in the assembly's celebrations (37, 74).[18] Finally, the banquet at the fiftieth day is directed by an ἐφημερευτής, recalling the Levitical divisions of temple service (66).[19]

The group's hieratic nature is also suggested by an interesting parallel from fragment 10 of the Chaeremon material, where Chaeremon the Egyptian priest, whose biographer Porphyry designates as a Stoic philospher, says of Egyptian priests, that they "devoted their whole life to contemplation and vision of the divine" (ἀπέδοσαν ὅλον τὸν βίον τῇ τῶν θείων θεωρίᾳ καὶ θεάσει).[20] In this text Chaeremon describes priests—ritual specialists—focused on contemplation and "vision of the divine."

Philo describes the experience of Therapeutae and Therapeutrides:

> But let the Therapeutic household, always taught beforehand to see (βλέπειν), aim at the vision of the Existent (τῆς τοῦ ὄντος θέας ἐφιέσθω) and ascend beyond the sense-perceptible sun (αἰσθητὸν ἥλιον), and never leave this position which leads to perfect happiness. Those, then, who desire this service (θεραπείαν), neither through custom nor the advice nor exhortation of anyone else, but because they have been seized by a heavenly desire, are possessed like Bacchants and Corybants, until they see the object of their longing. (*Contempl.* 11–12)

Philo combines here the language of ascent with that of vision and the mysteries that has come to him through Plato, who uses references to the Bacchants and Corybants—participants in the mysteries of Dionysius and Cybele—to describe

---

16. *Somn.* 1.216–218; see Lev 16:4. The biblical text says only that the robe is linen; it does not specify that it is white. Philo's description in *De somniis,* however, does say that it is white. See Jean Riaud, "Quelques Réflexions sur les Thérapeutes d'Alexandrie à la lumière de *De Vita Mosis* II.67," in *Heirs of the Septuagint: Philo, Hellenistic Judaism, and Early Christianity: Festschrift for Earle Hilgert* (ed. D. T. Runia, D. M. Hay, and D. Winston; Studia Philonica Annual 3. Atlanta: Scholars Press, 1991), 189.

17. Num 4:7; see Riaud, "Thérapeutes d'Alexandrie," 236–37.

18. On the prohibition against wine, see Riaud, "Quelques réflexions," 189.

19. 1 Chr 23:6 (LXX); 2 Esd 22:8–9; Luke 1:8; see Riaud, "Quelques réflexions," 188–89.

20. Pieter Willem van der Horst, *Chaeremon, Egyptian Priest and Stoic Philosopher: The Fragments Collected and Translated with Explanatory Notes* (EPRO 101; Leiden: Brill, 1984), 17. All references to the Chaeremon material will be according to page numbers in this collection. I have used van der Horst's translations. On the similarities between Philo and Chaeremon, see David M. Hay, "Foils for the Therapeutae: References to Other Texts and Persons in Philo's '*De Vita Contemplativa,*'" in *Neotestamentica et Philonica: Studies in Honor of Peder Borgen* (ed. D. E. Aune, T. Seland, and J. Henning Ulrichsen; Leiden: Brill, 2003), 340–41.

the mantic inspiration of the poets and oracle singers.[21] It is language found often in Philo's work to describe the goal of the philosophical life in general, as well as his own experience.[22]

2. Ascent

In *De vita contemplativa* Philo describes contemplative vision in terms of ascent. The Therapeutae and Therapeutrides, he says, "aim at the vision of the Existent, and ascend beyond the sense-perceptible sun" (*Contempl.* 11). Earlier comments signaled Philo's use of the image of ascent; its backdrop is his ideal of the "gradual removal of the psyche from the sensible realm and its ascent to a life of perfection in God."[23] Philo inherits that ideal from Plato, whose *Theaetetus* he quotes in *Fug.* 62–63.[24] Ascent takes the soul beyond the limits of sense perception (αἴσθησις) to the vision of the Existent.

Vision and ascent are combined with the imagery of the mysteries in *De vita contemplativa* in much the same way as they are in the surrounding culture.[25] The Therapeutae undertake their service (θεραπεία) "because they have been seized by a heavenly desire, [and] are possessed like Bacchants and Corybants, until they see the object of their longing" (*Contempl.* 12). Again, use of mystery terminology to describe mystical experience is a commonplace in Philo.[26] He uses terminology of possession and, through references to the Bacchants and Corybants, offers allusions to the mysteries of Bacchus and Cybele to describe contact

---

21. On the ascent in Plato, see *Theaet.* 176A; *Resp.* 7.514–521; *Sym.* 200e-212b; *Phaedr.* 246–257b. On the language of the mysteries as references to poetic and oracular inspiration, see *Ion* 533d–534e; on mantic inspiration or oracles as a model of the philosophical quest, see *Phaedr.* 243e–257b; cf. Taylor, *Jewish Women Philosophers*, 315.

22. See *Opif.* 69–71; *Cher.* 27–29, 48–52; *Ebr.* 146–147; *Migr.* 34–35; *Spec.* 3.1–6.

23. Winston, "Philo and the Contemplative Life," 213. For other examples of Philo's use of the metaphor of ascent, see *Leg.* 1.38; *QG* 4.20; *QE* 2.40; *Det.* 27–28; *Praem.* 30; *Deus* 151; *Plant.* 23–25.

24. Other examples from Plato are included above in note 21.

25. Burkert, *Ancient Mystery Cults*, 92. Burkert discusses here the text of *Phaedr.* 243e–257b as reflecting this language.

26. The classical treatment of the relation of Philo to Hellenistic mystery religion is Erwin R. Goodenough's *By Light, Light: The Mystic Gospel of Hellenistic Judaism* (New Haven: Yale University Press, 1935). See Luke Timothy Johnson, *Religious Experience in Earliest Christianity: A Missing Dimension in New Testament Studies* (Minneapolis: Fortress, 1998), 90–94; Arthur Darby Nock, "The Question of Jewish Mysteries," in *Essays on Religion and the Ancient World* (ed. Z. Stewart; Cambridge: Harvard University Press, 1972), 1:459–68. The metaphor of initiation was used by Greek and Roman philosophers. It occurs with the metaphors of vision and ascent in *Spec.* 3.1–6; see also *Migr.* 34–35; see Nock, "Jewish Mysteries," 467; David Winston, *Philo of Alexandria: The Contemplative Life, The Giants, and Selections* (CWSS; New York: Paulist, 1981), 332 n. 37.

with the divine. Use of language taken from ritual practice of the mysteries, as a metaphor for community members' experience of the divine, implies a ritual quality to that experience.

That language of ascent occurs together with that of the rites of Bacchus and Cybele seems paradoxical. On the one hand, there is the ascent of the one who has come to a state of ἀπάθεια, of equilibrium, the soaring beyond the limits of sense-perception, of the universe itself. On the other hand, there is language that evokes the frenzy of those mysteries, a language that suggests the sense-perceptible with its allusions to music and dance inducing altered states of consciousness.

3. Vision

In *Contempl.* 11 Philo uses two words that signify sight, vision. Members are taught to see (βλέπειν). They "fix their minds on the vision (θέας) of the Existent." Θέα is a cognate of θεωρέω, which signifies looking, observing, considering, beholding (*Contempl.* 1, 29, 58, 64, 67, 68, 78, 90). Philo frequently uses βλέπω metaphorically in a manner that suggests that in *Contempl.* 11 it is a synonym for θεωρέω.[27]

Even in the limited context of the *De Vita Contemplativa*, θεωρέω and its cognates have a range of objects. It refers to the vision of God, the Existent (*Contempl.* 11);[28] to the allegorical reading of texts (29, 78); to nature (90);[29] and, finally, to the teachings of wisdom under the power of divine illumination (68).

27. *Contempl.* 11, 13; for other examples of Philo's metaphorical use of βλέπω, see *Opif.* 53; *Leg.* 3.110; *Post.* 21; *Gig.* 31; *Agr.* 54; *Plant.* 38; *Ebr.* 157; *Congr.* 81; *Mut.* 40. In *Opif.* 53 Philo explains how physical vision can be used as a metaphor for the vision of intelligibles (νοητά). In *Post.* 21, the object of metaphorical vision is God the Existent One. In *Gig.* 31 it is the divine things or the heavens; in *Congr.* 81 the subject is reason (λογισμός) and the object is good and evil.

28. Philo speaks sometimes of the direct and unmediated vision of God; e.g., *Leg.* 3.172–173 (using ὁράω and βλέπω); *Praem.* 36–46. However, his understanding of God is also apophatic. Even in *Praem.* 40 he says that one cannot apprehend *what* God is but only *that* God is. See also *Mut.* 10. Ultimately God's essence "is in itself … beyond any possibility of human experience or cognition" (Winston, "Philo and the Contemplative Life," 208); one can know only the Logos or the potencies of God; e.g., *Mut.* 14–15. See Winston, *Philo*, 24–30; Gerhard Delling, "The 'One Who Sees God' in Philo," in *Nourished with Peace: Studies in Hellenistic Judaism in Memory of Samuel Sandmel* (ed. F. E. Greenspahn, E. Hilgert, and B. L. Mack; Chico, Calif.: Scholars Press, 1984), 28–42; C. T. Robert Hayward, "Philo, the Septuagint of Genesis 32:24–32 and the Name 'Israel': Fighting the Passions, Inspiration and the Vision of God," *JJS* 51 (2000): 209–26; Ellen Birnbaum, *The Place of Judaism in Philo's Thought: Israel, Jews and Proselytes* (BJS 290; Atlanta: Scholars Press, 1996), 61–127.

29. On nature as the object of contemplation, see *Her.* 246, 279; *Spec.* 2.45. In the context of Greek philosophy, contemplation of nature and of the world lead to knowledge of God; see Geoltrain, "Le traité," 57.

This last instance joins θεωρέω to yet another semantic field, the erotic and generative, specifically in relation to Sophia.[30] In *Contempl.* 68 Philo tells us that the women in the community are celibate out of their eagerness to have Sophia as a partner (συμβιοῦν). The result is impregnation by the Father and illumination with the vision of Sophia's teachings.[31]

A reading of *Fug.* 51–52 suggests that "Father" here refers to Sophia.[32] In that passage the "children" of the relation between sage and Sophia are virtues: learning (μάθησις), instruction (παιδεία), knowledge (ἐπιστήμη), prudence (φρόνησις), and good and commendable actions (καλὰς καί ἐπαινετὰς πράξεις). Usage in *Fug.* 51–52 suggests that in *Contempl.* 68 Philo is referring to the virgin Therapeutrides as sages who are "impregnated" by Sophia-Father and who will bear the "children" of the virtues suitable to sages. The contemplative life, in Philo's description, is—another paradox—a life of fruitful celibacy, in which aged virgins are visionaries whose metaphorical children are virtues.[33]

The convergence of ideas appears rather strange. A personified virtue, Sophia, usually cast as a female (bride, mother, nurse), appears here as Father "impregnating" a mostly aged group of virgins.[34] The erotic male imagery (bridegroom, husband, lover) associated with God does not appear.

Philo's gendering of both Sophia and sage explains the semantic puzzle. In the framework of Philo's thought, Sophia is male when active and female when passive. This follows a broader schema in the Greek and Hellenistic context in which the female is associated with the physical world, sense-perception, and passivity, while the male is associated with the rational, Sophia, Logos, the active.[35]

---

30. For other examples of such language in relation to Sophia, see *Det.* 115–116; *QG* 4.143–146. Use of sexual imagery for the intellectual life occurs in Plato (*Resp.* 6.490B); see David Winston, "The Sage as Mystic in the Wisdom of Solomon," in *The Sage in Israel and the Ancient Near East* (ed. J. G. Gammie and L. G. Perdue; Winona Lake, Ind.: Eisenbrauns, 1990), 390–91.

31. For other passages where Philo describes Sophia as impregnating the sage, see *Congr.* 9; *Fug.* 51–52.

32. See Sharon Lea Mattila, "Wisdom, Sense Perception, Nature and Philo's Gender Gradient," *HTR* 89 (1996): 108–12.

33. Cf. Kenneth L. Waters Sr., "Saved through Childbearing: Virtues as Children in 1 Timothy 2:11–15," *JBL* 123 (2004): 716–19.

34. This description of learned women at Lake Mareot would not have been unusual in the context of Hellenistic Egypt, where upper-class women were often highly educated; see Sarah B. Pomeroy, *Women in Hellenistic Egypt: From Alexander to Cleopatra* (New York: Schocken, 1984), 59–72.

35. See Mattila, "Wisdom, Sense Perception," 119. There is a growing body of literature on gender in relation to Philo's work. Some examples include Richard A. Baer Jr, *Philo's Use of the Categories of Male and Female* (ALGHJ 3; Leiden: Brill, 1970); Dorothy Sly, *Philo's Perception of Women* (BJS 209; Atlanta: Scholars Press, 1990); Colleen Conway, "Gender and Divine Relativity in Philo of Alexandria," *JSJ* 34 (2003): 471–91; on the Lake Mareot community, see Ross S. Kraemer, "Monastic Jewish Women in Greco-Roman Egypt: Philo Judaeus on the Therapeu-

In the context of the theory of vision presumed by Plato and inherited by Philo, visual language of contemplation, θεωρέω and its cognates, is about contact.[36] Sight is Philo's metaphor for apprehension and contemplation, sight understood not as external vision but as "internal visualization."[37] Certainly the sense of intimate contact is supported by *Contempl.* 68.

4. Space

In *De vita contemplativa*, space, both individual and collective, is "delineated and structured," in Bell's words cited earlier. Furthermore, Philo specifically uses ritual terms to describe space. Describing the community members' individual dwellings, he says: "In each one [house] there is a sacred chamber, which is called a sanctuary and a cell" (ἐν ἑκάστῃ δὲ ἐστιν οἴκημα ἱερόν ὃ καλεῖται σεμνεῖον καὶ μοναστήριον, *Contempl.* 25).[38] One should note especially the phrase οἴκημα ἱερόν ὃ καλεῖται σεμνεῖον, a "sacred chamber"; while this is the only occurrence of the adjective ἱερόν in *De Vita Contemplativa*, the noun ἱερεύς occurs in *Contempl.* 74 and 82, where it refers to the priestly character of the entire community joined in the fiftieth-day celebration. Further, σεμνείον occurs not only in reference to the solitary dwelling (25, 88), but also in *Contempl.* 32 to designate the sanctuary where the community assembles for worship each seventh day. Thus

trides," *Signs* 14 (1989): 342–70; G. Peter Richardson and Valerie Heuchan, "Jewish Voluntary Associations in Egypt and the Roles of Women," in *Voluntary Associations in the Graeco-Roman World* (ed. J. S. Kloppenborg and S. G. Wilson; London: Routledge 1996): 226–51; Joan E. Taylor, *Jewish Women Philosophers of First-Century Alexandria: Philo's 'Therapeutae' Reconsidered* (Oxford: Oxford University Press, 2003); idem, "The Women 'Priests' of Philo's *De Vita Contemplativa*: Reconstructing the Therapeutae," in *On the Cutting Edge: The Study of Women in Biblical Worlds: Essays in Honor of Elisabeth Schüssler Fiorenza* (ed. J. Schaberg, A. Bach and E. Fuchs; New York: Continuum, 2004), 102–22; idem, with Philip R. Davies, "The So-Called Therapeutae of *De Vita Contemplativa*: Identity and Character," *HTR* 91 (1998): 3–24.

36. David Chidester, *Word and Light: Seeing, Hearing, and Religious Discourse* (Urbana: University of Illinois Press, 1992), 3–4.

37. Werner H. Kelber, "Modalities of Communication, Cognition, and Physiology of Perception: Orality, Rhetoric, Scribality," *Semeia* 65 (1994): 204.

38. Richardson has provided diagrams of what these dwellings, as well as the communal structures might have looked like, drawing analogues from the later archaeological remains of the fifth- to seventh-century Christian monastery at Kellia. See G. Peter Richardson, "Philo and Eusebius on Monasteries and Monasticism: The Therapeutae and Kellia," in *Origins and Method: Towards a New Understanding of Judaism and Christianity: Essays in Honour of John C. Hurd* (ed. B. H. McLean; JSNTSSup 86; Sheffield: JSOT Press, 1993), 349–52. Richardson believes Philo's use of σεμνεῖον and μοναστήριον is confusing; use in *Contempl.* 25, 30, and 89 suggests a "'shrine' … within a special room for contemplation and devotion, within a somewhat larger house" (350). While the evidence of Kellia would support this, it is still not clear to me why Philo could possibly not be using these words to designate the same space, the sacred chamber.

the sacred chamber in the solitary dwelling is a sanctuary, a temple,[39] linked to the collective ritual space. Community members' lives are framed by the sacred spaces of individual as well as collective ritual performance.

More on that momentarily. At this point we simply note the fact that the designation of this chamber suggests that the member's house is not simply a human shelter but a ritual space. It is a "sacred chamber, which is called a sanctuary and a cell." With the individual's day framed by hours of prayer that parallel those of the Levites' temple services (*Contempl.* 27) and a dwelling that is a sanctuary, a spatial frame, Philo tells us that the whole life of the individual member is ritualized, made a "service," a θεραπεία. That is, temporal and spatial arrangements mark off even the solitary life of the Therapeutae as ritual, as "other," as distinct from other kinds of lives.

5. Text Work as Ritual Activity and Texts as Ritual Objects

Philo describes what happens in the "sacred chamber." In a play on the earlier μοναστήριον he says that in this sanctuary community members, isolated, are "initiated into the mysteries of the consecrated life" (ἐν ᾧ μονούμενοι τὰ τοῦ σεμνοῦ βίου μυστήρια τελοῦνται, *Contempl.* 25).[40] Again we meet the language of the mysteries, this time the vocabulary of initiation.[41] Immediately afterward Philo tells us that the Therapeutae and Therapeutrides bring into the sacred chamber of their homes only sacred texts and those books that will aid in their study (25, 28–29). The reference to text work echoes the place of text in some of the mysteries.[42]

The Therapeutae and Therapeutrides pass their days, between morning and evening prayers, in study of sacred texts, using the allegorical method to uncover the hidden meaning, a study that Philo associates with θεωρία (*Contempl.* 28–29), as we have seen. In the sacred chamber, the solitaries also compose hymns and psalms, an activity recalling the Levitical nature of their life as Philo describes it.[43] The "mysteries" of the Therapeutic life thus include text work as central to the way of life represented by that ritual term.

39. On the consecrated room as temple, see Geoltrain, "Le traité," 53. In this instance Geoltrain is thinking of "temple" as a place for the enacting of mysteries. I believe, however, that the designation οἴκημα ἱερόν suggests the nature of the individual dwelling as a temple.

40. In *Migr.* 190–191 Philo speaks of withdrawal and solitude as preparatory for visionary experience.

41. See Burkert, *Ancient Mystery Cults*, 18–22, 31–33.

42. Ibid., 69–71; see Plutarch, *Is. Os.* 352A-C; Apuleius, *Metam.* 11.22.

43. On the Levites as temple musicians and singers, see 1 Chr 15 and 25; Stefan C. Reif, *Judaism and Hebrew Prayer: New Perspectives on Jewish Liturgical History* (Cambridge: Cambridge University Press, 1993), 40.

Philo moves progressively inward in his description of the Therapeutae and Therapeutrides. He begins with the "inhabited world," the οἰκουμένη (*Contempl.* 21), turns to the Greeks and then to Egypt, growing ever more specific as he names the area around Alexandria and then Lake Mareot (21–22).[44] Finally he turns his attention to the individual houses, with their inner sanctuaries. The move inward focuses the reader's attention on that which is found in the chamber: the holy scriptures (ἱεροῖς γράμμασι, 28) as well as "anything else which will increase and perfect knowledge and piety" (25–26), including the writings of the community's founders who left memory aids (μνημεῖα) for training in allegorical interpretation (29).[45]

The μοναστήριον contains the texts that play so large a role in the mystical quest of the community at Lake Mareot, the object of which is the vision of God (*Contempl.* 11). Study is ritual, a performance set apart by a "delineated and structured space" and by "a special periodicity," the activity of those whose name and description designates them as "priests" (74, 81–82). The books are ritual objects, placed as they are in a sacred chamber.[46]

The text is ritual object, however, not only in the context of individual activity and dwelling. It is also the focus of ritual activity in the communal celebrations of the seventh and fiftieth days (*Contempl.* 30–33, 75–78). The solitary is thus joined to the collective through the ritual activity of studying texts sacred to the community and to the entire Jewish people. The member is also linked to the whole through the liturgical calendar and the ritual nature of private and communal space. The twofold text work of allegorical interpretation and composition of hymns and songs is set in a context that can be designated as "ritual" in the literal sense, with its particular spatial and temporal frames, ritual objects, and so forth. It can also be signified as "ritual" in the metaphorical sense, with designations drawn from the language of the Septuagint and Greco-Roman mystery religions.

6. Text and Interpretation

Study, a central practice in the lives of Therapeutae and Therapeutrides, focuses on a privileged body of texts: the "holy writings" and the writings of the group's founders (*Contempl.* 28–29). The method is ἀλληγορία (28–29), which allows the person "to contemplate the invisible through the visible" (τὰ ἀφανῆ διὰ τῶν φανερῶν θεωρεῖν, 78).[47] With these words Philo joins his community members

44. Taylor and Davies, "The So-Called Therapeutae," 4–8.

45. See Taylor, *Jewish Women Philosophers*, 130.

46. On the written copy of the sacred text as cultic object, see William A. Graham, *Beyond the Written Word: Oral Aspects of Scripture in the History of Religion* (Cambridge: Cambridge University Press, 1987), 59–62.

47. David M. Hay, "Things Philo Said and Did Not Say about the Therapeutae," *Society of Biblical Literature 1992 Seminar Papers* (SBLSP 31; Atlanta: Scholars Press, 1992), 681; Valentin

to an interpretive tradition that is already well established among Alexandrine Jewish thinkers, as seen in the work of Pseudo-Aristeas and Aristobulus.[48]

In *De vita contemplativa* Philo says little by way of defining allegory. He seems to presume that his reader knows exactly what he is talking about. He uses the term to refer to the search beyond the literal meaning of the text for a spiritual or hidden or deeper meaning. The allegorist reads the "manifest symbols of unseen things and the speech of the unspoken" (σύμβολα φανερὰ ἀφανῶν καὶ ῥητὰ ἀρρήτων).[49] In this work the founders' writings serve as models for imitation (*Contempl.* 29).

Philo does not consider "allegory" as a homogeneous category implying equivalent accuracy in all its practitioners. In fact, *Migr.* 89–93 suggests that there are allegorists in Alexandria who attend to the inner meaning of the text while abandoning the letter. This has practical consequences in relation to ritual matters, such as Sabbath observance (*Migr.* 91–92). Philo the allegorist attempts consciously to hold in tension letter and hidden meaning, understanding the letter of the text to be the body of the "soul," which is the inner meaning. As we care for the one, so too we should care for the other (*Migr.* 93). Indeed, in *De vita contemplativa* he will say that community members "consider the whole law book to be like a living being with the literal ordinances as the body, and the invisible meanings stored up in its sayings as its soul" (*Contempl.* 78).

It is difficult to ascertain the relation of the members of the Lake Mareot community to the literal meaning of the text and thus to Torah observance. For example, it is not clear just *how* Sabbath laws regarding labor were observed.[50] But the fact that Philo attributes to the Therapeutae and Therapeutrides a consideration of literal text and allegorical meaning to comprise one "being"—the very position he enjoins upon the extreme allegorists in *Migr.* 93—suggests that they are not among those disregarding or abandoning the literal text.[51]

Nikiprowetzky, *Le commentaire de l'Ecriture chez Philon d'Alexandrie: Son caractere et sa portee, observations philologiques* (ALGHJ 11; Leiden: Brill, 1977), 6; David Winston, *Philo*, 4–7. Geoltrain ("La contemplation à Qoumran et chez les Thérapéutes," *Sem* 9 [1959]: 54) doubts that the allegorical method used by the Therapeutae and Therapeutrides was similar to that of Philo but gives no reason for his question.

48. David Dawson, *Allegorical Readers and Cultural Revision in Ancient Alexandria* (Berkeley and Los Angeles: University of California Press, 1992), 74–82. Dawson discusses Gentile allegorical reading in a previous chapter (23–72). In the introduction to the volume, Dawson raises the pertinent literary and rhetorical issues.

49. *Spec.* 3.178; see also *Abr.* 217; *QG* 4.196. Cited by David M. Hay, "Philo's References to Other Allegorists," *SPhilo* 6 (1979–80): 44, 64 n. 11.

50. Taylor, *Jewish Women Philosophers*, 139–40.

51. Contra ibid., 145. Taylor relates the Mareotic understanding of text to their ascetical disregard of the body. One might, however, argue that ascetical practice regards the body with utmost seriousness.

Ἀλληγορία. Θεωρία, "allegorical method," is a way into the text. Certainly it is a way to read. It is also a way to *see*, to "*contemplate* the invisible through the visible." It is a vehicle for those activities at the very heart of the way of life of the community at Lake Mareot leading the contemplative life (βίος θεωρέτικος). The Chaeremon material, especially fragment 10, indicates the fact that one of tasks of some Egyptian priests—who were designated by θεραπεύω and its cognates—was the allegorical interpretation of myth and ritual.[52] This might suggest that, in the context of Egyptian ritual traditions, Philo interprets the allegorical work of the Therapeutae and Therapeutrides as ritual, priestly service. Through text work, especially allegorical interpretation, vision and ritual are inextricably linked in *De vita contemplativa*.

7. Text Work and Vision

Earlier Philo tells us that the desire of the Therapeutae and Therapeutrides is focused on the vision of the Existent (*Contempl.* 11). He describes their experience in the language of vision, ascent, and ecstasy, using categories from the mysteries. Bringing this passage into conversation with other passages from Philo's work suggests that contemplation of the text via allegory is related to that vision.

Philo believes the holy writings to be divinely inspired, and so the interpreter too must be inspired to read the text accurately.[53] In two autobiographical passages he describes textual interpretation as occurring in relation to mystical experience. The texts deserve to be quoted in full:

> I have no shame in describing my experience (τὸ ἐμαυτοῦ πάθος), which I have known from its happening ten thousand times. Having decided to follow customary procedure in writing on philosophical doctrines (φιλοσοφίαν δογμάτων), and knowing precisely what to compose, having found my understanding barren and sterile, I have put aside my ineffectual project, while reproaching my mind for its self-conceit while amazed at the might of the One Who Is, on whom depends the opening and closing of the wombs of the soul. There are times when I have come empty [i.e., to the task] and suddenly become full of thoughts falling like snow and invisibly sown from above, as though under the inspiration of Corybantic frenzy (ὡς ὑπὸ κατχῆς ἐνθέου κορυβαντιᾶν). I have become unaware of everything, place, people present, myself, things spoken, things written. I acquired possession of interpretation, enjoyment of light, the keenest vision, clear distinction of objects, such as might happen through the eyes as the result of the clearest manifestation. (*Migr.* 34–35)

52. Van der Horst, *Chaeremon*, 19. See references in other fragments: 5, 7, 11.

53. See David Hay, "Philo's View of Himself as an Exegete: Inspired, But Not Authoritative," *SPhilo* 3 (1991): 40–52.

Philo speaks of attending to "philosophical doctrines." While φιλοσοφία might indeed suggest the discourse that is the end of the school curriculum and that Philo describes as "the practice or study of wisdom" (*Congr.* 79), it can also refer to Jewish teaching, especially the study of the first five books of the Bible, which are the particular focus for Philo's attention throughout so much of his corpus.[54]

Here in *De migratione Abrahami* he tells us that he has often been helpless before the task of interpreting the sacred texts. He uses the language of human generativity, gendering himself as female, and describing his mind as barren and sterile. He then shifts metaphors, to use the ritual/ecstatic language of the mysteries. God seizes him, takes possession of him, leaves him frenzied, beyond normal consciousness and at the same time able to work the text with supranormal capacities.[55] In the framework of mystery language, Philo's interpretive work is not only a ritual act; it is identified with inspiration, contemplation, ecstasy.

There is another passage that is helpful to our reading of *De vita contemplativa*:

> There was a time [period, period of time] when I had the leisure for philosophy (φιλοσοφία) and contemplation of the universe (θεωρίᾳ τοῦ κόσμου) and everything in it.... I did not have lowly or base thoughts nor did I grovel about in search of reputation or wealth or bodily comfort, but I seemed (ἐδόκουν) to be carried up high in the air by some God-given inspiration of the soul (κατά τινα τῆς ψυχῆς ἐπιθειασμὸν) and to travel together with sun and moon and the heaven and indeed the whole universe.... But ... Envy, the hater of the good, suddenly fell upon me and plunged me into the sea of civic cares.... All the same, I endure, suffering, I have the yearning for Instruction (παιδεία), established in my soul from the earliest time of my life, which always has mercy and pity on me, taking me and raising and lifting me up.... And if unexpectedly there happens to me a brief spell of good weather and calm from civil turmoil, soaring [with wings] I ride on the waves not only borne by the air but breathed on by the breezes of Knowledge (ἐπιστήμη) who often persuades me to run away to spend my days with her.... Yet it is fitting for me to bring thanksgiving to God ... that I ... can also open the soul's eyes ... and am illumined by the light of Sophia, not being consigned to life in the darkness. So consequently, here I am not only

54. Cf. *Mos.* 2.215–216; *Spec.* 2.61–62. Philo's understanding bears its own logic. He assumes the Pentateuch to treat matters of nature, ethics, and the nature of the divine, the content of the curriculum. On Philo's understanding of Judaism as philosophy, see Steve Mason, "PHILOSOPHIAI: Graeco-Roman, Judean and Christian," in Kloppenborg and Wilson, *Voluntary Associations in the Graeco-Roman World,* 43–44. Mason sets Philo's considerations in the broader intellectual context of Greco-Roman thought.

55. Philo's description recalls Plato's descriptions of poetic inspiration, e.g., *Phaedr.* 245A; *Ion* 533D–36D; cited in John R. Levison, "Inspiration and the Divine Spirit in the Writings of Philo Judaeus," *JSJ* 26 (1995): 286.

> daring to read in the sacred messages of Moses, but loving knowledge, stooping to peep into each one and to unfold and make manifest those [meanings] which are not familiar to the multitude. (*Spec.* 3.1–6)

In *De specialibus legibus* Philo describes his experience of the ascent of the soul as allowing him to interpret the "sacred messages of Moses." The ascent is directly related to his practice of allegorical reading, empowering Philo to "make manifest those [meanings] which are not familiar to the multitude." Here Philo draws a direct correspondence between mystical experience, that of the ascent, and allegorical interpretation.[56] He does so in language that, once again, evokes the mysteries, with the illumination, sight, passage from darkness to light that are part of mystery language and praxis.[57]

The allegorical process, with its continuing interpretive play, might be understood to reflect Philo's belief that "God is essentially unknowable and language is not representationally reliable."[58] Similarly, one might say that the text that must be continually reinterpreted suggests a "saturated" quality mirroring the experience of the unspeakable Existent, a quality that demands continuous interpretation and reinterpretation, reading and rereading.[59]

The text provides matter for speculation, meditation, and visualization.[60] Reading the text, then, transforms the reader's consciousness.[61] The sacred writings with their accompanying texts, the privileged method of ἀλληγόρια, are both path to and site for θεωρία. And study is an occasion for visionary experience and experience of the divine.[62]

Philo leads us to believe that allegorical reading is the primary textual practice that he designates as "exercise" (ἄσκησις, *Contempl.* 28). There is another

56. See Levison, "Inspiration and the Divine Spirit," 288.

57. Mysteries such as the Isis initiation were often celebrated at night; see Apuleius, *Metam.* 11.23. Light and darkness formed part of the pattern of antithesis characterizing the mysteries; see Burkert, *Ancient Mysteries*, 93. Initiation brought sight, and the initiate *saw* the *dromena*, the *deiknymena* displayed in the sanctuary (Burkert, *Greek Religion*, 288; Meyer, *The Ancient Mysteries*, 11).

58. Dawson, *Allegorical Readers*, 92.

59. Jean-Luc Marion, "Introduction: What Do We Mean by 'Mystic'?" in *Mystics: Presence and Aporia* (ed. M. Kessler and C. Sheppard; Chicago: University of Chicago Press, 2002), 2–5; see idem, *Being Given: Toward a Phenomenology of Givenness* (trans. J. L. Kosky; Stanford, Calif.: Stanford University Press, 2002), 234–45.

60. Geoltrain, "La contemplation," 54–55.

61. On the transformative nature of religious reading, see Paul J. Griffiths, *Religious Reading: The Place of Reading in the Practice of Religion* (New York: Oxford University Press, 1999), 54.

62. See Michael Fishbane, "The Garments of Torah—Or, To What May Scripture Be Compared?" in *The Garments of Torah: Essays in Biblical Hermeneutics* (Bloomington: Indiana University Press, 1989), 42; Elliot R. Wolfson, *Through a Speculum That Shines: Vision and Imagination in Medieval Jewish Mysticism* (Princeton: Princeton University Press, 1994), 326–29.

textual practice, as noted earlier; Philo tells us that Therapeutae and Therapeutrides "compose chants and hymns to God in all kinds of meters and melodies, which they write down necessarily in very solemn rhythms" (29). The solitary composition and singing of hymns find their collective parallel in the celebration of the fiftieth day, in which first the president of the congregation and then the members take turns singing hymns (80), and then the whole congregation forms two choirs for singing, accompanied by dancing (84–88).

Composition and performance of singing and other forms of music have a rich background in the Bible that is at the center of the solitary dwelling and is the object of the ritualized activity of study. There is a proliferation of "hymnic, psalmic or poetic praises and the mystical formulations" appearing in the Second Temple period.[63] In the broader context of Greek and Hellenistic culture, musical composition also formed part of the classical education that many of the community members, coming as they did from elite circles, had received (*Contempl.* 69).[64] In addition, Philo's description of musical composition and performance at Lake Mareot evokes the Greco-Roman mysteries as well as the temple worship of Egyptian religion.[65]

Philo tells us that the sanctuary or μοναστήριον contains only the sacred texts and other books that aid "knowledge and piety" (*Contempl.* 25). He then comments that, not only does the community member remember God continually in her or his waking hours, but that even in their dreams there are "no phantasms but the beauty of the divine virtues and powers" (μηδὲν ἕτερον ἢ τὰ κάλλη τῶν θείων ἀρετῶν καὶ δυνάμεων φαντασιοῦσθαι, 26).[66] Aristotle had defined a dream as "an appearance [*phantasma*] that arises from the movement of the sense-impressions, while one is in the sleeping state."[67] In Hellenistic thought phantasms (φαντάσματα) are sense-impressions,[68] but in *their* dreams Therapeu-

63. Reif, *Judaism and Hebrew Prayer*, 47.

64. Taylor and Davies, "So-Called Therapeutae," 17–18. On the place of music in the curriculum, see Stanley F. Bonner, *Education in Ancient Rome: From the Elder Cato to the Younger Pliny* (Berkeley and Los Angeles: University of California Press, 1977), 77; Elizabeth Rawson, *Intellectual Life in the Late Roman Republic* (Baltimore: Johns Hopkins University Press, 1985), 167–69. On Philo's own education in music as part of the traditional curriculum, see *Congr.* 74–76. He also comments on music as part of the curriculum in *Congr.* 16.

65. Apuleius, *Metam.* 11.7–14; Plutarch, *Is. Os.* 372B.

66. On the Gentile and Jewish contexts for dreams as site for divine communication, see Geoltrain, "La traité," 53; idem, "La contemplation," 52. Elsewhere in Philo, see *Migr.* 190–191; *Somn.* 1.1–2; 2.1–4; *Spec.* 1.219.

67. *Insomn.* 462a29–31, quoted by Patricia Cox Miller, *Dreams in Late Antiquity: Studies in the Imagination of a Culture* (Princeton: Princeton University Press,1994), 43; citing David Gallop, *Aristotle on Sleep and Dreams: A Text and Translation with Introduction, Notes and Glossary* (Peterborough, Ont.: Broadview, 1990), 101.

68. Anthony A. Long, *Hellenistic Philosophy: Stoics, Epicureans, Sceptics* (2nd ed.; Berkeley and Los Angeles: University of California Press, 1986), 22, 123–31.

tae and Therapeutrides contemplate the Virtues and the Powers rather than sense images.[69]

Philo's juxtaposition of the description of the sanctuary's contents with his observation about members' dreams suggests that study transforms their vision across the whole spectrum of consciousness, sleeping and waking. That juxtaposition may also signal the textual nature of dreams, a possibility indicated by the fact that elsewhere Philo's interpretation of the text suggests that dreams are a metaphorical text that must be interpreted.[70]

Of course, Philo's understanding of dreams as a site for revelatory experience has precedent in the biblical texts that are the focus for much of his commentary: the patriarchal narratives about Abraham, Jacob, and Joseph. But the fact that dream activity is also part of Greco-Roman mysteries, as well as Egyptian temple worship, suggests the ritual as well as textual nature of the dreams of the Therapeutae and Therapeutrides.[71]

8. Text Work and Ascetical Practice

In *De vita contemplativa* Philo gives no description of the practical details of life in the solitary dwellings: source of livelihood, daily tasks, and so forth. But he does place text work and contemplative experience in a broader context of practices: divestment of material property (*Contempl.* 13–17), modified diet (34–37), simplicity of dress and shelter (38), solitude and silence (18–20, 24, 30, 89), celibacy (18, 68). There is also formal ritual: morning and evening prayer in solitude and communal worship on the seventh and fiftieth days.

Certainly the withdrawal and silence, the simplicity of life, dietary restrictions, and sexual restraint reflect the philosophical ideal, an ideal proffered not only in *De vita contemplativa* but elsewhere in Philo's work.[72] That ideal reaches back into the traditions around the figure of Socrates[73] and is exemplified in

---

69. The Virtues are most likely the virtues that Philo often allegorizes as women, e.g., Sarah as generic Virtue (ἀρετή) or Wisdom (σοφία) and Rebecca as Patience (ὑπομονή) and related to Reason (λόγος) or Knowledge (ἐπιστήμη). On Sarah as Virtue, see *Leg.* 2.82; 3.218, 244; *Cher.* 3–10; as Wisdom, see *Leg.* 2.82; *Cher.* 9–10, 45, 49–59; on Rebecca as Patience, see *Leg.* 3.88–89; *Sacr.* 4; *Congr.* 36, 111–113; on Rebecca as associated with Reason, see *Post.* 77–78; and Knowledge, see *Fug.* 195. Powers may represent those two entities Goodness (ἀγαθοτήτα) and Sovereignty (ἐξουσία), which are in his thought "supreme and immediate manifestations of God." See John Dillon, *The Middle Platonists, 80 B.C. to A.D. 220* (rev. ed.; Ithaca, N.Y.: Cornell University Press, 1996), 161; *Cher.* 27–31.

70. E.g., *Migr.* 190–191. See Philo's interpretation of Jacob's dream in *Somn.* 1.159–165.

71. E.g., Apuleius, *Metam.* 11.22, 27, 30; see Burkert, *Ancient Mystery Cults*, 10.

72. Cf. *Contempl.* 14–17; see Geoltrain, "La traité," 18–19. Elsewhere in Philo, e.g., see *Leg.* 3.142–159, 238–242; *Gig.* 15; *Plant.* 65–66; *Mos.* 1.152–159.

73. E.g., *Phaedo* 63e8ff., 64D, 66C, 67A; *Resp.* 4.430E–431A; see John M. Dillon, "Rejecting the Body, Refining the Body: Some Remarks on the Development of Platonist Asceticism,"

such divergent circles as those represented in traditions concerning Cynics[74] and Pythagoreans.[75]

Those practices also find interesting parallels in the Egyptian temple religion reflected in the Chaeremon fragments, particularly fragment 10.[76] Such practices provide a channeling of attention, or focus. Yet more, ongoing withdrawal is a permanent liminality, and the sensory deprivation of solitude and silence are vehicles of altering the practitioner's state of consciousness. Similarly, singing and chanting are exercises that could induce such alteration. Finally, study itself, with oral recitation as the method of reading, serves as an exercise conducive to altered states of consciousness and a propadeutic for contemplative or mystical experience.[77] What is more, textual study "provides the occasion for visionary experience," with the sacred text furnishing the Therapeutae and Therapeutrides with the metaphors for both expectation and visualization.[78] In other words, reading the sacred text informs readers what they may expect of their experience and yields the images with which to articulate those experiences.

All these practices—withdrawal, simplified lifestyle, silence, and solitude, reading—reflect the bodiliness that, paradoxically, is the correlative of θεωρία. Refashioning the individual and collective body through physical praxis and constructing a new intellectual and spiritual vision through text work create the possibility for contemplation, ascent, ecstasy—and these experiences become "texts" to be "read" as well as lenses through which the reader interprets sacred writings in yet new ways.

These practices are framed by the spatial boundaries of solitary and communal sanctuaries, as well as the communal dining hall (συμπόσιον, *Contempl.* 83).[79] They are also framed by the temporal boundaries of the community's ritual cal-

---

in *Asceticism* (ed. V. L. Wimbush and R. Valantasis; New York: Oxford University Press, 1995), 80–87.

74. E.g., Diogenes Laertius 6.13, 103–105; Epictetus, 3.22.1–109; *The Cynic Epistles* (ed. A. J. Malherbe; SBLSBS 12; Missoula, Mont.: Scholars Press, 1977).

75. E.g., Diogenes Laertius, 8:1–50; Iamblichus, *The Life of Pythagoras*, 16–17 in *The Pythagorean Sourcebook and Library* (ed. K. S. Guthrie; Grand Rapids: Phanes, 1987–88), 73–76.

76. Other sources can be found in Pieter W. van Der Horst, "The Way of Life of the Egyptian Priests according to Chaeremon," in *Studies in Egyptian Religion Dedicated to Professor Jan Zandee* (ed. M. H. van Voss et al.; Leiden: Brill, 1982), 61–71.

77. On the use of verbal exercises, mantras, and the use of music to induce altered states, see Stanley J. Tambiah, "A Performative Approach to Ritual," *Proceedings of the British Academy* 65 (1979): 141–42.

78. Wolfson, *Through a Speculum That Shines*, 326. See the work of Steven Katz, beginning with "The 'Conservative' Character of Mystical Experience," in *Mysticism and Religious Traditions* (ed. S. Katz; New York: Oxford University Press, 1983), 3–60.

79. See Taylor, *Jewish Women Philosophers*, 283–87. Richardson proposes a diagram in "Philo and Eusebius," 352.

endar: the six days, each of which begins and ends with prayer (27, 30); and the collective celebrations of the seventh day (30–37) and the fiftieth day (64–89).

9. Text Work and Communal Ritual

At the center of the solitary life of the six days is study of sacred texts. Study is also the center of the collective life on the seventh day, when the community gathers in the common sanctuary (κοινὸν τοῦτο σεμνεῖον, *Contempl.* 32). Seated separately, men and women hear the senior member "best versed in their doctrines" (τῶν δογμάτων ἐμπειρότατος) give a discourse (31). In this further "delineated and structured space" of the "common sanctuary" this person serves as "distinct and specialized personnel," and his or her discourse is ritualized. Assembled members respond with the most minimal of gestures, merely glances or nods. Those responses might be understood as suggesting the "restricted codes of communication to heighten the formality of movement and speech" characteristic of ritual, particularly since there are parallels in Egyptian practice (*Chaeremon*, 19, 21).

Philo does not say explicitly that the speaker's expertise in the community's "doctrines" (δογμάτων) refers to sacred texts. In other instances of δόγμα in *De vita contemplativa* (26, 31) the meaning is similarly not apparent. However, in *Contempl.* 35 and 68 it is associated with σοφία, which suggests that indeed the reference is to the interpretation of sacred texts, for the exposition of the biblical text is the privileged site for the pursuit of philosophy, as we saw earlier.[80] Here, in *Contempl.* 30, the seventh-day gathering is introduced by the remark that members seek wisdom (φιλοσοφοῦσι) by themselves for six days but come together on the seventh, implying group engagement in φιλοσοφία, that is, study of the sacred text (see also *Spec.* 2.61). Finally, the use of διαλέγομαι (31) with its connotations of discussion, even argument, suggests the question and answer method proper to exegetical and expository activity found elsewhere in Philo as well as in other Jewish and Hellenistic sources.[81]

The seventh day is marked not only by common study, described according to Greco-Roman rhetorical conventions, but by the rest of members and animals alike (*Contempl.* 36) and by a common meal (37).[82] Reference to the meal leads

80. *Mos.* 2.215–216; Nikiprowetzky, *Le commentaire*, 100–108; Geoltrain, "Le traité," 54; Taylor, *Jewish Women Philosophers*, 112–25.

81. Peder Borgen, *Philo of Alexandria: An Exegete for His Time* (NovTSupp 86; Leiden: Brill, 1997), 100–101. See also *Contempl.* 1, 33, 79. Other examples for use of διαλέγομαι in reference to exegesis of biblical texts include *Spec.* 1.194, 234; 2.1. Nikiprowetzky (*Le commentaire*, 179–80) believes that the synagogue was the background behind Philo's use of this method. With Borgen, I believe this to be too narrow a framework.

82. For various interpretations of the number 7, see *Leg.* 1.16–18; *Deus* 12; *Her.* 216; *Spec.* 2.59; see David Winston, "Philo and the Contemplative Life," in *From the Bible through the Middle Ages* (vol. 1 of *Jewish Spirituality*, ed. A. Green; New York: Crossroad, 1986), 206.

Philo into a lengthy excursus on Gentile banquets, including those in which such philosophers as Socrates, Xenophon, and Plato participated (40–64). The latter suffer by comparison, and the encomium segues into the lengthy description of the celebration of the fiftieth day (64–89).

It would appear that the Therapeutae and Therapeutrides celebrated cycles of seven Sabbaths, each ending with a fiftieth-day celebration.[83] Philo describes the fiftieth-day celebration in greater detail than he does that of the seventh day. At the fiftieth-day celebration, the president offers an exegesis of the sacred texts, laying before those assembled the "deeper sense conveyed in allegory" (αἱ δὲ ἐξηγήσεις τῶν ἱερῶν γραμμάτων γίνονται δι' ὑπονοιῶν ἐν ἀλληγορίαις, *Contempl.* 78). Those assembled respond in ritualized gestures, expressing approval or agreement by nods and facial expressions and difficulty with the exposition by moving the head more slowly and raising a fingertip of the right hand (77).

The president then sings a hymn, and others follow (*Contempl.* 80). All share an austere festival meal (69, 73–74, 81–82). We have already noted the priestly quality of the meal, with its allusions to the temple sacrifice as well as to the show-bread (73–74, 81–82). The contrast with Gentile philosophical banquets is explicit (64, 89), but the stylized ritual meal also evokes Philo's use elsewhere of the imagery of food and drink in reference to Wisdom and Logos (e.g., *Fug.* 137–139; *Somn.* 2.241–49), to study and learning (e.g., *Fug.* 183, 187; *QG* 4.191; *Dec.* 40–41), and to the encounter with the divine (e.g., *QG* 4.8; *QE* 2.39). Once again text work, mystical experience, and ritual converge.

The meal is followed by an all-night vigil (παννυχίδα, *Contempl.* 83). Participants form two choirs, one of women and one of men. They sing and dance, evoking the memory of the crossing of the Red Sea under the leadership of Moses and Miriam (85–87). Their performance enacts the narrative of Exod 15 with its account of Moses and Miriam singing and Miriam leading the women in dancing. In their ritual performance, members of the Lake Mareot community embody a text studied both in the μοναστήριον and in the assembly, individually and collectively, and interpreted in both places through ἀλληγορία. In ritual time and space, they *are* the people at the Red Sea; in their performance of the text they become a kind of embodied allegory.

The description of the fiftieth-day celebration suggests the celebration of the Feast of Weeks. There is an allusion to Lev 23:16, where the festival begins "the day after the seventh Sabbath, fifty days" (ἕως τῆς ἐπαύριον τῆς ἐσχάτης ἑβδομάδος ἀριθμήσετε πεντήκοντα ἡμέρας). The loaves of leavened bread not only stand in distinction to the unleavened show breads of the temple but also

83. See Nikiprowetzky, "Le 'De Vita Contemplativa' revisité," 123. Geoltrain ("Le traité," 25) notes a similar cycle at Qumran. There is evidence for a cycle of three festivals of weeks at Qumran; see James R. Davila, *Liturgical Works* (Eerdmans Commentaries on the Dead Sea Scrolls; Grand Rapids: Eerdmans, 2000), 10.

recall the offerings of the firstfruits of the wheat harvest at the Feast of Weeks.[84] However, there is no reference to Sinai in Philo's description. He draws attention, rather, to the parallels between the singing and dancing at the festival meal and that which was performed at the Red Sea under the leadership of Moses and Miriam (85–87). It is thus more likely that the fiftieth-day festival celebrates the firstfruits in cycles of seven weeks, evoking the Feast of Weeks, a pattern that the Lake Mareot community, like the Qumran community, extended beyond the demarcation of the agricultural cycle of three harvests.[85]

The dancing and singing that characterize the fiftieth-day celebration evoke Exod 15. They also function as a parallel to mystery rituals, as well as those of Egyptian temple cult, with their music and processions.[86] Philo uses language drawn from the mysteries as he describes the dancers "full of inspiration" (ἐπιθειάζοντες, *Contempl.* 84) and speaks of the choir as "having imbibed as in Bacchic rituals of the undiluted wine of God's love" (καθάπερ ἐν ταῖς βακχείαις ἀκράτου σπάσαντες τοῦ θεοφιλοῦς, 85).[87] Here, in the context of a communal festival, Philo uses the same language he used earlier to describe the fundamental experience impelling the Therapeutae and Therapeutrides to seek the way of θεραπεία (12). That language evokes the "mysteries" into which they are initiated in the sacred chambers of their solitary dwellings (24–25), and it evokes Philo's description of ἀλληγορία in *Migr.* 34–35. Given the use of mystery language in the philosophical tradition, Philo here claims authority over those other philosophers for the Therapeutae and Therapeutrides who similarly enjoy ecstatic experience. Rapture, mystical experience, θεωρία, are communal as well as individual. And they are related to text as a way to "see" the divine.

The meal, we recall, is a συμποσίον (*Contempl.* 71, 73, 83, 89), a banquet that is a philosophical gathering. It is an exegetical discourse followed by a meal and then by singing and dancing. All these elements reflect the embodiment of the text, of the foundation narrative, with its specific references to Moses and Miriam and to Exod 15. The text, the meal, the singing and dancing—ultimately all are

84. Lev. 23:15–21; see Joseph M. Baumgarten, "4Q Halakah[a] 5, the Law of Ḥadash, and the Pentecontad Calendar," *JJS* 27 (1976): 37–38.

85. Ibid., 36–46. There is evidence for other such "extra" local festivals, especially in Egyptian Jewish communities; e.g., 3 Macc 6:30–36, which recounts a festival of deliverance; Philo, *Mos.* 2.41–44, which describes a festival celebrating the completion of the Septuagint. See Jutta Leonhardt, *Jewish Worship in Philo of Alexandria* (TSAJ 84; Tübingen: Mohr Siebeck, 2001), 47–50.

86. Apuleius, *Metam.* 11.8–10; Apuleius does not mention dancing. This could be found in Greek religious traditions; see Burkert, *Greek Religion*, 102–3, 110, 234, 236.

87. On the theme of sober intoxication elsewhere in Philo, see *Opif.* 70–71; *Leg.* 1.82; 3.83; *Ebr.* 145; *Fug.* 32, 166; *Mos.* 1.187; *Prob.* 13; see Winston, "Philo and the Contemplative Life," 225–26.

about the text embodied in solitary oral reading, as well as in communal celebration. The fiftieth-day celebration is an enacted text.[88]

Philo concludes his description of the women and men of Lake Mareot at dawn following the fiftieth-day celebration, with members saying collectively the morning prayer. Then they withdraw to their private sanctuaries (ἑαυτῶν ἕκαστος σεμνεῖα ἀναχωροῦσι) and resume the solitary pursuit of philosophy (φιλοσοφία, *Contempl.* 89). Thus Philo describes the lives of the Therapeutae and Therapeutrides as framed spatially by the bounds of the solitary dwelling with its sanctuary, on the one hand, and the sanctuary and dining hall of the communal gathering, on the other. The focus of ritual in all three contexts is text work, and the document moves from individual study and composition (24–29) to collective study (30–33, 64–88) and performance, then returns to solitary study (89).[89]

Spatial and temporal frames, a variety of ascetical and meditative practices, communal rituals that include formal gestures, singing and dancing, group study under the guidance of a leader, and a symbolic meal—all focus our attention on the centrality of text work. That work itself is a ritual, framed by the periodicity of the calendar in solitary as well as communal settings and marked off spatially by the "sanctuaries" of the solitary dwelling and the assembly place as well as the dining hall. It is marked off as well by its place in the rituals of the seventh and fiftieth days, and it is further designated as ritual by the use of metaphors drawn from mystery traditions and Egyptian temple worship as well as the Septuagint.

None of this obscures the fact that the Therapeutae and Therapeutrides lead a contemplative life, the βίος θεωρέτικος. An experience that is vision, ascent, and bacchic fury is at the center of the contemplative life of those dwelling by Lake Mareot. That experience is closely associated with study of sacred texts and other writings, including those of the founders, both in the solitary dwelling and in the communal sanctuary. It is associated with an ascetical practice that includes solitude and silence and simplicity of life, text work that includes study of sacred texts as well as the composition of hymns. It is also associated with the communal singing and dancing that mark the celebration of the fiftieth day (*Contempl.* 85). *De vita contemplativa* thus displays an example of the relationship between study, ritual, and mystical experience.

Indeed ritual, including the ritual of study, serve that life and constitute its framework. The members of the Lake Mareot community are contemplatives, mystics. Philo describes their experience in the terms of vision, ascent, and the possession of participation in the mysteries and relationship with Σοφία.

---

88. On ritualization and the embodiment of cultural schemes, see Bell, *Ritual Perspectives and Dimensions*, 81.

89. See Engberg-Pedersen, "Philo's *De Vita Contemplativa*," 54.

10. Concluding Remarks

What is the function of *De vita contemplativa*? Certainly there is an apologetic function. As one commentator remarks, Philo spends more than a quarter of the work excoriating Gentiles.[90] The contrasts are patent. The Therapeutae and Therapeutrides are philosophers.[91] Their eminence exceeds even that of Socrates, Xenophon, and Plato (*Contempl.* 57). Like their Greek counterparts, they have divested themselves of material possessions, but they have exercised greater social responsibility in their manner of doing so (13–16). The austerity of the meals of the Therapeutae and Therapeutridae contrasts dramatically with the banquets of the Greeks.[92] On the one side there is but the simplest food and water, sobriety, the table service of young members of the community who render that service freely like sons of the family, the chastity of the Therapeutrides, discussion of sacred texts, the dignity of community gatherings. On the other side is gluttony, drunkenness, violence, ostentation, the service of young slaves, pederasty, and philosophical discourse on the merits of various forms of ἔρος. Philo makes his point in ways that are far from subtle!

I speak of his point, but it seems to me that Philo indeed tries to make several points.[93] Certainly he attempts to demonstrate, for Gentiles and Jews alike, that a group of Jews is living the philosophical ideal in dramatic ways in the nearby countryside. The title and opening paragraph suggest that he does this as part of a broader apologetic project discussing the virtuous life.[94] The second paragraph of *De vita contemplativa* refers explicitly to the Therapeutae and Therapeutrides as "philosophers," and his description of the Lake Mareot community's way of life recalls that of other idealized philosophical communities, as we have seen.

Parallels from mystery religions and descriptions of Egyptian priestly practices suggest that Philo's understanding of the philosophical life is both hieratic and contemplative, as well as intellectual. In the broader context of his world, the world of Greco-Roman Egypt, Philo represents in a dramatic fashion in *De vita contemplativa* the convergence of the hieratic and ritual with philosophy, understood as intellectual pursuit and way of life. To non-Jews and Jews alike this might

90. See Geoltrain, "Le traité," 14; David M.Hay, "Things Philo Said," 677–79.

91. *Contempl.* 2. Philo uses φιλοσοφέω and its cognates in *Contempl.* 14, 16, 26, 28, 30, 34, 57, 67, 69, 89. He uses it of Gentiles only in *Contempl.* 57 of Xenophon and Plato. On the Therapeutae and Therapeutrides as philosophers, see Manuel Alexandre, "The Eloquent Philosopher in Philo's *De uita contemplatiua*," *Euphrosyne* 29 (2001): 319–30.

92. On the Therapeutae, see *Contempl.* 37, 73–74; on the Greeks, see 40–56.

93. See Hay, "Foils for the Therapeutae," 347–48.

94. See Hay, "Things Philo Said," 677; Taylor and Davies, "So-Called Therapeutae," 7–10. Other components of the project have not survived, but his discussion of the Essenes as exemplars of the active life may have resembled that found in *Prob.* 75–91 or *Hypoth.* 11.1–18, cited by Eusebius in *Praep.ev.* 8.11.1–18; Taylor and Davies, "So-Called Therapeutae," 9.

suggest the excellence of Jewish philosophers whose lifestyle actually represents "a kind of 'fulfillment' of certain pagan ideals."[95]

An apologetic work is usually meant for the "inside" group as well as the external audience. *De vita contemplativa* holds up the Therapeutae and Therapeutrides as the most dramatic example of the ideal, not only of the philosophical life in general, but also of the contemplative life in particular. It is a way to legitimate, to Philo's Jewish audience, the authority of Judaism as a philosophy and the Therapeutae and Therapeutrides as worthy competitors of the likes of the great figures of the Greek philosophical tradition and the Egyptian priestly tradition.

De vita contemplativa is also a way for Philo to think about his own philosophical quest. Certainly, though Philo tells us that he sought out solitude and respite from urban life and proffered an ideal of restraint in the use of material possessions, he did not permanently withdraw from Alexandria and from his community responsibilities. His life included the activities of a member of the social, economic, and political elite, including banquets and chariot races (*Leg* 3.156; *Prov.* 2.58). Indeed, he reflects on his own struggle to achieve endurance and self-mastery at the banquet table (*Leg.* 3.156–157).

Because Philo was a member of one of the wealthiest and most prominent Jewish families in Alexandria, his life, at least externally, resembled in no way that of the community members at Lake Mareot. But Philo tells us that he knew what it was to see, to make the ascent, to be possessed by bacchic frenzy—and he knows this in relation to study of the sacred texts.[96] He withdraws periodically, seeking solitude for contemplation, occasionally discovering that solitude to be filled with the distraction of πάθος. Philo tells us that the contemplative experience he desires is dependent on God and can be had even in midst of the city's crowds (*Leg.* 2.85–87).

Philo, moreover, knows the framing of life by the liturgical cycle. Preeminently there is the seventh-day celebration in which the whole community assembles to "study philosophy" (*Spec.* 2.61–62; *Mos.* 2.215–216). Even those who are illiterate can learn the sacred text and its allegorical meaning, the "mysteries" of the text. Perhaps Philo is holding out—first of all, to himself—the hope that, even if the ideal is possible only for the very few, the philosophical life is possible, at least in some measure, for every Jew who studies the sacred writings. All who submit their gaze to the discipline of study, of ἀλληγορία, can *see*, can make the ascent, can be possessed of bacchic inspiration, can be united with Σοφία.

95. Hay, "Foils for the Therapeutae," 339. Hay refers here specifically to the community's dietary habits.

96. *Spec.* 3–6; *Migr.* 34–35; these refer to mystical experience in reference to study. There are other autobiographical descriptions of Philo's mystical experience, e.g., *Cher.* 27–28, 43–52; *Somn.* 2.251–253; *Her.* 69–74.

Philo's *De vita contemplativa* presents a description of a group that exemplifies the contemplative life in its most ideal form. According to that description, it is a community whose life is framed by the temporal boundaries of the liturgical cycle and the spatial boundaries of the sanctuaries, individual and communal. Those frames display clearly the sacred text and its study, which are inextricably associated with mystical experience through the oral reading that provides an aid to altered states of consciousness as well as the metaphors that serve as the content of the visualization process.

In the contexts of Greco-Roman mystery cult and Egyptian temple religion, literary activity is a site for contemplative experience.[97] It is associated with the category "philosophy" because the activity of the sacred scribes is part of a whole lifestyle—a "philosophy" in ancient terms.[98] Furthermore, the literary activity at the center of the priest's life, and so much the more the sacred scribe, has to do with ritual. Even the geometrical and astrological computations that occupy the night hours have to do with the calendar that governs the proper execution of cult, which cult preserves the order of the cosmos.[99] Written texts, and the labor associated with them, whether copying or interpreting, give access to the divine.

Philo's *De Vita Contemplativa* displays the ways in which Philo considers the relationship of text work to ritual and mystical experience. In the context of Roman Egypt we read a description of a Jewish philosophical community with text work as a central practice. Philo talks about their enterprise as priestly, as ritual praxis, and presents *Jews'* text work and lifestyle as superior to Greek philosophy, Greco-Roman mysteries, or Egyptian temple religion.

97. For a third-century example, see *P.Oxy*. 11.1381.32–52; see David Frankfurter, *Religion in Roman Egypt: Assimilation and Resistance* (Princeton: Princeton University Press, 1998), 238.

98. Mason, "PHILOSOPHIAI," 33–35.

99. Frankfurter, *Religion in Roman Egypt*, 240.

Jewish and Christian Heavenly Meal Traditions

Andrea Lieber

> Then Moses and Aaron, Nadab and Abihu, and the seventy elders of Israel ascended; and they saw the God of Israel: under God's feet there was the likeness of a pavement of sapphire, like the very sky for purity. Yet God did not raise a hand against the leaders of the Israelites; they beheld God, and they ate and drank. (Exod 24:9–11)

The relationship in ancient Jewish literature between sacrificial meals and eschatological banquets, both of which are meals that mediate between the human and divine realms, is largely unexplored in scholarly literature. Cultic sacrifice, grounded in the metaphor of a meal shared between God and humanity, established unity among the priestly community and affirmed God's presence. Like any ritual of communal solidarity, this symbolic priestly meal also served to exclude those not fit to be part of the group.

Similarly, the motif of a heavenly banquet, described in rabbinic midrash and in Hellenistic sources, is also represented as a meal consumed in God's presence, shared among the righteous of Israel. As with the sacrificial meal, participation in the heavenly banquet is limited to those who know the proper etiquette. Both cultic and eschatological meals mediate the boundaries of community and the boundaries that define the divine-human relationship.

Reading these traditions alongside one another suggests to me that the image of the heavenly banquet has its roots in the biblical institution of cultic worship. Indeed, the mythic image of the heavenly vision feast is a metaphorical transformation of the ancient sacrificial cult meal, a meal that was eaten at God's "table" (the temple altar) and in which God participated.[1] A central element of ancient cultic tradition—the cult meal—is thus transformed through biblical exegesis

1. This interdisciplinary approach, which brings together anthropological and sociological methods from the study of ritual with literary analysis of a textual tradition, is useful in highlighting the important relationship between two dominant expressions of religious experience in the history of Judaism: temple-centered cultic sacrifice and ecstatic visionary mysticism, which flourished in the Second Temple period and beyond and is centered around cultic imagery.

into a mythic, eschatological image that preserves a salient aspect of the cult: the careful maintenance of boundaries that structure the divine-human encounter. This symbolism then comes to play a significant role in early Jewish and Christian communal self-definition, as reflected in New Testament and rabbinic sources.

1. Philonic Exegesis of Exodus 24:11

My analysis begins with an important biblical theophany found in Exod 24. While not an explicitly temple-centered text, Exod 24:9–11 narrates a cultic episode that serves as an important exegetical base text for a number of the passages to be examined below. The text reads:

> Then Moses and Aaron, Nadab and Abihu, and the seventy elders of Israel ascended; and they saw the God of Israel: under God's feet there was the likeness of a pavement of sapphire, like the very sky for purity. Yet God did not raise a hand against the leaders of the Israelites; they beheld (*wayehezu*) God, and they ate and drank.[2]

In celebration of God's revelation at Mount Sinai, the leaders of the Israelites ascend the mountain and are permitted to gaze upon God's anthropomorphic form without harm coming to them.[3] The experience culminates in a communal meal, sealing the covenant between God and Israel in a sacred feast. The narrative context of Exod 24 suggests that this feast is indeed a covenant or cult meal.

Immediately preceding the ascent of Moses and his entourage, Moses performs a sacrifice and recites aloud the terms of the covenant. He sprinkles the blood of the slain animals both upon the altar and upon the Israelite people, a gesture that is here also symbolic of kinship in signifying "shared blood." He then ascends with his brother, nephews, and the seventy elders, where they enjoy a meal and a privileged vision of the divine *anthropos*. The meal affirms kinship among the Israelites and between God and Israel and performs a function similar to the sacrificial meal offered by Jacob in sealing his covenant with Laban in Gen 31:54.[4] Its power differentiates the Israelites from those nonparticipants in the covenant and simultaneously differentiates the exclusive patrilineal leadership of Moses, Aaron and his sons, and the elders.

According to Philo, who is the first proponent of a metaphorical interpretation of the feast, the leaders of Israel at Sinai experienced a heavenly ascent and

---

2. Exod 24:9–11; all biblical translations follow the NJPS.

3. The viewing of God's "feet" here is sufficient indication that this vision is of the divine *anthropos*, based on Ezekiel's enthroned vision in Ezek 1:26–28.

4. Gen 31:51–54; cf. 26:24–30. See also Gen 18:1–8 and Judg 6:21–22, where angelic theophany is accompanied by a meal.

their meal was, in fact, a taste of immortality.[5] His text, from *Quaestiones et solutiones in Exodum* (*Questions and Answers on Exodus*), reads:

> What is the meaning of the words, "they appeared to God in the place and they ate and drank"? [6] Having attained to the face of the father, they do not remain in any mortal place at all, for all such places are profane and polluted, but they send and make a migration to a holy and divine place, which is called by another name, *logos*. Being in this place, through the steward they see the master in a lofty and clear manner, envisioning God with the keen-sighted eyes of the mind. But this vision is the food of souls, and true partaking is the cause of a life of immortality. Wherefore, indeed, it is said, "they ate and drank." For those who are indeed very hungry and thirsty did not fail to see God become clearly visible, but like those who, being famished, find an abundance of food, they satisfied their great desire.[7]

Several things are notable about Philo's interpretation of the biblical scene. Most striking is his claim that the ascent upon Sinai was a heavenly ascent. Moses,

---

5. On heavenly ascent, see Wilhelm Bousset, "Die Himmelreise der Seele," *AR* 4:136–69, 229–73; Martha Himmelfarb, *Ascent to Heaven in Jewish and Christian Apocalypses* (New York: Oxford University Press, 1993; Alan Segal, "Heavenly Ascent in Hellenistic Judaism, Early Christianity and Their Environment," *ANRW* 2.23.2:1333–94; idem, *Two Powers in Heaven: Early Rabbinic Reports about Christianity and Gnosticism* (Leiden: Brill, 1977); Rebecca Macy Lesses, *Ritual Practices to Gain Power: Angels, Incantations, and Revelation in Early Jewish Mysticism* (HTS 44; Harrisburg, Pa.: Trinity Press International, 1998); David J. Halperin, "Ascension or Invasion: Implications of the Heavenly Journey in Ancient Judaism," *Religion* 18 (1988): 47–67; idem, *Faces of the Chariot: Early Jewish Reponses to Ezekiel's Vision* (TSAJ 16. Tübingen: Mohr Siebeck, 1988); Naomi Janowitz, *Poetics of Ascent: Theories of Language in a Rabbinic Ascent Text* (New York: State University of New York Press, 1989); M. Dean-Otting, *Heavenly Journeys: A Study of the Motif in Hellenistic Jewish Literature* (Frankfurt am Main: Lang, 1984); Morton Smith, "Ascent to Heavens and the Beginning of Christianity," *Eranos* 50 (1981): 403–29.

6. It is important to note that Philo is working with the Septuagint version of the biblical text, which translated *yehezu* as ὤφθησαν ἐν τῷ τόπῳ τοῦ θεοῦ. Hence Philo's reading, "they appeared in the place of God," rather than the Hebrew, "they saw God." Nonetheless, Philo does preserve the tradition that Moses and company "envisioned" God, and it is this vision that provides the "food of the soul." This reading is paralleled elsewhere in the Masoretic Text of the Hebrew Bible (Exod 23:17: "Three times in the year all males shall appear [lit., be seen] before [*lipne*] the Lord God") and in the various rabbinic sources that read it as a visionary episode. See Max Kadushin, *The Rabbinic Mind* (3rd ed.; New York: Bloch, 1972), 239–40.

7. *Quaestiones et solutiones in Exodum* is extant only in Armenian and Latin translations from the Greek. There are numerous Greek fragments, and I have provided relevant Greek text where it is available, but lack of an *Urtext* makes careful scrutiny of Philo's language in this document rather difficult. Manuscript variants are noted where pertinent. All texts cited in this essay are from Ralph Marcus, trans., *Philo: Supplements* (2 vols.; LCL; Cambridge: Harvard University Press, 1953). All other translations of Philo are from Francis H. Colson and George W. Whitaker, trans., *Philo* (10 vols.; LCL; Cambridge: Harvard University Press, 1932–62).

Aaron, Aaron's sons, and the elders "migrated" to a holy and divine place that is immortal and called *logos*. The *logos* here describes the *topos* that is before the "face of the father," perhaps referring to the intelligible nature of this realm. Like the philosopher who descends Plato's metaphorical cave and thus traverses the bounds between the sensible and intelligible spheres of reality, so Moses and the others have crossed into a higher stage of intelligible reality. In this place they are able to gaze upon God, but it is with the mind's eye. This transfer of place may be compared with the transfer of place experienced by the priest in the temple, thus suggesting that the ascent atop Sinai is functionally equivalent to the entry of the high priest into the holy of holies. In both *topoi* the seer is situated before the divine presence and is thus ontically transformed.

Second, the sacrificial meal is entirely "spiritualized" by Philo and replaced by an ecstatic vision of God that provides "food for the soul." No physical food is eaten, deemphasizing the stark physicality of the flesh-and-blood cultic ritual; rather, Israel's ability to gaze upon God and derive spiritual nourishment becomes the nation's own defining characteristic.[8]

Philo appears influenced by the tradition, witnessed also in rabbinic, patristic, and pseudepigraphic literature, that there is no "eating" in heaven; unlike humans, angelic beings do not require food, yet their "bodies" are nonetheless sustained by divine means. Philo's understanding of the ascent upon Sinai as *heavenly* ascent requires that the meal be understood as metaphorical, as there is no human food in the celestial realm.[9] His use of the verb τροφέω to describe this noetic nourishment connotes nurturing, the type of nourishment provided through the act of nursing. In ancient Greek philosophical literature, τροφέω was commonly employed as a synonym for παιδεία, implying that the cultivation of an individual mind through education parallels the physical nourishment of a child.[10] The image depicted is thus one of children being nourished or nursed by a mother, being raised to spiritual adulthood by means of this divine, contem-

8. Philo's metaphor also performs a "distancing" function. Unlike the senses of touch and taste, which demand direct contact of the subject with the sense-object (and in the case of taste, even internalization of the object), the sense of sight places one at a distance from the sense-object. Thus the visionary feast implies a necessary separation between the visionary and the *Shekhinah*.

9. This is a basic assumption shared by Philo and Josephus as well as a number of other ancient rabbinic, patristic, and pseudepigraphic sources. The underlying idea is that there is no eating in heaven. Rather, angels are sustained by the divine presence in the form of "spiritual" food. The need for food is explicitly bodily, and heavenly bodies are sufficently refined so as not to require food. See *Gen. Rab.* 48; 18:4; *Exod. Rab.* 47:4–5; Tob 12:19; *T. Abr.* 15; Justin, *Dial.* 56; *Did.* 9–10; Ignatius, *Rom.* 4; *Letter to the Smyrneans*. See also David Goodman, "Do Angels Eat?" *JJS* 37 (1986): 160–75

10. Werner Jaeger, *Paideia: The Ideals of Greek Culture* (trans. G. Highet; New York: Oxford University Press, 1963), vol. 3.

plative feast, despite Philo's explicit use of male imagery to describe the divine presence.[11]

The divine vision unifies the nation of Israel. This shared vision, which satiates by enabling the visionary to absorb the qualities of the divine image, unites the people much in the way sharing the flesh of a sacrificed animal victim united them. Replacing the sacrificial meal with an ecstatic vision radically transforms the activities of the sacrificial cult into a contemplative rite. The ecstatic vision of the divine *anthropos,* God's visible, human form, thus comes to replace the meal as the culmination of the sacrificial ritual.

According to Philo, the transfer of the covenant meal to this transcendent dimension is largely bound up with Israel's privileged status in the eyes of God.[12] Israel is distinguished from other nations of the world by its ability to "see" God. In his *Legatio ad Gaium* Philo says of Israel that "to behold the uncreated and divine, the prime good, the excellent, the happy, the blessed" is the gift of the people that "is called in the Hebrew tongue Israel, but expressed in our tongue, the word is 'he that sees God.'" Philo depicts Israel, the seeing nation, as a nation of philosophers: "Israel is the mind contemplative of God and the cosmos, for Israel means 'seeing God,'[13] while the house of the mind is the whole soul, and this is that most holy vineyard which has for its fruit that divine growth, virtue" (*Somn.* 2.173).

Israel is set apart from other nations by virtue of its ability to "see" or "contemplate" God. Yet Israel as a nation shares several other distinct traits that also link the themes of ecstatic vision, food, and sacrifice. According to Philo, Israel's talent for envisioning God is connected to its diet: Israel as a nation that eats manna, or angel's food. Peder Borgen's classic work on the subject demonstrated

11. Several studies have examined Philo's gendered language. See Sharon Lea Mattila, "Wisdom, Sense Perception, Nature, and Philo's Gender Gradient," *HTR* 89 (1996): 103–29; Richard Baer, *Philo's Use of the Categories Male and Female* (ALGHJ 3; Leiden: Brill, 1970); Judith Romney Wegner, "The Image of Women in Philo," in *Society of Biblical Literature 1982 Seminar Papers* (SBLSP 21; Chico, Calif.: Scholars Press, 1982), 551–63; Dorothy Sly, "Philo's Practical Application of *dikaiosyne,*" in *Society of Biblical Literature 1991 Seminar Papers* (SBLSP 30; Atlanta: Scholars Press, 1991), 298–308.

12. See Ellen Birnbaum, *The Place of Judaism in Philo's Thought: Israel, Jews and Proselytes* (BJS 290; Atlanta: Scholars Press, 1996).

13. The association of Israel with the *'ish* who sees God effects a masculinization of the nation. Several scholars have noted that Philo's use of gendered terms to describe the interplay of the sensible and intelligible worlds reflects a theme common among classical Greek thinkers. In Philo, the material world is typically associated with the feminine and the rational faculty that "tames" the material world of nature associated with a masculine potency. Indeed, Philo's consistent association of Israel, the nation of contemplative vision, with a highly evolved noetic ability is also a portrayal of the nation as masculine. The ability to contemplate God derives from Israel's ability to order properly the masculine faculty of reason and the feminine faculty of sense.

the connection between Israel's designation as a "nation of vision" with the notion that the vision is a source of spiritual nourishment. Manna and ecstatic vision of God are both sources of divine knowledge and angelic sustenance:

> while other men receive their food from earth, the nation of vision alone has it from heaven. The earthly food is produced with the co-operation of husbandmen, but the heavenly is sent like the snow by God the solely self-acting, with none to share his work. And indeed it says "behold I rain upon you bread from heaven" (Ex. 16:4). Of what food can he rightly say that it is rained from heaven, save of heavily wisdom which is sent from above on souls which yearn for virtue. (*Mut.* 259–260; cf. 137)

The miracle of manna, which provided bodily sustenance, is interpreted instead as having provided spiritual sustenance. But this nourishment is intimately linked to Israel's ability to envision or contemplate God. This food of the soul is knowledge and as such is associated also with Torah:

> When they sought what it is that nourished the soul ... they became learners and found it to be a saying of God, that is the Divine Word, from which all kinds of instruction and wisdom flow in perpetual stream. This is the heavenly nourishment, and it is indicated as such in the sacred records, when the First Cause in his own person says, "Lo, it is I that am raining upon you bread out of the heaven"; for in every deed God drops from above the ethereal wisdom upon minds which are by nature apt and take delight in contemplation; and they see it and taste it and are filled with pleasure, being fully aware of what they feel but wholly ignorant of the cause which produced the feeling. So they inquire "What is this" which has a nature making it sweeter than honey and whiter than snow? And they will be taught by the seer that "This is the bread, which the Lord hath given them to eat." ... This divine ordinance fills the soul that has vision alike with light and sweetness, flashing forth the radiance of truth and with the honied grace of persuasion imparting sweetness to those who hunger and thirst after nobility of character. (*Fug.* 137–139)

They "see it" (καὶ ἴδουσαι) and "taste it" (καὶ γευσάμεναι) and are "filled with pleasure." Israel's capacity for divine vision is linked to a consumption of "soul food," the acquisition of esoteric knowledge that nourishes the mind the way food nourishes the body. Manna has a mediating quality in Philo: the food mediates between the angelic/cognitive realm and the human realm of the senses. Manna is identified with both *logos* and *torah* and even with Moses himself in some cases.[14] This is an intriguing tradition, as both Moses and the heavenly bread perform mediating activities. Similarly, that the vision of God's form nourishes like manna suggests identification between manna and God's image.

---

14. Geza Vermes, "*He is the Bread*": *Targum Neofiti Exodus 16.15* (Post Biblical Jewish Studies; Leiden: Brill, 1975), 139–46.

Philo's biblical exegesis here reflects the influence of Hellenistic literature. Writing some years after Philo, Achilles Tatius also demonstrates the nourishing power of vision in his description of two lovers at dinner:

> The dinner she provided was sumptuous; she took a portion of the meats set before her, so as to appear to eat, but could swallow nothing of the food; she did nothing but gaze upon me. To lovers there is no delight save in the object of love, which occupies the whole of their soul, and leaves no place in it for the pleasures of the table. The pleasure which comes from vision enters by the eyes and makes its home in the breast; bearing with it ever the image of the beloved, it impresses it upon the mirror of the soul and leaves there its image.... I said to her, "How is this? Do you take nothing of the dainties you have yourself provided? You consume no more than those who are painted as eating." [And she replies] "What costly dish, what wine could be more satisfying to me than the sight of you?"[15]

As in Philo's text, we see here that the sight of the beloved substitutes for food. The lovers each emit an emanation of beauty that is mutually absorbed by the other.[16] The eyes are depicted as receptors of pleasure, and looking is a "taking in" that fills the self in the same fashion as food.[17] A second example of this device in Hellenistic literature is found in Philostratus: "So let the cups down and leave them alone, especially for fear of their fragility; and drink to me only with your eyes; it was such a draft that Zeus too drank—and took to himself a lovely boy to bear his cup."[18] It is an important feature of this text that drinking with the eyes is

15. Achilles Tatius, *Leuc. Clit.* 5.13; Stephen Gaselee, trans., *Leucippe and Clitophon* (rev. ed.; LCL; Cambridge: Harvard University Press, 1969). I am indebted to Jonathan Brumberg Kraus of Wheaton College for this reference.

16. Lucretius devoted almost an entire book of his *De rerum natura* to the study of the "effluences" that form the basis of sensory phenomena, most particularly the sense of sight. In this work, beauty is a physical emanation that radiates and flows in the form of a thin "membrane" from the body of the beloved into the eye of the beholder. Receiving this efflux of beauty stimulates in the eye of the beholder an appetitive desire that is only satisfied through physical "possession" of the beloved (*De rerum natura* 4.30–34; cf. Plato, *Phaedr.* 255c).

17. An analogous episode is witnessed in the gnostic text *Authoritative Teaching* in its description of the bride/heroine who is rescued from "the world": "Secretly her bridegroom fetched it [the word]; he presented it to her mouth to make her eat it like food and he applied the word to her eyes as a medicine to make her see with her mind and perceive her kinsmen and learn about her roots, in order that she might cling to her branch from which she had first come forth, in order that she might receive what is hers and renounce matter" (*Auth. Teach.* 22.23–25, cited in Madeline Scopello, "Jewish and Greek Heroines in the Nag Hammadi Library," in *Images of the Feminine in Gnosticism* [ed. K. L. King; Philadelphia: Fortress, 1988], 74). Ingesting the "word" here brings noetic enlightenment.

18. Philostratus, Ep. 32; Allen Rogers Benner and Francis H. Fobes, trans., *The Letters of Alciphron, Aelian and Philostratus* (LCL; Cambridge: Harvard University Press, 1949).

an act characteristic of Zeus. In putting down the cup and drinking with the eyes, one's thirst is quenched like that of the gods.[19]

While the Jerusalem temple occupies an important place in Philo's understanding of Judaism and the Jewish people, his radical spiritualization of the cult might be read as an effort to find daily moral and spiritual meaning in the prescriptions surrounding the cult. Israel, which is the nation who sees God, is also a nation of priests. Indeed, perhaps it is their priestly status that, in Philo's understanding, facilitates this extraordinary contemplative ability. But what is the meaning of a national priesthood that lives apart from the national temple? Philo's writing on this issue is evidence that, long before the destruction of the Jerusalem temple, many Diaspora Jews had learned to live without it.

Philo's spiritualization of the cult allows for the priesthood itself to become spiritualized and removed from the apparatus of temple sacrifice. Priestly status becomes a disciplined, moral, and spiritual ideal attainable by all Israel, which culminates, like the sacrifices in the temple, in the clear vision of God.

2. Temple and Cosmos

Interpreting sacrificial prescriptions in the Septuagint text, Philo attaches symbolic significance to the multiple components of the sacrificial rite.[20] Every detail of the cult is spiritualized as Philo transforms sacrifice into a contemplative journey. His references to sacrifice and the temple are scattered throughout his works, but the most extensive and detailed treatments are in *Quaestiones et solutiones in Exodum*, where he describes point by point the features of the tabernacle, and in *De specialibus legibus* (*On the Special Laws*), where he gives lengthy exegetical commentary on Leviticus. The entire geography of the temple as described in the

19. The erotic element, so blatant in these Greek texts, and perhaps implied in the Jewish texts, is not unimportant to the Jewish material. The depiction of God as nourishing or of the righteous as feeding on the divine presence employs distinctively feminine imagery. While the *Shekhinah* in later mystical sources represents the feminine aspect of God, the object of ecstatic vision in early Jewish mystical sources, the divine *anthropos*, is clearly described in the form of a male body. Indeed, we might view the image of the nourishing *Shekhinah* as a feminization of the *anthropos*.

20. It is important to note that the Septuagint itself allegorizes somewhat in its translation of some of the technical cultic apparatus. For example, the Urim and Thummim are translated as δήλωσις καὶ ἀλήθεια ("manifestation and truth") or σαφήνεια ("distinctness, perspicuity") καὶ ἀλήθεια (Philo, *Spec.* 3.132; 140; 4.69; *Mos.* 2.113; 128–129). Thus it is possible that Philo's own allegories were based upon similar ideas already circulating in Greek-Jewish culture.

One should also note that Philo employs allegory to "spiritualize" Jewish law as it is reflected in the text of the Septuagint. Philo reads the Bible on two levels: he reads contextually to provide a literal understanding of a text, but he also reads symbolically, abstracting the message of a biblical passage beyond its context to arrive at its homiletical or moral significance. Philo frequently calls these two components of scripture the "body" and "soul" of a text.

biblical text is fully allegorized. The temple itself symbolizes the cosmic meeting place of the sensible and intelligible worlds, and sacrifice becomes a contemplative activity by means of which these two aspects of reality are neatly bridged. The ark is itself a symbol of the incorporeal world (*QE* 2.59), and the table adjacent to it symbolizes the sense-perceptible world (*QE* 2.69).[21] The four rings that are fit onto the ark, two on each side, symbolize the division of the world into the sense-perceptible and the intelligible sides (*QE* 2.56); the cherubim are situated on two sides of the altar to indicate that the "bounds of the whole heaven and the world are fortified by the two highest guards," God's creative potency and God's ruling potency (*QE* 2.64). The temple is the sacred *topos* where divine and human, intelligible and sensible worlds meet.

Spiritual sacrifice, for Philo, is still a moment of divine revelation: "seeing God" means the contemplation God at the moment of true sacrifice. Indeed, vision of God actually becomes the culminating moment of the rite. Sacrificing together forges unity among the Jews. It is their collective experience at the altar that unifies the people as a single mind. Similar language is used when Philo speaks of Israel as a nation, ὁ γένος, who sees God. The visionary moment is functionally equivalent to the sacrificial meal. As a vehicle for divine perception, sacrifice ushers the soul before the luminous, divine presence:

> What is the meaning of the words, "Thou shalt make for me a sanctuary, and I shall appear among you"? … If however, thou art worthily initiated and canst become an animate shrine of the Father, then instead of having closed eyes, thou wilt see the First Cause [variant: First things] and in wakefulness thou wilt cease from the deep sleep in which thou has been held. Then will appear to thee that manifest one (ὁ ἐπιφανής).… For the beginning and end of happiness is to be able to see God. But this cannot happen to him who has not made his soul, as I said before, a sanctuary and altogether a shrine of God. (*QE* 2.51)

Every individual becomes a sanctuary, altar, and priest. Philo's understanding seems to endow one who contemplates noetic reality with a type of priestly ability. One whose soul is like an altar can see God and the secrets of creation. This text provides a vivid example of one of Philo's most extreme allegories of the cult. Philo spiritualizes the sacrificial process to such an extent here that he seems to describe an event that is almost entirely interior. Is Philo perhaps suggesting that metaphorical sacrifice is a contemplative experience that can be accessed without the temple and priestly apparatus? In this sense, Philo's allegory accomplishes a true democratization of the priesthood. A similar sentiment is expressed

---

21. Philo also attaches cosmic significance to many other pieces of the tabernacle's furnishings. The bowls on the branches of the menorah stand for zodiacal signs (*QE* 2.76); The mixing bowls on the lampstand represent the seasons of the year (*QE* 2.77). The lampstand in general seems to be associated with heavenly luminaries. See *QE* 2.78–80.

in Philo's discussion of the Passover sacrifice, which is distinguished from later sacrifices in that the people, rather than the priests, perform the rites for themselves. In this sense, according to Philo, "the whole people is honored with the priesthood" (*QE* 1.10). Philo says that in sacrificing together, the people join in a transcendent harmony:

> For when the whole multitude came together with harmonious oneness to give thanks for their migration, He no longer called them a multitude or a nation or a people, but a "congregation." And so it happened that they congregated and came together not only in body but also in mind as being about to sacrifice with one character and one soul.

Scholars have often assumed that it was lack of access to the temple that inspired tales of ascent to a heavenly temple and visions of a third, restored temple in the eschatological future. In Philo's time, however, the temple still stood and, as we have seen in the examples above, remained an institution of reverence in Philo's work. His need to attach moral and philosophical symbols to the detailed components of the rite reflects an attempt on his part to make these rites meaningful to a population that perhaps could not relate to them on the literal level. Though the temple still functioned in Jerusalem, Philo transformed sacrifice into an interior-focused, contemplative rite.

3. Early Christian Transformations of the Heavenly Banquet

In turning to the literature of early Christianity, it is clear that these ancient authors were also concerned with their relationship to the Judaism that continued to exist both in Palestine and throughout the Diaspora. While the Jerusalem temple stood, we must assume the need on the part of the earliest Christians to define their relationship to this important religious, social, and historical center of Jewish existence. Following the temple's destruction in 70 C.E., a generation after the very moments of Christianity's emergence, we must imagine this cataclysmic event had profound significance for sectarian communities. The heavy sacrificial symbolism that is the very backbone of Christian theology and New Testament narrative must be viewed in this light. Separating itself from the temple as a vehicle for religious expression and community self-definition necessitated the reworking of cultic tradition and the evolution of a new vehicle for divine revelation.[22]

---

22. Qumran provides yet another example of a community faced with this same issue. Convinced of the impurity of the Jerusalem temple, the members of the Qumran sect separated themselves from the Jerusalem cult and evolved a ritualized lifestyle that included ritual meals to replace the temple as cultic center. See Hannah K. Harrington, *The Impurity Systems of Qumran and the Rabbis: Biblical Foundations* (SBLDS 143; Atlanta: Scholars Press, 1993); Jacob

Hebrews, an epistle whose date and provenance are disputed, presents a vivid reworking of cultic imagery where Christ is figured as both high priest and sacrificial victim.[23] Likely composed in the Diaspora before the destruction of the temple, the text radically spiritualizes the temple cult, which finds its fulfillment in the most perfect sacrifice, Christ himself. In the letters of Paul, composed while the temple was still in existence and directed toward a largely Gentile audience, we see the symbolism of the temple transferred onto the body (the individual body and the body of Christ) in an effort to forge communal unity amidst a diverse group. The eucharistic meal here becomes a sacred rite that reaffirms communal unity in the same way the sacrificial cult did, yet it accomplishes this goal without the need for an external, centralized temple cult. Luke-Acts and John, on the other hand, written after the temple's destruction, reveal an entirely different set of concerns. For the author of Luke-Acts, table fellowship and the Passover sacrifice become central symbols of Christ's presence in the world, reversing key elements of traditional Jewish eschatology. Thus the Eucharist, which is in the Lukan narrative a sacred meal endowed with a clear visionary component, comes to replace sacrifice as a commemorative reenactment of its fulfillment in the sacrifice of Christ.[24] In John, our source chronologically most distant from the temple, the Eucharist is extremely spiritualized and almost completely removed from its cultic context. The consumption of Jesus' body is instead associated with Jewish manna traditions, witnessed also in Philo and other haggadic sources, and Christ is fully "angelified" as a source of heavenly nourishment.

The Eucharist in these early Christian sources can thus be understood as the actualization of the Philonic philosophical ideal: a substitute for sacrifice, or rather a manifestation of true sacrifice, the Jerusalem temple and cultic apparatus

---

Neusner, *Purity in Rabbinic Judaism: A Systematic Account* (South Florida Studies in the History of Judaism 95; Atlanta: Scholars Press, 1994); Krister Stendahl, *The Scrolls and the New Testament* (New York: Harper, 1957; repr., New York: Crossroad, 1992); Leonard F. Badia, *The Dead Sea People's Sacred Meal and Jesus' Last Supper* (Washington, D.C.: University Press of America, 1979).

23. Sidney Sowers, *The Hermeneutics of Philo and Hebrews: A Comparison of the Interpretation of the Old Testament in Philo Judaeus and the Epistle to the Hebrews* (Richmond, Va.: John Knox, 1965). While the *terminus ad quem* of the letter is no later than 100 C.E., its *terminus ad quo* is difficult to determine. Temple symbolism is central to the text, and as there is no mention of its destruction, a pre-70 C.E. date is possible. However, based on linguistic affinities with Luke-Acts, many scholars maintain a post-70 C.E. date. For a summary of the issues of date and authorship, see Harold Attridge, *The Epistle to the Hebrews* (Hermeneia; Philadelphia: Fortress, 1989), 5–10; Pamela M. Eisenbaum "The Jewish Heroes of Christian History: Hebrews 11 in Literary Context" (Ph.D. diss., Columbia University, 1995), 4–14; George Wesley Buchanan, *To the Hebrews* (AB 36; Garden City, N.Y.: Doubleday, 1972), 246–68.

24. Joachim Jeremias (*The Eucharistic Words of Jesus* [New York: Scribner, 1966], 240–55) argues that the memorial element of the Eucharist meal is a later development, derived from funerary rites.

become irrelevant. With the institution of the Eucharist, the ritual table becomes the altar, and all who partake in the meal might be viewed as priests.

3.1 The Epistle to the Hebrews

While Hebrews is not particularly concerned with the Eucharist or the cult meal, its detailed employment of sacrificial imagery is noteworthy for its parallels to the Philonic material. Chapters 7–9 of the letter establish Christ as an eternal priest, superior to the Levitical priesthood, and as one who exists "according to the order of Melchizedek."[25] Melchizedek is an enigmatic figure featured in Gen 14:17–20, who, as priest of El Elyon, "God on High," provides a victory meal of bread and wine before Abraham following his victory over Chedorlaomer. He is mentioned only one other time in the Hebrew Bible (Ps 110:4), and in this instance as well as the former he comes and goes without much notice.

However, for the author of Hebrews, Melchizedek becomes the paradigm for Christ's own high priesthood. Christ as high priest ministers not in the earthly temple at Jerusalem; rather, he serves as minister to the throne that is established in the "true tabernacle" established by God in heaven. The earthly sanctuary where mortal priests officiate is depicted as a "sketch and shadow of the heavenly one," made by Moses according to the pattern that was revealed to him at Sinai (Heb 8:5).[26] The author of Hebrews, like Philo, associates the outer sanctum of the temple, where the priests minister daily, with corporeal reality. That the priests may not enter the inner sanctum of the temple is symbolic of the limitations of the earthly priesthood, which is incapable of perfecting the "conscience" of the worshiper and instead deals with food and drink and other mundane bodily affairs (Heb 9:9–10).[27]

Christ's high priesthood, however, inaugurates a more perfected priesthood; while the Levitical priesthood purified the body, Christ's priesthood purifies the mind:

25. Fred L. Horton, *The Melchizedek Tradition: A Critical Examination of the Sources to the Fifth Century AD and in the Epistle to the Hebrews* (Cambridge: Cambridge University Press, 1976); Mathias Delcor, "Melchizedek from Genesis to the Qumran Texts and the Epistle to the Hebrews," *JSJ* 2 (1971): 115–35; Attridge, *Epistle to the Hebrews*, 192–95.

26. Compare Philo's discussion of the heavenly pattern according to which the tabernacle was constructed. Attridge (*Epistle to the Hebrews*, 223) notes that Hebrews' discussion of a paradigmatic heavenly temple situates the epistle within its Hellenistic-Jewish background. For comprehensive treatments, see also Ronald Williamson, *Philo and the Epistle to the Hebrews* (ALGHJ 4; Leiden: Brill, 1970); Sowers, *Hermeneutics of Philo*.

27. See Attridge, *Epistle to the Hebrews*, 231–43; Buchanan, *To the Hebrews*, 145–46. This contrast is of great significance to my reading of the Christian material.

> But when Christ came as high priest of the good things that have come, then through the greater and perfect tent (not made with hands, that is, not of this creation), he entered once for all into the holy place, not with the blood of goats and calves, but with his own blood, thus obtaining eternal redemption.... For this reason he is the mediator of a new covenant, so that those who are called may receive the promised eternal inheritance, because a death has occurred that redeems them from the transgressions under the first covenant. (Heb 9:11–16)[28]

The author of Hebrews describes the relationship between the heavenly and earthly temples in precisely the same terms as Philo. Christ, the most perfect high priest is, like Philo's high priest, an ambiguous figure who represents both the sacrificial victim and the priest who performs the rite. In both cases the identification between the priest and the sacrifice is carried to the utmost extreme, and their identities are thoroughly blurred.[29] The author of Hebrews provides an alternative to the temple for the early Christian community: the Levitical priesthood, which required daily offerings, has been superseded by Christ's supreme offering of his own blood. The slaughter of this divine priest/victim, having taken place on the altar of the heavenly temple rather than on the earthly altar, was required only once. The blood of bulls and goats could not take away sins; rather, this blood served as a reminder of sin. The blood of Christ, on the other hand, is supremely purifying. Christ's entry into the inner sanctum of the heavenly temple made bloody animal rites obsolete, and as in Philo's allegorical spiritualization of the cult, the author of this epistle decenters the significance of the Jerusalem temple. That Christ's entry into the holy of holies is contrasted with the high priest's inability to enter is of profound significance. Christ's presence collapses the very boundaries that were a central feature of the Judaic worldview.

It should be noted that this epistle does not make explicit reference to the Jerusalem temple in its references to the Levitical priesthood; its discussion of the cult is described, rather, in terms of the tabernacle in the wilderness. The point of reference, then, is the revelatory event at Sinai rather than the cultic institu-

---

28. Attridge, *Epistle to the Hebrews*, 245–56; Buchanan, *To the Hebrews*, 139–53.

29. The blurring of identity between priest and victim is an important component of the rite as it is described in Lev 8:22–36. The blood of the animal is dabbed on the body of the priests during their ceremony of consecration. Just as the animal is being dedicated to God, so is the priest in his consecration. The significance of this identification of priest and victim represents an important controversy in scholarship on biblical sacrifice. The question is whether the victim is actually a substitute for the priest himself. Levine maintains that the victim is representative of the priest, while Milgrom argues to the contrary. His refutation of the point is based on the sacrificial rites that are not centered around atonement and therefore do not contain that substitutive element. I side with Levine in affirming the consistent identification of the victim with the priest. This basic association is at the root of Hebrews' use of the sacrificial metaphor.

tion of the temple in Jerusalem. [30] Whether the letter was written before or after the destruction of the Jerusalem temple in 70 C.E., it is clear that the text represents an attempt by an early Christian community to define itself in relation to the Jewish temple cult. The striking similarities with the Philonic material suggest familiarity with his work. Christ's ministry as high priest represents the fulfillment of Philo's spiritual ideal:

> For Christ did not enter a sanctuary made by human hands, a mere copy of the true one, but he entered into heaven itself, not to appear in the presence of God on our behalf. Nor was it to offer himself again and again, as the high priest enters the holy place year after year with blood that is not his own; for then he would have to suffer again and again since the foundation of the world. But as it is, he has appeared once for all at the end of the age to remove sin by the sacrifice of himself. (Heb 9:23–26)[31]

Christ's entry into the heavenly temple effected the fullest transformation possible. Whereas Philo's high priest entered the earthly temple and was transformed temporarily into a divine being, Christ as high priest is fully transformed to immortality. The animal victim that served as a substitute for the Levitical high priest is not necessary for the cultic rite of this most perfect priest. Instead, Christ's own death in crossing the boundary of the holy of holies accomplishes an ontological change for all of humanity: they are freed from sin. The image seems to play with issues of boundary. The mechanics of the Levitical cult that navigated the boundaries between humanity and God are deemed unnecessary, suggesting the collapse of those boundaries in the death or ultimate consumption of the Christ/priest.

3.2. Luke's Last Supper

Luke's version of the Last Supper narrative is of special interest to this study because of the important role played by meals in that Gospel.[32] The meals scat-

---

30. James Swetnam, "Sacrifice and Revelation in the Epistle to the Hebrews: Observations and Surmises on Hebrews 7:6," *CBQ* 30 (1968): 227–34.

31. Attridge (*Epistle to the Hebrews*, 263) notes the use of cultic terminology here. "Entering" with the purpose of "appearing before the face of God" can be read cultically, in accordance with what we have seen above in section 2 of the present study.

32. The account of the Last Supper in Luke is preserved in two forms: a longer text, which is the more traditional reading, attested in all but one manuscript; and the shorter, or Western text, which omits verses 19b and 20. The major difference in reading affects the order of the meal. The longer reading posits a sequence of cup-bread-cup, and the shorter simply cup-bread. There are strong arguments for the originality of either version. See the discussion in Bruce M. Metzger *A Textual Commentary on the Greek New Testament* (2nd ed.; Stuttgart: Deutsche Bibelgesellschaft; United Bible Societies, 1994), 175–77; Willi Braun, *Feasting and Social Rheto-*

tered throughout the Gospel help set the stage for the climactic episodes of the Last Supper and the vision at Emmaus. Table fellowship is a dominant motif in Luke-Acts, employed most obviously to illustrate the social and communal component of Jesus' teaching.[33] The table, as we have seen, is a symbol of both inclusion and exclusion, serving symbolically to circumscribe the bounds of community. That Jesus eats with society's downtrodden is more than a gesture of acceptance; rather, it symbolizes the immanence of the anticipated divine kingdom and foreshadows the Lord's Supper, where those with inner righteousness feast on the divine presence embodied in Christ himself. I suggest that the author of this Gospel is familiar with the Jewish understanding of the world to come as a banquet for the righteous in the presence of God and that this heavenly banquet is in fact a heavenly cult meal. Aware of this Jewish tradition, the author of Luke consciously reworks this image, positing a reversal of the Jewish eschatological image.

In Luke's version of the Last Supper, Jesus charges Peter and John to arrange for the meal and his instructions bear the aura of prophecy:

> Then came the day of Unleavened Bread, on which the Passover lamb had to be sacrificed. So Jesus sent Peter and John, saying "Go and prepare the Passover for us, that we may eat it." They said to him, "Where will you have us prepare it?'" He said to them, "Behold, when you have entered the city, a man carrying a jar of water will meet you; follow him into the house which he enters, and tell the householder, 'the Teacher says to you, where is the guest room where I am to eat the Passover with my disciples?' And he will show you a large upper room furnished; there make ready." And they went and found it as he had told them; and they prepared the passover. (Luke 22:7–13; cf. Matt 26:17–19; Mark 14:12–16; Exod 12:18–20; Deut 16:5–8)

---

ric in Luke 14 (Cambridge: Cambridge University Press, 1995), 14–21; and Hans-Josef Klauck, "Lord's Supper" (trans. David Ewert), *ABD* 4:365–66. The book of Acts records "the breaking of the bread" on several occasions and has led some scholars to believe that the Lord's Supper may have been practiced with bread only.

On the date, unity, and provenance of Luke, see Joseph Fitzmyer, *The Gospel according to Luke* (2 vols.; AB 28–28A; Garden City, N.Y.: Doubleday, 1981, 1985). Scholars concur based on literary style, special emphases, and interests that the Gospel of Luke and the book of Acts together form a two-volume work composed by a single author. Most scholars agree that Luke-Acts was written outside of Palestine, sometime between 70 and 90 C.E.

33. Arthur A. Just Jr., *The Ongoing Feast: Table Fellowship and Eschatology at Emmaus* (Collegeville, Minn.: Liturgical Press, 1993). For other works on meals in Luke, see John Navone, "The Lukan Banquet Community," *TBT* 51 (1970): 155–61; David P. Moessner, *Lord of the Banquet: The Literary and Theological Significance of the Lukan Travel Narrative* (Minneapolis: Fortress, 1989); Dennis E. Smith, "Table Fellowship as a Literary Motif in the Gospel of Luke," *JBL* 106 (1987): 613–38; Braun, *Feasting and Social Rhetoric*. On the general subject of communal meals in early Christianity, see Dennis E. Smith, *From Symposium to Eucharist: The Banquet in the Early Christian World* (Minneapolis: Fortress, 2003).

While the Synoptic parallels agree that the Last Supper occurred at the Passover meal, none of the texts describe the details of the sacrifice or the lamb that should have been the central component of the meal. Rather, the focus is shifted from the lamb to the consumption of the body of Christ in the symbols of bread and wine:

> And when the hour came, he sat at table, and the apostles with him. And he said to them, "I have earnestly desired to eat this passover with you before I suffer; for I tell you I shall not eat it until it is fulfilled in the kingdom of God."[34] And he took a cup, and when he had given thanks he said, "Take this, and divide it among yourselves; for I tell you that from now on I shall not drink of the fruit of the vine until the kingdom of God comes." And he took bread, and when he had given thanks he broke it and gave it to them, saying, "This is my body which is offered[35] for you. Do this in remembrance of me." And likewise the cup after supper, saying, "This cup which is poured out for you is the new covenant in my blood." (Luke 22:14–20; cf. Matt 26:26–29; Mark 14:22–25)

In this climactic meal, the disciples feast on the body of Christ as if it is the Passover sacrifice. This association is rather explicit. But the text indicates further that the Passover feast also prefigures the eschatological banquet that is to take place in the kingdom of God. Jesus says that he desires to eat *this* Passover with his disciples before his suffering, as he will not eat it again until he sits at the heavenly banquet (and provides nourishment there?). The body is consumed like the flesh of the sacrificial victim, and the wine is poured out as a symbol of the covenant. The latter act echoes Moses' sacrifice following the revelation on Mount Sinai. Moses pours out the sacrificial blood upon the altar and designates it as blood of the covenant.[36] Jesus' instructions to "eat in remembrance" plays on the commemorative function of the Passover seder. This sacrificial meal supersedes that eaten on the eve of the exodus from Egypt. Moreover, this meal is a foretaste of the eschatological banquet, which is also linked to Passover imagery. By eating and drinking, Jesus gives his disciples a share in the atoning power of his own death.[37]

But if the Last Supper is, as I suggest, dependent upon Jewish traditions about the eschatological banquet, where is the visionary element in the New Tes-

---

34. The proper reading of this statement is debated by New Testament scholars because of multiple manuscript variants. Some texts read "I shall never eat it again." See Burton Throckmorton Jr., ed., *Gospel Parallels: A Comparison of the Synoptic Gospels* (Nashville: Nelson, 1992), 184.

35. I have altered the RSV translation here, changing from "is given" to "is offered." Attic usage of the verb was connected to sacrifice and offerings presented to the gods (see LSJ).

36. See Jeremias, *Eucharistic Words*, 222–25. Jeremias demonstrates philologically that Jesus' references to his body and blood reflect Jesus' own understanding of himself as a sacrifice. Paul calls Jesus "our Passover lamb" in 1 Cor 5:7.

37. Ibid., 233.

tament narrative? Luke's Gospel provides an answer in the vision at Emmaus. Here Christ's visionary presence provides both nourishment and revelation. Reading this episode in connection with the Last Supper, I suggest that Christ's presence at the dinner table be construed as endowed with an important visionary component.

Many scholars view the account of the Emmaus pilgrims and the meal they share with the risen Christ as the climax of that Gospel.[38] In the Lukan narrative, two disciples are headed toward Emmaus, a town outside of Jerusalem, shortly after Jesus' tomb has been discovered empty. On their journey, they discuss the events of the past few days (presumably the crucifixion, death, and resurrection of Jesus), when "Jesus himself came and went with them" (24:15).[39] The disciples did not perceive that it was Jesus, as "their eyes were kept from recognizing him."[40] They engage in conversation, and the disciples tell of the events that took place concerning "Jesus of Nazareth," as if Jesus were a stranger who has not heard of this "prophet." Upon hearing the disciples' description of the events, Jesus, still unrecognized to their eyes, explains the significance of all that has happened, apparently in "exegetical/midrashic" fashion. The meeting then culminates in a meal:

> Then beginning with Moses and all the prophets, he interpreted to them the things about himself in all the Scriptures. As they came near the village to which they were going, he walked ahead as if he were going on. But they urged him strongly, saying, "Stay with us, because it is almost evening and the day is now nearly over." So he went in to stay with them. *When he was at the table with them, he took bread, blessed and broke it, and gave it to them. Then their eyes were opened, and they recognized him; and he vanished from their sight.* They said to each other, "Were not our hearts burning within us while he was talking to us on the road, while he was opening the scriptures to us?" That same hour they got

38. See Just, *Ongoing Feast*. Just analyzes the nature of the Emmaus meal and demonstrates that the meals of Luke-Acts and the climactic meal at Emmaus form a matrix of events that have theological significance. Jesus' table fellowship in general is a manifestation of the eschatological kingdom present among the people. A work with a similar focus is Braun, *Feasting and Social Rhetoric*. Braun argues that the dinner scene in Luke 14 represents a rhetorical unit through which Jesus presents his argument for Luke's vision of society. He contends that the intended audience is the wealthy and elite of society, who are most in need of character transformation. Braun's study is based on the evidence of Greco-Roman banquet traditions. This study is typical of the sort that focuses on the pagan contributions to Christianity to the exclusion of Jewish influences. While the Hellenistic influences are apparent, there are clearly established Jewish traditions upon which this scene draws. To the extent that the Jewish eschatological banquet resembled the upper-class dinner party of the Hellenistic world, many of Braun's conclusions resonate with those outlined here.

39. This episode is peculiar to Luke. Compare Jerome, *Vir. ill.* 2.

40. Compare the way Manoah (Judg 6) and Abraham (Gen 18) did not recognize the angels.

> up and returned to Jerusalem; and they found the eleven and their companions gathered together. They were saying, "The Lord has risen indeed, and he has appeared to Simon!" *Then they told what happened on the road and how he had been made known to them in the breaking of the bread.* (Luke 24:27–35, emphasis added)[41]

Revealing scripture to his disciples, the risen Christ communicates esoteric knowledge about the Christ, but his own identity remains concealed. The revelation is incomplete because they do not know that they are in the company of the Messiah. The incident culminates in a meal, and it is the meal and the act of sharing bread that becomes the true moment of revelation. The disciples eat bread and see the Christ. I contend that this episode is an enactment of a Jewish motif. Although there is no sacrifice and no temple, the shared meal is the locus of revelation of God's anthropomorphic presence among humanity. It is as if the cult meal and the revelatory presence of God are no longer exclusively accessible in the temple.

What follows the Emmaus story is also fascinating. In it the risen Christ eats to prove his human reality. It is as if he returns from the grave with an appetite.[42]

> While they were talking about this, Jesus himself stood among them and said to them, "Peace be with you." They were startled and terrified, and thought that they were seeing a ghost. He said to them, "Why are you frightened? And why do doubts arise in your hearts? Look at my hands and feet; see that it is I myself. Touch me and see; for a ghost does not have flesh and bones as you see that I have." And when he had said this, he showed them his hands and feet. While in their joy they were disbelieving and still wondering, he said to them, "Have you anything to eat?" They gave him a piece of broiled fish, and he took it and ate it in their presence. Then he said to them, "These are my words that I spoke to you while I was still with you—that everything written about me in the law of Moses,

---

41. Compare traditions about Elijah and Moses. Jesus' ascent in prayer up the mountain is an echo of biblical tradition about both Elijah and Moses. Elijah is a second Moses, Jesus is the third. Also compare the narrative of the transfiguration in Matt 17:1–8; Mark 9:2–8 and Luke 9:28–36. In this episode, Jesus' divine transfiguration brings him into association with both Moses and Elijah. In all three traditions, Peter initiates the building of a "dwelling" for each semi-angelic being. Such a dwelling, perhaps a locus for a ritual meal, might be said to parallel the tabernacle or the temple.

42. A parallel in Jerome is equally cryptic. In his translation of Hebrews, Jerome writes: "after the resurrection of the Savior: The Lord, having given the linen cloth to the servant of the priest, went to James and appeared to him (for James had sworn that he would not eat bread from the time when he had drunk the Lord's cup until he saw the Lord risen from the dead). And shortly afterward, the Lord said, 'Bring a table and bread!' And immediately it is added, the Lord took bread, and blessed it, and broke it, and gave it to James the Just, and said to him, 'My brother, eat your bread, for the Son of Man is raised from the dead'" (*Vir. ill.* 2).

> the prophets, and the psalms must be fulfilled." Then he opened their minds to understand the scriptures." (Luke 24:41–43)[43]

In this passage Jesus demonstrates his corporeality, not his divinity, by the fact that he can be touched, is hungry, and can eat. Again, this meal is followed by Jesus' exegesis of scripture. These eating episodes cannot be separated from the Eucharist meal. Though the symbols of the bread and wine are not explicitly identified here with the body and blood of Christ, it is impossible to separate this meal from the Passover meal that took place just a few chapters earlier. In the Last Supper narrative, Jesus vowed not to eat again until he ate in the kingdom of God. At Emmaus, the revelation of the risen Christ, the fulfillment of scripture, culminates in a meal. Christ's participation in these meals indicates that scripture has been fulfilled and that the kingdom is thus manifest in human reality. These meals, like the Passover meal, are sacrificial feasts transformed and spiritualized. The eschatological redemption longed for at the Passover is fulfilled in the consumption of Christ's body as the ultimate sacrificial mediator. Sharing meals with God's presence, manifest in the risen Christ, the disciples are finally the privileged few who "see" God and understand the esoteric, hidden level of scripture.[44]

This last meal must be contrasted with the meals that preceded it in Luke. The nourishing vision at Emmaus and the Last Supper is foreshadowed throughout the Gospel narrative by the many meals Jesus eats among the Gospel characters. In the earlier episodes, as we will see below, Jesus' identity is hidden, and the meals serve to demonstrate the ignorance of the Pharisaic Jews. In Luke 22, how-

43. See also Ignatius, *Smyrn.* 3:2: "For my own part, I know and believe that He was in actual human flesh, even after His resurrection. When He appeared to Peter and his companions, He said to them, 'Take hold of me; touch me, and see that I am no bodiless phantom.' And they touched him then and there, and believed, for they had had contact with the flesh and blood reality of him.... Moreover, he ate and drank with them after fe was risen, like any natural man, though even then fe and the Father were spiritually one."

44. The ontological change effected by Christ's death is played out in Acts 10:9–16: "The next day, as they were on their journey and coming near the city, Peter went up on the housetop to pray, about the sixth hour. And he became hungry and desired something to eat; but while they were preparing it, he fell into a trance and saw the heaven opened, and something descending, like a great sheet, led down by four corners upon the earth. In it were all kinds of animals and reptiles and birds of the air. And there came a voice to him, 'Rise Peter; kill and eat." But Peter said, 'No, Lord; for I have never eaten anything that is common or unclean.' And the voice came to him again a second time. 'What God has cleansed, you must not call common.' This happened three times, and the thing was taken up at once to heaven." Note Ignatius, *Rom.* 4, in its use of the following imagery in a prayer for martyrdom: "pray leave me to be a meal for the beasts, for it is they who can provide my way to God. I am His wheat, ground fine by the lions' teeth to be made purest bread for Christ. Better still, incite the creatures to become a sepulcher for me; let them not leave the smallest scrap of my flesh, so that I need not be a burden to anyone after I fall asleep. When there is no trace of my body left for the world to see then I shall truly be Jesus Christ's disciple."

ever, Jesus makes his identity known, associating himself with the Son of Man and with the eschatological banquet. While there is no explicit vision here, Jesus' identity as the sacrificial victim and the priest who heads the meal evokes temple imagery that, as we have seen, is associated in Luke with angelic theophany.

3.3. John 6

John's chronology of Jesus' Last Supper, death, and resurrection departs from that of the Synoptic traditions.[45] The invitation to consume the body and blood of Christ comes earlier in this Gospel narrative than in the Synoptic parallels, and it is placed alongside the feeding of the five thousand in John 6. While the opening sentences of chapter 6 mention that the Passover festival is imminent, the consumption of Christ's body is removed from the setting of the Passover seder and is instead associated with the journey of the Israelites through the wilderness, culminating in the revelation of Torah at Mount Sinai. Manna rather than the sacrifice becomes the dominant symbol in John's treatment of the Eucharist, and the meal is allegorized in a fashion quite similar to that witnessed in Philo's work. Christ is still depicted as an angelic heavenly mediator, but instead of a slaughtered paschal lamb he is associated with symbols of revelation: Moses, manna, and Torah.

Initially Jesus' words concerning the bread of life resonate precisely with Philo's spiritualization of the cult meal. Jesus urges his followers to be concerned with spiritual rather than physical nourishment: "I say to you, you seek me because you ate your fill of the loaves. Do not labor for the food which perishes, but for the food which endures to eternal life, which the Son of Man will give to you; for on him God the Father has set his seal" (John 6:26–27).[46] Jesus does not yet identify himself with this spiritual food, and his words appear almost routinely

---

45. On the dating, provenance, and literary problems associated with John, see Ernst Haenchen, *John 1: A Commentary on the Gospel of John Chapters 1–6* (ed. and trans. R. Funk; Hermeneia; Philadelphia: Fortress, 1984), 67–70; Raymond E. Brown, *The Gospel according to John* (2 vols.; AB 29–29A; Garden City, N.Y.: Doubleday, 1966–70), xxi–l; J. Louis Martyn, *History and Theology in the Fourth Gospel* (New York: Harper & Row, 1968), xv–xxi. See also George Hogarth Carnaby MacGregor, "The Eucharist in the Fourth Gospel," *NTS* 9 (1962–63): 111–19. Klauck, "Lord's Supper," 366–67 provides a detailed summary of the problems surrounding the Fourth Gospel and its relation to the Synoptic account of the Eucharist.

46. See Haenchen, *John 1*, 288–90, for a thorough discussion of the many scholarly readings of this pericope. See Metzger, *Textual Commentary*, 212–23 on v. 27. Cf. *Did.* 10: "to all men thou hast given meat and drink to enjoy, that they may give thanks to thee, but to us thou hast graciously given spiritual meat and drink, together with life eternal, through thy servant." In this prayer Christ is identified as the source and provider of spiritual food and eternal life, but he is not identified with the actual food, as such. See Huub van de Sandt, "'Do Not Give What is Holy to the Dogs' (Did 9:5D and Mat 7:6a): The Eucharistic Food of the Didache in Its Jewish Purity Setting" *VC* 56 (2002): 223–46.

homiletic. Jesus continues by comparing this nonperishable food to the manna eaten by the Israelites in the wilderness:

> Our fathers ate the manna in the wilderness; as it is written, "He gave them bread from heaven to eat." Jesus then said to them, "Truly, truly, I say to you, it was not Moses who gave you the bread from heaven; my Father gives you the true bread from heaven. For the bread of God is that which comes down from heaven, and gives life to the world." They said to him, "Lord, give us this bread always.' (John 6:28–34)

Perhaps the author of this Gospel is familiar with Jewish traditions that associate Moses himself with the manna that was eaten in the desert.[47] Jesus reminds his disciples that this life-giving bread is the exclusive gift of God the Father. Nonetheless, the disciples solicit the bread from Jesus himself, recognizing him as its source. Jesus' response then departs from traditions observed in Philo; indeed, we might view John's narrative as a deliberate enactment of the Philonic scheme. Jesus claims that he is himself the source of eternal nourishment:

> Jesus said to them, "I am the bread of life;[48] he who comes [near][49] to me shall not hunger, and he who believes in me shall never thirst. But I said to you that you have seen me and yet do not believe: All whom the Father gives me will come to me; and him who comes to me I will not cast out. For I have come down from heaven, not to do my own will, but the will of him who sent me; and this is the will of him who sent me, that I should lose nothing of all that he has given me, but raise it up at the last day. For this is the will of my Father, that every one who sees the Son and believes in him should have eternal life; and I will raise him up at the last day." (John 6:35–40)

Jesus makes the radical claim that he himself is the bread of life. In this passage, however, it is seeing Christ and believing in him as the source of eternal life that in itself brings that eternal life. It appears that consumption of the bread of life is a visionary or cognitive act. Gazing at Jesus and deriving spiritual nourishment from his presence, one is included in the kingdom of heaven. Again, this image is comprehensible against the background of the Jewish eschatological meal. Here the disciples derive eternal life by feasting on Christ's divine presence.

But as the narrative continues we see that the eschatological image does not end here, and Jesus' proclamation that he is himself the bread of eternal life is not the last of his controversial claims. Faced with the disapproval of the Jews, Jesus

---

47. See Vermes, "He Is the Bread," 139–46.

48. Brown has suggested (*Gospel according to John*, 1:274–75) that bread of life should be understood as an exegetical interpretation of Isa 55.

49. This phrase might imply a journey rather than a gathering, a fact that could have significance related to mystical ascent traditions.

becomes even more radical in his interpretation of the eschatological meal. The Jews do not understand Jesus' claim. As in the Synoptic traditions, the Jews do not recognize Jesus as the Christ, God's angelic mediator. Rather, they interpret Jesus' speech too literally and are thus confused:

> The Jews then murmured at him, because he said, "I am the bread which came down from heaven." They said, "Is this not Jesus, the son of Joseph, whose father and mother we know? How does he now say, 'I have come down from heaven'? Jesus answered them, "Do not murmur among yourselves. No one can come to me unless the Father who sent me draws him;[50] and I will raise him up at the last day. It is written in the prophets, 'And they shall all be taught by God.' Everyone who has heard and learned from the Father comes to me. Not that anyone has seen the Father except him who is from God; he has seen the father. Truly I say to you, he who believes has eternal life. I am the bread of life. Your fathers ate the manna in the wilderness, and they died. This is the bread which comes down from heaven, that a man may eat of it and not die. I am the living bread which came down from heaven; if any one eats of this bread, he will live for ever; and the bread which I shall give for the life of the world is my flesh." (John 6:41–51)

Only those who hear and learn the deeper meaning of Jesus' words are called to the Father, admitted to the eschatological banquet. The manna that the Jews ate in the wilderness (and, by analogy, the Torah that was revealed there) is superseded by the bread of life embodied in Christ. Manna, which was like but not equivalent to the food of angels, did not provide eternal life to those who ate it. By contrast, consuming the bread of Jesus' flesh will bring immortality. Christ's identity with the bread of life is not merely metaphorical; rather, his body is the actual edible substance that will bring eternal life to those who eat it.

When the Jews still do not understand, Jesus responds to their murmuring with his most radical formulation of his claim. Here the sacrificial symbolism returns as Jesus transforms the idea of the spiritual eschatological banquet, which centered around visionary or noetic consumption of God's body, back into a sacrificial meal at which the mediating body of the sacrificial victim is consumed in its flesh and blood.

> The Jews then disputed among themselves saying, "How can this man give us his flesh to eat?" So Jesus said to them, "Truly, truly I say to you, unless you eat the flesh of the Son of Man and drink his blood, you have no life in you; he who eats my flesh and drinks my blood has eternal life, and I will raise him up at the last day. For my flesh is food indeed and my blood is drink indeed. He who eats my

50. It has been suggested that this and similar assertions in the Gospel refer to a polemic against the practice of mystical ascent to heaven. See April D. DeConick, *Seek to See Him: Ascent and Vision Mysticism in the Gospel of Thomas* (VCSup 33; Leiden: Brill, 1996), 72–73.

> flesh and drinks my blood abides in me, and I in him. As the living Father sent me, and I live because of the Father, so he who eats me will live because of me. This is the bread which came down from heaven, not such as the fathers ate and died; he who eats this bread will live forever." (John 6:52–58)[51]

This passage seems to be a conflation of two traditions: Christ's identification with both the paschal lamb and the manna. Eating here is not symbolic; indeed, Jesus' body is actually edible and potable. He is the nourishing divine presence. The boundaries of the eschatological banquet as formulated by Jewish tradition are collapsed, and the presence of God is wholly consumed. This consumption effects a breach of boundaries that is akin to the incarnation: God becomes flesh, and flesh likewise becomes God, because in consuming the body and blood of Christ, one assimilates the divine attribute of immortality.[52] As such, this image represents a radical enactment of the Jewish eschatological meal. This transformation is one that moves away from the spiritualized interpretation and is perhaps even a reaction against it.

John's narrative of the Eucharist asserts a somewhat antinomian character. On the one hand, distance between humanity and the invisible Father God is repeatedly affirmed, and Christ is positioned as mediator between these two realms. The passages that describe the disciples as "coming near" to Christ, seeing him, and believing in him underscore his role as mediator, yet the implied visionary component and the mystery in which the figure of Jesus is shrouded imply a similar distance between the realms of human and divine.

However, the outright devouring of the body of Christ that is required to access eternal life is in fact a radical transgression of boundaries that effectively collapses those very boundaries. It is as if the violent destruction of the mediator obliterates the distinction between mortality and immortality: just as the boundaries were violated through the incarnation of God in the person of Jesus Christ, the consumption of that incarnated God further collapses such distinctions. It is also fascinating to note that the consumption of Christ's blood along with his flesh is in itself a departure from Jewish cultic practice, where the blood of the victim is drained and poured out on the altar and the flesh is eaten without its life blood. In the eucharistic image, the sacrificial victim is consumed with the blood, the very way in which it is offered to God and presumably consumed by God. Perhaps it is the consumption of the blood that truly symbolizes one's access to immortality.

---

51. Variants noted in Metzger, *Textual Commentary*, 214–15.

52. Klaukc, "Lord's Supper," 367.

4. Rabbinic Exegesis of Exodus 24:11

Rabbinic tradition agrees with Philo that the meal described in Exod 24 did not consist of ordinary food. *Leviticus Rabbah* is an exegetical midrashic collection redacted in the fifth century but that, like most midrashim, likely has a very long prehistory.[53] In its discussion of Exod 24:11, this text reads:

> R. Joshua said: Did provisions go up with them to Sinai, that you should be able to say: And they beheld God, and ate and drank? No, but it teaches you that they fed their eyes upon the *Shekhinah*. "And they beheld God," as a man looks upon his neighbor while in the act of eating and drinking. R. Johanan says: They derived actual nourishment; as is proved by the citation, "in the light of the king's countenance is" life (Prov 16:15). (*Lev. Rab.* 20:10)[54]

The rabbis claim, like Philo, that it was the vision of the *Shekhinah* that provided nourishment to its beholders: they fed their eyes on the brilliance of the *Shekhinah*. Rabbi Johanan's remark confirms that this vision provided "actual nourishment." A distinctive element of the rabbinic interpretation, however, and one that also resonates with passages in other Hellenistic sources, is the comparison of the vision-feast to the phenomenon of looking at a neighbor while in the act of eating and drinking. In other words, the *Shekhinah* can be understood here as a participant in the meal, sitting across the table from one who is eating and drinking, yet, paradoxically, the *Shekhinah* is also the nourishing substance that is "ingested" through the eyes.

The metaphor of feasting on the divine presence appears in numerous other contexts in rabbinic literature and often bears eschatological significance.[55] To feast on the *Shekhinah* is the privilege both of angelic beings and of the righteous in the world to come. As in Philostratus's *Epistulae*, to experience the nourishing gaze is to be fed like a divine being. It is implied that those who experience such a meal during their actual lifetimes are in fact experiencing a "taste" from the plate

53. All dates for midrashim are based on Hermann L. Strack and Günther Stemberger, *Introduction to the Talmud and Midrash* (trans. and ed. M. Bockmuehl; Minneapolis: Fortress, 1992).

54. Translation excerpted from Harry Freedman and Maurice Simon, eds., *Midrash Rabbah: Translated into English with Notes, Glossary, and Indices* (10 vols.; London: Soncino, 1961), 4:261. For a summary of textual issues and dating, see Strack and Stemberger, *Introduction to the Talmud*, 342–43. Hebrew text from Mordecai Margulies, ed., *Midrash Wayyikra Rabbah: A Critical Edition Based on Manuscripts and Geniza Fragments with Variants and Notes* (2 vols.; New York: Jewish Theological Seminary of America, 1993). Cf. *Num. Rab.* 2:25.

55. Ira Chernus, *Mysticism in Rabbinic Judaism* (Berlin: de Gruyter, 1982). For a full list of sources, see also Arnold M. Goldberg, *Untersuchungen über die Vorstellung von der Schekhinah in der früen Rabbinischen Literatur: Talmud und Midrasch* (Berlin: de Gruyter, 1969), 267–85, 527–29.

of the righteous in the messianic era, who feast like the angelic ministers of God's throne.

While the theme of the eschatological banquet is not what one might call a "major" motif in rabbinic thought, nonetheless it is one that reappears with some regularity throughout the corpus of rabbinic literature. Perhaps the most vivid picture of the eschatological meal is preserved in those traditions dealing with the Leviathan and Behemoth, the two mythic beasts engaged in primordial struggle and whose corpses are consumed by the righteous in the world to come.[56] After the resurrection, judgment, and cosmic wars have taken place, the righteous will be entertained at God's table, where God joins them in this festive meal.

Given the centrality of the slain animal within this tradition, it is likely that it has important connections to cultic sacrifice and may itself be a type of mythic transformation of that rite.[57] God is unequivocally considered a part of the meal and is described in vivid anthropomorphic terms. In one midrashic exposition of Song 1:3, God is depicted as dancing among the righteous: "R. Berekhya and R. Helbo said: 'The Holy One, blessed be He, will act as the head dancer for the righteous in the future to come.... Righteous on this side and righteous on that side and the Holy One, blessed be He in the middle.'"[58] In another formulation of the myth, after God's righteous guests have been served a meal of Behemoth and Leviathan, God "fulfills the wishes of the pious" by rising from the throne of Glory and sitting with them at the table. The narrative continues: "And each pious man will see God's Glory, and each of them will point with his finger and say, 'This is god, our God, forever and ever!' and they will eat and drink and rejoice."[59] God is not consumed at this meal but is a participant in the banquet, eating among the righteous.

The eschatological banquet in rabbinic literature, where humans feast like angels, is consistently linked to exegesis of Exod 24:11. *Genesis Rabbah*, another exegetical midrashic collection, discusses the meaning of the phrase *tohu wabohu*

56. E.g., *b. B. Bat.* 74b–75a. See Kenneth William Whitney Jr., "Two Strange Beasts: A Study of Traditions concerning Leviathan and Behemoth in Second Temple and Early Rabbinic Judaism" (Ph.D. diss., Harvard University, 1992). On later developments of meal symbolism in Jewish mysticism, see Joel Hecker, *Mystical Bodies, Mystical Meals: Eating and Embodiment in Medieval Kabbalah* (Detroit: Wayne State University Press, 2006).

57. Whitney's dissertation hints at themes throughout the work.

58. *Cant. Rab.* 1, 3:3. Translation excerpted from Freedman and Simon, *Midrash Rabbah,* 9:40. For a summary of textual issues and dating, see Strack and Stemberger, *Introduction to the Talmud,* 342–43.

59. Compare *Alphabet of Rabbi Akiba,* in Adolf Jellinek, ed., *Bet ha-Midrasch: Sammlung kleiner Midraschim und vermichster Abhandlungen aus der ältern jüdischen Literatur* (6 vols.; 1853–77; repr., Jerusalem: Bamberger & Wahrmann, 1938), 3:33–34. For a summary of textual issues surrounding this late work, see Strack and Stemberger, *Introduction to the Talmud,* 381.

in Gen 1 and offers the following midrash to explain why the earth at the time of creation was in a state of confusion:

> So did the earth sit unformed and void. The earth said, "The creatures of the upper world and those of the lower were created at the same instant. But the creatures of the upper world draw sustenance from the splendor of the presence of God (*nizonim mi-zib hashekhinah*), while as to the lower realm of creation, if the created ones do not work, they will not eat." (*Gen. Rab.* 2:2)[60]

It is indeed characteristic of the angelic beings that they are privileged to feast on the divine presence, and it is characteristic of the human condition to toil for food. Yet in the messianic age, the righteous too will enjoy a heavenly meal, as we see in in a saying attributed to Rav from *b. Ber.* 17a:

> Rav was in the habit of saying: The coming aeon is not like this aeon. In the coming aeon there is neither eating nor drinking nor procreation nor trade and commerce, nor is there jealousy or hatred or competition; rather the righteous sit with their crowns on their and feed upon the splendor of the *shekhinah*, as it is said, "And they beheld God and ate and drank" (Exod 24:11).[61]

In the world to come there is no eating or drinking in the conventional sense, but there is a heavenly banquet at which the righteous feed on the divine presence.

Yet the eschatological banquet described in these sources does not collapse the boundaries between human and divine in the way our New Testament sources do. In fact, these Jewish traditions appear very concerned with the maintenance of the divine-human boundaries that were symbolized concretely in the structure of the Jerusalem temple.

This preoccupation with boundaries is illustrated in the way that midrashic exposition of Exod 24:9–11 is linked to the fates of Nadab and Abihu, the two sons of Aaron, who die sometime after the Sinai theophany, as punishment for having *offered sacrifices* at an improper time. In Lev 10, the text indicates that they offered "strange fire" that God had not commanded. Yet the midrash in several of its versions attributes the death of Nadab and Abihu to their inappropriate behavior at the meal atop Mount Sinai with Moses, Aaron, and the seventy elders. The *Leviticus Rabbah* version reads, with reference to Nadab and Abihu:

---

60. Text from Hanokh Albeck, ed., *Midrash Bereshit Rabbah: Critical Edition with Notes and Commentary* (2nd ed.; 3 vols.; Jerusalem: Wehrman, 1965). Translation from Freedman and Simon, *Midrash Rabbah*, 1:15.

61. On the issue of reading *lehanot* as a feeding metaphor, see Goldberg, *Untersuchungen über die Vorstellung*, 286; and Chernus, *Mysticism in Rabbinic Judaism*, 79 n. 34. The strongest argument for this reading is the midrash itself, which associates the verb with the eating and drinking of the Exodus episode.

> Rabbi Tanhuma said, the text teaches us that they uncovered their heads, became presumptuous and fed their eyes on the *Shekhinah*. R. Joshua of Siknin in the name of R. Levi observed: Moses did not feed his eyes on the *Shekhinah* and derived benefit from the *Shekhinah*. Moses did not feed his eyes on the *Shekhinah*, as it says, "And Moses hid his face" (Exod 3:6)... and he derived benefit from the *Shekhinah*, as it says, "Moses knew not that the skin of his face sent forth beams." (Exod 24:29) ... Nadab and Abihu, however, fed their eyes on the *Shekhinah* and did not derive benefit therefrom, as may be inferred from the following: "And Nadab and Abihu died before the Lord" (Num 3:4). (*Num. Rab.* 20:10 Vilna)[62]

What is the difference is between the behavior of Nadab and Abihu, on the one hand, and Moses, on the other? Moses looked away and thus received nourishment. Nadab and Abihu, by contrast, acted inappropriately. Their feeding on the *Shekhinah* is symbolized as a type of sinful gluttony. In another version of this tradition from *Numbers Rabbah,* the phrase "they uncovered their heads" instead reads "they stood upon their feet." In both cases the text offers these gestures as a sign of arrogant behavior, of overstepping the appropriate boundaries of the feast.

The heavenly meal in its rabbinic context is thus not an utter devouring of God by the adept but rather is one that entails limits and prescriptions for propriety. That the midrash associates the inappropriate offerings of Nadab and Abihu described in the biblical text with the improper viewing of God's anthropomorphic form presents further evidence supporting a connection between the sacrificial meal and the metaphor of the nourishing vision.

Reading this mythic tradition alongside the early Christian sources, we can see the way in which heavenly meal imagery functions to articulate powerful statements about the divine-human relationship. Philo uses cultic meal imagery to affirm the legitimacy of a pious life apart from the Jerusalem temple; in New Testament sources meal symbolism is used to assert a collapsing of the boundaries that formerly structured humanity's relationship to the divine; and in rabbinic sources, the eschatological meal provides a model of the divine-human encounter that necessitates the maintenance of the very boundaries that are challenged in the emergent Christian tradition.

---

62. For parallels, see *Exod. Rab.* 45; *Num. Rab.* 2:25. Note the subtle distinction between the use of active and passive verb forms in this text. The arrogant behavior of Aaron's sons is described in the active sense, while a passive form describes Moses' way of deriving benefit from the divine presence. Again, it is worthwhile to note the attribution of this text to the late Tanhuma midrashim. This later layer of tradition focuses in on the difference between the behaviors of Moses, on the one hand, and the sons of Aaron, on the other. Perhaps it is this later tradition that notes the subtle distinction between the active and passive forms of the verb *zun* and the passive behavior of Moses.

Baptismal Praxis and Mystical Experience in the Book of Revelation

Charles A. Gieschen

> There shall no more be anything accursed, but the throne of God and of the Lamb shall be in it, and his servants shall worship him; they shall see his face, and his name shall be on their foreheads. (Rev 22:4)

One of the reasons that interpreters sometimes overlook evidence of baptismal praxis in the book of Revelation is because two important actions in early baptismal rites are not connected with depictions of similar actions in this apocalypse.[1] These two actions are the marking of the Divine Name on the baptismal initiate and the placing of a white garment on the newly baptized. Did mention of marking and giving of names as well as the wearing of white garments in the book of Revelation become the source of this baptismal praxis in the early church, or do these depictions reflect already existing first-century baptismal praxis?

There are two compelling reasons to see these depictions as reflecting already-existing baptismal rites. First, these practices are not completely new rituals but an adaptation of the priestly ordination rites of ancient Israel. Second, the visions of this apocalypse communicate to early Christians more readily if the imagery used is grounded in the actual experience of the hearers.

---

1. Robert H. Mounce (*The Book of Revelation* [rev. ed.; NICNT; Grand Rapids: Eerdmans, 1998], 157), for example, denies any connection between the sealing in Rev 7 and baptism. In spite of G. K. Beale's (*The Book of Revelation* [NIGTC; Grand Rapids: Eerdmans, 1999], 409–16, esp. 409 n. 105) excellent discussion of the seal, he only briefly notes that Jewish Christians connected the seal with baptism. Scholars who see an allusion to baptism in Rev 7 or even a reflection of baptismal praxis include Pierre Prigent, *Commentary on the Apocalypse of St. John* (Tübingen: Mohr Siebeck, 2001), 283–84; Massey H. Shepherd Jr., *The Paschal Liturgy and the Apocalypse* (Richmond: John Knox, 1960), esp. 85–91; Jean Daniélou, *The Theology of Jewish Christianity* (Philadelphia: Westminster, 1964); Joseph Ysebaert, *Greek Baptismal Terminology: Its Origins and Early Development* (Nijmegan: Dekker & Van de Vegt, 1962), 285–88; and Margaret Barker, *The Revelation of Jesus Christ* (Edinburgh: T&T Clark, 2000), 159–63.

Revelation 7:1–8 depicts a scene in which the elect of God are "sealed" before destructive activities are carried out. It is evident from other texts in Revelation that this seal represents the sacred four-letter Divine Name of the Hebrew Bible: יהוה (hereafter YHWH).[2] This study will demonstrate that Revelation evinces early Christian baptismal praxis wherein the initiate received a mark that was the bestowal of the Divine Name as a seal. Furthermore, it will be argued from the text of Revelation that this reception of the Divine Name, washing, and clothing in a white garment was understood to be the foundational priestly preparation for early Christian mystical experience of the presence of God, especially in the Eucharist.

1. The Seal with the Divine Name

Revelation shows a great interest in the marking or receiving of a name or names. Three key texts in Revelation speak about this:

> He who conquers, I [Christ] will make him a pillar in the temple of my God; never shall he go out of it, and I will write on him the name of my God, and the name of the city of my God, the new Jerusalem which comes down from my God out of heaven, and my own new name. (Rev 3:12)

> Then I [John] looked, and lo, on Mount Zion stood the Lamb, and with him a hundred and forty-four thousand who had his name and his Father's name written on their foreheads. (Rev 14:1)

> There shall no more be anything accursed, but the throne of God and of the Lamb shall be in it, and his servants shall worship him; they shall see his face, and his name shall be on their foreheads. (Rev 22:4)

Two foundational questions arise from these texts: How many names do the followers of the Lamb receive, and what is each name? Revelation 3:12 speaks of writing the name of God, the name of the new Jerusalem, and the new name of Christ on those who are faithful. Revelation 14:1 states that the elect had the name of the Lamb and the Father's name written on their foreheads. Revelation 22:4 testifies that the servants of God will have the name of God on their foreheads. The fact that these texts exist alongside each other in the same document supports the conclusion that they each are speaking of a singular name that is shared by God,

2. This is argued below as well as in Charles A. Gieschen, *Angelomorphic Christology: Antecedents and Early Evidence* (AGJU 42; Leiden: Brill, 1998), 252–56; and idem, "The Divine Name in Ante-Nicene Christology," *VC* 57 (2003): 115–58. For a thorough discussion of the Divine Name in Second Temple Judaism and early Christianity, see Sean M. McDonough, *YHWH at Patmos: Rev. 1:4 in Its Hellenistic and Early Jewish Setting* (WUNT 2.107; Tübingen: Mohr Siebeck, 1999), 59–194. For a discussion of sealing as baptism, see Geoffrey W. H. Lampe, *The Seal of the Spirit: A Study in the Doctrine of Baptism and Confirmation in the New Testament and the Fathers* (London: SPCK, 1967), esp. 284–96.

the Lamb (the Son/Jesus), and the new Jerusalem (the bride/church as the visible manifestation of the Holy Spirit).[3] What, then, is this singular name?

The place to start in solving this puzzle is Rev 19:12–13, a text that gives insight into the mysterious or hidden name of the Son:

> His eyes are like blazing fire, and on his head are many crowns. He has a name written on him that no one knows, but he himself. He is dressed in a robe dipped in blood, and his name is the Word of God.

There is solid evidence to support the conclusion that the unknown or hidden name of Jesus is YHWH, the personal name of God in the Hebrew Bible.[4] Furthermore, this conclusion is supported by the fact that the name by which Christ is known according to this text is "the Word of God" (19:13). The identification of Christ as the Word is founded upon the identification of Christ with the Angel of YHWH who is present in several theophanies in the Pentateuch, Joshua, and Judges. Exodus 23:20–22 states that this angel has the Divine Name "in him":

> Behold, I [YHWH] send an angel in front of you, to guard you on the way and to bring you to the place that I have prepared. Be attentive to him and listen to his voice; do not rebel against him, for he will not pardon your transgression; for my Name is in him. (Exod 23:20–21)

Since this "angel" has the name YHWH in him, he is not from among the myriads of created angels; he is YHWH in a visible form.[5]

It is not surprising that Israelites and Jews, long before and during the first century C.E., referred to this "angel" who possessed the most important word of the world as "the Word of YHWH," "the Word of God," or simply "the Word."[6] Note the following varied texts that evince this phenomenon:

> After these things the Word of YHWH came to Abram in a vision, "Fear not, Abram, I am your shield; your reward shall be very great." But Abram said, "O Lord God, what will you give me, for I continue childless, and the heir of my house is Eliezer of Damascus?" And Abram said, "Behold, you have given me no offspring; and a slave born in my house will be my heir." And behold, the Word

3. The understanding that the new Jerusalem is a personal reality in Revelation is evident in the identification of this "city" also as "the bride" of the Lamb (19:7–8; 21:2). The church as the Holy Spirit in the visible form of a woman is also an aspect of the pneumatology of the Shepherd of Hermas; see esp. *Vis.* 4.2.1.

4. See Gieschen, *Angelomorphic Christology*, 253.

5. See esp. Jarl E. Fossum, *The Name of God and the Angel of the Lord: Samaritan and Jewish Concepts of Intermediation and the Origins of Gnosticism* (WUNT 36; Tübingen: Mohr Siebeck, 1985); see also Gieschen, *Angelomorphic Christology*, 51–69.

6. Exod 23:20–21 is a text used frequently by Philo in his discussion of the Word. For further evidence, see Gieschen, *Angelomorphic Christology*, 103–13.

of YHWH came to him, "This man shall not be your heir; your own son shall be your heir." (Gen 15:1–3)

For while gentle silence enveloped all things, and night in its swift course was now half gone, your all-powerful Word leaped from heaven, from the royal throne, into the midst of the land that was doomed, a stern warrior carrying the sharp sword of your authentic command, and stood and filled all things with death, and touched heaven while standing on earth. (Wis 18:14–16)

"Stay, Moses, best of men, do not come near until you have loosed the bindings from your feet; the place on which you stand is holy ground, and from this bush the Divine Word shines forth to you." (Ezekiel the Tragedian, *Exag.* 96–99)

But if there be any as yet unfit to be called a son of God, let him press to take his place under God's Firstborn, the Word, who holds eldership among the angels, an archangel as it were. And many names are his for he is called: the Beginning, the Name of God, His Word, the Man after His Image, and "He that sees," namely Israel. (Philo, *Conf.* 146)

This identification of the hidden name of Christ as YHWH may appear to go against the clear testimony of Rev 19:12: "He has a name written on him that no one but he himself knows." This assertion, however, does not imply that the name that "no one but he himself knows" cannot be revealed. Revelation 19:12 is evidence that an important aspect of early Christian teaching, probably prebaptismal instruction, was the revelation of the true name of Christ, as can be seen already in the foundational Christian creed: "Jesus is Lord" (Phil 2:11).[7] Such revelation of Jesus' hidden name as the Divine Name is also visible in the prayer at the close of the farewell discourse in the Gospel of John:

Holy Father, protect them in your Name that you have given me, so that they may be one, as we are one. While I was with them, I protected them in your Name that you have given me.... I made your Name known to them and will continue to make it known. (John 17:11b, 26)

The understanding that the Son and the Holy Spirit share the Divine Name is also evident in the baptismal formula in Matt 28:19: individuals are to be baptized in the (singular Divine) Name shared by the Father, Son, and Holy Spirit.[8] The revelation of Jesus' hidden name is also a significant topic in some gnostic texts.[9]

---

7. The relationship between the Divine *Name* and the *title* κύριος has been widely recognized but sometimes challenged; see Gieschen, "Divine Name in Ante-Nicene Christology," 116–18.

8. Ibid., 143–46.

9. E.g., *Gos. Truth* 38:7–40:29; *Gos. Phil.* 54:5–8; see further Gieschen, "Divine Name in Ante-Nicene Christology," 153–56.

Therefore, the three references in Revelation to the Name on the forehead speak about the Divine Name and appear to be linked to baptism. Although 3:12 speaks about the writing of the Name as a future reality ("He who conquers . . . I will write on him the Name of my God"), both 14:1 and 22:4 imply that the Name was written on the people of God before the eschatological events and certainly before these people entered the New Jerusalem. This Name gave them identity and protection during earthly tribulations as well as assured them of their heavenly inheritance. Note the relationship between the Name and being faithful to Christ in two texts from the seven letters to the churches: "I know you have fortitude even to endure on account of my Name" (Rev 2:3); "I know that you have but little power, and yet you have kept my word and have not denied my Name" (3:8). This language and imagery is grounded in the fact that the Divine Name is written, spoken, and imparted in baptism.

The primary text that supports connecting this language of the writing of the Name on the forehead with baptism is the vision of the sealing of the elect:

> Then I saw another angel ascend from the rising of the sun, with the seal (σφραγῖδα) of the living God, and he called with a loud voice to the four angels who had been given power to harm earth and sea, saying, "Do not harm the earth or the sea or the trees, till we have sealed (σφραγίσωμεν) the servants of our God upon their foreheads." (Rev 7:2–3)

The historical background of this sealing imagery in Revelation is Ezek 9, where the prophet sees "the Glory," who is the visible YHWH, command a man in white linen and his six associates to mark the faithful of Jerusalem and then carry out a Passover-style purge of all the unfaithful who do not bear YHWH's mark.[10]

> And the LORD said to him, "Go through the city, through Jerusalem, and put a mark upon the foreheads of the men who sigh and groan over the abominations that are committed in it." And to the others he said in my hearing, "Pass through the city after him, and kill; your eye shall not spare, and you shall show no pity; slay old men outright, young men and maidens, little children and women, but touch no one upon whom is the mark." (Ezek 9:4–6)

The Hebrew word translated "mark" here is *taw*, which also signifies the specific mark made for the last letter of the Hebrew alphabet. Therefore, the mark to be placed upon the faithful remnant is probably the Hebrew letter *taw*. It was placed upon the forehead for visibility. As the last letter of the Hebrew alphabet, it functioned as a mark of YHWH's ownership because it was considered shorthand for his Name, much like the Greek letter *omega* does in early Christian symbol-

10. This relationship with Ezek 9 is acknowledged by most commentators; see, e.g., Beale, *Revelation*, 409–10.

ism, including Revelation, where both God and Christ are known as the Alpha and Omega (Rev 1:8; 22:13). Like the blood on the Israelite doorposts during the night of the tenth plague, this mark was a protecting sign or seal that shielded its bearer from the purge of the unrighteous that YHWH ordered in the vision of Ezek 9. Furthermore, it is not insignificant that in ancient Hebrew script and even in the first century C.E. a Hebrew *taw* looked like two equal lines crossed, either erect like + or at an angle like X.[11]

This imagery from Ezek 9 is the pattern used in both depicting and recording the vision of the sealing of the righteous in Rev 7. The "angel" who ascends "from the rising of the sun, with the seal of the living God" in 7:2, therefore, appears to be a depiction of the angelomorphic Glory, since the Glory was to return from the East (Ezek 43:1–2), and he bears the seal, which is the Divine Name (Exod 23:21; cf. 28:36).[12] The identification of the Son of Man/Glory as the risen Christ in Rev 1 makes a christological identification of this angel possible. This sealing in Revelation does not necessarily imply that the name was actually written on the initiate but was probably sealed with a mark, possibly a Hebrew *taw*, that represented the Divine Name.[13] This is also apparent from the contrasting *mark* of the Beast, which represents nothing other than the *name* of the Beast: "so that no one can buy or sell unless he has the mark, that is, the name of the beast or the number of its name" (Rev 13:17).

Some have argued against understanding the sealing in Rev 7 as baptism, since it is depicting this group as already Christians who then are sealed before the eschatological tribulations.[14] It must be remembered, however, that John is given a vision that encompasses a lengthy period of time. There had already been a few generations of Christians who had been reborn in baptism, had experienced the chaos of this world as described in John's visions, and then had died in the faith. John is not given multiple individual visions of these Christians but one encompassing vision that depicts the sealing of the church of various generations

---

11. For a discussion of this mark and its transformation into the sign of the cross, see Jack Finegan, *The Archaeology of the New Testament: The Life of Jesus and the Beginning of the Early Church* (Princeton: Princeton University Press, 1978), 220–60.

12. See Robert H. Gundry, "Angelomorphic Christology in Revelation," in *Society of Biblical Literature 1994 Seminar Papers* (SBLSP 33; Atlanta: Scholars Press, 1994), 662–78; and Barker, *Revelation of Jesus Christ*, 159–63; see also John 6:27.

13. Daniélou, *Theology of Jewish Christianity*, 329–31. Daniélou (*The Bible and the Liturgy* [Notre Dame: University of Notre Dame Press, 1956], 54–69) details evidence of the sign of the cross as the *sphragis* (seal) in the early church fathers.

14. For example, Ysebaert (*Greek Baptismal Terminology*, 28) argues that this scene depicts the bestowal of the "eschatological seal" that is a development of the first-century "baptismal seal." Revelation is not developing a new "eschatological seal" but is depicting the eschatological significance of the seal Christians receive in baptism. For other important New Testament evidence, see 2 Cor 1:22 and Eph 1:13; 4:30.

with the Divine Name in baptism. In other words, it is precisely in the individual baptismal sealings throughout history that this eschatological sealing dramatized in Rev 7 is taking place.

Another Christian apocalypse, the second-century *Shepherd of Hermas*, provides abundant support for this understanding of sealing with the Divine Name in baptism. Notice what the following text says about the building of the church:

> Hear, then why the tower has been built upon the water: because your life was saved and shall be saved through water, and the tower has been founded by the utterance of the almighty and glorious Name, and is maintained by the unseen power of the Master. (*Herm. Vis.* 3.3.5)

This text is vivid testimony that the church, which is the tower, is built by baptism, which is depicted as water and the utterance of the Divine Name. *Hermas*, furthermore, speaks specifically of baptism with water and the Name as the seal:

> "So these also who had fallen asleep received the seal of the Son of God and entered into the kingdom of God. For before," said he, "a man bears the Name of the Son of God, he is dead. But when he receives the seal he puts away mortality and receives life. The seal, then, is the water." (*Herm. Sim.* 9.16.3–4)

There are also several hymns in the Jewish-Christian *Odes of Solomon*, dated between the late first to the third century, which understand the sealing as the marking of the Divine Name with oil in baptism. Although it cannot be determined that the author of *Odes* actually knew the book of Revelation, the eighth ode could function as a fine commentary on the scene in Rev 7:

> And before they existed, I [Christ] recognized them and imprinted a seal on their faces.... And my righteousness goes before them; and they will not be deprived of my Name; for it is with them. Seek and increase, and abide in the love of the Lord. You who are loved in the Beloved, you who are kept in him who lives, you who are saved in him who was saved, you shall be found uncorrupted in all ages, on account of the Name of your Father. Hallelujah. (*Odes Sol.* 8.13, 19–22)

Although Ezek 9 with its roots in the Passover is the primary text shedding light on the vision depicted in Rev 7, some of the background for the significance of the Divine Name as a protecting agent has its origin in the high-priest traditions of ancient Israel. The high priest, who entered the holy of holies on Yom Kippur, bore the Divine Name on his turban (Exod 28:36–38). This Name was understood as an important element of what protected the high priest as he came into the presence of YHWH. The protection of the priestly garb, including the Divine Name, from the punishing presence of YHWH is especially vivid in Wisdom of Solomon's description of Aaron's intervention on behalf of Israel (cf. Num 16:41–50):

> He conquered the wrath not by strength of body, and not by force of arms, but by his word he subdued the Punisher, appealing to the oaths and covenants given to our fathers. For when the dead had already fallen on one another in heaps, he intervened and held back the wrath, and cut off its way to the living. For upon his long robe the whole world was depicted, and the glories of the fathers were engraved on the four rows of stones, and thy majesty [i.e., the Divine Name] on the diadem upon his head. To these the Destroyer yielded, these he feared; for merely to test the wrath was enough. (Wis 18:22–25)

The priests of Israel were also anointed with oil as part of their ordination rite (Exod 29:7). A relationship between priestly rites and early baptismal practices involving the baptismal formula is explicitly expressed in some second- and third-century texts concerning baptismal praxis:

> After this pouring the consecrated oil and laying of his hand on the head, he shall say: "I anoint thee will holy oil in God the Father Almighty and Christ Jesus and the Holy Ghost." And sealing him on the forehead, he shall give him the kiss of peace.[15] (Hippolytus, *Trad. ap.* 22.2–3)

> Then having come up from the font we are thoroughly anointed with a blessed unction, in accordance with the ancient discipline whereby, since the time when Aaron was anointed by Moses, men were anointed unto the priesthood with oil from a horn.[16] (Tertullian, *Bapt.* 7)

> But where there is a woman, and especially a deaconess, it is not fitting that women should be seen by men, but with the imposition of the hand do thou anoint the head only. As of old the priests and kings were anointed in Israel, do thou in like manner, with the imposition of the hand, anoint the head of those who receive baptism, whether of men or women.[17] (*Did. apost.* 16)

In summary, these texts support the understanding that the texts from Revelation that speak of sealing or writing the Name on the forehead are depicting the baptismal rite and the resultant baptismal reality. Jean Daniélou has even argued that early Jewish Christians placed the *taw* upon the forehead of the baptismal initiate with oil as the seal of the Divine Name spoken when the water was poured.[18] It was the sign of ownership, protection, and enlistment into the church. Christians then bore the Name, had the power of the Name, called upon the Name, and willingly suffered on account of the Name.

---

15. Translation from Edward C. Whitaker, *Documents of the Baptismal Liturgy* (London: SPCK, 1960), 6.

16. Ibid., 8.

17. Ibid., 10.

18. Daniélou *Theology of Jewish Christianity*, 329–31; also idem, *Primitive Christian Symbols* (trans. D. Attwater; Baltimore: Helicon, 1964), 136–45; Lampe, *Seal of the Spirit*, 284–96.

The Divine Name was also a significant element in later Jewish mystical experience of the Divine Presence.[19] Neither was this seal a mere symbolic abstraction for many early Christians; the outer mark was a tangible reminder that Christ, the incarnation of YHWH, tabernacles in the Christian even as the Name dwelt in the tabernacle and temple of ancient Israel. This understanding of the Name as the personal reality of Christ dwelling in the believer is evident in the postcommunion prayer found in the *Didache:* "We give you thanks, Holy Father, for your holy Name, whom you have caused to dwell in our hearts" (10.1). Therefore, the focus on the marking with the Divine Name in Revelation probably is reflecting extant first-century baptismal praxis.

2. The Wearing of White Garments

In addition to this focus on the Divine Name, a second aspect of Revelation's testimony to early baptismal praxis is evident in the repeated imagery of white "garments" (3:4–5, 18; 4:4; 16:15; 19:13, 16) or "robes" (6:11; 7:9, 13–14; 22:14). Because of the frequency of depictions of saints and angels in heaven clothed in white, it could be argued that the white clothing is simply a symbol of glorification. Revelation, however, appears to make a distinction between the white "garments" (ἱμάτια) worn by the followers of the Lamb on earth and the white "robes" (στολαί) worn by the saints in heaven.[20] Several texts testify that the white garment is already a possession of followers of Jesus on earth, long before their glorification in heaven:

> Yet you still have a few names in Sardis, people who have not soiled their garments; and they shall walk with me in white, for they are worthy. He who conquers shall be clad thus in white garments, and I will not blot his name out of the book of life. (Rev 3:4–5)
>
> Therefore, I counsel you to buy from me … white garments to clothe you and to keep the shame of your nakedness from being seen. (Rev 3:18)
>
> Lo, I am coming like a thief! Blessed is he who is awake, keeping his garments that he may not go naked and be seen exposed! (Rev 16:15)

There is clear testimony from the third century forward that the baptismal initiate was stripped naked, washed, and then clothed in a white garment.[21]

---

19. Rachel Elior, "From Earthly Temple to Heavenly Shrines: Prayer and Sacred Song in the Hekhalot Literature and Its Relation to Temple Traditions," *JSQ* 4 (1997): 217–67.

20. It also appears that the vesting with "robes" happens at the parousia, since the elders of heaven in 4:4 are wearing white "garments" (not "robes").

21. See Thomas M. Finn, *Early Christian Baptism and the Catechumenate* (Collegeville, Minn.: Glazier, 1992), 7–21.

Anointing with oil was also part of the baptismal rite in some locales. These two texts from very significant church fathers are representative evidence of this baptismal praxis:

> After Baptism, you have received white garments, that they may be a sign that you have taken off the clothing of sin and that you have been clad in the pure garments of innocence.[22] (Ambrose, *Myst.* 34)

> Now that you have taken off your old garments and been clad in white garments, you must also in spirit remain clothed in white. I do not mean to say that you must always wear white garments, but that you must always be covered with those that are truly white and shining, so that you may say with the prophet Isaiah: "He has clothed me with the garment of salvation, and he has covered me with the vestment of joy."[23] (Cyril of Jerusalem, *Mystagogic Catheches*)

It has been already demonstrated that early baptismal practice of anointing is rooted in the priestly ordination rites of ancient Israel. It is very probable that the clothing with white also has its roots in priestly clothing.[24] According to Exod 29, YHWH commanded Moses that Aaron and his sons be washed with water, anointed, and clothed at the door to the tent of meeting:

> You shall bring Aaron and his sons to the door of the tent of meeting, and wash them with water. And you shall take the paraments, and put on Aaron the coat and the robe of the ephod, and the ephod; and the breastpiece, and gird him with the skillfully woven band of the ephod; and you shall set the turban on his head, and put the holy crown upon the turban. And you shall take the anointing oil, and pour it on his head and anoint him. Then you shall bring his sons, and put coats on them, and you shall gird them with girdles and bind caps on them; and the priesthood shall be theirs by a perpetual statute. Thus you shall ordain Aaron and his sons. (Exod 29:4–9)

These ordination rites clearly informed early Christian baptismal practice and theology.[25] The many divine theophanies of the Hebrew Bible, as well as the careful priestly rituals, all testify concerning the difficulties involved with sinners coming into the presence of a holy God. Like the faithful of ancient Israel, Jewish

22. Danielou, *Bible and the Liturgy*, 49.

23. Ibid.

24. White linen appears to be a central aspect of the garb of every priest (Exod 28:42). This is reflected in Revelation, where the priestly elders of the heavenly throne room are clad in white (Rev 4:4; cf. 1 Chr 24:3–19; 26:17–19).

25. Margaret Barker (*On Earth as It Is in Heaven* [Edinburgh: T&T Clark, 1995], 71) identifies the Name and clothing on the elect in Revelation with the Divine Name and clothing of the high priest.

Christians had a healthy understanding and respect for the holiness of God. Baptism in Revelation, therefore, can be understood as the salvific event that purifies sinners to be "a kingdom and priests to our God who reign on earth" (Rev 5:10). This evidence supports the conclusion that later baptismal praxis in the church is not rooted primarily in the visions of Revelation but is a continuation of extant baptismal praxis that is reflected in Revelation and was influenced by the ancient ordination practices of the Israelite priesthood. The priestly nature of baptism in cleansing and clothing individuals to enter and serve in God's Presence is also visible in this text from the Epistle to the Hebrews:

> Therefore, brethren, since we have confidence to enter the [heavenly] sanctuary by the blood of Jesus, by the new and living way that he opened for us through the curtain, that is, through his flesh, and since we have a great high priest over the house of God, let us draw near with a true heart in full assurance of faith, with our hearts sprinkled clear from an evil conscience and our bodies washed with pure water. (Heb 10:19–22)

This priesthood of the baptized, according to Revelation, is lived out in mystically gathering around the heavenly throne to sing the unceasing liturgy with the angels and saints, then going into the chaotic world to be a faithful and uncompromising witness like Jesus, "the faithful witness" (Rev 1:5; 3:14; 17:6).

In addition to this priestly background, the white-garment imagery in Revelation also reflects how baptism was understood as a wedding ceremony in which a person is cleansed, clothed as a bride, and joined with the Bridegroom, Jesus Christ. The church as Christ's bride is the prominent image of the closing chapters of Revelation (19:7–9; 21:2, 9). Although 19:8 states that the fine linen of the Bride is "the righteous deeds of the saints," this should not be viewed as distinct and disparate from the understanding of the white garments elsewhere as baptismal. This, rather, reinforces one of the themes of Revelation that the baptized saints indeed bear the fruit of their life in Christ. The white garment of baptism, therefore, shows forth the individual foretaste of the corporate experience of the eschatological wedding between Christ and the church. A similar understanding of baptism is the foundation for Paul's discussion of marriage in Ephesians:

> Husbands, love your wives as Christ loved the church and gave himself for her, in order that he sanctify her, having cleansed her by the washing of water with the Word [i.e., the Divine Name], that he present the church to himself in splendor, without spot or wrinkle or any such thing, that she be holy and without blemish. (Eph 5:25–27)

Therefore, the white-garment imagery of Revelation probably reflects both baptismal praxis and theology. The white garment depicts the purity from sin and the priestly vocation that individuals receive in holy baptism. It is a reminder that this baptismal purity allows individuals to experience the presence of God in the present and is the basis for their future service before the throne in eternity.[26]

3. The Mystical Experience of the Divine Presence

What, finally, is the relationship between this baptismal praxis in Revelation and mystical experience of the Divine Presence? If one accepts the relationship between baptism and priestly ordination rites proposed above, then the marking with the Divine Name, washing, and clothing of baptism prepares for the experience of the Divine Presence. Revelation gives significant focus to the experience of the Divine Presence in John's mystical ascent through the "open door" of heaven (4:1), especially his experience of the heavenly throne room in Rev 4–5. Was John, however, the only individual on earth whom Revelation expects mystically to experience the Divine Presence?

Some scholars have drawn attention to how the reading of Revelation allows the hearers to have an experience that parallels John's.[27] There is validity for this assertion in terms of experiencing all the scenes of Revelation. The experience of the Divine Presence, however, does not appear to result solely from the reading of Revelation. It is not insignificant that John had this experience on "the Lord's Day" (1:10), the typical day for Christians to gather for worship that included the Eucharist.[28] The understanding that other faithful Christians could pass through the "open door" of heaven in the context of Lord's Day worship appears to be the basis for these two invitations of Christ in the seven letters: (1) "Behold, I set before you an open door which no one is able to shut" (Rev 3:8); (2) "Behold, I stand at the door and knock; if any one hears my voice and opens the door, I will come in to him and eat with him and he with me (3:20).

A common metaphorical interpretation of the second text emphasizes that Jesus is standing at the door of hearts and calling people to repentance; people must only open their hearts to him so that he can enter.[29] Such an interpretation

26. It is noteworthy that purification is accomplished in baptism as preparation for the experience of the Divine Presence. Some Jewish mystical ascent traditions emphasize the transformation happening as part of the ascent experience; see Christoper Morray-Jones, "Transformational Mysticism in the Apocalyptic-Merkavah Tradition," *JJS* 48 (1992): 1–31.

27. David Aune ("The Apocalypse of John and the Problem of Genre," *Semeia* 36 [1986]: 65–96) speaks of "actualizing" the experience of the vision. Leonard Thompson (*The Book of Revelation: Apocalypse and Empire* [New York: Oxford University Press, 1990], 53–73) emphasizes that the use of this book in worship enabled the congregation to experience eschatological deliverance in the here and now.

28. Richard Bauckham, "The Lord's Day," in *From Sabbath to Lord's Day* (ed. D. A. Carson; Grand Rapids: Zondervan, 1982), 197–220.

29. For example, Richard C. H. Lenski, *The Interpretation of St. John's Revelation* (Columbus: Lutheran Book Concern, 1935), 164.

ignores the context and also the meal imagery. If this text is interpreted in its immediate context, however, there is a door and a voice described only two verses later: the door to heaven and the voice of the Spirit who beckons John to come into the Divine Presence. This text, moreover, echoes Song 5:2 ("the voice of my beloved, he knocks at the door: Open to me, my beloved"), a document that had significant use in Jewish mystical tradition. Given the context and meal imagery, there are grounds for understanding both of these "door" texts as allusions to the experience of the Divine Presence in the context of the Eucharist. In the Eucharist, participants are invited to have a mystical experience of the Divine Presence: the door to heaven is open as Christ, the Paschal Lamb, comes to eat with them by giving them his own flesh and blood for a blessed feast.[30] The Lamb Christology of this apocalypse is congruent with the way early Christians experienced Christ in the eucharistic worship. The hymns found in Rev 4–5, especially the use of the song of the seraphim from Isa 6, would have helped hearers of this apocalypse "see" the relationship between John's Lord's Day experience of the Divine Presence and their own experience of the Divine Presence in the Eucharist each Lord's Day.[31]

Therefore, Rev 4–5 and the other scenes of worship that follow can be understood as visual depictions of the hidden-to-the-naked-eye heavenly worship that early Christians participated in each Lord's Day as the church on earth. These chapters are not only depicting a past or future reality; they are showing forth a present reality for John and the congregations of his day. As such, they served as a vivid commentary on what was happening in eucharistic worship where the Paschal Lamb who shed his blood and gave his body is present sharing his victory through this meal. It is no coincidence that Christ as the having-been-slaughtered-and-now-standing Lamb is the focus of worship in heaven according to Revelation, not Christ as the glorified "one like a Son of Man" who is seen in other scenes of this apocalypse. A congregation who listens to this apocalypse from start to finish is reminded that heaven is an accessible and present reality that the baptized enter and mystically experience in worship, especially in the celebration of the Eucharist.

This access of the baptized who dwell on earth to the heavenly sanctuary is also discussed in Heb 10:19–22, as quoted above. The author later goes on to discuss the mystical experience within this heavenly sanctuary:

> But you have come to Mount Zion and to the city of the living God, the heavenly Jerusalem, and to innumerable angels in festal gathering, and to the assembly of the Firstborn who are enrolled in heaven, and to a judge who is God of all,

30. For interpreting the Lamb imagery primarily in light of the Passover, see Prigent, *Commentary on the Apocalypse*, 43–44 and 249–51.

31. See Shepherd, *Paschal Liturgy*, 92–97. The song of Isa 6 appears to have been incorporated into eucharistic worship at a very early date.

> and to the spirits of just men made perfect, and to Jesus, the mediator of a new covenant, and to the sprinkled blood that speaks more graciously than the blood of Abel. (Heb 12:22–24)

Although the "sprinkled blood" here certainly alludes to the Day of Atonement sacrifice offered by Christ himself (Heb 10:12–14), it probably is pointing primarily to the presence of this atoning sacrifice in Christ's eucharistic blood offered in worship. A priest in the temple of ancient Israel would no doubt get blood from the sacrifices on his linen garments. It is possible that Revelation understands the eucharistic blood as the source for the regular cleansing of the Christian's white baptismal garment: "they have washed their robes and made them white in the blood of the Lamb" (Rev 7:14). Therefore, Revelation depicts baptism and the Eucharist as sacred rites that facilitate the temporal experience of the Divine Presence for Christians on earth and are the foundation for the eternal experience of God at the parousia.

Divine Secrets and Divination

Daphna Arbel

> R. Ishmael said: Metatron said to me: Come and I will show you the letters by which heaven and earth were created ... seas and rivers ... mountains and hills ... trees and grasses ... stars and constellations ... the orb of moon and the disk of sun ... Orion and the Pleiades and all the various luminaries.... and I saw water.... I saw fire.... I saw snow.... I saw hailstones.... I saw ... lightning.... I saw thunder. (*3 En.* 41–42).

Correspondences between Near Eastern divinatory traditions and early Enochic literature have long been demonstrated.[1] In contrast, relatively little scholarly attention has been given to *3 Enoch*.[2] Moreover, *3 Enoch*, in its present form,

---

1. On the impact of Mesopotamian divinatory traditions on early Enochic literature, see Heinrich Zimmern, "Urkönige und Uroffenbarung," in *Die Keilinschriften und das Alte Testament* (ed. E. Schrader; 2 vols.; Berlin: Reuther & Reichard, 1903), 2:530–43; Herman Lundin Jansen, *Die Henochgestalt: Eine vergleichende religionsgeschichtliche Untersuchung* (Oslo: Dybwad, 1939); Pierre Grelot, "La légende d'Hénoch dans les apocryphes et dans la Bible: Origine et signification," *RSR* 46 (1958): 5–26, 181–210; Otto Neugebauer, "The 'Astronomical' Chapters of the Ethiopic Book of Enoch (72–82)," in *The Book of Enoch or 1 Enoch* (ed. M. Black; Leiden: Brill, 1985), 387; Helge S. Kvanvig, *Roots of Apocalyptic: The Mesopotamian Background of the Enoch Figure and of the Son of Man* (Neukirchen-Vluyn: Neukirchener, 1988); John J. Collins, *The Apocalyptic Imagination: An Introduction to the Jewish Matrix of Christianity* (New York: Crossroad, 1992), 24–36, 44–45; idem, "The Sage in Apocalyptic and Pseudepigraphic Literature," in: *The Sage in Israel and the Ancient Near East* (ed. G. Gammie and L. G. Perdue; Winona Lake, Ind.: Eisenbrauns, 1990), 343–54; idem, *Seers, Sibyls and Sages in Hellenistic-Roman Judaism* (Leiden: Brill, 1997), 44–48, 341–43; James C. VanderKam, *Enoch and the Growth of an Apocalyptic Tradition* (SBQMS 16; Washington, D.C.: Catholic Biblical Association of America, 1984), idem, *Enoch: A Man for All Generations* (Columbia: University of South Carolina Press, 1995), 1–22.

2. *3 Enoch*, or *Sefer Hekhalot*, is included in Peter Schäfer, Margaret Schlüter, and Hans George von Mutius, *Synopse zur Hekhalot Literatur* (TSAJ 2; Tübingen: Mohr Siebeck, 1981), §§1–80. A German translation of *3 Enoch* with text-critical notes has been provided by Peter Schäfer, ed., *Übersetzung der Hekhalot-Literatur* (4 vols.; TSAJ 17, 22, 29, 46; Tübingen: Mohr Siebeck, 1995), 1:1–82. The English translations of *3 Enoch* used here is that of Philip S. Alex-

has been dissociated from divinatory or magical traditions. For instance, Peter Schäfer has compared the existing *3 Enoch* with an earlier Genizah fragment of *3 Enoch* (T.-S. K 21.95.L = G12).[3] He has suggested that the present form of *3 Enoch*, following its redaction by Ashkenazi Jewry in the Middle Ages, displays close similarities with the conventional theology and anthropology of classical rabbinic Judaism. It contrasts with the earlier Genizah fragment, which displays interest in the arts of astrology and physiognomy and therefore, according to Schäfer, "turns this basic tendency of the 'classical' *3 Enoch* upside down."[4]

Taking a different position, I suggest that the existing *3 Enoch*, parallel to the Genizah fragment, contains echoes of Mesopotamian divinatory traditions, even after its redaction by Ashkenazi Jewry.[5] As I intend to demonstrate, *3 Enoch*'s

---

ander, "3 (Hebrew Apocalypse of) Enoch," *OTP* 1:223–315. Another translation may be found in Hugo Odeberg, *The Hebrew Book of Enoch or Third Enoch* (New York: Ktav, 1928; repr. with a prolegomenon by Jonas C. Greenfield; New York: Ktav, 1973). On *3 Enoch* in the context of the parallel traditions, see Alexander, "3 (Hebrew Apocalypse of) Enoch"; idem, "The Historical Setting of the Hebrew Book of Enoch," *JJS* 28 (1977): 156–80; Vita Daphna Arbel, *Beholders of Divine Secrets: Mysticism and Myth and the Hekhalot and Merkavah Literature* (Albany: State University of New York Press, 2003), 97–102; James R. Davila, *Descenders to the Chariot: The People behind the Hekhalot Literature* (JSJSup 70; Leiden: Brill, 2001), 9–10; Rachel Elior, *The Three Temples: On the Emergence of Jewish Mysticism* (Oxford: Littman Library of Jewish Civilization, 2004), 234–35, 237–47; Ithamar Gruenwald, *Apocalyptic and Merkavah Mysticism* (AGJU 14; Leiden: Brill, 1980), 191–208; David J. Halperin, *The Faces of the Chariot: Early Jewish Responses to Ezekiel's Vision* (TSAJ 16; Tübingen: Mohr Siebeck, 1988), esp. ch. 9; Andrei Orlov, *The Enoch-Metatron Tradition* (TSAJ 107; Tübingen: Mohr Siebeck, 2005), 85–146; Christopher Rowland, *The Open Heaven: A Study in Apocalypticism in Judaism and Early Christianity* (New York: Crossroad, 1982), 98–113; Peter Schäfer, *The Hidden and Manifest God: Some Major Themes in Early Jewish Mysticism* (Albany: State University of New York Press, 1992), 123–38; Gershom Scholem, *Major Trends in Jewish Mysticism* (3rd ed.; New York: Schocken, 1954), 40–79; idem, *Jewish Gnosticism, Merkabah Mysticism and Talmudic Tradition* (2nd ed.; New York: Jewish Theological Seminary of America, 1965), 43–55; Alan F. Segal, *Two Powers in Heaven: Early Rabbinic Reports about Christianity and Gnosticism* (Leiden: Brill, 1977), 60–72; idem, "The Risen Christ and the Angelic Mediator Figures in Light of Qumran," in *Jesus and the Dead Sea Scrolls* (ed. J. Charlesworth; New York: Doubleday, 1992), 308–13; Elliot R. Wolfson, *Through a Speculum That Shines: Visions and Imagination in Medieval Jewish Mysticism* (Princeton: Princeton University Press, 1994), 82–98.

3. Peter Schäfer, ed., *Geniza-Fragmente zur Hekhalot-Literatur* (TSAJ 16; Tübingen: Mohr Siebeck, 1984), 136–37.

4. Schäfer, *Hidden and Manifest God*, 136–38; 147–48.

5. Schäfer has discussed the extensive redactional process of the *hekhalot and merkabah* literature, including *3 Enoch*, and identified four stages and contexts in which *3 Enoch* developed: (1) a formative stage in Babylonia; (2) a stage of development in "eastern circles" manifested in fragments from the Cairo Genizah; (3) an intermediary Byzantine stage; and (4) a final stage in which the text was edited and redacted by Ashkenazi Jewry in the Middle Ages, which formed the existing *3 Enoch*. See Schäfer "Research on Hekhalot Literature: Where Do We Stand Now?" in: *Rashi 1040–1990: Hommage à Ephraïm E. Urbach* (ed. G. Sed-Rajna; Paris: Cerf, 1993), 231–

conceptualization of "authorized" divine secrets and their revelation is consonant with a series of features rooted in divinatory traditions of the Mesopotamian *ṭupšarru* scribe-scholars.[6] These were accessible, directly and indirectly, in the prevailing cultures of late antiquity and may have been absorbed by early and late writers and redactors of *3 Enoch*, who in turn transformed them to construct their own views.[7]

In the following discussion I will treat these issues in three parts. First, making use of recent observations regarding the Mesopotamian divinatory lore and its continued vitality in subsequent cultures of late antiquity, I will examine several conceptual and thematic conventions rooted in traditions of the *ṭupšarru* scribe-scholars. These are associated particularly with notions of divine secrets and their revelation. Second, I will consider several of *3 Enoch*'s accounts associated with "authorized" divine secrets and revelation, which seem to echo Mesopotamian divinatory traditions both explicitly and implicitly. Third, I will discuss the manner in which *3 Enoch* modifies and alters such concepts and themes in order to construct and express its own ideologies in a different context and in a much later time.

1. Mesopotamian Scholarly Divination

In order to explain my broad reference to Mesopotamian divinatory lore, it is important to recognize its ongoing vitality and influence. Regarded as a secret of the gods, the art of divination was included in the Mesopotamian scribal

---

32, idem, ed., *Hekhalot Studien* (TSAJ 19; Tübingen: Mohr Siebeck, 1988), 228–29. Compare Scholem, *Major Trends in Jewish Mysticism*, 45–46.

6. In this context I will not treat traditions of unlawful revelation of forbidden secrets. On traditions of illicit revelation of secrets and their reception, see a recent comprehensive study by Annette Yoshiko Reed, *Fallen Angels and the History of Judaism and Christianity: The Reception of Enochic Literature* (New York: Cambridge University Press, 2005). For her discussion of *3 Enoch* and the *hekhalot* and *merkabah* mysticism, see 233–72.

7. On Mesopotamian traditions, including the divinatory lore, and their vitality and presence in late antiquity and beyond, see discussions and references in Stephanie Dalley, ed., *The Legacy of Mesopotamia* (Oxford: Oxford University Press, 1998); Markham J. Geller, "The Influence of Ancient Mesopotamia on Hellenistic Judaism," in *Civilizations of the Ancient Near East* (ed. J. M. Sasson; New York: Scribner; 1995), 1:43–54; For the ongoing presence of Mesopotamian astrology and omen literature see David Pingree, "Legacies in Astronomy and Celestial Omens," in Dalley, *The Legacy of Mesopotamia*, 125–37; Francesca Rochberg, *The Heavenly Writing: Divination, Horoscopy, and Astronomy in Mesopotamian Culture* (Cambridge: Cambridge University Press, 2004), 15–29. On links between Jewish legal practice, halakah, and the Akkadian term *alaktu* "oracular decision," as well as Mesopotamian traditions of divination, see a remarkable analysis by I. Tzvi Abusch, "Alaktu and Halakhah, Oracular Decision, Divine Revelation," *HTR* 80 (1987): 15–42.

scholarship known as *ṭupšarrūtu* (literally, "the art of the scribe").[8] This tradition spanned three millennia, roughly from the old Babylonian to the Seleucid periods, and covered various practices. By the end of the second millennium there was what A. Leo Oppenheim called "the stream of tradition": a fairly well-defined body of tradition that was transmitted from that time onward by scribes and scholars over a wide geographical area within the Mesopotamian cultural sphere of influence. Several of these traditions continued to surface in the Hellenistic world and beyond.[9]

A number of conceptual and thematic notions rooted in the Mesopotamian lore of the *ṭupšarru* scribe-scholars are relevant to our discussion of *3 Enoch*. These can be organized under three headings: (1) accessing divine secrets; (2) initiation into secrets and their disclosure; and (3) guarding divine secrets. In the following discussion I will examine a series of characteristics associated with each of these three headings. Since this essay focuses on the ideological stance of the Mesopotamian divinatory lore rather than on its inner developments, the loss of historical details implied by the wide scope of the discussion will not detract from its conceptual and thematic examination.

1.1. Accessing Divine Secrets

One common feature shared by most Mesopotamian scholarly divinatory traditions is the notion of an ongoing communication between the gods and humans

8. *Ṭupšarrūtu*, literally "the art of the scribe," is an abstract nominal form from the term *ṭupšarru*, scribe-scholar. It refers to the learned repertoire of the scribe-scholars, which mainly includes scholarly divination, magical texts, scholastic lists of word and commentaries, and liturgical and ritual prescriptions. See Rochberg, *Heavenly Writing*, 3–4, 210–11; A. Leo Oppenheim, "Divination and Celestial Observation in the Last Assyrian Empire," *Centaurus* 14 (1969): 97, 99. As Rochberg has noted, a scribe trained in omen literature, and thereby a diviner by artifice, was designated by the title *ṭupšarru* "scribe" (an Akkadian term derived from the term *ṭuppu* "tablet" or "text," which is a loanword from Sumerian [dub]). Another term was *ummanu* "scholar" or "literatus." See Rochberg, *Heavenly Writing*, 48; idem, "Scribes and Scholars: The *ṭupšar* Enūma Anu Enlil," in *Assyriologica et Semitica: Festschrift für Joachim Oelsner anläßlich seines 65. Geburtstages am 18. Februar 1997* (ed. J. Marzahn and H. Neumann; Münster: Ugarit-Verlag, 2000), 359–75.

9. On the ongoing "stream of tradition," see A. Leo Oppenheim, *Ancient Mesopotamia: Portrait of a Dead Civilization* (Chicago: University of Chicago Press, 1977), 13. For discussions of an "ideological stream of tradition," see Rochberg, *Heavenly Writing*, 3–13; Ulla Koch-Westenholz, *Mesopotamian Astrology: An Introduction to Babylonian and Assyrian Celestial Divination* (Copenhagen: Carsten Niebuhr Institute of Near Eastern Studies, Museum Tusculanum Press, University of Copenhagen, 1995), 74–76. For discussion of Mesopotamian divination from a social-historical perspective, see Frederick H. Cryer, *Divination in Ancient Israel and Its Near Eastern Environment* (JSOTSup 142; Sheffield: Sheffield Academic Press, 1944), 124–215. On the presence of Mesopotamian divination in late periods, see discussion and references in Koch-Westenholz, *Mesopotamian Astrology*, 162–79; Rochberg, *Heavenly Writing*, 15–29.

accessed through methods of divination. As Francesca Rochberg has made clear, "The conception of a divinely created order underlies the various forms of Mesopotamian divination, which functioned as a system of divine communication with human beings by means of perceptible patterns of phenomena."[10] The gods' cosmic order, plans, and decisions as they pertained to the past, present, and future were traditionally seen as divine secrets. These were envisioned, as elements of divine discourse, in images of divine pictograms or cosmic designs, encoded and inscribed on various phenomena above and below.[11] Countless visible terrestrial, celestial, and physiognomic phenomena were regarded as potential vehicles for divine messages. The earth, sun, moon, stars, changes in the weather, human behavior and bodies, and other phenomena were all seen as coded signs, or omens, through which knowledge about the gods' intentions could be accessed by qualified human diviners.[12] Records of these omens as well as methods for their interpretation were compiled, standardized, and arranged in series according to schematic categories, several of which are relevant for this study.[13]

For instance, the well-known series of celestial omens entitled *Enūma Anu Enlil* illustrate the significance ascribed to celestial and weather phenomena as mediums through which knowledge about the gods' plans could be reached. It consists of seventy tablets and perhaps seven thousand omens, including lunar omens, solar omens, omens drawn from thunderclaps and lightning flashes, rainbows, clouds, rain, and earthquakes, as well as omens drawn from the fixed stars, the five lesser planets, meteors, and comets. All are seen as coded signs from which one could decode and derive meaning.[14] Astronomical and astrological data were used also in horoscopes. Seen as indicative of the gods' plans about human affairs, the heavens were thought to bear meaning for the king as well as

10. Rochberg, *Heavenly Writing*, 45. Compare Oppenheim, *Ancient Mesopotamia*, 394.

11. On the common use of metaphors of writing in the context of divination, see Jean Bottéro, *Mesopotamia: Writing, Reasoning and the Gods* (Chicago: University of Chicago Press, 1992), 92. For specific examples of metaphors of a graphic model or a written discourse, see Rochberg, *Heavenly Writing*, 1–2, 197–99.

12. This conception gave rise to the entire system of the so-called "deductive divination," including unprovoked omens. A classification of divinatory genres of "inspired" and "deductive" divination was introduced by Bottéro, based on Cireco's classification in *De divinatione* (1.11; 2.26). See Jean Bottéro, "Symptômes, signes, écritures en Mésopotamie ancienne," in *Divination et rationalité* (ed. J. P. Vernant et al.; Paris: Éditions du Seuil, 1974), 70–197. Unlike provoked omens, which included messages from the gods given in response to questions posed to them by various methods of manipulation, unprovoked omens were observed by the diviner without any request or manipulation.

13. For survey of the unprovoked omen texts, see Rochberg, *Heavenly Writing*, 66–97.

14. On the celestial omens entitled *Enūma Anu Enlil*, see Rochberg, *Heavenly Writing*, 66–78; Koch-Westenholz, *Mesopotamian Astrology*, 97–136; Erica Reiner, "Babylonian Celestial Divination," in *Ancient Astronomy and Celestial Divination* (ed. N. M. Swerdlow: Cambridge: MIT Press, 1999), 21–37.

for the individual.[15] The majority of personal horoscopes do not name the person for whom the horoscope was cast but simply use the phrase "the child" and specify the date and time of birth, as well as the planetary positions in the zodiac and the zodiacal signs as indicators of the gods' decisions.

Humans' physical, facial, and behavioral features were also perceived as signs that could potentially disclose the gods' decisions. As the series known as "diagnostic" omens demonstrates, "a person's nature seems to have been conceived of as the result of the allotment by a god of the characteristics and qualities possessed, as well as the length of life itself. Such was the individual's share or 'lot' in life."[16]

In principle, all systems of deductive divination assumed that omens could be accessed through the act of observation and typically employed the verb "to observe" to indicate the act of deciphering coded messages.[17] Although a collected set of rules for the observation and interpretation of signs was specified in various omen texts, the rules were not mechanically applied, as the tradition assumed that the act of observation was not simply a mechanical ability but laid a special stress on the request that diviners would be able to see what was hidden or obscure and behold meanings that lay beyond ordinary perception.[18]

A related notion is the concept of *šīmtu,* often translated as "destiny" or "fate." This term gives expression to the nature, characteristics, and functions of all physical and ontological phenomena of the orderly cosmos, in the past, pres-

---

15. On horoscopes, see Rochberg, *Heavenly Writing,* 98–120; idem, *Babylonian Horoscopes* (TAPS 88.1; Philadelphia: American Philosophical Society, 1998); Abraham J. Sachs, "Babylonian Horoscopes," *JCS* 6 (1952): 49–74.

16. On "diagnostic" omens, whose apodoses do not predict the future but function as diagnosis, see Erica Reiner *Astral Magic in Babylonia* (TAPS 85.4; Philadelphia: American Philosophical Society, 1995), 84–85; Rochberg *Heavenly Writing,* 49–53; Cryer, *Divination in Ancient Israel,* 167–68. On personal prognostications from heavenly phenomena in horoscopes, see Rochberg, *Heavenly Writing,* 202–8.

17. On accessing messages through the act of observation, see Rochberg, *Heavenly Writing,* 250, 254–55. As she has clarified, phenomena were observable not in our sense of being subject to sense perception but in the sense of being objects of empirical interest to the diviners.

18. On the hermeneutical techniques of interpretation, see Koch-Westenholz, *Mesopotamian Astrology,* 149–51. On divination as a form of hermeneutics, see Jonathan Z. Smith, "Sacred Persistence: Toward a Redescription of Canon," in idem, *Imagining Religion: From Babylon to Jonestown* (Chicago: University of Chicago Press, 1982), 36–52; Michael D. Swartz, "Divination and Its Discontents: Finding and Questioning Meaning in Ancient and Medieval Judaism," in *Prayer, Magic, and the Stars in the Ancient and Late Antique World* (ed. S. Noegel, J. Walker, and B. Wheeler; University Park: Pennsylvania State University Press, 2003), 155–66; Abusch, "Alaktu and Halakhah." On the similarity between kabbalistic hermeneutical techniques and divinatory methods of interpretation, see Piotr Michalowski "Presence at Creation," in *Lingering Over Words: Studies in Ancient Near Eastern Literature in Honor of William Moran* (ed. T. Abusch, J. Huehnergard, and P. Steinkeller; HSS 37; Atlanta: Scholars Press, 1990), 395.

ent, and future, that were "fixed" and decided by the gods in primeval times.[19] "Destinies" were thought to be inscribed on cosmic phenomena.[20] They were also seen to be inscribed on the "Tablet of Destinies," *ṭuppi šimâti*, seen as a medium through which one could gain access to the gods' plans.[21] A number of scholars have emphasized the significance of the Tablet of Destinies for divination. According to Wim van Binsbergen and Frans Wiggermann, for example, "the canonical interpretation of divination links up with this view, by presenting the signs … as divine operation of the unanimated world. These operations encode messages concerning the governmental decisions of the gods."[22] In a similar vein, Geo Widengren has asserted: "through the Tablet of Destinies divine powers communicated their will and their decisions to the king and nation."[23]

That divination was thought to be the way to gain access into the hidden dimensions of reality and to the gods' secret cosmic plans can be seen from the variety of practices and methods perceived as channels of communication between gods and humans. These include terrestrial, celestial, and weather phenomena, humans' physical, facial, and behavioral features, as well as the Tablet of Destinies—all seem to be of cosmic significance that only initiated experts can decode. The manner in which these experts were initiated into the art of divination will be explored next.

---

19. On the concept of *šīmtu* (Sumerian NAMTAR), which denotes "that which was determined by decree," including the decreed nature of phenomena and the lot of humans, see Jean Bottéro, *Religion in Ancient Mesopotamia* (Chicago: University of Chicago Press, 2001), 92–95; Rochberg, *Heavenly Writing*, 50–51, 196–200, 202–3; Oppenheim, *Ancient Mesopotamia*, 201–6; Jack Newton Lawson, *The Concept of Fate in Ancient Mesopotamia in the First Millennium: Toward an Understanding of Šīmtu* (Wiesbaden: Harrassowiotz, 1994). On the option of undoing the destinies by *namburbi* ritual, see Oppenheim, *Ancient Mesopotamia*, 210, 226.

20. On destinies inscribed on natural phenomena, see Francesca Rochberg, "Heaven and Earth: The Divine-Human Relations in Mesopotamian Celestial Divination," in Noegel, Walker, and Wheeler, *Prayer, Magic, and the Stars*, 176–82; idem, *Heavenly Writing*, 195–200.

21. On the Tablet of Destinies, *tuppi simati*, see Bottéro, *Religion in Ancient Mesopotamia*, 93; Jeremy Black and J. Anthony Green, *Gods, Demons and Symbols of Ancient Mesopotamia: An Illustrated Dictionary* (Austin: University of Texas Press, 1992), 173; Cornelis Van Dam, *The Urim and Thummim: A Means of Revelation in Ancient Israel* (Winona Lake, Indi.: Eisenbrauns, 1997), 46–50; see 56 n. 32 for discussion of and references to the frequent scholarly discussions regarding the singular or plural nature of the tablet(s). For the tablet of the gods associated with celestial and terrestrial secrets, see Andrew R. George, "Sennacherib and the Tablet of Destinies," *Iraq* 48 (1986): 138–46.

22. See Wim van Binsbergen and Frans Wiggermann, "Magic in History: A Theoretical Perspective and Its Application to Ancient Mesopotamia," in *Mesopotamian Magic: Textual, Historical, and Interpretive Perspectives* (ed. T. Abusch and K. van der Toorn; Groningen: Styx, 1998): 20–25.

23. Geo Widengren, *The Ascension of the Apostle and the Heavenly Book* (Uppsala Universitets Årsskrift 1950.7; Uppsala: Lundequistska, 1950), 25.

1.2. Initiation to Secrets and Their Disclosure

Recording and systematizing the varied divinatory practices and the empirical collections of omens and their interpretations obviously required the trained application of the human intellect. Nonetheless, the art of divination itself was also perceived as involving divine secrets revealed by a divine agent only to the ranks of the *ṭupšarru* scribe-scholars.[24] Unlike other groups of scribes, whose primary responsibilities included reading and writing, the *ṭupšarru* scribe-scholars were the beholders and interpreters of unprovoked omens. Through these they accessed and ascertained the wills, plans, and intentions of the gods.[25]

Many traditions associate the origin of divination with the ancient mythological history of the cosmos. According to several traditions, the first human to be initiated into the knowledge of divination was an antediluvian sage who was chosen by the gods to be privy to these secrets and subsequently to disclose them to other humans. A number of traditions identify this figure as the legendary Adapa, while other traditions affirm that the first human to whom knowledge of divination was revealed was King Enmeduranki of Sippar.[26] A well-known tradition found in a mythological-explanatory text from Nineveh describes King Enmeduranki's initiation into divine secrets:

> Shamash in Ebabbarra [appointed] Enmeduranki [king of Sippar], the beloved of Anu, Enlil [and Ea]. Shamash and Adad [brought him in] to their assembly. Shamash and Adad [honored him], Shamash and Adad [set him] on a large throne of gold. They showed him how to observe oil on water, a mystery of Anu [Enlil and Ea]. They gave him the tablet of the gods, the liver, a secret of heaven

24. On secrecy associated with of divination, see van Binsbergen and Wiggermann, "Magic in History," 24–25; Paul Alain Beaulieu, "New Light on Secret Knowledge in Late Babylonian Culture," *ZA* 82 (1992): 98–111; Rochberg, *Heavenly Writing*, 212–19; Koch-Westenholz, *Mesopotamian Astrology*, 95–96; Joan Goodnick-Westenholz, "Thoughts on Esoteric Knowledge and Secret Lore," in *Intellectual Life in the Ancient Near East: Papers Presented at the 43rd Rencontre assyriologique internationale, Prague, July 1–5, 1996* (ed. J. Prosecky; Prague: Academy of Sciences of the Czech Republic, Oriental Institute, 1998), 451–62.

25. On responsibilities of different groups of scribes, see Oppenheim, "Divination and Celestial Observation," 97, 99; David Brown, *Mesopotamian Planetary Astronomy-Astrology* (Groningen: Styx, 2000), 34; Koch-Westenholz, *Mesopotamian Astrology*, 48.

26. For traditions related to Adapa, see Wilfred G. Lambert, "A Catalogue of Texts and Authors," *JCS* (1962): 59–77; Peter Machinist and Hayim Tadmor, "Heavenly Wisdom," in *The Tablet and the Scroll: Near Eastern Studies in Honor of William W. Hallo* (ed. M. E. Cohen, D. C. Snell, and D. B.Weisberd; Bethesda, Md.: CDL, 1993), 146–51. For discussions and references regarding Adapa, see Rochberg, *Heavenly Writing*, 182; Koch-Westenholz, *Mesopotamian Astrology*, 95. For traditions related to Enmeduranki and divination, see Wilfred G. Lambert, "Enmeduranki and Related Matters," *JCS* 21 (1967): 126–38, esp. 132; Rochberg, *Heavenly Writing*, 215–16; Koch-Westenholz, *Mesopotamian Astrology*, 58; Ivan Starr, *The Rituals of the Diviner* (Malibu, Calif.: Undena, 1983), 55–56.

and [underworld]. They put in his hand the cedar-(rod), beloved of the great gods.[27]

After the gods initiated Enmeduranki into several divinatory methods, he passed on this knowledge to his successors and instructed them, like a master teaching a novice (literally, his beloved son), the lore of the profession: "the scholar, the one who knows, who guards the secrets of the gods, will bind his son, whom he loves ... and will instruct him."[28]

This text has been often linked exclusively to the cult of the *baru* and their methods of extispicy. Yet recently scholars have also associated this tradition with the *ṭupšarru* scribe-scholars, particularly with their methods of celestial divination.[29] Consequently, several insights related to the initiation of the *ṭupšarru* scribe-scholars into divinatory knowledge can be derived from this text. (1) A mythological antediluvian figure, King Enmeduranki, who is characterized as the "beloved of the gods" as well as a "learned servant" and the "guardian of secrets," is depicted as the first human who was initiated into divinatory knowledge.[30] (2) The initiation process is said to involve several features: joining the celestial inner circle of deities, sitting on a celestial throne in heaven, receiving the tablets containing secret knowledge of divination, and transmitting the secret knowledge to successor initiated seers. (3) Divinatory knowledge was transmitted from this antediluvian sage to his successors, the scribe-scholars, who swore an oath to guard the secrets of the great gods and keep them within their circle.

Closely related to this tradition is the ritual of the diviners depicted in several divinatory reports. According to these accounts, the human diviner, who was initiated into the heavenly realm, also played a judicial role in heaven. He was seated on a golden chair, witnessed the decisions of the gods, and adopted the role of a celestial judge.[31] Starr has directed attention to this symbolic legal role:

---

27. Lambert, "Enmeduranki and Related Matters," 132.

28. Ibid. On the view that experts of divination are seen as the offspring of Enmeduranki, see Koch-Westenholz, *Mesopotamian Astrology*, 58; Starr, *Rituals of the Diviner*, 55–56. As Starr has suggested, "it may be argued that the professional competence of the diviner and his qualifications were here 'legitimized' by grounding his origins in hoary antiquity.... The diviner's 'legal mandate' as it were, flows from that bestowed upon his putative ancestor, Enmeduranki, by the gods of divination, and which he in turn submitted to the people of three privileged cities" (56).

29. On links to celestial divination, see Rochberg, *Heavenly Writing* 183, 215. As Starr has noted, the term *bārû* does not occur in this text before line 22, and the appurtenances of divination are evidently the properties of others as well (*Rituals of the Diviner*, 55–56).

30. According to Starr (*Rituals of the Diviner*, 57), the title "son" indicates a novice. From the third to the first millennium, the term was often used as the epithet or title for kings or individuals chosen by a specific god.

31. See text A (HSM 7494) in ibid., 37–44, in particular, lines 18–19, pp. 37–38.

> There is a marked interplay between the celestial and the terrestrial judicial roles in the rituals of the diviner. The one played by the gods in the celestial sphere is transferred to the diviner in the terrestrial sphere, where the latter is depicted as a judge, just as the gods are in their assembly. Like them he seats in the judge's seat and makes oracular pronouncements. The action is symbolic: the diviner sits in the judge's seat to "duplicate" the role of the gods in the assembly.[32]

The tradition about King Enmeduranki of Sippar as well as the ritual of the diviners have served as our primary examples in this section, in which we have examined the manner in which the *ṭupšarru* scribe-scholars were initiated into the secret knowledge of divination. Their role as the exclusive guardians of these secrets will be discussed next.

1.3. Guarding Divine Secrets

As noted, the art of divination was considered a secret of the great gods. However, this secret was also perceived as the secret of the *ṭupšarru* scribe-scholars.[33] Colophons on several divinatory tablets designate a particular body of knowledge, including the content of scholarly divination, as "secret," "exclusive," and "guarded" knowledge, restricted to initiated scribe-scholars.[34] This was often expressed in a common formula of secrecy, the so-called *Geheimwissen* formula, which ensured that divinatory knowledge was passed on exclusively to other *ṭupšarru* scribe-scholars and guarded by them.[35] Although this formula was not altogether standardized, its various versions agree in asserting that divinatory knowledge was forbidden to the uninitiated and reserved only to the initiated, literally, "the ones who know." For example, a colophon from the Middle Assyrian period states: "Exclusive knowledge: the one who knows may show it to another who knows.…" Similarly, a Neo-Assyrian colophon of an incantation text from Assur's temple states:

> Secret knowledge of the great gods
> The one who knows may show [it] to another one who knows.
> The one who does not know may not see it.
> It [belongs] to the forbidden things of the great gods.[36]

32. Ibid., 57–58.

33. Joan Goodnick-Westenholz ("Thoughts on Esoteric Knowledge," 451–62) has demonstrated the notion of privileged exclusive knowledge within the community of scribes already in the third millennium.

34. Terms often used are *niṣirtu* "guarded" (from the root *nsr* "to guard") and *pirištu* (from the root *prs* "to cut off" or "to separate"), which denote exclusivity. See Rochberg, *Heavenly Writing*, 212.

35. See R. Borger, "*Geheimwissen*," *RlA* 3:188–91.

36. See discussions and references in Rochberg, *Heavenly Writing*, 211–19; Koch-Westenholz, *Mesopotamian Astrology*, 95–96.

The meaning of secrecy has been the subject of some ambivalence among astrologists. Beaulieu has raised the possibility that an esoteric tradition existed in the sense of "an intellectual approach seeking to comprehend the hidden relationship between the constituent elements of knowledge and the cosmic order."[37] From a different perspective, others scholars have emphasized that secrecy is associated more with notions of exclusivity and social control. Alasdair Livingstone, for example, has maintained that, while there is no doubt that certain texts or doctrines were understood or held only by a select few, these texts are not esoteric in a sense of being abstruse or recondite.[38] In Nuegebauer's view, "the [*Geheimwissen*] formula merely expresses the tendency of the scribes to keep the knowledge of their arts within their own circles."[39] Rochberg has likewise emphasized this point: "The interdiction against persons outside the circle of 'knowers' reflects the efforts of a particular scribal body to maintain control over its tradition and to protect a particular body of knowledge."[40]

From a theological perspective, this view of divination as secrets of the gods may suggest a specific perception of the divine as the ultimate source of all knowledge. Yet, on the other hand, divination seems also to be regarded as a technique that could be acquired by human endeavors. Unlike the mythological traditions about the first human sages who received secret knowledge from the gods, most divinatory traditions do not indicate the necessity of divine revelation or inspiration for acquiring divinatory knowledge. Instead, according to numerous records, divinatory knowledge was acquired directly through studying textual records: the omen compendiums.[41] From this point of view, it appears that the emphasis on the secrecy of the diviners' knowledge does not reflect a specific theological stance but rather a social concern. It demonstrates the interests of the *ṭupšarru* scribe-scholars to protect the knowledge of their learned society from the uninformed, to demarcate their identity as the exclusive recipients and guardians of divine secrets, and to authorize their claims and status by an appeal to revealed knowledge.

In order to gain pertinent background to the following discussion of *3 Enoch*, I have thus far examined several notions rooted in the divinatory lore of the *ṭupšarru* scribe-scholars that are associated with divine secrets and their revelation. First, I have examined the notion of accessing divine secrets, which typically involved the gods' cosmic order and plans, through various visible terrestrial, celestial, and physiognomic phenomena, as well as on the "Tablet of Destinies."

---

37. Beaulieu, "New Light on Secret Knowledge," 108; see also Otto Nuegebauer, *Astronomical Cuneiform Texts* (London: Humphries, 1955), 1:12; Alasdair Livingstone, *Mystical and Mythological Explanatory Works of Assyrian and Babylonian Scholars* (Oxford: Clarendon 1986), 1.

38. Livingstone, *Mystical and Mythological Explanatory Works*, 1.

39. Nuegebauer, *Astronomical Cuneiform Texts*,12.

40. Rochberg, *Heavenly Writing*, 217.

41. Ibid., 181, 217–19.

Second, since the knowledge of decoding the hidden meanings of such phenomena through divination was also considered divine secrets, I have examined the process of initiation into this exclusive knowledge. This process, which was often associated with the ancient mythological time before the flood, entailed an initiation into the celestial divine council of the gods, sitting on a heavenly throne, receiving tablets containing secret knowledge from the gods, and transmitting these secrets to successor seers. In this context I have also examined the rituals of the diviner, which describe the role of a human diviner as a heavenly judge who was invested with the authority and role of divine judges.

Finally, I have examined a common formula of secrecy that was often associated with the divinatory knowledge. According to this formula, the art of divination was restricted only to the initiated *ṭupšarru* scribe-scholars. By this appeal to secrecy, they possibly attempted to secure the knowledge of their learned society, to maintain control over their tradition, and to validate their agenda and authority.

2. Divine Secrets and Revelation in *3 Enoch*

Can a case be made for associating these divinatory traditions of the *ṭupšarru* scribe-scholars with *3 Enoch*? I am not assuming a simple correlation. Yet, as I will suggest in the following discussion, explicit and implicit echoes of these traditions resonate in *3 Enoch* with different degrees of clarity.[42] This resonance allows the possibility that the authors and redactors of *3 Enoch*, in accordance with their methods of utilizing a variety of traditions, may have re-employed and transformed available Mesopotamian divinatory traditions, among other sources, to construct their views and ideologies.

In its present form, *3 Enoch*, attributed to the fifth or sixth century C.E., combines threads from a variety of sources to introduce conflicting views regarding divine secrets and their revelation. As mentioned earlier, this essay treats only accounts associated with "authorized" revelation of divine secrets. These describe the revelation of secrets to three figures: Enoch-Metatron, Rabbi Ishmael, and Moses. Accounts of the revelation of secrets to Enoch-Metatron occur in *Synopse* §§4–20 and in an analogous account in *Synopse* §§72–78. Accounts of revelation of divine secrets to Rabbi Ishmael, by Enoch-Metatron, occur in *Synopse* §§59–68 and in the Genizah fragment of *3 Enoch* mentioned above. Accounts of the rev-

42. In my discussion I treat echoes as nonexplicit references of Near Eastern sources. I adopt methodological observations made by Richard B. Hays, *Echoes of Scripture in the Letters of Paul* (New Haven: Yale University Press, 1989), esp. 15–33; and Devorah Dimant, "Use and Interpretation of Mikra in the Apocrypha and Pseudepigrapha," in *Mikra: Text, Translation, Reading and Interpretation of the Hebrew Bible in Ancient Judaism and Ancient Christianity*. (ed. M. J. Mulder and H. Sysling; CRINT 2.1; Assen: Van Gorcum; Philadelphia: Fortress, 1988), 379–419, esp. 410–419.

elation of secrets to Moses, by Enoch-Metatron, occur in a concise account in *Synopse* §§79–80.[43] Although there are variations in detail, a consistent conceptualization of divine secrets and their revelation emerges in these accounts. In what follows I examine both the major and minor features that correspond to the Mesopotamian divinatory traditions examined earlier.

2.1. Accessing Divine Secrets

The divine secrets that Enoch-Metatron attains often seem to be associated with God's created order and cosmic plan. This is evident, for instance, in Enoch-Metatron's first-person statement that equates revealed secrets with God's manifested order: "All mysteries [רזי] of the world and all the orders [סדרי] of nature stand

43. On Enoch-Metatron, see Daniel Abrams, "The Boundaries of Divine Ontology: The Inclusion and Exclusion of Metatron in the Godhead," *HTR* 87 (1994): 291–321; Alexander, "Historical Setting," 156–80; idem, "3 (Hebrew Apocalypse of) Enoch," 223–315; Daphna Arbel, "Seal of Resemblance, Full of Wisdom and Perfect in Beauty: The Enoch/Metatron Narrative of *3 Enoch* and Ezekiel 28," *HTR* 98 (2005): 121–42; Joseph Dan, "The Seventy Names of Metatron," in idem, *Jewish Mysticism* (4 vols.; Northvale, N.J.: Aronson, 1998): 1:229–34; idem, *The Ancient Jewish Mysticism* (Tel-Aviv: MOD Books, 1993), 108–24; James R. Davila, "Of Methodology, Monotheism and Metatron," in *The Jewish Roots of Christological Monotheism: Papers from the St. Andrews Conference on the Historical Origins of the Worship of Jesus* (ed. C. C. Newman, J. R. Davila, and G. S. Lewis; JSJSup 63; Leiden: Brill, 1999), 3–18; idem, "Melchizedek, the 'Youth,' and Jesus," in *The Dead Sea Scrolls as Background to Postbiblical Judaism and Early Christianity: Papers from an International Conference at St. Andrews in 2001* (ed. J. R. Davila; Leiden: Brill, 2003), 248–74; Rachel Elior, "You Have Chosen Enoch from Among Human Beings: Enoch the Scribe of Righteousness and the Scroll's Library of The Priests the Sons of Zadok," in *Creation and Re-creation in Jewish Thought: Festschrift in Honor of Joseph Dan on the Occasion of His Seventieth Birthday* (ed. R. Elior and P. Schafer; Tubingen: Mohr Siebeck, 2005), 15–64; Crispin Fletcher-Louis, *All The Glory of Adam: Liturgical Anthropology in the Dead Sea Scrolls* (STDJ 42; Leiden: Brill, 2000), 244 n. 56, 278–79, 363; Halperin, *Faces of the Chariot*, 420–27; Gruenwald, *Apocalyptic and Merkavah Mysticism*, 195–206; Martha Himmelfarb, "A Report on Enoch in Rabbinic Literature," in Society of Biblical Literature 1978 Seminar Papers (SBLSP 13–14; Missoula, Mont.: Scholars Press, 1978), 259–69; Moshe Idel, "Enoch Is Metatron," *Immanuel* 24/25 (1990): 220–40; Saul Lieberman, "Metatron, the Meaning of His Name and His Functions," appendix in Gruenwald, *Apocalyptic and Merkavah Mysticism*, 235–41; Christopher R. A. Morray-Jones, "Transformational Mysticism in the Apocalyptic-Merkabah Tradition," *JJS* 43 (1992): 1–31; Odeberg, *Hebrew Book of Enoch*, 79–146; Orlov, *Enoch-Metatron Tradition*, 86–147; Schäfer, *Hidden and Manifest God*, 29–32; Scholem, *Jewish Gnosticism, Merkabah Mysticism*, 43–55; idem, *Major Trends in Jewish Mysticism*, 43–55; Segal, *Two Powers in Heaven*, 60–72; idem, "Risen Christ," 308–13; Gedaliahu G. Stroumsa, "Form(s) of God: Some Notes on Metatron and Christ," *HTR* 76 (1983): 269–88; Loren T. Stuckenbruck, *Angel Veneration and Christology* (WUNT 2.70; Tübingen: Mohr Siebeck, 1995), 71–87; Wolfson, *Through a Speculum That Shines*, 113, 334; Elliot R. Wolfson, "Metatron and *Shi'ur Qomah* in the Writings of *Haside Ashkenaz*," in *Mysticism, Magic and Kabbalah in Ashkenazi Judaism* (ed. K. E. Groezinger and J. Dan; Berlin: de Gruyter, 1995), 60–92.

revealed before me as they stand revealed before the creator."[44] What is particularly noticeable is that divine secrets and mysteries are envisioned as being engraved upon or encoded in terrestrial and celestial phenomena in the natural world. These in turn are associated with cosmological, astrological, astronomical, and meteorological occurrences.

For instance, *Synopse* §15 associates Enoch-Metatron with celestial phenomena (the sun and constellations) by describing how Enoch-Metatron was endowed with a robe on which "all kind of luminaries were set" as well as with a crown on which forty-nine stones, "each like the sun's orb," were placed.[45] *Synopse* §16 further depicts a crown inscribed with the letters associated with the creation of cosmic: "He wrote ... upon the crown which was on my head the letters by which ... seas and rivers ... stars and constellations, lightning, and wind, thunder and thunderclaps, snow and hail hurricane and tempest ... and all the necessities of the world and all orders of creation were created." [46]

---

44. *Synopse* §14; Alexander, "3 (Hebrew Apocalypse of) Enoch," 264. Compare similar descriptions of the seer's achievements as recorded in *Hekhalot Rabbati* (*Synopse* §§81–86).

45. *Synopse* §15; Alexander, "3 (Hebrew Apocalypse of) Enoch," 265.

46. *Synopse* §16; Alexander, "3 (Hebrew Apocalypse of) Enoch," 265–56. The list of revealed "secrets" bears a close resemblance to revelations mentioned in apocalyptic literature and early Enochic texts, esp. the Astronomical Book in *1 En.* 72–82, the Book of the Watchers in *1 En.* 1–36, and the Similitudes in *1 En.* 37–71. See Michael E. Stone's important observations in "Lists of Revealed Things in the Apocalyptic Literature," in *Magnalia Dei: The Mighty Acts of God* (ed. F. M. Cross, W. E. Lemke, and P. D. Miller, Jr.; New York: Doubleday, 1967), 414–52. See further Neugebauer, "The 'Astronomical' Chapters," 386–414; George W. E. Nickelsburg, "The Nature and Function of Revelation in *1 Enoch, Jubilees,* and Some Qumranic Documents," in *Pseudepigraphic Perspectives: The Apocrypha and Pseudepigrapha in Light of the Dead Sea Scerolls* (ed. E. G. Chazon and M. E. Stone; Leiden: Brill, 1999), 96–99; VanderKam, *Enoch,* 76–114; A. Yoshiko Reed, "Heavenly Ascent, Angelic Descent, and Transmission of Knowledge in 1 Enoch 6–16," in *Heavenly Realms and Heavenly Realities in Late Antique Religions* (ed. R. Boustan and A. Yoshiko Reed; Cambridge: Cambridge University Press, 2004), 47–66. On revealed secrets in the Hebrew Bible, the pseudepigrapha, early rabbinic sources, and Qumran texts, see further Markus N. A. Bockmuehl, *Revelation and Mystery in Ancient Judaism and Pauline Christianity* (Tübingen: Mohr Siebeck, 1990), 7–126; B. Reicke, "Da'at and Gnosis in Intertestamental Literature," in *Neotestamentica et Semitica: Studies in Honor of Matthew Black* (ed. E. E. Ellis and M. Wilcox; Edinburgh: T&T Clark, 1969), 245–55. On revealed secrets in *2 Enoch,* see Andrei Orlov, "Secrets Of Creation in 2 (Slavonic) Enoch," *Hen* 22 (2000): 45–62. Different views have been offered regarding the revelation of secrets in the *hekhalot* and *merkabah* literature: according to Scholem, for example, "the mysteries of creation and the hidden connection between all things existing in the universe are the ongoing riddles, whose solution is of deep interest to the authors of the literature.... yet, these secrets are not revealed" (*Major Trends in Jewish Mysticism,* 56); Odeberg has associated divine secrets with creation and the Torah and with Metatron's role as the prince of wisdom who brought down the divine secret doctrine to humanity (*Hebrew Book of Enoch,* 31); in Dan's view, depictions of divine mysteries that were revealed to Enoch-Metatron intend to emphasize his closeness and similarity to God (*Ancient Jewish Mysticism,* 199); Elior has associated secrets with angelic and priestly knowl-

There is no doubt that the concept of a secret creation by letters found in this passage is in accord with the esoteric Jewish rabbinic lore found in *Ma'aseh Bereshit* traditions and with traditions about the creative power of the Hebrew alphabet found in *Sefer Yetzirah,* among other sources.[47] Yet *3 Enoch* emphasizes additional elements that are not developed in these traditions. In particular, the work expands considerable effort on presenting systematic lists organized according to precise and detailed categories of revealed phenomena. These consist of terrestrial phenomena, including seas and rivers, and predominantly celestial and meteorological phenomena, including stars and constellations, lightning, wind, thunder and thunderclaps, snow and hail, and hurricane and tempest.

Moreover, in *3 Enoch* the letters by which cosmic aspects were created seem to be conceived not only as the creative power behind creation but also as something inseparable from natural phenomena. For instance, according to *Synopse* §17–18, when Enoch-Metatron is endowed with divine secrets, he receives the letters by which these phenomena were created but also gains knowledge and some power over these particular phenomena, as he rules over angels and princes whose names correspond to the natural manifestations above and below, which they seem to embody: "Even the angel of fire, the angel of hail, the angel of wind ... lightning ... whirlwind ... thunder ... snow ... rain ... day ... night ... sun ... moon ... stars ... constellations trembled and shrank back in alarm from me when they saw me."[48] The linking of letters with natural phenomena is also found in *Synopse* §59–60. Here Rabbi Ishmael not is not simply an observer of letters but also a beholder of natural phenomena on which, plausibly, God's secrets are inscribed and codified as signs.[49]

> R. Ishmael said: Metatron said to me: Come and I will show you the letters by which heaven and earth were created ... seas and rivers ... mountains and hills ... trees and grasses ... stars and constellations ... the orb of moon and the disk of sun ... Orion and the Pleiades and all the various luminaries.... and I saw

---

edge, which includes the secret of the solar calendar, the cycle of seven-based cosmic time, and the deterministic progressions of meta-history (*Three Temples,* 234–35, 237–47); Alexander has correlated divine secrets and letters with *Ma'aseh Merkavah* speculations ("3 [Hebrew Apocalypse of] Enoch," 265).

47. See Alexander, "3 (Hebrew Apocalypse of) Enoch," 239, 265; Dan, *Ancient Jewish Mysticism,* 25–38; Odeberg, *Hebrew Book of Enoch,* 34–35; Rowland, *Open Heaven,* 344. The classic statement about the power of the twenty-two letters of the Hebrew alphabet is in *Sefer Yetzirah* 2.2. See Ithamar Gruenwald, ed., "A Preliminary Critical Edition of *Sefer Yezira,*" *IOS* (1971): 148 n. 19; Yehuda Liebes, *Ars Poetica in Sefer Yetsira* [Hebrew] (Jerusalem: Schocken, 2000), 16–30.

48. *Synopse* §§17–18; Alexander, "3 (Hebrew Apocalypse of) Enoch," 266–67.

49. It is interesting to note that the Hebrew term for a letter, אות, can also be translated as a sign, a visible marker, or an omen (e.g., Gen 1:14).

water.... I saw fire.... I saw snow.... I saw hailstones.... I saw ... lightning... I saw thunder.[50]

Enoch-Metatron and Rabbi Ishmael thus emerge as the ones who gain access to God's secrets through natural phenomena above and below. Terrestrial phenomena (seas, mountains, hills), celestial phenomena (moon, sun, constellations), and weather phenomena (wind, thunder, thunderclaps, hail hurricanes, and tempests) are all filled with meaning, embodying inscribed divine secrets that could be observed and deciphered. Clearly, in *3 Enoch* these are not overtly associated with divination. Nevertheless, the records of detailed, observable, terrestrial and celestial phenomena, introduced as mediums of manifested divine secrets, may suggest a conceptual correspondence with divinatory principles.

These descriptions may also reflect some familiarity with conventions found on particular omen lists, such as the celestial omens *Enūma Anu Enlil* mentioned above, according to which divine communication is inscribed on various phenomena that take place in the sky. Moreover, it is clear from these accounts that in *3 Enoch* divine secrets are not seen as mysteries that are to be fully protected from all humans. Instead, secrets are declared for the sake of their revelation. *Synopse* §14, for instance, emphasizes the revelation of divine secrets through natural and cosmic phenomena: "All mysteries of the world and all the orders of nature stand revealed before me as they stand revealed before the creator. From that time onward I looked and beheld deep secrets and wonderful mysteries.... there is nothing in heaven or deep within the earth concealed from me.[51] For Enoch-Metatron, the world of phenomena, "the orders of nature," is inherently semiotic. Heaven and earth are filled with hidden meanings that he can decode.

Moreover, this description conveys another noteworthy concept that may be reminiscent of divinatory concepts and vocabulary. It employs synonymous terms such as "beholding," "seeing," and "looking" (לצפות, לראות, להסתכל) to indicate the act of accessing divine secrets, as *Synopse* §72, for example, states: "I [God] committed to him [Enoch-Metatron] wisdom and understanding so he should behold the secrets of heaven above and earth below."[52]

These terms, which are used throughout *3 Enoch*, often seem to function as technical terms pertaining to the process through which Enoch-Metatron and Rabbi Ishmael gain access to God's coded secrets.[53] Their skills of observation are put in the service of beholding various phenomena, through which they ascertain God's secrets about his cosmic creation and plans. Furthermore, the authors

50. *Synopse* §§ 59–60; Alexander, "3 (Hebrew Apocalypse of) Enoch," 292– 93.

51. *Synopse* §14; Alexander, "3 (Hebrew Apocalypse of) Enoch," 264.

52. See *Synopse* § 72; Alexander, "3 (Hebrew Apocalypse of) Enoch," 311. Compare *Synopse* §§1, 2, 3, 14, 59–70.

53. On terms pertain to the act of beholding in the context of *hekhalot and merkabah* mysticism, see Arbel, *Beholders of Divine Secrets*, 24–29.

and redactors of *3 Enoch* appear to assume that the act of beholding was not a mechanical act. They stress the unique and superior ability of certain individuals to look at visible cosmic manifestations of the created order (סדרים) and behold their concealed meanings (סתרים). Moreover, they associate this unique perception with a quasi-divine elevated perspective that discerns the inner nature of things.[54]

A description in the Genizah fragment of *3 Enoch* mentioned above presents a parallel method by which divine secrets could be attained. This is the earliest existing fragment of *3 Enoch* that suggests affinities with Mesopotamian divinatory modes of thought and with its specific omen lists. Entitled "Good Omen" (סימן טוב), the description recounts how Enoch-Metatron revealed divine secrets to Rabbi Ishmael and makes note of the twelve constellations and their zodiacal signs, which are associated with an individual's physiognomy:

> And he showed me twelve constellations and also their zodiacs.... He said: One who is born in the constellation of Libra, on the first day, in Jupiter or in the moon: when he, the child, is born in these two hours, he is only born little and small and sallow. And he shall have a sign on the fingers of his hands and toes of his feet, or an extra finger (or "toe") on his hands or on his feet. And he shall be a fast and will have three lines in (the form of) crowns are wide lines. And he is one of the good. And at the age of seven months and ten days he shall become sick and shall be in hot waters.[55]

Reminiscent of both Mesopotamian horoscopes and the "diagnostic" omens mentioned earlier, the description emphasizes the significance ascribed to constellations as well as to a human's physical features. These seem to be regarded as mediums through which divine plans and decisions regarding the characteristics and "lots" of individuals can be ascertained.

---

54. It is worth noting that some manuscripts of *3 Enoch* use the term "secrets" (סתרי), "mysteries" (רזי), and "orders" (סדרי) interchangeably. In *Synopse* §14, for instance, three manuscripts mention "orders" of nature, two mention "mysteries of creation, one mentions "secrets" of creation. In *Synopse* §16 two manuscripts mention "orders" of creation, and two mention "secrets" of nature. See Alexander, "3 (Hebrew Apocalypse of) Enoch," 264 n. c, 266 n. d.

55. See Genizah fragment G12 (T.-S. K 21.95.L), discovered and published by Schäfer, *Geniza-Fragmente,* 136–37. Compare Gershom Scholem, "Physiognomy and Chiromancy" [Hebrew], in *Sepher Assaf: Festschrift for Simha Assaf* (ed. M. D. Cassuto et al.; Jerusalem: Mossad HaRav Kook, 1953), 459–95; idem, "Ein Fragment zur Physiognomik und Chiromantik aus der Tradition der spatantiken judischen Esoterik," in *Liber Amicorum: Studies in Honour of Professor Dr. C. J. Bleeker* (Leiden: Brill, 1969), 175–93; Ithamar Gruenwald, "New Passages from Hekhalot Literature" [Hebrew], *Tarbiz* 38 (1968–69): 354–72; idem,"Further Jewish Physiognomic and Chiromantic Fragments" [Hebrew], *Tarbiz* 40 (1971): 301–19. See the discussion in Schäfer, *Hidden and Manifest God,* 137–38.

Another theme associated with divine secrets is the revealed *Pargod* (פרגוד) "on which the course of human history was written." Traditionally scholars have interpreted the *Pargod* as a celestial curtain or veil,[56] yet in the context of *3 Enoch* the *Pargod* seems more a heavenly tablet on which God's plan is inscribed. The image is of an engraved, blueprinted plan pertaining to human history, past, present, and future, as we see in *Synopse* §64:

> R. Ishmael said: Metatron said to me: Come and I will show you the *Pargod* of the Omnipresent One, which is spread before the holy one blessed be He, and on which are printed all the generations of the world and all their deeds … whether done or to be done in the time to come, to all generations, till the end of time, were all printed on the *Pargod* of the Omnipresent One. I saw them with my own eyes.[57]

It seems that the *Pargod* of *3 Enoch* functions in a manner similar to the Mesopotamian Tablet of Destinies. It contains hidden knowledge about God's decisions and plans regarding the course of human history. These includes norms, deeds, and thoughts pertaining to the past, present, and future, which are all engraved on the *Pargod*'s surface and could be observed by those who were qualified.[58]

2.2. Initiation to Secrets and Their Disclosure

The characterization of Enoch-Metatron and descriptions of his initiation to divine secrets likewise suggest some affinities with Mesopotamian traditions of scholarly divination. In particular one can single out the tradition of King Enmeduranki, the human seer who was initiated to the secrets of the gods as well as to the rituals of the diviner. The following features are particularly suggestive.

First, similar to the Mesopotamian prototype, Enoch-Metatron is characterized as a mythological antediluvian figure (*Synopse* §§5–8), the "beloved of God" (§15), the "learned servant" (§13), and the "guardian of secrets" (§73) who was chosen by God to be taken to heaven and be privy to his secrets.

56. On the *Pargod* (a loanword from Persian) as a heavenly curtain, see Alexander, "3 (Hebrew Apocalypse of) Enoch," 296 n. a; Odeberg, *Hebrew Book of Enoch*, 141; Scholem, *Major Trends in Jewish Mysticism*, 72; Compare images of heavenly tablet in the Astronomical Book of *1 En.* 81:1–2; 93:2; 103:2; 106:19.

57. *Synopse* §§64–65; Alexander, "3 (Hebrew Apocalypse of) Enoch," 296–99. On the exegetical feature of the act of beholding, see Arbel, *Beholders of Divine Secrets*, 135–38. See descriptions of what seems to be an illuminated perception in *Synopse* §§81, 104, 335 (MS M22), 414, 421, 424, 544, 547, 550, 595.

58. Compare *Synopse* §78, which describes the twenty-two seals by which all *orders* and *destinies* were sealed.

Second, the initiation process is said to be involve several aspects that correspond to those in the Mesopotamian account: (1) an initiation to the celestial inner circle (*Synopse* §5–10); (2) the act of sitting on a celestial throne ("After all this, the Holy One, blessed be he, made for me a throne like the throne of glory.... He placed it at the door of the seventh heaven and sat me down upon it"); and (3) the reception of a divine tablet, "the *Pargod* of the Omnipresent," which contains secrets that otherwise are reserved for God alone.

Third, like the Mesopotamian tradition, *3 Enoch* establishes a tradition of transmission of secrets from a mythological ancient sage, Enoch-Metatron, the "knower of secrets," to his followers, the seers/beholders of the *merkabah*. *Synopse* §59–68 describes the transmission of secrets from Enoch-Metatron to Rabbi Ishmael. Using the same formulaic sentence "Come and I will show you," it recounts how Enoch-Metatron reveals mysteries to him, discloses heavenly treasures, exposes celestial archives, and unveils divine secrets, including the content of the *Pargod*.[59] In a similar vein, §64 presents Enoch-Metatron as a master of secrets who instructs a novice, Rabbi Ishmael of the *merkabah* circle:

> Rabbi Ishmael said, Metatron said to me: "Come and I will show you the *Pargod* ...on which are printed all the generations of the world and all their deeds, whether done or not done, till the last generation. I went and he showed them to me with his finger, like a father teaching his sons the letters of the Torah, and I saw.[60]

After his initiation, Enoch-Metatron not only sits on a celestial throne in heaven but also, perhaps in a manner reminiscent of the Mesopotamian depiction of the diviner's judicial role, adopts the divine persona of a heavenly judge. It is interesting to note that, unlike in the Targums, in the *b. Hag.* 15a, and in early Enochic sources, *3 Enoch* does not emphasize the standard, well-known scribal features and duties of Enoch-Metatron.[61] He is never identified by the title scribe

59. Compare similar conceptions in Genizah fragment T.-S. K 21.95.L, which presents the transmission of secrets from Enoch-Metatron to Rabbi Ishmael, and in *Synopse* §79, which recounts the transmission of secrets to Moses.

60. *Synopse* §§64–65; Alexander, "3 (Hebrew Apocalypse of) Enoch," 296.

61. Compare early depictions of Enoch-Metatron as a scribe in *Targum Pseudo-Jonathan* on Gen 5:24 (Michael W. Maher, trans., *Targum Pseudo-Jonathan: Genesis* [Collegeville, Minn.: Liturgical Press, 1992], 36). Compare *b. Hag.* 15a (Isodore Epstein, ed, *Soncino Hebrew-English Talmud.* [London: Soncino:, 1960–], *b. Hag.* 12b). Compare early Enochic sources that mention titles such as "scribe of righteousness" "scribe of truth," "skilled scribe," and "distinguished scribe," which stress the scribal features of Enoch (e.g., *1 En.* 12:3–4, 14:24–15:1, 81:1–2, 92:1; *2 En.* 23:4, 6, 4QEnGiants 4:16–24). For a discussions of Enoch's scribal roles in the Enochic literature, see Orlov, *Enoch-Metatron Tradition*, 50–59, 98–101; David E. Orton, *The Understanding Scribe: Matthew and the Apocalyptic Ideal* (JSNTSup 25; Sheffield: Sheffield Academic Press, 1989), 77–97; Christine Schams, *Jewish Scribes in the Second Temple Period* (JSOTSup 291; Shef-

(סופר). Moreover, several accounts explicitly present other celestial creatures as being engaged in the scribal acts of reading and writing.[62] Instead, *3 Enoch* often accentuates the scribal position of Enoch-Metatron as an expert of divine wisdom and a mediator of revealed secrets who partakes in the celestial judicial assembly. In a manner reminiscent of the Mesopotamian diviners, Enoch-Metatron sits on a heavenly throne to render a verdict on behalf of God: "At first I sat upon a great throne at the door of the seventh palace, and I judged all the denizens of the heights on the authority of the Holy One, blessed be he.[63]

2.3. Guarding Divine Secrets

In *3 Enoch* God reveals divine secrets to Enoch-Metatron, who in turn discloses them to selected adepts. The recipients of secrets include Rabbi Ishmael and Moses, both portrayed in this context as members of the *merkabah* group.[64] The revelation of secrets, however, is not limited to these qualified individuals. *Synopse* §74 introduces a noteworthy tradition regarding the human guardians of divine secrets. Endowed with the title the "knower of secrets," Enoch-Metatron is instructed in this account to reveal secret knowledge only to exclusive individuals, designated as the "wise of the world" and "those who understand." It states: "To give wisdom to all the wise of the world, and understanding and knowledge to those who understand, to reveal to them the secrets of my word, and to instruct them in the decree of my judgment."[65] The text refers to Dan 2:21 as the source behind this statement. Nonetheless, both the meaning and significance of this statement in the context of *3 Enoch* raise some doubts: What kind of wisdom is to be revealed, and of what does it consist? What is Enoch-Metatron's role as the one to whom these exclusive secrets are disclosed? Who are these "wise of the world" and "those who understand"?

The description does not provide direct answers. However, in light of conventions rooted in the Mesopotamian divinatory traditions, is it plausible to

field: Sheffield Academic Press 1998), 90–98. On the scribal features of Enoch in the context of early Judaism, see Frances Flannery-Dailey, *Dreamers, Scribes, and Priests: Jewish Dreams in the Hellenistic and Roman Eras* (JSJSup 90; Leiden: Brill, 2004), 139–47. On scribal roles of Enoch-Metatron in the context of priestly traditions, see Rachel Elior, "You Have Chosen Enoch," 15–64.

62. See *Synopse* §§26, 41, 43, 50, which describe various divine figures engaged in the acts of writing reading as scribes.

63. *Synopse* §20; Alexander, "3 (Hebrew Apocalypse of) Enoch,"268.

64. On the transmission of secrets from Enoch-Metatron to exclusive figures, see *Synopse* §80. As Alexander has noted ("3 [Hebrew Apocalypse of] Enoch," 315), the chain is similar to the chains of tridents of the oral law but has many missing links.

65. *Synopse* §74; Alexander, "3 (Hebrew Apocalypse of) Enoch," 312.

suggest that the statement of *Synopse* §74 is reminiscent of the divinatory secrecy formula, which, as we have seen, states:

> Secret knowledge of the great gods
> The one who knows may show [it] to another one who knows.
> The one who does not know may not see it.
> It [belongs] to the forbidden things of the great gods.[66]

The juxtaposition of similar concepts, styles and structures found in the two statements suggest certain affinities between the two traditions. Both are concerned with three key notions: divine wisdom, secrecy, and group identity. They also seem to employ a similar formulaic mode of expression to convey these matters.

Both sources classify divine wisdom or knowledge as secrets by using a formula of secrecy. Both use the notion of secrecy and revelation in order to identify a specific excusive group whose members are qualified to be the guardians of revealed secrets. The Mesopotamian divinatory formula confines the secrets of the gods to "the ones who know," the *ṭupšarru* scribe-scholars. The formula in *Synopse* §74 limits the knowledge of God's secrets to the "wise of the world," the "ones who understand," the members of the *merkabah* circle. It is possible that, as with the divinatory tradition, an appeal to secrecy and exclusivity in *3 Enoch* reflects the efforts of the particular *merkabah* group to demarcate their distinctiveness. Similarly, by employing a conventional formula of secrecy, members of the *merkabah* circle could have safeguarded their tradition and legitimized their claims, status, and authority.

To conclude this section, it is apparent that *3 Enoch*'s accounts of "legitimate" revelation of secret do not include direct references to divination. Yet these accounts, found in the existing *3 Enoch* after its redaction by Ashkenazi Jewry as well as in the early Genizah fragment of *3 Enoch*, seem to contain both explicit and implicit echoes of concepts and themes rooted in the Mesopotamian divinatory lore of the *ṭupšarru* scribe-scholars.

One can disregard the significance of specific analogous themes, yet the cumulative and specific nature of the evidence suggests a deliberate approach. Reminiscent of Mesopotamian divinatory conceptions, *3 Enoch* associates divine secrets with God's cosmic order and plans, envisioned as coded and inscribed on visible and observable terrestrial, celestial, and physiognomic phenomena, as well as on the *Pargod*. These are seen as mediums or channels through which qualified humans such as Enoch-Metatron or Rabbi Ishmael can gain access to God's plans and cosmic decisions. Descriptions of the initiation to secrets in *3 Enoch* are likewise reminiscent of themes found in the Mesopotamian divinatory lore. Enoch-Metatron is the beloved antediluvian sage, a learned servant who is initi-

66. See n. 36 above.

ated to divine secrets through a specific process. First, he is accepted into the celestial realm. He is then seated on a celestial throne, presented with secrets as well as with the *Pargod*, and transmits these secrets to qualified individuals.

Finally, *3 Enoch*'s presentation of secrecy through a specific formula seems to reflect not only a conceptual or thematic correspondence to divinatory conceptions but also a shared formulaic style. In its terms, structure, and mode of expression, *Synopse* §74 is reminiscent of the Mesopotamian *Geheimwissen* formula. Through this standard formula divine secrets are limited to "wise of the world" or "the ones who understand," including Rabbi Ishmael, Moses, and presumably other members of the *merkabah* circle, who may have defined their identity and validated their tradition and authority through an appeal to a revealed secret knowledge.

3. A Distinctive Conceptualization

Where, then, do all these considerations lead? To what extent do notions of divine secrets and their revelation in *3 Enoch* correspond to notions rooted in the Mesopotamian divinatory lore of the *ṭupšarru* scribe-scholars? In his discussion of the impact of Mesopotamian mantic traditions on the early Enochic literature, John J. Collins has observed that, despite clear links between the two traditions, "the Jewish sages who produced the Enochic literature were by no means diviners of the Babylonian type.… what one finds in the Enochic apocalypses is ultimately a new phenomenon which draws motifs and patterns from many sources but which cannot be understood as the sum of its sources."[67]

In my view, *3 Enoch* displays similar tendencies. It re-employs concepts and themes rooted in the divinatory lore of the *ṭupšarru* scribe-scholars, yet it also alters such notions and reintroduces them in an alternative context in order to assert its own perspectives regarding divine secrets and their revelation. While the scope of this essay does not allow an extensive investigation of this development, it is helpful to consider, albeit briefly, one noticeable difference by way of example.

As noted above, in the Mesopotamian tradition divinatory knowledge the secrets of the gods were ultimately derived from a divine source in ancient times. Yet the tradition also makes it clear that successive diviners gained access to these divine secrets by studying the textual omen collections, not through direct communication with the divine.[68] Moreover, the personal, interior experiences of the diviners were not thought to play any role in this context. Rochberg has made this point clear: "as no testimony to the necessity of divine revelation as the method of access to 'secrets' is extant for the Mesopotamian diviners and scholars

67. See Collins, *Seers, Sibyls and Sages*, 343.

68. On divination as an intellectual activity, see Rochberg, *Heavenly Writing*, 265–73.

themselves, study would seem to be the only route.... the authority of the interpretation was grounded in the text not on a claim to divine inspiration."[69] Thus, the wisdom of the *ṭupšarru* scribe-scholars was primarily dependent on intellectual activities and was achieved through scholarly pursuits.

In contrast, as I have demonstrated in a previous publication, *3 Enoch* appeals to notions of experiences and revelations whether they fictional, literary, or authentic.[70] As part of *hekhalot* and *merkabah* mysticism, *3 Enoch* introduces a religious outlook, recognized as mystical, according to which qualified humans could attain personal experiences of God and the heavenly realm through elevated perception and altered consciousness. According to several macroforms of this literature, including *3 Enoch*, members of the *merkabah* circle practiced various techniques and spiritual exercises, elevated their human perception beyond its ordinary limits, and underwent inner transformations, thus gaining a new awareness. They were then initiated into God's secrets, attained divine revelations, and beheld and interpreted their concealed meanings and hidden truths.[71]

For instance, Enoch-Metatron's experience of transformation is presented metaphorically in *Synopse* §11. In this account Enoch-Metatron attains superior and elevated inner abilities and undergoes a transformation from one level of existence to another before he attains knowledge of divine secrets:

> Before the Holy One blessed be he, set me to serve the throne of glory, he opened for me 300,000 gates of understanding, 300,000 gates of prudence, 300,000 gates of life, 300,000 gates of grace and favor, 300,000 gates of love, 300,000 gates of Torah, 300,000 gates of sustenance, 300,000 gates of mercy.[72]

Enoch-Metatron is then granted an altered, exceptional, quasi-divine perception, illuminated wisdom, and understanding: "I [God] have committed to him [Enoch-Metatron] the Prince of Wisdom and the Prince of Understanding to teach him the wisdom of those above and below."[73]

Enoch-Metatron's cosmic experience is presented in *3 Enoch* as well in the wider context of the *hekhalot* and *merkabah* literature as a model for all members of the *merkabah* circle. These adepts gain access to divine secrets only after they undergo similar experiences. For instance, in *3 Enoch* Rabbi Ishmael's experience of inner transformation and an altered, enlightened state of consciousness is presented metaphorically in *Synopse* §2: he ascends to heaven, falls down and

---

69. See ibid., 217.

70. See Arbel, *Beholders of Divine Secrets*, 21–50.

71. See ibid., 37–44; Daphna Arbel, "Understanding of the Heart—Mystical Experiences in the Hekhalot Literature," *JSJ* 6 (1999): 319–44; Morray-Jones, "Transformational Mysticism," 1–31.

72. *Synopse* §12; Alexander, "3 (Hebrew Apocalypse of) Enoch," 256.

73. *Synopse* §13; Alexander, "3 (Hebrew Apocalypse of) Enoch," 256.

faints, only to be revived by Enoch-Metatron, and later illuminated by God, who enlightens his eyes and his heart:

> I shrank back trembling and fell down … until the Holy One, blessed be he, rebuked them.… At once Metatron, Prince of the Divine Presence, came and revived me and raised me to my feet.… after an hour the Holy One, blessed be he, opened to me the gates of *Shekhinah*.… He enlightened my eyes and my heart.[74]

Following this experience, Rabbi Ishmael is led on a tour through the celestial realm by Enoch-Metatron, who discloses to him hidden divine secrets that he is now able to behold. Enoch-Metatron constantly uses the same formula before he lists the concealed divine secrets: "Come and I will show you."[75] Consequently, he describes visions that are normally beyond perception, emphasizing thereby Rabbi Ishmael's new, enlightened ability to access the hidden dimensions of reality.[76]

As noted, the accounts of *3 Enoch* seem to re-employ available conventions rooted in Mesopotamian divinatory traditions in order to convey ideas about a direct communication between the human and the divine. Further, *3 Enoch* embraces ideological concepts about ascertaining concealed divine truths through manifested phenomena. Likewise, it incorporates specific concepts and themes related to divine secrets and revelation that correspond to distinct divinatory traditions of the *ṭupšarru* scribe-scholars. Yet all these are altered and reintroduced in *3 Enoch*, in the context of its specific religious outlook. This outlook emphasizes primarily the human's interior experience and awareness as keys to knowing God and beholding his secrets.

The Mesopotamian divinatory tradition asserts that a mythological antediluvian sage gained secrets from the gods. Successor diviners, however, are seen more as technical diviners who acquire divine secrets through study of the special textual lore of divination, which was largely inaccessible to others. Parallel to the Mesopotamian lore, *3 Enoch* characterizes Enoch-Metatron as an ancient sage who gained divine secrets from God. This macroform, however, introduces different concerns by emphasizing Enoch-Metatron's experiences and divine revelations. It presents him as an inspired seer who undergoes experiences of transformation that, in turn, enable him to attain divine secrets. Moreover, Enoch-Metatron is depicted as a model for all successor adepts, an archetype of a pneumatic exegete who is guided by experiences and divine revelations into the meaning of secrets. Like him, Rabbi Ishmael and other members of the *merkabah*

---

74. *Synopse* §11; Alexander, "3 (Hebrew Apocalypse of) Enoch," 256.

75. *Synopse* §59; Alexander, "3 (Hebrew Apocalypse of) Enoch," 292. Compare *Synopse* §§60–62, 64–68.

76. *Synopse* §11; Alexander, "3 (Hebrew Apocalypse of) Enoch," 256.

circle are portrayed as inspired seers who gain access to God's secrets through an enlightened state of consciousness and direct divine revelations.[77]

Analogous to the Mesopotamian lore, *3 Enoch* assumes that humans are able to access deeper and concealed dimensions of reality. Yet behind the two traditions are two different conceptual modes of thought. One tradition emphasizes that these can be attained through study and learning, while the other accentuates the inner experiences and direct divine revelation as highly significant.

In this essay I have suggested that, in its distinctive presentation of divine secrets and their revelation, *3 Enoch*, even in its present form, is not completely divorced from concepts of divination, particularly not from the Mesopotamian divinatory lore of the *ṭupšarru* scribe-scholars. Rather, a different reading of *3 Enoch* reveals that several of its key concepts and themes correspond, both explicitly and implicitly, to Mesopotamian divinatory notions. As such, it seems plausible to suggest that early and late authors and redactors of *3 Enoch*, in accordance with their method of mixing up traditions, have also appealed to traditions of the *ṭupšarru* scribe-scholars in order to formulate their views. These divinatory traditions were available in the cultural context of the Greco-Roman world of late antiquity. They may have been embraced, altered, and reapplied in *3 Enoch* in order to formulate and express certain notions in a different context and in a much later time.

At the same time, however, *3 Enoch* introduces a conceptual change regarding the relationship between the divine and humans that seems to reflect the sensibilities of both early and later Jewish authors and redactors. Unlike the secrets of divination, which could be acquired by successor diviners by studying the ancient omen compendiums, *3 Enoch* emphasizes the inner experiences of altered states of consciousness that ultimately lead to beholding God and his secrets. Utilizing the discourse of the diviner scribe-scholars, *3 Enoch* thus seems to introduce Enoch-Metatron as a different ideal figure. He is an inspired seer, a pneumatic exegete who attains divine secrets and gains access into the deeper dimensions of reality though direct divine revelations and personal experiences of God.

77. On experiences of transformation that enable the *merkabah* adepts to cross conceptual boundaries and behold divine secrets in an enlightened perspective, see, e.g., *Synopse* §§11, 124, 247–251, 580–581, 585, 595.

Bibliography

Abrams, Daniel. "The Boundaries of Divine Ontology: The Inclusion and Exclusion of Metatron in the Godhead." *HTR* 87 (1994): 291–321.

Abusch, I. Tzvi. "Alaktu and Halakhah, Oracular Decision, Divine Revelation." *HTR* 80 (1987): 15–42.

———. "Ascent to the Stars in a Mesopotamian Ritual: Social Metaphor and Religious Experience." Pages 15–39 in *Death, Ecstasy, and Other Worldly Journeys*. Edited by John J. Collins and Michael Fishbane. Albany: State University of New York Press, 1995.

———. "Mesopotamian Anti-Witchcraft Literature: Texts and Studies. Part I: The Nature of Maqlû: Its Character, Divisions, and Calendrical Setting." *JNES* 33 (1974): 251–62.

Abusch, Ra'anan. "Rabbi Ishmael's Miraculous Conception: Jewish Salvation History in Anti-Christian Polemic." Pages 307–43 in *The Ways That Never Parted: Jews and Christians in Late Antiquity and the Middle Ages*. Edited by A. H. Becker and A. Y. Reed. TSAJ 95. Tübingen: Mohr Siebeck, 2003.

Afzal, Cameron. "The Communal Icon: Complex Cultural Schemas, Elements of the Social Imagination (Matthew 10:32//Luke 12:8 and Revelation 3:5, A Case Study." Pages 58–80 in *Putting Body and Soul Together: Essays in Honor of Robin Scroggs*. Edited by Virginia Wiles, Alexandra Brown, and G. F. Snyder. Valley Forge, Pa.: Trinity Press International, 1997.

———. "Time Revealed: The Eschatology of Revelation Chapters 6–7." Ph.D diss. Columbia University, 1993.

Albeck, Enoch, ed. *Midraš Berešit Rabbati ex Libro R. Mosis hadDaršan*. 1940. Repr., Jerusalem: Mĕqiẓei-Nirdamim, 1966/67.

Albright, William F. "A Catalogue of Early Hebrew Lyric Poems [Psalm LXVIII]." *HUCA* 23 (1950–51): 24–25.

———. "The Location of the Garden of Eden." *AJSL* 38 (1922): 15–31.

Alexander, Philip. "From Son of Adam to Second God: Transformation of the Biblical Enoch." Pages 102–11 in *Biblical Figures Outside the Bible*. Edited by Michael E. Stone and T. A. Bergen. Harrisburg, Pa.: Trinity Press International, 1998.

———. "The Historical Setting of the Hebrew Book of Enoch." *JJS* 28 (1977): 156–80.

———, ed. and trans. "3 (Hebrew Apocalypse of) Enoch." *OTP* 1:223–315.

Alexander, Philip, and Geza Vermes, eds. *Qumran Cave 4.XIX: 4QSerekh Ha-Yaḥad and Two Related Texts*. DJD 26. Oxford: Clarendon, 1998.

Alexandre, Manuel, Jr. "The Eloquent Philosopher in Philo's De uita contemplatiua." *Euphrosyne* 29 (2001): 319–30.

Ali, Ahmed, trans. *Al-Qur'an: A Contemporary Translation.* Princeton: Princeton University Press, 1988.

Amusin, Iosif D. *Kumranskaja Obshchina.* Moscow: Nauka, 1983.

Andersen, Francis. "2 (Slavonic Apocalypse of) Enoch." *OTP* 1:102–221.

Aptowitzer, Avigdor. "Bet hamMiqdaš šel Ma'alah 'al Pi ha'Aggadah." *Tarbiz* 2 (1931): 137–53, 257–77.

Arbel, Vita Daphna. *Beholders of Divine Secrets: Mysticism and Myth and the Hekhalot and Merkavah Literature.* Albany: State University of New York Press, 2003.

———. "Seal of Resemblance, Full of Wisdom and Perfect in Beauty: The Enoch/Metatron Narrative of 3 Enoch and Ezekiel 28." *HTR* 98 (2005): 121–42.

———. " 'Understanding of the Heart'—Mystical Experiences in the Hekhalot Literature." *JSJ* 6 (1999): 319–44.

Ashton, John. *The Religion of Paul the Apostle*. New Haven: Yale University Press, 2000.

Attridge, Harold. *The Epistle to the Hebrews.* Hermeneia. Philadelphia: Fortress, 1989.

———, ed. *Qumran Cave 4.VIII: Parabiblical Texts, Part 1.* DJD 13. Oxford: Clarendon, 1994.

Auffarth, Christopher, and Loren Stuckenbruck, eds. *The Fall of the Angels*. Leiden: Brill, 2004.

Aune, David E. "The Apocalypse of John and the Problem of Genre." *Semeia* 36 (1986): 65–96.

———. "The Influence of Roman Law Court Ceremonial on the Apocalypse of John." *BR* 18 (1983): 5–26.

———. "Luke 20:34–36: A Gnosticized Logion of Jesus?" Pages 187–202 in vol. 3 of *Geschichte-Tradition-Reflexion: Festschrift für Martin Hengel zum 70. Geburtstag.* Edited by Hubert Cancik, Hermann Lichtenberger, and Peter Schäfer. Tübingen: Mohr Siebeck, 1996.

Austin, James H. *Zen and the Brain: Toward an Understanding of Meditation and Consciousness.* Cambridge: MIT Press, 1998.

Avigad, Nahman, and Yigael Yadin. *A Genesis Apocryphon: A Scroll from the Wilderness of Judaea*. Jerusalem: Magnes, 1956.

Badia, Leonard F. *The Dead Sea People's Sacred Meal and Jesus' Last Supper.* Washington, D.C.: University Press of America, 1979.

Baer, Richard. *Philo's Use of the Categories Male and Female.* ALGHJ 3. Leiden: Brill, 1970.

Baillet, Maurice. *Qumrân grotte 4.III (4Q482–4Q520).* DJD 7. Oxford: Clarendon, 1982.

Balentine, Samuel. *The Hidden God: The Hiding of the Face of God in the Old Testament.* Oxford: Oxford University Press, 1983.

Barker, Margaret. *The Gate of Heaven: The History and Symbolism of the Temple in Jerusalem*. London: SPCK, 1991.

———. *The Older Testament: The Survival of Themes from the Ancient Royal Cult in Sectarian Judaism and Early Christianity*. London: SPCK, 1987.

———. *On Earth as It Is in Heaven*. Edinburgh: T&T Clark, 1995.

———. *The Revelation of Jesus Christ*. Edinburgh: T&T Clark, 2000.

Barr, James. "Theophany and Anthropomorphism in the Old Testament." Pages 31–38 in *Congress Volume: Oxford, 1959*. VTSup 7. Leiden: Brill, 1960.

Bauckham, Richard. *The Climax of Prophecy: Studies on the Book of Revelation*. Edinburgh: T&T Clark, 1993.

———. *The Fate of the Dead: Studies on the Jewish and Christian Apocalypses*. NovTSup 93. Leiden: Brill, 1998.

———. "The Lord's Day." Pages 197–220 in *From Sabbath to Lord's Day*. Edited by D. A. Carson. Grand Rapids: Zondervan, 1982.

Baumgarten, Joseph M. "4Q Halakah[a] 5, the Law of Ḥadash, and the Pentecontal Calendar." *JJS* 27 (1976): 35–46.

———. "The Qumran-Essene Restraints on Marriage." Pages 13–24 in *Archaeology and History in the Dead Sea Scrolls*. Edited by Lawrence Schiffman. Sheffield: Sheffield Academic Press, 1990.

———. "The Qumran Sabbath Shirot and Rabbinic Merkabah Traditions." *RevQ* 13 (1988): 199–213.

Beale, Gregory K. *The Book of Revelation: A Commentary on the Greek Text*. NIGTC. Grand Rapids: Eerdmans, 1999.

Beaulieu, Paul Alain. "New Light on Secret Knowledge in Late Babylonian Culture." *ZA* 82 (1992): 98–111.

Bell, Catharine. *Ritual: Perspectives and Dimensions*. New York: Oxford University Press, 1997.

———. *Ritual Theory, Ritual Practice*. Oxford: Oxford University Press, 1992.

Bietenhard, Hans, trans. *Midrasch Tanhuma B: R. Tanhuma über die Tora, genannt Midrasch Jelammedenu*. 2 vols. Judaica et Christiana 5–6. Bern: Lang, 1980–82.

Binsbergen, Wim van, and Frans Wiggermann. "Magic in History: A Theoretical Perspective and Its Application to Ancient Mesopotamia." Pages 20–25 in *Mesopotamian Magic: Textual, Historical, and Interpretive Perspectives*. Edited by Tzvi Abusch and Karel van der Toorn. Groningen: Styx, 1998.

Birnbaum, Ellen. *The Place of Judaism in Philo's Thought: Israel, Jews and Proselytes*. BJS 290. Atlanta: Scholars Press, 1996.

Black, Jeremy, and J. Anthony Green. *Gods, Demons and Symbols of Ancient Mesopotamia: An Illustrated Dictionary*. Austin: University of Texas Press, 1992.

Black, Matthew. *The Scrolls and Christian Origins: Studies in the Jewish Background of the New Testament*. New York: Scribner, 1961.

———, ed. *Apocalypsis Henochi Graece*. PVTG 3.1. Leiden: Brill. 1970.

———. *The Book of Enoch, or 1 Enoch*. SVTP 7. Leiden: Brill, 1985.

Blake, William. *Milton: A Poem*. Blake's Illuminated Books 5. Edited by R. N. Essick and J. Viscomi. London: Blake Society/Tate Gallery, 1993.

Bloch, R. "Die Gestalt des Moses in der rabbinischen Tradition." Pages 95–171 in *Moses in Schrift und Überlieferung*. Edited by Henri Cazalles et al. Düsseldorf: Patmos, 1963.

Boccaccini, Gabriele. *Beyond the Essene Hypothesis: The Parting of the Ways between Qumran and Enochic Judaism*. Grand Rapids: Eerdmans, 1998.

———. *Enoch and Qumran Origins*. Grand Rapids: Eerdmanns, 2005.

Bockmuehl, Markus N. A. *Revelation and Mystery in Ancient Judaism and Pauline Christianity*. Tübingen: Mohr Siebeck, 1990.

Bodnar, John. *Remaking America: Public Memory, Commemoration, and Patriotism in the Twentieth Century*. Princeton: Princeton University Press. 1992.

Boesak, Allen A. *Comfort and Protest: Reflections on the Apocalypse of John of Patmos*. Philadelphia: Westminster, 1987.

Bogaert, Pierre. *Apocalypse de Baruch*. 2 vols. Paris: Cerf, 1969.

Bokser, Baruch M. *Philo's Description of Jewish Practices*. Center for Hermeneutical Studies in Hellenistic and Modern Culture, Colloquy 30. Berkeley and Los Angeles: Graduate Theological Union; University of California Press, 1977.

Bonner, Stanley F. *Education in Ancient Rome: From the Elder Cato to the Younger Pliny*. Berkeley and Los Angeles: University of California Press, 1977.

Bonwetsch, G. Nathanael. *Die Bücher der Geheimnisse Henochs: Das sogenannte slavische Henochbuch*. TU 44. Leipzig: Hinrichs, 1922.

———. *Das slavische Henochbuch*. AGWG 1. Berlin: Weidmannsche Buchhandlung, 1896.

Borgen, Peder. *Philo of Alexandria: An Exegete for His Time*. NovTSup 86. Leiden: Brill, 1997.

Borger, R. "Geheimwissen." *RlA* 3:188–91.

Boring, M. Eugene. *Revelation*. IBC. Louisville: John Knox, 1989.

Bottéro, Jean. *Mesopotamia: Writing, Reasoning and the Gods*. Chicago: University of Chicago Press, 1992.

———. *Religion in Ancient Mesopotamia*. Chicago: University of Chicago Press, 2001.

———. "Symptômes, signes, écritures en Mésopotamie ancienne." Pages 70–197 in *Divination et rationalité*. Edited by J. P. Vernant et al. Paris: Éditions du Seuil, 1974.

Böttrich, Christfried. *Adam als Mikrokosmos: Eine Untersuchung zum slavischen Henochbuch*. Frankfurt am Main: Lang, 1995.

———. *Das slavische Henochbuch*. Gütersloh: Gütersloher Verlaghaus, 1995.

———. *Weltweisheit, Menschheitsethik, Urkult: Studien zum slavischen Henochbuch*. WUNT 2.50. Tübingen: Mohr Siebeck, 1992.

Bousset, Wilhelm. "Die Himmelreise der Seele." *AR* 4:136–69, 229–73.

Boustan, Ra'anan S. *From Martyr to Mystic: Rabbinic Martyrology and the Making of Merkavah Mysticism*. TSAJ 112. Tübingen: Mohr Siebeck, 2005.

———. "Response to Rachel Elior's 'The Three Temples.'" Paper presented at the Society of Biblical Literature Annual Meeting. San Antonio, 22 November 2004.

Bowker, John W. "'Merkabah' Visions and the Visions of Paul." *JJS* 16 (1971): 157–73.

Braude, William G., and Israel J. Kapstein, trans. *Pěsikta dě-Rab Kahăna: R. Kahana's Compilations of Discourses for Sabbaths and Festal Days*. London: Routledge & Kegan Paul, 1975.

Braun, Willi. *Feasting and Social Rhetoric in Luke 14*. Cambridge: Cambridge University Press, 1995.

Brewer, Raymond R. "Revelation 4.6 and Translations Thereof." *JBL* 71 (1952): 227–31.

Brock, Sebastian. "The Holy Spirit as Feminine in Early Syriac Literature." Pages 73–88 in *After Eve: Women, Theology and the Christian Tradition*. Edited by J. Martin Soskice. London: Collins, 1990.

Brooke, George, et al., eds. *Qumran Cave 4.XVII: Parabiblical Texts, Part 3*. DJD 22. Oxford: Clarendon, 1996.

Brown, David. *Mesopotamian Planetary Astronomy-Astrology*. Groningen: Styx, 2000.

Brown, Raymond E. *The Gospel according to John*. 2 vols. AB 29–29A. Garden City, N.Y.: Doubleday, 1966–70.

Brownlee, William H. "The Scroll of Ezekiel from the Eleventh Qumran Cave." *RevQ* 4 (1963–64): 11–28.

Buber, Solomon, ed. *Midrasch Tanchuma: Ein agadischer Commentar zum Pentateuch von Rabbi Tanchuma ben Rabbi Abba*. 6 vols. 1885. Repr., Jerusalem: Ortsel, 1963.

———, ed. *Solomon Midrash Eikhah Rabbah*. Vilna: Romm, 1899.

———, ed. *Pesiqta de-Rav Kahana*. Lvov: Meqitzei Nirdamim, 1868.

Buchanan, George Wesley. *To the Hebrews*. AB 36. Garden City, N.Y.: Doubleday, 1972.

Burkert, Walter. *Ancient Mystery Cults*. Cambridge: Harvard University Press, 1987.

———. *Greek Religion: Archaic and Classical*. Translated by John Raffan. Oxford: Blackwell, 1985.

Butler, Judith. *Excitable Speech: A Politics of the Performative*. New York: Routledge, 1997.

Cadbury, Henry J. "A Qumran Parallel to Paul." *HTR* 51 (1958): 1–2.

Caird, George Bradford. *The Revelation of St. John the Divine*. HNTC. New York: Harper & Row, 1966.

Caquot, André. "La Divinite Solaire Ougaritique." *Syria* 36 (1959): 90–101.

Carmignac, Jean. "Les Dangers de l'Eschatologie." *NTS* 17 (1981): 365–90.

———. "Description du phénomène de l'Apocalyptique dans l'Ancien Testament." Pages 163–170 in *Apocalypticism in the Mediterranean World and the Near East: Proceedings of the International Colloquium on Apocalypticism Uppsala, August 12–17, 1979*. Edited by David Hellholm. Tübingen: Mohr Siebeck, 1983.

———. "Règle des Chants pour l'Holocauste du Sabbat: Quelques détails de lecture." *RevQ* 4 (1964): 563–66.

Carr, Wesley. *Angels and Principalities: The Background, Meaning, and Development of the Pauline Phrase "Hai Archai kai hai Exousai."* SNTSMS 42. Cambridge: Cambridge University Press, 1997.

Carrithers, Michael, et al., eds. *The Category of the Person: Anthropology, Philosophy, History*. New York: Cambridge University Press, 1985.

Carruthers, Mary. *The Book of Memory: A Study of Memory in Medieval Culture*. Cambridge: Cambridge University Press, 1990.

———. *The Craft of Thought: Meditation, Rhetoric, and The Making of Images, 400–1200*. Cambridge: Cambridge University Press, 1998.

Cassin, Elena. *La splendeur divine: Introduction à l'étude de la mentalité mésopotamienne*. Paris: Mouton, 1968.

Cavell, Stanley. *Philosophical Passages: Wittgenstein, Emerson, Austin, Derrida*. Cambridge: Blackwell, 1995.

Chadwick, Henry. "St. Paul and Philo of Alexandria." *BJRL* 48 (1966): 286–307.

Charles, R. H. *The Book of Enoch or 1 Enoch*. Oxford: Clarendon, 1912.
———. *A Critical and Exegetical Commentary on the Revelation of St. John*. 2 vols. ICC. Edinburgh: T&T Clark, 1920.
———. *The Greek Versions of the Testaments of the Twelve Patriarchs*. 1908. Repr., Oxford: Oxford University Press; /Hildesheim: Olms, 1960.
Charles, Robert H., and William Richard Morfill. *The Book of the Secrets of Enoch*. Oxford: Clarendon, 1896.
Charlesworth, James H. *The Old Testament Pseudepigrapha and the New Testament: Prolegomena for the Study of Christian Origins*. SNTSMS 54. Cambridge: Cambridge University Press, 1985.
———. "The SNTS Pseudepigrapha Seminars at Tübingen and Paris on the Books of Enoch (Seminar Report)." *NTS* 25 (1979): 315–23.
Chernus, Ira. *Mysticism in Rabbinic Judaism*. Studia Judaica 11. Berlin: de Gruyter, 1982.
Chidester, David. *Word and Light: Seeing, Hearing, and Religious Discourse*. Urbana: University of Illinois Press, 1992.
Childs, Brevard S. *The Book of Exodus: A Critical, Theological Commentary*. OTL. Philadelphia: Westminster, 1974.
Coblentz Bautch, Kelley. *A Study of the Geography of 1 Enoch 17–19: "No One Has Seen What I Have Seen."* JSJSup 81. Leiden: Brill, 2003.
Cohen, Martin Samuel, ed. *The Shi'ur Qomah: Texts and Recensions*. TSAJ 9. Tübingen: Mohr Siebeck, 1985.
Collins, John J. "Apocalyptic Eschatology as Transcendence of Death." *CBQ* 36 (1974): 21–43.
———. *The Apocalyptic Imagination: An Introduction to the Jewish Matrix of Christianity*. New York: Crossroad, 1992.
———. "Apocalyptic Literature." Pages 345–70 in *Early Judaism and Its Modern Interpreters*. Edited by Robert A. Kraft and George W. E. Nickelsburg. SBLBMI 2. Atlanta: Scholars Press, 1986.
———. "Apocalyptic Literature." Pages 432–447 in *The Blackwell Companion to the Hebrew Bible*. Edited by Leo Perdue. Malden, Mass.: Blackwell, 2001.
———. *Daniel*. Hermeneia. Minneapolis: Fortress, 1993.
———. *Daniel, with an Introduction to Apocalyptic Literature*. FOTL 20. Grand Rapids: Eerdmans, 1984.
———. "The Genre Apocalypse in Hellenistic Judaism." Pages 531–49 in *Apocalypticism in the Mediterranean World and the Near East: Proceedings of the International Colloquium on Apocalypticism Uppsala, Aug. 12–17, 1979*. Edited by David Hellholm. Tübingen: Mohr Siebeck, 1983.
———. "Inspiration or Illusion: Biblical Theology and the Book of Daniel." *ExAud* 6 (1990): 31–33.
———. "Introduction: Towards the Morphology of a Genre." *Semeia* 14 (1979): 1–20.
———. "The Jewish Apocalypses." *Semeia* 14 (1979): 21–59.
———. "The Sage in Apocalyptic and Pseudepigraphic Literature." Pages 343–54 in *The Sage in Israel and the Ancient Near East*. Edited by G. Gammie and L. G. Perdue. Winona Lake, Ind.: Eisenbrauns, 1990.

———. *The Scepter and the Star: The Messiahs of the Dead Sea Scrolls and Other Ancient Literary.* ABRL. New York: Doubleday, 1995.
———. 1997. *Seers, Sibyls and Sages in Hellenistic-Roman Judaism.* JSJSup 54. Leiden: Brill.
———, ed. *Apocalypse: The Morphology of a Genre. Semeia* 14 (1979).
Colson, Francis H., and George W. Whitaker, trans. *Philo.* 10 vols. LCL. Cambridge: Harvard University Press, 1932–62.
Conway, Colleen. "Gender and Divine Relativity in Philo of Alexandria." *JSJ* 34 (2003): 471–91.
Cooke, George A. *A Critical and Exegetical Commentary on the Book of Ezekiel.* 2 vols. ICC. New York: Scribner, 1937.
———. "The Paradise Story of Ezekiel 28." Pages 37–45 in *Old Testament Essays.* London: Griffin, 1927.
Cothenet, Edouard. "Influence d'Ézéchiel sur la spiritualité de Qumrân." *RevQ* 13 (1988): 431–39.
Cross, Frank Moore. *Canaanite Myth and Hebrew Epic: Essays in the History of the Religion of Israel.* Cambridge: Harvard University Press, 1973.
———. "The Council of Yahweh in Second Isaiah." *JNES* 12 (1953): 274–77.
Cry, L. "Quelques noms d'anges ou d'êtres mystérieux en II Hénoch." *RB* 49 (1940): 195–203.
Cryer, Frederick. H. *Divination in Ancient Israel and Its Near Eastern Environment.* JSOTSup 142. Sheffield: Sheffield Academic Press, 1994.
D'Andrade, Roy. *The Development of Cognitive Anthropolgy.* Cambridge: Cambridge University Press, 1995.
Dalley, Stephanie, ed. *The Legacy of Mesopotamia.* Oxford: Oxford University Press, 1998.
Dan, Joseph. *The Ancient Jewish Mysticism.* Tel Aviv: MOD Books, 1993.
———. "The Gate to the Sixth Palace" [Hebrew]. *Jerusalem Studies in Jewish Thought* 6 (1987): 197–220.
———. *Jewish Mysticism.* 4 vols. Northvale, N.J.: Aronson, 1998–99.
———. "Melchizedek, the 'Youth,' and Jesus." Pages 248–74 in *The Dead Sea Scrolls as Background to Postbiblical Judaism and Early Christianity: Papers from an International Conference at St. Andrews in 2001.* Edited by James R. Davila. Leiden: Brill, 2001.
———. "The Religious Experience of the Merkavah." Pages 289–307 in *From the Bible through the Middle Ages.* Vol. 1 of *Jewish Spirituality.* Edited by Arthur Green. New York: Crossroad, 1986.
———. *Three Types of Ancient Jewish Mysticism.* Cincinnati: University of Cincinnati Press, 1984.
Daniélou, Jean. *The Bible and the Liturgy.* Notre Dame: University of Notre Dame Press, 1956.
———. *The Origins of Latin Christianity.* London: Darton, Longman & Todd, 1977.
———. *Primitive Christian Symbols.* Translated by D. Attwater. Baltimore: Helicon, 1964.
———. *The Theology of Jewish Christianity.* Philadelphia: Westminster, 1964.

———. "Trinité et angélologie dans la théologue judéo-chrétienne." *RSR* 45 (1957): 5–41.

Davila, James R. "The Animal Apocalypse and Daniel." Pages 35–38 in *Enoch and Qumran Origins: New Light on a Forgotten Connection*. Edited by Gabriele Boccaccini. Grand Rapids: Eerdmans, 2003.

———. "The Dead Sea Scrolls and Merkavah Mysticism." Pages 249–64 in *The Dead Sea Scrolls in Their Historical Context*. Edited by Timothy H. Lim et al. Edinburgh: T&T Clark, 2000.

———. *Descenders to the Chariot: The People behind the Hekhalot Literature*. JSJSup 70. Leiden: Brill, 2000.

———. "The Hekhalot Literature and Shamanism." Pages 767–89 in *Society of Biblical Literature 1994 Seminar Papers*. SBLSP 33. Atlanta: Scholars Press, 1994.

———. "The Hodayot Hymnist and the Four Who Entered Paradise." *RevQ* 17/65–68 (1996): 457–78.

———. *Liturgical Works*. Eerdmans Commentaries on the Dead Sea Scrolls 6. Grand Rapids: Eerdmans, 2000.

———. "The Macrocosmic Temple, Scriptural Exegesis and the Songs of the Sabbath Sacrifice." *DSD* 9 (2002): 1–19.

———. "Of Methodology, Monotheism and Metatron." Pages 3–18 in *The Jewish Roots of Christological Monotheism: Papers from the St. Andrews Conference on the Historical Origins of the Worship of Jesus*. Edited by C. C. Newman, J. R. Davila, and G. S. Lewis. JSJSup 63. Leiden: Brill, 1999.

———. "The Old Testament Pseudepigrapha as Background to the New Testament." *ExpTim* 117 (2005): 53–57.

———. *The Provenance of the Pseudepigrapha: Jewish, Christian, or Other?* JSJSup 105. Leiden: Brill, 2005.

———. "Ritual in the Jewish Pseudepigrapha." Pages 158–83 in *Anthropology and Biblical Studies: Avenues of Approach*. Edited by Louise J. Lawrence and Mario I. Aguilar. Leiden: Deo, 2004.

Dawson, David. *Allegorical Readers and Cultural Revision in Ancient Alexandria*. Berkeley and Los Angeles: University of California Press, 1992.

Dean-Otting, Mary. 1984. *Heavenly Journeys: A Study of the Motif in Hellenistic Jewish Literature*. Judentum und Umwelt 8. Frankfurt am Main: Lang.

DeConick, April D. "The Great Mystery of Marriage: Sex and Conception in Ancient Valentinian Traditions." *VC* 57 (2003): 307–42.

———. "Heavenly Temple Traditions and Valentinian Worship: A Case for First-Century Christology in the Second Century." Pages 308–41 in *The Jewish Roots of Christological Monotheism: Papers from the St. Andrews Conference on the Historical Origins of the Worship of Jesus*. Edited by C. C. Newman, J. R. Davila, and G. S. Lewis. JSJSup 63. Leiden: Brill, 1999.

———. *Recovering the Original Gospel of Thomas: A History of the Gospel and Its Growth*. JSNTSup 286. London: T&T Clark, 2005.

———. *Seek to See Him: Ascent and Vision Mysticism in the Gospel of Thomas*. VCSup 33. Leiden: Brill, 1996.

———. "The True Mysteries: Sacramentalism in the Gospel of Philip." *VC* 55 (2001): 225–61.

———. 2001. *Voices of the Mystics: Early Christian Discourse in the Gospels of John and Thomas and Other Ancient Christian Literature.* JSNTSup 157. Sheffield: Sheffield Academic Press.

———, ed. "'Early Jewish and Christian Mysticism': A Collage of Working Definitions." Pages 278–304 in *Society of Biblical Literature 2001 Seminar Papers.* SBLSP 40. Atlanta: Society of Biblical Literature, 2001.

DeConick, April D., and Jarl E. Fossum. "Stripped before God: A New Interpretation of Logion 37 in the Gospel of Thomas." *VC* 45 (1991): 123–50.

Delcor, Mathias. "Melchizedek from Genesis to the Qumran Texts and the Epistle to the Hebrews." *JSJ* 2 (1971): 115–35.

Delling, Gerhard. "The 'One Who Sees God' in Philo." Pages 28–42 in *Nourished with Peace: Studies in Hellenistic Judaism in Memory of Samuel Sandmel.* Edited by Frederic E. Greenspahn, Earle Hilgert, and Burton L. Mack. Chico, Calif.: Scholars Press, 1984.

Dennys, Nicholas B. *The Folklore of China and Its Affinities with That of the Aryan and Semitic Races.* London: Trubner, 1876. Repr., Detroit: Tower, 1971.

Deutsch, Nathaniel. *The Gnostic Imagination: Gnosticism, Mandaeism, and Merkabah Mysticism.* Brill's Series in Jewish Studies 13. Leiden: Brill, 1995.

———. *Guardians of the Gate: Angelic Vice Regency in Late Antiquity.* Brill's Series in Jewish Studies 22. Leiden: Brill, 1999.

Dillmann, August. *Das Buch Henoch Übersetzt und Erklärt.* Leipzig: Vogel, 1853.

Dillon, John M. *The Middle Platonists, 80 B.C. to A.D. 220.* Rev. ed. Ithaca, N.Y.: Cornell University Press, 1996.

———. "Rejecting the Body, Refining the Body: Some Remarks on the Development of Platonist Asceticism." Pages 80–87 in *Asceticism.* Edited by Vincent L. Wimbush and Richard Valantasis. New York: Oxford University Press, 1995.

Dimant, Devorah. "Dualism at Qumran: New Perspectives." Pages 55–73 in *Caves of Enlightenment: Proceedings of the ASOR Dead Sea Scrolls Jubilee Symposium.* Edited by J. H. Charlesworth. N. Richland Hills, Tex.: Bibal, 1998.

———. 1996. "Men as Angels: The Self -Image of the Qumran Community." Pages 93–103 in *Religion and Politics in the Ancient Near East.* Edited by Adele Berlin. Potomac: University Press of Maryland.

———. "Use and Interpretation of Mikra in the Apocrypha and Pseudepigrapha." Pages 379–419 in *Mikra: Text, Translation, Reading and Interpretation of the Hebrew Bible in Ancient Judaism and Ancient Christianity.* Edited by M. J. Mulder and H. Sysling. CRINT 2.1. Assen: Van Gorcum; Philadelphia: Fortress, 1988.

Dimant, Devorah, and John Strugnell. "The Merkabah Vision in Second Ezekiel (4Q385 4)." *RevQ* 14 (1990): 331–48.

Dimant, Devorah, and John Strugnell, eds. *Qumran Cave 4.XXI: Parabiblical Texts, Part 4: Pseudo-Prophetic Texts.* DJD 30. Oxford: Clarendon, 2001.

Dobroruka, Vicente. "Stories about Chemical Induction of Visions in 4 Ezra in the Light of Comparative Persian Material." *JSQ* (forthcoming).

Dozeman, Thomas. "Masking Moses and Mosaic Authority in Torah." *JBL* 119 (2000): 21–45.

Dunn, James D. G. *The Epistles to the Colossians and to Philemon.* Grand Rapids: Eerdmans, 1996.

Edelstein, Emma Jeannette, and Ludwig Edelstein. *Asclepius: A Collection and Interpretation of the Testimonies.* 2 vols. Baltimore: Johns Hopkins University Press, 1945. Repr., New York: Garland, 1975.

Eichrodt, Walther. *Ezekiel: A Commentary.* Translated by Coslett Quin. OTL. Philadelphia: Westminster, 1970.

———. *Theology of the Old Testament.* Translated by J. A. Baker. 2 vols. Philadelphia: Westminster, 1967.

Eisenbaum, Pamela M. "The Jewish Heroes of Christian History: Hebrews 11 in Literary Context." PhD. diss. Columbia University, 1995.

Elior, Rachel. "The Concept of God in Hekhalot Mysticism." Pages 97–120 in *Binah: Studies in Jewish Thought II.* Edited by Joseph Dan. New York: Praeger, 1989.

———. "From Earthly Temple to Heavenly Shrines: Prayer and Sacred Liturgy in the Hekhalot Literature and Its Relations to Temple Traditions" [Hebrew]. *Tarbiz* 64 (1995): 421–80.

———. "From Earthly Temple to Heavenly Shrines: Prayer and Sacred Song in the Hekhalot Literature and Its Relation to Temple Traditions." *JSQ* 4 (1997): 217–67.

———. "Hekhalot and Merkavah Literature: Its Relation to the Temple, the Heavenly Temple, and the 'Diminished Temple'" [Hebrew]. Pages 107–42 in *Continuity and Renewal: Jews and Judaism in Byzantine-Christian Palestine.* Edited by Lee I. Levine. Jerusalem: Yad Ben-Zvi, 2004.

———. "Merkabah Mysticism: A Critical Review [David J. Halperin, *Faces of the Chariot* Tubingen 1988]." *Numen* 37 (1990): 233–49.

———. "The *Merkavah* Tradition and the Emergence of Jewish Mysticism." Pages 101–58 in *Sino-Judaica: Jews and Chinese in Historical Dialogue: An International Colloquium, Nanjing, 11–19 October, 1996.* Edited by Aharon Oppenheimer. Tel-Aviv: Tel-Aviv University Press, 1999.

———. "Mysticism, Magic, and Angelology—The Perception of Angels in Hekhalot Literature." *JSQ* 1 (1993/94): 3–53.

———. "The Priestly Nature of the Mystical Heritage in Heykalot Literature." Pages 41–54 in *Expérience et écriture mystiques dans les religions du livre: Actes d'un colloque international tenu par le Centre d'études juives, Université de Paris IV-Sorbonne 1994.* Edited by R. B. Fenton and R. Goetschel. EJM 22. Leiden: Brill, 2000.

———. *Sifrut haHekhalot uMasoret haMerkavah.* Tel Aviv: Miskal, 2004.

———. *The Three Temples: On the Emergence of Jewish Mysticism.* Translated by David Louvish. Oxford: Littman Library of Jewish Civilization, 2004.

———. "You Have Chosen Enoch from among Human Beings: Enoch the Scribe of Righteousness and the Scroll's Library of the Priests the Sons of Zadok." Pages 15–64 in *Creation and Re-creation in Jewish Thought: Festschrift in Honor of Joseph Dan on the Occasion of His Seventieth Birthday.* Edited by Rachel Elior and Peter Schäfer. Tubingen: Mohr Siebeck, 2005.

———, ed. *Hekhalot Zutarti, Ms. New York 8218 (828)*. Jerusalem Studies in Jewish Thought Supplement Series 1. Jerusalem: Magnes, 1982.

Elliott, James K. *The Apocryphal New Testament*. Oxford: Oxford University Press, 1999.

Elm, Susanna. *Virgins of God: The Making of Asceticism in Late Antiquity*. Oxford: Clarendon, 1994.

Engberg-Pedersen, Troels. "Philo's *De Vita Contemplativa* as a Philosopher's Dream." *JSJ* 30 (1999):40–64.

Engell, Ivan. *The Call of Isaiah: An Exegetical and Comparative Study*. Uppsala Universitets Årsskrift. Uppsala: Lundequistska, 1949.

Enoch Zondel ben Joseph. *Midraš Tanhuma'*. 2 vols. Jerusalem: Eshkol, 1990.

Eshel, Esther. "4Q471b: A Self-Glorification Hymn." *RevQ* 17/65–68 (1996): 175–203.

Eshel, Esther, et al., eds. *Qumran Cave 4.VI: Poetical and Liturgical Texts, Part 1*. DJD 11. Oxford: Clarendon, 1998.

Farrer, Austin. *The Revelation of St. John the Divine*. Oxford: Clarendon, 1964.

Feen, Ralph. "Nedyia [*sic*] as Apocalypse: A Study of Cicero's Dream of Scipio." *JRS* 9 (1981): 28–34.

Fekkes, Jan. *Isaiah and Prophetic Traditions in the Book of Revelation: Visionary Antecedents and Their Development*. JSNTSup 93. Sheffield: JSOT Press, 1994.

Finegan, Jack. *The Archaeology of the New Testament: The Life of Jesus and the Beginning of the Early Church*. Princeton: Princeton University Press, 1978.

Finn, Thomas M. *Early Christian Baptism and the Catechumenate*. Collegeville, Minn.: Glazier, 1992.

Firestone, Reuven. "Jewish Culture in the Formative Period of Islam." Pages 267–304 in *Cultures of the Jews*. Edited by David Biale. New York: Schocken, 2002.

Fischer, Ulrich. *Eschatologie und Jenseitserwartung im hellenistischen Diasporajudentum*. BZNW 44. Berlin: de Gruyter, 1978.

Fishbane, Michael. "Arm of the Lord: Biblical Myth, Rabbinic Midrash, and the Mystery of History." Pages 271–92 in *Language, Theology, and the Bible: Essays in Honour of James Barr*. Edited by Samuel E. Balentine and John Barton. Oxford: Clarendon, 1994.

———. *Biblical Interpretation in Ancient Israel*. Oxford: Clarendon, 1985.

———. *Biblical Myth and Rabbinic Mythmaking*. Oxford: Oxford University Press, 2003.

———. "The Book of Zohar and Exegetical Spirituality." Pages 105–22 in idem, *The Exegetical Imagination: On Jewish Thought and Theology*. Cambridge: Harvard University Press, 1998.

———. "Form and Reformulation of the Biblical Priestly Blessing." *JAOS* 103 (1983): 115–21.

———. "The Garments of Torah—Or, To What May Scripture Be Compared?" Pages 33–46 in idem, *The Garments of Torah: Essays in Biblical Hermeneutics*. Bloomington: Indiana University Press, 1989.

———. " 'The Holy One Sits and Roars': Mythopoesis and the Midrashic Imagination." Pages 60–69 in *The Midrashic Imagination: Jewish Exegesis, Thought, and History*. Edited by Michael Fishbane. Albany: State University of New York Press, 1993.

———. "'Measures' of God's Glory in the Ancient Midrash." Pages 70–73 in *Messiah and Christos: Studies in the Jewish Origins of Christianity Presented to David Flusser on the Occasion of His Seventy-Fifth Birthday*. Edited by Ithamar Gruenwald, Saul Shaked, and Gedaliahu G. Stroumsa. TSAJ 32: Tübingen: Mohr Siebeck, 1992.

Fitzmyer, Joseph. 1968. "A Feature of Qumran Angelology and the Angels of 1 Cor 11:10." Pages 31–47 in *Paul and Qumran*. Edited by Jerome Murphy-O'Connor. London: Chapman.

———. *The Gospel according to* Luke. 2 vols. AB 28–28A. Garden City, N.Y.: Doubleday, 1981.

Flannery-Dailey, Frances. *Dreamers, Scribes and Priests: Jewish Dreams in the Hellenistic and Roman Eras.* JSJSup 90. Leiden: Brill, 2004.

———. 2005. "Lessons on Early Jewish Apocalypticism and Mysticism from Dream Literature." Lecture presented at the Institute for Antiquity and Christianity, Claremont Graduate University. IAC 2005 Fall Lecture Series.

Fletcher-Louis, Crispin H. T. *All the Glory of Adam: Liturgical Anthropology in the Dead Sea Scrolls.* STDJ 42. Leiden: Brill, 2002.

———. "Apocalypticism." In *The Handbook of the Study of the Historical Jesus.* Edited by Thomas Holmén and Stanley E. Porter. 4 vols. Leiden: Brill, forthcoming.

———. "Heavenly Ascent or Incarnational Presence? A Revisionist Reading of the Songs of the Sabbath Sacrifice." Pages 367–99 in *Society of Biblical Literature 1998 Seminar Papers.* SBLSP 37. Atlanta: Scholars Press, 1998.

———. *Luke-Acts: Angels, Christology and Soteriology*. Tübingen: Mohr Siebeck, 1997.

Ford, J. Massyngberde. *Revelation: Introduction, Translation, and Commentary.* AB 38. Garden City, N.Y.: Doubleday, 1975.

Fossum, Jarl E. "The Adorable Adam of the Mystics and the Rebuttal of the Rabbis." Pages 529–39 in vol. 1 of *Geschichte-Tradition-Reflexion: Festschrift für Martin Hengel zum 70. Geburtstag*. Edited by Hubert Cancik, Hermann Lichtenberger, and Peter Schäfer. Tübingen: Mohr Siebeck, 1996.

———. "Glory." *DDD*, 348–52.

———. *The Image of the Invisible God: Essays on the Influence of Jewish Mysticism on Early Christology.* NTOA 30. Göttingen: Vandenhoeck & Ruprecht, 1995.

———. *The Name of God and the Angel of the Lord: Samaritan and Jewish Concepts of Intermediation and the Origins of Gnosticism*. WUNT 36. Tübingen: Mohr Siebeck, 1985.

Francis, Fred O. "Humility and Angelic Veneration in Col 2:18." Pages 163–95 in *Conflict at Colossae.* Edited by Fred O. Francis and Wayne A. Meeks. SBLSBS 4. Missoula, Mont.: Scholars Press, 1975.

Frank, Karl Suso. *Angelikos Bios: Begriffsanalytische und begriffsgeschichtliche Untersuchung zum 'engelgliechen Leben' im frühen Mönchtum.* Beiträge zur Geschichte des alten Mönchtums und des Benediktinerordens 26. Münster: Aschendorff, 1964.

Frankfurter, David. *Elijah in Upper Egypt: The Apocalypse of Elijah and Early Egyptian Christianity.* Minneapolis: Fortress, 1993.

———. *Religion in Roman Egypt: Assimilation and Resistance.* Princeton: Princeton University Press, 1998.

Freedman, Harry, and Maurice Simon, eds. *Midrash Rabbah: Translated into English with Notes, Glossary, and Indices.* 10 vols. London: Soncino, 1961.

Freud, Sigmund. "The Interpretation of Dreams." Pages 181–552 in idem, *Basic Writings.* Translated by A. A. Brill. New York: Modern Library, 1938.

———. *The Interpretation of Dreams.* 8th ed. Translated by J. Strachey. New York: Basic Books, 1965.

Gallop, David. *Aristotle on Sleep and Dreams: A Text and Translation with Introduction, Notes and Glossary.* Peterborough, Ont.: Broadview, 1990.

García Martínez, Florentino. "L'interprétation de la Torah d'Ézéchiel dans les ms. de Qumrân." *RevQ* 13 (1992): 441–52.

———. *Qumran and Apocalyptic.* STDJ 9. Leiden: Brill, 1988.

———, ed. *The Dead Sea Scrolls Translated: The Qumran Texts in English.* Leiden: Brill, 1994.

García Martínez, Florentino, and Julio Trebolle Barrera. *The People of the Dead Sea Scrolls: Their Writings, Beliefs and Practices.* Leiden: Brill, 1995.

Garside, Bruce. "Language and Interpretation of Mystical Experience." *International Journal for the Philosophy of Religion* 3 (1972): 93–102.

Geiger, M. "Einige Worte über das Buch Henoch." *Jüdische Zeitschrift für Wissenschaft und Leben* 3 (1864/65): 196–204.

Geller, Markham J. "The Influence of Ancient Mesopotamia on Hellenistic Judaism." Pages 43–54 in vol. 1 of *Civilizations of the Ancient Near East.* Edited by Jack M. Sasson. New York: Scribner, 1995.

Geoltrain, Pierre. "La contemplation à Qoumran et chez les Thérapeutes." *Sem* 9 (1959): 49–57.

———. "Le traité de la Vie Contemplative de Philon d'Alexandrie: Introduction, traduction et notes." *Sem* 10 (1960): 5–67.

George, Andrew R. "Sennacherib and the Tablet of Destinies." *Iraq* 48 (1986): 138–46.

Giblin, Charles Homer. *The Book of Revelation the Open Book of Prophecy.* Good News Studies. Collegeville, Min.: Liturgical Press, 1991.

Gieschen, Charles A. *Angelomorphic Christology: Antecedents and Early Evidence.* AGJU 42. Leiden: Brill, 1998.

———. "The Divine Name in Ante-Nicene Christology." *VC* 57 (2003): 115–58.

Ginsberg, H. L. "The Oldest Interpretation of the Suffering Servant." *VT* 3 (1953): 400–404.

Ginzberg, Louis. *The Legends of the Jews.* 7 vols. Philadelphia: Jewish Publication Society, 1928.

Gnuse, Robert. *The Dream Theophany of Samuel: Its Structure in Relation to Ancient Near Eastern Dreams and Its Theological Significance.* Lanham, Md.: University Press of America, 1984.

Goldberg, Arnold M. "Einige Bemerkungen zu den Quellen und der Redaktionellen Einheiten der grossen Hekhalot." *FJB* 1 (1973): 1–49. Repr. in *Mystik und Theologie des rabbinischen Judentums: Gesammelte Studien.* Edited by Margarete Schlüter and Peter Schäfer. TSAJ 61. Tübingen: Mohr Siebeck, 1997.

——. *Untersuchungen über die Vorstellung von der Schekhinah der Früen Rabbinischen Literatur (Talmud und Midrasch)*. Berlin: de Gruyter, 1969.

——. "Der Vortrag des Ma'asse Merkawa: Eine Vermutung zur frühen Merkavamystik." *Jud* 29 (1973): 9–12.

Goodblatt, David. *The Monarchic Principle: Studies in Jewish Self-Government in Antiquity.* TSAJ 38. Tübingen: Mohr Siebeck, 1994.

Goodenough, Erwin R. *By Light, Light: The Mystic Gospel of Hellenistic Judaism*. New Haven: Yale University Press, 1935. Repr., Amsterdam: Philo, 1969.

Goodman, David. "Do Angels Eat?" *JJS* 37 (1986): 160–75.

Goodnick-Westenholz, Joan. "Thoughts on Esoteric Knowledge and Secret Lore." Pages 451–62 in *Intellectual Life in the Ancient Near East: Papers Presented at the 43rd Rencontre assyriologique internationale, Prague, July 1–5, 1996*. Edited by J. Prosecky. Prague: Academy of Sciences of the Czech Republic, Oriental Institute, 1996.

Goshen-Gottstein, Alon. "The Body as Image of God in Rabbinic Literature." *HTR* 87 (1994): 171–95.

Graham, William A. *Beyond the Written Word: Oral Aspects of Scripture in the History of Religion*. Cambridge: Cambridge University Press, 1987.

Green, Arthur. *A Guide to the Zohar.* Stanford, Calif.: Stanford University Press, 2004.

Greenfield, Jonas. "Ba'al's Throne and Isa. 6:1." Pages 193–98 in *Mélanges bibliques et orientaux en l'honneur de M. Mathias Delcor.* Edited by André Caquot, Simon Légasse, and Michel Tardieu. AOAT 215. Neukirchen-Vluyn: Neukirchener, 1985.

Greenfield, Jonas C., and Michael E. Stone. "Books of Enoch." *Numen* 26 (1979): 89–103.

Grelot, Pierre. "La géographie mythique d'Hénoch et ses sources orientales." *RB* 65 (1958): 33–69.

——. "La légende d'Hénoch dans les apocryphes et dans la Bible: Origine et signification." *RSR* 46 (1958): 5–26, 181–210.

Griffiths, Paul J. *Religious Reading: The Place of Reading in the Practice of Religion.* New York: Oxford University Press, 1999.

Grözinger, Karl-Erich. *Musik und Gesang in der Theologie der frühen jüdischen Literatur.* TSAJ 3. Tübingen: Mohr Siebeck, 1982.

——. "The Names of God and the Celestial Powers: Their Function and Meaning in the Hekhalot Literature." *Jerusalem Studies in Jewish Thought* 6 (1987): 53–69.

Gruenwald, Ithamar. *Apocalyptic and Merkavah Mysticism*. AGJU 14. Leiden: Brill, 1980.

——. *From Apocalyptic to Gnosticism*. BEATAJ 14. Frankfurt am Main: Lang, 1988.

——. "Further Jewish Physiognomic and Chiromantic Fragments." *Tarbiz* 40 (1971): 301–19

——. "Knowledge and Vision: Towards a Clarification of Two 'Gnostic' Concepts in Light of Their Alleged Origins." *Israel Oriental Studies* 3 (1973): 257–77.

——. "New Passages from Hekhalot Literature." *Tarbiz* 38 (1968–69): 354–72.

——. "The Place of Priestly Traditions in the Writings of Merkavah Mysticism and the *Shi'ur Qomah*" [Hebrew]. *Jerusalem Studies in Jewish Thought* 6 (1987): 65–120.

———, ed. "A Preliminary Critical Edition of Sefer Yezira." *Israel Oriental Studies* 1 (1971): 132–77.

Gundry, Robert H. "Angelomorphic Christology in Revelation." Pages 662–78 in *Society of Biblical Literature 1994 Seminar Papers*. SBLSP 33. Atlanta: Scholars Press, 1994.

Guthrie, Kenneth S. "The Life of Pythagoras." Pages 16–17 in *The Pythagorean Sourcebook and Library*. Edited by David R. Fideler. Grand Rapids: Phanes, 1987.

Haenchen, Ernst. *John 1: A Commentary on the Gospel of John Chapters 1–6*. Edited and translated by Robert Funk. Hermeneia. Philadelphia: Fortress, 1984.

Hafemann, Scott. "Moses in the Apocrypha and Pseudepigrapha: A Survey." *JSP* 7 (1990): 79–104.

Halbwachs, Maurice. *The Legendary Topography of the Gospels in the Holy Land* Translated by Lewis A. Coser. Chicago: University of Chicago Press, 1992.

———. *On Collective Memory*. Translated by Lewis A. Coser. Chicago: University of Chicago Press 1992.

Hall, Robert G. "The Ascension of Isaiah: Community, Situation, Date, and Place in Early Christianity." *JBL* 109 (1990):289–306.

———. "Living Creatures in the Midst of the Throne: Another Look at Revelation 4.6." *NTS* 36 (1990): 609–13.

Halperin, David J. "Ascension or Invasion: Implications of the Heavenly Journey in Ancient Judaism." *Religion* 18 (1988): 47–67.

———. *Faces of the Chariot: Early Jewish Reponses to Ezekiel's Vision*. TSAJ 16. Tübingen: Mohr Siebeck, 1988.

———. "Heavenly Ascension in Ancient Judaism: The Nature of the Experience." Pages 218–32 in *Society of Biblical Literature 1987 Seminar Papers*. SBLSP 26. Atlanta: Scholars Press, 1987.

———. *The Merkabah in Rabbinic Literature*. New Haven: American Oriental Society, 1980.

———. "Merkabah Midrash in the Septuagint." *JBL* 101 (1982): 351–63.

———. "Origen, Ezekiel's Merkabah and the Ascension of Moses." *CH* 50 (1981): 261–75.

Hamerton-Kelly, R. G. "The Temple and the Origins of Jewish Apocalyptic." *VT* 20 (1970): 1–15.

Haran, Menahem. "The Shining of Moses's Face: A Case Study in Biblical and Ancient Near Eastern Iconography [Ex 34:29–35; Ps 69:32; Hab 3:4]." Pages 159–73 *In the Shelter of Elyon: Essays on Ancient Palestinian Life and Literature in Honor of G. W. Ahlström*. Edited by W. Boyd Barrick and John R. Spencer. JSOTSup 31. Sheffield: JSOT Press, 1984.

Harrington, Hannah K. *The Impurity Systems of Qumran and the Rabbis: Biblical Foundations*. SBLDS 143. Atlanta: Scholars Press, 1993.

Harvey, Susan Ashbrook. "Feminine Imagery for the Divine: The Holy Spirit, the Odes of Solomon, and Early Syriac Tradition." *SVTQ* 37 (1993): 111–40.

Hay, David M. "Foils for the Therapeutae: References to Other Texts and Persons in Philo's 'De Vita Contemplativa.'" Pages 330–48 in *Neotestamentica et Philonica: Studies in Honor of Peder Borgen*. Edited by David E. Aune, Torrey Seland, and Jarl Henning. NovTSup 106. Leiden: Brill, 2003.

———. "Philo's References to Other Allegorists." *SPhilo* 6 (1979–80): 41–75.
———. "Philo's View of Himself as an Exegete: Inspired, But Not Authoritative." Pages 40–52 in *Heirs of the Septuagint: Philo, Hellenistic Judaism, and Early Christianity: Festschrift for Earle Hilgert*. Edited by David T. Runia, David M. Hay, and David Winston. Studia Philonica Annual 3. Atlanta: Scholars Press, 1991.
———. "Things Philo Said and Did Not Say about the Therapeutae." Pages 673–83 in *Society of Biblical Literature 1992 Seminar Papers*. SBLSP 31. Atlanta: Scholars Press, 1992.
Hays, Richard B. *Echoes of Scripture in the Letters of Paul*. New Haven: Yale University Press, 1989.
Hayutin, Michael. *Milhamat luhot ha-šanah bi-tequfat bayit šeni. Tel* Aviv: Modan, 1993.
Hayward, C. T. Robert. "Philo, the Septuagint of Genesis 32:24–32 and the Name 'Israel': Fighting the Passions, Inspiration and the Vision of God." *JJS* 51 (2000): 209–26.
Hecker, Joel. *Mystical Bodies, Mystical Meals: Eating and Embodiment in Medieval Kabbalah*. Detroit: Wayne State University Press, 2006.
Heimpel, Wolfgang. "The Sun at Night and the Doors of Heaven." *JCS* 38 (1986): 127–51.
Heinemann, Joseph. "Once Again melekh ha-ʿolam." *JJS* 15 (1964): 149–54.
———. *Prayer in the Talmud: Forms and Patterns*. Berlin: de Gruyter, 1977.
Hemer, Colin J. *The Letters to the Seven Churches of Asia in Their Local Setting* JSNTSup 11. Sheffield: Sheffield Academic Press, 1986.
Hempel, Johannes. "Die Grenzen des Anthropomorphismus Jahwes im Alten Testament." *ZAW* 57 (1939): 75–85.
Hieatt, Constance B. *The Realism of Dream Visions: The Poetic Exploitation of the Dream-Experience in Chaucer and His Contemporaries*. The Hague: Mouton, 1967.
Hillers, Delbert R. "Delocutive Verbs in Biblical Hebrew." *JBL* 86 (1967): 320–24.
Himmelfarb, Martha. "Apocalyptic Ascent and the Heavenly Temple." Pages 210–17 in *Society of Biblical Literature 1987 Seminar Papers*. SBLSP 26. Atlanta: Scholars Press, 1987.
———. *Ascent to Heaven in Jewish and Christian Apocalypses*. New York: Oxford University Press, 1993.
———. "From Prophecy to Apocalypse: The *Book of the Watchers* and Tours of Heaven." Pages 145–65 in *From the Bible through the Middle Ages*. Vol. 1 of *Jewish Spirituality*. Edited by Arthur Green. New York: Crossroad, 1986.
———. "Heavenly Ascent and the Relationship of the Apocalypses and the Hekhalot Literature." *HUCA* 59 (1988): 73–100.
———. "Levi, Phinehas, and the Problem of Intermarriage at the Time of the Maccabean Revolt." *JSQ* 6 (1999): 1–24.
———. "A Report on Enoch in Rabbinic Literature." Pages 259–69 in *Society of Biblical Literature 1978 Seminar Papers*. SBLSP 13–14. Missoula, Mont.: Scholars Press, 1978.
———. "Revelation and Rapture: The Transformation of the Visionary in the Ascent Apocalypses." Pages 79–90 in *Mysteries and Revelations: Apocalyptic Studies since*

the Uppsala Colloquium. Edited by John J. Collins and James H. Charlesworth. JSPSup 9. Sheffield: Sheffield Academic Press, 1991.

———. "Sexual Relations and Purity in the Temple Scroll and the Book of Jubilees." *DSD* 6 (1999): 11–36.

———. "The Temple and the Garden of Eden in Ezekiel, the Book of the Watchers, and the Wisdom of ben Sira." Pages 63–78 in *Sacred Places and Profane Spaces: Essays in the Geographics of Judaism, Christianity, and Islam*. Edited by James Scott and Paul Simpson-Housley. Contributions to the Study of Religion 30. New York: Greenwood, 1991.

———. *Tours of Hell: An Apocalyptic Form in Jewish and Christian Literature*. Philadelphia: University of Pennsylvania Press, 1983.

Holladay, Carl R. *Fragments From Hellenistic Jewish Authors*. 4 vols. SBLTT 20, 30, 39–40. Atlanta: Scholars Press, 1983–96.

Hooker, Morna. "Authority on Her Head: An Examination of I Cor XI.10." *NTS* 10 (1964): 410–16.

Hornblower, Simon, and Antony Spanforth. *The Oxford Classical Dictionary*. New York: Oxford University Press, 1996.

Horowitz, Wayne. *Mesopotamian Cosmic Geography*. Winona Lake, Ind.: Eisenbrauns, 1998.

Horst, Pieter Willem van der. *Chaeremon, Egyptian Priest and Stoic Philosopher: The Fragments Collected and Translated with Explanatory Notes*. EPRO 101. Leiden: Brill, 1984.

———. "Images of Women in the Testament of Job." Pages 93–116 in *Studies on the Testament of Job*. Edited by Michael Knibb and Pieter Willem van der Horst. Cambridge: Cambridge University Press, 1989.

———. "Moses' Throne Vision in Ezekiel the Dramatist." *JJS* 34 (1983): 21–29.

———. "The Way of Life of the Egyptian Priests according to Chaeremon." Pages 61–71 in *Studies in Egyptian Religion Dedicated to Professor Jan Zandee*. Edited by M. Heerma van Voss et al. Leiden: Brill, 1982.

Horton, Fred L., Jr. *The Melchizedek Tradition: A Critical Examination of the Sources to the Fifth Century AD and in the Epistle to the Hebrews*. SNTSMS 30. Cambridge: Cambridge University Press, 1976.

Hübner. Wolfgang. *Zodiacus Christianus: Jüdisch-christliche Adaptationen des Tierkreises von der Antike bis zur Gegenwart*. Königstein: Hain, 1983.

Hutton, Patrick H. "Collective Memory and Collective Mentalities: The Halbwachs-Aries Connection." *RHist* 15 (1988): 311–22.

Hyman, Arthur B., Isaac Nathan Lerer, and Isaac Shilon, eds. *Yalqut Šimʿoni*. 5 vols. in 9. Jerusalem: Mossad haRab Quq, 1973–91.

Idel, Moshe. "Enoch is Metatron." *Imm* 24/25 (1990): 220–40.

———. 1988. *Kabbalah: New Perspectives*. New Haven: Yale University Press.

Irshai, Oded. "The Priesthood in Jewish Society in Late Antiquity" [Hebrew]. Pages 67–106 in *Continuity and Renewal: Jews and Judaism in Byzantine-Christian Palestine*. Edited by Lee I. Levine. Jerusalem: Yad Ben-Zvi, 2004.

Irwin-Zarecka, Iwona. *Frames of Remembrance: The Dynamics of Dollective Memory*. New Brunswick, N.J.: Transaction, 1994.

Jacob, Edmond. *Théologie de l'Ancient Testament.* Neuchâtel: Delachaux, 1955.
Jaeger, Werner. *Paideia: The Ideals of Greek Culture.* Translated by Gilbert Highet. New York: Oxford University Press, 1963.
Janowitz, Naomi. *Icons of Power: Ritual Practices in Late Antiquity.* University Park: Pennsylvania State University Press, 2002.
———. *The Poetics of Ascent: Theories of Language in a Rabbinic Ascent Text.* Albany: State University of New York Press, 1989.
Jansen, Herman Lundin. *Die Henochgestalt: Eine vergleichende religionsgeschichtliche Untersuchung.* Oslo: Dybwad, 1939.
Jaubert, Annie. *The Date of the Last Supper.* New York: Alba House, 1965.
Jellinek, Adolf, ed., *Bet ha-Midrasch: Sammlung kleiner Midraschim und vermichster Abhandlungen aus der ältern jüdischen Literatur.* 6 vols. 1853–77. Repr., Jerusalem: Bamberger & Wahrmann, 1938.
Jeremias, Joachim. *The Eucharistic Words of Jesus.* New York: Scribner, 1966.
Johnson, Luke Timothy. *Religious Experience in Earliest Christianity: A Missing Dimension in New Testament Studies.* Minneapolis: Fortress, 1998.
Johnson, M. D. "Life of Adam and Eve." *OTP* 2:249–95.
Jonge, Marinus de. "Notes on Testament of Levi II–VII." Pages 247–60 in *Studies on the Testaments of the Twelve Patriarchs.* Edited by M. de Jonge. Leiden: Brill, 1975.
Just, Arthur A., Jr. *The Ongoing Feast: Table Fellowship and Eschatology at Emmaus.* Collegeville, Minn.: Liturgical Press, 1993.
Kadushin, Max. *The Rabbinic Mind.* 3rd ed. New York: Bloch, 1972.
Kanagaraj, Jey J. *"Mysticism" in the Gospel of John: An Inquiry into Its Background.* JSNTSup 158. Sheffield: Sheffield Academic Press, 1998.
Kapferer, Bruce. "The Ritual Process and the Problem of Reflexivity in Sinhalese Demon Exorcisms." Pages 179–213 in *Rite, Drama, Festival, Spectacle: Rehearsals Toward a Theory of Cultural Performance.* Edited by John J. MacAloon. Philadelphia: Institute for the Study of Human Issues, 1984.
Katz, Steven T. "The 'Conservative' Character of Mystical Experience." Pages 3–60 in *Mysticism and Religious Traditions.* Edited by Steven T. Katz. New York: Oxford University Press, 1983.
———. "Language, Epistemology and Mysticism." Pages 22–74 in *Mysticism and Philosophical Analysis.* Edited by Steven T. Katz. London: Sheldon, 1978.
———, ed. *Mysticism and Language.* New York: Oxford University Press, 1992.
Kelber, Werner H. "Modalities of Communication, Cognition, and Physiology of Perception: Orality, Rhetoric, Scribality." *Semeia* 65 (1994): 193–216.
Keller, Carl A. "Mystical Literature." Pages 59–67 in *Mysticism and Philosophical Analysis.* Edited by Steven T. Katz. London: Sheldon, 1978.
Kimelman, Reuven. "The Conflict between the Priestly Oligarchy and the Sages in the Talmudic Period (PT *Shabbat* 2:3, 13c = *Horayot* 3:5, 48c)" [Hebrew]. *Zion* 48 (1983): 135–48.
Kister, Menahem. "5Q13 and the *Avodah:* A Historical Survey and Its Significance." *DSD* 8 (2001): 136–48.
Knibb, Michael A. *The Ethiopic Book of Enoch: A New Edition in the Light of the Aramaic Dead Sea Fragments.* 2 vols. Oxford: Clarendon, 1978.

———. "The Use of Scripture in 1 Enoch 17–19." Pages 165–178 in *Jerusalem, Alexandria, Rome: Studies in Ancient Cultural Interaction in Honour of A. Hilhorst.* Edited by Florentino García Martínez and Gerard P. Luttikhuizen. JSJSup 82. Leiden: Brill, 2003.

Knights, Chris H. "The Rechabites of Jeremiah 35: Forerunners of the Essenes?" *JSP* 10 (1992): 81–87.

Knohl, Israel. "Between Voice and Silence: The Relationship between Prayer and Temple Cult." *JBL* 115 (1996): 17–30.

———. *The Messiah before Jesus: The Suffering Servant of the Dead Sea Scrolls.* Translated by David Maisel. Berkeley and Los Angeles: University of California Press, 2000.

Koch-Westenholz, Ulla. *Mesopotamian Astrology: An Introduction to Babylonian and Assyrian Celestial Divination.* Copenhagen: Carsten Niebuhr Institute of Near Eastern Studies, Museum Tusculanum Press, University of Copenhagen, 1995.

Koester, Craig R. *The Dwelling of God: The Tabernacle in the Old Testament, Intertestamental Jewish Literature and the New Testament.* CBQMS 22. Washington, D.C.: Catholic Biblical Association of America, 1989.

Kohn, Livia. *The Taoist Experience: An Anthology.* Albany: State University of New York Press, 1993.

Korpel, Marjo C.A. *A Rift in the Clouds: Ugaritic and Hebrew Descriptions of the Divine.* Münster: Ugarit-Verlag, 1990.

Kraemer, Ross Shepard. "Monastic Jewish Women in Greco-Roman Egypt: Philo Judaeus on the Therapeutrides." *Signs* 14 (1989): 342–70.

———. *When Aseneth Met Joseph: A Late Antique Tale of the Biblical Patriarch and His Egyptian Wife Reconsidered.* New York: Oxford University Press, 1998.

Kraft, Heinrich. *Die Offenbarung des Johannis.* HNT. Tübingen: Mohr Siebeck, 1974.

Kraft, Robert A. "The Pseudepigrapha and Christianity Revisited: Setting the Stage and Framing Some Central Questions." *JSJ* 32 (2001): 371–95.

———. "The Pseudepigrapha in Christianity." Pages 55–86 in *Tracing the Threads: Studies in the Vitality of Jewish Pseudepigrapha.* Edited by John C. Reeves. SBLEJL 6. Atlanta: Scholars Press, 1994.

Kuyt, Annelies. *The "Descent" to the Chariot: Towards a Description of the Terminology, Place, Function and Nature of the Yeridah in Hekhalot Literature.* TSAJ 45. Tübingen: Mohr Siebeck, 1990.

———. "Once Again: Yarad in Hekhalot Literature." *FJB* 18 (1990): 45–69.

Kvanvig, Helge S. *Roots of Apocalyptic: The Mesopotamian Background of the Enoch Figure and of the Son of Man.* WMANT 61. Neukirchen-Vluyn: Neukirchener, 1988.

Lambert, Wilfred G. *Babylonian Wisdom Literature.* Oxford: Oxford University Press, 1960.

———. "A Catalogue of Texts and Authors." *JCS* 16 (1962): 59–77.

———. "Enmeduranki and Related Matters." *JCS* 21 (1967): 126–38.

Lampe, Geoffrey W. H. *The Seal of the Spirit: A Study in the Doctrine of Baptism and Confirmation in the New Testament and the Fathers.* London: SPCK, 1967.

Lane Fox, Robin. *Pagans and Christians*. New York: Penguin, 1986.

Lang, Birgit. *Gott als "Licht" in Israel und Mesopotamien: Eine Studie zu Jes. 60:1–3.19f.* ÖBS 7. Klosterneuburg: Österreichische Katholische Bibelwerk, 1989.

Lawson, Jack Newton. *The Concept of Fate in Ancient Mesopotamia in the First Millennium: Toward an Understanding of Šīmtu*. Orientalia Biblica et Christiana 7. Wiesbaden: Harrassowitz, 1994.

Lenski, Richard C. H. *The Interpretation of St. John's Revelation*. Columbus: Lutheran Book Concern, 1935.

Leonhardt, Jutta. *Jewish Worship in Philo of Alexandria*. TSAJ 84. Tübingen: Mohr Siebeck, 2001.

Leslau, Wolf. *Comparative Dictionary of Ge'ez*. Wiesbaden: Harrassowitz, 1991.

———. *Concise Dictionary of Ge'ez (Classical Ethiopic)*. Wiesbaden: Harrassowitz, 1989.

Lesses, Rebecca. "The Adjuration of the Prince of the Presence: Performative Utterance in a Jewish Ritual." Pages 185–206 in *Ancient Magic and Ritual Power*. Edited by Marvin Meyer and Paul Mirecki. Religions in the Greco-Roman World 129. Leiden: Brill, 1995.

———. "Ritual Practices to Gain Power: Adjurations in the Hekhalot Literature, Jewish Amulets, and Greek Revelatory Adjurations." Ph.D. diss. Harvard University, 1995.

———. *Ritual Practices to Gain Power: Angels, Incantations, and Revelation in Early Jewish Mysticism*. HTS 44. Harrisburg, Pa.: Trinity Press International, 1998.

Levenson, Jon D. "The Jerusalem Temple in Devotional and Visionary Experience." Pages 32–59 *From the Bible through the Middle Ages*. Vol. 1 of *Jewish Spirituality*. Edited by Arthur Green. New York: Crossroad, 1986.

———. *Sinai and Zion: An Entry into the Jewish Bible*. Minneapolis: Winston, 1985.

———. "The Temple and the World." *JR* 64 (1984): 275–98.

Levine, Lee I. *The Rabbinic Class of Roman Palestine in Late Antiquity*. Jerusalem: Yad Izhak Ben-Zvi, 1989.

Levison, John R. "Inspiration and the Divine Spirit in the Writings of Philo Judaeus." *JSJ* 26 (1995): 271–323.

———. *The Spirit in First Century Judaism*. AGJU 29. Leiden: Brill, 1997.

Lewin, Bernard, ed. *Tractate Jom-Tow, Chagiga and Maschkin*. Vol. 4 of *Otzar ha-Geonim*. Haifa: Hebrew University Press Association, 1931.

Liddell, Henry George, and Robert Scott. *A Greek-English Lexicon*. Oxford: Clarendon, 1940.

Lieb, Michael. *The Visionary Mode: Biblical Prophecy, Hermeneutics and Cultural Change*. Ithaca, N.Y.: Cornell University Press, 1991.

Lieber, Andrea. "Voice and Vision: Song as a Vehicle for Ecstatic Experience in Songs of the Sabbath Sacrifice." Pages 51–58 in *Of Scribes and Sages: Early Jewish Interpretation and Transmision of Scripture*. Edited by Craig A. Evans. London: T&T Clark, 2004.

Lieberman, Saul. "Mišnat Šir ha-Širim." Apendix D of Gershom Scholem, *Jewish Gnosticism, Merkabah Mysticism, and Talmudic Tradition*. 2nd ed. New York: Jewish Theological Seminary of America, 1965.

Liebes, Yehuda. "*De Natura Dei*: On the Development of the Jewish Myth." Pages 1–64 in idem, *Studies in Jewish Myth and Jewish Messianism*. Translated by Batya Stein. Albany: State University of New York Press, 1993.

———. "How the Zohar was Written." Pages 85–138 in idem, *Studies in the Zohar*. Translated by Stephanie Nakache. Albany: State University of New York Press, 1993.

Livingstone, Alasdair. *Court Poetry and Literary Miscellanea*. SAA 3. Helskini: Helsinki University Press, 1989.

———. *Mystical and Mythological Explanatory Works of Assyrian and Babylonian Scholars*. Oxford: Clarendon, 1986.

Lods, Adolphe. *Le Livre D'Hénoch: Fragments Grecs, Découverts à Akhmîm [Haute-Égypte] Publiés Avec Les Variantes du Texte Éthiopien*. Paris: Leroux, 1892.

Long, Anthony A. *Hellenistic Philosophy: Stoics, Epicureans, Sceptics*. 2nd ed. Berkeley and Los Angeles: University of California Press, 1986.

Longenecker, Bruce W. *Eschatology and the Covenant: A Comparison of 4 Ezra and Romans 1–11*. JSNTSup 57. Sheffield: JSOT Press, 1991.

Lust, Johan. "Ezekiel Manuscripts in Qumran." Pages 90–100 in *Ezekiel and His Book: Textual and Literary Criticism and Their Interrelation*. Edited by Johan Lust et al. BETL 74. Leuven: Leuven University Press, 1986.

Luttikhuizen, Gerard P. *The Revelation of Elchasai*. Tubingen: Mohr Siebeck, 1985.

MacDermot, Violet. *The Cult of the Seer in the Ancient Middle East*. Berkeley and Los Angeles: University of California Press, 1971.

MacGregor, George Hogarth Carnaby. "The Eucharist in the Fourth Gospel." *NTS* 9 (1962–63): 111–19.

Machinist, Peter, and Hayim Tadmor. "Heavenly Wisdom." Pages 146–51 in *The Tablet and the Scroll: Near Eastern Studies in Honor of William W. Hallo*. Edited by M. E. Cohen, D. C. Snell, and D. B.Weisberd. Bethesa, Md.: CDL, 1993.

MacRae, George W. "The Jewish Background of the Gnostic Sophia Myth." *NovT* 12 (1970): 86–101.

Maher, Michael W., trans. *Targum Pseudo-Jonathan: Genesis*. Collegeville, Minn.: Liturgical Press, 1992.

Maier, Johann. "Das Gefährdungsmotiv bei der Himmelsreise in der jüdischen Apokalyptic und 'Gnosis.'" *Kairos* 5 (1963): 18–40.

———. "Šire Olat Haššabbat: Some Observations on Their Calendric Implications and on Their Style." Pages 543–60 in vol. 2 of *The Madrid Qumran Congress: Proceedings of the International Congress on the Dead Sea Scrolls, Madrid 18–21 March, 1991*. Edited by Julio C. Trebolle Barrera and Luis Vegas Montaner. 2 vols. Leiden: Brill, 1992.

———. *Vom Kultus zur Gnosis*. Salzburg: Müller, 1964.

Malamat, Abraham. "A Forerunner of Biblical Prophecy: The Mari Documents." Pages 33–52 in *Ancient Israelite Religion: Essays in Honor of Frank Moore Cross*. Edited by Patrick D. Miller, Paul D. Hanson, and S. Dean McBride. Philadelphia: Fortress, 1987.

Malherbe, Abraham J. *The Cynic Epistles*. SBLSBS 12. Missoula, Mont.: Scholars Press, 1977.

Malina, Bruce J. *On the Genre and Message of Revelation: Star Visions and Sky Journeys*. Peabody, Mass.: Hendrickson, 1995.

Mandelbaum, Bernard. *Pesikta de-Rav Kahana*. 2 vols. New York: Jewish Theological Seminary of America, 1962.

Mann, Jacob. "An Early Theologico-Polemical Work." *HUCA* 12–13 (1937–38): 411–59.

Mara, Maria Grazia. 1973. *Évangile de Pierre: Introduction, text critique, traduction, commentaire et index*. Paris: Cerf.

Marcus, Ralph. *Philo: Supplements*. 2 vols. LCL. Cambridge: Harvard University Press, 1953.

Margaliot, Reuven. *Sefer ha-Zohar*. 3 vols. Jerusalem: Mossad ha-Rav Kook, 1984.

Margulies, Mordecai, ed. *Midrash Wayyikra Rabbah: A Critical Edition Based on Manuscripts and Geniza Fragments with Variants and Notes*. 2 vols. New York: Jewish Theological Seminary of America, 1993.

Marion, Jean-Luc. *Being Given: Toward a Phenomenology of Givenness*. Translated by Jeffrey L. Kosky. Stanford, Calif.: Stanford University Press, 2002.

———. "Introduction: What Do We Mean by 'Mystic'?" Pages 1–7 in *Mystics: Presence and Aporia*. Edited by Michael Kessler and Christian Sheppard. Chicago: University of Chicago Press, 2002.

Martyn, J. Louis. *History and Theology in the Fourth Gospel*. New York: Harper & Row, 1968.

Mason, Steve. "PHILOSOPHIAI: Graeco-Roman, Judean and Christian." Pages 31–58 in *Voluntary Associations in the Graeco-Roman World*. Edited by John S. Kloppenborg and Stephen G. Wilson. London: Routledge, 1996.

Mattila, Sharon Lea. "Wisdom, Sense Perception, Nature, and Philo's Gender Gradient." *HTR* 89 (1996): 103–29.

Maunder, Annie S. D. "The Date and Place of Writing of the Slavonic Book of Enoch." *The Observatory* 41 (1918): 309–16.

McDonough, Sean M. *YHWH at Patmos: Rev. 1:4 in Its Hellenistic and Early Jewish Setting*. WUNT 2.107. Tübingen: Mohr Siebeck, 1999.

McGinn, Bernard. *The Foundations of Mysticism*. New York: Crossroad, 1991.

McNamara, Martin. *The New Testament and the Palestinian Targum to the Pentateuch*. AnBib 27. Rome: Pontifical Biblical Institute, 1966.

McNeil, Brian. "The Narration of Zosimus." *JSJ* 9 (1978): 68–82.

McNicol, Allan J. "The Heavenly Sanctuary in Judaism: A Model for Tracing the Origin of the Apocalypse." *JRelS* 13 (1987): 66–94.

Meeks, Wayne. "Moses as God and King." Pages 354–71 in *Religions in Antiquity: E. R. Goodenough Memorial Volume*. Edited by Jacob Neusner. Numen Supplements 14. Leiden: Brill, 1968.

———. *The Prophet-King: Moses Traditions and the Johannine Christology*. NovTSup 14. Leiden: Brill, 1967.

———. "Social Functions of Apocalyptic Language in Pauline Christianity." Pages 687–706 in *Apocalypticism in the Mediterranean World and the Near East*. Edited by David Hellholm. 2nd ed. Tübingen: Mohr Siebeck, 1989.

Meier, Gerhard. "Studien zur Beschwörungssammlung Maqlû." *AfO* 21 (1966): 70–81.

Merkur, Daniel. *Gnosis: An Esoteric Tradition of Mystical Unions.* New York: State University of New York Press, 1993.

———. "The Visionary Practices of Jewish Apocalyptists." Pages 119–48 in *The Psychoanalytic Study of Society 14: Essays in Honor of Paul Parin.* Edited by L. Bryce Boyer and Simon A. Grolnick. Hillsdale, N.J.: Analytic, 1989.

Meshcherskij, Nikital. "Sledy pamjatnikov Kumrana v staroslavjanskoj i drevnerusskoj literature (K izucheniju slavjanskih versij knigi Enoha)." *Trudy otdela drevnerusskoj literatury* 19 (1963): 130–47.

———. "K voprosu ob istochnikah slavjanskoj knigi Enoha." *Kratkie soobshchenija Instituta narodov Azii* 86 (1965): 72–78.

Mettinger, Tryggve N. D. *The Dethronement of Sabaoth: Studies in the Shem and Kavod Theologies.* ConBOT 18. Lund: Wallin & Dalholm, 1982.

Metzger, Bruce M. *A Textual Commentary on the Greek New Testament.* 2nd ed. Stuttgart: Deutsche Bibelgesellschaft; United Bible Societies, 1994.

Michaeli, Frank. *Dieu à l'image de l'homme: Étude de la notion anthropomorphique de Dieu dans l'Ancient Testament.* Neuchâtel: Delachaux, 1950.

Michalowski, Piotr. "Presence at the Creation." Pages 391–96 in *Lingering Over Words: Studies in Ancient Near Eastern Literature in Honor of William L. Moran.* Edited by Tzvi Abusch, John Huehnergard, and Piotr Steinkeller. HSS 37. Atlanta: Scholars Press, 1990.

Milik, Jozef T. "The Dead Sea Scrolls Fragment of the Book of Enoch." *Bib* 32 (1951): 393–400.

———. "Milkî-ṣedeq et Milkî-reša' dans les anciens écrits juifs et chrétiens." *JJS* 23 (1972): 135–37.

———. *Ten Years of Discovery in the Wilderness of Judaea.* SBT 26. Naperville, Ill.: Allenson, 1959.

———, ed. *The Books of Enoch: Aramaic Fragments of Qumrân Cave 4.* With the collaboration of Matthew Black. Oxford: Clarendon, 1976.

Miller, Patricia Cox. *Dreams in Late Antiquity: Studies in the Imagination of a Culture.* Princeton: Princeton University Press, 1994.

Moessner, David P. *Lord of the Banquet: The Literary and Theological Significance of the Lukan Travel Narrative.* Minneapolis: Fortress, 1989.

Montefiore, Claude G., and Herbert Loewe, eds. *A Rabbinic Anthology.* London: Macmillan, 1938.

Moore, Peter. "Mystical Experience, Mystical Doctrine, Mystical Technique." Pages 101–31 in *Mysticism and Philosophical Analysis.* Edited by Steven T. Katz. London: Sheldon, 1978.

Morray-Jones, Christopher R. A. "Merkabah Mysticism and Talmudic Tradition." Ph.D. diss. Cambridge University, 1988.

———. "Paradise Revisited (2 Cor 12:1–2): The Jewish Mystical Background of Paul's Apostolate, Part 1: The Jewish Sources." *HTR* 86 (1993): 177–217.

———. “Paradise Revisited (2 Cor 12:1–2): The Jewish Mystical Background of Paul’s Apostolate, Part 2: Paul’s Heavenly Ascent and Its Significance.” *HTR* 86 (1993): 265–92.

———. Review of Saul M. Olyan, *A Thousand Thousands Served Him: Exegesis and the Naming of Angels in Ancient Judaism*. *JSS* 42 (1997): 154–59.

———. “The Temple Within: The Embodied Divine Image and Its Worship in the Dead Sea Scrolls and Other Early Jewish and Christian Sources.” Pages 400–431 in *Society of Biblical Literature 1998 Seminar Papers*. SBLSP 37. Atlanta: Scholars Press, 1998.

———. “Transformational Mysticism in the Apocalyptic-Merkabah Tradition.” *JJS* 43 (1992): 1–31.

———. *A Transparent Illusion: The Dangerous Vision of Water in Hekhalot Mysticism: A Source-Critical and Tradition-Historical Inquiry*. JSJSup 59. Leiden: Brill, 2002.

Mounce, Robert H. *The Book of Revelation*. Rev. ed. NICNT. Grand Rapids: Eerdmans, 1998.

Moyise, Steve. *The Old Testament in the Book of Revelation*. JSNTSup 115. Sheffield: Sheffield Academic Press, 1995.

Mullen, E. Theodore, Jr. *The Divine Council in Canaanite and Early Hebrew Literature*. HSM 24. Chico, Calif.: Scholars Press, 1980.

Munoa, Phillip B., III. *Four Powers in Heaven: The Interpretation of Daniel 7 in the Testament of Abraham*. JSPSup 28. Sheffield: Sheffield Academic Press, 1998.

Murmelstein, Benjamin. “Adam, ein Beitrag zur Messiaslehre.” *WZKM* 35 (1928): 242–74.

Najman, Hindy. “Interpretation as Primordial Writing: Jubilees and Its Authority Conferring Strategies.” *JSJ* 30 (1999): 379–410.

———. *Seconding Sinai: The Development of Mosaic Discourse in Second Temple Judaism*. Leiden: Brill, 2003.

———. “The Symbolic Significance of Writing in Ancient Judaism.” Pages 139–73 in *The Idea of Biblical Interpretation: Essays in Honor of James L. Kugel*. Edited by Hindy Najman and Judith E. Newman. Leiden: Brill, 2004.

———. “Torah of Moses: Pseudonymous Attribution in Second Temple Writings.” Pages 202–16 in *The Interpretation of Scripture in Early Judaism and Christianity: Studies in Language and Tradition*. Edited by Craig.A. Evans. Sheffield: Sheffield Academic Press, 2000.

Navone, John. “The Lukan Banquet Community.” *TBT* 51 (1970): 155–61.

Nemoy, Leon. “Al-Qirqisani’s Account of the Jewish Sects and Christianity.” *HUCA* 7 (1930): 317–97.

Neugebauer, Otto. “The ‘Astronomical’ Chapters of the Ethiopic Book of Enoch (72–82).” Pages 386–419 in Matthew Black, *The Book of Enoch, or 1 Enoch*. SVTP 7. Leiden: Brill, 1985.

———. *Astronomical Cuneiform Texts*. Vol 1. London: Humphries, 1955.

Neusner, Jacob. *A Life of Yohanan ben Zakkai, ca. 1–80 C.E.* 2nd ed. Leiden: Brill, 1970.

———. *Purity in Rabbinic Judaism: A Systematic Account*. South Florida Studies in the History of Judaism 95. Atlanta: Scholars Press, 1994.

———, trans. *Pesiqta deRab Kahana: An Analytical Translation.* 2 vols. BJS 122–123. Atlanta: Scholars Press, 1987.

Newberg, Andrew, Eugene d'Aquili, and Vince Rause. *Why God Won't Go Away: Brain Science and the Biology of Belief.* New York: Ballantine, 2001.

Newsom, Carol. "He Has Established for Himself Priests: Human and Angelic Priesthood in the Qumran Sabbath Shirot." Pages 100–120 in *Archeology and History in the Dead Sea Scrolls.* Edited by Lawrence H. Schiffman. JSPSup 8. Sheffield: Sheffield Academic Press, 1990.

———. "Merkabah Exegesis in the Qumran Sabbath Shirot." *JJS* 38 (1987): 11–30.

———. "'Sectually Explicit' Literature from Qumran." Pages 167–87 in *The Hebrew Bible and Its Interpreters.* Edited by William H. Propp, Baruch Halpern, and David Noel Freedman. Biblical and Judaic Studies from the University of California, San Diego 1. Winona Lake, Ind.: Eisenbrauns, 1990.

———. *Songs of the Sabbath Sacrifice: A Critical Edition.* HSS 27. Atlanta: Scholars Press, 1985.

Nickelsburg, George W. E. *1 Enoch 1: A Commentary on the Book of 1 Enoch, Chapters 1–36; 81–108.* Hermeneia. Minneapolis: Fortress, 2001.

———. "The Apocalyptic Construction of Reality in *1 Enoch.*" Pages 50–64 in *Mysteries and Revelations: Apocalyptic Studies since the Uppsala Colloquium.* Edited by John J. Collins and James H. Charlesworth. Sheffield: JSOT Press, 1991.

———. "Enoch, Levi, and Peter: Recipients of Revelation in Upper Galilee." *JBL* 100 (1981): 575–600.

———. *Jewish Literature between the Bible and the Mishnah.* Philadelphia: Fortress, 1981.

———. "The Nature and Function of Revelation in *1 Enoch, Jubilees,* and Some Qumranic Documents." Pages 91–119 in *Pseudepigraphic Perspectives: The Apocrypha and Pseudepigrapha in Light of the Dead Sea Scrolls.* Edited by Esther G. Chazon and Michael E. Stone. Leiden: Brill, 1999.

———. "Where Is the Place of Eschatological Blessing?" Pages 53–71 in *Things Revealed: Studies in Early Jewish and Christian Literature in Honor of Michael E. Stone.* Edited by Esther G. Chazon, David Satran, and Ruth A. Clements. JSJSup 89. Leiden: Brill, 2004.

Nickelsburg, George W. E., and James C. VanderKam. *1 Enoch: A New Translation.* Minneapolis: Fortress, 2004.

Nikiprowetzky, Valentin. *Le commentaire de l'Ecriture chez Philon d'Alexandrie: Son caractere et sa portee, observations philologiques.* ALGHJ 11. Leiden: Brill, 1977.

———. "Le 'De Vita Contemplativa' revisité. Pages 205–25 in *Sagesse et Religion: Colloque de Strasbourg.* Paris: Presses Universitaires de France, 1979.

Nitzan, Bilhah. "4QBerakhot (4Q286–290): A Preliminary Report." Pages 53–71 in *New Qumran Texts and Studies: Proceedings of the First Meeting of the International Organization for Qumran Studies, Paris 1992.* Edited by George J. Brooke with Florentino García Martínez. STDJ 15. Leiden: Brill, 1994.

———. *Qumran Prayer and Religious Poetry.* STDJ 12. Leiden: Brill, 1994.

Nock, Arthur Darby. "The Question of Jewish Mysteries." Pages 459–68 in vol. 1 of *Essays on Religion and the Ancient World*. Edited by Zeph Stewart. Cambridge: Harvard University Press, 1972.

Noort, Edward. "Gan-Eden in the Context of the Mythology of the Hebrew Bible." Pages 21–36 in *Paradise Interpreted: Representations of Biblical Paradise in Judaism and Christianity*. Edited by Gerard P. Luttikhuizen. Leiden: Brill, 1999.

Noth, Martin. *A History of Pentateuchal Traditions*. Translated by Bernhard W. Anderson. Englewood Cliffs, N.J.: Prentice-Hall, 1972.

Odeberg, Hugo. *The Hebrew Book of Enoch or Third Enoch*. Cambridge: Cambridge University Press, 1928. Repr. with a prolegomenon by J. C. Greenfield. New York: Ktav, 1973.

Olson, Daniel. *Enoch: A New Translation: The Ethiopic Book of Enoch, or 1 Enoch, Translated with Annotations and Cross-References*. North Richland Hills, Tex.: BIBAL, 2004.

Olyan, Saul M. *A Thousand Thousands Served Him: Exegesis and the Naming of Angels in Ancient Judaism*. TSAJ 36. Tübingen: Mohr Siebeck, 1993. Reviewed in detail by C. Morray-Jones. *JSS* 42 (1997): 154–59.

Oppenheim, A. Leo. "Akkadian pul(u)h(t)u and melammu." *JAOS* 63 (1943): 31–4.

———. *Ancient Mesopotamia: Portrait of a Dead Civilization*. Chicago: University of Chicago Press, 1977.

———. "Divination and Celestial Observation in the Last Assyrian Empire." *Centaurus* 14 (1969): 97–135.

———. *Interpretation of Dreams in the Ancient Near East: With a Translation of an Assyrian Dream-Book*. TAPS 46.3. Philadelphia: American Philosophical Society, 1956.

Orlov, Andrei. *The Enoch-Metatron Tradition*. TSAJ 107. Tübingen: Mohr Siebeck, 2005.

———. "Melchizedek Legend of 2 (Slavonic) Enoch." *JSP* 32 (2000): 23–38.

———. "Secrets of Creation in 2 (Slavonic) Enoch." *Hen* 22 (2000): 45–62.

———. "Titles of Enoch-Metatron in 2 Enoch." *JSP* 18 (1998): 71–86.

———. "'Without Measure and Without Analogy': The Tradition of the Divine Body in *2 (Slavonic) Enoch*." *JJS* 56 (2005): 224–44.

Orton, David E. *The Understanding Scribe: Matthew and the Apocalyptic Ideal*. JSNTSup 25. Sheffield: Sheffield Academic Press, 1989.

Osiek, Carolyn. *Shepherd of Hermas: A Commentary*. Hermeneia. Minneapolis: Fortress, 1999.

Otero, Aurelio de Santos. "Libro de los secretos de Henoc (Henoc eslavo)." Pages 147–202 in vol. 4 of *Apócrifos del Antiguo Testamento*. Edited by Alejandro Díez Macho. Madrid: Cristiandad, 1984.

Patai, Raphael. *Man and Temple in Ancient Jewish Myth and Ritual*. 2nd ed. New York: Ktav, 1967.

Pate, C. Marvin. *Communities of the Last Days: The Dead Sea Scrolls, the New Testament, and the Story of Israel*. Leicester: Apollos, 2000.

Petersen, David L. "Eschatology, Old Testament," *ABD* 2:575–79.

Pétrement, Simone. *A Separate God: The Origins and Teachings of Gnosticism*. New York: HarperCollins, 1990.

Petuchowski, Jakob J. *Theology and Poetry: Studies in the Medieval Piyyut.* London: Routledge & Kegan Paul, 1978.

Pfann, Stephen J. *Qumran Cave 4.XXVI: Cryptic Texts;* Philip S. Alexander et al., *Miscellanea, Part 1.* DJD 36. Oxford: Clarendon, 2000.

Pines, Shlomo. "Eschatology and the Concept of Time in the Slavonic Book of Enoch." Pages 72–87 in *Types of Redemption.* Edited by Raphael J. Zwi Werblowsky. SHR 18. Leiden: Brill, 1970.

Pingree, David. "Legacies in Astronomy and Celestial Omens." Pages 125–37 in *The Legacy of Mesopotamia.* Edited by Stephanie Dalley. Oxford: Oxford University Press, 1998.

Polen, Nehemiah. "Divine Weeping: Rabbi Kalonymos Shapiro's Theology of Catastrophe in the Warsaw Ghetto." *Modern Judaism* 7 (1987): 253–69.

———. *The Holy Fire: The Teachings of Rabbi Kalonymus Kalman Shapira, the Rebbe of the Warsaw Ghetto.* Northvale, N.J.: Aronson, 1994.

Polzin, Robert. *Moses and the Deuteronomist: A Literary Study of the Deuteronomic History.* New York: Seabury, 1970.

Pomeroy, Sarah B. *Women in Hellenistic Egypt: From Alexander to Cleopatra.* New York: Schocken, 1984.

Prigent, Pierre. *L'Apocalypse de Saint Jean.* CNT. Paris: Delachaux & Niestlé, 1981.

———. *Commentary on the Apocalypse of St. John.* Tübingen: Mohr Siebeck, 2001.

Propp, William H. "The Skin of Moses' Face—Transfigured or Disfigured?" *CBQ* 49 (1987): 375–86.

Puech, Émile, ed. *Qumrân Grotte 4.XXII: Textes araméens, première partie: 4Q529–549.* DJD 31. Oxford: Clarendon, 2001.

Qimron, Elisha. "Celibacy in the Dead Sea Scrolls and the Two Kinds of Sectarians." Pages 287–94 in vol. 1 of *The Madrid Qumran Congress: Proceedings of the International Congress on the Dead Sea Scrolls, Madrid 18–21 March, 1991.* Edited by Julio C. Trebolle Barrera and Luis Vegas Montaner. 2 vols. Leiden: Brill, 1992.

Qimron, Elisha, and John Strugnell, eds. *Qumran Cave 4.V: Miqsat Maase Ha-Torah.* DJD 10. Oxford: Clarendon, 1994.

Quispel, Gilles. "The Demiurge in the Apocryphon of John." Pages 1–34 in *Nag Hammadi and Gnosis.* Edited by Robert McL. Wilson. Leiden: Brill, 1978.

———. "Ezekiel 1:26 in Jewish Mysticism and Gnosis." *VC* 34 (1980): 1–13.

———. "Gnosticism and the New Testament." *VC* 19 (1965): 70–85.

———. "The Origins of the Gnostic Demiurge." Pages 271–76 in vol. 1 of *Kyriakon: Festschrift Johannes Quaesten.* Edited by Patrick Granfield and Josef A. Jungmann. 2 vols. Münster: Aschendorff, 1970.

Rad, Gerhard von. *Theologie des Alten Testaments.* 2 vols. 2. 4th ed. Munich: Kaiser, 1965.

———. *Wisdom in Israel.* Nashville: Abingdon, 1972.

Ramsey, William M. *The Letters to the Seven Churches in Asia Minor and Their Place in the Plan of the Apocalypse.* London: Hodder & Stoughton, 1904.

Rawson, Elizabeth. *Intellectual Life in the Late Roman Republic.* Baltimore: Johns Hopkins University Press, 1985.

Reed, Annette Yoshiko. *Fallen Angels and the History of Judaism and Christianity: The Reception of Enochic Literature*. New York: Cambridge University Press, 2005.

———. "Heavenly Ascent, Angelic Descent, and Transmission of Knowledge in 1 Enoch 6–16." Pages 47–66 in *Heavenly Realms and Earthly Realities in Late Antique Religions*. Edited by Ra'anan Boustan and Annette Yoshiko Reed. Cambridge: Cambridge University Press, 2004.

Reeves, John C. *Jewish Lore in Manichaean Cosmogony: Studies in the* Book of Giants *Traditions*. HUCM 14. Cincinnati: Hebrew Union College Press, 1992.

Reicke, Bo Ivar. "Da'at and Gnosis in Intertestamental Literature." Pages 245–55 in *Neotestamentica et Semitica: Studies in Honor of Matthew Black*. Edited by E. Earle Ellis and Max Wilcox. Edinburg: T&T Clark, 1969.

———. *The Disobedient Spirits and Christian Baptism*. Copenhagen: Munksgaard, 1946.

Reif, Stefan C. *Judaism and Hebrew Prayer: New Perspectives on Jewish Liturgical History*. Cambridge: Cambridge University Press, 1993.

Reindl, Joseph. *Das Angesicht Gottes im Sprachgebrauch des Alten Testaments*. ETS 25. Leipzig: St. Benno, 1970.

Reiner, Erica. *Astral Magic in Babylonia*. TAPS 85.4. Philadelphia: American Philosophical Society, 1995.

———. "Babylonian Celestial Divination." Pages 21–37 in *Ancient Astronomy and Celestial Divination*. Edited by Noel M. Swerdlow. Cambridge: MIT Press, 1999.

Riaud, Jean. "Quelques Réflexions sur les Thérapeutes d'Alexandrie à la lumière de De *Vita Mosis* II.67." Pages 184–91 in *Heirs of the Septuagint: Philo, Hellenistic Judaism, and Early Christianity: Festschrift for Earle Hilgert*. Edited by David T. Runia, David M. Hay, and David Winston. Studia Philonica Annual 3. Atlanta: Scholars Press, 1991.

———. "Les Thérapeutes d'Alexandrie et l'idéal Lévitique." Pages 221–40 in *The Teacher of Righteousness: Literary Studies*. Part 2 of *Mogilany 1989: Papers on the Dead Sea Scrolls Offered in Memory of Jean Carmignac*. Edited by Zdzusław J. Kapera. Cracow: Enigma, 1993.

Richardson, G. Peter. "Philo and Eusebius on Monasteries and Monasticism: The Therapeutae and Kellia." Pages 334–59 in *Origins and Method: Towards a New Understanding of Judaism and Christianity: Essays in Honour of John C. Hurd*. Edited by Bradley H. McLean. JSNTSup 86. Sheffield: JSOT Press, 1993.

Richardson, G. Peter, and Valerie Heuchan. "Jewish Voluntary Associations in Egypt and the Roles of Women." Pages 226–51 in *Voluntary Associations in the Graeco-Roman World*. Edited by John S. Kloppenborg and Stephen G. Wilson. London: Routledge, 1996.

Ricoeur, Paul. "Preface to Bultmann." Pages 49–72 in *Essays on Biblical Interpretation*. Edited by Lewis S. Mudge. London: SCM, 1981.

———. *Time and Narrative*. Translated by Kathleen McLaughlin and D. Pellauer. 3 vols. Chicago: University of Chicago Press, 1983–86.

———. *The Rule of Metaphor: Multi-disciplinary Studies of the Creation of Meaning in Language*. Translated by Robert Czerny, Kathleen McLaughlin, and John Costello. Toronto: University of Toronto Press, 1977.

Robertson, R. G. "Ezekiel the Tragedian." *OTP* 2:803–19.

Rochberg, Francesca. *Babylonian Horoscopes.* TAPS 88.1. Philadelphia: American Philosophical Society, 1998.

———. "Heaven and Earth: The Divine-Human Relations in Mesopotamian Celestial Divination." Pages 176–82 in *Prayer, Magic, and the Stars in the Ancient and Late Antique World.* Edited by Scott Noegel, Joel Walker, and Brannon Wheeler. University Park: Pennsylvania State University Press, 2003.

———. *The Heavenly Writing: Divination, Horoscopy, and Astronomy in Mesopotamian Culture.* Cambridge: Cambridge University Press, 2004.

———. "Scribes and Scholars: The tupsar Enuma Anu Enlil." Pages 359–75 in *Assyriologica et Semitica: Festschrift für Joachim Oelsner anläßlich seines 65. Geburtstages am 18. February 1997.* Edited by Joachim Marzahn and Hans Neumann. Münster: Ugarit-Verlag, 2000.

Rowland, Christopher. "Apocalyptic Visions and the Exaltation of Christ in the Letter to the Colossians." *JSNT* 19 (1983): 73–83.

———. "The Influence of the First Chapter of Ezekiel on Jewish and Early Christian Literature." Ph.D. diss. Cambridge University, 1974.

———. *The Open Heaven: A Study of Apocalyptic in Judaism and Early Christianity.* New York: Crossroad, 1982.

———. "The Vision of the Risen Christ in Rev. 1:13ff: The Debt of Early Christology to an Aspect of Jewish Angelology. *JTS* 31 (1980): 1–11.

———. "The Visions of God in Apocalyptic Literature." *JSJ* 10 (1979): 145–50.

Rubinstein, A. "Observations on the *Slavonic Book of Enoch.*" *JJS* 15 (1962): 1–21.

Ruiten, Jacques van. "The Garden of Eden and Jubilees 3:1–31." *Bijdr* 57 (1996): 305–17.

Ruiz, Jean-Pierre. *Ezekiel in the Apocalypse: The Transformation of Prophetic Language in Revelation 16,17–19,10.* European University Studies Theology Series 23. Frankfurt: Lang, 1989.

Russell, David S. *The Method and Message of Jewish Apocalyptic.* Philadelphia: Westminster, 1964.

Sachs, Abraham J. "Babylonian Horoscopes." *JCS* 6 (1952): 49–74.

Saggs, Henry W. F. *The Encounter with the Divine in Mesopotamia and Israel.* London: University of London, Athlone, 1978.

Sanders, James A., ed. *The Psalms Scroll of Qumran Cave 11 (11QPs).* DJD 4. Oxford: Clarendon, 1965.

Sanders, Seth. "Old Light on Moses' Shining Face." *VT* 52 (2002): 400–407.

———. "Performative Utterances and Divine Language in Ugaritic." *JNES* 63 (2004): 161–81.

Sandt, Huub van de. "'Do Not Give What Is Holy to the Dogs' (Did 9:5D and Matt 7:6a): The Eucharistic Food of the Didache in Its Jewish Purity Setting." *VC* 56 (2002): 223–46.

Sasson, Jack. "Mari Dreams." *JAOS* 103 (1983): 283–93.

Sauneron, Serge. "Les songes et leur interprétation dans l'Égypte ancienne." Pages 17–61 in *Les songes et leur interpretation.* Edited by Serge Sauneron. Sources orientales 2. Paris: Seuil, 1959.

Schäfer, Peter. "The Aim and Purpose of Early Jewish Mysticism." Pages 289–95 in *Hekhalot-Studien*. Edited by Peter Schäfer. TSAJ 19. Tübingen: Mohr Siebeck, 1988.

———. "Ein neues Fragment zur Metoposkopie und Chiromantik." Pages 84–95 in *Hekhalot-Studien*. Edited by Peter Schäfer. TSAJ 19. Tubingen: Mohr Siebeck, 1988.

———. *Hidden and Manifest God: Some Major Themes in Early Jewish Mysticism*. Translated by A. Pomerance. Albany: State University of New York Press, 1992.

———. "Merkavah Mysticism and Rabbinic Judaism." *JAOS* 104 (1984): 537–54.

———. "New Testament and Hekhalot Literature: The Journey into Heaven in Paul and in Merkavah Mysticism." *JJS* 35 (1984): 19–35.

———. "Research on Hekhalot Literature: Where Do We Stand Now?" Pages 229–35 in *Rashi 1040–1990: Hommage à Ephraïm E. Urbach*. Edited by Gabrielle Sed-Rajna. Paris: Cerf, 1993.

———. "Tradition and Redaction in Hekhalot Literature." *JSJ* 14 (1983): 172–81.

———, ed. *Geniza-Fragmente zur Hekhalot-Literatur*. TSAJ 6. Tübingen: Mohr Siebeck, 1984.

———. *Hekhalot-Studien*. TSAJ 19. Tübingen: Mohr Siebeck, 1988.

———. *Konkordanz zur Hekhalot-Literatur*. 2 vols. TSAJ 12–13. Tübingen: Mohr Siebeck, 1986–88.

———. *Übersetzung der Hekhalot-Literatur*. 4 vols. TSAJ 17, 22, 29, 46. Tübingen: Mohr Siebeck, 1987–95.

Schäfer, Peter, Margaret Schlüter, and Hans George von Mutius. *Synopse zur Hekhalot Literatur*. TSAJ 2. Tübingen: Mohr Siebeck, 1981.

Schams, Christine. *Jewish Scribes in the Second Temple Period*. JSOTSup 291. Sheffield: Sheffield Academic Press, 1998.

Schenke, Hans-Martin. *Der Gott "Mensch" in der Gnosis: Ein religionsgeschichtlicher Beitrag zur Diskussion über die paulinische Anschauung von der Kirche als Leib Christi*. Göttingen: Vandenhoeck & Ruprecht, 1962.

Schiffman, Lawrence H. "*Merkavah* Speculation at Qumran: The 4Q Serekh Shirot 'Olat ha-Shabbat.'" Pages 15–47 in *Mystics, Philosophers, and Politicians: Essays in Jewish Intellectual History in Honor of Alexander Altmann*. Edited by Jehuda Reinharz and Daniel Swetschinski. Durham, N.C.: Duke University Press, 1982.

———. "The Recall of Rabbi Nehuniah Ben Ha-Qanah from Ecstasy in Hekhalot Rabbati." *AJS Review* 1 (1976): 269–81.

Schlüter, Margarete. "Die Erzählung von der Rückholung des R. Nehunya ben Haqana aus der *Merkava*-Schau in ihrem redaktionellen Rahmen." *FJB* 10 (1982): 65–109.

Schniedewind, William. *Society and the Promise to David: The Reception History of 2 Samuel 7:1–17*. New York: Oxford University Press, 1999.

Scholem, Gershom. "Ein Fragment zur Physiognomik und Chiromantik aus der Tradition der spatantiken judischen Esoterik." Pages 175–93 in *Liber Amicorum: Studies in Honour of Professor Dr. C. J. Bleeker*. SHR 17. Leiden: Brill, 1969.

———. *Jewish Gnosticism, Merkabah Mysticism and Talmudic Tradition*. 2nd ed. New York: Jewish Theological Seminary of America, 1965.

———. *Kabbabah*. Jerusalem: Keter, 1974.

———. *Major Trends in Jewish Mysticism*. 3rd ed. 1954. Repr., New York: Schocken, 1961.

———. "Major Trends in Jewish Mysticism." Pages 25–86 in *Gershom Scholem's* Major Trends in Jewish Mysticism *Fifty Years After: Proceedings of the Sixth International Conference on the History of Jewish Mysticism*. Edited by Peter Schafer and Joseph Dan. Tübingen: Mohr Siebeck, 1993.

———. *On the Kabbalah and Its Symbolism*. Translated by Ralph Manheim. New York: Schocken, 1965.

———. *On the Mystical Shape of the Godhead: Basic Concepts in the Kabbalah*. Edited by Jonathan Chipman. Translated by Joachim Neugroschel. New York: Schoken, 1991.

———. *Origins of the Kabbalah*. Edited by Raphael J. Zvi Werblowsky. Translated by Allan Arkush. Princeton: Princeton University Press, 1987.

———. "Physiognomy and Chiromancy." Pages 459–95 in *Sepher Assaf: Festschrift for Simha Assaf*. Edited by M. D. Cassuto et al. Jerusalem: Mossad HaRav Kook, 1953.

Scopello, Madeline. "Jewish and Greek Heroines in the Nag Hammadi Library." Pages 71–90 in *Images of the Feminine in Gnosticism*. Edited by Karen L. King. Philadelphia: Fortress, 1988.

Schüssler Fiorenza, Elisabeth. *Revelation: Vision of a Just World*. Proclamation Commentaries. Minneapolis: Fortress, 1991.

Segal, Alan F. "Apocalypticism and Life after Death." *PIBA* 22 (1999): 41–63.

———. "Heavenly Ascent in Hellenistic Judaism, Early Christianity and Their Environment." *ANRW* 2.23.2:1333–94.

———. *Life after Death: A History of the Afterlife in the Religions of the West*. New York: Doubleday, 2004.

———. *Paul the Convert: The Apostolate and Apostasy of Saul the Pharisee*. New Haven: Yale University Press, 1990.

———. "The Risen Christ and the Angelic Mediator Figures in Light of Qumran." Pages 302–28 in *Jesus and the Dead Sea Scrolls*. Edited by James H. Charlesworth. New York: Doubleday, 1992.

———. "Ruler of This World: Attitudes about Mediator Figures and the Importance of Sociology for Self-Definition." Pages 245–68 in *Aspects of Judaism in the Greco-Roman Period*. Vol. 2 of *Jewish and Christian Self-Definition*. Edited by E. P. Sanders. Philadelphia: Fortress, 1981.

———. *Two Powers in Heaven: Early Rabbinic Reports about Christianity and Gnosticism*. Leiden: Brill, 1977.

Segal, Moshe Zvi. *Sefer ben Sira ha-Shalem* (*The Complete Book of Ben Sira*). 2nd ed. Jerusalem: Bialik Institute, 1958.

Segert, Stanislav. "Observations on Poetic Structures in the Songs of the Sabbath Sacrifice." *RevQ* 13 (1988): 215–23.

Seim, Turid Karlsen. *The Double Message: Patterns of Gender in Luke-Acts*. Edinburgh: T&T Clark, 1994.

Sekki, Arthur Everett. *The Meaning of Ruach at Qumran*. SBLDS 110. Atlanta: Scholars Press, 1989.

Shaffer, Elinor S. *"Kubla Khan" and the Fall of Jerusalem*. Cambridge: Cambridge University Press, 1972.

Shepherd, Massey H., Jr. *The Paschal Liturgy and the Apocalypse*. Richmond: John Knox, 1960.

Shils, Edward. *Tradition*. Chicago: University of Chicago Press, 1981.

Silverstein, Michael. "Language Structure and Linguistic Ideology." Pages 193–247 in *The Elements: A Parasession on Linguistic Units and Levels*. Edited by Paul R. Clyne, William F. Hanks, and Carol L. Hofbauer. Chicago: Chicago Linguistic Society, 1979.

Simon, Marcel. "L'ascétisme dans les sectes juives." Pages 393–426 in *Tradizione dell'enkrateia: Motivazioni ontologiche e protologiche, atti del Colloquio Internazionale Milano, 20–23 aprile 1982*. Edited by Ugo Bianchi. Rome: Edizioni dell'Ateneo, 1982.

Slater, Thomas B. "On the Social Setting of the Revelation to John." *NTS* 44 (1998): 232–56.

Sly, Dorothy. *Philo's Perception of Women*. BJS 209. Atlanta: Scholars Press, 1990.

———. "Philo's Practical Application of *dikaiosyne*." Pages 298–308 in *Society of Biblical Literature 1991 Seminar Papers*. SBLSP 30. Atlanta: Scholars Press, 1991.

Smelik, Willem. "On Mystical Transformation of the Righteous into Light in Judaism." *JSJ* 26 (1995): 122–44.

Smith, Dennis E. *From Symposium to Eucharist: The Banquet in the Early Christian World*. Minneapolis: Fortress, 2003.

———. "Table Fellowship as a Literary Motif in the Gospel of Luke." *JBL* 106 (1987): 613–38.

Smith, Jonathan Z. *Imagining Religion: From Babylon to Jonestown*. Chicago: University of Chicago Press, 1982.

———. *Map Is Not Territory*. Leiden: Brill, 1978.

Smith, Mark S. *The Early History of God: Yahweh and the Other Deities in Ancient Israel*. San Francisco: Harper & Row, 1990.

———. "The Near Eastern Background of Solar Language for Yahweh." *JBL* 109 (1990): 29–39.

———. " 'Seeing God' in the Psalms: The Background to the Beatific Vision in the Hebrew Bible." *CBQ* 50 (1988): 171–83.

Smith, Morton. "Ascent to Heavens and the Beginning of Christianity." *Eranos* 50 (1981): 403–29.

———. "Ascent to the Heavens and Deification in 4QMa." Pages 81–88 in *Archaeology and History in the Dead Sea Scrolls*. Edited by Lawrence Schiffman. JSPSup 8. Sheffield: Sheffield University Press, 1990.

———. "Palestinian Judaism in the First Century." Pages 67–81 in *Israel: Its Role in Civilization*. Edited by Moshe Davis. New York: Jewish Theological Seminary, 1956.

———. "Two Ascended to Heaven—Jesus and the Author of 4Q491." Pages 290–301 in *Jesus and the Dead Sea Scrolls*. Edited by James H. Charlesworth. New York: Doubleday, 1992.

Sokolov, M. I. "Materialy i zametki po starinnoj slavjanskoj literature. Vypusk tretij, VII. Slavjanskaja Kniga Enoha Pravednogo. Teksty, latinskij perevod i izsledovanie. Posmertnyj trud avtora prigotovil k izdaniju M. Speranskij." *Chtenija v Obshchestve Istorii i Drevnostej Rossijskih* 4 (1910): 1–162.

Sommer, Benjamin. *A Prophet Reads Scripture: Allusion in Isaiah 40–66.* Stanford, Calif.: Stanford University Press, 1998.

Sowers, Sidney. *The Hermeneutics of Philo and Hebrews: A Comparison of the Interpretation of the Old Testament in Philo Judaeus and the Epistle to the Hebrews.* Richmond, Va.: John Knox, 1965.

Speiser, Ephraim A. *Genesis.* AB 1. Garden City, N.Y.: Doubleday, 1964.

Staerk, Willy. *Die Erlösererwartung in den östlichen Religionen.* Stuttgart: Kohlhammer, 1938.

Stähli, Hans-Peter. *Solare Elemente im Jahweglauben des Alten Testaments.* OBO 66. Fribourg: Universitätsverlag; Göttingen: Vandenhoeck & Ruprecht, 1985.

Starr, Ivan. *The Rituals of the Diviner.* Malibu: Undena, 1983.

Stendahl, Krister. *The Scrolls and the New Testament.* New York: Harper, 1957. Repr., New York: Crossroad, 1992.

Stone, Michael E. "Apocalyptic—Vision or Hallucination." *Milla wa-Milla, The Australian Bulletin of Comparative Religion* 14 (1974): 47–56. Repr. as pages 415–28 in *Selected Studies in Pseudepigrapha and Apocrypha with Special Reference to the Armenian Tradition.* Edited by Michael E. Stone. Leiden: Brill, 1991.

———. "Apocalyptic Literature." Pages 383–441 in *Jewish Writings of the Second Temple Period: Apocrypha, Pseudepigrapha, Qumran Sectarian Writings, Philo, Josephus.* Edited by Michael E. Stone. CRINT 2.2. Philadelphia: Fortress, 1984.

———. "Enoch, Aramaic Levi and Sectarian Origins." *JSJ* 19 (1988): 160–69.

———. "The Fall of Satan and Adam's Penance: Three Notes on the Books of Adam and Eve." Pages 43–56 in *Literature on Adam and Eve: Collected Essays.* Edited by Gary Anderson, Michael Stone, and Johannes Tromp. SVTP 15. Leiden: Brill, 2003.

———. "Lists of Revealed Things in the Apocalyptic Literature." Pages 414–52 in *Magnalia Dei: The Mighty Acts of God.* Edited by Frank Moore Cross, Werner E. Lemke, and Patrick D. Miller Jr. New York: Doubleday, 1976.

———. "A Reconsideration of Apocalyptic Visions." *HTR* 96 (2003): 167–80.

———, ed. *Jewish Writings of the Second Temple Period: Apocrypha, Pseudepigrapha, Qumran Sectarian Writings, Philo, Josephus.* CRINT 2.2. Philadelphia: Fortress, 1984.

Strack, Hermann L., and Günther Stemberger. *Introduction to the Talmud and Midrash.* Translated and edited by Markus Bockmuehl. Minneapolis: Fortress, 1992.

Stroumsa, Gedaliahu (Guy) G. "Le couple de l'ange et de l'esprit: Traditions juives et chrétiennes." *RB* 88 (1981): 42–61.

———. "Form(s) of God: Some Notes on Metatron and Christ." *HTR* 76 (1983): 269–88.

———. *Hidden Wisdom: Esoteric Traditions and the Roots of Christian Mysticism.* NumenSup 70. Leiden: Brill, 1996.

Strugnell, John. "The Angelic Liturgy at Qumran—4QSerek Šîrôt 'Ôlat Haššabbāt." Pages 318–45 in *Congress Volume: Oxford, 1959.* VTSup 7. Leiden: Brill, 1959–60.

Strugnell, John, and Devorah Dimant. "4Q Second Ezekiel (4Q385)." *RevQ* 13 (1988): 45–58.

Strugnell, John, and Lawrence H. Schiffman. "Merkavah Speculation at Qumran: The 4QSerekh Shirot Olat Ha-Shabat." Pages 15–47 in *Mystics, Philosophers, and Politicians: Essays in Jewish Intellectual History in Honor of Alexander Altmann.* Edited by Jehuda Reinharz and Daniel Swetschinski. Durham, N.C.: Duke University Press, 1982.

Stuckenbruck, Loren T. *Angel Veneration and Christology.* WUNT 2.70. Tübingen: Mohr Siebeck, 1995.

———. *The Book of Giants from Qumran.* TSAJ 63. Tübingen: Mohr Siebeck, 1997.

Sullivan, Kevin. *Wrestling with Angels: A Study of the Relationship between Angels and Humans in Ancient Jewish Literature and the New Testament.* AGJU 55. Leiden: Brill, 2004.

Suter, David. "Why Galilee? Galilean Regionalism in the Interpretation of *1 Enoch.*" *Hen* 25 (2003): 167–212.

Sutin, Lawrence. *Divine Invasions: A Life of Philip K. Dick.* New York: Harmonym 1989.

Swartz, Michael D. "Divination and Its Discontents: Finding and Questioning Meaning in Ancient and Medieval Judaism." Pages 155–66 in *Prayer, Magic, and the Stars in the Ancient and Late Antique World.* Edited by Scott Noegel, Joel Walker, and Brannon Wheeler. University Park: Pennsylvania State University Press, 2003.

———. *Mystical Prayer in Ancient Judaism: An Analysis of Ma'aseh Merkavah.* TSAJ 28. Tübingen: Mohr Siebeck, 1992.

———. *Scholastic Magic: Ritual and Revelation in Early Jewish Mysticism.* Princeton: Princeton University Press, 1996.

Swete, Henry Barclay. *The Apocalypse of John.* 3rd ed. London: Macmillan, 1909.

Swetnam, James. "Sacrifice and Revelation in the Epistle to the Hebrews: Observations and Surmises on Hebrews 7:6." *CBQ* 30 (1968): 227–34.

Talmon, Shemaryahu. "The Community of the Renewed Covenant: Between Judaism and Christianity." Pages 1–24 in *The Community of the Renewed Covenant: The Notre Dame Symposium on the Dead Sea Scrolls.* Edited by Eugene Ulrich and James C. VanderKam. Christianity and Judaism in Antiquity Series 10. Notre Dame: University of Notre Dame Press, 1994.

———. *The World of Qumran from Within: Collected Studies.* Jerusalem: Magnes, 1989.

Talmon, Shermaryahu, Jonathan Ben-Dov, and Uwe Glessmer, eds. *Qumran Cave 4.XVI: Calendrical Texts.* DJD 21. Oxford: Clarendon, 2001.

Tambiah, Stanley J. "A Performative Approach to Ritual." *Proceedings of the British Academy* 65 (1979): 113–69.

Taylor, Joan E. *Jewish Women Philosophers of First-Century Alexandria: Philo's 'Therapeutae' Reconsidered.* Oxford: Oxford University Press, 2003.

———. "The Women 'Priests' of Philo's *De Vita Contemplativa:* Reconstructing the Therapeutae." Pages 102–22 in *On the Cutting Edge: The Study of Women in Biblical Worlds: Essays in Honor of Elisabeth Schüssler Fiorenza.* Edited by Jane Schaberg, Alice Bach, and Esther Fuchs. New York: Continuum, 2004.

Taylor, Joan E., and Philip R. Davies. "The So-Called Therapeutae of *De Vita Contemplativa:* Identity and Character." *HTR* 91 (1998): 3–24.

Theodor, Julius, and Chanoch Albeck, eds. *Bereshit Rabba mit kritischem Apparat und Kommentar.* 2nd ed. 3 vols. Jerusalem: Wahrmann, 1965.

Thiering, Barbara. "The Biblical Source of Qumran Asceticism." *JBL* 93 (1974): 429–44.

Thompson, Leonard L. 1990. *The Book of Revelation: Apocalypse and Empire.* New York: Oxford University Press.

Throckmorton, Burton, Jr., ed. *Gospel Parallels: A Comparison of the Synoptic Gospels.* Nashville: Nelson, 1992.

Tigchelaar, Eibert. *Prophets of Old and the Day of the End: Zechariah, the Book of the Watchers and Apocalyptic.* OtSt 35. Leiden: Brill, 1996.

Tiller, Patrick A. *A Commentary on the Animal Apocalypse of I Enoch.* SBLEJL 4. Atlanta: Scholars Press, 1993.

Tishby, Isaiah. *The Wisdom of the Zohar.* Translated by David Goldstein. 3 vols. Oxford: Littman Library, 1989.

Tov, Emanuel, ed. *The Text from the Judaean Desert: Indices and an Introduction to the* Discoveries in the Judaean Desert *Series.* DJD 39. Oxford: Clarendon, 2002.

Trapnel, Anna. *The Cry of a Stone.* Edited by Hilary Hinds. Tempe: Arizona Center for Medieval and Renaissance Studies, 2000.

Uhlig, Siegbert. *Das äthiopische Henochbuch.* Jüdische Schriften aus hellenistisch-römischer Zeit 5. Gütersloh: Mohn, 1984.

Ullendorff, Edward. *The Ethiopic Book of Enoch: A New Edition in the Light of the Aramaic Dead Sea Fragments.* Oxford: Clarendon, 1978.

Urbach, Ephraim E. "Ha-Masorot ʿal Torat ha-Sod bi-Tequfat ha-Tannaim." Pages 2–11 in *Studies in Mysticism and Religion: Presented to G. G. Scholem on His Seventieth Birthday.* Edited by Alexander Altmann. Jerusalem: Magnes, 1967.

Vaillant, André. *Le livre des secrets d'Henoch: Texte slave et traduction française.* Paris: Institut D'Etudes Slaves, 1952.

Van Buren, E. Douglas. "The Seven Dots in Mesopotamian Art and their Meaning." *AfO* 13 (1939–41): 277–89.

Van Dam, Cornelis. *The Urim and Thummim: A Means of Revelation in Ancient Israel.* Winona Lake, Ind.: Eisenbrauns, 1997.

VanderKam, James C. "The Angel of the Presence in the Book of Jubilees." *DSD* 7 (2000): 378–93.

———. *Calendars in the Dead Sea Scrolls: Measuring Time.* Literature of the Dead Sea Scrolls. London: Routledge, 1998.

———. *The Dead Sea Scrolls Today.* Grand Rapids: Eerdmans; London: SPCK, 1995.

———. *Enoch: A Man for All Generations.* Studies on Personalities of the Old Testament. Columbia: University of South Carolina Press, 1995.

———. *Enoch and the Growth of an Apocalyptic Tradition.* CBQMS 16. Washington, D.C.: Catholic Biblical Association of America, 1984.

———. "The Origin, Character and Early History of the 364 Day Calendar: A Reassessment of Jaubert's Hypotheses." *CBQ* 41 (1979): 390–411.

———, ed. and trans. *The Book of Jubilees.* 2 vols. CSCO 510–11. Scriptores Aethiopici 87–88. Leuven: Peeters, 1989.

Venter, Pieter. "Spatiality in Enoch's Journeys (1 Enoch 12–36)." Pages 211–30 in *Wisdom and Apocalypticism in the Dead Sea Scrolls and the Biblical Tradition*. BETL 168. Edited by Florentino García Martínez. Leuven: Peeters, 2003.

Vermes, Geza. *"He is the Bread": Targum Neofiti Exodus 16.15*. Post Biblical Jewish Studies. Leiden: Brill, 1975.

Vieyra, Maurice. "Les songes et leur interprétation chez les Hittites." Pages 87–98 in *Les songes et leur interpretation*. Edited by Serge Sauneron. Sources orientales 2. Paris: Seuil, 1959.

Virolleaud, Charles. *L'astrologie chaldéenne*. Paris: Geuthner, 1905–12.

Volten, Aksel D. F. *Demotishe Traumdetutung*. Analecta Aegyptiaca 3. Copenhagen: Munksgaard, 1942.

Wacholder, Ben Zion. "Ezekiel and Ezekielianism as Progenitors of Essenianism." Pages 186–96 in *The Dead Sea Scrolls: Forty Years of Research*. Edited by Devorah Dimant and Uriel Rappaport. STDJ 10. Leiden: Brill; Jerusalem: Magnes, 1992.

Wacker, Marie-Theres. *Weltordnung und Gericht: Studien zu I Henoch 22*. Würzburg: Echter, 1982.

Waters, Kenneth L., Sr. "Saved through Childbearing: Virtues as Children in 1 Timothy 2:11–15." *JBL* 123 (2004): 703–35.

Wegner, Judith Romney. "The Image of Women in Philo." Pages 551–63 in *Society of Biblical Literature 1982 Seminar Papers*. SBLSP 21. Chico, Calif.: Scholars Press, 1982.

Weinfeld, Moshe. *Deuteronomy and the Deuteronomic School*. Oxford: Clarendon. 1972.

Wenham, Gordon J. *Genesis 1–15*. WBC 1. Waco, Tex.: Word, 1987.

Werman, Cana. "The Sons of Zadok." Pages 623–30 in *The Dead Sea Scrolls Fifty Years after Their Discovery*. Edited by Lawrence W. Schiffman, Emanuel Tov, and James C. VanderKam. Jerusalem: Israel Exploration Society, 2000.

Whitaker, Edward C. *Documents of the Baptismal Liturgy*. London: SPCK, 1960.

Whitney, Kenneth William, Jr. "Two Strange Beasts: A Study of Traditions concerning Leviathan and Behemoth in Second Temple and Early Rabbinic Judaism." Ph.D. diss. Harvard University, 1992.

Widengren, Geo. *The Ascension of the Apostle and the Heavenly Book*. Uppsala Universitets Årsskrift 1950.7. Uppsala: Lundequistska, 1950.

———. "Early Hebrew Myths and Their Interpretations." Pages 165–69 in *Myth, Ritual and Kingship: Essays on the Theory and Practice of Kingship in the Ancient Near East and in Israel*. Edited by Samuel H. Hooke. Oxford: Clarendon, 1958.

Wiesenberg, Ephraim Jehudah. "Gleanings of the Liturgical Term Melekh Ha-'olam." *JJS* 17 (1966): 47–72

———. "The Liturgical Term Melekh Ha-'olam." *JJS* 15 (1964): 1–56.

Wiggermann, Frans. "Mythological Foundation of Nature." Pages 279–306 in *Natural Phenomena: Their Meaning, Depiction and Description in the Ancient Near East*. Amsterdam: Royal Netherlands Academy of Arts and Sciences, 1992.

Williamson, Ronald. *Philo and the Epistle to the Hebrews*. ALGHJ 4. Leiden: Brill, 1970.

Winston, David. "Philo and the Contemplative Life." Pages 198–231 in *From the Bible through the Middle Ages*. Vol. 1 of *Jewish Spirituality*. Edited by Arthur Green. New York: Crossroad, 1986.

———. "The Sage as Mystic in the Wisdom of Solomon." Pages 383–97 in *The Sage in Israel and the Ancient Near East*. Edited by John G. Gammie and Leo G. Perdue. Winona Lake, Ind.: Eisenbrauns, 1990.

———, trans. *Philo of Alexandria: The Contemplative Life, The Giants, and Selections*. CWS. New York: Paulist, 1981.

Witherington, Ben. *Women in the Ministry of Jesus: A Study of Jesus' Attitudes to Women and Their Roles as Reflected in His Earthly Life*. Cambridge: Cambridge University Press, 1980.

Wolfson, Elliot R. "Metatron and Shi'ur Qomah in the Writings of Haside Ashkenaz." Pages 60–92 in *Mysticism, Magic and Kabbalah in Ashkenazi Judaism*. Edited by Karl-Erich Grözinger and Joseph Dan. Berlin: de Gruyter, 1995.

———. "Mysticism and the Poetic-Liturgical Compositions from Qumran: A Response to Bilhah Nitzan." *JQR* 85 (1994): 185–202.

———. *Through a Speculum That Shines: Visions and Imagination in Medieval Jewish Mysticism*. Princeton: Princeton University Press, 1994.

———. "*Yeridah la-Merkavah*: Typology of Ecstasy and Enthronement in Ancient Jewish Mysticism." Pages 13–44 in *Mystics of the Book: Themes, Topics, and Typologies*. Edited by Robert A. Herrera. New York: Lang, 1993.

Woolard, Kathryn A. "Introduction: Language Ideology as a Field of Inquiry." Pages 14–15 in *Language Ideologies: Practice and Theory*. Edited by Bambi B. Schieffelin, Kathryn A. Woolard, and Paul V. Kroskrity. New York: Oxford University Press, 1998.

Wright, J. Edward. *The Early History of Heaven*. New York: Oxford University Press, 2000.

Yadin, Yigael. *The Temple Scroll*. 3 vols. and supplement. Jerusalem: Israel Exploration Society, 1977–83.

Yahalom, Joseph. *Poetry and Society in Jewish Galilee of Late Antiquity* [Hebrew]. Tel Aviv: Hakibbutz Hameuchad, 1999.

Yarbro Collins, Adela. "The Seven Heavens in Jewish and Christian Apocalypses." Pages 62–66 in *Death, Ecstasy and Other Worldly Journeys*. Edited by John J. Collins and Michael Fishbane. Albany: State University of New York Press, 1995.

———, ed. *Early Christian Apocalypticism: Genre and Social Setting*. *Semeia* 36 (1986).

Ysebaert, Joseph. *Greek Baptismal Terminology: Its Origins and Early Development*. Nijmegan: Dekker & Van de Vegt, 1962.

Zelizer, Barbie. "Reading the Past against the Grain: The Shape of Memory Studies." *Critical Studies in Mass Communication* 12 (1995). 204–39.

Zimmerli, Walther. *Ezekiel*. 2 vols. Hermeneia. Philadelphia: Fortress, 1983.

Zimmern, Heinrich. "Urkönige und Uroffenbarung." Pages in 530–43 in vol. 2 of *Die Keilinschriften und das Alte Testament*. Edited by Eberhard Schrader. 2 vols. Berlin: Reuther & Reichard, 1903.

Zonabend, Françoise. *The Enduring Memory: Time and History in a French Village.* Translated by Anthony Forster. Manchester: Manchester University Press, 1984.

Contributors

Cameron Afzal is Professor of Religion at Sarah Lawrence College (Bronxville, New York). He specializes in biblical studies, teaching Hebrew Bible, early Christian literature, and the origins of Christian mysticism in late antiquity. Currently he is writing a book on Revelation.

Daphna Arbel teaches in the Classics Department at the University of British Columbia (Vancouver, Canada) as an Associate Professor of Religion. She has authored *Beholders of Divine Secrets: Myth and Mysticism in Hekhalot and Merkavah Literature* (2003) and several significant articles on various aspects of Near Eastern mythology and Jewish mysticism.

Ra'anan S. Boustan (né Abusch) is Visiting Assistant Professor in the Departments of History and Near Eastern Languages and Cultures at the University of California, Los Angeles. A scholar of early Judaism, he has published studies on early Jewish mysticism, the relationship between Jews and Christians in late antiquity, and the role of gender and sexuality within Judaism. His publications include *From Martyr to Mystic: Rabbinic Martyrology and the Making of Merkavah Mysticism* (2005) and a co-edited volume, *Heavenly Realms and Earthly Realities in Late Antique Religions* (2004).

Kelley Coblentz Bautch is Assistant Professor in the Department of Religious Studies at St. Edward's University (Austin, Texas). Her areas of specialization include apocalypticism, eschatology, mysticism, and spirituality. She has published several papers on Enochic literature and a book, *A Study of the Geography of 1 Enoch 17–19: "No One Has Seen What I Have Seen"* (2003).

James R. Davila is a Reader in Early Jewish Studies at the University of St. Andrews (Scotland). He specializes in the Dead Sea Scrolls, ancient Jewish and Christian parabiblical literature, and early Jewish mysticism. His books include *The Jewish Roots of Christological Monotheism: Papers from the St. Andrews Conference on the Historical Origins of the Worship of Jesus* (co-edited with Carey C. Newman and Gladys S. Lewis, 1999); *Liturgical Works* (Eerdmans Commentaries on the Dead Sea Scrolls 6, 2000); *Descenders to the Chariot: The People behind the Hekhalot Literature* (2001); *The Dead Sea Scrolls as Background to Postbiblical Judaism and Early Christianity: Papers from a*

Conference at St. Andrews in 2001 (ed., 2003); and *The Provenance of the Pseudepigrapha: Jewish, Christian, or Other?* (2005).

April D. DeConick is the Professor of New Testament and Early Christianity and the Isla Carroll and Percy Turner Professor of Biblical Studies in the Department of Religious Studies at Rice University (Houston, Texas). She specializes in early Christian theology, noncanonical Gospels, and gnostic and mystical traditions. Her books include *Seek to See Him: Ascent and Vision Mysticism in the Gospel of Thomas* (1996); *Voices of the Mystics: Early Christian Discourse in the Gospels of John and Thomas and Other Ancient Christian Literature* (2001); *Recovering the Original Gospel of Thomas: A History of the Gospel and Its Growth* (2005); and *The Original Gospel of Thomas in Translation, with Commentary and New English Translation of the Complete Gospel* (2006).

Celia Deutsch teaches at Barnard College and Columbia University (New York City, New York), where she is an Adjunct Associate Professor in the Religion Department. She focuses on early Judaism and early Christianity and their relationship to mysticism. Her books include *Hidden Wisdom and the Easy Yoke: Wisdom, Torah and Discipleship in Matthew 11.25–30* (1987) and *Lady Wisdom, Jesus, and the Sages:Metaphor and Social Context in Matthew's Gospel* (1996).

Rachel Elior is John and Golda Cohen Professor of Jewish Philosophy and Jewish Mystical Thought at the Hebrew University (Jerusalem, Israel). She is the chair of the Department of Jewish Thought in the Hebrew University of Jerusalem and the recipient of The Gershom Scholem Award for the study of Kabbalah 2006 awarded by the Israel Academy of Sciences and Humanities. She has been a research fellow and visiting professor at University College London, the University of Amsterdam, Oberlin College, the University of Michigan, the Oxford Center for Hebrew and Jewish Studies, Case Western University, Yeshiva University, Tokyo University, and Princeton University. She is the author of numerous works on Jewish mysticism and Hasidism, *The Paradoxical Ascent to God: The Kabbalistic Theosophy of Habad Hasidism* (1992) and *The Three Temples: On the Emergence of Jewish Mysticism* (2004).

Frances Flannery-Dailey teaches biblical studies, Judaism, and religion and culture courses at Hendrix College (Conway, Arkansas) as Associate Professor of Religion in the Department of Religion. She specializes in Second Temple Judaism, particularly in dreams, visions, rituals, the temple cult, and constructions of worlds, with related interests in religion and monsters. She is author of *Dreamers, Scribes, and Priests: Jewish Dreams in the Hellenistic and Roman Eras* (2004).

Charles A. Gieschen teaches at Concordia Theological Seminary (Fort Wayne, Indiana) as Professor of Exegetical Theology (New Testament) and chair of the Department of Exegetical Theology. He specializes in Second Temple Jewish literature, early Christology, and early sacramental practices. He is author of *Angelomorphic*

Christology: Antecedents and Early Evidence (1998) and editor of a collection of essays entitled *The Law in Holy Scripture* (2004).

Rebecca Lesses is Assistant Professor of Jewish Studies at Ithaca College (Ithaca, New York). Her research interests span *hekhalot* literature, theories of ritual, late antique Judaism, Jewish women's history, and the comparative study of magic in late antiquity. She has published many articles on these subjects as well as a monograph, *Ritual Practices to Gain Power: Angels, Incantations, and Revelation in Early Jewish Mysticism* (1998).

Andrea Lieber is the Sophia Ava Asbell Chair of Judaic Studies and Associate Professor of Religion at Dickinson College (Carlisle, Pennsylvannia). Her courses and publications explore the transformations of Judaism as a living religion and evolving culture from its origins in antiquity through its varied manifestations in the twentieth century, including rabbinic literature and kabbalah.

Christopher Morray-Jones (Ph.D., University of Cambridge), was formerly a research fellow of Oxford University. He has taught in the Religious Studies Program of the University of California, Berkeley, and holds a J.D. from U.C. Berkeley School of Law. He is currently the Legal Services Coordinator of Bay Area Police Watch, a program of the Ella Baker Center for Human Rights in Oakland, California.

Andrei A. Orlov teaches at Marquette University (Milwaukee, Wisconsin) as Assistant Professor of Christian Origins. He specializes in the study of Christian origins, with special attention to the formative influences of the Second Temple pseudepigrapha, Jewish apocalyptic literature, and early Jewish mysticism. He has published twenty articles in edited volumes and scholarly journals such as *Journal for the Study of Judaism, Journal for the Study of the Pseudepigrapha, Henoch, Vigiliae Christianae, Journal of Jewish Studies,* and *Catholic Biblical Quarterly.* He is the author of a monograph entitled *The Enoch-Metatron Tradition* (2005).

Christopher Rowland is Dean Ireland Professor of the Exegesis of Holy Scripture, University of Oxford. He has written extensively on apocalypticism, including *The Open Heaven* (1982) and *Revelation* (with Judith Kovacs, 2004). He has a long-standing interest in the visionary in radical and prophetic groups in Christian history and the British artist, poet, and visionary William Blake.

Seth Sanders has held teaching and research posts at Hebrew University and the University of Chicago and is currently Visiting Assistant Professor of Hebrew Bible at Cornell University. He is the editor of *Margins of Writing, Origins of Cultures: New Approaches to Writing and Reading in the Ancient Near East* (2005) and co-editor of *Cuneiform in Canaan: Cuneiform Sources from the Land of Israel in Ancient Times* (2006).

Alan Segal teaches at Barnard College, Columbia University (Manhattan), as Professor of Religion and Ingeborg Rennert Professor of Jewish Studies. He specializes in Judaica, Christian origins, and rabbinics. Professor Segal's publications include *Two Powers in Heaven* (1977), *Rebecca's Children: Judaism and Christianity in the Roman World* (1986), *The Other Judaisms of Late Antiquity* (1987), *Paul the Convert: The Apostasy and Apostolate of Saul of Tarsus* (1990), and *Life after Death: A History of the Afterlife in Western Religion* (2004).

Kevin Sullivan is an Assistant Professor in the Religion Department at Illinois Wesleyan University (Bloomington, Illinois). He specializes in late Second Temple Judaism and early Christianity. He is the author of a monograph entitled *Wrestling with Angels: A Study of the Relationship between Humans and Angels in Ancient Jewish Literature and the New Testament* (2004). He is the current chair of the Early Jewish and Mysticism Group in the Society of Biblical Literature.

Index of Ancient Sources

Old Testament/Hebrew Bible

New Testament

Apocryphal/Deuterocanonical books

Old Testament Pseudepigrapha

DEAD SEA SCROLLS

Josephus and Philo

New Testament Apocrypha and Nag Hammadi Codices

Apostolic Fathers and Patristic Writers

Mishnah, Talmud, and Related Literature

Mishnah

Tosefta

Babylonian Talmud

Jerusalem Talmud

Targumic Texts

Other Rabbinic Texts

Jewish Mystical Literature

Greek and Latin Authors

Other Literature

Index of Modern Authors

Printed in the United States
84661LV00003B/1-12/A

9 781589 832572